MY OPPOSITION

This is a truly unique account of Nazi Germany at war and of one man's struggle against totalitarianism. A mid-level official in a provincial town, Friedrich Kellner kept a secret diary from 1939 to 1945, risking his life to record Germany's path to dictatorship and genocide and to protest his countrymen's complicity in the regime's brutalities. Just one month into the war he is aware that Jews are marked for extermination and later records how soldiers on leave spoke openly about the mass murder of Jews and the murder of POWs; he also documents the Gestapo's merciless rule at home from euthanasia campaigns against the handicapped and mentally ill to the execution of anyone found listening to foreign broadcasts. This essential testimony of everyday life under the Third Reich is accompanied by a foreword by Alan Steinweis and the remarkable story of how the diary was brought to light by Robert Scott Kellner, Friedrich's grandson.

Robert Scott Kellner discovered his grandfather's diary in 1960 and has worked tirelessly to bring it to the attention of the world through exhibits at the Dwight D. Eisenhower and George H. W. Bush Presidential Libraries, a documentary film screened at the United Nations, and the publication of a complete edition of the diary in German and abridgments in Russian and Polish.

MY OPPOSITION

The Diary of Friedrich Kellner – A German
against the Third Reich

Translated and Edited by
ROBERT SCOTT KELLNER

With a Foreword by
Alan E. Steinweis

CAMBRIDGE
UNIVERSITY PRESS

CAMBRIDGE
UNIVERSITY PRESS

University Printing House, Cambridge CB2 8BS, United Kingdom

One Liberty Plaza, 20th Floor, New York, NY 10006, USA

477 Williamstown Road, Port Melbourne, VIC 3207, Australia

314–321, 3rd Floor, Plot 3, Splendor Forum, Jasola District Centre, New Delhi – 110025, India

79 Anson Road, #06–04/06, Singapore 079906

Cambridge University Press is part of the University of Cambridge.

It furthers the University's mission by disseminating knowledge in the pursuit of education, learning, and research at the highest international levels of excellence.

www.cambridge.org
Information on this title: www.cambridge.org/9781108418294
DOI: 10.1017/9781108289696

First published 2018
Reprinted 2018
Paperback edition first published 2020

Printed in the United Kingdom by TJ International Ltd. Padstow Cornwall

A catalogue record for this publication is available from the British Library.

Library of Congress Cataloging-in-Publication Data
NAMES: Kellner, Friedrich, 1885–1970, author. | Kellner, Robert Scott, editor.
TITLE: My opposition : the diary of Friedrich Kellner – a German against the Third Reich / edited by Robert Scott Kellner ; with a foreword by Alan E. Steinweis.
Other titles: Vernebelt, verdunkelt sind alle Hirne. German
DESCRIPTION: Cambridge, United Kingdom; New York, NY : Cambridge University Press, 2017. | Includes bibliographical references and index.
IDENTIFIERS: LCCN 2017030752 | ISBN 9781108418294 (hardback : alkaline paper)
SUBJECTS: LCSH: Kellner, Friedrich, 1885–1970 – Diaries. | World War, 1939–1945 – Personal narratives, German. | Kellner, Friedrich, 1885–1970 – Political and social views. | Germany – Officials and employees – Diaries. | Germany – History – 1933–1945 – Biography. | Anti-Nazi movement – Germany – Laubach (Giessen) | Jews – Persecutions – Germany – Laubach (Giessen) – History – 20th century. | World War, 1939–1945 – Germany – Laubach (Giessen)
CLASSIFICATION: LCC D811.5 .K4513 2017 | DDC 943.086/4092 [B]–dc23
LC record available at https://lccn.loc.gov/2017030752

ISBN 978-1-108-41829-4 Hardback
ISBN 978-1-108-40696-3 Paperback

Hitler has risen to be a glaring example of abomination for mankind.

For me he has always been what he was: a brigand, a beast!

Friedrich Kellner, December 17, 1942

CONTENTS

FOREWORD

In 1933, Friedrich Kellner relocated from his home city of Mainz to the small town of Laubach. Located on the river Wetter on the western edge of the Vogelsberg mountain region, Laubach had a population of slightly less than 2,000 in 1933. The town lies about 75 kilometers northeast of Frankfurt and about 25 kilometers directly east of Giessen, an important university town and administrative center in Upper Hesse, the northern section of the German province then known as the People's State of Hesse (*Volksstaat Hessen*).[1] Laubach dates from the eighth century and is known for its impressive medieval castle, winding alleys, and half-timbered houses. The town had been connected to the wider region by the Hungen-Mücke railroad line since 1890. The local courthouse, where Friedrich Kellner assumed his professional duties in 1933, had been established in 1822.[2]

A committed Social Democrat and steadfast opponent of Nazism, Kellner went to Laubach to escape retribution from Nazi activists in Mainz. Ironically, his destination was itself a stronghold of Nazism. In the Reichstag election of July 1932, the NSDAP had received 62.9 percent of the votes cast in Laubach, in contrast to the 37.3 percent of the vote attained by the Nazis nationally. The Social Democrats, who in the closing days of the Weimar Republic had constituted the only real opposition to Nazism in Laubach and the surrounding region, had received only 18.7 percent of Laubach's votes. The electoral success of the Nazis in July 1932 was even more dramatic in the county (*Kreis*) to which Laubach belonged, *Kreis Schotten*, where Hitler's party received 77.4 percent of the vote. In all of Germany, only one county had given the Nazis a higher percentage of the vote than Schotten. In the city of Mainz, where Kellner had lived almost his entire life before 1933, the Nazis received 31 percent of the vote in July 1932, lower than the national average and far less than the combined result for the Social Democrats and the Communists.[3] Kellner nevertheless considered the move from Mainz to Laubach to be to his advantage. In his new base in Laubach, he would benefit from the protections accorded by a promotion in his civil service rank. He was also, at first, not known for his anti-Nazi activism in Laubach, as he had been in Mainz, although the local Nazi officials in Laubach would eventually come to regard him as a troublemaker.

In 1938, Laubach was integrated into the county of Giessen. The area bore many of the hallmarks of rural Upper Hesse. The population was overwhelmingly Protestant and drew its livelihood from occupations related to agriculture. Of the 69,000 people in the county (not including the city of Giessen), 55,000 – about 80 percent – lived in towns of 2,000 inhabitants or fewer.[4] One of the most notable conclusions to have been posited by historians who have analyzed the elections of the Weimar Republic is that the Nazis achieved their greatest support in the Protestant countryside, so in this regard the area around Laubach corresponded to a broader pattern. Like in other Nazi strongholds, rural Upper Hesse lacked the two segments of the German population that had been least enthusiastic about Nazism before 1933: the industrial working class and Catholics, whose well-established party loyalties and political subcultures had made these two groups less susceptible to the attraction of Nazism than other segments of German society.[5] The fact that these groups were largely absent from the region accounts for a lower level of resistance to Nazism there after 1933. Had Kellner landed in Berlin or the Ruhr industrial region in 1933 rather than in Laubach, his assessment of his fellow Germans in his diary may well have been less severe.

Kellner's diary begins in late 1939 and therefore tells us relatively little about the actual events of the pre-war years of Nazi rule. But in several entries made during the war, Kellner did summarize in general terms his analysis of the death of German democracy and the rise of the Nazi dictatorship. On October 7, 1939, he described what he regarded as eighteen "cardinal errors" that "this Nazi tyranny" had made since coming to power. These included "the enforced greeting, 'Heil Hitler'"; "one-sided control of public opinion"; "suppressing free expression of opinion"; "protecting the Old Fighters and Party members, even if they are criminals"; "persecuting decent citizens only because they once had another opinion and perhaps referred to the Nazis as an abscess"; "persecution and extermination of the Jews"; "disrespect for people's religious convictions"; "unbelievable over-organization in the nation and, in particular, in the Party and its institutions"; "dreadfully unproductive offices (and a bloated bureaucracy)"; "easy sinecures and benefits for Nazi Party members (minor offices, utensils, uniforms, toys, circus, fanfares: Sieg-Heil, Sieg-Heil)"; "The Führer commands and we follow"; and "we owe everything to our Führer."

Despite these offensive attributes of the regime, the German people, in Kellner's estimation, had supported it enthusiastically. In the very same early entry in the diary, Kellner attempted to explain why: "Too many of my fellow men allowed themselves to be deluded by National Socialist propaganda," which, he believed, amounted to little more than "bluff and swindle; base public fraud." He gave vent to this same exasperation two days later: "What our ancestors had fought to achieve over centuries was forfeited in 1933 by inane carelessness, incomprehensible gullibility, and the damned blasé attitude of the German middle class." Kellner's contempt not only for the immorality of the Nazi leadership, but also for the stupidity (a term he used often) of so many of his countrymen runs as a leitmotif through the diary.

One unusual characteristic of rural Hesse that helps explain the high level of support for Nazism in the region was its significant population of Jews who resided in small towns. These Jewish communities had been there for centuries. Many of the Jews had been "Schutzjuden" who had enjoyed the protection of local rulers during periods when Jews had been expelled from other parts of Germany. By the beginning of the twentieth century, over 400 towns in all regions of Hesse were homes to officially recognized Jewish communities. These included Laubach, which had forty-one Jewish residents (as of 1925) and a seventy-eight-seat synagogue dating from 1780.[6] The level of Jewish integration was lower in such towns than in the major cities. Intermarriage, for example, was a good deal less common than in Berlin or Frankfurt. Many of the small town Jews in Hesse ran small businesses specializing in household goods, clothing, or tools. Others engaged in "middleman" occupations, most notably cattle trade. The complex economic interdependencies between Jewish cattle dealers and their Christian customers had historically been a source of anti-Semitism in the region. In tough economic times, farmers were confronted with the threat of repossession when experiencing difficulty making payments on cattle they had bought on credit. When in the late 1920s, after a severe downturn in the German agricultural economy, the inhabitants of many Hesse towns mobilized to pressure local courts to block repossessions, Jewish cattle dealers were stigmatized as the greedy, unforgiving face of capitalism.[7]

Peasant anti-Semitism had, in fact, long played an important role in the politics of rural Hesse, eventually emerging as an important factor in the success of Nazism there. The region had been a bastion of the peasant movement led by the populist agitator Otto Böckel in the 1880s and 1890s. A librarian and folklorist by training, Böckel analyzed the difficulties faced by farmers as a result of the transformation of German agriculture from a manorial system to modern capitalism. He laid much of the blame for their suffering at the feet of Jewish money lenders, cattle dealers, and grain speculators. He published a virulently anti-Semitic newspaper, the

Reichsherold, and was elected to the Reichstag in 1887 on the platform of "Against Junkers and Jews." A little while later Böckel founded the Hesse-based Antisemitic People's Party (*Antisemitische Volkspartei*), which throughout its existence until 1919 advocated the disenfranchisement of Jews.[8]

One of the political spinoffs of Böckel's movement was the German Social Party, which before World War I enjoyed its highest level of support in the precise area where Laubach was located. During the Weimar period, this particular political tradition was carried forward first by the Hessian Peasant League (*Hessischer Bauernbund*) and then by the Christian National Peasant and Rural People's Party (*Christlich-Nationale Bauern- und Landvolkpartei*). In the Reichstag election of September 1930, the latter party received slightly fewer votes than the NSDAP in Schotten County, where Laubach was located, but by the July 1932 election its supporters had abandoned it for the NSDAP. One can, in other words, identify a direct historical continuity between the anti-Semitic Böckel movement of the late nineteenth century and the rise of the Nazi Party in rural Hesse.[9]

This continuity was underscored by the leader of the Nazi Party organization in southern Hesse – the so-called Gau Hesse-Nassau – Jakob Sprenger, a figure mentioned several times in the Kellner diary.[10] A self-styled champion of German peasants (and the German common man more generally), in 1933 Sprenger co-authored a book titled *The Development of the Völkisch Movement: The Antisemitic Peasant Movement in Hesse from the Time of Böckel until National Socialism*, the purpose of which was to depict Nazism as the logical culmination of the history of his region. Sprenger was without question the dominant political figure in the People's State of Hesse during the Nazi period. As Hitler and the members of the Führer's immediate circle had no personal connections or interests in Hesse, Sprenger was given a free hand in his Gau.[11]

Even by the standards of the Nazi Gauleiter, who were mainly "Old Fighters" from the early days of the party, Sprenger was an ideologically zealous anti-Semite and racist. This fanaticism exhibited itself during the war in ways that provide important background to several observations made by Friedrich Kellner in his diary. One illustration of Sprenger's fanaticism relates to the Hadamar sanatorium, one of the major facilities associated with the killing of disabled Germans, which was located about 80 kilometers west of Laubach. During the war, Hadamar was the site of the murder of about 15,000 disabled Germans.[12] On June 10, 1941, Kellner noted that "notifications about deaths in the mental care facility in Hadamar have recently increased. Supposedly incurable patients are being brought to this institution. And they are soon to begin building a crematorium." Gauleiter Jakob Sprenger had an active interest in the operation at Hadamar, and there is strong evidence to suggest that he personally issued the order to have sick and injured patients killed at Hadamar in order to free up hospital beds in his region during the war.[13]

The deportation of German Jews to the ghettoes and death camps in the east was implemented faster and more thoroughly in Sprenger's Gau than almost anywhere else in the Third Reich. In other regions, some Jews were exempted from deportation in order to be deployed as workers in war-related industries. But Sprenger did his best to prevent this from happening in his own Gau, working hand-in-glove with the local Gestapo to thwart efforts by industrial managers to acquire Jewish workers. Once the deportation of the Jews from Sprenger's Gau had been completed in September 1942 – a measure noted by Kellner in his diary on September 16 – the only Jews who remained were those who had "Aryan" spouses. The Nazi leadership in Berlin had decided to delay the deportation of intermarried Jews, fearing negative effects on the morale of the non-Jewish relatives. But in the autumn of 1942, Sprenger defied Berlin by authorizing deportations of intermarried Jews from his Gau. Only after being admonished by the Reich Security Main Office in Berlin did Sprenger cease the deportations in June 1943. Notably, Sprenger's Gau was the only one in the entire Reich that deported intermarried Jews in a systematic manner.[14]

Friedrich Kellner may not have been aware of the unique character of the anti-Jewish measures in his region, but he did record quite a few entries about the persecution and murder. On three occasions, he referred retrospectively to the November 1938 pogrom (often referred to as Kristallnacht, although not by Kellner). Two of these observations were entered into the diary over three years after the actual event, underscoring the shock and disgust engendered by the pogrom in anti-Nazis such as Kellner. Only a few Jews remained in Laubach by November 1938, the majority having either emigrated abroad or moved to larger communities in Germany in the meantime. Nevertheless, on November 10, a substantial mob vandalized the synagogue, packed the interior furnishings onto the hearse owned by the local Jewish community, transported the hearse to a public square in front of the local sport hall, and set the hearse and furnishings ablaze.[15] Such violent public rituals of anti-Semitic purification were a common feature of the Kristallnacht and help to explain why Kellner's outrage was so enduring.[16] In other entries, Kellner describes the anti-Semitic propaganda efforts of the

Nazi regime, the anti-Semitic sentiments of some of his townspeople, the imposition of forced labor on German Jews, and the deportation of the local Jews.

The ultimate fate of the deported German Jews, and of Jews throughout Nazi-dominated Europe, was clear to Kellner. On October 28, 1941, he wrote the following in his diary:

A soldier on leave here said he personally witnessed a terrible atrocity in the occupied part of Poland. He watched as naked Jewish men and women were placed in front of a long deep ditch and, upon the order of the SS, were shot by Ukrainians in the back of their heads, and they fell into the ditch. Then the ditch was filled in as screams kept coming from it!!

These inhuman atrocities are so terrible that even the Ukrainians who were used for the manual labor suffered nervous breakdowns. All soldiers who had knowledge of these bestial actions of those Nazi subhuman beings were of the same opinion that the German people should already be trembling in their shoes because of the coming retribution.

This entry is significant for two reasons. First, it shows how knowledge of the mass murder of the Jews, which took place mainly in German-occupied eastern Europe, filtered back into German society. Second, it exemplifies a not uncommon reaction among Germans who learned of the killings, namely a combination of disgust, guilt, and certainty that there would be a price to pay for this atrocity. Kellner's diary is not the only evidence we have of knowledge about the "Final Solution" among Germans who lived very far away from the Nazi killing fields in Poland and the Soviet Union.[17]

Kellner was also disturbed by the fate of other targeted groups. He bemoaned the imprisonment and mistreatment of Germans in concentration camps. A number of foreign workers who had been pressed into forced labor by the Third Reich were deployed to locations near Laubach, and Kellner noted the brutal way in which they were treated. He also took note of the so-called "labor and education camp" (*Arbeits- und Erziehungslager*) set up in 1944 in the village of Freienseen, just a couple of kilometers from Laubach. The camp in Freienseen housed mainly foreign laborers who produced fittings for V-1 and V-2 rockets.[18]

Laubach was spared from Allied bombardment on account of its small size and rural location. On August 6, 1940, Kellner wrote, "Hardly anything of war is to be felt locally. Above all, we have not seen or heard air attacks. Enemy fliers flew over Laubach once, but that was not an attack of any sort. The war is not thought of unfavorably here because we have felt little or no effects of it." Kellner often reported on the optimism of his neighbors, who were confident that the British would fold. Even the expansion of the conflict to include the Soviet Union and the United States failed to disabuse them of their delusional confidence in a German victory. Over time, the once distant war was brought home to the residents of Laubach in a variety of ways. Kellner reported on the deaths of German soldiers who had come from Laubach. In August 1941, explosions from British air raids in the region could be heard, and a couple of bombs even fell in the town. On September 1, 1943, "endless columns of enemy airplanes flew over Laubach" on their way to drop bombs on Berlin. In 1944, the male population of Laubach (including Kellner) was drafted into the *Volkssturm*, a people's militia intended to defend the Fatherland against the impending invasion of its territory. After the nearby city of Giessen was bombarded in December 1944, the men of Laubach were ordered to help clean the rubble. In April 1945, homes in Laubach were commandeered by American soldiers. Kellner had no objections to this, but did complain that the homes of the local Nazi bosses had not been targeted for confiscation.

Friedrich Kellner's impassioned dissent translated into acts of actual resistance on a number of occasions, such as when he distributed Allied leaflets, told friends about what he had learned from BBC broadcasts, or discouraged co-workers from joining the Nazi Party.[19] As a low-level civil servant in a small town, he was limited in what he could do. There was little in the way of organized resistance in the vicinity of Laubach. As a former Social Democrat who was known as an anti-Nazi among local Nazi Party officials, Kellner had to exercise extreme caution. As the war progressed, and the country's military situation deteriorated, the regime intensified its crackdown on Germans who criticized the leadership or expressed doubts about the ultimate victory. Although Kellner wrote down his own criticisms and doubts almost every day, he only rarely attributed similar sentiments to others. In part this may have been to protect his friends and acquaintances from retribution were his diary to fall into the hands of the Gestapo, which he understood was a genuine possibility.

While there can be no doubt that the Nazi regime enjoyed overwhelming popularity among the German population, the support was not universal. Kellner, living as he did in a stronghold of Nazism, and understandably furious with the obtuseness of his countrymen, overlooked the limited, but real, dissatisfaction in the country. The Reich Security Service (SD) compiled substantial documentation of popular discontent with the behavior of party bosses, the prosecution of the war, and the mendacity of official propaganda.[20] Such dissatisfaction rarely translated into active opposition, much less organized resistance, because people feared for their own safety and that of their loved ones in the face of a ruthless apparatus of repression, especially during the war years. A small percentage of Germans did, nonetheless, engage in organized opposition activity, which often took the form of printing and distributing leaflets, or providing assistance to victims of persecution. Opposition groups drew their members from the Communist Party, the Social Democratic Party, and the labor unions, all of which had been outlawed by the regime in 1933, and from church circles. The Rhine-Main area centered on Frankfurt was an important center of labor-oriented opposition on account of its highly developed industrial economy.[21] That region, in addition to other locations in Gau Hesse-Nassau, including the city of Giessen, were bases for Social Democratic cells loosely organized under the leadership of Wilhelm Leuschner, a former interior minister in Weimar-era Hesse who acted as a liaison between the Social Democratic opposition and the military-aristocratic conspiracy to kill Hitler. After the failed July 20, 1944 assassination attempt, Leuschner was arrested, tried before the People's Court, and executed. The members of the cells in his organization had focused their efforts on helping to form a new government in Germany after Hitler's removal.[22]

Critics and opponents of the Nazi regime in Hesse frequently paid a high price for their dissent or opposition. Between November 1938 and 1945, sixty-nine men and women from Hesse were sentenced to death by the People's Court for treason and other political offences. Some among the executed had been involved in organized opposition activity, while others had simply publicly expressed the kinds of criticism that Kellner had committed to his diary and shared with his friends.[23] It should be emphasized that prosecutions for such transgressions were not limited to the People's Court. Lower courts handled similar cases. A so-called Special Court in Darmstadt, which only adjudicated cases from Hesse, presided over the prosecutions for political crimes of 2,316 defendants between 1933 and 1944. Most of the trials did not result in executions, but time in a concentration camp or a Nazi-era prison certainly qualified as a harsh punishment.[24] The opponents of the regime also included those who were arrested and sent to concentration camps without prosecution or trial, as well as those who were never arrested, like Friedrich Kellner himself.

German citizens had good reason to fear the consequences of opposing the regime, but some did so anyway, despite the risks. While Friedrich Kellner's harsh blanket condemnations of his countrymen may have been unfair to the others who, like him, dissented and resisted, his righteous anger at his countrymen was most definitely well founded.

Alan E. Steinweis

PREFACE

The long effort to bring my grandfather's diary to the public was rewarded by the reception it received when published in Germany in 2011. "Eine grosse Entdeckung" was the general view: "A major discovery." The reviewer in *Der Spiegel* wrote, "Kellner fashioned an image of Nazi Germany that has never existed before in such a vivid, concise and challenging form," and added, "the diary belongs in every German library and on every bookshelf possible." The history magazine *Damals* named it Autobiography of the Year.[1] A major facet for German readers of this anti-Nazi diary was the conclusion it brought to many decades of controversy. If an ordinary person such as Friedrich Kellner, a mid-level official with a high school education, living in a small country town far from any major city, could know so much about what was happening in the supposedly secretive Third Reich, then people everywhere had to have known far more than they admitted of the brutality and genocide waged by their forces in every precinct of a ravaged Europe. The post-war meme that the general population knew little or nothing of what the Nazi Party was up to (suggested as late as 2005 by former German president Richard von Weizsäcker) could finally be laid to rest.[2]

Friedrich Kellner predicted the people would lie about it if they lost the war: "All of the small-minded people will say they always knew National Socialism would end in this manner and that none of them had ever been a National Socialist. In reality, only one percent of Germans at most were true opponents of Hitlerism."[3] His notes show that soldiers returning from the front were speaking openly about massacres they had witnessed of Jews and of Russian prisoners of war. From the beginning he knew Jews were facing genocide. Just one month after German forces invaded Poland, he alluded to the "Verfolgung und Ausrottung der Juden," persecution and extermination of Jews.[4]

He also documented atrocities within the homeland: the murder of patients in mental hospitals, and the executions of Germans who listened to foreign radio programs or read airplane leaflets. He described these dreadful events in the context of past and future, the mistakes made in the Weimar Republic that elevated a depraved Adolf Hitler to power, and the miscalculations of leaders in the democratic nations that abetted the dictator in his drive for world mastery. Friedrich wrote for the entire period of war, filling ten notebooks, almost nine hundred pages, with his meticulous script, supplementing his observations with hundreds of newspaper clippings. Had he been discovered, he would have been branded a traitor and executed. His wife, Pauline, whose own moral integrity reinforced Friedrich's determination to give a true accounting of events, would have shared his fate.

I learned about the diary when I was nineteen years old, in 1960, the year I met Friedrich and Pauline. Their only child was my father. They had sent him to America in 1935, when he was nineteen, to clear his mind of Nazi doctrine, a move that unfortunately had no effect. My mother, who married Fred William Kellner two years after his arrival in New York, spoke of him only as "that Nazi bastard."[5] Although Freda Schulman, according to Nazi racial theories, was a "subhuman" on two counts – a Jew and of Slavic origin – such odious invective could not compete with the young woman's compelling good looks, and the troubled German immigrant fell in love. They had three children in four years, who, at his insistence, were baptized Lutheran. Disinclined to work, Fred hung out with his friends from the German-American Bund, distributing pro-Nazi pamphlets. In April 1943 the Federal Bureau of Investigation opened a case against him to determine if he was spying for Germany. Fred had gone to Norfolk, Virginia, where it was thought he was seeking information about ship movements.[6] The evidence, presented in November 1943 to the US Attorney's Office, was inconclusive and unlikely to lead to a trial, yet Fred prudently took the FBI's unofficial advice to join the US Army to prove his loyalty to his adopted country. One week after the army accepted him, the FBI case was shelved. For most of his enlistment, Fred was stateside, but in February 1945, after being busted in rank to private for some unspecified misconduct, he was shipped to France to serve as an MP, guarding captured Germans in an Allied prisoner-of-war camp. Honorably discharged in January 1946, Fred remained in Europe using the forged credentials of an officer in the Occupation Forces to support himself in the black market.

When the monthly allotment checks stopped arriving from the army in 1946, Freda rejected the prospect of moving in with her parents and working as a waitress or sales clerk to pay for expenses. It was an era of lavish MGM and RKO musicals, of beautiful leggy women filling the screens of movie theaters, and she had long-held notions of becoming another Ginger Rogers or Cyd Charisse. Opportunities for a twenty-seven-year-old mother of three, however, with no dancing experience, were found mostly in tawdry venues. Applying to the World of Mirth Carnival, which followed a circuit from Maine to Georgia and was known for its hoochie-coochie "girlie shows," Freda took her three children to the Jewish Home for Children in New Haven, Connecticut, and left them there. I was four years old. My sister was seven, my brother six.

We were in the Home for seven years, a long stretch under a troubled superintendent. "For the least small infraction of the rules, a kid was usually severely beaten," recounted a former inhabitant in his memoirs.[7] We infrequently saw our mother. Our father came only once with a promise to bring us "home" to his parents in Germany, but we never saw him again. In time the Connecticut welfare department shut down such privately run homes, and we were back with our mother and her new husband, a carnival roustabout, in 1953, the year we learned of my father's death. The cold facts in the death certificate were numbing: in 1951 Fred had re-enlisted in the US Army in Germany; in 1952 he went AWOL and was declared a deserter; in 1953 he committed suicide in France.[8]

I was a wild youth with a juvenile record. I dropped out of high school at sixteen and ended up homeless on the streets of New York. At seventeen I was in the navy. Military service was salvation for boys like me, and I earned a high school equivalency degree and rose in the ranks to second-class petty officer. In 1960 orders came for special shore duty in Ras Tanura, Saudi Arabia. The travel plans included a two-day layover at Frankfurt Air Force base in Germany. My father's death had not affected me, yet I felt a need to know about him, to meet his parents – if they were still alive. I applied for leave but was refused, so upon arriving in Frankfurt I went AWOL. I knew from my mother that Friedrich and Pauline Kellner lived in a town named Laubach, where my grandfather worked in the courthouse, but there were six towns in Germany with that name. In a train station near the fourth Laubach, while worrying I had overlooked my grandparents in the previous three, I met a young woman and told her of my search. She was on her way to visit her parents in Laubach, she said, where an old couple named Kellner lived just around the corner.

I could not have imagined them any better – my tall grandfather and petite grandmother, both with gray hair, and with some lines of sadness engraved on their faces. He was seventy-five, and she seventy-two, and they held themselves with such dignified reserve it made me stand straighter. I braced for disappointment as I took from my wallet a photograph of my father holding his infant daughter, my sister, on his knee (one of the few pictures of him my mother had not destroyed). The old woman sighed, and in moments I was looking in their album at an enlarged copy of that photograph. Then my grandparents excitedly turned the pages in the album, pointing from one photo to another. I could not understand their words, but I knew they were introducing me to my family.

I stayed with them for four days in their small retirement cottage on a wooded hill. My grandfather knew some English, and I began my German studies. The first evening, after dinner, he covered the dining table with a series of notebooks that held hundreds of pages handwritten in a cryptic Old German script with newspaper clippings pasted among his writing. He explained it was a diary he had written during the war when he was the court administrator. He pointed to the title, *Mein Widerstand* (My Opposition) and my relief was great; for months, since receiving my transfer orders, I had been preparing myself to forgive my grandfather, if I should find him, for a myriad of Nazi crimes I assumed he must have committed.

One of the first entries my grandparents helped me read described a letter-telegram from my mother, sent through the Red Cross, telling them of my birth. They asked me numerous questions and learned some of the truth of what happened with their son in America. They were grieved to hear about the children's home, having been told by my father that Freda had run off with another man and we children were happy. Another surprise was their son's deception about my mother's religion, that she was not a German-American Lutheran. Speaking more to my grandmother than to me, my grandfather said slowly, so I could understand, "At least in this he acted well, letting love rule over prejudice."

They each elicited a promise from me before I returned to Frankfurt. My grandfather wanted me to go to college and study history and German so I could return for the diary someday and use it to counter totalitarian ideologies – at that time Communism and neo-Nazism. My grandmother wanted me to devote some time to helping children because I had needed help as a child. "We must pay our debts to society," she insisted. I wanted to please them, and so I agreed, though I had no idea how it would be achieved.

I was placed under arrest at Frankfurt until I could be put on the next flight to the navy liaison office on Bahrain Island. I was so overdue in Arabia there was no time even for a captain's mast, and the Bahrain commander made do with a tongue-lashing and sent me on my way. My unauthorized sojourn went unpunished.

We wrote frequently to each other, my grandparents and I. My brother and sister also wrote but stopped after a few letters, preferring to keep the past behind them. After the navy, I had ambitious college plans: four years of undergraduate study and six years in graduate school. They were delayed, however, by an early marriage that produced a bright and spirited little girl but did not succeed otherwise, ending in divorce. During this period my grandparents moved to Mainz to be closer to my grandmother's sisters. In July 1966 my grandfather shared with me a letter that held deep meaning for him: the German government acknowledged his open stance against the Nazis.[9] When I received the letter, I was enrolled at the University of Massachusetts. I planned to spend a summer in Germany when I graduated, to study the diary with my grandfather, and bring the notebooks home with me. But at the end of my junior year I received an urgent summons from him. Concerned that I would have difficulty deciphering the old-style script, he had given Notebook 1 and the pre-war writings to my grandmother's sister Katie to type into modern German. The papers disappeared from her apartment, where Katie lived with her common-law husband, Willi Weber, a former and unrepentant Nazi soldier. Though Weber denied taking them, my grandfather knew the rest of the diary was no longer safe.

Despite their stress over the missing papers, our reunion in the summer of 1968 was joyful. Friedrich, with his stately and yet good-natured manner, was unbowed even at eighty-three. Pauline looked frail but was charming and energetic. My college courses had enlarged my German vocabulary, and though my grammar was shaky it was fun to talk with them. Our readings in the diary during the five weeks of my stay gave rise to fascinating stories about the people and places that had shaped their perilous existence in the Third Reich. My grandfather described the contents of the missing notebook and dictated to me from memory the sentences that began the first entry, that of September 1, 1939.[10]

My grandmother's sisters, Katie and Lina, came often to visit, bringing pastries for our family breakfasts and dinners. Katie apologized for the notebook's loss. Lina apologized, too, because Willi Weber was related to her husband, Heinrich Fahrbach. I met Weber – a sullen block of a man. At my grandfather's caution I said nothing about the diary. Regarding Heinrich Fahrbach, my grandfather showed me an entry describing Heinrich and Lina's narrow escape during the bombing of Mainz in September 1941. He showed me a photograph he had taken of their bombed apartment building and told me how Heinrich had wanted to destroy all of London in retaliation.

My grandfather tapped me on the shoulder and in a somber tone added, "His nephew Willi would destroy London today."

Visitors arrived from Laubach for an afternoon: Ludwig and Elfrieda Heck and their two daughters. Ludwig had worked for my grandfather in the courthouse and was like a son to my grandparents. But like their real son, Heck had been inspired by the Nazi doctrine, an ardent believer from his membership in the Hitler Youth to his frontline service in a panzer corps. In a 1942 entry about Heck being home on leave for Christmas, my grandfather noted his protégé's "arrogant" insistence that the Nazis were invincible.

I learned much about the various branches of my family: the Kellners in Arnstadt, the Vaigles in Bissingen, and the Preusses in Mainz. I learned of my grandfather's political campaigns during the Weimar Republic and my father's susceptibility to the poisonous lure of National Socialism. I saw post-war photographs of Fred with his second wife, whom he had met in France in 1945, and my half-sister, Margrit, who was twenty-one and living near Versailles. Having embraced the counter-culture movement that marked the 1960s, Margrit was no longer in touch with her family, and my grandfather gave me her address and asked me to write to her when I was home.

One afternoon when my grandmother lay down for a nap, my grandfather – better able to handle his own emotions when he did not have to see my grandmother in distress – told me more about my father, mostly about happier moments from his childhood. He described his and my grandmother's deep depression in the years after my father's death and how he had thrown away his collection of Nazi documents and even considered destroying the diary. He added, almost nonchalantly, that my appearance in Laubach in October 1960 had saved more than the diary from destruction. Several months earlier he had resigned from political office, and he and my grandmother, thinking there was nothing and no one left to live for, had planned to end their own lives before Christmas.[11]

I took countless notes during our conversations, writing sometimes in German but mostly in English, always in an abbreviated form because everyone spoke rapidly. Although my vocabulary increased daily, I was not able to keep up with everything fully, so each evening in my room, I would spend an hour or more working on my notes, making a list of questions to ask everyone the next day. With list in hand, my entrance at breakfast always got a laugh.

We did not spend all our time studying the diary and talking about the past. We took a trip on the Rhine to see the Lorelei; had a picnic in the

Lenneberg Forest with my cousin Erwin Ganglberger and his family; went to Bad Münster for lunch with some friends; visited cousins in Frankfurt; and one evening we attended a musical at the Mainz Electoral Palace. I marveled at my grandparents' stamina. But they did need to rest. They sent me to spend a day and night in Laubach and gave me a list of people to meet. There I spoke with my grandfather's former employee, court bailiff Ludwig Brunner, and a number of others from that generation soon to take their memories with them to the grave. They praised my grandparents' courage during the war and my grandfather's political work afterward.

On July 31 my grandfather placed the nine remaining diary notebooks and other writings and documents inside a handbag for me to carry on the airplane. "This was my resistance to terror and lawlessness," he reminded me, "my way to give your generation – and generations to come – a weapon of truth against any repeat of such terror." I promised to find a way to get the diary to the public. I also renewed my promise to my grandmother to help children.

Back home I wrote to Margrit in France and was pleased when she quickly replied. But when I asked for information about our father, and any photographs she could provide – and I mentioned my hope she would write to our grandparents – she did not respond. I wrote several more times but never heard from her again.

Two months after I left Mainz, my grandmother fell and broke her hip. A long stay in the hospital was followed by a challenging period of recovery that required most of her strength – and my grandfather's strength, too. "She slowly has to learn to walk again," he wrote to me on December 15, 1968. "She links her arm with mine, and with a cane in hand she makes progress." To which he added, "We miss your young arms." She was not able to fully recover, and a year later my grandfather sent heartrending news. "Your gentle grandmother is dying," he wrote. "Despite every effort, her physical and mental condition has lately become mercilessly bad. Can you believe such a marvelous woman must meet such an undeserved end?"

My grandfather was at her bedside during the day and on an adjacent cot during the fitful nights when even morphine could not stifle the pain for long. In the last week of Pauline Kellner's life, Friedrich turned once more to pen and paper to record their final days together. On February 1, she had the presence of mind to wish him a happy birthday: he was eighty-five. Three days later the pain was so bad she begged him to release her. Later that day, when she was calmer, she reached out for his hand. Her eyes "shone again with the same brilliance as when I first fell in love with her. In this moment she was saying farewell." On February 8, 1970, Friedrich wrote this melancholy sentence: "On Carnival-Sunday in 1910 we first met each other, and on Carnival-Sunday in 1970 death has parted us." Karolina Paulina Preuss Kellner, who had stood with her husband during those fearful days of Nazi rule and faced his every risk, had died at eighty-two. Her most fitting epithet would be something Friedrich wrote about her refusal to join the Nazi Women's League: "A monument should be erected to my brave wife."

A macabre irony exists in Germany's *Lebensraum* dilemma. They gained not an inch of territory in their murderous quest for it, but they caused their neighbors to use otherwise good farmland for tens of millions of new graves. Because of space limitations, Germans may not own the plot they are buried in; they pay annual rent on it, and only for a limited time. Unless their graves are considered special, their bones eventually are *abgeräumt* – dug up for reburial in a communal grave – and someone else picks up the lease on their old place. After paying the rent for over forty years on his parents' graves, and knowing their bones would be *abgeräumt* after he and Pauline died, Friedrich had the Mainz cemetery move the large natural stone that marked their graves to the plot he had rented for Pauline and himself. Beneath that stone he placed her ashes.

He returned then to Laubach where Pauline and he had faced down so many challenges, where he best could feel her presence.

On June 22, 1970, I introduced my wife, Bev, to my grandfather. She and I had met in college and graduated together. My grandfather was living in an apartment building close to the Laubach courthouse. He looked his years and, for the first time, vulnerable. He and I acutely felt my grandmother's absence, but he was charmed by Bev: petite, dark-haired, and lovely, like his memory of a young Pauline. I gave him a copy of a letter from the University of Massachusetts accepting me into their doctoral program. He insisted on a champagne toast, and we went to the restaurant at our hotel where he took a few drops of wine mixed in a glass of water. "*Wasserwein*," he laughingly called it, and raised his glass: "The first white-collar worker of our family salutes the first professional." And to Bev: "His Oma and I knew this would come to pass."

We took my grandfather for drives into the country. We visited my cousin Erwin Ganglberger and went to dinner at Ludwig Heck's house. I had many questions for my grandfather about people and places in diary entries, and he seemed happiest when speaking. He went from one subject to the next, not bound by chronology. When he described his political activities in the Social Democratic Party and his campaigns against the Communists and Nazis, he took a book from the table and, as he used to do with Hitler's *Mein Kampf*, shook it angrily above his head and called out, "Gutenberg, your press has been violated by this evil book!" Bev worried about him becoming overly impassioned, as did I. But these were not an old man's ravings. My grandfather's travails in the midst of a destroyed Europe had shattered his religious beliefs. To him, death was final, with no comforting tomorrows in heaven. All that would be left of Friedrich Kellner were his ashes – and his grandson. Therefore, he was transferring into his grandson's mind as many of his memories as possible, and he fully expected me to pass them on with his diary.

He was not feeling well on our last day together but insisted on talking about the diary's purpose and its relevance to current events. He complained about the Soviet Union increasing its support for Palestinian militants, who that year had brought their terrorism to Germany, attacking Israeli passengers at the Munich airport. He called the connection between atheist Russia and jihadist Islam "an unholy alliance of totalitarian fanatics" that would seriously challenge the democracies in the future.

Our parting was agony. Despite the brave pretense of our *Auf Wiedersehen*, we knew we would never see each other again. Bev and I had traveled by ship to Europe, and during the five-day voyage home to New York, I had much to think about. My father had made the same voyage to the same destination in 1935. What if he had been wiser and not gone so far adrift into troubled waters and not caused such unending grief? And what if wiser men had ruled the democracies in his time and given no ground to evil? That question was the very essence of the diary.

I received a few more of my grandfather's beautifully penned letters, but in less than three months after our goodbyes he was gone. November 4, 1970, was the last day of life for Justice Inspector August Friedrich Kellner: soldier, administrator, poet, politician, and historian. In the darkest time of Germany's history, when madmen and murderers ruled, this man did not lose sight of all that was great in centuries of German culture. He carried that within him. He passed that on. He was one of Germany's truest patriots.

Ludwig Heck, the executor of my grandfather's will, arranged for the cremation, and for the ashes to be placed alongside Pauline's in the Mainz Hauptfriedhof. A small amount of money, ten thousand dollars, was divided equally among the four grandchildren. Most of the other possessions were for me: all his papers and the family documents, and his oil paintings. And though I already had the diary notebooks in my possession, they were specifically listed for me in his will. Heck sent the money within the first year, but despite my repeated requests, he delayed for many years sending anything else. After six years a wooden crate of documents and belongings arrived with a note from Heck: "It is a comfort for me to know I have fulfilled your grandfather's wish and the family belongings are in good hands."[12] But Friedrich Kellner's wish had not been fulfilled, which I would discover thirty years later.

Further attempts to contact my half-sister in France were unsuccessful. I eventually would learn that on April 12, 1970 – between the deaths of our grandparents that year – Margrit gave birth to a son out of wedlock and named him Alexandre William Kellner. Giving her child over to foster care, she moved to the Montparnasse area on the left bank of the Seine, where, among its artist colonies and unrestrained nightlife, she would live but five more years. The specifics of her death in the certificate sent to me from Paris were few but profoundly sad: On the Sunday morning of December 21, 1975, Margrit's lifeless body was found on a street not far from her apartment. She had died six or seven hours earlier, around 2 a.m., evidently of exposure to the freezing night air. She was twenty-eight.

Promises to Keep

The diary project, which included supplemental essays, documents relating to Friedrich's resistance, and family histories, was daunting: thousands of pages of handwritten Sütterlin script had to be transcribed into modern German; research was needed for the people, places, and events in the diary; and the source of each news clipping had to be determined. Moreover, I would need to create a biographical narrative to provide the vital context, the tragedies and triumphs of Friedrich and Pauline Kellner's lives. Friedrich had deliberately left out personal matters from his diary in order to focus on the important issues.

Easier to fulfill was the promise I made to my grandmother. While teaching at Texas A&M University, I formed a student club to sponsor an entire village of children through the Christian Children's Fund. The actress Sally Struthers, spokesperson for the Fund, came to the campus to help get the "Village of Hope" campaign started.[13] Thousands of students participated in the fundraising and sponsored 125 children in a village near Amaga, Colombia, for a two-year period. News stories in the *Houston Chronicle* and elsewhere about our efforts inspired other American universities to lead similar campaigns, and I could imagine Pauline Kellner's nod of approval.

Eventually I was able to persuade the editor of the *Chronicle* to take an interest in the diary. On February 21, 1993, the newspaper published a four-page feature article in its Sunday magazine, replete with photographs of diary pages and of my grandparents. The headline declared the diary "may have parallels for today's Germany." I sent copies to the newly built United States Holocaust Memorial Museum in Washington, DC, and to Yad Vashem in Jerusalem. With anti-Semitism and Holocaust denial on the rise, I felt certain these institutions would help me transcribe the diary and get it published. The museum archivists, keen to add the diary to their collections, responded quickly but offered no guarantee to publish it.

I sent the article to the movie actor and producer, Kirk Douglas, asking if he would produce a documentary about it. "I agree with you – the content of these diaries should be revealed to the world," he wrote in his positive response of April 2, 1993. But in concert with Michael Berenbaum, a director of the Holocaust Museum in Washington, Mr. Douglas pressured me to give the diary to the museum. On April 21 he wrote, "I would continue my interest in this diary when it goes to Washington." I was tempted. It seemed an honorable way to be relieved of a heavy responsibility: to give it into the care of an important institution and a legendary personality. But the museum had already turned down my request to publish the diary, and Hollywood producers often sat on scripts and projects for years, only to abandon them. As it happened, Mr. Douglas suffered a stroke and had to drastically reduce his workload. Had I agreed to his terms, Friedrich Kellner's writings, his warnings to the generations, might have been consigned to oblivion among the tens of thousands of other unpublished documents in the museum's archives.

In 2001, on September 11, America was brutally reminded of Pearl Harbor. I spurred my efforts to finish my transcriptions and collect the information I needed for the biography. My father's army records arrived with an explanation that numerous documents had been damaged or destroyed in a major fire at the National Personnel Records Center in St. Louis in 1973.[14] What remained of my father's file (with the burned edges visible in the photocopies) gave evidence to his duplicity and wrongdoing: being reduced in rank from sergeant to private, stealing from his comrades, deserting his post. The twenty-page FBI report was particularly helpful as it detailed his movements in America from 1935 until 1943. For oral histories, I located Ursula Cronberger, the young woman from the train station in 1960 who had led me to my grandparents, and Else Gross, the Laubach courthouse maid, who knew my grandparents well; she was living in Baltimore. In San Diego lived John Peter Abt, whom my grandparents had helped when he was nine months old, along with his parents, to safely leave Germany. I renewed correspondence with Ludwig Heck and others in Laubach; and I wrote to Vaigle, Preuss, and Kellner cousins in Germany, Switzerland, and Sweden. The compact biographical narrative I had anticipated grew in scope.

The difficulties of getting the diary into print were not overcome until I sent my narrative and numerous pages of transcriptions to an American leader who had piloted combat aircraft in World War II, and who, as president of the United States fifty years later, forged a worldwide military coalition to restore sovereignty to Kuwait. George H.W. Bush realized the perceptive observations in the diary needed to be brought to the public. In April and May 2005, Friedrich Kellner's diary and assorted memorabilia were on display in the rotunda of the George Bush Presidential Library and Museum in College Station, Texas, to commemorate the sixtieth anniversary of V-E Day, Victory in Europe.

News stories about the exhibit led to a collaboration with the Holocaust Literature group at Giessen University to complete the transcription into modern German, do the necessary research, and obtain funding for publication. At my suggestion, members of the group sought an oral history from eighty-five-year-old Ludwig Heck, executor of my grandfather's will. During the interview Heck revealed he had the missing diary notebook and a few pre-war essays, saying he had received them from my grandfather shortly before he died. He had no explanation for the many questions that arose: who returned the stolen items in those final days of my grandfather's life when he was too ill to communicate with me; what happened to the bulk of the pre-war essays and the missing pages from the notebook; why were the papers not sent to me immediately in 1970, or at least in 1976 after the six-year delay in getting the other material to me – or sent to me any time during the following decades; and why was there no mention of the notebook and essays in the highly detailed nine-page inventory Heck had made of my grandfather's effects, an inventory verified and countersigned by Erwin Ganglberger (my aunt Katie's son, and therefore stepson of her partner, Willi Weber, who had stolen the papers)?

Well acquainted with each other, Heck, Ganglberger, and Weber had been comrades in arms in the Wehrmacht and could not have been happy with Friedrich Kellner's depiction of the army's depredations. But whatever the circumstances for the long delay in the documents' return, I am chastened by my father's similar allegiance to the Nazi banner. The diary now is mostly whole, and there is wisdom in the old adage, "Be grateful for what you have."

Other exhibits followed the one in the Bush Library, including seven months at the Dwight D. Eisenhower Presidential Library in Abilene, Kansas. A film company in Toronto made a documentary for Canadian television, which was given a special screening in the Hammarskjöld Auditorium at United Nations Headquarters in New York to commemorate the seventieth anniversary of Kristallnacht.[15] Exhibits of the original notebooks in Berlin and Bonn preceded the complete diary's publication in Germany in two volumes. Abridged translations were published in Poland and Russia.

The diary's reception in its homeland can be measured by honors awarded the Kellners. In Mainz, where Friedrich had campaigned against the Nazis, his and Pauline's burial site in the Hauptfriedhof bears the status of *Ehrengrab*, Grave of Honor – never to be *abgeräumt*.[16] In Laubach, students on their way to school each day pass by the Kellners' small retirement home. Their school and the cottage have a new address: Friedrich-Kellner-Strasse.[17]

Although the diary comes to us belatedly, it does so at a critical time. Friedrich Kellner had presented *Mein Kampf* to his contemporaries as an example of the very worst in human thinking. We now have Friedrich Kellner's own book, and the example of his life, to challenge those in our century who would disturb the world's peace. Readers of the diary will have no difficulty seeing the similarities between Friedrich's world and our own. And with Friedrich they will wonder with alarm why the pillars of civilization are so meager they can be pulled down by brutes.

BIOGRAPHICAL NARRATIVE

Early Years

In an apartment above Georg Kellner's pastry shop in Vaihingen-an-der-Enz in southern Germany, Georg's wife, Wilhelmine, gave birth to their son. It was February 1, 1885. The father, born out of wedlock twenty-two years earlier in Arnstadt, Thuringia, conferred an overdue legitimacy upon his family line by naming his son August Friedrich, after his mother's lover, August Friedrich Schonert, the man who had sired him. In the next three years, Wilhelmine – from the large Vaigle family in nearby Bissingen – bore two more children, but neither survived infancy.[1]

When their son was four, the Kellners moved to Mainz, "City of Gutenberg," where Georg was employed as a master baker. Young Friedrich was educated in a breathtaking era of human ingenuity that brought radios, telephones, electric lighting, phonographs, movies, automobiles, and airplanes into everyday lives. He was an outgoing child, bright in his studies, particularly math, and talented in music and art. Sensible to his parents' wishes, he agreed to a career that would make him the first white-collar worker in the family. He attended public elementary school and vocational high school, and when he turned eighteen in 1903, Friedrich began a three-year unpaid apprenticeship as an office clerk in the Mainz courthouse. His immediate goal was to become a justice inspector (*Justizinspektor*), a supervisor of law records and court accounting, including registrar duties. His greater hope was someday to become an administrative manager of a courthouse.

An added benefit for employees in the bureaucracy of Wilhelm II's German Empire was a more flexible military requirement: one year of active duty, with occasional training over the next six years. Friedrich began his full year in October 1907 when he was twenty-two. Lucky to have missed the Reich's participation in China's Boxer Rebellion and the brutal skirmishes in Wilhelm's colonial territories in southwest Africa, the young man safely marched and drilled with his regiment, practiced shooting, and hit the bull's-eye often enough to earn a marksman's lanyard for his jacket.

At a Carnival-Fastnacht party in 1910, Friedrich was introduced to the woman he would marry, a petite young lady he had seen for the first time a few days earlier skating on a pond. Energetic and independent, Karolina Paulina "Pauline" Preuss was three years younger than her admirer. Her father, Karl Preuss, was a tinsmith; her mother, Johanna née Martin, was a robust woman who raised seven children amid the grueling chores of the German housewife.[2] Pauline graduated from vocational high school and was employed as an office clerk at Schöfferhof Brewery. After a year of courtship, Pauline and her office mates drew Friedrich with them to Frankfurt for the first International Women's Day, where he wisely cheered in support of women's suffrage. On the train back to Mainz they became engaged. They were married on January 18, 1913, one day before Pauline's twenty-fifth birthday and two weeks before Friedrich would turn twenty-eight. He still was intent on becoming a justice inspector, and she would keep working at Schöfferhof for two more years before starting a family.

War and Politics

On August 4, 1914, called from his desk at the courthouse to be with his army reserve unit, Sergeant Friedrich Kellner mustered with Prince Carl Infantry Regiment, No. 118, to march into a war that would embroil much of the world. Helpless to intervene in the unfolding events, a stoic Pauline comforted her in-laws and her parents. Her brothers Franz and Ludwig had also been drafted.

There was some solace in the hope this would be "the war to end all wars," but Friedrich was not beguiled by the slogans or the municipal bands and cheering crowds gathered to see them off. He had reason not to be. A page in his military passbook, with the handwritten heading "Battles Participated In," soon would have the names of towns where deadly engagements had played out. His marksman's lanyard had become a hangman's noose; his shooting skills put him at the front of every fight.

His first action was at Neufchâteau on August 22. By mid-September he had survived eight battles, including the series of fights known as the First Battle of the Marne, where the French and British put an end to the German advance on Paris. He experienced the humiliation of retreat, but instead of maneuvering homeward, the Prince Carl Infantry Regiment headed into northwest France.[3]

For two months Friedrich lived in muddy sand-bagged trenches in the area west of Reims, dreading the futile daytime charges and the eerie nighttime crawls through barbed wire to toss hand grenades into enemy dens while earth and air shook with the thunder of artillery. He questioned the High Command's inept strategy and the Kaiser's ruinous quest for glory – and even the concept of monarchical rule. He saw no sense in a German soldier shedding blood in France because a Serbian killed an Austrian in Bosnia. He would readily take a stand at the Reich's borders, protecting home and country with his life. But the men protecting their country in this instance were those he was firing upon and killing. Try as he might, he could not square his actions with the simple tenet, "Treat others the same way you want them to treat you."

In November Friedrich was struck by shrapnel from a bursting shell and became one of the 4 million German men wounded in that war; 2 million would be killed. Packed into an overloaded train soaked with the blood of groaning soldiers, the pain in Friedrich's torn leg, and the likelihood it might fester and have to be amputated, brought a temporary halt to his philosophical musings.

Recovery took place in Mainz's St. Rochus Hospital. By spring he was fit for the front lines but instead was assigned to quartermaster headquarters in Frankfurt, where he had a broad picture of warfare and its ruinous costs. Close to Mainz, he could be with Pauline often. On February 29, 1916, as an affirmation of life amid the pestilence of war, their only child was born in their Mainz apartment on Mosel Street, a few blocks from the Rhine River. They named him Karl Friedrich Wilhelm and called him Fritz.

Whether it was the singularity of being a Leap Year's Day child that cast a shadow on this newborn, or the general state of nihilism that gripped the world during the first half of the twentieth century – or a hedonistic gene passed down from his great-grandmother who had brought Georg illegitimately into the world – Karl Friedrich Wilhelm Kellner would seldom know happiness in his adult life and never become inured to the absence of it. Friedrich and Pauline had not the slightest foreboding of the ineffable sorrow tiny Fritz eventually would bring them.

Heroic posters and popular jingles were not enough to maintain enthusiasm for a losing war. The reduced bread rations and growing casualty lists affected almost every family. Pauline's youngest brother, Ludwig, was missing in action, later declared dead. In 1907 Friedrich had posed for a photograph with the men in his reserve squad, each man holding a glass of beer, proud and content. No such élan is seen in the 1917 photograph of Friedrich with the staff at quartermaster headquarters. What Friedrich intuitively had understood in August 1914 about the realities of war was now plainly visible on the dour faces of his comrades. The old German order was fast approaching its end.

For Friedrich and Pauline the Weimar Constitution was exhilarating, giving her the right to vote and inspiring him to participate in the newly created Republic's self-governance. He joined the Social Democratic Party (SPD) in 1920 and became a local organizer to increase party membership.[4] In April he was promoted to justice inspector, a major step toward his goal of courthouse administrator. And in that year he and Pauline formally withdrew from the Lutheran Evangelical Church "because it and a great many of their ministers behaved un-Christianly" by siding with the military in continuing a lost war instead of surrendering and saving lives.[5]

Friedrich handed out SPD leaflets and addressed crowds at Schiller Square and in the marketplace at St. Martin's Cathedral. Extremists on both ends of the political spectrum harassed speakers like Friedrich and stoked anger about the Versailles Treaty's heavy reparations. The collapse of Germany's currency in early 1923 threatened the government's downfall, but the economy improved as 1924 approached. The nation's renewed optimism confounded the plans of an ambitious politician who tried to take over the Munich government by force. The would-be usurper's putsch failed, but his subsequent courtroom theatrics were closely followed in the press, and Adolf Hitler emerged after a year in prison with popularity, rich patrons, and a manuscript outlining a master Aryan race whose master nation would eject Jews and Slavs and confiscate the lands and resources of its neighbors.

In the summer of 1925 Friedrich's father gave him a recently published book that held a harsh prescription for forging a true German nationality through the ruthless extermination of its enemies – including Germans who would not conform.[6] Georg encouraged his son to take a stand against its author. At his rallies after that, Friedrich would hold aloft *Mein Kampf* and cry out, "Gutenberg, your printing press has been violated by this evil book!"[7] His scorn for Adolf Hitler raised the ire of the Nazi Party's paramilitary "stormtroopers," but Friedrich held his ground against them, having contended with worse in Belgium and France.

As Georg's and Wilhelmine's health began to decline, they spent more time with their grandson, Fritz, encouraging him to take his studies seriously. The child possessed a quick mind and excellent memory, but he put forth minimal effort, passing tests with what he recalled of classroom lessons. He considered homework an intrusion on his playtime and required prompting and scolding to get it done. "There is something in the boy," Georg said to Friedrich and Pauline, "that makes me think of my mother."

In the autumn of 1925, a few months before her forty-second wedding anniversary, Wilhelmine died. As Friedrich mourned his mother, he watched carefully over his ailing father. They had long discussions about young Fritz's future – and about the unsettled Republic's also. Georg urged Friedrich to write his own book to challenge the absurdities in *Mein Kampf.* In November 1926 Georg died and was laid to rest beside his wife in the Mainz Hauptfriedhof. A large rough-hewn stone placed at the grave held a simple bronze plaque bearing a single word: "Kellner."

At the end of that year the second volume of *Mein Kampf* was published with this conclusion: "In this age of racial poisoning, a state that dedicates itself to the care of its best racial elements must someday become lord of the earth." Sensing the terrible implications in the book and how it would appeal to deeply ingrained German prejudices and militarism, the grieving justice inspector wondered how long he would have to campaign against its dangerous author. "I knew from the beginning Hitler and his politics meant war."[8]

The Social Democrats kept the National Socialists to less than 3 percent of the vote in 1928, but the loss of jobs and savings during the 1929 global depression perfectly suited the Nazis. The belligerent but charismatic Nazi Party leader railed against capitalism and communism, blamed the Jews for every social ill, and vowed to restore Germany's greatness, not merely the former empire, but a Greater Germany, which would begin with the annexation of Austria. By 1930 the Nazis had the second largest party in the nation, and fourteen-year-old Fritz, at an age when teenagers naturally rebelled against their parents, was among those caught up in the budding national fascination with Adolf Hitler, whose notion of Aryan supremacy elevated within the Darwinian hierarchy even the scrawniest of German boys and gave them leave to tread upon the "subhumans." When Fritz came home from school whistling a popular song about SA stormtroopers marching through the land, and he wanted to join the Hitler Youth, it required all of Friedrich's skills and a rebuke from the normally calm Pauline to persuade him from it. "The youth have been contaminated through and through by the spirit of Hitler," Friedrich later would write sadly.[9]

Hitler's visit to Mainz for a large rally had Pauline's sisters and their husbands preaching about the need for "a strong man" to restore order. Her brother Franz admitted to voting for the National Socialists. "Victims of Nazi propaganda," Friedrich described his in-laws.[10] But nothing disturbed him more than those in the courthouse, including attorneys and judges, who were seriously considering Hitler's views. Friedrich angered a chief inspector when he predicted Hitler would start another war. A colleague warned him to be careful because no one knew who was turning toward "Hitlerism" and such people could be dangerous.[11]

The July 1932 elections gave the Nazis almost 40 percent of the vote and the largest party in the Reichstag. In January 1933, after six months of tense political intrigues, Adolf Hitler was chancellor. From that position he launched a dictatorship that would make his name a synonym for Monster. "Who carries the blame?" cried Friedrich, after having fought for so many years against this outcome. "The people without a brain! To trample democracy with one's feet and give power to a single man over almost eighty million people is so terrible that one can really tremble over the things that will come."[12]

The Errant Son

Under no illusions about what the Mainz Nazis would do to those who had opposed them, Friedrich moved with his family to the small castle town of Laubach, 40 miles north of Frankfurt, where no one was aware of his political activities. The high position available in the Laubach court offered some security against overbearing local Nazi officials. As the courthouse administrative manager, he had one of the two apartments in the building. The chief judge and his family lived on the upper floor.

The Kellners found little difference between the city and the country when it came to Hitler zealots. More than 60 percent of Laubach's votes had gone to the National Socialists, and they ruled the town council.[13] The professional class kowtowed shamelessly to the new powers and pressured Friedrich and Pauline to join the Nazi Party. Joining was not mandatory, but in a town of only eighteen hundred their refusal was conspicuous and placed them under a cloud of suspicion. Friedrich did not help matters when he expressed disapproval of the Nazis' enactment of oppressive laws: the Enabling Act granting Hitler dictatorial powers, a civil service law restricting Jews, and a law to sterilize people with hereditary diseases.

Their son, unhappy about leaving his friends in Mainz, was unco-operative. When Fritz graduated from high school, he balked at finding a job. It was senseless to start a career, he said, when he soon would be drafted into national work service or the army. He spent his time tinkering with radios, earning money repairing them. To get him away from Nazi influence, his parents arranged for a relative in New York to sponsor him there. A few months before he was to leave, Fritz went to London to take courses in radio repair and English at Polytechnic University. Back in Germany he worked part-time at the courthouse. When a small amount of money, 2 marks, disappeared from a countertop where it had been left as payment for a fine, the judge blamed Fritz. There was no proof, and Fritz denied taking the money; nevertheless, the judge threatened an investigation, not so much to punish the son as to humiliate the anti-Nazi father.

On August 14, 1935, Fritz departed Hamburg for New York on the steamship SS President Roosevelt. His name on the passenger list was Fred William Kellner. He was nineteen and ready for a new start. As the ocean liner steamed toward the North Sea, his distraught parents comforted each other. Friedrich thought of his father, who, despite the stigma of his birth, had created a respectable life through hard work. He prayed Georg's grandson would do the same.

It would be eleven years before they would see each other again, terrifying years when the dock upon which Friedrich and Pauline stood, and the shipyards around them, and all of Hamburg and much of Germany would be smashed beneath the weight of powerful bombs. Not even the perceptive justice inspector could imagine the broken world in which they and their son would reunite.

A few weeks after the SS President Roosevelt departed for New York, the masters of Germany announced new racial laws. Jews, no matter how far back they could trace their German ancestry, were arbitrarily stripped of their citizenship and rights.[14] This, to Friedrich, was an unthinkable villainy. "If the Jews, who over the centuries contributed demonstrable achievements in the economic life for the total development of the nation, can be made a people without rights, then that is an act unworthy of a cultured nation."[15]

The government's official contempt for Jews encouraged the basest mistreatment of them among the general population, resulting in brutal harassment even in school classrooms. Such actions were made known to the world by the many foreign correspondents in Berlin reporting on the "new Germany." But condemnations were few and feeble. Bolstered by unwitting politicians, celebrities, and industrialists in the democracies that pandered to him, Hitler and his henchmen drew up their plans for mass mayhem.

Friedrich's compassion for Germany's Jews did not stem from friendships or work-related associations. Jews comprised less than 1 percent of the population, so it was not unusual he would have little intimate knowledge of them. He simply felt no one should be attacked for being different, and he was angry such a simple truth could be obscured so easily by racial propaganda designed to stir up primordial tribal hatreds. His principles would be tested when a Jewish family named Heynemann approached Pauline in the spring of 1935 to seek Friedrich's help. The Heynemanns' son-in-law, Julius Abt, and their daughter, Lucie, were being harassed by the police and local Nazi office. When Friedrich learned a case had been fabricated against Julius to confiscate his property, he helped the harried man get safely from Laubach and passage to America. Lucie Abt was due to give birth in June, so she remained behind. The next year, when her child, John Peter, was nine months old, Friedrich and Pauline helped them get away. They tried to persuade her parents, Salli and Hulda Heynemann, to emigrate while it was still possible for Jews to do so, but the older couple remained behind, certain their neighbors would do them no harm.[16]

Sensing another European war was coming, the Kellners were thankful their son would not be in it. Fred's cheerful letters from New York confirmed their judgment in sending him there. He found a job in an import company, became engaged to a young German-American woman and married her in St. Mark's Lutheran Church. In wedding photographs, the young couple looked like motion picture stars: he in a tuxedo, and the bride in a white gown. A year later he sent a photo of himself and his baby daughter.

Only the child was true. He was not working; their daughter-in-law was neither German nor Lutheran; the marriage had been by a justice of the peace, and the wedding photos staged in a photography studio. But considering all that Friedrich and Pauline would have to contend with in the dreadful years ahead, it was a blessing they did not have to know of their son's real activities.

The Diarist

"Every mind is clouded and darkened," wrote Friedrich of his brainwashed countrymen: "Vernebelt, verdunkelt sind alle Hirne!"[17] He felt the same about the minds of foreign leaders who continued to be duped by Joseph Goebbels's lies and cowed by Hitler's threats. He made short trips with Pauline into France – to Strasbourg in 1937 and Forbach in 1938 – to mail letters to Cordell Hull, Franklin Roosevelt's Secretary of State, describing the oppressive methods in Germany. He urged Hull to end America's neutrality.[18] On their return from Forbach, Friedrich began a series of essays about the "mood and images" of his surroundings. His first essay, written on

September 26, 1938, described his countrymen's nervousness about Hitler's claim on Czechoslovakia's Sudetenland; they were not ready for another war with England and France. But the leaders of those nations misread the situation and gave in to Hitler's menacing bluster, "An unbelievably pathetic nincompoop," was Friedrich's assessment of the British prime minister.[19]

Following the success of their belligerent foreign policy, the Nazis increased their internal malice. Persecution of Germany's Jewish citizens in the large cities had taken place for years, with SA brownshirts damaging Jewish businesses and harassing individuals on the streets. Late in the night of November 9, 1938, the stormtroopers launched a co-ordinated pogrom nationwide where even the smallest towns could participate in the frenzy and hatred that had become commonplace in Berlin and Munich. On this "Night of the broken glass" (Kristallnacht), the Laubach schoolteacher, Albert Haas, head of the local SA, led a mob past the courthouse toward the Heynemann house.[20] Friedrich demanded that the chief judge, Ludwig Schmitt, order the police to escort the Jewish families of Laubach and the surrounding villages to the courthouse. The judge refused.[21] Pauline fared no better with the Nazi women's group leader, Frau Desch. Jews were beaten wherever they were found, and the contents of Jewish homes were tossed into the streets to be stolen or smashed. The Torah scrolls and books from the Laubach synagogue were burned in the marketplace. The next day the police took the battered Jewish men into custody – not to protect them but to intimidate them further.

Friedrich wanted to press charges against Haas and another riot leader, Wilhelm Rühl. Judge Schmitt said he needed sworn statements from corroborating witnesses – and no Jew would be allowed to submit an affidavit.[22] That proved impossible. When Friedrich offered his own and Pauline's written testimonies, Schmitt angrily responded that Pauline was under investigation herself and would be sent to a concentration camp. "And the same for you," the judge added ominously.

Pauline's refusal to join the women's group, and her sympathetic attitude to Jews – and having sent her son to America – meant one thing to the Nazi mind: the courthouse administrator's wife had a Jew in her family. At the instigation of Frau Desch, Judge Schmitt ordered a secret investigation into Pauline's ancestry and submitted the matter to Regional Court President Hermann Colnot in Giessen. On the day of Kristallnacht, November 9, Colnot approved the investigation and forwarded his recommendations to his superior in Darmstadt, Chief Regional Court President Ludwig Scriba.

Furious at the action against his wife, Friedrich gathered Pauline's family documents to take to Darmstadt. On the cover page of a thick file of his own family papers, he wrote, "To prove the Aryan ancestry of Justice Inspector Kellner in Laubach." The birth and death certificates and baptism papers detailed Pauline and Friedrich's lineage back to the early seventeenth century and were enough to satisfy Court President Scriba. On November 18, Scriba sent a curt memorandum (signed on his behalf by Judge Dr. Meier) to President Colnot and Judge Schmitt that ended the matter. The subject of his memo was "Justice Inspector Kellner in Laubach – Concerning the report from the regional president in Giessen of November 9, 1938." The text had two sentences: "I ask that you return the attached documents to the subject of this report. Doubts about his wife's German bloodlines cannot be validated." When this document later came into Friedrich's possession, he used his fountain pen to insert two additional words in the margin above the text: "Doubts about his and his wife's German bloodlines cannot be validated."

After a full year of writing, Friedrich composed a final essay on August 30, 1939, and signed his name after this concluding paragraph: "As a preacher in the wilderness I felt compelled to write down the thoughts that dominated my mind in this nerve-wracking time so that later – should it still be possible – I could convey a picture of the true reality to my descendants." He was emotionally exhausted, under surveillance for speaking out, and lucky not to be in a concentration camp. Their son was across the Atlantic, and they might never get to see their grandchildren. Moreover, Friedrich was fifty-four years old, his injured leg ached from sciatica, and he was developing an asthma condition.

But the "nerve-wracking time" was just beginning. Two days after Friedrich signed off on his essays, the German army invaded Poland. Blitzkrieg! The terrible events of war required not sporadic essays but a disciplined kind of reporting. His father had urged him to respond to Hitler's *Mein Kampf*. This would be his answer, a wartime diary he named *Mein Widerstand* (*My Opposition*). He wrote the first entry on September 1, 1939, the day the troops marched into Poland, and no matter how dangerous his self-imposed task would become, he continued until his nation's unconditional surrender in May 1945. Like a war reporter on the front lines, he maintained his position in the courthouse, directly engaging the town's Nazi functionaries to gain information for his journal.

For his essays before the war he used loose sheets of blank paper. For his diary he chose accounting notebooks with lined pages bound together with string. Occasionally he felt the need to write a supplemental essay to expand on a topic or describe an event not in the diary. For those he used the blank sheets of paper.

Shortly after the invasion of Poland, Friedrich wrote such a supplemental essay to sum up the first few weeks of his diary and titled it "Early September 1939." It is fortunate he wrote it. His first diary notebook and the pre-war essays would be stolen many years later, and when they were recovered, the first pages of the notebook with his entries for September 1–12 were missing. Only three pre-war essays remained.

Notable in the "Early September 1939" essay is Friedrich's awareness of being spied on by the most fanatical and dangerous of Nazi organizations, the *Schutzstaffel* (Protection Squadron) under Heinrich Himmler. An SS man named Willi Wolf was trying to find out from Friedrich's employees if he greeted everyone with the Hitler salute. Slighting the Führer could cost people not only their jobs but even their lives.

More than one Nazi was keeping an eye on him. On November 15, 1939, Friedrich wrote of "a new attempt to take action against me." The court attendant and acting constable, Heinrich Scherdt, wanted to know why Friedrich and Pauline had turned away a soldier they were supposed to quarter in their apartment. Part of Friedrich and Pauline's passive resistance was to limit, whenever possible, their help to the war effort. But they were obliged to provide a room, and Scherdt later checked with the soldier to see if he was pleased with them. "This former policeman's painstaking efforts to get something explicit and unfavorable against us will one day receive their deserved award."[23]

When collectors for the National Socialist People's Welfare (NSV) came to their door for contributions, they gave little or nothing at all. In January 1940 the NSV Block Warden, Georg Walter, sent Friedrich a letter questioning the small amount of his contribution. Friedrich unwisely responded with sarcasm, which he regretted after mailing his reply. "I must always assume [as in the matter of contributing more to the NSV] that something else is being devised against me . . . Caution is the mother of wisdom."[24] Judge Schmitt's maid, Else Gross, who turned to Pauline for comfort when the mercurial Frau Schmitt got too overbearing, warned Pauline, "Herr Kellner should speak less about politics; Dr. Schmitt has informed on him to Nazi Party Leader Pott."[25]

Pauline, too, remained under the microscope. In one of his separate essays, Friedrich wrote a tribute to her: "For several years now, the leaders of the Nazi Women's League and the Women's Block Warden Group have brought their admission forms to my wife to persuade her to join their organizations, bringing the forms personally to our apartment with the stern admonition they would be back for them in a few days. Despite their repeated efforts and intimidations, my wife never filled out a single form or became a member of any such organization. I would suggest that in all of Germany there are to be found few wives of officials who showed the same courage. Yes, she is most definitely courageous. The reader will understand when I propose here that a monument should be erected to my brave wife."[26]

The Great Risk

On February 19, 1940, Friedrich was summoned to Giessen by Regional Court President Hermann Colnot and District Leader Heinrich Backhaus to answer complaints against him and Pauline.[27] Later that day Friedrich would describe this meeting in a supplemental essay, partly using a dialogue format.

Backhaus: "I have heard nothing good about you."

Kellner: "I see that, unfortunately. But yet I cannot understand why."

Backhaus: "The Party and National Socialist Welfare have often complained about you. You are not a member of any organization. Your wife has not attended the women's organizations."

President Colnot: "It is out of the question for an official's wife to stand apart in the manner she is doing. Officials are expected to set a good example."

Backhaus opened a folder to give Friedrich a two-page complaint letter against him by Block Warden Walter.

"If you socialized more and had friendly personal relationships with officials like Walter," continued President Colnot, "there would be no friction."

Friedrich's attention was on a piece of paper beneath the second page of the letter, a memorandum the paper clip had inadvertently snagged when the letter was slid from the folder. He read the chilling words penned by the local NSV leader, Ernst Mönnig: "Kellner's attitude exerts a bad influence on the rest of the population, and in our view he should be made to disappear from Laubach."[28]

Alarmed, Friedrich responded forcefully, declaring that Walter's behavior and attitude had contravened the rules for block wardens "enacted by the president of the Reichstag." Colnot and Backhaus stiffened at the reference to the Führer's favorite field marshal, Hermann Göring, who commanded the Luftwaffe and ruled over the parliament.

"Block wardens have been charged by the highest authorities to treat every citizen with respect, and so I made that clear to Walter," continued Friedrich. Then he alluded to another of Hitler's closest aides. "I am sorry you had to be bothered by this small incident. It could easily have been handled in Laubach between Walter and me. But if this disagreement must proceed further, it cannot be done this way. I would request a formal hearing – at which I could defend myself with even a stronger voice." The "stronger voice" would not only be his own. If the wheels of the Nazi state were to be kept in motion, officials in the bureaucracy could not be placed arbitrarily into the Gestapo's hands. They had the right to a trial – and Hitler had ordered his deputy, Rudolf Hess, to review all judgments against officials. The three men in that tense room knew the top executive in Berlin would not look lightly on being presented with such a petty dispute.

"We will not take this any further," President Colnot responded, adding he had accomplished what he wished, merely to advise Friedrich of certain complaints. The dark look on District Leader Backhaus's face, though, suggested it was not over.

In spite of his bravado in Giessen, Friedrich was in low spirits when he wrote about the meeting. He knew the cruel mishandling that befell those who disturbed the Nazis' sense of absolute authority. He ended his essay with the depressing observation, "Law and justice have disappeared!"[29]

More menacing was the confrontation a month later. On March 22 Scherdt appeared in Friedrich's office to summon him to the town hall for questioning by Mayor Högy and Nazi Local Group Leader Pott. Insisting on first going downstairs to his apartment, Friedrich told Pauline to leave for Mainz if he did not return by noon. With the court attendant hovering in the apartment doorway, Pauline could see what was at stake.

The mayor, though younger than Friedrich by several years, was adept at getting what he wanted and firmly wielded his authority. He and Ortsgruppenleiter Otto Pott had profited well in the Third Reich by compelling Jews to sell their properties at cheap prices. They interrogated Friedrich about his views on National Socialism, Adolf Hitler, and other Nazi leaders. More specifically, they wanted to know why he had refused to be a volunteer treasurer for the local Colonial League, had been reluctant to quarter soldiers in his apartment, and had displayed a lack of comradeship by avoiding celebrations, including the Führer's birthday. Pott referred to anonymous complaints about Friedrich unfavorably comparing Germany to England and America. "One more of those," the Nazi leader threatened, "and you and your wife will be sent to a concentration camp."

Friedrich angrily admonished Pott for using anonymous complaints, and he took the mayor to task for bringing up old matters like the Colonial League. "I made it clear to District Leader Backhaus my court-house duties took precedence over being treasurer in this local club."[30] Repeating his Giessen tactic, Friedrich threatened to call for a formal trial in which he, too, would submit complaints. "Mine will not be hearsay or anonymous," he pointedly said. "And they are thoroughly documented." He knew of their wrongful appropriations of land, their failure to pay taxes, and even Pott's unwanted lecherous attentions to women. "Your charges against me are petty and personal. But what I have against you – and against some of your relatives – will be of great interest to those in Berlin who assure the German people their local Party leaders are honest and sincere." That brought the meeting to an end, but not without a final outburst by Pott that Friedrich was the most unpatriotic person he had ever met. Infuriated, the former sergeant rolled up his right trouser leg and demanded the Nazi leader address his accusations to the wound he received fighting in the service of the Kaiser.

Friedrich found Pauline picking up papers and books from the apartment floor. Georg Walter and Ernst Mönnig, the men who had lodged complaints against him to President Colnot and District Leader Backhaus, had arrived unannounced to search the apartment. It was likely Backhaus had ordered the interrogation and the search. Fortunately Pauline had been prompted by Friedrich's warning – and in particular the look on Scherdt's face – to gather up the loose sheets of an essay he was writing and other incriminating notes and burn them in the cellar furnace. When the expected knock came at the door, the diary notebook was in her hand, and she placed it beneath her blouse and sweater. The two men, searching without due authority, gave wide berth to the petite woman with blazing eyes.

Despite the scare, Friedrich had no intention of stopping his writing. The Nazis had the power to still his voice in the present, but he could fight them in the future; his diary would be a weapon for coming generations to use against any resurgence of Nazi types and their totalitarian ideologies. He sat at his desk and rewrote everything he could remember of the destroyed notes. Then he constructed a hidden compartment in the dining room cabinet in which to keep them.

Only after the war would he and Pauline learn the depth of the conspiracy against them. Four days before the confrontation at the town hall, NSDAP

Political Director Hermann Engst had replied to Otto Pott's request to send Friedrich to a concentration camp:

I have read the notices related to the Kellner case a number of times, and I have considered the nature of the report's allegations. I was not able to come to a resolution because he did not exhibit a lack of interest in Germany, nor did he reveal his ultimate aims ... We should not forget people of Kellner's type are too intelligent to allow themselves to be caught off guard, and for that reason are never in a position to be charged with disciplinary indiscretions by the court. Only after these kinds of people have expressed their opinions or behaved in a manner for which the Secret Police can indict them on a charge, is there a possibility to turn them over to the Gestapo. Then they are subject to Party discipline and, with the approval of a representative of the Führer, can be sent to a concentration camp. If we want to catch people such as this character Kellner, we will have to entice them out of their hiding-place and allow them to incriminate themselves. At present, there is no other way open to us. The time is not yet ripe to take measures similar to those being taken against the Jews. That can occur after the war. Therefore, I assume the District Leader [Heinrich Backhaus] will reject a report of the type we have been thinking about; and thus it is pointless. Heil Hitler, Engst.[31]

The Terror War

Political Director Engst had good reason to expect Germany to win the war and then to settle with the likes of Friedrich Kellner. The rapid seizure of Poland and the torpid response by the League of Nations and Poland's dilatory allies augured even greater victories to come. Denmark, Norway, Belgium, Luxembourg, and the Netherlands were quickly conquered. France surrendered after a mere six weeks of fighting.

Friedrich was appalled by France's and England's lack of preparedness before the war, and that France would give in without a real fight, and the British would pretend their haphazard retreat at Dunkirk was an illustrious achievement. He blamed pre-war greed for their defeat, for continuing to sell raw material to Germany while knowing Hitler was re-arming the nation. And he abhorred his fellow citizens' lack of regard for civilian deaths and the destruction of Europe's architectural treasures. "To the shame of my countrymen, it definitely must be said they are completely dazzled by the military successes."[32]

Since his interrogations in Giessen and Laubach, Friedrich confined such observations to his diary. According to the maid, Else Gross, one more person was spying on him. Friedrich's newly hired typist, Fräulein Helga Elbe, a recent high school graduate, was reporting Friedrich's statements to Judge Schmitt, who was home on an extended leave from the army.

Each of Germany's successes, particularly in Russia, darkened Friedrich's mood. He knew the killing and destruction would be for nothing once the United States discarded its posture of neutrality and drove Germany back to its borders. The worst claimants of neutrality, in Friedrich's view, were not far across the ocean but close to home: Switzerland and Sweden, who supplied vital war material to Germany for almost the entire war. "Those who supported an aggressor should be treated exactly the same as the aggressor. Death to the supplier!"[33]

His diary entries reflected a new, horrific tone to the fighting, the indiscriminate murders in the East – kept from official reports but revealed by soldiers home on leave or in hospitals. Other abominations were but an hour's drive from Laubach, in the mental hospital in Hadamar. "What would he have said," asked Friedrich, in the single reference in his diary to his father, "to these awful slaughterers of mankind?"[34]

On August 4, 1941, two bombs landed without damage in Laubach. Mainz was not as lucky, and the next month Friedrich and Pauline went to see how her relatives were holding up. On the way, they examined various areas bombed by the Royal Air Force. The inaccuracies of the strikes and the questionable value of the targets did not impress Friedrich. If England intended to win, it would have to put infantry and tank divisions on German soil.

Near the end of their stay with Pauline's mother, air raid sirens woke them in the middle of the night. At dawn Pauline's sisters, Katie and Lina, and Lina's husband, Heinrich Fahrbach, appeared at the door.[35] Their apartment building had been hit. Friedrich went with his brother-in-law to photograph the building and see what could be salvaged. Heinrich Fahrbach kicked at the rubble and swore the Luftwaffe would destroy all of London in revenge. Friedrich asked if Heinrich would destroy an entire city and kill a million people for the sake of one apartment building. "London is filled with Jews," was the surly response in the affirmative.

The irrational hatred of Jews was the subject of diary entries the next month. A massacre of Jewish men and women in Poland revealed to what level his countrymen had sunk, giving rise to Friedrich's angry declaration that "There is no punishment that would be hard enough to be applied to these Nazi beasts."[36] With each piece of distressing news he recorded, he wondered how long the reign of terror would continue.

The terror found America when the Japanese launched their surprise attack against the US fleet at Pearl Harbor. Although masterfully planned and executed, it was the same kind of hubristic military decision Germany had made in attacking Russia. Friedrich now was certain how the war would end.

The Inevitable End

Friedrich and Pauline had a small circle of friends they could trust. They shared news, relished the freedom to speak their minds, and lamented the dangers of doing so in public. They were not young or daring enough to blow up trains. Even their small acts of active resistance, like leaving Allied leaflets in public places, could get them executed. For the most part, they gave each other reassurance that bad people eventually ran out of good luck.

When working hours were increased to six days a week, there was little time for friends to get together. On their Sundays off, Friedrich and Pauline would walk through the country and forests or climb the foothills of the Vogelsberg (Bird Mountain). They looked for a place to build their retirement home. They intended to remain in Laubach after the war and re-establish the local branch of the Social Democratic Party and do what they could to keep Nazis from governing again.

In March 1942 they went for a few weeks to Freudenstadt in southern Germany, surrounded by the Black Forest's dramatic hills and woodlands. They had vacationed there a few times with Fritz. The army's prioritized needs strained the railway system; passenger cars were overcrowded, and the delays doubled the usual time of their journey. The normally bright and lively city had the somber appearance of a massive hospital. Instead of carefree tourists strolling from shop to shop, convalescing soldiers with expressionless faces limped down the sidewalks and filled the park benches. The large hotels had been converted into military hospitals. Most shops were shuttered; others were open for only a few hours each day. "All in all, a gloomy picture."[37]

The bleak atmosphere, contrary to the thrilling news accounts of victorious German soldiers, gave Friedrich hope the turning point was close. It was not – still three years away. But he received some welcome deliverance from his personal enemies. Mayor Högy was sent to Mosina in occupied Poland to prepare for post-war occupation and settlement. Judge Schmitt was granted fewer leaves from the Russian front. The Kristallnacht mob leaders, Willi Rühl and Albert Haas, were learning firsthand how "subhuman" Slavs defended their motherland against the master race. And Heinrich Scherdt had been called up for army duty.

One of Friedrich's most persistent enemies was still at home. Group Leader Pott wanted to commandeer half of the Kellners' apartment for a family of displaced bombing victims, but Friedrich managed to thwart the attempt.[38] A new danger was a judge named Bischoff, frequently at the Laubach courthouse, who would probe Friedrich for defeatist remarks. Friedrich knew to be wary of this "pure type of a molded Nazi: arrogance personified."[39]

To replace military casualties, German workers were drafted into the army, and their jobs were filled by concentration camp inmates and forced labor from the occupied countries. White-collar workers, however, in the overlapping layers of governmental bureaucracies, could not be replaced by outsiders and had to fill empty slots within their ranks by taking on additional work. In March 1943 Friedrich became responsible for a second courthouse. He would have to spend three days a week in Altenstadt, near Frankfurt. Pauline would not be alone during his absence. The heavy bombing in Mainz had persuaded her mother to move in with them. And Pauline's sisters found refuge in Laubach when needed.

The 26-mile train journey to Altenstadt, with transfers at Hungen and Stockheim, took less than two hours in normal times. Bomb attacks on rail lines and depots, and the army having first priority, had turned the trip into six hours and longer. During these travels, Friedrich sometimes took the grave risk of placing Allied leaflets on the trains and in the waiting rooms – "intended for wavering Party members" – to watch their reactions when they read the bold statements:[40]

"Germany has lost the war. We know it, Hitler knows it."

"How can Germany yet be saved?"

"Every five minutes a new airplane is built in America."

Friedrich never doubted the rightness of his actions. The Allies had a duty to the entire world to conquer a Germany that had metamorphosed into a monstrosity. But that did not allay his deep sorrow at what was happening to his country and countrymen. He was pained by the prospect of his nation being torn to shreds to be rid of its cancer. Within Friedrich's heart lay the Deutschland of his childhood, a nation of enlightenment and accomplishment, a world leader in science and art, a symbol of what it meant to be civilized. "It is unspeakably sad," he wrote on June 24, 1943, "that Germany has run into such a dead end from which an escape appears to be, as far as one can tell, no longer possible."

A rare moment of happiness came to the Kellners when a twenty-five-word Red Cross letter-telegram arrived from America that gave Friedrich a chance to write something good in his diary. "Can there be such a thing?" he wondered of the joy he and his wife were feeling that day, December 2, 1943.

After years of chafing at the Allies' slow pace, Friedrich greeted their massive landing on the French coast of Normandy in June 1944 with the word "*ENDLICH!*" written in large letters: "FINALLY!" Another long year lay ahead as the Americans and British closed in from the west, liberating Paris, while the Russians made their push for Germany's eastern border and Berlin. A clique of German officers, believing Germany's best hope was to sue for peace with the western Allies, tried to kill Adolf Hitler. Early in the war Friedrich had longed for such an action, but now he was glad they failed. He did not want the German people to pretend they could have won the war "if only Hitler had lived."

Friedrich included more obituaries of soldiers and civilians in his diary in that last year. But one particular death was not mentioned. On October 7, 1944, he wrote about the navy's shortage of ships, a sighting of a V-1 flying bomb over Frankfurt, and the execution of four men in Bielefeld for listening to foreign radio broadcasts; and he augmented the entry with newspaper clippings. But in keeping with his usual policy of omitting personal matters, Friedrich wrote nothing of the acute sorrow in his apartment. Pauline's mother, Johanna Karolina Preuss, living with them for the last year of her life, died on that day. Grieving in private with his wife, he would not write for the next ten days.

Soon afterward, Friedrich did include something personal because it heralded Germany's fast-approaching defeat. In November 1944, thirty years after being wounded in France, the old veteran was called up once more for military service. A new militia, the *Volkssturm* (People's Attack Force), had been formed under the control of the increasingly desperate Nazi Party. It was comprised of old men and boys: veterans of earlier wars and teenagers from Hitler Youth, who could do no more than prolong the defeat by a few days or weeks. They were to assist regular army units defending the Home Front and also to be deployed along the front lines with *Panzerfaust* weapons (bazookas) to shoot at enemy tanks. Friedrich's Volkssturm unit met for Sunday on his only time off, to drill fruitlessly in the park near the old castle. He would march, but he would not fight to keep the Nazis in power.

Overworked and physically ill, Friedrich did not write in his diary for almost three months, from mid-December 1944 until March 7, 1945. By then the Allies had reached Remagen on the Rhine's west bank and captured the bridge before it could be destroyed. Two more weeks and the entire river would come under their control, and the fickle Lorelei would not sink the enemy's boats. The Party members were doing everything to hold onto their beliefs and hopes, but when a miracle was not forthcoming from the Führer, the Nazi leaders of Laubach went to hide out with distant relatives. Friedrich convinced the members in his Volkssturm unit to consider themselves discharged from service. He expected the thoroughly brainwashed Hitler Youth boys to protest and call him a traitor, but even they grasped the reality when Group Leader Otto Pott destroyed his papers and burned his uniform. When that happened, the townsfolk found a new North for their moral compass, which pointed directly at the courthouse, and they eagerly sought approval from Friedrich and Pauline.

On March 28, 1945, Friedrich was at his desk, writing in his diary. Faint percussive booms of artillery came from the west where the Americans were crushing last-ditch efforts of resistance near Giessen. Overhead suddenly an airplane engine roared, and two bombs exploded in the street, shattering the courthouse windows. The maid, Else, rushed into the apartment to find Friedrich and Pauline coated with plaster dust but otherwise unharmed. Broken glass and ceiling tiles were scattered everywhere. Describing the scene years later, she said, "Herr Kellner was the only one who had anything nice to say about the Americans, and they dropped a bomb on him. It was good they did not kill him. Everyone in Laubach was counting on him to protect them from the Allies."

The bombs had exploded while Friedrich was midway through a sentence. When he returned to his diary, he placed an ellipsis of five dots where he had left off, and in parentheses briefly described the attack. Then he completed the original sentence, and added, "We can hold up under everything if only we have the certainty the monster Hitler with his insatiable bloodletting and plundering will have committed soon his last shameful deed."

The next day Friedrich and Pauline sat in the courthouse cellar with Else, Mrs. Schmitt and her three children, the courthouse employees, some neighbors, and wounded soldiers from the courthouse infirmary, listening to the approaching sounds of Allied troops. Judge Schmitt would not be returning from the war; the Russian army had overrun his field post, and he was sent to a draconian prison camp in Tbilisi. When the sound of jeeps and other vehicles were close, Friedrich and Pauline went outside to see their liberators.

The American commander in Giessen, upon learning the courthouse administrator in Laubach was a known anti-Nazi, sent District Administrator Theodor Weber to offer Friedrich the position of mayor. Friedrich declined, but not for the reasons he gave Weber: health and work. For as long as Adolf Hitler remained alive and in charge – even though hiding in a bunker in Berlin – he would not be associated with that class of National Socialist officials, Germany's mayors, who had so shamelessly done Hitler's bidding.

On May 1 a special announcement came over the radio. Hitler was dead. Several weeks later Laubach's new mayor, Heinrich Schmidt, offered Friedrich the position of first town councilman and deputy mayor. He accepted and played a substantial role determining which local Nazi Party members should be disqualified from their professions and from public service. He had often raged in his diary about the blind acceptance of National Socialism and hoped everyone involved would be punished. The war itself had accomplished much of that. More than a hundred men in Laubach and the nearby villages had been killed or severely wounded by an enemy they had mocked. Some, like Judge Schmitt, would die in captivity. In Giessen, District Leader Backhaus was dead, and President Colnot was under arrest and would go to prison. Tempering justice with understanding, Friedrich used his diary not for revenge but for reconciliation. His nation and millions of its citizens were destroyed; now it was necessary to rebuild. But he was harsh with former Nazis who tried to profit from the reconstruction. On November 22, 1945, in a letter rejecting a bid from a contractor named Johann Pipping, he wrote, "You are a sly businessman. If it had to be, you would step upon corpses. You make contracts with the devil without batting an eye. Whenever necessary, you were an excellent National Socialist. Today, that is certainly not the thing to be, so now you want to prove you were not a Nazi."

When his work as deputy mayor was completed, he returned the diary to its hiding place and went on about the business of rebuilding his political party. He gathered around him former Social Democratic Party members and recruited new ones for the small Laubach branch. They elected Friedrich Kellner their chairman.[41]

Return of the Prodigal Son

On April 1, 1946, Fred William Kellner arrived in Laubach in an army jeep, dressed in the uniform of his country's occupier, with stolen lieutenant bars denoting his rank. He was not the nineteen-year-old youth who had left but a gaunt thirty-year-old, with eyes reflecting the shock of what he had seen that day traveling through the rubble and ruins of his homeland. He embraced his surprised parents tentatively at first, almost formally, until his parents pulled him close.

With him was a young woman of twenty, Leonie Nassiet, nicknamed Liliane, from France. In a single breath Fred introduced his new wife to his perplexed parents and told them Freda had left him for another man, which was why he had joined the army. He said he took part in the 1944 invasion of Normandy and would remain in Germany as a civilian interpreter for the American Occupation Forces. Liliane's parents had disowned her for marrying a German, so he asked if she could stay with Friedrich and Pauline while he traveled in the region.[42]

Friedrich decried the harsh judgment against Liliane, insisting Fred was as much American now as German. Pauline exclaimed that Freda, having left her husband for another man, could not be trusted to care for her children properly and wanted Fred to go to America to check on their welfare. Fred reassured his mother, saying he would go soon. And to his father, his doleful response was, "I no longer know what I am."

For several months their son was in and out of Laubach, not in an army uniform but wearing civilian clothes and driving a large sedan. On each return his car would have cartons of food for the food supply committee Friedrich had formed with two other council members.[43] If in 1935 Fred really took the two marks from the courthouse, he now redeemed himself.

In 1947 Fred went for a brief visit to America. Upon his return he said nothing about Freda dancing in a carnival and the children being in a home. He said Freda was newly married and all were content. In June that year, Liliane gave birth to a daughter, Margrit, easing some of Friedrich's and Pauline's sadness at losing their American grandchildren; however, Margrit's birth caused Liliane's parents to relent, and Fred moved his family to Paris.

Friedrich was promoted to chief justice inspector and accepted a transfer to the district auditor's office in Giessen. At age sixty-five in 1950, he retired. He and Pauline built their small retirement home on an unpaved road on the Ramsberg, a foothill of the Vogelsberg, a brief walk from the courthouse by way of the castle park where Friedrich had marched with the Volkssturm. He remained politically active on the town council, and Pauline volunteered her time with the Red Cross. His spare time was spent writing a history of the Third Reich, in which he planned to incorporate parts of his diary.

Fred, Liliane, and Margrit came for visits on the holidays, and Friedrich and Pauline visited them in Paris. In early 1951 Fred told his parents he had lost his job in France and wanted to start over in Germany. Liliane was not happy being away from France again, and from loud arguments with her husband, Friedrich and Pauline learned their son was involved in the black market and in trouble with his French partners. After an especially serious argument, Liliane took Margrit back to France, and Fred left for a job prospect in Munich. After a year of little contact, he reappeared in Laubach in obvious distress, borrowing money from his parents so he could go to his wife and child.

In one of her infrequent letters, Liliane confirmed Fred was in Paris. Then a letter arrived with grievous news. On May 30, 1953, in Liliane's apartment on the outskirts of Paris, their son was found dead. The gas oven had been turned on without being lit, and he died of asphyxiation.

The photographs in their 1953 passport show Friedrich's and Pauline's anguish. When they arrived in France, they learned Fred had not gone to Munich in 1951 for a job offer but to re-enlist in the US Army, hoping to find protection from his criminal black market confederates. When he came to Laubach for money – the last time they saw him – he was AWOL from his post and on the run. The civilian and military authorities investigating his death had reason to suspect foul play but concluded he had ended his own life. Their son's body passed through the crematorium and his ashes were interred in the American Legion Tomb in the Cimetière Nouveau (New Cemetery) in the city of Neuilly on the Seine River. The boundary line that separates the cities of Neuilly and Puteaux runs directly through the center of the cemetery; even in death, Fred William Kellner – born in Germany, naturalized in America, and desolated in France – would reside in a kind of No Man's Land. "I no longer know what I am," he had told his father.

Friedrich and Pauline Kellner had survived two world wars that took the lives of millions of their countrymen, but this one single death, the death of their only child, removed their last vestige of hope. Friedrich managed somehow to continue his participation in the Social Democratic Party and serve the community as a legal adviser. When called upon, he even wrote poems and was the master of ceremonies at children's Carnival parties. He played his role without revealing the void in his heart. He witnessed history repeating itself: neo-Nazis raising their fists and voices on every continent; the totalitarian Soviet Union spreading its insidious propaganda throughout the world; dictators and fanatics in the Middle East using Jews as scapegoats; and the democracies again impotent, fighting with half their might. He stopped working on his history of the Third Reich. Each day he threw into his furnace something from the stacks of newspapers and magazines, the remains of Goebbels's propaganda, or from the boxes of documents he had collected. He discarded the "Watchword of the Week" posters mentioned in his May 5, 1945, diary entry, and the memorabilia of his political campaigns during the time of the Republic. He even threw away photographs that brought back painful memories. He burned his research notes for his history book, and the day came when Friedrich placed the book manuscript itself, more than a hundred pages, in the fire. Who was he to save the world when he had been unable to save his own son? He would have placed the diary notebooks on the burning manuscript, but he had no energy to crawl into the cabinet to take them from their hiding place.

Pauline was in an even worse state, having spent so many years during Hitler's regime rejoicing that her son had been spared the most senseless and horrible of all wars, only to lose him in such a way. She withdrew from everyone. Only a rare visit from Liliane and Margrit brought her to life. But Margrit presented problems. She did not get along with her stepfather and would not help her mother with the new children. Liliane bitterly complained to her former in-laws that Margrit was like Fred: lazy and self-centered. One more calamity for the saddened couple to bear.

Seven years would pass before a young American sailor, searching for the Kellners of Laubach, would appear at their door with a photograph of their son in his pocket.

ABOUT THE TRANSLATION

The two-volume German edition of Friedrich Kellner's diary, *"Vernebelt, verdunkelt sind alle Hirne": Tagebücher 1939–1945*, is a complete presentation of every word in the diary, including the entire texts of the hundreds of newspaper articles pasted among the entries. Further editions can well serve the reading public through abridgments. For this translation the news clippings were the first and primary targets for reduction, although with care to preserve the diary's unique atmosphere of the Third Reich's unrelenting propaganda. In diary entries where Friedrich made no reference to the news article – and the article did not add essential information to the entry's topic – it was removed. Where multiple articles covered the same topic, the most instructive was retained. In many instances, articles were condensed to headlines and relevant paragraphs. The occasional long lists of news headlines pasted on some diary pages could be truncated without diminishing their dramatic impact. The obituaries were decreased in number without losing their somber effect.

Reducing Friedrich's writing was the greater challenge. The various themes and lines of discourse had to be pruned of repetitions without harming emphasis and balance, especially in entries where Friedrich's forceful tone and earthy choice of words underscore the topic's significance for him: e.g., his fellow Germans' "idiotic" faith in Nazi propaganda; the "cowardly" West's failure to act swiftly; and the "bestial" slaughter of innocents. The diary is noted for its author's early recognition of the intention to exterminate (*Ausrottung*) the Jews of Europe, a word that first appears October 7, 1939. Friedrich mentions Jews in forty entries (less than 5 percent of the diary), which makes it a minor theme, albeit one of major historical importance, and one that elicits strong empathy from the diarist. This abridgment retains the majority of those entries without exaggerating Friedrich's interest in this subject, as it still remains a minor theme among the many other subjects. The impressive variety of topics in the author's wide coverage of the war years is evident in even a cursory glance at the index section, which carries over 1,500 entries. The omission of entire diary entries is denoted by an ellipsis on its own line, placed flush with the left margin. The omission of news articles from within diary entries is denoted by an ellipsis on its own line, indented from the left margin. Considering the interwoven nature of Kellner's observations and news articles, the indented ellipsis occasionally denotes such a combination.

The research section in this volume is one third that of the German edition. It might have been reduced further except many notes are still needed to describe people, places, and events of an era fast receding from living memory and increasingly less familiar to the public. As for the references to Friedrich Kellner's letters and memoranda and other documents, all such material, along with the notebooks of the diary, are privately held by me in College Station, Texas.

Robert Scott Kellner

PRE-WAR WRITINGS
September 26, 1938 – August 30, 1939

September 26, 1938

Laubach, Hesse.

I want to capture in writing the immediate mood and images of my surroundings so people in the future will not be tempted to fabricate a great event out of them – a "Heroic Period" or the like. To begin with, there is a complete lack of enthusiasm.[1] Everyone hopes, trusts in miracles, and fashions in their own little minds a picture of the world that has nothing whatsoever to do with foresight. (Whoever wants to learn about the souls of the "good Germans" in my contemporary society should read my notes. But I harbor the misgiving that once these events have come to pass only a few decent people will remain and the guilty will have no interest in seeing their disgrace written down on paper.)

On Sunday, September 25, men and horses of a veterinary detachment assembled here, though it cannot be said their exercise went smoothly. They were all in low spirits – older men, 35–45. Some had seen service; some had not.

What are people saying? A variety of opinions: France and England will stay neutral; Poland and Hungary are meddling in Czechoslovakia. No one mentions Russia. "Suddenly and swiftly we will move against the Czechs, and in just two or three days – a very short time – Czechoslovakia is in our hands." Hardly anyone thinks about possible counter-actions. I frequently bring my opinion into these conversations to point out a person should never underestimate his opponents. No one listens. Arrogance has been raised to the highest power.

It will take war to bring the entire population to reason. Unfortunately the few Germans with sense and understanding will have to suffer through it, but such is fate. We will have to experience and feel what it is like to have war upon our own soil before a new generation can arise that perhaps will bring an end to cocky, loudmouthed, and brutal Germans.

Says Dr. Schmitt: "No enemy pilot will cross the border and live." And "The military demonstrations at the Nuremberg Party Rally went

<u>Laubach, den 26. September 1938.</u>

Der Sinn meiner Niederschrift ist der, augenblickliche Stimmungsbilder aus meiner Umgebung festzuhalten, damit eine spätere Zeit nicht in die Versuchung kommt, ein „großes Geschehen" daraus zu konstruieren. (eine „heroische" Zeit od. dergl.)

Vor allem: es herrscht keinerlei Begeisterung. Alle Menschen „hoffen", glauben an Wunder und machen sich ein Weltbild in ihren Köpfchen zurecht, das mit Weitblick aber auch gar nichts zu tun hat.

Am Sonntag, den 25.9.1938, wurden hier Mannschaften u. Pferde einer Veterinär-Abteilung zusammengestellt. Man kann nicht sagen, daß die Sache wie am Schnürchen geklappt habe. Die Mannschaften befanden sich durchweg in gedrückter Stimmung. Es handelte sich teils um gediente, teils um ungediente Männer im vorgerückten Mannesalter (35–45).

Aber die zeitgenössische Gesellschaft, die Taten der „guten" Deutschen kennen lernen möchte, der Sinn meiner Aufzeichnungen. Aber ich hege die Befürchtung, daß nach dem Ablauf der Geschehnisse werden nur wenig aufrechte Menschen übrig bleiben u. die Schuldigen haben kein Interesse, ihr Benehmen festgehalten zu sehen.

Was sagen die Leute: bunte Meinungen. Frankreich u. England bleiben neutral. Polen u. Ungarn greifen gegen die Tschechoslowakei ein. Von Rußland redet niemand. „Wir gehen schlagartig gegen die Tschechen vor und in ganz kurzer Zeit (2–3 Tage) ist die Tschechei in unseren Händen." ~~Nicht~~ ein einziger Mensch denkt an die Kosten) Gegenwirkungen. Ich bringe in Gesprächen immer wieder meine Warnung zum Ausdruck, daß man seine Gegner nie unterschätzen dürfe. Aber das hört niemand. Die Überheblichkeit ist bis zur höchsten Potenz gesteigert.

<u>Meine Auffassung</u>: Der Krieg muß das gesamte Volk zur Vernunft bringen. Leider müssen die wenigen Deutschen mit Vernunft u. Verstand darunter leiden. Das ist Schicksal. Nur wenn allen einmal

splendidly."[2] This same man once spoke of "a little war" with Russia. I am sorry to have to say the primitive thinking of the German people has reached a degree utterly impossible to surpass. That is your work, Propaganda Minister! Every mind is clouded and darkened! [*Vernebelt, verdunkelt sind alle Hirne!*] One must despair of the people. Critical thinking is bad for us. Everything is wonderful.[3]

Wait and see. From heavenly joy to deadly sorrow – we will yet experience it.[4]

The Lardenbach mayor [Otto Keil] – a Nazi Party member! – purportedly has a gun, and if the war is lost, he will "shoot himself."

We absolutely must win the war.

These elevated ones, the *Parteigenossen* [Nazi Party comrades], expect the second-class human beings, the *Volksgenossen* [national comrades who have not joined the Party], to help them achieve victory for their policies![5] What a "noble" idea. You will get the shock of your lives, you Party comrades!

October 1, 1938

After finding ourselves on the brink of a world war because of Germany's behavior, and when Propaganda Minister Goebbels's badgering could not have become any worse, an "agreement" on Czechoslovakia was reached through the initiative of the English prime minister. Problem now solved in Munich.[6] Still, to keep the upper hand, Goebbels states insolently, "Peace has been preserved *only* by Hitler's peaceful demeanor." And what is worst of all: the German people blindly repeat it. Against stupidity the gods themselves contend in vain![7]

August 1939

We live through days of tremendous tension. Unmistakable signs of secret mobilization have shaken even the greatest optimists. The various military measures taking place underscore the increasing seriousness of the situation.

How we came to know this: At 4 in the morning on August 26, Franz Schüler, the courthouse night watchman, knocked on our bedroom window. He had just received call-up papers, effective immediately, to report for duty in Giessen. Altogether 120 such orders were delivered during the night. The senior magistrate, Dr. Schmitt, was among the recipients.

Naturally the people do not yet have a uniform opinion about this situation. Their views cover a wide range, depending on their own circumstances. It is worth noting that the overwhelming majority truly believe in the newspaper articles and other opinions being fed to them: that our armed forces have an almost fairy-tale strength and striking ability, and our army will swallow Poland in a lightning-quick assault. Whenever it has anything to do with something to be "taken," you can scarcely hear a voice of reason. What tragic traits of mankind are revealed here: Robbery and Greed! No one bothers to think that by this same "right," he himself can be driven from his own place tomorrow.

Scarcely anyone really believes France and England will back Poland. As the ominous pact with Russia was being concluded, the stock of the federation of the "takers" rose. The "alliance" with this nation seems rather bizarre after the long and drawn-out campaign the Nazis waged against Russia in word and writing, in particular against the "subhumans" there. The victory of National Socialism can be traced solely to its harsh campaign against Communism. No Reichstag session or Party rally took place where there was not a tremendous battle cry raised against the "world enemy, Stalin." It is not surprising even those with less tender natures have been knocked off balance, at least for a day or two, by the reversal of opinion regarding the danger from Russian "common bloodstained criminals" and the "scum of humanity" – as Adolf Hitler put it in *Mein Kampf*.[8] On the other hand, only a few people seem to wonder about Russia's motives for signing the pact. Will Russia use its "neutrality" pact with Germany to insidiously seduce us into declaring war on Poland and only later throw its own unscathed forces onto the scale for the final decision?

Adolf Hitler wrote that if Germany should ever ally with Russia against England and France, "Its outcome would be the end of Germany."[9] What should a simple man say about this, and what should the believers in National Socialism think? Is Prophet Hitler wrong and Chancellor Hitler correct, or the reverse? History will know how to tell it. Perhaps the last word in wisdom is this: The mills of God grind slowly but surely.

As a preacher in the wilderness I felt compelled to write down the thoughts that dominated my mind in this nerve-wracking time so later – should it still be possible – I could convey a picture of the true reality to my descendants.

August 30, 1939
Fr. Kellner

The Diary

1939

September 1, 1939

Hitler ordered the invasion of Poland. The German officers did not object. The German troops did not rebel. The German people did not protest. Now they and the entire world will pay for their indifference to tyranny and terrorism.[1]

Early September 1939 [Supplemental essay]

The foolish people are intoxicated by the German army's exaggerated initial successes in Poland. Tales of atrocities of the worst kind are buzzing in the air and inside the heads of the armchair warriors.[2] Certain regulatory measures at home – in particular the introduction of food ration cards – has somewhat dampened the assurance of victory. And those measures are compulsory! Nevertheless, nothing has yet shaken the childlike faith in the infallibility of the gods and demigods. What can one say when even those who always formed opinions based on their own experiences now ravenously devour ridiculous gossip and asinine rumors – which have been planted and purposely circulated – and then use such nonsense to prop up the shaky image of their hero?

If one considers all that has been babbled and written about the "Axis Powers." What a circus, with official receptions for each other, and so on. Many Germans believe in the tremendous power of the legendary "Axis" regardless of our bad experiences in 1915.[3] Whenever I spoke up in close circles about the Anti-Comintern Pact and said Italy would never enter a war for Germany, I received mostly silence – scarcely any agreement.[4] What were my considerations in forming this opinion? At the outbreak of war in 1914, the Triple Alliance consisted of Germany, Austria-Hungary, and Italy, with Bulgaria and Turkey also siding with Germany. Today Turkey is allied with England and France (as are Greece and Romania). Under such circumstances, it would be suicidal for Italy to enter a war against England and its allies. Why? Italy would be a prisoner in the Mediterranean, cut off from the rest of the world, particularly its suppliers of raw material (oil!). What's more, it would have to write off Abyssinia, Libya, Albania, and the Dodecanese Islands.[5] France, England, and Turkey would control the

Anfang September 1939. 1

Das blöde Volk berauscht sich an den aufgebauschten ~~übertriebenen~~ Anfangserfolgen der deutschen Armeen in Polen. Kriegslüsternheit übelster Art durchschwirren den Aether u. die Köpfe der Heimkrieger. Die Siegesgewissheit wird allerdings sehr und da etwas herabgedrückt ~~gedämpft~~ durch die gesetzlichen Maßnahmen. Insbesondere ist es die Einführung der Lebensmittelkarten. ~~Die sich~~ Das sind unerwünschte Dämpfer! Allerdings ist der kindliche Glaube an die Unfehlbarkeit der Götter und Halbgötter noch nicht erschüttert. Was soll man auch schon sagen einem selbst Menschen, die kraft ihres Lebensganges sich eine eigene Meinung bilden müssten, jedes dümmste Geschwätz u. jeden dümmsten Aufschlag in Umlauf gebracht, Gerücht mit wahren Hoffnungen verschlungen und ihre wankende Haltung daran aufrichten.

Wenn man bedenkt was über die „Achsenmächte" geschwätzt u. geschrieben worden ist. „Welch' ein Zirkus von bedauernswerten Geschöpfen usw. (~~Jeder Landsknecht~~) Viele Deutsche haben trotz der Erfahrungen von 1915 an die ungeheure Gewalt der sogenannten „Achse" geglaubt. Wenn ich im andern Laufe von Abschluß des Kommunistenpaktes ab der Auffassung vertreten habe, daß Italien niemals in einem Krieg für Deutschland eintreten ~~wird~~ würde so habe ich höchstens Achselzucken aber kaum einmal Beifall geerntet. Aus welchen Erwägungen heraus bildete ich mir meine Meinung über Italien. Bei Ausbruch des Krieges 1914 bestand der Dreibund: Deutschland, Österreich-

Mediterranean. Italy's entire shipping industry would be condemned to death. Can anyone possibly believe Italy is crazy enough to do itself in?

And there is another question: If Italy kept its power and strength intact and behaved decently toward England, would it not then get a little piece of the pie when the war was over?

These are but assumptions and assertions. It will be the future that instructs us.

Our leaders have taken leave of their senses. [...] How can anyone conduct and win a war with people who are being treated like slaves? It is such today that life overall is no longer worth living. A harassed, tormented, intimidated, and extremely subjugated people are supposed to let themselves be shot dead for a tyrant. Terror without equal! The Party bosses as police informers. The decent German has hardly any courage left to think, let alone to speak. For instance, Mayor Högy warned Herr Heusing to be more circumspect in his conversations because Heusing had mentioned to a woman that we were using colonial troops on the Western Front.[6] Is that not outrageous?

As for the Western Front, that is a subject in itself: the "impregnable" Siegfried Line. What nonsense is there that has not been said? I am absolutely convinced the Siegfried Line is our greatest misfortune. Without the Siegfried Line in the West, we could never have provoked a conflict in the East. We waged war in the East in order to liberate the "ethnic Germans" in Poland – or so we were told. But in doing so, we destroyed much of the property that belonged to the "ethnic Germans," and we removed hundreds of thousands from their homeland to bring them here to the West. We are learning this from the refugees. What an unbelievable insanity! If we had been of good will, we would have first determined who among the bribed "ethnic Germans" really wanted to become German? Surely, a pitiful number would have come forth. It happened exactly this way in Corsica for Mussolini. There was much drum beating but few recruits; and the reality was only a measly handful of Corsicans prepared to return to their "beloved motherland." And see how Italian demands for Corsica have grown silent.

We have the same sham along the border between Germany and Poland. Whoever is complaining within each of these countries is a troublemaker and needs to be kicked out! Then peace can be established. We have an historical example of this when Turkey made all the Greeks leave Asia Minor in 1922.[7] After that, Turkey and Greece buried the war hatchet. At some point in time, permanent borders have to be drawn. And then, enough!

It is exactly the same with the colonial question.[8] Who goes voluntarily to the colonies? Why is that not clearly and officially recorded? Who considers themselves fertilizers of culture? Go ahead, you ranters, but you might want to look before you leap! In my circle of acquaintances, I have never come across anyone who felt the desire to move to a colony. The only type still bringing up the colonial question is someone who fancies himself a colonial minister – and perhaps others who are on the prowl for sinecures. That is the gist of the matter.

If the government would like to accomplish a great feat, there is but one way:

Dissolution of the Nazi Party and its entire organizational structure!

No more First and Second Class Germans (Parteigenossen and Volksgenossen) but only Germans – just as there are only soldiers in the trenches. But since this concept is not National Socialist (i.e., obdurate), it is out of the question. And Fate strides quickly on.

For illustration, I will tack on here some statements by a few people:
Major Goldmann, September 7, 1939: "The war will be over in six days."
[Josef] Hessler: "French soldiers have set up signs along the Western Front with the words, 'We will not shoot.'"
SS Wolf to Heck: "Does your supervisor [Friedrich Kellner] greet you in the morning with 'Heil Hitler'?"[9]
Frau Anna Steller Jochem: "This is really a great and glorious time!"
Weisel, the gardener: "Mussolini is going after the Suez Canal, Tunis, and Corsica."

Various regulatory measures:
Complete permanent blackouts (a cemetery-like silence on the streets in the evening).[10]
Motor vehicle traffic is forbidden beginning September 20, 1939.
Imprisonment or even death for deliberately listening to forbidden foreign broadcasts.

September 13, 1939

Everyone I come across lately asks, "What do you think about the situation?" Naturally, extreme caution must be used. A candid response is possible only in the smallest circles among good friends; just a small minority have been able to maintain a clear view – at least here in the country: an oasis in the National Socialist desert. The optimism of the first days is no longer one hundred percent, but the people continue to believe only too gladly in everything they are wishing for: particularly a quick and victorious end to the war. I let fall a droplet of doubt when I refer to the war of 1914, which also was going to be finished in six weeks. But faith in miracles is extremely strong. Six years of National Socialist propaganda has totally befogged the German people's brains. Unbelievable but unfortunately true.

Lindemeyer speaks gingerly with me. He sings songs of praise about the planning and organization and apparently has set his hopes on the presumed assistance from Russia. Russia has called up two million reservists and surely will "take" the remainder of Poland. (Thus Lindemeyer no longer builds upon our own strength.)

Now and then I throw "Italy" into the debate. No one wants to openly express his disappointment.[11]

Naturally, there are completely crazy military cadets too. And in the Laubach train station, Wetzel (with some others) said to me, "Hopefully the Führer will conquer France." He rages about the English [naval] blockade. I tell him that is war and remind him Germany is carrying on unrestricted submarine warfare. I detect little understanding for justice; overall, a feeling for justice is decidedly the weakest side of our people.

A windbag in a broadcast from Munich speaks about the abominations the English committed against the Boers.[12] Hasn't he heard that those in glasshouses shouldn't throw stones? Why doesn't he bemoan the victims of the hateful and bloodthirsty National Socialists in the deep tranquility of the German concentration camps? Even a harmless utterance has brought our fellow countrymen into such a place. And how many were shot "during an attempt to escape"? Has this idiot heard nothing about November 9 and 10, when all the synagogues were destroyed?[13]

September 14, 1939

6:45 in the morning. Frau Schüler tells me she is driving to Giessen to see her husband [Franz, the courthouse night watchman] before he is transferred. In the name of our courthouse working staff, I will say here in writing, "Fare thee well." It turned out harmlessly, though. Schüler was sent merely from Giessen to Marburg.

A few days ago two batteries of heavy artillery were quartered in Laubach.[14] They came from Landsberg, Bavaria, but were told to say they were from Landshut. Nonsense! At their departure one could see very glum faces – no morale whatsoever. A bad omen!

Among the men who have not yet been called up, a strange manner of thinking can be found. Not that they take a position against the war. No, it is just they all hope for a rapid end (meaning none of them would have to be called up). Nice people, are they not? [War is fine, but] just no consequences! For God's sake!

A discussion with Dr. Hemeyer reveals complete agreement with my own opinions. Why are there not more like this one? It is a calamity for our pitiful native land that the best must live like hermits, and common brutal hangmen have power!

The Praetorian Guard (Wolf, Dirlam, Leidner) has placed itself every-where in the background and watches decent Germans.[15] *Pfui!*

Frau Becker heard from the Schmitts' housemaid [Else Gross] that Judge Schmitt wrote a long letter home.[16] Schmitt is with a communications staff at the Western Front. From the letter's contents the maid knew only that there would be no war; the French and the Germans are playing cards together in the trenches! Either this academic Schmitt is a complete blockhead, or he regards us as first-class idiots.

A rumor going around is that a veterinary surgeon in Grünberg was arrested for passing around leaflets of Chamberlain's speech.[17] I made a phone call, and the courthouse in Grünberg knew nothing about arrests. The fact that enemy airplanes can casually fly over Germany and drop leaflets has astounded the people (who had it pounded into their heads no enemy airplane would ever cross the border). So the poisonous rumormongers would like the simple-minded folk to believe the leaflets were not from enemy planes but printed by German traitors. Yet Hermann Göring expressly pointed out in his speech in the first days of September the English were indeed dropping leaflets onto German territory.[18] It does not matter. The people are so forgetful everything can simply be changed from one day to the next.

France and England's military alliance is not going to shake the Nazi Party members' confidence. If Poland is completely devastated, the Western powers will have to reproach themselves for not having done enough before the outbreak of war to protect Poland from being overrun. At the least England and France should have stationed their air forces in Poland.

September 16, 1939

Depressed mood: the war measures are burdening people's minds. In particular, the strictly carried-out blackouts greatly discomfort everyone. Those in agriculture are extra encumbered. To make up for the shortage of day laborers [who have been called into the military], they have to work late into the evening, but they are not allowed to illuminate their house, yard, cellar, barn, or stable as in former times. In the evenings now, a dead silence reigns throughout our entire small town. The old folks are afraid to go out on the streets because of the darkness. An unusual peace prevails on the highways. "Motorized" Germany sleeps. Beginning September 20, only vehicles designated as having special permission may be driven.

The poison of the Nazis' "sun politics" has penetrated deeply into the human organism.[19] Each fostered rumor is believed. Everyone clings to the still-coming "great miracle." When spirits become dampened, "Thirty thousand German airplanes are going to attack England." A herald of such news who can spin a convincing fairy tale about attacking England gathers a large number of believers. [. . .]

September 17, 1939

Sunday. I have on-call duty from 2–10 p.m. We received a letter from Katie – the first sign of life since she had to leave Saarbrücken – and in no way am I delighted with her selected place of residence: Weisskirchen, region of Trier.[20] Her choice reflects a carefree attitude – if not even an overly brave one. People's views are so varied: one wants to take a rest on the railway tracks, and the other one is afraid of white mice. In the center lies caution. Caution has yet to cause any great damage.

Suspense: how does the commenced war go? We now have gone through the beginnings of two wars. Who dares to forecast the end of this one? Because of our experience with the war of 1914–18, [Pauline and I] are extremely skeptical. A burnt child fears the fire. What all can yet occur? The undreamed of, the unexpected. The land maps have been thrown out of joint. Has nothing even once been said of [Oswald Spengler's] *The Decline of the West*?[21]

Who carries the blame? The people without a brain! To trample democracy with one's feet and give power to a single man over almost eighty million people is so terrible one can really tremble over the things that will come. A people allow an idea to be poured and hammered into them, narrow-mindedly follow every suggestion, let themselves be stepped on, tormented, conned, exhausted – and must, in addition, under national control, call out "Heil Hitler." One can feel only deep mourning in his heart over such a dreadful age and over the sheep-like patience of an entire population. Are there no men left at all? I believe I can answer this question in the negative. These people can be compared only with a herd being led to the slaughterhouse, and like this herd not even conscious of their strength and their misery.

Oh God, let your light shine – and be merciful unto these people!

September 18, 1939

According to official reports, Russian troops supposedly invaded Poland. The sinking of the exchange rate will coincide with the rapidly rising stocks of war profiteers, beer hall strategists, and gamblers. These types already view the fourth division of Poland as an already accomplished fact.[22]

That is how the situation presents itself in the minds of my fellow men, but once again I stand apart because I simply cannot imagine Russia undertaking anything in favor of Germany. When Hitler quite openly points out in *Mein Kampf* that the future of Germany can be found only in the East – where we will solve our requirements for *Lebensraum* – every reasonable human being realizes we are heading for a tremendous argument with the Slavs: if not tomorrow, then at some definite point in time.[23] Yet now the Russians are in the process of creating strategic positions for themselves, and the German "Michel" is all inspired about it.[24]

It is completely evident our foreign policy has been carried along or driven by irrationality. For twenty years we had raging paper battles over Russia, but now, overnight, we have the "stoutest" friendship. We made anti-Communist pacts with Japan, Italy, Spain, and Hungary. But today we are arm-in-arm with the same Russia we depicted a thousand times over as the world's enemy. An entire Nazi Party Congress was devoted to presenting Germany as the bulwark of culture and humanity against a hostile Bolshevism.[25] "Explain to me, Count Oerindur, the duplicity of nature!"[26] Even if such things are permitted as policy, we must not employ the methods of medieval robbers. I believe it was Bismarck who once said history will nail down every political error and provide a correction more precise than anything found in a Prussian audit office.[27]

The hardheaded obstinacy of our "Führer" alone has steered us into the situation today. A nation, just like an individual, cannot expect to totally fulfill every one of its desired plans; it cannot actually move into every castle it builds in the air. True mastery is being able to work and succeed within limitations, not in establishing a dictatorship to conquer a continent and subjugate other people.

We have indeed learned nothing from history. The world might be conquered through peaceful actions by free thinkers in an open economy – but not by a corrupt monetary economy and excessive armaments.

September 25, 1939

Frau Anna Jochem, née Steller, wants to report to the Ortsgruppenleiter [Local Group Leader] anyone who claims shooting has begun at the Siegfried Line.[28] A profound peace may now reign: the lunatic asylum is complete! Germans may no longer speak even about German army reports. Although the army is telling us belatedly, their report clearly states fighting is underway. According to Steller-Jochem, however, no one may say that freely.

Everything blithely goes on. You Nazi women are on the right track.

October 2, 1939

A cloudy and rainy day. With much persuasive vigor, senior clerk Becker has just developed a fanciful plan.[29] German troops will seek to land in England, supported by submarines and thirty thousand airplanes. My few objections bounce off without success. I begin to see the complete futility in speaking with my fellow creatures about military matters. Success in Poland has deranged the majority of the people. At the least, it has strongly impaired their power to comprehend.

October 4, 1939

We have been ordered to fly flags on the building for one week to mark the occasion of German troops entering Warsaw.[30] Such gestures, I have to say, make no impression on the population. The people feel nothing now from all these "victories." The breadbasket will be hung higher and out of reach, the portions will become smaller, and the struggle to obtain a ration card for doing an essential laundry – or purchasing a piece of clothing – is what really will stir up their blood.[31] The situation is that these small things of daily life generally exert a substantial influence on the people's mood. The artifice of "culture" cannot stand disturbances because people feel it immediately; the smallest change makes them think their way of life has been impaired. The higher the culture, the further away must be war.

October 6, 1939

I no longer hear as many hopeful expressions as in the first days, and I find it interesting no one speaks any more of "Axis Power" Italy. All wait for Hitler's speech today in the Reichstag.

After so many years of experience, I personally do not think anything of the so-called "peace offer," which is allegedly to come. Indeed it will not be, as the National Socialists believe, that the world will dance to their tune. Furthermore, it is the tone that determines the music, and in that regard our governing officials display an unusually poor lack of feeling. Why must they always speak to the world in such a threatening manner? "Fear guards the forest" was their prescription for within Germany. But no one should expect countries like England and France to simply crawl into a mouse hole because of our loud shouting. Such a view is more than ridiculous. That might work with a small nation, but the British Empire is not going to be made docile in this way or forced to its knees. And mankind's sympathies will go without question to those who do not use the openly brutal methods we inflicted upon the people of Austria, Czechoslovakia, and Poland – true nations of culture.

Are countries like Switzerland, Belgium, Holland, Denmark, and others to be delighted with what has been occurring around them – the annihilation of nations?

I just spoke with Becker about the defense pact Russia made with Lithuania and Latvia and told him such an action was directed against Germany.[32] After all, we are the one and only country that might attack Lithuania in the future. What had we written in the past about German interest in the Baltic States? Volumes! So now Russia, with its fleet in the Gulf of Riga, is "defending" the German Baltic Sea! That really is an ironic joke. Nevertheless, Herr Becker has hopes we will be supported by Russia. Hope is the walking-stick from the cradle to the grave. Nothing can be done about that – except to wait and see.

What effect did Hitler's speech have in my immediate area? To get right to the point: it did not convince anyone peace was moving closer. The young and politically inexperienced generation understandably desires to see the world bow to the words of Adolf Hitler. In my opinion, the speech was not a masterpiece. It sounded as though the foreign ministry had composed it: issues tossed about in a hodge-podge fashion without clearly outlined formulas and proposals; blurred and washed out; murky suggestions that a nation of "Poland" might be rebuilt, but then, "the Poland of the Versailles Treaty will never arise again."[33]

If no more Poland, then please specify how, where, and when the Polish "people" will govern themselves. The Polish language has not yet been stamped out. One shall have to attend to the problem of "Poland," whether one wants to or not! It is sheer nonsense to try to mislead the world that Europe will now have peace because Poland has been destroyed. The opposite is the case. Every Pole will harbor an indelible hatred against Germany that will produce blazing flames of revenge – if not tomorrow, then the day after tomorrow. This prophecy is a safe bet. My descendants will have the opportunity to see the proof, and they will certainly be pleased and proud there were Germans who did not for a moment agree with such politics as 1933–1939. Unfortunately, it must be said, however, that those who never wavered were such small handfuls within the abyss they had to live like hermits.

October 7, 1939

Too many of my fellow men allowed themselves to be deluded by National Socialist propaganda. The "Sun" politics ensnared those who should have looked more critically on the Fata Morgana mirage and recognized it for what it was: bluff and swindle; base public fraud. The major guideline was "Just do not think." And it was so charmingly "beautiful" that the "Leader" makes everything clear for those too lazy to think. What was the common saying, "The Führer will yet make it right"? Or as a pitiful contemporary once said to me, "You should not be bothering with such thoughts; that will all be taken care of."

Jugglers, dazzlers, bigwigs, and position seekers are in influential positions. Terror is trump. Methods of common brutal suppression are considered sanctified laws. "Old Fighters" are saints, and from the district leader upwards there are only Gods![34] And all this has been going on already for almost seven years.

How can a reasonable person think there can be any eternal values carried within such a cagey and criminal system?

What cardinal errors has this Nazi tyranny made?

1. The enforced greeting, "Heil Hitler."
2. Splitting the people into Party members and non-Party members.
3. One-sided control of public opinion – meaning a press with just one voice.
4. Suppressing free expression of opinion.
5. Protecting the Old Fighters and Party members, even if they are criminals.
6. Persecuting decent citizens only because they once had another opinion and perhaps referred to the Nazis as an abscess.
7. Persecution and extermination of the Jews.[35]
8. Disrespect for people's religious convictions.
9. Continuously changing the laws: new laws in great volumes, and thousands of regulations. Even specialists can no longer keep up with their own subjects.
10. Unbelievable over-organization in the nation and, in particular, in the Party and its institutions.
11. Dreadfully unproductive offices (and a bloated bureaucracy).
12. Irresponsible expenditures without taking income into consideration.
13. Protecting the worst people in the state (pardons, etc.).
14. Tax burden without end.
15. Mendicants in bulk (NSV, WHW).[36] Badges, etc.
16. Easy sinecures and benefits for Nazi Party members (minor offices, utensils, uniforms, toys, circus, fanfares: Sieg-Heil, Sieg-Heil).
17. "The Führer commands and we follow!"[37]
18. "We owe everything to our Führer."

Another sick spirit is the retired justice secretary Ferdinand Stotz. In a discussion with Dr. Matting at the stamp counter in the Laubach post office, Stotz said, "We will not have peace as before until the English are destroyed." Dr. Matting responded, "You are a warmonger. The Führer wants the exact opposite: a compromise." Stotz continued, "Let the Russians lend us their airplanes against England, and within fourteen days the French will break away from the English."

Such dumb chatterboxes belong under lock and key.

October 8, 1939

We received a letter from Pauline's sister Lina. Pauline and I should be happy to be in Laubach, she wrote, because it was terrible in the city. She stood for two hours at the butcher's waiting for meat.

October 9, 1939

Folks like us find themselves constantly asking the question, "How was it possible a cultured people like the Germans could have handed absolute authority to a single man?" One must despair over the total obtuseness and cowardliness. What our ancestors had fought to achieve over centuries was forfeited in 1933 by inane carelessness, incomprehensible gullibility, and the damned blasé attitude of the German middle class. Our freedom poets lived altogether in vain. In the past, youths with ideals fought for liberty. Today, within a direful tyranny, they allow and defend a juggler and pied piper's abuse. Such a people are not worthy of continued existence.

[Albrecht] Marx received a field-post letter from his brother-in-law stationed in the Saar. A dark mood emerges from the letter: "Hopefully the swindle will not last much longer. We are filled up to the neck with it . . . Where are the Old Fighters? Here is where they could fight . . . Don't leave home. Be content even if you must eat from the cat's dish."
  Enough said.

In 1932 the editor in the *Frankfurter Zeitung* wrote, "The German people will yet again long for democracy – on their knees." But before the great mass of Germans can be ready again for democracy, they will have to drink to the very last drop from the bitter cup of National Socialism. That was my point of view from the beginning. Only when hope in the conjured castles in the air and other miracles finally gives out will the entire house of cards collapse. Everyone, naturally, will then say he knew it would turn out that way, and no one will say he was involved with the NSDAP. During the economic boom, ninety-nine percent were screaming "Heil Hitler" and "Sieg Heil" [Hail Victory]. One person might have gone along because it promised personal advantages for him or his children; another because he was a weakling and did not want to swim against the current. The craftsman saw only profits. The farmer believed Hitler would free him from taxes. Each had something that suited his own purpose, and this entire brew was called "National Socialism." The worst part of it was the newspaper smearers. Babblers and smooth talkers were allowed to put in their two cents, as long as their bombastic phrases praised either the Nazi system or its satellites, and if they declared everything flowing from the "Nuremberg funnel" was simply marvelous.[38] Never the smallest word of doubt or criticism. Like gods, the rulers could hourly applaud their own work and heap tremendous quantities of praise upon themselves. They heard nothing but the thudding clang of their own voices. No sound of the people penetrated their barricaded castles or their Brown House.[39] They did not see the clenched fists nor feel the hatred from those they oppressed. Herr Goebbels said during the Kampfzeit [Time of Struggle] before they came to power that the National Socialists could be proud they would always have the ear of the people and would know their distresses and desires.[40] But once these men had power and sat in their armchairs and feathered their own nests, only the most brutal force governed – without any leniency. Except there was the greatest indulgence for their own Party members, who had to be kept content lest they unravel the whole system.

October 10, 1939

To keep the people from directing their rage at their actual oppressor, rulers in every age have used diversionary tactics to shield their own guilt. The entire action against the Jews was no different from throwing down a piece of meat for the beasts. "The Jews are our misfortune," cry out the Nazis.[41] The correct answer of the people would have been, "No, not the Jews, but the Nazis are the misfortune for the German people."

It is exactly the same today, except the drums now beat against the English. Every reasonable person knows that if we had behaved in a decent manner we could have achieved a satisfactory relationship with England, at least to some extent. Everything with us is weapons and shouts of war and continuous threats – with no suitable middle ground. The purpose is to intimidate the alleged or real opponent to want to be on good terms with us. But eternal saber rattling leads to one thing, and that is war.

The lack of good will on our side is clear to see from all of our propaganda. We take a spiteful swipe at the English at every single opportunity. I need only think of Palestine. At the same time we were throwing Jews out of Germany, we roused up the Arabs through radio and press to resist Jewish settlement.[42] Is this a coherent foreign policy? This mania to make things more difficult for the English everywhere, and then to exult over it, makes us look ridiculous. [. . .]

October 11, 1939

[Pauline's sister] Anna and some others were here visiting for two days.[43] She is a victim of National Socialist propaganda, but a representation of my views on how things were tied together was fruitful. At least I planted a seed for a better insight. Anyone who is informed about only one side is really an impoverished creature. Franz fancies himself an inspired "conqueror."[44] It is a shame this fellow does not have to use his own bones for it. But he, too, will receive his just reward.

October 12, 1939

The guessing games have begun: "What is happening in the West?" Here behind the front lines, several hundred kilometers from the shooting, the people have no impression a war is even going on. But they will feel the economic impact: food ration cards (which perhaps might have come even without war); coupons for purchasing certain goods; and a lack of agricultural workers. All these features are not sufficient, however, to cause the population even for a moment to consider shaking off the yoke. By their slavish nature, Germans today have lost everything all of the earlier freedom movements brought about. Such a nature almost gives the impression of enjoying being regularly suppressed. Cowardice celebrates its triumph: simply do not resist. People have been turned into worms.

Sometimes I come close to letting my own hopes sink. Then I convince myself again there must be at least some men within the armed forces who are preparing to put an end to the tyranny. Good things take time, though. Because of a lack of any kind of organization, nothing at all can be expected from the civilians. Taking charge requires people to come together, whether they want to or not, in order to face the dangers. A palace revolution is therefore unlikely.

Actually it is very difficult for someone situated off the beaten track, as I am, to judge whether different groups will come together for such an undertaking. And usually nothing is achieved with conjectures, which so often are supported merely by our own wishes. But my close examination and rational consideration show me but one possibility [for a resolution]: the failure of the German armed forces, which can happen only from depleted supplies or defeats.

Perhaps the same interpretation has influenced our opponents' leaders to choose the kind of warfare they are waging. But their choice will not impress the part of German society that suffers from pride and arrogance. Only a much more brutal procedure, similar to what the German populace welcomed and cheered against Poland, can impress this class. No doubt the destructive effects of war would contribute substantially to stifling voices for war and strengthen the desire for peace, though the lawful among us already suffer so much. We must be grateful England and France have preferred, so far, a humane warfare – to the extent such a description can even be applied to war.

Pastor [Ferdinand] Scriba from Wetterfeld, a convinced Hitlerist, had a discussion with August Högy of Ruppertsburg. The "small number" of fatalities in the Polish campaign (naturally Scriba is convinced Hitler's figures of 10,000 are true) is for him "praiseworthy."[45] These are the church-men. They do not notice at all they hunt in their own forest [ultimately eroding faith]. If these ministers truly have an inner religious conviction (and not just because it earns them money for bread), they must be against war. They preach, "Thou shalt not kill," on one day, and then bless weapons on the next. That is an irony of religion, an internal contradiction, and the Church need not be surprised if the sheen from their former splendor has completely worn off. What remains is a wasteland of stammering and murmuring.

Hopefully after this war a foreign corporal will not take power again and have generals pass before him in review. Oh holy simplicity![46]

October 13, 1939

[. . .] I dread to imagine how matters yet to come will turn out. Too much was taken on during these past six years, and not a single thing was solved. The Jewish question was approached with a singularly brutal nature and in a radical form.[47] Where are the Jews supposed to live? The Nazis do not think about it. They generously leave that problem to the other nations. The Jew is plundered according to the regulations, and then he can go to a gang of robbers.[48] Not even Gypsies are proceeded against in such a way.[49] These at least are sent to specific places. And from the inviolable state's point of view, no complaints can be made against it. However, if the Jews, who over the centuries contributed demonstrable achievements in the economy for the total development of the nation, can be made a people without rights, then that is an act unworthy of a cultured nation. The curse of this evil deed will indelibly rest on the entire German people. The authors, the National Socialists, will have disappeared some day; their deeds, however, will live on.

October 14, 1939

After the failure of their "measures to bring about peace," it appears the Party will apply other little methods to stimulate internal war activity and direct the people's rage toward England. The newspapers provide the slogans; for example, a headline in the *Hessische Landes-Zeitung* reads, "Chamberlain Mocks Peace – He Wants to Destroy Germany."[50]

The Party bigwigs of course know this written puffery is not enough to kindle a combative spirit. Something needs to be occurring. For now, they employ mysterious hints. The barbershop is a suitable place for spreading fairy tales. The barber [Fritz] Kircher says to his customers, "We surround their island [with ships], and then we fly there with an overwhelming supremacy and destroy England." My colleague Karl Paul is also with the annihilators (albeit only with words).[51] He heard from a traveler we have airplanes that can carry forty-five fully equipped soldiers. Clerk Becker parrots that, then turns toward me and says, "You can say what you want; we are undertaking something big against England." All such utterances show how they must desperately sustain the belief in Germany's impregnable position and invincibility. The newspapers eagerly help. Grandiose victories of our fliers against the English fleet are announced daily. "Hits" on warships are the main agenda. [. . .]

When I am in the circle of my acquaintances and profusely rant against the national and financial ruin painted on the wall, I might have listeners, but I am far from certain my words are convincing. I more often get the impression one or the other is convinced Hitler will succeed in establishing a burgeoning empire. I must admit that starting from 1933 many new regulations were put into effect without the slightest resistance. The aggressive National Socialists' numerous successes brought the majority of the people to believe in an omnipotent Adolf Hitler. A faith in miracles explains the groveling attitude of Hitler's subjects: a cringing obedience to all instructions. External affairs went perfectly: one victory after another. The necessary drum beats and actors standing by in the wings were never missing. And the radio broadcasts wagged their tails too.

All of this came out of a single kitchen: Dr. Goebbels's! This "Conqueror of Berlin," as he has named himself, has completely conquered Germany. And not only that: many Germans living abroad – all too many of them, unfortunately – have fallen for the cunning propaganda.

October 16, 1939

The sinking of the "Royal Oak," an English battleship, has established a feeding frenzy for the press.[52] The will to resist England's campaign to destroy Germany (what the Nazis maintain England is planning) has increased noticeably. At any rate, the faith in England's coming defeat has been strengthened. The neutral observer must also come to the realization that the image of England's might is not furthered here. The English navy still has not supplied any apparent proof of its strength.

Approximately 800 sailors went down with the battleship. That amount is equal to the crews of 200 large airplanes. Was it not possible for the English navy to cause substantial damage to the submarines' main bases and ship-yards? If they do not have the ability to do this, then the English should not be offering their warships on a platter to the German navy and helping them get cheap triumphs.

Up to now, no one can be convinced of the English navy's capability. Shall England's tactic of blockading the German coast be its only war measure? That would be nothing much and hardly sufficient for victory.

October 19, 1939

It was admitted today the negotiations between Russia and Turkey [over Black Sea access] failed. Turkey rejected Russia's demands, which shows Turkey has finally placed itself on the side of England and France. These countries can book this as a great success. It also appears the Balkan states – supported by Turkey's firm attitude – will carry out resistance against the Russians and Germans.[53] The near future will give us a look at how these situations turn out.

Also, the situation in the North (Finland, Sweden, Norway, and Denmark) will have to be fleshed out.

Soon, "Neutral" will certainly no longer be given. It will have to be called, Either/Or! Either these countries give themselves over to the German and Russian dictatorships, or they follow the democratic countries and thereby keep their liberty and independence as in the past. Considering the overall situation, it would seem something will surely emerge and crystallize – slowly but surely – from the chaos of this period: a revolt against raw force! Is it not a brutality to ship people, like some commodity, out of their second homeland (South Tyrol, the Baltic), where their ancestors established themselves centuries ago, simply to artificially establish "the borders of the Reich"? I do not believe people are obligated for all eternity to endure staying where they are told to stay. At the first promising opportunity, they will look for a "homeland" suited to their own taste.[54]

Again the Nazis make "policy." On Sunday a meeting is to be held, during which the regional group leader will give the awed Volksgenossen the prescribed "Explanations." What mental poverty. No one may say anything.

The nonsensical stuff must be swallowed down without opposition. The entire people must take the blame for this mistake. The Party members get the whipped cream. The thin broth is for the dumb folks.

October 25, 1939

Foreign Minister von Ribbentrop spoke yesterday in Danzig.[55] Such a way of speaking can be done if one wants to intensify a situation. But it must not be. It is no special feat for a Party member to rage against England: the speaker must merely clench his fists, grumble loudly, discharge wild threats, and he will find inspired listeners. I do not know if it is this way with all people. That certainly would not have advanced culture and civilization. Herr von Ribbentrop has mixed together events of the last war with accusations from the past and hereby set up England as an exclusive scapegoat.[56]

But who destroyed Austria, Czechoslovakia, and Poland? Who said he did not have more territorial demands but hid the truth about Poland? Who gives absolutely no security for the future?

Before the war, England and France stated their alliance and daily warned Germany against attacking Poland. Herr von Ribbentrop did not believe the two nations would keep their promise – and in that lies the tragedy of the outbreak of war.

[. . .]

October 29, 1939

Sunday. There is a meeting this afternoon at 4:00 in the Traube restaurant. The Nazi Local Group Leader and the mayor spoke.[57] The group leader selected the topic: "We march against England." It should be said at the outset not many citizens were enthusiastic about the matter; they remained home or worked in the field, which was more useful. The speech was a collection of gleaned subjects [from news reports], essentially to encourage the Home Front to endure. "Either we triumph or we are completely broken," spoke Group Leader Pott.

We appear already to be half broken.

Pott also said we would get supplies from our allies.

The mayor spoke about the economic emergency regulations. The ration cards are causing him trouble. The population is admonished to practice the strictest restraint because recently only five percent of ration cards were authorized in line with population figures. He guards himself against the rumors that he and his family provide plenty of ration cards for themselves and declares he has not requested a ration card yet and also presumably needs none! (This brother must have hoarded.) That was not very clever, Herr Mayor. There are some people who have small incomes, and even with the best intentions cannot make do economically.

Naturally, that is something a 150-percent National Socialist does not want to know.

Keep going a little further, gentlemen! You are doing great – and that in just two months of war. Nothing like this was felt in 1914. Pardon me – I always forget we now have lightning war and lightning victory [*Blitzkrieg* and *Blitzsieg*].

For a whole three days we had the appearance of being equipped for the task.

October 30, 1939

Today Sergeant Schmitt – our chief judge, who is home on leave – visited our office. He acts like an inspired soldier. I do not believe him, but what else can he do – admit that enough absurd things have been prattled already and we have been completely hoodwinked? He lacks the audacity for that. He knows nothing of his coming assignment, whether he will be sent to Spain, Italy, or to a landing corps. (Enjoy yourself!)

What an ability these men have for defiant thoughts.

[. . .]

November 8, 1939

Already much is being spoken about "Lebensraum," and it is time to give out hints this means the living space of the Polish people.[58] And are the people in these smaller nations to be exterminated? For sure, the smaller nations are now aware of their recent errors and the consequences they wrought. It made no sense, for example, for Poland and Czechoslovakia not to have been more prudent. Had they forged a union and stood together, they would not have been overrun. The future organization of Europe must result in a union of smaller states. I am thinking about something similar to Austria-Hungary, a confederation of states under the guidance of a larger country. Each inhabitant of such a country must be reminded daily to realize it cannot exist without its neighbor – and not that the Hungarians should fight the Serbs, and the Serbs should fight the Romanians, and the Romanians go against the Bulgarians or Greeks.

Also, the problem of population growth must be regulated internationally. We simply cannot put up with unrestrained propagation (as in Japan). Nature can tolerate just a few animals like the rabbit.

November 9, 1939

At the Bürgerbräukeller beer hall in Munich yesterday, Hitler gave a speech to his Party members – the usual glorification of members of the "Movement" who were killed.[59] The German government of 1923 failed to act decisively against this political movement, and so it must be said the 1923 government bears a huge responsibility for the graves in Germany. The NSDAP clearly showed at the beginning it intended to create a tremendous general disturbance. Every fanatic and every brutal egoist was accepted into its ranks with open arms: charmers, con men, convicted criminals, and murderers. Everyone against the government then, whether in words or with deeds, was called a revolutionary and held up as a "hero." The worst sort of criminals, fools, and position seekers became known in time as the "Old Fighters," whose self-glorification brought them into the highest government positions – or into important Party positions – with a virtuoso's ease. Here they could be let loose on the unfortunate people. Today we are seized by a distinct sadness over the development of this terrible Party – today, when thinking itself has become dangerous. [. . .]

November 10, 1939

The alleged bomb assassination attempt in the Bürgerbräukeller caused no great impression.[60] The people are tired and worn-out. Too much has already been made of it. The mentally nimble part of the population has its own thoughts and does not believe it was a real assassination attempt but rather another kind of "Reichstag fire" charade to enable Nazis to pursue disagreeable elements among them.[61] It cannot be denied some in the Party, who for twenty long years honestly believed in the struggle against Bolshevism, consider the new Russian course as having upended everything. Now Hitler must look upon such idealistic National Socialists as adversaries. The NSDAP edifice shows cracks! If Germany also experiences a failure now outside its borders, the artfully constructed house of cards can be brought to a collapse.

I fear some reckless chess move is possibly in preparation, and its execution will bring us new opponents. The road to reason is not passable through propaganda.

November 11, 1939

The way the newspapers are howling furiously against England, blaming it for the explosion in the Munich Bürgerbräukeller, it is evident this incident will be fully used to stir up the flagging war mood.[62] Without batting an eye and without the slightest proof, they make England the suspect in the attempted assassination of the Führer.

This affair will not be solved with presumptions and conjectures. One day the truth will become known, we hope.

November 13, 1939

All the newspapers are reporting more details about the explosion in the Bürgerbräukeller. The *Völkischer Beobachter* even published photos of the seven fatalities – all immemorial Old Fighters.[63] It is interesting the first reports – without any investigation – directed suspicion at a foreign country. Moreover, a foreign fuse was used on the bomb. Today it is made known we ourselves deal with companies that manufacture parts of this type of fuse. Not a word even hints a Party member could be behind the attempt – which actually would be the most obvious possibility. But the public is not supposed to think about such things, let alone know.

We quietly wait and see.

Hundreds of [suspected] people are being denounced and harassed. The sadists need to keep busy.

November 14, 1939

[. . .] The shop assistant in the grocery store was called up for military service, so the company owner, Reiss, came into town to take care of the customers. When it was time for an old woman's turn in the line, Reiss asked "What is your name?"

"Katz."[64]

"You are a Jewess?"

"Yes."

"Then you will not receive anything from me; I am a National Socialist and do not sell to Jews."

The old Jewess was intimidated but said the police directed her there. The noble Nazi stood by his refusal.

Why have we become so cruel a people? Here we see the inhuman harvest of all the wretched incitement. How woefully sad the implanted hatred can cause such raving against an old, defenseless woman. Abysmal meanness and pathetic cowardliness! Herr Reiss, you will receive your wages!

November 15, 1939

Herr Scherdt wants to find out from Pauline and me why we sent away a soldier who was to be quartered with us.[65] No soldier had come by to see us. Once again, a new attempt to take action against me. [...]

[...]

December 7, 1939

A first lieutenant appeared at the office with a sergeant and wanted to place the sergeant in one of our cells for punishment. One cannot argue with the armed forces, and so their demands must be met. The soldier has strict detention because he had eaten his entire iron ration [of canned meat]. In an unheated cell with the straw mattress removed, and no chair to sit on, he was to get only water and bread to eat!

This punishment must be called barbaric – and still this soldier is expected to exert himself with enthusiasm for his fatherland!

December 9, 1939

Russia shows its face unmasked. These scoundrels have attacked small Finland.[66] The whole world must condemn Russia for these actions. Germany will have to put a good face on this evil game of its pitiful "alliance." Russia's actions will prove to be expensive. The dictator Stalin knows the pretense of sitting on the sidelines is finished. World conquest arm in arm with Hitler. Enjoy yourselves!

The future will show these accursed power politics could not endure forever. It is high time for the neutral nations to abandon their simple-minded "neutrality" and place themselves on the side of those nations that can guarantee them independence.

December 16, 1939

Clothing drive – despite clothing ration cards! Toy collections, too. In short, nationally organized begging.

The clothing collector, Fräulein Röschen, says she also takes money.

We respond we cannot give clothes, as we do not know how long the war will last.[67]

Fräulein Röschen: "The war will not last a long time."

Frau Kellner: "They said that in 1914, and yet the war went on until 1918."

Fräulein Röschen: "Except now we have the Führer!"

December 19, 1939

After it was briefly reported to the German people that we had to scuttle our own heavy cruiser Graf Spee at the mouth of the River Plate estuary, it was impossible a "victory" would not immediately follow.[68] An air battle over the North Sea provided an opportunity to report thirty-four of forty-four English bombers were shot down, and merely two German planes were hit. The English, however, say they shot down twelve German Messerschmitts and lost seven of their own airplanes. The prize question: Which is the truth?[69]

December 20, 1939

Today we learn the German passenger ship Columbus (32,000 tons) was sunk by its own crew.[70] Goebbels had predicted a naval victory for the Graf Spee and the demise of England's control of the sea. But now in quick succession the Graf Spee and Columbus, two German ships, have committed suicide. Suicide is usually chosen when absolutely no other way is at hand. [...]

December 31, 1939

The end of the year! The German people will be punished for continuing to offend against all understanding and reason.

1940

January 12, 1940

I received a "love letter" from the Winter Aid Organization of the NSV (National Socialist People's Welfare) with a request for an "appropriately higher" amount, signed by Local Group Leader Pott and Mayor Högy. Pott has the audacity to pressure others to pay higher contributions when he is not even an NSV member.

At the last meeting in the Solmser Hof Inn, the district leader, [Heinrich Backhaus], with head held high, ignored the war collection box.[1] Following this example, I behaved exactly the same.

January 13, 1940

The 14th Company of Infantry Regiment No. 25 was to be ready for departure at 4.30 a.m. The departure order was cancelled, so Corporal Ehlert returned to our apartment for continued lodging.

January 14, 1940

The required Sunday stew.[2] Mr. Collector did not appear.

January 15, 1940

I must always assume [as in the matter of contributing more to the NSV] that something else is being devised against me. So I sent Katie to Ernst Mönnig of the NSV with 1 RM for cards. Caution is the mother of wisdom.[3]

Herr Scherdt asked the soldier we are quartering if he was pleased with us! This former policeman's painstaking efforts to get something explicit and unfavorable against us will one day receive their deserved award.

[...]

January 27, 1940

I waive my claim to be a German if I no longer may act like a human being! Yesterday evening Local Group Leader Pott gathered his little flock of sheep

14. Jan. 1940	Sintoffsonntag. Das Haar Sinfommeler ist nicht erschienen.
15. Jan. "	Da die Vermutung nahe liegt, daß in diesem Falle wieder etwas geschehen muß erkommen werden ist, habe ich durch Kutti i.e. von Mönnig gezahlt. Vorsicht ist die Mutter der Weisheit. —
	Diese fingerartigungsbommen rund von Herrn schürdt gefangt wie ob ihn bei uns gefällt!
	Diese „sorgfältigen" bemühungen dieses ehemaligen Schützenamts übedingt irgend etwas ungünstiges gegen uns zu premeln werden unes durch die merkwürdige Trone aufgehalten. —
18. Jan. 1940	Die Blockwalter der N.S.T. haben ein Schreiben erhalten, worin sie aufgefordert werden bei den Volksgenossen übrig gebliebene brotkorten zu sammeln auch wenn es sich um erbgleichhaue handelt. Eine weine Ort von Gauftabewirtschaft wird hier sichtbar. Die brotkartenzuteilungen sind von vornherein schon so erfolgt, daß keine Überschüssung zu beobachten ist. Diese raffinierte Methode einen Grund zu finden, irgendwelche

once again for a "comforting lecture" about the scarcity of coal. According to him we have enough coal (we have none at all!); it is merely a question of transportation; and the severe winter can also be blamed (the frozen rivers and railway switches). Then he mentioned Polish prisoners would soon come to Laubach.[4] They could only be treated as "prisoners" and may not – under any circumstance – sit at the same table to eat with the farmers and servants. At most, they can eat in the hallway.

In former times one would not have invited a vagrant to the table either, but the "prisoner" makes his work skills available, and at least for that he must be treated humanely to some degree. The Nazi leader has no feelings at all!

Why have we sunk so low as a people?

January 29, 1940

This morning the 14th Company of Infantry Regiment No. 25 (Armored Defense) moved out of Laubach. Corporal Ehlert from Stargard-in-Pommern was quartered with us from December 10. He was a decent man who never spoke one word too many. He did not seem one hundred percent convinced about National Socialism, but on the other hand he believed German weapons would be victorious. All in all, he still would have agreed with an immediate peace treaty.

February 5, 1940

The Russians are sending their planes to bombard villages and cities inside Finland, and the rest of mankind calmly looks on – an example of the unbelievable cowardice of everyone! Each nation must fight without further ado against Russia's breaches of law because tomorrow they themselves will become victims of this brutal lust for power. If Russia would feel a bomb attack on its cities in its own country, then perhaps there would be a change of its attitude regarding "method of civilizing." No one will get through to such beasts with "protests" and witless phrases. Just with: How you treat me, I will treat you! And with a dose of pepper. Retaliate like for like! That is the only possible policy. Repay with interest and compound interest.

February 6, 1940

A secret corps [commanded by General Erwin Rommel] has been in Laubach since the middle of January 1940. But here like elsewhere, the greater the intrigue of the mystery-mongers, the faster the veil is lifted. They belong to the defense force of Führer Headquarters (Regiment Greater Germany). Similar troops are connected with the SS in the Castle District in Prague. Such troops are designated as "The Führer's Personal Adjutancy."[5]

March 7, 1940

My writing has had a one-month rest. What is to be noted?[6] The war cries and threats on all sides will not be enough to terminate this strange "war."[7] Nothing but the effects of war in one or the other country – devastation, fires, destruction of war materials – can bring about a weakening and thereby a change. Airplane leaflets are not a replacement and have no effect.

Nazi propaganda, with its promise of many tremendous things, has not impaired the war machines in France, England, Canada, Australia, and New Zealand. And within Germany the propaganda is often so ridiculous even small children are not taken in.

For example, the English merchant fleet's destruction! Even if it is assumed the given numbers correspond to reality, much more still would need to be done to force England to its knees. We conceal the enemy's growing strength and our own fleet's losses. We further conceal that England has crippled nearly our entire overseas trade. That kind of damage will persist for a long time past the war. The markets in America, Western Europe, Africa, Australia, and Asia are lost to us at least for the foreseeable time. That alone is a plus for the enemy nations, not to be underestimated. And then our currency! That is a black chapter. With what do we buy our raw materials after the war? As our inventory dwindles, and we need to order goods to manufacture, what currency will be used? I would like to know, just once, what our leaders really think. They probably no longer know up from down – and they wait for miracles. But there are no miracles in the present. At most, they appeared in legends of the past.

Our newspapers are likewise a chapter in themselves. Every idiotic babbler – whether he is an Old Fighter, flatterer, hypocrite, or salivating bootlicker – presumes to let loose with his muck. People who remain even minimally perceptive do not read this completely foul stuff anymore. The headlines, written by carnival barkers, are sufficient for the thinkers. The entirely dumb readers can gorge themselves. They are beyond hope.

I will record here some newspaper headlines for the future; they are from the March 5, 1940, *Völkischer Beobachter*:

PILOT RETURNS AFTER BREACHING THE MAGINOT
LINE FOR AN EMERGENCY LANDING[8]

(Thus, dear Musketeer, there is no special art in breaking through France's defensive line. Is that what you are trying to say, Mr. Newspaper Scribbler?)

TWELVE FRENCH AIRCRAFT FLEE BEFORE
FOUR GERMAN HUNTER PLANES

(The new generation of German pilots need only seat themselves in a German airplane and victory is already there.)

SUBMARINE ANNOUNCES: 36,000 TONS SUNK

(And if things continue much longer this way, final victory cannot be far off. That is probably the intent of these accumulated messages. Which ships did this U-boat sink – that cannot be said for the sake of secrecy.)

It is an indelible disgrace and dishonor how and in which way the German people are treated under this "glorious" tyrannical dictatorship. Human rights cannot have been besmirched any worse in the darkest period of the Middle Ages and in the deepest jungle.

March 10, 1940

Part of the German people has lost any and all feeling for right and justice – and that is definitely the most dreadful aspect of what is happening here. They do not even notice they are the same as cattle in a barn. [My wife and I] came across such an example in a woman, Frau Monfang, in the Hesse Courtyard Restaurant in Grünberg. "Adolf needs only to press on the button and then everything is finished." And "The Italians know to the minute when they have to attack." And similar prophecies, all readily offered by Frau Monfang.

Hopefully he presses the button soon, so I can reply to her.

March 15, 1940

The peace between Finland and Russia proves again that some "neutral" states are governed by unusually cowardly and weak people. Instead of supporting Finland with all their might, Sweden and Norway refused to allow Finland's determined troops to march through their countries. The Swedes and Norwegians have taken leave of their senses. How is it possible to be so uncommonly shortsighted? Do their leaders believe they can feed a lion with mosquitoes? Even a small nation can resist a large nation's desire to rob it. In any case, the entire world could have shown, in this situation with Finland, there were still ideals. There should have been more support. But the same error made with Abyssinia repeated itself.

All people must stand together if they want to punish an aggressor. Everybody! That would be a League of Nations. What does experience show? Tiresome talk and tokens of sympathy without follow-up action. If bomber aircraft had struck Russia immediately on its own territory after Russia's attack on Finland, the correct answer would have been given, and then the whole affair would have taken a substantially different turn.

I have nothing but scorn for a League of Nations that cannot even once make bombers available to a threatened member or provide some sort of active help.[9]

At 12:30 noon today, the Führer's Escort Battalion left Laubach – destination unknown.

March 16, 1940

Since the outbreak of war the uniformly controlled German newspapers are filled only with "heroic acts" of the fliers, the submarine crews, reconnaissance troops, etc. It is a systematic attempt to show the enemies as incapable fools. This portrayal of heroes definitely produces the desired effect on the average naïve person. But, my dear Propagandists, this alone cannot win a war. The most empty-headed of my contemporaries will come to see this in time; or at least they will begin to take notice.

What practical application is derived from this attempt to build a warlike spirit? And if we really broke the enemy into pieces, then why did we not, on the second day of war, put into play all of our conceited skills [and win]? This is where an enormous difference shows up between promises and practice.

In any case, one thing is certain: the enemies were not prepared enough. Otherwise the strange "war" would have gotten a rather different kind of coloring. It is clear from the orders for American airplanes that France and England are either not able to manufacture enough airplanes or the quality of their own airplanes had been left to wishful thinking. Either – or.

March 17, 1940

"Today Germany belongs to us, and tomorrow the whole world," sings our nice young boys as they march along the roads.[10] What should one say about this? Ignorance? Thoughtlessness? No, it is the spirit of the leading class, which needs a herd, and no thinking people. This witless arrogance brought us war in 1914, and it carries even more guilt for this war. When the German Empire crumbled, where did the Pan-German movement leaders hide themselves?[11] They all burrowed into the NSDAP where, with Indian whoops, they could put across their plans for world conquest. Banning free expression of opinion was especially helpful to them. In former times, such machinations could be challenged, at least by word and writing. But today? A united press – and every word superfluous! An extremely sad chapter in mankind's history. Instead of further progress, a plunge backward into darkness. [...]

March 19, 1940

The Führer's Escort Battalion troops, quartered here in our area with a great deal of secrecy, have been gone for exactly four days, and already it is well known they are billeted now near Limburg, in bad accommodations. It is completely impossible to keep a secret. If two people know something, a third will know it soon. If this third is female, it is over; the "secret" will then roll through city and country like an avalanche.

Adolf Hitler and Mussolini met together with their ministers of foreign affairs near the Brenner Pass on Italian soil. The people in both nations will get only a doctored version of their conversation. What value is it to experience mere fragments? It almost is better to hear nothing at all. "What you do not know won't hurt you," says a proverb. And that applies here.

Well, no one should get excited. The Italians will restrain themselves and not haul the chestnuts for us from the fire. The Italian leaders, who advertised "Axis politics" a little too much, must make a show of independence for their people. It takes time to change direction, especially for Italy with its decidedly and extremely weak spots: coal and oil – and raw materials in general – which must be delivered to Italy by sea. The French and English fleets are capable of keeping the Italian fleet in check, and that is paramount, as it could put all of Italy's holdings (Libya, Eritrea, Abyssinia) in the greatest danger. [...]

March 27, 1940

The propaganda ministry's convulsive attempts to transform the English air raid on [our northern island of] Sylt into a defensive victory for Germany will leave people cold who are even only halfway reasonable. The army report states Sylt was attacked for several long hours and a "house" was destroyed. One cannot expect the German Army Corps to admit to everything. Everyone is left to draw his own conclusions. A bomb attack lasting several hours can easily bring about all kinds of destruction. And it means nothing when so-called "neutral" correspondents on just one part of the island coincidentally tell us there was very little damage. That is blarney. The army report mentioned one English airplane was downed. Dr. Goebbels maintained six airplanes were brought down this week because parts of at least six airplanes washed ashore.[12] Absolute garbage!

This is of course an extraordinarily unpleasant matter for a large segment of the populace – and in particular the professional brainwashers and swindlers – who had so profusely praised our anti-aircraft artillery flak. They went so far as to arrogantly proclaim not a single enemy airplane would ever fly over German soil. All kinds of mysterious remarks about our inviolability were passed around. There is nothing so stupid that it cannot always find its public.

Mental work is not for my contemporaries at all. Reason can only be pounded into them with thick clubs. It was too bad the 1914–18 war played itself out on foreign soil. Most Germans have absolutely no conception of what war means. Only experience can teach them. It is a hopeless enterprise to try to build upon their thinking.

On the way from Laubach to Freienseen we came across a truck with the sad remains from a fallen airplane shot down over Wohnfeld. Two officers and two enlisted men were found by some Wohnfeld citizens after the crash. Two other airplanes crashed during the night near Giessen. That adds up to three planes within twenty-four hours in our area alone. There are no propaganda reports about these losses. These victims are not appreciated. How much senseless loss of people and material has this unnecessary war brought about?

We had an opportunity a little later on in Freienseen to meet a singular example of a Third Reich contemporary in the person of the innkeeper Kratz, a crazy fellow. With grandiose phrases in High German, he told us of his heroic acts as a submariner. This phrase-beater of the first rank "overawes" his listeners with the exuberance of a hero. He rages against Freemasons and Jews, and it will be their fault if we lose the war.[13] Aha, my dear friend, you have anxiety about your own mastery. "If we lose the war," you striplings will be back on your own, having to provide for yourselves. Your exuberant "spirit" will be driven out of you! This innkeeper/submariner drives around the country giving lectures about his conceited acts and makes fools out of the youth. He is the worst sort of poisoner of people's souls. His brother-in-law is the equally bad Local Group Leader Emil Hofmann in Freienseen.[14]

March 28, 1940

[. . .] The highways, which are obviously maintained, lie so beautifully quiet. "Motorized" Germany, as the National Socialist salesmen called it several years ago, has turned away from the automobile. My forecast promptly arrived: "When the autobahns are finished we will have no gasoline." But no one believed me.

When I said these highways would be the best guides for enemy airplanes, I was immediately hushed. All roads were to be camouflaged to match the surroundings by way of a fabulous spray-painting technique (a National Socialist concoction).[15] Yes, a true Nazi is one-in-a-thousand for whom there are no difficulties at all. Their incessant self-compulsion has accomplished much, but in the end everything has its limits. It is not done with the big mouth alone.

March 30, 1940

It is being said Russian Minister of Foreign Affairs Molotov, in a speech given in Moscow, declared Russia would remain "neutral" as long as the war does not continue to expand.[16] The Nazis certainly had a different conception of the Russian alliance, but it is absurd to believe Russia would sacrifice itself for Germany after receiving no respect whatsoever over the past years from the German side. Russia's behavior is repayment for the common way our leaders treated it from 1933 to 1939. I never agreed with the method of "statesmen" talking in a vulgar way about statesmen of other countries. Everything that was written about Russia and its government is available to read: continuous volumes of offensiveness and slander. That is precisely the dreadful "policy" we put forth. Why only hate? Where does love remain? Or at least a little decency toward other people? We think we can behave against everyone in the exact same rabid way we did against the Jews: to smash, crush – and even exterminate. (Look at Poland.)

April 1, 1940

Today we begin the eighth month of war. Neither the "Blitzkrieg" nor "Blitzsieg" proved to be true. The German people were lulled to sleep by these slogans. It is so unbelievably easy to tell this herd another fairy tale every day. Gullibility seems to be a German congenital defect.

Waging war with words. Apart from the destruction of Poland, that is how war is being conducted today. England and France have not yet undertaken to restrain us, or to convince us our politics of force is directed against all of humanity.

April 9, 1940

Aha! The Germans have taken parts of Denmark and ports in Norway. "We just want to protect these countries and forestall the others [from taking them]" (Belgium in 1914!). Or so it flows from the press.[17]

Now what voices assail my ears? The average German swims in his element with two more nations under "the sovereignty of the Third Reich!" One person declares, "It will go the same with Belgium and Holland." To have to remain quiet while hearing such things is excruciating.

The whole world seems to have become mad, and nobody can be found to take hold of it. Does the world consist only of cowards?

[. . .]

April 11, 1940

The Supreme Command of the German Armed Forces' report of April 10 includes the following self-praise: "The German troops' successful landing in every position from Oslo to Narvik is an achievement unlike anything else before in the history of naval warfare."[18]

That is true. It is completely true this is a singular achievement of your vileness. It would be more appropriate if fewer bombastic words were used for such dark acts. Besides that, it would be even smarter not to blow one's horn to the world until first you knew what steps the others were going to take. Perhaps it will turn out to be one of the most preposterous attacks ever undertaken by a power against a neutral state. The German troops in Norway depend on supplies from the homeland. In a matter of days it will be shown to what large measure military enterprises in foreign lands depend on supply. Each delay can have fatal consequences. Time will reveal whether it was a stroke of genius or an act of insanity.

April 12, 1940

Now he was here – he, most splendid of all. We received a call from the Grünberg courthouse that the Giessen regional court president was on his way to us and would be here at three in the afternoon – and everything must be done punctually. After the president arrived and had a long consultation with Assessor Graefling [the auxiliary judge], we were commanded to appear in the judge's chamber.[19] The president, who is well known to me, gave a lame speech, reminding those of us "who make up the inner front lines" of our duty to help bring about the final victory – of which, naturally, there could be no doubt.

This Nazi Party member, Regional Judge President Colnot, put forth his little maxims and said goodbye at five o'clock with the remark that he no doubt had made himself quite unpopular. This self-realization is actually the only thing I liked about this bigwig.[20]

His criticisms were those of a bureaucratic nature (period calendar, expenditure for documents, registration department). He did not forget to declare he would appear again before the next prescribed audit.

April 13, 1940

I learned from Assessor Graefling that President Colnot took particular pains to speak "affectionately" about me, and to make inquiries about me. I am accustomed now to such things in this glorious time of 1933–1940. How often already has the attempt been made to rein me in? These despisers of human rights have not succeeded in getting me to lie down. And that is because I shy away from their neighborhood as though it were fire. And among like-minded acquaintances I pull out all the stops. I criticize every action of these Nazi subhumans with the strongest persuasive power I can muster. Every error they make in the world that they attempt to conceal with diseased eagerness, I pull into the daylight and express my doubts and hack at it with my opposition. Not a single convinced Nazi remains in my circle. This fight is nerve-wracking but must be done nevertheless. Such preliminary work to bring about a collapse is of tremendous importance.[21]

"The bondage will last only a short time," isn't that so, Horst Wessel?[22] Isn't that what you sang? You are a prophet, Herr Horst Wessel!

What does our "ingenious" corporal think about that, this clown in world history? When this murderer of mankind receives his just punishment, I will experience the most beautiful days of my life. The vast, terrible suffering of so many people, for which he is responsible, unfortunately can never be set right. Nevertheless, they have not endured it in vain. And how will that be brought home to the silly German people? Only through painful experience – otherwise through nothing. They have no understanding or reason. The German people have to be instructed as if they were little children:

Treasures of wickedness profit nothing!

Do unto others, as you would have others do unto you! [. . .]

In our small country town, an epidemic of hoof-and-mouth disease has broken out. Hitler's "Providence" seems to have withdrawn his benevolent hand. We hope for the best. The main thing is the epidemic has also reached the con artist and deceiver Röder. This fellow deserves it.

April 14, 1940

Sunday rest. It is 11 a.m. and I have not yet heard the columns of singing marchers – supposedly a medical company but really an out-and-out circus. When I used this description in talking with a non-commissioned officer, he heartily confirmed it. For several hours this group marches in circles in the high school courtyard, continually singing marching songs. I have named this military unit, "The Warring Glee Club." These songsters have a room in our courthouse for supplies. We had an alert late in the night of April 9, and they went traipsing up and down the stairs with crates and boxes. Any more rest that night was over – and we found out early in the morning the alert was merely a test. But behind this activity is the suggestion they might be moving away in a few days. A medical officer whispered something about an offensive being needed in the West to provide relief. Relief? Where do we have to be relieved? In Norway? I believe the entire dictatorship of the swastika will soon be relieved.

The agriculture section has problems finding enough skilled workers, but yet in the cities and villages millions of people just hang about and wait for miracles. World Conqueror, you have been robbed of your reason!

At seed distribution time, farmers received just fifty percent of the clover seeds they ordered. Yet Herr Darré will nevertheless win the "Production Battle."[23] On paper, that is. If only there were no more paper – what a lucky thing that would be for our people. But the paper war stands in full bloom – and the Party appears to have tremendous supplies of it.

April 15, 1940

Mankind would sigh in relief if there were no more Hitler, this unemployed immigrant from Austria who wants to control the world. It is impossible to understand how the entire German people, with all their five senses intact, could allow themselves to be led to the slaughterhouse. Eighty million people believe in miracles that cannot happen. How will it end?

I have the dark feeling we are at the turning point. The collection of scrap metal is underway, accompanied by the usual propaganda. As always, pressure is applied when anything is supposedly "voluntary." Police Sergeant [Wilhelm] Lauber went to [the Jewish merchant] Heynemann's house and threatened to send him to a concentration camp if he did not hand over his metal goods.

I can understand if a foreigner is confused about why the German people simply do not take hold of this dictator and his henchmen and send them to the devil. An outsider does not see the jumble of interconnections that make up the Nazi Party's organization, its federations and associations at ground level – all devilishly cunning in the way it is drawn up – in which the many department heads have total command and grind down the people. Such power arouses the criminal nature, and there are no noble men among them: to be the proper fighter one must be brutal. Naturally, once these wretches get a post, they will strive to keep it. So the sum of such creatures (job seekers, materialists, lazy bums) results in a strong bloc, where one supports the other. Everyone realizes that everything depends on the whole. And that is where their strength lies. And also their weakness, as the large number of Party members includes a large number of scoundrels. However, the chief commander himself has said, the more that are connected with him, the smaller becomes the probability of a downfall. But now we approach a critical stage. The daily "victories" are not enough any longer to mask the coming defeat.

Madmen or criminals? Criminally insane, I say.

April 16, 1940

[...] How much different could it have been in Europe if the cowardly North American people had shown themselves to be more heroic? How can a people be so shortsighted and tell themselves, "I sit on an island, and do not concern myself with the rest of the world"? Did it really not come to mind Hitler would not be content with a poor Europe but intended – no matter what – to go where there was still something to rob and to steal? Do the Americans really not see that?

More idealism, my rulers! Where humanity and justice are crushed by Hitler and his cohorts with such cruel means as in Europe, the entire world must rise up against them and disarm them. Again I think of Abyssinia: if Mussolini had been taught a lesson there, perhaps everything would have turned out differently.

I admit it still might have come out the same because mankind knows no other way to do things. No one wants to reason. Conquests are surely so beautiful – let happen what may, we will burn our bridges. "Heil Hitler!"

A more suitable greeting would have been "*Heilt* Hitler" [Heal Hitler].

[. . .]

April 18, 1940

After the war, we must ask the English – who broadcast almost every day that they control the seas – how it was possible for Germany to land troops in six places in Norway. In Narvik alone, in northern Norway, we have ten German warships and a large number of transport ships. Extremely bad English air reconnaissance, and a not much better "control of the seas."[24]

April 19, 1940

"Today, Germany belongs to us, and tomorrow the whole world," bellow the youth. "Next we go against England," shout the rest.

Some have already gone to England – but as prisoners. And not a few have paid for their insanity with their lives and gone to the bottom of the sea. And so ends what was undertaken with élan and senselessness. What happens to those responsible? How will the base lies of a Goebbels be punished?

April 24, 1940

Mayor Otto Högy of Laubach was appointed Mayor of Mosina in Poland, near Poznan. I wish much luck to this "noble" man! Party member = Party wallower![25]

April 25, 1940

The war takes humorous forms. The English claim they have attacked Sylt and some airfields in German-occupied Denmark and Norway. They have already attacked the airfield at Stavanger, Norway, twelve times. Airfields are attacked. Why not the factories that manufacture the airplanes?

It is exactly the same with submarines. Hunt submarines in the ocean but, by God, do not attack the shipyards; it would be just dreadful if your enemy could not build any more ships, and then the hunting would have to end, and then the war would have to be terminated. So instead of destroying the most important railway lines and bridges, they undertake hundreds of pleasure flights.

Whoever wants to interpret this war may do so, but that does not mean they will be any good at it. A French broadcaster announced that two French fighter pilots went after a German seaplane that barely managed to escape from them. The correct statement would have been: Today we learned German engines are better than ours because two of our planes were not capable of destroying one of theirs.

May 10, 1940

Luxembourg, Belgium, and Holland were attacked during the night, as we learned in a proclamation by Dr. Joseph Goebbels over the radio this morning.[26]

A huge excitement seizes those Germans who have but a flickering spark of decent feeling left within them. Brutality celebrates triumph. The Nazis puff up their chests once again and babble about a campaign that will be decisive for a thousand years. It would indeed be high time for these rulers to finally get a smack on their criminal fingers. If the English leaders still do not know what is happening, God himself can no longer help them.

May 11, 1940

Mr. Chamberlain finally resigned from office. With that, an unbelievably pathetic nincompoop has finally disappeared. Now the crackpot Nazis will be shown what it is like to become an enemy of the entire world. It will cost many victims until reason slowly awakens our memories to what was better in the past. This will be a harsh lesson for a generation that has become so crazy. If only they can be cured, then these victims will not have died without meaning.

Woe to these criminals! Woe to these beasts in the form of people!

May 12, 1940

Word is that the Germans try to cause confusion by dropping paratroopers behind the lines in Belgium and Holland. The insidiousness of this Russian invention naturally pleased the Nazis, and they have copied this tactic. I can imagine such a method having some success against the Hottentots, but against a modern, well-equipped, and intelligent opponent it will remain a gimmick and will end with the destruction of the jumpers. Unless one can place an entire division at a chosen spot, such a childlike undertaking should not even be considered. [. . .]

May 20, 1940

Very eventful days lie behind us. The total failure of our opponents' military leaders made it possible for German troops to overrun Holland and Belgium and penetrate into France. The seriousness of the situation for France need hardly be stressed. It is unbelievable how little that country prepared for its defense. They needed to be able to launch overwhelming attacks with bomber aircraft on Germany. If it were not absurd to believe, one might assume certain circles in France had worked hard behind the scenes to place their country in the hands of Hitler the Conqueror.

In 1914 France was in position along the Marne River to bring the German assault to a halt. But it appears France will not be able to do that in 1940. There is but one way now for them: France must gather its entire armed forces from wherever they are stationed [in the world] and throw them against the advancing German troops.

Just now I learned General Weygand has taken over the French Supreme Command. So we have before us clear proof regarding my assessment of General Gamelin's incapability.[27] All the ambassadors and attachés have likewise failed. Were these men not in the position to see into the tremendous re-arming of Germany? In every German illustrated newspaper one could see pictures that exposed everything. Every small child here knew at least something about the armament.

And the entire world looked on! Poor world!

It is almost impossible to believe how the French and English committed so many tremendous errors these past years:

a. It began with Abyssinia, a League of Nations member totally left in the lurch by the other members. (Why didn't some resolute leaders close the Suez Canal?)
b. Demilitarization of the Rhine country!
c. Rearmament of Germany!
d. Occupation of Austria. (The "Guaranteeing Powers" look on.)
e. Occupation and destruction of Czechoslovakia. (The ally France does nothing.)
f. Crushing Poland. (The Allies "promise" assistance.)
g. Russia attacks Finland. (The Western powers "want" to help.)
h. Germany attacks Norway. (The "helping" English flee.)

Exactly where is the English fleet? This fleet should have been placed in position on September 1, 1939, primarily to assist Poland. Instead this fleet lies at anchor at Scapa Flow [Scotland], and allows one loss after another to occur. Is the entire world governed by idiots?

May 21, 1940

The world's democracies have failed so far, just as Germany's democracy failed. The world bows down to three tyrants: Mussolini, Stalin, and Hitler.

In particular, the world undertook no counter-action against the militarization of German youth in HJ and BdM [Hitler Youth and League of German Girls]. And they did nothing at all to stop the SA [Assault Division, stormtroopers] and SS [Protection Squadron]. All the German youth are militarized beginning on their tenth birthday.

What did your Houses of Commons and your Senates undertake against this power?

[. . .]

May 29, 1940

The carnage will eventually come to an end, but the Western powers will carry the historical guilt for not promptly providing the most intensive preventive measures against Germany's incessant politics of aggression. Possibilities existed, but no actions were taken. Spineless policies do not change the mind of a tyrant. The sharpest means would still be too mild. Where is the English fleet?

Yet another aspect of this failure is seen in how the small Polish fleet could find its way from the Baltic Sea to England, but not even a single rowboat went from England to Poland! Sad, extremely sad, but unfortunately true.

By the time these Englishmen wake up, the greater part of Europe will be a heap of rubble.

May 30, 1940

The king of Belgium [Leopold III] gave his troops orders to lay down their weapons. Only a madman could do that. His failure to better reinforce their small border was already highly deplorable. Under no circumstance should Belgium's collapse have come about so quickly. Needless to say, England is greatly to blame. After all, England's best protection was a strong Belgium that should have been supported with all means, particularly large armies, on a twenty-four hour basis. But if one waits as England did until May 1939 to establish a feeble and limited military conscription, nobody needs to wonder at the great weakness of England. All omissions, all errors will painfully take their toll, and the fight will become only crueler.

Of what use is it for us to continue swallowing up these nations? Digestive pains are going to show up very soon.

The destruction in our own country by enemy airplanes will have an effect one of these days. They can substantially disrupt the transportation of coal for our winter needs and endanger the population's food supplies. The railroad plays a large role in peacetime. And today we cannot even get fuel. We approach glorious times![28]

May 31, 1940

I need to write down two local opinions:

"What occurs now will be decisive for one thousand years" (in the favorable sense for Germany): Laubach Air Defense "General" Hessler.

"After the war Germany will be the richest country on earth": Local Group Leader Pott's wife.

June 12, 1940

Mussolini has now rolled the dice.[29] It is not easy to evaluate Italy's combat capability; without doubt there are many weak points. The extent to which it can help Germany will have to be proven.

Perhaps the ruling government in France will realize how foolishly it behaved on September 1, 1939. A vigorous French attack against Germany would have brought them victory because the German–French borders were poorly protected. France's behavior cannot be understood at all. Perhaps they counted on rebellion within Germany or on a greater effect from the English blockade. Maybe they believed the Germans were bluffing about their arms. In any case, a nation must build up its own strength and not just count on possibilities.

Our enemies are not clever! They saw the tremendous way Germany armed itself, yet they supplied Germany with even more raw material so they could be better killed. Is this how a person with a healthy understanding of human nature should reckon?

Monsieur Maginot built a fortified line. If he were still alive, he could see he committed a major error. He should have gone the whole distance and extended the fortifications all the way from the sea to the Alps – and not stopped at Sedan. A reasonable General Staff, after the experiences of 1870–71 and 1914–18, would have put the strongest fortifications behind Luxembourg and Belgium. And made them fortifications no army could run over. There had to be dynamite, hydrochloric acid pits, tank traps of the largest extent, spring-guns, electrically charged fences, poisoned wells in the fields, and thousands of heavy caliber cannons in the major role. Not to mention underground airfields and ammunition chambers. In place of infantrymen, only machine gunners in swiveling steel towers – covering areas 400 × 400 meters. And the exact same thing with the artillery (in particular, anti-tank defense).

June 14, 1940

The fate of France, so it appears, is sealed: the death of their democracy. They know very well they brought it upon themselves. It is impossible to fight a dictator by democratic methods. The stronger one will triumph, and that means the German dictatorship. The French government's suicidal behavior in September 1939 was the decisive factor. No one in Germany could understand why France stood nonchalantly at ease. An unbelievable error! An idiocy! Hitler was correct in what he once said: If the democracies had been good for anything, I would not be standing here before you today! Very correct! German democracy was so tolerant of everything: the creation of a private army, the worst terror, and even the National Socialists' meetings, which they protected into the bargain. The Nazis really could not have asked for more. French foreign policy was also responsible, and not in a small way. It would not help the Weimar government with food supplies, and that created the fertile soil for National Socialism. In addition they watched calmly, beginning in 1933, as Hitler re-armed Germany without anything resembling a consequence. Now the French can learn about the weapons from close range.

Only a single man among the opponents, in my opinion, recognized the danger, and that was Churchill. So naturally the fine German propaganda treated this man "affectionately." The propaganda aimed at France and England was quite the most deplorable I had ever heard about other people. Contemptible is not enough to describe it.

France's and England's failure might have been understandable if their leaders had not been warned. Hitler clearly designated France in *Mein Kampf* as the hereditary enemy.[30] Didn't the French believe that – not even somewhat? Senate President Dr. Rauschning, formerly from Danzig, published a book in France that should have been a warning for all mankind.[31] Was that also not considered? It is uncommonly difficult to imagine what the governing powers in France and England were thinking and planning. I realize they might have erred anyhow in some way, and still been deceived in the end. But the truth should have been obvious when Germany and Russia concluded their pact. The Russians, who harp about helping the "proletarians of all countries," allowed the German tanks to crush the working folk in Poland, etc. This same Russian spirit could clearly be seen in the Spanish Civil War when they broadcast calls over the radio for Spanish workers to fight but then did nothing to assist them.

Refrain from fine phrases.

How will everything end now? What does the German "Versailles" look like? I admit my imaginative powers fail here. As is well known, war is won only by making peace. If one takes their behavior from 1933 to 1940 as an example, the National Socialists' intoxication with victory will be of an unrestrained nature. Unless a miracle happens, that is what it will be now. In any case, "Providence" is one hundred percent on the side of Hitler. How the believers in the world interpret this is up to them. It is a strange God who spreads his benediction and grace upon those who plan the premeditated murder of mankind.

Not everything is to be understood with simple human reasoning. Billions of dollars of goods destroyed, millions of people killed, and uncountable broken hearts. And some individuals sun themselves in the gloss of this "fame!" That is a world that has actually earned its downfall.

In Mainz, a French general from Gram killed himself. The entire French General Staff has earned the death penalty. An inconceivable incompetence along the entire line, in particular by the air force and anti-tank defense. The main German railway lines near the French border are still intact today in the tenth month of war, completely undisturbed! And for an entire year now, a large French force has been kept in Syria. The French have lost their minds. The motherland is conquered by Germany, and yet large units of troops float around in the universe.

Just now, at two in the afternoon, an announcement over the radio tells us German troops have marched into Paris.[32] France is lost.

There will be another Versailles Peace Treaty – but this second one will have a reversal of roles. That is a triumph for Hitler-Germany that does not show up in history very often.

June 17, 1940

[. . .] He who dares, wins. So far the English have only disgraced themselves. They might try to justify their escape from Norway and northern France as a "strategy," but there is no place in that category for achievements and heroism. One cannot recall often enough their common and mean behavior during the Polish campaign. Completely deplorable. Instead of granting Poland every possible assistance, the English acted as though nothing were occurring. Every little bit of help would have strengthened Poland's fighting spirit, and the campaign would have been of a longer duration. A protracted fight in Poland would have had a heavy impact upon further German aims. After all, the preparations had been for a Blitzkrieg – and it was with the speed of lightning Poland was defeated. Not a single Polish airplane saw German territory! Was it not possible to have based some Polish airplanes in France or England? Such a question is actually redundant, considering the proven ineptitude of our opponents. Their answer would be only a dazed stammering.

Whoever wants to triumph must attack. That is what Germany proved on nine occasions: Austria, Czechoslovakia, Poland, Denmark, Norway, the Netherlands, Belgium, Luxembourg, and France. No nation in Europe is carrying out a resistance. The tyrant divides Europe, and the slaves have no right to complain.

June 24, 1940

Frankfurt am Main. [Pauline and I] made a trip to Frankfurt to find out more about the rumors of "bomb attacks." I saw damaged houses only in the Rebstock section.[33] A woman from there told me four people were killed in those houses, and seven more were killed on the roadside as they were giving technical help to clear out the bombs. Almost every night the people of Frankfurt are in the air raid shelters.

We had a salad lunch for 80 Rpf [Reich pfennigs] in the restaurant at the stock exchange. It was a meat-free day. The businesses are completely closed one day of the week. The activity in the shops cannot be compared with former times. I searched without success in different stores for sandals. Many electric streetcars are being run by women conductors.

In response to a question I asked at the Schumann restaurant, I was told they now serve meals only starting at six in the evening. We bought some of our favorite pretzels and happily traveled home to the Vogelsberg hills. City life is not very charming. Our "flight from the city" was definitely the wise thing to do.

June 27, 1940

Giessen. Herr Köhler stated, "In eight days we will go up against England. We will finish them off even faster [than the French]. We will have to keep ration cards for clothing for one more year at least. We will get imports from Argentina." As for my sandals, I found and "conquered" a pair in Giessen at Darré shoe store. (It was just by good fortune: the saleslady said they had received merely three pairs altogether!)

June 28, 1940

Laubach. [Karl] Klein said, "In four to five weeks we will be finished with the English." His wife added, "Then everything will be available again."

July 13, 1940

The mayor of Karlsruhe boasted how businesses in his city had "spontaneously" donated 100,000 RM for a fourth "Karlsruhe" cruiser.[34] The third cruiser was torpedoed near Norway. It surely would have been more valuable for the people of Karlsruhe had the millions wasted on building four ships been used for building homes. When does reason finally return?

July 18, 1940

Dr. [Werner] Vogels, Section Leader in the Reich Ministry of Justice, writes in the *Deutsche Justiz* journal,

The population's return into the vacated and disengaged areas [around Saarbrücken, etc.] has begun; it can be carried out only gradually because in the liberated areas the houses first must be made habitable again. The weather – in particular frost – caused damage, but the destruction the enemy brought about is relatively small. Therefore, it can be counted on that resettling the recaptured cities and villages will be finished in a matter of weeks.[35]

For eight months of the war, the French troops lay before these vacated areas and sat there doing nothing until they were forced out. They certainly did not learn such "warfare" from Napoleon. Just one explanation is possible: the entire French General Staff consisted either of the mentally ill or criminals. France was "allied" with Czechoslovakia and Poland yet tranquilly watched these nations being wiped from the earth. For this breach of trust, a just punishment overtook them. The French are not worth the spit one can direct at them!

July 20, 1940

The people were summoned to the Solmser Hof Inn to listen to one of the Reich's traveling speakers. This babbler brought up, among other things, an example from Grünberg: a laborer gave 20 marks to the Red Cross but a mid-level official merely half a mark: 50 pfennigs. Group Leader Pott then added his view about collections, saying that "maybe after the war the soldiers who fought at the front will be shown the lists, and those who did not give enough will have their faces smashed!" A fine man this Herr Pott. After the war we shall want to converse about this point in detail.

This is the same Herr Pott no young girl will work for, and who swindled his employees in the distribution of food supplies.

July 21, 1940

Bad Salzhausen. As Pauline and I sat in front of the spa building, the Hellwig family greeted us. Herr Hellwig, a senior inspector in Mainz, believes the English will be totally beaten quickly, and after the war we will be in a very good position for natural resources because we occupy every country with raw materials. The worst sort of business-oriented politician, he sees his wheat in bloom. In former times he was a Social Democrat. Today, 250 percent Nazi.

July 24, 1940

After France's extraordinary collapse, the broad mass of Germans do not in the slightest resent the total imposition upon them by Nazi propaganda. Ninety-nine percent of the German people have turned off thinking for themselves. A boundless arrogance can be seen in all layers of the population – an indestructible faith in the power of weapons. There are but a handful of people who concern themselves critically with what may yet develop. It is useless to try to convince the average German that the situation with England could become more difficult. They give no consideration at all to the ocean and the English Channel. I have hardly met a German who believes we might possibly fail in our attack against England – or even that the attack could possibly be cancelled. On the contrary, everyone says England will be "beaten down" in a very short period of time or that it will be "destroyed." Dr. Goebbels has already sunk the entire English fleet, so no one among the silly crowd needs to worry his head about England's "destroyed" navy. Now and then the realization comes that we indeed will have to reckon with losses in such a fight, "but such things are simply the price one must pay." One could say such "humanity" is an inherited Germanic trait.

[. . .]

August 6, 1940

[. . .] Hardly anything of war is to be felt locally. Above all, we have not seen or heard air attacks. Enemy fliers flew over Laubach once, but that was not an attack of any sort. The war is not thought of unfavorably here because we have felt few or no effects of it. An individual casualty is also not going to get the masses down (says Becker). We know little of those other areas that are exposed to air attacks. The Ruhr district and the Rhineland are too far away. It may be a different mood prevails in those places. The war situation might be judged quite harshly there. Purely by the feel of things, it is likely a long war is in prospect because we have yet to defeat the main opponent, England. My understanding tells me it is utterly impossible to defeat England outright. To do that, one needs something we do not have: a large fleet.

[. . .]

August 21, 1940

A dreary, rainy day. We will have to begin heating the house today! That is a bad sign. Is "Providence" no longer on Germany's side?

Would it not be possible, by the way, to omit the daily threats against England? Usually only children make threats – and then run away. So far only one thing has been achieved by it: England has armed itself to the teeth. There can be no doubt about that. And why is the Englishman (who, it must be noted, is also Teuton) not going to learn how to handle weapons exactly the same as the Germans? If the serious intention existed, or still exists, to attack England, i.e. with land troops, then it was and is a great stupidity to be sounding our trombones in the world, as we have been doing this past year with every kind of variation, arousing the maddest hopes in our own weak and hollow heads. If I want to attack a powerful opponent, my only possibility for initial success can come through perfect surprise. Not even the smallest child among us would be "surprised" if today or tomorrow we attempted a landing in England. If our troops did make such a landing at some place, the entire English army would attack those poor fellows. I do not even have to mention the worst problem: keeping supplied.

The one success I will not deny our propaganda is the entire German people, with few exceptions, believe in an attack on England and in its destruction. In particular, I find this childlike faith most shamefully among academically educated people. To me, the deeds of these teachers are especially woeful – poverty of spirit unlike anything else. Unparalleled.

Accompanying this mental aberration is a lack of heart or soul. One could just scream at these people. Nothing remains of their earlier virtue. Now only crudeness, brutality, and the quest for power reign. And arrogance.

August 23, 1940

The newspaper states, "In an air attack against Germany, English planes bombed historical churches near Derichsweiler, classified as protected ancient monuments, and destroyed them completely."[36] It is the first time we admit to a complete destruction of anything. Naturally it is only because the English pilots had the bad luck to strike a church, and the propagandists hope to nurture hatred for England within any Hitler believers who so far had remained peace-loving.

We have yet to hear announcements about the destruction of factories. "Protector and Defender of Churches" – that is the latest characterization of Nazis. They are such nice guys!

[Otto] Roll, a bank manager and currently a private first class in an armored division, visited us and told of the glorious campaign against France. He spoke with a boundless arrogance and a glorification of dive-bombers and armored forces. He said, among other things, we would have to be even more brutal. Even more brutal! This is a human being, yes, but he will have to take his place in line among the beasts.

August 24, 1940

"Somaliland Liberated from English Rule" is the newspaper's front-page headline.[37] This time an Italian victory must take the credit. Hear, hear! I can imagine there is not much difference for the inhabitants of Somalia whether their miserable existence is under English or Italian "rule." A lash is a lash.

August 27, 1940

A furniture truck drove by, carrying Mayor Högy's furniture to Poland. Farewell! You have my blessing. An entire truck filled with a bunch of unnecessary items being delivered to Poland. Away with you worms! Hopefully the payback will not be missing.

August 28, 1940

"In fourteen days the war will be over," proclaims mortgage broker Fischer, a militarist from Hungen.

August 29, 1940

A letter from [our daughter-in-law] Freda in the USA, written on February 9, 1940, arrived here today![38] It took over six months for this letter to come into the hands of the addressee. Poor progressive mankind!

August 31, 1940

Tonight marks the third time English airplanes have flown over Berlin. The war has taken a turn so that the masters in Berlin finally can feel something of it firsthand. The "inviolability" of Berlin, so plentifully given out in speeches, has proved to be a vain illusion. How much other nonsense and gossip has come out of this year of war? It is truly beyond counting.

The bombardments between London and Berlin perhaps may develop into something positive for the future. The English must fly approximately 2,000 kilometers roundtrip to strike Berlin – a laudable achievement, after all. If in the future long distances no longer present a safety problem for pilots, a would-be aggressor could be punished in such a way he would lose his desire to plot war. It is not absurd to believe wars might be prevented just by maintaining a large force of bomber aircraft (which in peacetime could be put to peaceful uses). I imagine it this way: Orders are given in Berlin one morning for troops to invade a neighboring country. The following night Berlin is destroyed. The war is over. When such a possibility exists, every government will think three times before beginning a war.

[. . .]

September 6, 1940

Just after it became known America was delivering fifty destroyers to England, the Supreme Command of the German Armed Forces issued an immediate response through their propaganda office. "Six British Destroyers Sunk," shouted the army report's September 5, 1940, headline.[39] Now,

German people so beautifully safe in your air raid shelters, you need just count the days until every one of the fifty destroyers will be wiped off the surface of the sea. Dr. Goebbels will have managed that by October 1, 1940, at the latest.[40]

The following news is amusing: "Warplanes approaching the Hamburg blockade zone came under heavy artillery fire, and merely a few were able to come near the city's center. The enemy was hindered from dropping his bombs." Thus spoke the Reich Propaganda Office in Hamburg on September 5, 1940.[41]

"Hindered from dropping his bombs," says the propagandist. Who hindered the enemy? Nobody can hinder him. The only hindrance was that the pilots probably had orders to unload their bombs close to Stettin.[42] The height of ridiculousness is to try to comfort the inhabitants of a metropolitan city like Hamburg with dumb statements. Had the bombing squadron been ordered to attack Hamburg, neither the propaganda chief nor any anti-aircraft flak could have prevented it from doing so. Their numerous attacks on the Ruhr district prove this. If that area could actually have been protected, it definitely would have been from the beginning.

September 8, 1940

I was busy today as a collector for the winter war effort.[43] I received 13.20 RM from eighteen donors. I did not notice any "joyous" givers. They all want to know what the others were giving so they would not give more than that. The Party members, supposed to set good examples, do not stand at the head of the line when it comes to donations. I am making a note of this here only because history may want to report the opposite.

September 11, 1940

Guard duty on the turret of the secondary school.[44]

I stood at the warning signal with Demmer (Dörnis's son-in-law) from 11 p.m. to 1 a.m. in the moonlit night while two other guards (including Scherdt!) were patrolling in order to catch the blackout transgressors. Two professional watchmen could have handled this whole thing, but that would have been too clever – in no way should ingenuity occur in the Third Reich. Always obstinate! When the entire population is tormented, the dictator is content. It was exactly the same during the search for potato beetles. Every week one member of each household had to report for an afternoon's work.[45] Columns of searchers went through the potato fields. Nothing was ever found, yet the search went on until September. I would not have wondered at all if the search had gone on after all the potato plants had withered and winter had set in. [...] A single guard, focusing on the potato fields, would have been sufficient to detect any danger. Had he seen potato beetles anywhere, he could have alerted all the field owners, who then would have given it immediate attention. Every farmer would have done his utmost to protect his potatoes. That is clear to every reasonable person.

But reason will not answer the question, "How can we torment our vassals?" Therefore, it was done as it was done, and that is an end to it!

September 15, 1940

When English pilots fly to Berlin, it is piracy. When German pilots bomb London, it is heroism. At least that is what we read in the newspapers. If there is any chance our people might become angry, the impudent news writers use every means to direct their anger away from the truly guilty ones and onto others. Since the masses are unbelievably dimwitted, the brainwashers quickly achieve their desired goal without much effort. "What is written in the newspaper is true," said a farm lady from the Schlitz area. Nothing can counter this mentality. It is a losing battle, trying to educate people who believe no one would lie to them before an election, during a war, and after a hunt.

September 16, 1940

As soon as an official or Party member falls victim to an air raid, the Party line in the obituaries reads, "English air pirates" and "Cowardly bomb attacks by British night pirates." One or the other naïve German might fall for this, but it will not impress even halfway reasonable people outside the Third Reich who see no difference between our bombing London and their retaliation on German cities. It is ludicrous to utter even a word of discontent about their attacks. If one does not want to be bombed, then one should not make war.

By the way, who attacked the residents of Poland with airplanes? Were those airmen also pirates? What about Holland (Rotterdam)?[46]

[...]

September 19, 1940

A report from a regional economic ministry states, "Because of increased export commitments, the coal situation, which primarily was a transportation problem this past winter, will be a major quantity problem in 1940–1941."

It requires little insight to see the coming coal problem will be both one of transportation and shortages. We can thank our Führer for that. If things were going right, such announcements would not be necessary. Understandably the shortages have to be addressed. The responsibility remains the same.

October 7, 1940

German troops moved into Bucharest – but just "to protect the oil," of course! Something always has to be protected. First, there was neutrality; then butter and eggs in Denmark; ore in Norway; food supplies in Holland; iron in Luxembourg and Belgium; war supplies in France; and now oil in Romania. [...] Will we not get into trouble with another powerful nation at some point – if not tomorrow, then the day after? Making Germany bigger will not limit potential conflicts of interest. Russia, in particular, will take measures soon to strike up its own "friendship treaties." Our pact with Japan was to put pressure on America, but undoubtedly an inner motive was aimed also at Russia.[47] The world's continents are being affected and forced into final decisions. Is that favorable for Germany? Never!

If America, Russia, and England would only provide China a little more support, our partner Japan would become very busy and cease to be a means of pressure against America and Russia. Then the Allies would be taking matters into their own hands. [...]

October 9, 1940

No sooner did I suggest the opponents' next campaign should be to support China, when such support was confirmed over the airwaves. England had earlier agreed with Japan to close the only road between Burma and China for three months to war supplies. England has declared it will not extend the deadline that was to end the middle of this month. Burma Road will be open, and China will be able to receive support from all countries capable of providing it and willing to do so. The Chinese power of resistance certainly has been reinforced, giving the Japanese less opportunity to plunder. Chinese fortitude will decide the results of this struggle. If Chiang Kai-shek knows to give his soldiers the right inspiration, the Chinese will be victorious – and justifiably so.[48] If Russia has not lost its common sense, it, too, will help the Chinese. Russia will have no future prospects in Asia if Japan wins.

What prompts Germany to stand at the side of Japan is totally beyond comprehension. Japan can bring us neither political nor economic advantages. It is and remains a robber state of the foremost rank. When someone makes a pact with a thief, he had better reckon from the beginning on being robbed himself someday. [. . .]

After an English air attack on Berlin, the following headline appeared in the *Hessische Landes-Zeitung* on Oct. 9, 1940: "The British Killer-Beast Rampages in Berlin."

   I assume the English newspapers use similar language about German attacks on London. Such presentation does little to change the situation. The root of evil is war. Who can maintain we tried with all our means to avoid war? Over-armament has always led to war. There was an upstanding German woman who once wrote a booklet called, "Armament and Over-Armament."[49] Would this book be something the officials might circulate and recommend? Or would it indeed be damned in "national" circles and destroyed? "Leave it to the experts," they say. Always the same game.

October 10, 1940

The announcement of opening the trade routes in Burma scored a hit:

JAPAN READY FOR ANY ENEMY
WHO COMES AGAINST THEM

Responsibility of the USA

Report by our representative, Copenhagen, October 8, 1940

[. . .] An article in the Kokumin Shimbun newspaper argues the United States is behind England's plan to open the Burma Road again. Should this situation lead to complications between Japan and the United States, the government in Washington alone must carry the responsibility. Just at this moment the position is especially critical. It depends exclusively on America whether the Burma Road should be opened again or not. The United States needs to clearly realize Japan is ready to advance against every enemy with a terrible and destructive blow. Japanese troops are already in Indo-China and thereby close to Burma. The Japanese are already concluding their preparation for any action that might become necessary. [. . .]

Source: "Japan bereit, jedem Feind entgegenzutreten" *Hamburger Fremdenblatt* [*HF*], October 8, 1940, p. 2.

In Japanese eyes, it is a crime if a zealous patriot like Chiang Kai-shek arouses the Chinese people in order to protect them from Japanese enslavement. This example clearly shows Imperialist-Nationalism has not even the least spark of social justice. Prince Konoe of Japan is in for a nasty shock. Blindness appears to be a consequence of national egotism. For over three years already the Chinese have offered a heroic resistance under Chiang Kai-shek's outstanding leadership. Such an achievement cannot be for nothing. Chinese freedom fighters will be a shining example of a new kind of strength, and it will lead to a deserved victory.

If I were convinced prayers brought help, I would pray daily for a free China – and also pray everyone on earth would be moved to offer every possible aid to the Chinese. Their truly unique courage and idealism should inspire mankind, and that inspiration can be the death blow to every kind of tyranny.

October 11, 1940

[. . .] How many German farmers were enticed by the most absurd inducements in the years before the National Socialists' "Seizure of Power" when the Nazi Party told them exactly what they wanted to hear. how they would break up the domination of invested capital, go against the Jews, lower the taxes, and keep government salaries limited to 1,000 Reichsmarks per month, etc.?[50] "If Hitler wins, the corn will develop faster and the cows will cheerfully give milk," said a speaker in 1932 at Solmser Hof Inn. And at a campaign meeting in Ruppertsburg, the teacher, B., from Gonterskirchen, stated, "If we (that is, the Nazis) come to power, the finance ministry will disappear." Loud calls of "Bravo" thundered throughout the hall. That was before the Seizure of Power. And today? Does not Reich Marshal Göring chuckle about his fellow Party members in Hesse who in 1932 proposed in the state parliament ministerial salaries should be lowered to 1,000 RM a month? He, the most masterful of all, earns more than 1,000 RM per day. What is a measly one thousand marks? Small change.

October 12, 1940

Does Germany have weak points? Readers of German newspapers would say no without hesitation. Day after day, a strong and defiant Greater Germany is portrayed before their eyes. Boastfulness is an essential NSDAP component. Nevertheless, observant and thoughtful Germans (their number is not large) realize not everything that glitters is gold.

At the war's very beginning, all-encompassing restrictions were placed throughout the land on oil and gasoline. A large number of trucks of every kind had to be turned over to the army, which resulted in limited public traffic. Gasoline supplies were confiscated. The sale of gasoline was placed under federal control. Controls were placed on the use of motor vehicles: only those with a red triangle sign were allowed on the road. Such is motorized Germany after one year and forty days of war.

All these restrictions on commercial traffic show how much we are feeling the pinch. Fuel is our problem child. The deepest well is empty. We were always dependent on many kinds of raw material, which we imported in huge quantities even during peacetime. Because of a lack of storage here, our supplies were limited and always in need of replenishment. We might be able to advance the manufacture of fuel from coal, but with war increasing our consumption, we will not be able to do without imports. It does not require any further investigation to see how widely the deficiencies are felt; measures taken by our war administration speak volumes. The military occupation of important strategic positions in Romania and securing waterways at the Danube and Black Sea show we have the same motives as when we last waged war against Romania in 1916.

[. . .]

October 17, 1940

If it is true German squadrons continue to bomb London, then it must be said England did not sufficiently prepare its defensive ability, particularly against air raids.

But there is also an old saying that applies: "Attack is the best defense." Where is the English fleet?

October 18, 1940

Today is an historical day within my small circle. Not because the Battle of Leipzig took place on this day [in 1813]. No. This is the day my hunting partners, Herr Becker, and Herr Fritz from Giessen, prophesied the end of the war. Herr [Otto] Fritz is the type who snaps up information without any question, adds the necessary embellishments, and passes it on to the crowd – and becomes infuriated if anyone dares express a doubt. He has launched countless prophecies during the course of this war. One cannot cure such people. They have to be beaten down with a thick club until they cannot get back up. No one ever takes a position against these outrageous latrine rumors. On the contrary, the Party has lent a hand, dredging up as many phrases as possible in order to intoxicate the people.

Last Sunday, October 13, in the Geist Inn in Altenhain, a soldier home on leave said in front of everyone he believed all the stories about the attacks against England were lies, and he would not believe anything else unless he personally could see it. Now that is a rare bird! It is encouraging that despite everything, small rays of light are visible.

[. . .]

October 28, 1940

Still no move against England! Instead, things are becoming lively in the Balkans, where we have something to rob. How long yet, Herr Hitler, will you abuse wretched humanity that has displayed the patience of Job? You can carry the pitcher to the well only so often before it breaks. We Germans may depend on that. Now the war goes into its last phase. Now the decline of Europe develops. There can be no more rest for those who trample others underfoot, breed confusion, and root up continents. Power-hungry Germany and Italy can obtain cheap victories through brute force and the incredibly indecent nature of their tactics. But as far as it can be determined, we have not won a single friend through that method. An inextinguishable hatred has been created in the hearts of the poor oppressed people, and one day it will come against us as a blazing flame.

It has been reported Italy has given unacceptable conditions to Greece – just as Austria gave the Serbs in 1914. Everything repeats. This can turn out positively. Now is the time for Turkey to take action, to take up arms. Or do they also not know what must be done? The Turks must help the Greeks with all their means, whatever the cost. That is the only way to save themselves. Do not wait until the floodwater is up to the neck. Not a single nation yet has understood the right way to handle things. The basic procedure was apparent with Finland – except simple-minded "friends" and neighbors behaved stupidly.

October 29, 1940

The teacher Bechtold's son is home on leave. When a young woman asked him about his depressed mood, he told her he was to become a paratrooper, and it would be terrible until he got accustomed to murdering women and children. This child-assassin explained that his group was assigned to attack

a certain factory during the forthcoming assault against England. They were
to kill everyone who got in their way.[51]

November 2, 1940

Judge Boländer thinks an attack by Germany and Italy against Turkey is
imminent. Russia would attack the Turks at the same time! I disagreed with
these very optimistic views. I believe Russia will not offer a hand to help the
powers of Germany and Italy rule Europe. If Russia, in spite of everything,
acts in favor of Germany and Italy, I will have to say Russia is governed by
madmen!

It is said differences of opinion prevail among the highest people. Göring
would be for executing the attack against England though one third of the
pilots are dead, one third are sick, and one third not trained enough yet to
use.

November 3, 1940

Now we are writing November 3, 1940. One year and sixty-four days of war
already. Where does the time go? The Blitzkrieg, as the Nazis so happily
called their war in 1939, is lasting pretty damned long. Recently a high-
positioned person asked me, "How long will this war last now?" Without
thinking about it I answered, "Until 1943." He replied, "Well, that is at least a
positive response." Approximately half a year ago I mentioned this to my
friend Hellwig in Krakow who responded with a ringing prophecy I would
still be debating this with him in 1943, and he would produce all of our letters.
Speaking of 1943, I would like to say this world war has already lasted longer
than prophesied by various official German circles at the beginning.

So what is next? The last land is not yet "conquered." The war must
continue to be "obligatory" (a word the Führer uses often). And that is
because the enemy is not going to acquiesce to the fate being forced upon
him. The struggle goes on. The real chaos begins in 1941.

I might predict decisive events will occur in Africa. Above everything else,
I believe Abyssinia will once again arise. With England's support, the Italians
will be chased out of Abyssinia. The war will end in Asia, and China will win.
Japan's prestige has been greatly damaged by not being able to overcome the
Chinese after three years of war. Japan's armory has been used up. From the
start, I have been enthusiastically on China's side. Attacked as it was and so
brutally treated by the robber nation Japan, China has one hundred percent
of my sympathy. The Japanese fiends ruthlessly bombed towns and cities; the

number of victims must have been enormous.[52] The heroic struggles of the Chinese will bear much fruit. Another China will arise from this and remember who stood by its side: the United States of America, Russia, and England.

And where does the German jackass stand? With the robber Japan, of course, who, in a "subtle" way, removed the Germans in 1914–18 from their eastern colonial territories.[53] And out of gratitude, we are creeping behind this loathsome nation – naturally in the supposition we will catch a crumb from these crooks. In truth, we have never understood how to promote an intelligent foreign policy.

Applying power by itself always leaves wisdom and humanity in the lurch. In the end, reconciliation requires decorum, culture, and morality. Germany knows only brutal suppression: "If you don't want to be my brother, I'll smash in your skull." The handling of Alsatians after the war of 1870–71 was a typical example of this. Today it is even worse. Overnight the Alsatians and Lothringers were "transformed" into National Socialists. What colossal nonsense.[54]

November 5, 1940

The curse of the evil deed is it will give birth to future evils: Italy has invaded Greece.[55] They intend to teach the Greeks about the "New Order," as prescribed by the "Axis Powers."

It is difficult to imagine these positions reversed: the nations now under attack overrunning Italy, Germany, and Japan in the same way. There would be such screaming and lamentation about the infringement of the people's rights the entire globe would hear it. Yet they are the same ones today who would subjugate the world, who have made right and justice itself bend to their might. A "New Order" cannot be built upon such principles!

November 6, 1940

Yesterday on November 5 the United States held its presidential elections. Roosevelt, the candidate of the Democratic Party (where my own sympathies lie), was elected.

This election will soon change everything quite noticeably to England's advantage. Domestic politics in the USA made them cautious in many things. Now these considerations can be set aside, and America's foreign policy can enter into a decisive phase. It will be called: Oppose Japan and totalitarian Germany and Italy. America does not need to enter the war at all;

if it inserts itself with its entire industrial skills for China and England, the war is decided.

November 8, 1940

Our propaganda derides the nations that call for England to help them, and it laughs at the extent and value of England's guarantees. The mockery is being revived just now in light of Italy's attack against Greece.[56]

Irrespective of one's sympathies, for or against, the fact remains Greece has been attacked. And Greece must decide whether to cowardly give up or heroically defend itself. What would men in Italy and Germany do? Would they not defend themselves? What is good for one is good for the other. It is understood Greece's resistance does not suit Germany's aims and is therefore unpleasant. Through their resistance, they make it clear they have no inclination to allow meddling tyrants to rule over them. The rest of the world knows that and judges accordingly.

[. . .]

November 10, 1940

Italian army reports have become subdued. Greece is continuing its resistance. Perhaps it will be clear soon that Italy has launched a capital stupidity. Also, England has won a foothold [in North Africa] it can exploit: southern Italy may receive unpleasant visitors in the coming months.

Did Mussolini not realize when he frivolously began to make war the position could be turned around upon him? Has he, too, been taken in by German propaganda? Italy entered into the war in June 1940 but accomplished nothing (except for the occupation of British Somaliland) that could shake the English. The Italian fleet has not undertaken anything. They should have engaged the English Mediterranean fleet when France collapsed. Nothing was done. The reason is hard to know. Should Italian bragging not have included quite so many fibs? Does its "huge" navy exist merely on paper? Or is something else rotten here? Time will instruct us about these points too.

If the Italian fleet is weakened, the entire cardboard house will collapse. The army in Albania is dependent on constant supply. The same goes for the Italian occupation in Africa. In light of such concerns, I would not be inclined, if I were an Italian statesman, to move against England. History will show whether the present Italian authority or I, the ordinary man in the Vogelsberg hills, had a better grasp of the possibilities of world politics.

November 12, 1940

A few days ago former Prime Minister Neville Chamberlain died. It was clear to me the falsifiers of history would go straight to work to shift the blame for this war onto this old man. Just how is seen below:

CHAMBERLAIN IS DEAD

Met Up With His Own Curse

Stockholm, November 10, 1940

According to a Reuters news report, Neville Chamberlain died on Saturday evening. With Neville Chamberlain's death, one of the war's first firebrands has left the political world stage. Although one may not overestimate his significance as a politician, he was even more dangerous in his role as English Prime Minister, and he is the real arsonist who has to answer with his name for the dreadful crime of transforming Europe and the world into a theatre of war. At this moment, one also recalls one of Chamberlain's most monstrous sayings, how he hoped to experience the day when Hitler would be destroyed. Now he has met up with his own dreadful curse. Indeed, through his continuing government work he tried to escape the heavy responsibility and guilt, but in vain. The judgment of history has very quickly fallen upon this man, this typical English plutocrat.

> Source: "Chamberlain gestorben," *Hessische Landes-Zeitung* [HLZ], November 11, 1940, p. 1.

Were I an Englishman, I, too, certainly would place a heavy blame on Chamberlain but in a manner other than this German writer. Chamberlain and the entire subsequent government carry the blame for not having taken equivalent steps when they discovered Germany's preparations for war. A world power must always be prepared to successfully and energetically repulse any attack.[57] [. . .]

November 21, 1940

Herr Hessler gave me two gas masks and told me we are now counted in the danger zone. "If the English run out of ammunition, they will come after us with gas! That will be the last straw on which they themselves will be sunk!" declared Hessler, retired insurance agent from Frankfurt who now lives in Laubach. A genuine Party man and possessor of several official positions (air defense and supply officer), he is the type of narrow-minded fellow for whom politics shapes his horizon and who becomes enraptured by propaganda that daily offers what he so gladly would hear. Dear Joseph Goebbels, you are doing excellently. How well you know them!

County Court Judge [Fritz] Boländer is yet another breed: son of a highly placed customs officer and a sworn enemy of Jews, First Class. Prior to 1933, he was a fraternity member and belonged to the Pan-German League and the National Liberal Party. He is convinced of a total German victory but unable to describe what peace will be like. He is dead certain of victory. One more zealot among Third Reich men.

We will have to talk about this in 1943. Nothing can be gained from arguing with a person who has absolutely no concern for the human rights of other people. Germany is trump. Everything and everyone must submit. That truly is a damned simple policy, but it is also one people outside of Germany will not accept. Whether Herr B. would be as zealous if he had to take weapon in hand and subdue the world by himself remains to be seen. For the time being, he intoxicates himself with the heroic deeds of others.

November 23, 1940

Yesterday the radio reported two Italian divisions in Albania had taken up new positions. Instead of conquering Greece, they retreat to "new" positions in Albania. It is plain the Italians were not able to withstand the pressure from the Greek resistance.

The Italians are dependent in Albania on supplies from home. That is a decisive factor because the Italian fleet will have to neglect other important duties as it protects the transports from Italy to Albania. This is why Italy was unable to undertake anything decisive in Africa. With English troops now stationed on Crete, it is impossible for Italy to succeed in Africa. It is their own fault. By attacking Greece, Italy's strategic position has visibly deteriorated.

With some skillful operations by the Greeks, the Italians will be forced out of Albania. That would be a triumph of justice, almost too good to believe.

December 5, 1940

On October 30 the newspapers reported, "Italians March into Greece."[58] On November 1 they were proclaiming, "The Italians Advance 70 Kilometers" and "Italian Air Force Controls Greek Air Space."[59]

And today? The press is silent. No Italian soldier stands any longer on Greek soil. Greece turned the tables and invaded the Italian positions in Albania, causing them to lose emplacement after emplacement. Where is the much-celebrated Italian Fascist pluck? Nothing at all is solved with the big mouth alone. A spirited determination decides. The Greeks defend their fatherland. And the Italians – they wanted to invade and plunder a small country.

A ray of hope finally appears within the European chaos.

An opportunity for England begins to show itself on the horizon. But do they realize that in England? They have shown such an unbelievable policy of irresolution one is tempted to assume they are entirely incapable of making any military chess moves. Attack! They must attack in every place they can in Africa – and at any cost. Now that Italy finds itself in a bad situation in Albania, we will see whether England finally knows what it has to do.

December 8, 1940

All of South Albania should already be in Greek hands. Italy's position is unusually bad, and the next few days will clarify the ground campaign's outcome. If English and Greek air forces immediately attack the retreating Italians, and if Albanians in the rear sabotage the Italian forces, the Italian army's fate in Albania is sealed.

December 13, 1940

An unlucky day for the Fascists in Italy. Over twenty thousand Italian prisoners, including three generals, can now contemplate – while in English custody – the Suez Canal and recall how they bragged for so many years about conquering it.

Dear Duce! You are a complete dunce. If you had correctly kept your friendship with England, you would have been spared an African defeat. But when things are going well for a jackass, he goes dancing on ice.[60]

Finally, justice is being served.

The English army in Egypt is attacking the Italians who are trying to push into Egypt from Libya. The first day of the offensive has already brought substantial strategic advantages to the English. With such favorable progress, we might yet anticipate several surprises. It is entirely possible the Italians will be checkmated in quite a short time. Whoever enters so frivolously into a completely unnecessary war – as Mussolini did – should not wonder if someone gives him a good lesson with a bomb or two. Did this dictator really run out of possibilities to work for peace? This "Duce" was for me always a bandit. History will also treat him as such.

[. . .]

December 24, 1940

One more step and the second Christmas of the war is here. Though nothing can be felt of "Peace on Earth," I believe I discern a faint outline of a beginning change in the situation. Italy continues to retreat in Albania. And instead of being on the offensive in Egypt, they are being forced out of Egypt by the English army, which is also attacking them in Libya. England's successful follow-up operations in both Albania and Libya have placed it in a favorable military position. [. . .]

The Fascist edifice staggers!! Mankind, overthrow it!!

December 31, 1940

Today 1940 will be laid to rest. What great, unspeakable suffering it has brought to the enslaved world. And what is yet to come? It is not to surmise. Nobody can know. The prophecy in 1939 was for a quick victory: "Blitzsieg." Tomorrow we write "1941."

Friedrich and Pauline Kellner, with grandson Robert Scott Kellner, 1968.

Robert Scott Kellner in US navy uniform, 1960.

Friedrich and Pauline Kellner outside their retirement cottage, 1955.

Friedrich Kellner (front row, second from right) on the courthouse steps, 1948.

Laubach courthouse with the Kellner's apartment, 1938.

Fred William Kellner in US army uniform, 1946.

Friedrich Kellner playing a violin, 1938.

Friedrich Kellner painting, 1938.

Friedrich Kellner, 1938.

Friedrich and Pauline Kellner, with their son Fred, 1927.

Friedrich and Pauline Kellner, with their son Fred, 1934.

Friedrich and Pauline Kellner, with their son Fred, 1916.

Friedrich Kellner, 1923.

Friedrich and Pauline Kellner, first anniversary, 1914.

Friedrich Kellner in uniform, 1913.

Friedrich Kellner and Pauline Preuss, engagement photo, 1911.

Pauline Preuss, 1912.

Friedrich Kellner (seated second from right) and comrades, 1908.

Friedrich Kellner with his parents, 1903.

Friedrich Kellner, 1892.

1941

January 7, 1941

Australian troops stormed the fortified town of Bardia in Libya and supposedly captured thirty thousand Italian soldiers. Our propaganda machine
was doing somersaults [in September] when the Italian troops penetrated
Egypt and advanced to Sidi Barani, about 180 kilometers from the Libyan
border, to give us the screaming impression Egypt would be conquered in a few
more days. Then all at once silence reigned. Now and then a conjuror would
help the waiting folk with a newspaper article about the difficulties in Africa –
like a quack doctor tranquilizing the frantic. Suddenly the English attacked
before Christmas, and the entire Italian cardboard house in Africa immediately
came down. It is evident to the entire world Italians in Africa will not be going
on the offensive, not when they can no longer support themselves.

Of what benefit to Germany is this noble ally and "Axis partner"? The end
result will be our having to support Italy in everything if it is going to remain
standing, just as we had to do for Austria in the last war. [. . .]

January 8, 1941

We are in a strange state of mind. I well remember reading in the newspapers
just before war began in 1939 that we would not have a long war. No one
speaks of that anymore. How does the ostrich do it – he sticks his head in the
sand so he does not have to see anything. We are just like that.

According to the pronouncements, the National Socialist German Workers'
Party (NSDAP) places only the most noble of the land in authoritative
positions. Yet the most noteworthy criminal offenses in Laubach from
1933–1940 were committed by Party members:

Reuter: False witness, embezzlement (one year in the penitentiary).
Döll: Embezzlement (nine months in prison).
Leidner: Bodily injury, insult.
Hans Högel: Hitler Youth leader. Theft, embezzlement (ten days in prison).
And some of the highest Party members committed tax fraud. These were
sentenced to pay fines:

8. Jan. 1941. Wir befinden uns in einer merkwürdigen geistigen Umfassung. Ich kann mich gut erinnern, daß im Jahre 1939 — von Beginn des Krieges — oft in den Zeitungen zu lesen stand, daß wir einen langen Krieg nicht führen könnten. Heute spricht niemand mehr davon. Wie macht es der Nazel Kreis? Er packt den Kopf in den Sand damit er nicht sieht. Wir sehen es ihm nach. —

Nur die Edelsten der Nation sind nach den Nachrichtberichten maßgebender Stellen in der Nationalsozialistischen-Deutschen-Arbeiter-Partei (NSDAP).

In den Jahren 1933 bis 1940 sind zu höheren Strafen bemerkenswerte Straftaten in Laubach ausschließlich von Parteigenossen begangen worden:

  Reuter. Urkundenfälschung, Amtsunterschlagung (1 Jahr Zuchthaus)

  Döll. Amtsunterschlagung (9 Monate Gef.)

  Leidner. Körperverletzung, beleidigung

  Hans Högel (HJ führer) Diebstahl, Amtsunterschlagung
    (10 Tage Gef.)

  Immer so ist es bei den Parteiführern.
Zu der Parteiführer Pg.
Zu Geldstrafen wegen Parteiuntersuchung
wurden verurteilt:

  Högy (20000 RM)
  Reichen (6000 RM)
  W. Michel (6000 RM)
  Holz (2000 "

10. Jan 1941 Der Wehrmachtsbericht v. 8.I.41 spricht von Kreisen u. Artillerie tätigkeit zwischen Derna u. Tobruk in der Cyrenaika. Das klingt nicht sehr optimistisch. Dieses Gebiet wird bald im Besitze der Engländer sein. Das ist eine ungeheure Schlag für die Großmannsucht eines Mussolini. Liegen wir immer

Högy (fined 20,000 RM). The Nazi mayor's son; he hid assets of 50,000 RM.
Kreicker (fined 6,000 RM).
W. Michel (fined 6,000 RM).
Stotz (fined 2,000 RM).

January 10, 1941

[. . .] I find it amusing how the Italian public is informed. The ministry calls
for "resolute purpose," applauds "the heroic defenders of Bardia," and tells
the people about "the unshakeable resolve of those who will fight until
victory."[1] What humbug! Rome says the Fascists are "fighting," but entire
divisions in Africa are heading into prisoner-of-war camps.

I can hardly wait until the Italians receive their payment in Abyssinia for
the vile acts they have been committing for five years. To invade and annex a
country twice as large as Germany is the height of brutal shamelessness.
These damned Fascists carry the guilt for knocking the entire world out of
joint. And for that they must atone.

I feel the war will soon be wound up in Abyssinia. A properly executed and
concentrated attack, along with the people rising up, and the Italians will be
wiped out. The hour of freedom will soon strike. This defeat will not occur
without consequences in the motherland. The guilty men will be brought to
the public square. The king of Italy will place his rusty Abyssinian crown in the
junkyard of history and with tears in his eyes realize it might have been better
had he abdicated after Mussolini's 1922 March on Rome. This pitiful figure of a
king is a good-for-nothing not worth the rope to hang him, a wretched coward
without example in history. He played the role of a straw puppet and set the
crowns of Albania and Abyssinia – a king and an emperor – on his degenerate
head. Such a clown!

January 24, 1941

The Italian army report admits Australian troops have captured Tobruk in
Libya. I think the report exaggerates the details about the attacking troop
strength to make their defeat more palatable.[2] Such hokum. Was anyone
holding back the "heroic" Fascist army leaders from sending reinforcements
to Libya and attacking the English troops with airplanes? Italy has said often
enough it and not England rules the Mediterranean. Not to mention what I
have read about the Italian soldier who fights so bravely that he puts the
Australians "out of commission."

It is a favorite tactic in this war to hold up the individual soldier as an
unqualified hero whose actions are heroic deeds without example in the

history of warfare. Continually present this image to the overweening German people, and what little character they have left goes completely to the devil. The opponents, according to the propaganda makers, have nothing but gangs, bandits, snipers, and so on.

When will the sensible Germans be allowed to speak out again?

January 25, 1941

I keep wondering what the Italian leaders must have been thinking when they decided to tie themselves to Germany. A neutral observer can see the German dictator will endure no other god besides himself. There can be but one Napoleon. What role did Mussolini believe he would have if Hitler became ruler of Europe? That is a rather dark matter. Every Italian child would fear the German in his subconscious. After a victorious war, how would a covetous Germany deal with its Italian "friend"? Every slumbering German chauvinist would leap to his feet and let out a scream for a German corridor to the Mediterranean (at the seaport of Trieste) that would be heard in all nooks and crannies. This is reality. Everyone who knows the National Socialist soul knows that. Only the Fascist lords in Italy run around the universe like blockheads.

Everyone is allowed to make mistakes – except for statesmen. Italy has no statesmen: merely braggarts and megalomaniacal idiots.

[. . .]

February 6, 1941

Today's *Hessische Landes-Zeitung* includes a small map. The caption says fighting is occurring in Eritrea between Agordat and Barentu and both sides have taken heavy casualties.

DIFFICULT FIGHTING IN ITALIAN EAST AFRICA

> In the northern part of Italian East Africa, intense battles are taking place in the western plains of Eritrea between Agordat and Barentu. As announced in the Italian army reports, the fighting at Agordat and Barentu involves heavy losses for both sides.
>
> *Source:* "Harte Kämpfe in Italienisch-Ostafrika," *HLZ*, February 6, 1941, p. 1.

This is the first time both sides have casualties. Before this, only the enemy had heavy losses. Yet, the information in this case is coming from the Italian army reports. The Italian people are slowly being prepared for ill tidings.

Goebbels, with his endless sunshine, would not let such a report out of his incubator.

February 7, 1941

In the *Hamburger Fremdenblatt* of January 27, 1941, a certain K.A.v.W. writes about "The Fall of Tobruk." He states, among other things,

Obviously the events in Libya have confused some of the English; they are no longer rooted in reality if they think Benghazi is to be the next objective for the Wavell offensive. If they but look on a map of Libya, they will realize deeds of such fantasy cannot succeed. It is farther from Tobruk to Benghazi than from Sidi Barani to Tobruk, almost twice as far if one goes not as the birds fly but on the coastal roads. And between Tobruk and Benghazi, Marshal Graziani awaits with fresh divisions not used in the smaller battles.[3]

The author of this article, sitting in his study, has invented the situation as he would like it to be. But he had uncanny bad luck. The English plan was not pulled out from a fantasy. Marshal Graziani, who perhaps at one time did stand between Tobruk and Benghazi, is today no longer there.[4]

Benghazi, the capital of Cyrenaica, is now in the hands of the "fantasizing" English. This occurred exactly ten days after the above-mentioned article's appearance. [...]

February 10, 1941

A request came today to report immediately the names of those who had served in the navy and were still capable of shipboard service. The last resort! With what kind of enthusiasm will those poor guys go onboard?

February 12, 1941

Apparently widespread transgressions are occurring against the ban on feeding animals grains used in making bread (Regulation for the Guarantee of Bread Cereals Requirements from July 22, 1937).[5] So word has come from on high that posters have to be hung to remind us of the fodder prohibition and to point out its relevance to the war. It is worth noting precautions for the guarantee of bread cereals were announced back in 1937. Now posters have to be put up to achieve this: the paper war shall help. Clearly, if farmers had other food supplies for their animals, there would not have to be a prohibition on bread grains. That is exactly the crucial point. Instead of informing the farmers of what is yet available to feed their animals, they hang these posters in front of their noses.

Posters instead of animal feed!

February 13, 1941

Speaking of animal feed, bird feed for our canaries is no longer available. We have this "Greater Germany," indeed, and plan to create a New Order in Europe (Order = Robbery), yet so many things of daily living are scarce or not obtainable at all. I am not referring to luxuries; for example, even cleaning rags are not to be found. Hundreds of other articles require "substitutes" or are entirely gone. Where have you gone, you good old days?

February 22, 1941

A Local Group Leader, [Karl] Naumann, an Old Fighter from the early Nazi Party, who works as an accountant at the district savings bank, applied to the regional office to be exempted from military service. Naumann was formerly a typically inept clerk in the county government earning 100 RM per month. His petition was approved by all the various offices. Nevertheless, Naumann is currently assigned to a military unit – although doing his "fighting" from their office. He said the army unit did not exempt him because he earlier had stated a strong desire to take part in the coming fight against England.

Naumann is not the only one who would like to "participate" in the glory but only at the greatest possible distance from the shooting. Unfortunately more people than can be counted benefit materially during the war. This sort would prefer we never again had peace. Another example is our courthouse watchman, Schüler, presently a master sergeant in nearby Bebra. He has already garnered a thick paunch and thick skull.

February 26, 1941

Many speeches have been made these past few days concluding with the call for "final victory" [Endsieg]. I recall the mouthing of such empty phrases at the end of 1918: always the same old song. The ignorant masses willingly accept everything. Three hundred years ago a Swedish statesman wrote to his son, "You would scarcely believe with how little intelligence the world could be ruled."[6] On this point, nothing has changed. Hitler laid out in Mein Kampf his disdain for the general public; yet despite that the masses go to him and howl "Heil Hitler."[7] Or maybe it is because of that – because only the stupidest calves elect their own butcher.

English Commonwealth troops are penetrating Italian East Africa from all sides and establishing one position after another. Italian resistance will be possible for just a short period. For months, they have been cut off and fighting in hopeless positions. A modern war with its tremendous demand for supplies requires, above all else, sufficient material reserves – which the Italians lack. They are entirely dependent on themselves for supplies. Their fate shall now be carried out. A first-class divine judgment! Someone who handles things as frivolously as Mussolini does deserves no other punishment.

As to whether or not the people will learn from this? No! The successors and imitators will always think they are smarter. They will not make the same mistakes – or so they say – but they make others, and the comedy goes on and on, while glory and military marches are not uprooted.

[. . .]

March 28, 1941

A refreshing vacation allowed me to take a break from describing events and setting down my thoughts. A stay in Freudenstadt in the Black Forest has brought a longed-for recuperation. The treadmill begins again.

Since I last wrote, National Socialist diplomacy in the Balkans has been busy and achieved new "successes." Bulgaria – another nation that knows nothing about freedom and honor – willingly bowed to the dictator Hitler. And an article, "Victory Without Weapons," in the March 25 *Hamburger Fremdenblatt* glowingly describes Yugoslavia's agreement to join the Tripartite Pact, presenting it as the crowning conclusion of a great diplomatic campaign. Before Bulgaria and Yugoslavia signed on, Hungary, Romania, and Slovakia joined in November 1940.[8] [. . .]

What is happening in the theaters of war?

England's strategic position has suddenly become better because England splendidly understood to strengthen its positions in the Eastern Mediterranean. The conquest of Cyrenaica dealt a blow to the threat against Egypt and the Suez Canal. Not only has Italy been made militarily impotent in Africa, but its reputation has been so damaged it definitely cannot be revived in this war. Italy cannot list any success at all in Albania; and in the meantime, it has lost Italian Somaliland. Even British Somaliland, which the Italians occupied in August 1940, is firmly back in English hands. The German newspapers print nothing, of course, about these English successes. [Radio broadcaster] Fritzsche must be wondering how he can explain this to his dependent children, the German people.[9] Children who are served only overwhelming victories and kept in the dark about mistakes are naturally very delicate. The slightest draft of fresh air can become quite unpleasant.

The East African drama is heading toward its end. I mentioned to a friend in January the Italian colonies in East Africa would be in English hands by April 1. My prophecy was correct almost to the day. Yesterday, the Italian army reported they were withdrawing from two places of major strategic significance: Keren in Eritrea and Harar in Abyssinia. It can be just a short while before the Italians discontinue their resistance. Every further loss of men is clearly crazy. I do not put the blame on the individual Italian soldiers who stand in lost outposts, cut off from their homeland and left to their own resources. The collapse was merely a question of time and only hastened by the British attacks. The soldiers and settlers are to be pitied. They can give thanks to the insane Mussolini!

Germany's Balkan adventure will also be seen as a definite mistake. Bismarck had it instinctively correct when he told the Reichstag the Balkan Peninsula was not worth the bones of a single Pomeranian grenadier.[10] [...]

April 2, 1941

English troops now occupy Asmara, the capital of Italian Eritrea. This cuts off any remaining Italians inside Abyssinia from the harbor of Massawa.

The *Völkischer Beobachter* of March 27 has a running series of reports about the Yugoslavian Minister Zwetkowitsch's visit to Vienna.[11] For the German philistine, his visit is supposedly "joyous" news. The editors make a great effort to keep such events from being overlooked or forgotten. [...] But contrary to what Herr von Ribbentrop wants, it often comes out otherwise.[12] The National Socialists have had an unusual amount of success due to their not-so-gentle methods, but with far too many unnatural successes being achieved so quickly, a bad end is definitely yet to come.[13]

April 3, 1941

After the shameful reverses German diplomacy brought to Yugoslavia, something else was needed to continue Germany's victory delirium. This time it is not happening in our vicinity; it is another continent's turn: Africa! We have been hearing for some time about German troop transports [Erwin Rommel's Africa Corps] heading to Italy and from there to Africa (Libya). Their landing in Tripoli was filmed. So theatrical! I do not like that; a genuine soldier does not show off.[14]

The first news indicates German troops have advanced against Cyrenaica. The English are pulling back.

April 5, 1941

The English have evacuated Benghazi! Are they trying to lure us into the vicinity of their consolidated positions? I do not believe Germany will earn laurels in Africa. [. . .]

And what are we to do about the Balkans? It is a mistake for Germany not to seize it – but it is a bigger mistake if we do seize it.

April 6, 1941

Sunday. My question of yesterday already can be answered: German troops have crossed the Bulgarian border and are invading Greece. German planes have dropped bombs on Yugoslavian territory. Two more nations must experience the horror of war. Two more peoples have become Germany's enemies.[15] [. . .]

April 8, 1941

An enormous effort was made for Japanese Foreign Minister Matsuoka's visit to Berlin and Rome. "The overwhelming reception the German people prepared for our Japanese friends is being lively celebrated in Japan as a spontaneous expression of the two people's unity for future decisions," so heralded the leading article writer of a newspaper.[16]

The German people did absolutely nothing: it was the scene-shifter [Goebbels] who created both the politics and the "spirited" reception. In the last war, the Japanese were "slant-eyed bandits" because they robbed us of Kiautschou Bay. Today they are "friends." How mutable your soul, German newspaper writer! [. . .]

What does it imply when we use all our diplomatic arts to seek Japanese assistance? Would it not be more conceivable that Japan needs our help? Japan is in no position to undertake anything against America or England. If it were otherwise, then Japan should have attacked immediately in 1939. But there never was an apparent point in time Japan was in a position to make the Americans bow their heads to them. I do not consider the Japanese that dumb. They are never going to pull the chestnuts out of the fire for us. That will have to be verified soon.

April 14, 1941

England's position has been improved. The United States will allow their merchant ships to travel on the Red Sea now that the Italians are defeated in East Africa. In addition, the Danish envoy had a covert meeting with the American government, and they agreed on a temporary base in Greenland for American troops. That creates a landing field for planes patrolling the Atlantic.[17] Both significant occurrences.

With that, America has taken on provisioning the English troops in Africa, Asia, and the Balkans.

April 19, 1941

Yugoslavia has laid down its weapons. Strong German forces are attacking Greece. After the Greeks' outstanding resistance against the Italians, they must retreat in the face of Germany's craven attacks. The strongest will naturally win, but Germany will not reap any glory from this. The same drama keeps repeating: one land after another overrun. No nation helps the other one but waits quietly until it also is attacked. Why does Turkey not come to the aid of Yugoslavia and Greece?

So now, German troops occupy the Balkans. That completes the picture. The war has seriously hurt that region, and it will take a long time for their economy to recover.

Since 1938 Germany has conquered or occupied the following nations: Austria, Czechoslovakia, Poland, Denmark, Norway, Netherlands, Luxembourg, Belgium, France, Hungary, Romania, Bulgaria, Yugoslavia, and Greece. Together these countries have a population of approximately 180 million. [...] We can stifle the spirit of freedom in the Europeans with tanks and airplanes, but the day will come when the brook will rise and send out its floods. [...]

England must carry through with this life and death struggle because its entire existence is in jeopardy. Just the *idea* of world domination by Germany is a danger.

April 21, 1941

If in the near future Germany does not dominate the seas, it will be "forced" to search for another way out, which will be in the East. All the raw materials Adolf Hitler so urgently needs are there. On this basis, and if Russia does not volunteer to give us everything we want, Hitler will start the war in the East. Militarily, a favorable alliance would be with Turkey, before they are given other "submit or fight" alternatives. Turkey might receive support from other embattled countries, such as Russia or England. England could send troops to Turkey through India and Iraq. Russia, being Turkey's neighbor, would not find it difficult to assist in a number of ways.

In broad outline, it is easy to see the war's end nearing at a rapid pace. A series of battles, one after another, is taking place in Asia, Africa, and Europe. The final victory remains to happen on every continent. The only consolation is to wait.

May 1, 1941

First of May, how you have changed: no official festivities, not even a flag. Does this First of May not suit the war profiteers, or do they hope the people will not notice we have nothing at all to celebrate with – a shortage of supplies? An increased consumption of food and drink would perhaps disturb the equilibrium. Who knows?

German troops now occupy Yugoslavia and Greece, and the war goes on until we are victorious over England. Are we in a better position to overcome England today than a year ago? After considering all the possibilities, I still say Germany cannot defeat England militarily. We would need a superior fleet to do that.

The main determining factor will be how much Canada and the United States can increase their production of war materials and place them at England's disposal. This is just like 1917 when all the officials said help from America was impossible. "No troop ships would reach Europe," they stated repeatedly. They all came. Not a single ship was sunk. And today? America does what it can and knows how to defend its transports. We can depend on that. In the last war our navy was a little larger than today. They also accomplished much but had considerable damage too. Their abilities were limited. Nothing has changed in that regard.

Enemy action has definitely and grievously disrupted the production we had in peacetime. England's continuing methodical attacks against Emden, Wilhelmshafen, Bremen, Hamburg, and Kiel will certainly not be without consequences. The shipyards in Canada and in the United States, on the other hand, operate undisturbed. This will be a daily increasing factor in conducting the war. [...]

May 2, 1941

Adolf Hitler shows no sentimentality in *Mein Kampf* about foreign policy. His words offer unambiguous proof of that. National Socialists can take up from where the Germans left off six hundred years ago, he writes. "We stop the endless German movement to the south and west, and turn our gaze toward the land in the east ... If we speak of soil in Europe today, we can primarily have in mind only Russia and her vassal border states."[18]

Hitler calls the Russians an inferior race yet was not averse to making a pact with this inferior race in August 1939. This was merely of the moment, of course, and the Russians fell for it. When Germany wanted to bring the German settlers in Estonia, Latvia, Lithuania, and Bessarabia back home to the Reich, I realized they were being brought out to be used in a coming war against Russia and not fall victim to Russian revenge. It is almost a year since the Nazis have written anything about Russia. This is suspicious.

May 3, 1941

When we bombed English cities this past year, almost every German believed the attacks would soften up the English and victory would be that much sooner in coming. Dreadful stories and photographs told about the terrible results of German bombings. The photographs gave the impression everything was destroyed: ruins in the foreground, with the background of each picture blurred and unrecognizable. The propaganda was raised to its highest levels, especially after the bombing of Coventry.[19] But considering a second attack had to be made on Coventry, one must assume the first attack was not quite so drastic – or the English had rebuilt everything between attacks. I will let Party members decide that. Before the war, airplane attacks were a thing born of a fearful imagination. Just by itself, the word "bomb" could evoke fear or horror. I now assert a bomb is not such a dangerous thing. It can cause terrible damage, but the earth has many places left where no bomb attacks, or not many attacks, occurred.

Let us consider the total results of English attacks on German targets this year. As far as my own eyes can see, I have not yet perceived results. The cities I visited during this time show not the slightest trace of destruction. A toll may have been taken to some extent on our war machine, but the English were not able to stop us from anything. The war actually expanded when we launched assaults against Yugoslavia, Greece, and North Africa. Attacks by English planes have been without effect so far. I have not yet had to revise my opinion about the air war. If the English continue in the same way, I will advise them to save their fuel.

May 12, 1941

The Army Command report of May 9, 1941, states, among other things, "Besides some industrial damage [in Hamburg], most destruction occurred in residential areas. The loss of civilian dead and wounded is considerable."[20] This is the first time I can remember them using the phrase "considerable losses." Usually it is "simple property damage" or "no military damage."

However, it would be a pretty poor National Socialist propaganda office that could not make something out of such an effective English attack. And see here:

EFFECTIVE DEFENSE

The Reich Propaganda Office of Hamburg reports:

The British air raid during the night of May 9 encountered an effective defense that kept most of the planes from flying over the city. At least five planes attacking Hamburg and its neighboring areas were shot down. The attack's results clearly show it was primarily a terrorist campaign against the civilian population. Residential houses in densely populated areas were destroyed or damaged, and in several places a large number of civilians were killed or injured. A hospital, two schools, and a scientific institution were also hit. Incendiary or high-explosive bombs were dropped on several factories and also in the harbor at Dresden. However, the damages have not hindered production in the medium-sized operations. Also, supplying the population has in no way been affected. The fires caused by incendiary bombs were extinguished by volunteer defense groups, police, and the Security and Assistance Service.

The simple German citizen may continue to sleep in peace because our defense is A-1 First Class. This effusive news article admits "some factories" had been bombed but declares the attack did not bring about any falling-off in production or adversely affect the supplies for the population.

Thus it is written, and your pack of sheep can readily believe it.

May 13, 1941

It appears the English attacks in the last eight days against Hamburg, Bremen, Berlin, Mannheim, and so on, have been somewhat heavier than before. I do not have the childish belief these attacks were designed as terror actions against civilians. The intention is to stop production, whether it is at the workplace or the worker's living quarters. And when we take every opportunity to announce how the raids caused no slack in production and how every fire was immediately extinguished, we are actually exposing our weak points to any thinking person.

If our opponents succeed in disrupting important production, there is no doubt about the outcome of this war. My wife and I belong to the few Germans who, from the beginning, were convinced of a German defeat.

It was broadcast over the radio yesterday, on May 12, Deputy Führer Rudolf Hess has been missing since May 10.[21] When last seen he was not of sound mind. And in spite of that Hess was still a man of position and authority? Are there any more unsound minds in action? It seems so to me.

Thus, the first man to climb out of the government carriage is Rudolf Hess. That is an especially heavy blow for this system. Is the building swaying? What is going on? Was Hess no longer certain of victory? Did it dawn on him we were not going to be able to conquer the entire world? Today we are not hearing the pure truth, but that day will come, and then the scales will fall from the blind German people's eyes!

It has been some time already since I felt the National Socialists were no longer firmly in the saddle. The quest for conquest apparently has made them a bit nervous. In any case, they walk along with muffled steps and look about nervously. Thoughts begin to rise within them. How arrogantly and brutally these brothers behaved. The German people learned nothing from the 1914–1918 war. Will they learn anything from these terrible years of 1933–1941? The Nazis have always said, "We will not have another November 1918."[22] We can agree such a feeble November 1918 is unthinkable. These lords can depend on that.

This afternoon around 2:15, the radio reported Rudolf Hess was in Scotland. An extremely interesting situation: the Party chief flies to England. Hess was a respected man because he belonged to the less aggressive Party members. That is a great triumph for England. If now the adherents of Hess follow their friend, there will be a jolly bunch of fliers heading for the

British Isles. But even without Hess's departure, we can see our position is not rosy. We are experiencing an almost unbearable shortage in many of our daily necessities and already there is talk about coming reductions in meat and bread rations. The farmers, too, will have shortages. Oh, well, the more victories, the more sorrows. Everything would be much simpler with a little less lust for expansion and a little more love for peace. The joy of militarism is a fixed horse for the majority of my countrymen. The catastrophe of 1918 had not the least beneficial effect. The people's spiritual strength was not strong enough to make them peace-loving. Their base instincts were awakened – a lust for power, irrationality, and a thirst for revenge – which brought them to a monstrous employment. Gamblers, position seekers, and rat catchers, with skills akin to swindlers and felons, elevated themselves to "statesmen."

May 14, 1941

Everyone is talking about Rudolf Hess, the man who escaped from the madhouse of Germany. No one believes he was deranged. An insane person does not fly himself from Augsburg to Scotland. Opinions about his motives range widely. My own opinion: Hess made that flight after a lot of deliberation. He was the Führer's best friend and a fanatical National Socialist, so there must have been unusually grave reasons for him to give up the Party and betray it. Perhaps Hess realized the Führer was a completely unenlightened person, and he wanted to open the German people's eyes, hoping to yet create some way for the German people's deliverance before they reached the abyss. Perhaps the next few days will bring an explanation.

The regional directors and leading bigwigs are in Berlin for discussions, and they have repeated their sworn allegiance to the Führer. If Hess really was of unsound mind, as the official explanation puts it, why then this charade? Hess simply would be designated as sick and relieved of his duties. Any procedure that does not include this will cause the remaining colleagues to wonder about the truth. But in any case, the worm is in the apple.

[. . .]

May 21, 1941

As reported in *Deutsches Recht* (German Law) and in other sources, Reich Minister Governor General Dr. Frank spoke at the International Lawyers' Conference in Berlin in April and said:

A national order can endure only if it satisfies the people's longing for justice. Brutality, despotism, force, and tyranny have already produced many nations; none have lasted. The National Socialist ideal of justice is not government-oriented but people-oriented. We think beyond the state. At the head of the German people stands not only the greatest statesman we ever have had, not only the most gifted Commander-in-Chief, whose strategic plans demolished great nations in a matter of days, but also in Adolf Hitler resides the greatest civilized man who ever stood at the head of the German people.[23]

It is futile to open a discussion with a National Socialist over these soaring words. National Socialist thinking gives no heed to other opinions. It is interesting a national order can last only if the people's longing for justice is satisfied. Does Dr. Frank really believe the German people's longing for justice will be satisfied only in the distant future? Who established the longing for justice? Perhaps Gauleiter Frank? These are terrible clichés.

Even more interesting is Frank's statement that a tyranny does not last. There is yet a glimmer of hope for Europe. We can simply cross off the list his words, "statesman, commander-in chief, and civilized man." If a person who ruthlessly demolishes other nations with tanks and dive-bombers can be labeled a "civilized man" in world history, I would like to call that into question.

May 22, 1941

As reported, our paratroopers have landed in Crete. The war is becoming a circus. Attacking an island solely from the sky is not only foolhardy but also strange. I cannot imagine an island can be held for long if the occupier cannot dispatch a supporting fleet. The best example is England: unimaginable without a fleet. English troops have occupied the Isle of Crete for some time. As long as England considers the island's occupation important, the Germans will not easily conquer it with a wave of the hand. If they do succeed, it will have taken so many men to accomplish it that the losses would bring little joy. If the invasion of Crete miscarries, we will definitely have to abandon similar attacks, and we can finally silence the refrain, "Next, we are going to England."

Assume we also conquer Gibraltar, Malta, and Cyprus – what would we gain? England yet remains.

Three months from now, we begin the third year of war!

May 26, 1941

It is being reported with special joy the German battleship Bismarck has destroyed the largest English battle cruiser Hood (42,000 gross tons) near Iceland.

May 27, 1941

Today we learn English naval forces sank the Bismarck (35,000 tons). Bismarck was launched on Feb. 4, 1939, from the Blohm and Voss wharf in Hamburg and placed in service at the beginning of 1941. On its first trip, this warship, under the leadership of Fleet Admiral Lütjens, has been sunk.[24] Lütjens led the group of German battleships (Scharnhorst, Gneisenau) that operated for some time in the Atlantic and attacked convoys.

May 29, 1941

I was informed in a private letter a considerable number of newspapers will discontinue publication soon to slow down the already perceptible depletion of paper. First in line to disappear will be those papers the Party does not control. Anything not one hundred percent for National Socialism is finished. It would have been much better had they shown a strong character in 1933 and stopped publishing, rather than the cringing servility and toadyism they have gone through during this sad time. Everyone gets his due! And when the last drop has been emptied from the cup of sorrows, Germany will awaken. [. . .]

The next meat-rationing card will be good for a total of 1,600 grams from June 2 through June 29 – the amount of meat for one person for that four-week period. That means a reduction of 400 grams (100 grams weekly) compared to what we now get.

May 30, 1941

BACK FROM GERMANY

Copenhagen, May 29, 1941.

As reported from Oslo, the Norwegian Nationalsamling [National Unity Party] leader, Quisling, returned from a stint in Germany, accompanied by SS Standartenführer Lie and Staff Leader Laether of the Norwegian Hird [paramilitary group]. Quisling visited the volunteer Norwegian soldiers in their training camps in Germany, and received excellent impressions there. Quisling reported the Norwegians' military training and fighting spirit were excellent, and they would undoubtedly do honor to Norway's traditions. The Norwegians who came with the first transport to Germany are now together in one place and stay in private accommodations. They are inspired by their German hosts.

Source: "Aus Deutschland zurück," HF-Abend, May 29, 1941, p. 1.

The Norwegian officer Quisling, who swore to be true to his king, is nothing other than an entirely low-life traitor to his country.[25] For his own advantage and against the majority of his countrymen, Quisling placed himself under the command of Germany. This Quisling is the type of man we try to win over in all countries for our own purpose. As long as the German army protects these traitors from their own people, the wheels will keep turning for them. But these elected leaders are doomed when the day comes the German soldiers must return to their homeland. Then the firm of Quisling and Company will be quickly extinguished. As seen from this angle, current politics are myopic without equal.

May 31, 1941

To assess the availability of bicycles, the head of every household must fill out a form. And because of a noticeable shortage of beverages in many inns, only beer will be available on Sundays. Also, 0.2 liters of wine [6.5 oz.] costs 60 or 70 pfennigs despite the price commissioner.

A rumor is spreading that Germany wants to lease the Ukraine from Russia on a ninety-nine year lease and in return will support Russia's seizing possession of India. The Party has never been shy about enrapturing folks with plans for future conquests. It is certain troops are being massed in the East. What will occur there nobody can foretell. Everything is possible with the leaders of Germany and Russia because they want to hold onto, under all circumstances and at whatever cost, their precious feeding troughs. In the end they will use a piece of straw as a life preserver.

June 3, 1941

German propaganda has greeted the revolution in Iraq with unrestrained joy and celebrates the revolution's leader, Rashid Ali al-Gaylani, as a national hero.[26] National Socialist sympathies go less to the inhabitants of Iraq and much more to the abundance of oil. The press goes to great lengths to stir up the entire Arab world to rebel against England. [. . .] Even from this distance National Socialist leaders claim to know "Iraq is solidly behind Rashid Ali al-Gaylani." That is the essence of propaganda. They will write something about this every day, and in a short time the gullible folks will believe there is a distinct revolt against England throughout Arabia. The real matter is that Iraq is obliged to England for its independence because Mesopotamia was placed under British mandate after the First World War. Before 1914 this territory belonged to Turkey. Yet all methods of German-Italian intrigues are employed here to make many difficulties for the English. [. . .]

German troops have conquered Crete. That is a serious English defeat of which there can be no doubt. They must guard against this victory being expanded and England becoming viewed as beaten. Crete is not an English island but a Greek island. German air force superiority in this case determined the outcome of the attack. The distance for the English fighter planes (from Egypt) was too far. Germany slowly approaches the positions where England will be forced to exert its full strength. But it is vital to realize we distance ourselves ever farther from our own base. In North Africa it is evident we were not able to follow up on our initial success. The English continue to hold onto Tobruk in the Marmarica region and to stand fast at the Egyptian border.

June 4, 1941

The conquest of Crete was decidedly an expensive matter. The huge German commitment shows the operations in the Near East [Middle East] are not yet over. With all the military successes so far, it is not particularly significant our preparations went completely unhindered. But that page now has been turned. The enemy can look at the maps and undertake attacks on our reinforcements.

The armed forces in North Africa have difficult conditions. These troops are not able to take anything they need from the land, so everything must be brought to them. The damage to our ships (troop transports, munitions ships) is deeply felt because replacements must operate under the same unfavorable circumstances. The enemy can take good advantage of our lost material and the waste of time. Our plan appears to be to attack the English in Egypt and Asia Minor. Any surprise has been ruled out. Our first attacks (in Libya and Crete, and provoking unrest in Iraq) have made our strategic preparations evident. The English have enough time to take preventive military measures. If they are able to create reserve divisions, they can dispatch them to places not particularly advantageous for us, and that can have a bad outcome.

For fourteen days we have had 131 women and 175 children from Düsseldorf in Laubach. At first they were to be treated as evacuees. Then it was said they will recuperate here. Finding accommodations was not easy, in spite of NSV promising to pay 3.50 RM daily for a woman and 2 RM for a child. The propaganda was a little exaggerated, as always. The Düsseldorf women were told milk and honey flows here, and they would not have to work. The local people believed they were going to get additional help for agriculture. Both parties were deceived. Already there are loud complaints here and there. Even among the genuine Nazis. A leading Nazi woman, Anna Steller Jochem, said to another woman she felt deeply unlucky to have to quarter two women, but she cannot complain because many will then say, "That serves the Nazi wife right."

I must surely confirm Frau Jochem has this correct. Practical National Socialism has its dark side. Only with experience do they get smart. The Nazi wife is finally having her eyes opened wide. Not just here: in all of Germany.

June 10, 1941

Notifications about deaths in the mental care facility in Hadamar have recently increased. Supposedly incurable patients are being brought to this institution. And they are soon to begin building a crematorium.[27]

The local newspapers have reports, dated May 31, about Iraq:

FIERCE BATTLE FOR BAGHDAD

16 British tanks destroyed

Damascus, May 31.

The battle for Baghdad has further intensified. With the help of powerful motorized forces British troops were able to advance after fierce fighting to Kadhimain in the vicinity of Baghdad. The Iraqi troops continue to resist fiercely. They captured more than 400 prisoners in the course of battle and destroyed 16 armored vehicles.

The production of oil continues to be carried out without interruption and is completely in Iraqi hands. Also the oil pipeline to the English in Haifa is still closed. Palestine reported new acts of sabotage against British petroleum and munitions camps, causing visible fires. It has been made known from Amman there have been new arrests of Transjordanian officers who refused to fight with British troops against Iraqi troops. Transjordanians aligned with England continue to flee. Emir Abdullah is expected to arrive in Jerusalem.

> Source: "Erbitterter Kampf um Bagdad," HLZ, June 1–2, 1941, p. 3.

[. . .]

All reports of this sort are to be read with great care. A June 5 article in the *Hamburger Fremdenblatt* says England – for the time being – has suppressed the uprising in Iraq. "For the time being" is simply a little band-aid. Germany's joy over the national strike in Iraq was for nothing.

The English have pushed into Syria. With their flank no longer threatened from Iraq, it can be assumed they will quickly occupy Syria. With that, England's position in the Near East will improve considerably. The Suez Canal will no longer be threatened with attack from this side.

For some time rumors have been spread about how good our relationship is with Russia – and in particular how our troops were going to pass through Russia toward objectives in Iraq and India. The fact is, we have many troops in the East. And it goes without saying there are plans regarding such deployment. I think they are meant to pressure Russia, a kind of extortion. That would be Hitler's thanks to Russia for its foolish restraint in 1939. If Russia bows to the demands of Germany, it will prove Stalin and his comrades want merely to hold on to their own positions. Naturally, it is also possible we will invade Russia, using one of our well-known fabrications as justification. This will give the capitalists of all countries an incentive to flock to Hitler.

[. . .]

June 16, 1941

[. . .]

According to a Reuters news report from London, the Luftwaffe attacks on London during May resulted in 5,394 deaths, 5,181 wounded, and 75 missing. Of the latter, one assumes they are dead. Although the numbers are less than those of April, the overall count in May is nevertheless the second highest since November of last year.

> Source: "40 000 Tote in England," HLZ, June 14, 1941, p. 3.

A considerable number of civilians in Great Britain were killed by German air attacks last month. The dreadful evidence of gruesome modern warfare is registered in these 5,394 deaths. If Germany were to suffer a similar amount of victims by an air attack, a strong, loud howling would break out in the German press. It must not be forgotten Germany started all this with its bombing of Warsaw and Rotterdam, and no one had the slightest compassion for the defenseless civilians in those cities. On the contrary, the reports enthusiastically lauded the capability of our "glorious" Luftwaffe.

Retribution will come. I have never doubted that. But to the shame of my countrymen, it definitely must be said they are completely dazzled by the military successes, and they simply do not or will not believe that today or tomorrow the enemy will ultimately return our blows, turning our own method against us once he has a sufficient number of his own long-distance bombers.

Rumors keep buzzing about things to come. One is that Russia will assent to the Tripartite Pact; another says Stalin will visit Berlin. The tendency is to promote the belief Russia has things in common with Germany. By God and dictators, everything is possible. Russia's behavior since 1939 clearly shows an exchange of fire is not inevitable between Russia and Germany. It is quite possible the two dictators, to preserve both their thrones, will join forces against plutocratic Anglo-Saxon world domination.

If they did that, the entire world would be set aflame.

June 19, 1941

The news writer, Erich Glodschey, concludes his article, "The Atlantic Battle," with the following:

> The transport of war supplies across the ocean has caused a splintering of England's naval forces. It compels the enemy to use even its battleships as armed escorts to protect the transports. Because of that, the giant battleship "Malaya," heavily damaged by a German U-boat while in escort service, had to be brought to America for long months of repair. Our surface warships and submarines complement each other effectively in their employment.
>
> The navy on the whole provides a potent addition for Luftwaffe attacks in this commercial aspect of the war. [. . .] The English Isle may have accumulated a large stock of supplies, the English people may be able to put up with many deprivations, and they may still get some assistance from the outside, or expect to get some; nevertheless, England cannot turn back on the way to its final downfall.

Source: "Die Atlantik-Schlacht," *HLZ*, June 12, 1941, p. 2.

English merchant ships have already sustained enormous and decisive damage in this war. But as easy as Mister Article Writer makes England's "final downfall" out to be, it certainly is not so in reality. Instead of presenting wishful thinking as facts to his hopeful readers, the author should have described the development of England's merchant fleet production since the outbreak of war. [...]

The retired clergyman Goldmann is a good example of a special kind of contemporary: the fantasy-endowed barstool strategist.[28] He fills out any pause in military reporting with fantastic blabbering. We should go through Russia to India and from there to Africa, he says. In this way, the mother country England would be deprived of its colonial supplies and surrender in two months. This addle-minded blockhead has not mentioned even once that the conquest of England – if it is going to take place – might be attempted in a direct way. I would not be astonished if a prophet showed up tomorrow proclaiming that by July 1 the sun would shine only for National Socialists.

The Reich Transportation Minister [Dorpmüller] notes the increasing demand for the railways to transport war and living necessities, and he has requested the postponement of all conferences and congresses, whose members for the most part have to use the trains.[29] The railroad will be in such a lovely condition after the war's end; by then we will not even know what is most urgent to repair. Charming prospect.

Looking over the present situation, one can only be depressed by the thought that since 1933 the vast majority of intellectual leaders – with university professors in the forefront – shoved aside everything they had previously stood up for and taught, and devoted themselves entirely to the new political direction. Almost all of them relinquished their own wills and their own reasoning, and exalted in a servile and spineless way everything the Party prescribed for them. What can a simple man say of these scholars and scientists who no longer dare to give expression to their better judgment? What will the rest of the world think about German scholarship corroded by Nazi politics?

June 21, 1941

When Germany – with the support of Italy – undertook to create a New Order in Europe, the knowledgeable inhabitants of this continent knew from the beginning a coerced union could not have an eternal existence. We get but sporadic reports from the German-occupied lands, but such articles as the following make people realize the fight against this "New Order" is not over yet.

BURNING FORESTS

Copenhagen, June 9, 1941.

A number of reports give information about extensive forest fires in Norway. After already having incurred heavy damage during Pentecost by open fires that were carelessly handled, a fire broke out on Wednesday of this past week in a sawmill in Storelvdalen that was stirred up by heavy winds and spread to the nearby forest. In the course of only a few hours, approximately 2,000 hectares were ablaze. Fire fighters arrived by car, other vehicles, and special trains. At last count 1,500 people were busy fighting the flames.

HALF OF SEMENDRIA DESTROYED

2,500 Dead after the Explosion

Budapest, June 9, 1941.

The Budapest papers from Neusatz report an explosion Thursday in Semendria [Smederevo]. A former Serbian ammunition depot within the Semendria fortress blew up. Further details about the catastrophe have come in from Belgrade. The Serbian ammunition depot explosion destroyed almost half the city. The number of dead has increased to 2,500. Clearing of debris is in full course. The detonation force mostly destroyed the historical Roman fortress on the Danube, a Semendria landmark.

Source: "Halb Semendria zerstört," HLZ, June 10, 1941, p. 1.

It appears more freedom fighters exist in the occupied lands than did in Germany in 1933. How quickly so many Germans emerged then from the cocoon as quick-change artists: today liberal, tomorrow despotic. To possess principles was not a noteworthy attribute. And where was the pride of these newly enthroned gods when the mad rush for positions seized even the few Nazis who had some ideals? Where there were not enough posts to go around, they created a mass of auxiliary posts.

The German possesses a sick weakness – it could be called a craving for recognition. It is seen in his need to have a little more than the other. The army has taken this into account: private, private-first-class, lance-corporal, senior lance-corporal, etc. Just a simple soldier is hard to find. A little stripe, a little star, or a medal: everyone has one. Take a look at the civilians today! One hardly dares to appear in a simple citizen's suit of clothing. The Party members must (God be thanked) wear the Party badge. Others hang little decorations on themselves: medals, ribbons, union pins, or – at the least – an NSV badge.

When you begin a conversation with a stranger, your first glance is not anywhere in the face but at the heroic breast to ascertain what kind of spiritual offspring he is. A noteworthy age!

What will the United States do? A year ago, Dr. Joseph Goebbels wrote their help would not come in time. No one here can make a correct assessment about whether or not America will help, but I recall how Germans laughed in the same way about America in 1917. A year later America's participation was a significant contribution to victory for the other side. [. . .]

I have just heard Judge Schmitt (presently a war judge in the East) wrote home that it might be several weeks before he could write home again. He is enthused by something "big" soon to happen. When it does, we will talk about it.

Something is in the air.

June 22, 1941

Sunday. Early this morning German troops crossed the Russian border![30]

Again a nation has become the victim of its own non-aggression pact with Germany. The friendship between Germany and Russia, which was so loudly extolled before the astonished world, lies in pieces before us.

Without being able to ascertain what went on behind the scenes, we may never know which side exemplified the greatest hypocrisy, maliciousness, and baseness. In any case, the fact is we have attacked our "friend."

My wife and I have often said to acquaintances and friends Germany would be at war with Russia in a foreseeable time. No one believed us. Judge Boländer sought me out more than once to remind me everything was in good order with Russia, and we were receiving many supplies from them. Whatever reasons we give for our advance into Russia, the simple truth is we want their products. Raw materials are trump. "And if you are not willing, I will take it by force."[31] The worshiper of power has again conquered. The army seeks places to plunder, and the lords of industry want cheaper raw materials. However, every narrow-minded townsman will embrace whatever the official interpretation is of our actions.

I would love to ask this power-wielding horde how they would feel if another nation wanted to take over the coal-rich German Ruhr district because that nation, having no coal of its own, decided to claim ours. Their response would be some sort of dumb rhetoric that twisted reality. But the simple truth is, what Germany is doing today should not be done. This is not a solution to the people's problems. It is war without end. A real, actual world war!

Germany and Russia's friendship pact in 1939 surprised not only those who had some knowledge about the political fighting method of both sides. Very seldom has a diplomatic deed stirred up a greater sensation. No one quite knew what to make of it or how it would play out. In politics everything is possible, yes, but a little character and honesty must be there or people will lose all belief in treaties.

What did the two partners have up their sleeves in 1939? Germany needed to be sure Poland could not look to Russia for support, or Germany would have to toss its plans on the dump heap. The German dictator had far-reaching military designs, and he needed a quick victory against Poland to win the people's trust for them.

Russia gained almost all of the territory it lost in 1918 – and without firing a shot. It especially created for itself a strategic forward position.

At that point both partners supposedly were completely satisfied. Then various things occurred that showed the "friends" were not friends. Our push into the Balkans, attacking Yugoslavia, was vastly disturbing to the Russians and a direct challenge to them. The Slavic soul was offended. The Russians could not ignore Hitler's push for conquest, which was backed by Mussolini. Then came the conspicuous efforts to relocate into Germany those Germans who had settled in the nations bordering Russia (Latvia, Estonia, Lithuania, the Volga region, and Bessarabia). Why would not the friend leave a friend alone?

Today we have the explanation. It is called War.

June 23, 1941

The people's opinion! Such opinion does not come from within the individual. This is formed "from on high" and implanted in a person's brain. From now on I will record more of what is being said around here, so I can be in a position later to offer a picture of the German people's state of mind.

Fräulein Helga Elbe, 18 years old: "It is completely fine with me that we attacked Russia, otherwise they would have attacked us. Two years ago they took territory we had conquered."[32]

Court Judge Dr. Hornef is depressed about the war spreading.[33]

Court Bailiff [Ludwig] Brunner: "We will not have an easy task with Russia, and the war will no longer be ended this year." Brunner has become a skeptic.

Since Sunday, there has been no mail from the field posts. Paratrooper Bechtold, the misled youth, has written he now has an insight into why the adults tried to dissuade him from joining. I hope he will not have to see action again. Theory versus experience. If the youth are getting some experience, perhaps we will be able to speak with them again.

June 25, 1941

According to the wish of our dictator, the war on the second front, in the East, is now underway. War with all its terrible suffering spreads over more areas. The sufferers are not only the inhabitants of Russia; we too in Germany will come to feel the widening of the war. When will this insanity be brought to an end? When will the intoxication of victory turn into a terrible hangover?

Now is a unique chance for England and America to take the initiative, but not only with empty promises and insufficient measures. America will not be able to bring about a utopia here, but if it sincerely has the will to throw its entire might into the fray, America could tip the balance and bring back peace. At the height of their insane power, the German people cannot be brought to reason with words. Only a tremendous force and the commitment of all war material can bring the wild steer to its senses.

I would like to assume that at least some men in the world are energetically working to do for humanity what all the other statesmen – through unbelievable short-sightedness – neglected or failed to do.

Mankind, awake!

Concentrate all your might against the destroyers of peace!

Do not let any airplane or vehicle merely sit around. England and Russia must receive active help from all nations. Everyone must view the situation exactly as if he were being attacked. Is that really so difficult to grasp?

No deliberations, no resolutions, no rhetoric, no "neutrality." Advance against the enemy of mankind!

In the East, huge victories are imminent. So far Germany has found no one who can present an energetic resistance. How is it to be explained Germany could overcome all of Europe?

A very iniquitous Europe was sleeping, and Adolf Hitler punished it with his arsenal. In the first place, France: this country missed every chance for a real defense. It learned absolutely nothing from 1918. It did not monitor the sly preparations of its neighbor and took no military measures. Do not tell me "this is easier said than done." France should have adjusted its manufacturing output of bombers, artillery, tank units, and flak to keep up with a strong Germany. French Colonial Minister Mandel said he would "consider" training the colonial troops as pilots. "Consider." Incompetent imbecile. Does anyone believe Germany would merely "consider," if it had colonies? No, it would be done. And that is the great secret.

Everyone could see tanks had become Germany's chief weapon. And what did the rest of the governments do? They looked about sheepishly and hoped it would be somebody else gobbled up. Lacking a sense of solidarity is the second cardinal error. Except for Churchill, and perhaps also Eden, I know of no statesman who even approached realizing what we were about.[34] So the National Socialist press poured its entire scorn and anger on the head of Churchill.

Even today there are idiots in America who talk nonsense about some compromise with Germany under Adolf Hitler. They are the most atrocious dummies. As Churchill said, whoever feeds the crocodile will also be devoured.[35] If Hitler wins, there will be an enormous slave empire with the name "Europe."

The world was in a placid slumber when we created our mammoth war machine, which we did indeed begin in 1934. How well-behaved everybody acted: this one believed we would go only against Russia, while this other eagerly licked the soles of Adolf Hitler's boots, astounded by his "genius" and content with a promise of continued sunshine if he kept silent while watching his neighbors being slaughtered.

Most abhorrent was England, allowing itself to be stupefied under the leadership of a contemptible senile man, Chamberlain. This is the man who said in 1936 (or around then), "Peace at any price."[36] I will not reproach him for espousing peace, but he should have been a parson in a small village. As the foremost statesman of a world power, he had the damned duty and obligation to ensure any attack would be immediately countered.

June 28, 1941

A woman said: "On Sunday (when the war began against Russia) I had some hesitation, but today things appear favorable. Unlike the former war, we now have allies, and so far everything has worked out well. This war will end quickly when the Russians in the interior rebel."

Thus spoke the lady with the Prussian accent. Always the same song. We have had good luck, so we can covet more. Without much ado, war will cover the entire world – precisely because "so far everything has worked out well." Such is the German: not a single feeling for the fate of other people. The entire world can be demolished if only he – the magnificent German – can live on the debris.

Worthy contemporaries, how will it be if the page is turned and we stand against a singularly strong Russia, one that defends itself stubbornly? Then will I contemplate your stupid faces. Never in the entire history of mankind have a people been more deserving of punishment than the Germans – for boundless arrogance.

Helga Elbe said her brother wrote from Holland, and at the end of the letter, he declared, "On to Moscow!" Such is the haughty pride that goes before a fall.

Hungary declared war against Russia yesterday. It has finally come that major capitalists in every country, faithful to the call of their leader Hitler, seek to finish off the hated regime in Russia. The German friendships forged these past years with Spain, Italy, Hungary, Slovakia, Romania, and Vichy France were simply and solely nourished to create a confederacy against Russia. Dr. Joseph Goebbels immediately lets the cat out of the bag: "European Front against Moscow," "The Continent on a Crusade." These are the editorials in the newspapers, trying once again to frighten the enemy at the front.[37]

"Neutral" Sweden, I should also point out, has allowed the passage of German troops to go to the assistance of Finland [against Russia].[38]

Military officer [Lieutenant Wilhelm] Ott says, "Russia is finished soon. If we take Moscow, the war with Russia is over. Then we go to England."

Most Germans were surprised by our military operation against Russia. To account for all the movements and activity taking place in the East, the propaganda line had convinced folk that Russia was allowing us to cross its borders. Our soldiers were told in their daily briefings: "Everything is in great shape with Russia; German troops are already there. We will march through and attack India." The goal was to convince our soldiers, beginning to tire of war, that things yet to come would be an easy walk.

And before the initial successes could wear off and the people become concerned about the outcome, the propaganda revived their intoxication with victory. "Our armed forces are carrying out this fight with all the granite-hard determination and energy they displayed in every campaign in this war," declares Alfred Kästner in today's *Frankfurter General-Anzeiger*.[39]

"The successes are simply fabulous," says a woman from Düsseldorf.

Are the Russians aware of the boundless stupidity they committed in 1939? For the Russian dictator to seal a treaty of friendship with an enemy that had worked day and night to stir up his allies to fight Russia was a dreadful, a really monstrous, "achievement." For that, this nation is punished.

June 30, 1941

In Dr. Koch's anteroom, the upholsterer [Otto] Schneidt says, "The Russian armies will be captured in eight days."

An army radio report yesterday (Sunday) announced the initial successes against Russia in twelve special dispatches that sounded like the hawking at an annual county fair. Cities, villages, and fields are devastated, soldiers lose their lives, and hundreds of thousands become homeless, but no final words are said over the gravestone. Only fame and glory, and again fame![40] The manner and various ways in which the Army High Command copies the methods of its teacher, Goebbels, are too many to mention. It remained for the German army to make a variety show of war. Tasteless drumming. [. . .]

July 1, 1941

A good place to hear the daily news is a doctor's waiting room. Everyone in the room is pleased more conquests are occurring in Russia. The true soul of the people. With huge satisfaction they name the "taken" cities. I am certain hardly anyone troubles himself to locate these places on the map and get a real picture of the situation. The opinions about military matters are mostly primitive. What particularly infuriates me is the ruthless brutality of human beings. Hardly anyone thinks about the thousands of young men left on the battlefields so one victory after another can be celebrated. A mania for victory rules the nation. From their expectations they see the war coming to an end. But even if Russia were militarily defeated, it would be a long time before anyone could speak about the war coming to an end. Not to mention the technical impossibility of occupying all of Russia.

The decision shall be made in the West! England, with the USA's support, cannot and will not permit Adolf Hitler and his crowd to enslave Europe. [...]

Our terrible foreign policy has its tradition. Before 1914, Pan-Germanism, with its various people and associations (Heinrich Class, von Reventlow and company, and the Fatherland Party) brought the whole world's hatred upon us.[41] The bad experiences of the World War of 1914–18 temporarily silenced the leaders who were completely responsible for the length of that war. Then came the most shining period for the chauvinists and the politicians of force. The NSDAP, with plans that knew no boundaries, was the most marvelous breeding place for violent politicians and military officers. A collection of ruthless conquerors could spin their unrestrained propaganda. The final result was the inevitable war of 1939, a world conflagration without example in the history of mankind, born of National Socialist brains and protected through the elimination of free expression of opinion. No criticism, no doubts, no material objections. Everyone who dared express even the smallest thing against the Party line was a public enemy.

There must be a complete collapse of National Socialist institutions – and nothing less. No intermediate thing. No compromise must turn away the calamity. Let it be Either/Or. People who ignore their nation's Constitution, as did the Germans, have nowhere to go but completely down. People who relinquish their fundamental rights are a heap of shit: unprincipled scoundrels, cowardly rabble.

July 2, 1941

[...] The authorities have forbidden people to listen to foreign radio broadcasts and are imposing severe punishments. It is commonly known the military itself whistles at this ban. Is this to protect the German people's weak nerves, to keep them from losing their balance? Or is it conceivable foreign radio stations are not spreading lies?

A great and mature people, a worthy people, would not allow such prohibitions. If we were truthful with ourselves about our successes and our failures, outsiders could not dim our confidence. Because everything is presented to us as pretty pictures, it is understandable a seeker of truth would defy this ban.

[...]

July 5, 1941

Forester [Rudolf] Ritter of Giessen should have been arrested because he said the war would last another three years. Two years ago R. was *executed* because he said the war would last two years. The truth may not be said.

July 6, 1941

This is the fifteenth day of war with Russia. The propaganda is not demure at all. On the same newspaper page that mentions the Russians' determined resistance is an article about twenty thousand Russian refugees. The wish is father of the thought. I wonder if our vainglorious General Staff thought the engagement with Russia would be little more than a childish game. It is well known – and it cannot be kept secret – that the Russians are bringing stubborn resistance to bear in many places. Even those who do not know much about that country have to be aware of Russia's size. Russia can bring a continuous supply of reserves to the front. It is highly probable Russian troops in the Ural region and in Siberia were nowhere near the front lines during the beginning battles.

Germany has been spoiled by its conquests. It threw itself with all of its might into various countries and gained victory in a relatively short time. Holland and Belgium were beaten down in merely a few days. But it needs to be said these countries were not very adept and did not make a courageous defense. Only one exception can be noted: Greece. All these wars were ended by simple occupation of the country. In those regions of France not occupied by German troops, the occupation is carried out by French politicians who bow down to Hitler like so many lackeys. They are the gravediggers of Free France.[42]

But now Germany has come up against a country that gives the appearance it will offer a tenacious defense. Russia is the kind of country that will teach our rulers the meaning of limited possibilities. Just how do the Nazis imagine they will ever dominate the vast territory of this nation and its huge reserves of people? He who lays Russia in ruins today must reckon with its resurrection tomorrow. Of that there is no doubt. The masters may look over Russia as they will, but Russia will never irrevocably relinquish its possessions. Adolf Hitler has laid the cornerstone for war without end.

Beside these considerations is the memory of how we occupied the Ukraine in 1918, and half the peninsula of Crimea, and the Caucasus, and we still lost the war. It was likely because of such incursions that we lost. The general proverb in those days was, "We occupy ourselves to death."

We must keep in mind that Germany's main opponent, England (not my opponent), continues to arm itself and organize the opposition against us. The industries of Australia, America, and Canada support England, and this block of countries will one day – I assume in 1942 or 1943 – announce its presence. Then all those we lost on the battlefields of Russia will have been sacrificed for nothing at all – absolutely nothing.

Oh, Germany, what has become of you? Wake up![43]

July 7, 1941

Today my father would have celebrated his 80th birthday.[44] What would he have said, this friend of peace, to these awful slaughterers of mankind? How many times did he remind me of how I invariably predicted Germany would lose the war of 1914–18? Cautious and temperate people in Germany have the rank only of speakers in the wilderness. Those who scorn mankind, the reckless and merciless aggressors: they are the heroes of present-day Germany.

A turning point is still not in sight.

Fräulein Helga Elbe just told me she was in Traisa [near Darmstadt] to visit a relative in a field hospital. I asked her about the mood there. The patients and doctors in the hospital believe we will be finished with Russia this year and go after England next year! This sort of people never seems to get enough of war – which is almost incomprehensible but yet a fact. This is the psyche the rest of the world will never understand.

[...]

July 15, 1941

[...] When I saw the clique of ex-military men Hitler surrounded himself with, I could see what was to come. I knew everything they were doing served but one purpose: a coming war. The Hitler Youth, the League of German Girls, the SA stormtroopers, the SS, and the Motor Corps – these were the pre-schooling. Then came labor service and the military. Since

Hitler knew weapons alone would not be decisive, he focused on molding the people's spirit, breeding something singular in history: bravado, blind obedience, ruthlessness, and brutality. There was contempt for every noble human emotion; contemptible disregard for the thinking of others; destruction of religion and religious establishments.

And there was the extermination of the Jews because they were wiser than the German people.

[...]

July 24, 1941

The regional forester from Ruppertsburg, who presently is in Lorraine, says, "These people are not for Germany. Everyone in the region will have to be relocated."

Whoever on this planet is not for Germany will be removed. Well, this is still a humane concept. I have often had to hear that other people (Poles, for example) were simply to be exterminated. The real German is not sentimental, and when he takes on a task he is thorough.

Senior Magistrate Gross from Grünberg is very victory oriented; he has no other way of thinking. The Russians are not intelligent enough, he says, to counter our attacks. And he does not concern himself about peace. Wars must be! Period! It is to be expected such bureaucratic academicians would have minimal resistance to our regime. Their only concern is the horse they are riding must win. Their total attitude is directed toward that, and they entertain no possibility of things going wrong. I always attempt to interpose my opposite perceptions in these discussions of current events, but only occasionally do I get my colleagues to voice any doubts. Most people prefer not to occupy themselves with uncomfortable things. It is just too wonderful to remain and live in the glow of victory. The followers, who so spiritedly abandoned their own natures and decent attitudes in 1933 and wholeheartedly accepted Hitler's ideas and uncritically adopted "Heil Hitler," shall find it very embarrassing when the course of events takes another direction.

When I think back on these many doleful figures and place-seekers who altered their own views and became Hitler followers to obtain material things, I know that respectable people can feel only shame for such men: a totally sad chapter of self-serving rogues.

Leaders within the large industries and banks, the nobility, major farmers, teachers, public officials, all these noble characters who showed little understanding for [the laborers in] the social process before 1933, were suddenly converted and transformed and became spirited supporters of the National Socialist German *Workers'* Party (NSDAP). White-collar and blue-collar workers [*Stirn und Faust*] went arm-in-arm.[45] Meaningless phrases were thrashed around day and night until the laborers lost their backbone, forgot their political schooling, and gave up their independent work spirit. The conservatives and reactionaries had their greatest triumph when the common worker gave up and sank to the level of a slave. The A to Z of this "socialist" creation was to craftily draw the "Old Fighters" away from the capitalistic class. The Nazis offered unimagined possibilities, with Hitler impressing the upper classes with fairy tales about world domination: a vision to which the German has absolutely no resistance. So the largest military buildup of all times came about and, of course, the desired war.

The German people will someday sleep off this intoxication, but the hangover will not go away as easily. When the curtain finally opens and the theater is visible to the audience without impostors and stage directors, there will be a frightful awakening. Never in the history of a nation have the guilty ones been more evident than now.

It may be that one or the other bandit will have a higher degree of blame, but in general it is the entire bunch that is guilty. In my view the people of industry and the military officers will be at the head of the line. With few exceptions, they went through thick and thin with Hitler and gave him counsel.

July 25, 1941

The widow Frau Emmelius received news that her son August was killed. He is the first casualty from Laubach on the Eastern Front. Reports came today of other casualties: Philippi, Kammer, and von Eiff.[46]

What I hear is August Emmelius was no Nazi. Naturally the respectable always have to die. The "most valuable" elements of the populace – Haas, Naumann, Haack, and other Party members – are still among the living.

July 26, 1941

I cannot remember how peace once looked. National Socialists waste no time thinking about it. They see a Europe ruled by Germans.

Hitler's Europe: a police state.

And in every country rogues handle things for Hitler.

Hitler: tyranny in its greatest measure. [...]

July 27, 1941

Today the sixth week of the campaign against Russia begins. The army reports leave out many specifics. The operation's "scheduled" progress is hogwash. The knowledgeable person knows something is amiss. The reports rang out optimistically in the beginning for the people's benefit, but that approach is a dangerous game to play. We experienced the same thing once before, in the second half of 1918. The main liar then was Ludendorff.[47] But how did the German people penalize him? Most unfortunately this rascal was allowed to continue on about his business. The dimwitted Germans allow anything to happen. It leads one to despair. [...]

Do you have any idea, German people, why your sons had to be sacrificed throughout all of Europe, and in the regions of ice, and in the deserts of Africa?

You, people of Germany, gave yourselves up in 1933. That is the sin of which you are guilty. Indict yourself, Germany. Cry over your own stupidity, submissiveness, fear, and cowardice. In the future keep your hands off foreign possessions. Stay home and take care of yourselves honestly!

July 28, 1941

The mental hospitals have become murder centers. As I learned, a family brought their mentally deranged son back home from an institution. After some time, they received a letter from the sanatorium informing them their son had died and his cremated ashes were being sent to them! The office clerk had forgotten to strike this boy's name from the death list. From that oversight, the intended and premeditated murder came to light.

July 29, 1941

Wounded soldiers in the field hospital in Giessen are saying Russian prisoners of war are to be killed![48]

Barbarous gangsters!

Are the German people a people of culture? No! A cultured people must be able to think as individuals and behave properly, but our people have repeatedly allowed themselves to be controlled and guided by their "infallible" Führer without participating in the slightest degree in their own fate. "The Führer is always right; the Führer never errs." [...]

Hitler correctly assessed England in *Mein Kampf*, but he has never followed up on his written word. Hitler said we could have come to an understanding with England in the past and further wrote about the most disastrous self-deception that occurred around 1914 in underestimating England's place in the world. [...] "In the predictable future there can be only two allies for Germany in Europe: England and Italy." And in another place, he said, "When the German nation wants to end a state of affairs that threatens its extermination in Europe, it must not fall into the error of the pre-war period and make enemies of God and the world."[49]

Between these thoughts and his later actions is an irreconcilable chasm of contradiction. Today our enemies are England, Russia, and America. "My dearest, what more do you want?"[50]

Today is the thirty-eighth day of the Russian campaign. France surrendered on the thirty-seventh day. The battle in the East appears to be more difficult, with more casualties and less effectiveness than that in the West. Herr Hitler, have you deceived yourself about the Russians? Have you and your accomplices underestimated them? Did you really foresee and "calculate" this Russian resistance?[51] Is it still your opinion today that the war will be ended by 1941? And what do the granaries of the Ukraine look like?

You had it right when you told the German people one should not make an enemy of God and the world. Or did you, Adolf Hitler from Braunau, really think God would be only on the side of German tanks and fighter planes?

All guilt is avenged on earth![52] The horrific crimes the army has brought to bear, especially those of the SS Verfügungstruppe, will have to be accounted for.[53]

[...]

August 1, 1941

[...] Regional Farm Leader Metzger from the village of Röthges asserted to me yesterday things would soon happen in the West. We are in this hard arena with Russia, and this man already begins to think about further undertakings. The German people have an incurable craze to conquer. One day they will fall from the clouds of seventh heaven – and crash. [. . .]

[. . .]

August 4, 1941

An old farmer from Lardenbach: "When we take the Ukraine, then we will have grain. And the Russians still will have enough land."

This old rogue represents the typical Germanic concept of justice. It appears this guy has never heard the phrase, "Thou shalt not steal." It will be the main task after the war to restore the general public's spiritual condition based on decency and proper morality. It remains to be seen, though, if such can be done with the animalistic tendencies of our youth, who have become thoroughly depraved. I do not have much hope. Almost a hundred percent of today's crimes are ascribable to youth. On Thursday, there is a sentencing session for four juvenile defendants.

Last night two incendiary bombs were dropped on Laubach. One landed in Helle Square, and the other in a garden on Roten Berg Street.

August 6, 1941

Two English planes flew over Laubach last night. We could hear strong explosions from 1–2 a.m. Based on the direction of the anti-aircraft fire, the attack was in the Frankfurt area.

August 12, 1941

We learned from a young woman living in Frankfurt-Rodelhcim that part of Rodelheim was under heavy attack on August 6 and 7 and many homes were destroyed. It is said few were killed. Yet again reliable objective reports are not received. Most inhabitants of a city under attack do not want to hear about the damage; the head-in-the-sand policy prevails. Next month, if I receive a vacation, I will go to the areas hit by thcsc aircraft and learn, at least to some extent, what "minimal damage" means.

A certain type has only the appearance of being a German judge. The Federal Finance Court passed a judgment on July 23 that Jewish hospitals were not to be tax free. The chief finance president decided "populace" is to be understood as German [Aryan] populace. According to the judgment, it is not a matter of interpreting the law but merely a question of deciding the facts in accordance with the National Socialist world view.[54]

So no longer does the "independent" and "superior" German judge need to concern himself with justice. He need only consult the Nazi world view – which has absolutely nothing at all to do with "justice." In today's Nazi Germany, justice is composed purely and simply of Power and Despotism.

August 14, 1941

In Cafe Göbel a vacationer from Düsseldorf gave a loud and clear report of the war situation to the astonished customers there. He declared the war with Russia will end within three weeks. According to him, we will occupy Russian territory only up to Moscow, which then would be incorporated into a United States of Europe (under German leadership, naturally). Then we will go against England. Everything is already prepared.

Whether this warrior really believes everything he says is not for me to decide; yet it could be possible because a large number of the faithful are the same way. Just do not think; it could destroy illusions, and it is so-o-o lovely to conquer the whole world. The German Master Race! How such Germans consider mastering other countries is seen in an article in today's *Das Schwarze Korps* [*The Hour of Europe*]."[55]

August 15, 1941

The author [of yesterday's *Das Schwarze Korps* article] writes, among other things, "There are difficult ethnic questions to be resolved in the East, and they cannot be handled with sentimental or romantic notions. This must be pounded into the public's consciousness. The only thing that is going to work there is severity."[56]

Hard and brutal, ruthless and mean: such are the trump cards of National Socialism. Here is more from the article in *Das Schwarze Korps* (which is the SS official newspaper):

When Adolf Hitler on June 22, 1941, committed the German armed forces to the crucial battle, countless optimists both inside and outside the German borders believed the Red Army terror would be ended within a few days. They expected a Blitzkrieg that would end with a result even faster than the campaign in France. The Führer was far removed from such overly bold calculations. It was clear to him what kind of enemy we were facing in the East. Today, after seven weeks of bloody battles, almost a million Bolsheviks have been taken prisoner, several million are dead or wounded, thirteen thousand tanks and nine thousand airplanes have been destroyed, but the Monster of the East continues to defend itself in spite of its fatal injuries. Its material reserves have not been exhausted. It can still throw new divisions into the campaign, men driven on by fanatical commissars, nothing more than soulless wheels in the gigantic Bolshevik war machine.

So now in the middle of August, *Das Schwarze Korps* has come to realize many Russians will defend themselves. According to National Socialist thinking, that is a gross insult. The optimists (meaning the Nazis) truly thought the Russian people devoutly wished for nothing other than to be liberated from the Bolshevik yoke. This was assumed from the start, and even today after eight weeks, these swindlers try to deceive the German people with "the Führer was far removed from such overly bold calculations."

But Ladies and Gentlemen, not a single person was singing this tune at the start of this campaign – that there would be difficult battles ahead and the Germans would encounter such a strong defense. Today it is presented as the most understandable thing in the world and something the leaders and everyone else had expected. The opposite is true. The official Supreme Command reports handed out exorbitant exaggerations. [. . .]

Platoons of Italy's Blackshirt battalions went on the march on August 5 to take up positions at the Eastern Front. The Duce gave a speech and told them, "A great honor and high privilege awaits you. I am convinced you volunteers feel this in your hearts. It is an honor and privilege to participate in a real colossal battle."[57]

El Duce Mussolini, most glorious of all, prudently [to be on the safe side with Hitler] dispatched fools into this "real colossal battle" while he himself stays comfortably at home.

Another of those army reports: "On August 7, 1941, the Army Group von Bock victoriously ended the great Battle of Smolensk. With moderate losses of their own, the enemy's bloody losses are unusually high."[58] In previous wars it was the aggressor who always had the higher losses. It is exactly the reverse with the Nazi war. What I would like to know is who killed the people whose names are in the obituaries?

August 16, 1941

Otto Dirlam has fallen in battle. Only a few will cry for him in mourning. He was the typical SS man – an informer – and useful for nothing but denunciation. At one time he was employed briefly by the police, and then he returned into the arms of the SS black bandits. We are rid of this parasite.

Many people are surprised officers who served under the Kaiser could place themselves without any reservations at the Third Reich's disposal. It does not amaze me at all. Military officers were the Republic's greatest opponents, regarding it as a system unsuitable for leading their besotted war of revenge. They correctly saw in Hitler a man who perfectly and in every way took into account their wishes and pursuits: unprecedented career opportunities, as well as honors and positions in great measure. [...]

August 27, 1941

The army report of July 13 said German troops were massed before Kiev and in action at Leningrad.[59] The Russian forces were supposedly disintegrating then and their troops were demoralized; Kiev and Leningrad would soon be captured. It is obvious the optimistic reports were founded on considerable error. The Russians continue to stubbornly defend themselves. Apparently they still have the necessary reserves. It was utterly foolish to report on July 17 Russia was on its "last" reserves. The Russians can solve any manpower emergency by bringing millions of men into battle. So the real analysis needs to focus on material rather than people. If the Russian military command can supply its fighting troops with the war material, there will be no quick end to the engagements.

Russia's vastness should have given pause to the German army command. Russia can afford to give up territory to the enemy without becoming overly weakened. They withdraw the men fit for duty – along with all industry and manufacturing – and re-establish everything in the hinterland. China did the same. The Japanese still have not won the war after four years of taking over vast areas of China.

September 1941

I was on vacation September 1–13 and visited Mainz, Mannheim, Ludwigshafen, and Mühlacker. In Mannheim I wanted to find out about the extent of damage caused by air raids. The inner city showed very little damage. Some residents told me houses in the suburbs had been hit. Except for the Lanz Agricultural Equipment Company, factory buildings were not damaged. I feel certain air raids, to the extent they have occurred so far, will have no influence on the war's outcome. The people affected by air raid

alarms complain about their stay in air raid shelters – and without doubt
their nerves are affected – but this is of little significance. Air raids will not
end the war sooner by even half a day.

In the night of September 12–13 there was an air raid in Mainz. Pauline and
I were staying overnight [with her mother] at 2 Wallau Street on the second
floor. Shortly after 11 p.m., the siren on the tower of Christ Church sounded
and we could already hear airplanes. The hissing sound of a falling bomb was
discernible, and from the explosion I guessed it struck in the area of the
railroad station. We would soon know. At 5 a.m., after the all-clear sounded,
the doorbell rang. Pauline's sisters, Katie Ganglberger and Lina Fahrbach,
and Lina's husband, Heinrich, stood before us and told us what happened.
Katie was dressed only in nightgown and coat. The first bomb had fallen on
their apartment house at 13 Erthal Street just a minute after Lina and
Heinrich made it safely to the basement. Katie was on her way from the
second floor to the basement. The bomb's impact caught her by surprise and
she landed on beams and debris inside the inn on the first [ground] floor.

The house was completely destroyed down to the second floor and ten
people died. Except for Katie and two girls, all the others who lived in the
upper floors but stayed in their apartments, including a father, mother, son,
and daughter on the fourth floor, were killed. Katie was injured.

My in-laws were very concerned about their belongings and furniture on
the second floor. The things Katie had stored on the top floor were completely destroyed.[60]

Additional bombs landed at the corner of Bonifazius Street and Bahnhof
Square (in front of the Central Hotel), and on the second-class waiting room
in the railroad station. It is said the total number of dead is forty-seven.
Officially this was reported as follows: "There was some damage and small
losses among the civilians."[61]

October 2, 1941

Reinhard Heydrich, SS Senior Group Leader, will conduct the business in the
Reich Protectorates of Bohemia and Moravia for the duration of Reich Minister
Freiherr von Neurath's illness. The Führer's September 27 edict on this appoint-
ment has been published in the *Reichsgesetzblatt* [*Reich Law Gazette*].[62]

This signifies a change in how the Czech population will be treated. The SS
is now in power there. Poor "Protectorates."

[. . .]

October 10, 1941

A powerful German offensive is taking place along the entire Russian front.[63] If the German reports are correct, a Russian defeat is possible. On June 28, I wrote that the Russian nation would be punished for its terrible behavior during the past years. That has been completely fulfilled. For years, in speeches and publications, the Russians had stormed against the "aggressors" Hitler and Mussolini. They had correctly recognized the approaching danger of Germany's and Italy's reactivation of their armed forces. Suddenly in August 1939 the world's proletariats were given a drama never seen before, a sight for the gods: Stalin arm-in-arm with Hitler and Mussolini. A decent man could but turn away and retire to a remote island, mourning for everything that makes us human. Where were Truth and Honor?

There must be traitors in Russia at work in large numbers. The population of 200 million should have been able, twenty years after their revolution, to at least defend its own country with more success. It is most evident something is amiss with their navy, which should have attacked immediately at the beginning of the war.

Today in the early morning hours two governmentally protected robbers, the courthouse attendant Scherdt and the swimming teacher Scharf, appeared at the door of the Jewish families Strauss and Heynemann and on the basis of a secret order confiscated all their fruit preserves and linens.[64] Only the essential linens were left for the families.

When I criticize the Russian navy's inaction, I do not forget the inability of all our opponents. England especially is burdened with an incomprehensible laziness and paucity of ideas. If anything is to be done at all militarily against Germany, the time is right now when our armies are deep in Russia. Germany's and Italy's fronts are unbelievably extended. Any halfway educated soldier in former times would have seen this as an ideal situation to seek out and find the weak points. England has nearly all of Africa on its side but is unable to do anything with it. It has not shown any initiative with its colonial empire that might have commanded some respect from the Germans. It is a pathetic and shameful stain on their reputation if the so-called British "World Empire" can only defend itself rushing about hither and yon with foreign (American) help.

Without this foreign aid, England would be a shambles instead of a world power. Can anyone there imagine what National Socialism, with its productive capabilities, would have done with a colonial empire such as England's?

October 11, 1941

Yesterday the *Völkischer Beobachter* had the following headline: "Offensive in the East Decided."[65] It can be assumed "decided" does not mean "ended." "Decided" can be an undesirably long situation. It will depend on whether the Russian nation gives up as France did, or if intact forces still remain that will keep resisting.

In my opinion, support for Russia will not be lacking from outside (America and India, by way of England). This factor should not be underestimated. We will wait and see.

October 17, 1941

Karl Poth, a master watchmaker, became the victim of an air raid in Boulogne. I was talking to him one day before his induction into the military; it was hard on him to leave. Poth was a decent man. Others, who are not worth keeping, are still with us.

The Führer has ordered the retention of the sharp-s (ß) in our alphabet to designate a double-s (ss), except when it is capitalized, in which case the regular-s will be used (SS). His decision, according to a Ministry of the Interior circular dated September 10, applies to anything published. It is really grand, and certainly unique, that during battles in the East the Führer still can attend to the sharp-s.

October 19, 1941

The fanfares are blaring out a different tune about the decisive offensive in the East. Once again they have to rectify the overflow from their mouths. When the propagandists shouted, "The campaign is decided," it was quite natural for the gullible to think it meant the end of the war. It is time to calm down what they stirred up.

The highest source now confirms what I wrote on October 11. It is Herr Goebbels's turn to speak:

THE EASTERN CAMPAIGN IS DECIDED
BUT NOT YET ENDED

Dr. Goebbels speaks to the Berlin SA leadership

Berlin, October 15, 1941.

Reich Minister Dr. Goebbels explained to a roll-call of the Berlin SA leadership that never before in our history has the nation found itself in such a favorable position. On our side stand all the factors that guarantee victory: ingenious leadership, the best armed forces, powerful weaponry potential; no more problems with food supplies in the Reich; also an unassailable economy. The enemy has undertaken in his confusion a hopeless attack against the German soul, against which the national leadership has shielded its people. The war against the Soviet Union is indeed decided, but it is not yet ended. Any dangerous threat from the East is finally struck down thanks to the Führer's commanding artistry, our brave soldiers, and the unshakeable homeland.

Source: "Ostfeldzug entschieden, aber noch nicht beendet," *VB-Süd*,
October 16, 1941, p. 2.

Herr Juggler Dr. Goebbels, as long as fighting is going on, the war is not yet decided.

October 20, 1941

Count von Galen, Bishop of Münster, turned to his diocese on July 13, 1941, and spoke of afflictions. He described how monks and nuns were being driven from their establishments and made homeless.[66]

And that was done in this moment when everybody trembles and shakes from night attacks that could kill us all or make every one of us a homeless refugee. They are chasing countless innocent and even highly regarded men and women from their humble dwellings and making national comrades, our fellow citizens, into homeless refugees . . .

Repeatedly and even very recently we have seen the Gestapo arrest highly ranked and innocent people without a court judgment or a defense, to deprive them of their freedom and place them in prison . . .

Every German citizen is completely defenseless and helpless against the Gestapo's physical power. Many German citizens have suffered this during the course of the past years – like our beloved religious instructor Friedrichs who is being kept prisoner without process and without sentencing . . .

My dear Christians, the imprisonment of many blameless people without the possibility of defense and without any indictment, the emptying of the abbeys, and the eviction of innocent people of the cloth, our brothers and sisters, compel me to remind you today of the old truth: Justice is a fundamental right. Justice is the basic foundation of our state. The right to life, the inviolability of freedom is an essential part of the moral order within society. Maybe the state has a right to limit these rights of its citizens in punishment but only when faced with unlawfulness. And guilt must be proven by means of a non-partisan process of law. The state that surpasses these God-given limits and tolerates the punishment of innocent people undermines its own authority and the respect in the mind of the citizens ...

Due to Gestapo orders and edicts this process is excluded. Since we therefore do not know any way we can counter in a non-partisan way Gestapo measures, their infringement on freedom, their methods of imprisonment, their placing of German citizens into concentration camps creates a great feeling of helplessness, even cowardly fear, in the far reaches of the German people, and has greatly damaged national unity ...

We demand justice. If this call remains unheard and the reign of justice is not reinstated, the German people and the German nation will perish in spite of the great victories, in spite of the bravery of our soldiers; it will perish because of internal rot and decay.

Thus spoke a noble, heroic man, this Bishop Count von Galen in Münster. He is considered a shining star in Germany's deepest darkness and will be an example for coming generations.[67]

The German people must sink even lower. They have to be brought to the point of despair, and then perhaps they will turn against their tormentors. Perhaps!

October 23, 1941

Das Schwarze Korps newspaper today is upset that a Swedish professor, Herbert Tingsten, has given a lecture about the race problem, and during the lecture he said the difference between a Swede and a Bantu Negro consisted only in the skin color; with education there was nothing to hinder a nigger-baby from being made into a completely acceptable Swede.[68]

The Swedish professor – with whom I completely agree, by the way – has grabbed hold of a Nazi wasp nest, and the answer of Das Schwarze Korps is clear and unmistakable. The editor writes, "If today anyone goes up against the race theory we cannot but consider this as a political aggression against National Socialism. Whoever thunders against the race theory uses a roundabout method, a sleight of hand, in the struggle against the New Germany and the reorganization and cleansing of the European continent. Through our own rebirth, through our policies, and through our war of extermination against Judaism, Bolshevism, and plutocracy, we have become the carriers of the battle of Nordic self-determination against every organized form of subhumanity. In this regard, Herr Tingsten has come up against us."

The editor has forgotten to mention the Nazis also are conducting a war of extermination against the Christian religions, in particular against the Catholic Church.[69]

The Nazis are completely incapable of realizing every race can be changed to an equal family of nations by emancipation – as this has come about in North America in relation to the Negro race. If certain Germans consider other races as creatures without value, then this has its source only in a sick arrogance. If these men were to be honest, they would have to pronounce a final abandonment of German colonial politics; with these Nordic theories you just cannot colonize. But the German is incapable of that.

October 26, 1941

In Nantes and Bordeaux in France, two German officers were shot by unknown culprits. Fifty citizens in each of these towns were apprehended and executed in retribution. To let people who are completely innocent suffer for the deed of another is reminiscent of the horrific deeds of wild beasts in times long gone. It remained to General von Stülpnagel to revive one of the most gruesome deeds. The world will rightfully be outraged over so much inhumanity, and it will ignite a hatred that can never be extinguished.[70]

It would do Germans good to remember our pathetic hypocrisy in producing our own martyrs [when France occupied us on occasion]. People like Schill, Palm, Andreas Hofer, and Schlageter. All were rightly condemned for breaking the law, and they were lawfully judged. But they were turned into national heroes in order to breed even more hatred against the French.[71]

The Germans conquered France and have occupied a large part of it for over a year. So it is understandable crimes against the occupation forces are committed here and there. Whoever makes their own criminals into heroes may not, under any condition, be as intolerant as we are being in France. What would the National Socialists say if their opponent exacted a similar revenge?

How long will this reign of terror continue?

October 28, 1941

A soldier on leave here said he personally witnessed a terrible atrocity in the occupied part of Poland. He watched as naked Jewish men and women were placed in front of a long deep ditch and, upon the order of the SS, were shot by Ukrainians in the back of their heads, and they fell into the ditch. Then the ditch was filled in as screams kept coming from it!![72]

These inhuman atrocities are so terrible that even the Ukrainians who were used for the manual labor suffered nervous breakdowns. All soldiers who had knowledge of these bestial actions of those Nazi subhuman beings were of the same opinion that the German people should already be trembling in their shoes because of the coming retribution.

There is no punishment that would be hard enough to be applied to these Nazi beasts. Of course, in the case of retribution the innocent will have to suffer along with them. Ninety-nine percent of the German people, directly or indirectly, carry the guilt for the present situation. Therefore we can only say this: Those who travel together, hang together.

[. . .]

November 1, 1941

Lieutenant Colonel [Werner] Mölders, a pilot frequently named in the army reports, is supposed to have been withdrawn from action with his whole squadron. The reasons are secret and given under a seal of silence. Mölders's sister was supposedly a member of a Catholic order in Münster, Westphalia, and the SS forced her to leave her cloister. It is said her brother spoke to the Führer and demanded retribution for this injustice. Since nothing happened, Mölders returned his medals and said he could no longer fly because of his emotional state.

It is hard to check the accuracy of this report. However, non-commissioned officer Gaub, a member of Mölders's squadron at the time, is presently here on leave. Gaub said the airplanes needed to be overhauled but something else was probably the matter.[73]

November 2, 1941

All Souls' Day: to commemorate those who have died. This is an annual excursion, especially in Catholic areas, where people go to the flower-bedecked graves of their relatives and remember them. Not all graves are being visited; many are far from home in foreign soil. Young people full of hope had to give their lives before they could fulfill the purpose of their existence. Why is death so prominent? Why is the young woman robbed of her husband? Why do parents lose their only son, and children their fathers? Why? Whose fault is it?

Almost all of humanity carries the blame. The bad and the evil prevail over the good. Hate is triumphant. Plundering is celebrated. Destruction is enthusiastically and proudly proclaimed to the astonished world. Revenge rages. Terror rules. Human lives are extinguished as if they were nothing but animals pre-ordained by God for destruction. Nationalism and militarism are the sources of this mind-set that stands in the way of mankind's peaceful progression! It begins with tin soldiers – and mass graves are the closing act.

[. . .]

November 7, 1941

There are special employment conditions for Jews, announces the executor of the Four Year Plan [Hermann Göring] on October 3, 1941.[74] Jews placed in work are to be considered in a special category. The order states the conditions:

Jews are outsiders and cannot become members of German workers' associations.
Jewish workers have no right to paid sick leave.
Jews will receive no subsidies for dependents.
Jews will receive no monetary assistance for births, marriage, or death.
Jews will not have special allowances (bonuses, maternity benefits, anniversaries, etc.).
Jews must take the employment the labor office gives them.
Jewish laborers may be used only in groups and are to be separated from other employees. Jews may not be employed as apprentices.

Why so many words? Just say, "Jews are not people but slaves." This would not be nice but truthful. From this official order breathes the spirit and essence of National Socialism. The Jews who emigrated from Germany should thank God. The treatment of Jews who remained is cruel, relentless, and inhuman. Their fate is pitiful.

November 8, 1941

I wanted to send an eight-pound parcel of apples by express at the railroad station but was told the shipment needed the approval of the local Farm Leader [Franz Gäbisch]. The Thousand Year Third Reich does not make life easy. I had to go and obtain his permission. Thankfully Genesis has already taken place. It would have been quite portentous had Eve been required to seek out the Farm Leader.

November 11, 1941

[. . .] Young people are enticed by all conceivable means into paramilitary education. It is not difficult to make them excited about military things. To them it is more like play. By providing the ambitious youngsters with permits for radio licenses, and certificates for horse-back riding and news gathering, the armed forces affect a moral educational foundation for the entry of these children into military service. Then it becomes grimly serious. And the parents have to write of the "inconceivable news" in the obituary.

Have parents told their children anything before they entered those special training groups? They were proud their children were learning about broadcasting, flying, or riding, but at the drama's end, they are shattered by the loss on the battlefield. Very few parents are logical in how they think and act about this.

November 12, 1941

[. . .] On November 9 Adolf Hitler talked in the Löwenbräu beer hall in Munich about "the decisive battle of our century."[75] He widely denigrated our opponents' leaders in his talk, saying this about Churchill: "This insane drunkard, who has now led England for years, considered my offer of peace as a new sign of my weakness."

I do not think Bismarck ever said anything like this about an opposing statesman.

During Hitler's speech nothing was said about our losses. Last month I counted 281 obituaries in the *Hamburger Fremdenblatt*. Suppose there are currently 250 newspapers in Germany, each publishing an average of five obituaries per day. By that alone we would count about 30,000 killed every month. But there actually are more because not every soldier gets an obituary.

I have the feeling many German soldiers will die this winter in Russia. In no way is Russia beaten! The German High Command should have refrained from bragging.

[...]

November 16, 1941

The United States' law of neutrality has been replaced with a law allowing the arming of merchant ships.[76] This puts the US practically in the middle of the war. England's situation has been essentially improved. Previously England had to transport its own materials, protected by a large number of warships. Now the Americans bring them the war material and food, freeing up many English ships for other tasks.

The situation in the Far East must also clear up soon. According to Japanese politicians, Japan feels encircled by China, Dutch East Indies, England, and America. If Japan wants to change its position, it has to attack. Since Japan has sent troops to Indo-China, I assume the attacks will be against Siam [Thailand], Burma, and the Malacca Peninsula. A Japanese attack against Siberia would bring big advantages to Germany. It would tie down large Russian army forces on their eastern border. But Japan has always preferred Japanese interests exclusively, and it will be guided by the principle of what is the greatest advantage for them.

It will be welcomed if England and America are finally forced to abandon their delaying tactics and put their rusting arsenal and forces into use and strengthen any weak points. Then world war really comes into play.

The development in 1942. The end in 1943.

November 20, 1941

Each year when winter has arrived and people again are bound to their homes, the National Socialist press under Joseph Goebbels begins its racist campaign against the Jews. "The Jewish enemy has to be eradicated."

Would the Nazis then be quiet? They are giving the people a scapegoat so that the originators of all the atrocities, the men of the NSDAP, will not be called to account. A great number of mentally inert German people succumb to this cunning deception. [...]

December 1, 1941

German troops have pulled out of Rostov-on-Don.[77] Battles are ongoing in Africa. For the first time the Army High Command had to headline unfavorable news. It has taken a long time to find out the army cannot handle every assignment.

It is impossible to constantly maintain the initiative from Norway's North Cape down to Africa. The weak links now become apparent. And the decision to continually attack in the area of Moscow this time of year is unwise. The army should have taken up good positions early on and lowered the hostilities. What more should have to be conquered? Now every retreat, wherever it happens to be, means a big loss of prestige, gives the enemy new hope, and increases the prospect of a longer war. Any gain in time is to the enemy's advantage. This was so in 1914–18 and is also the case today. Once again the people in their blindness do not want to admit it.

Punishment for the German people's arrogance, coupled with Adolf Hitler's excesses, will not be lacking.

December 2, 1941

The Army's retreat in southern Ukraine continues. It is remarkable Dr. Goebbels provides no bombastic explanations about the war material the German army had to leave behind. Is it not true a person becomes very discreet when his own head is on the block?

There is no denying our army has failed at the moment; and this because it has not had one minute's rest since June 22, 1941. A retreat this time of year is very dangerous. The rearguard will not be able to dig gun-emplacement trenches, which they need for defense. It takes good positions to hold off an enemy pushing from behind. If the Russians have well-armed troops for a successful pursuit, the entire front's dissolution is entirely possible. Someday November 1941 will be considered in German history the black month of this war. It was August 1918 in the last war.

The rather strange mishaps in the Luftwaffe might be an indication of approaching disaster – or is it coincidence that within the course of a few days high-ranking officers have met with bad accidents? Lieutenant General Udet, General of the Aviators Wilberg, Colonel Mölders, and Lieutenant

Colonel Kürbs were killed in three air accidents! We may have to find the solution to this mystery after the war.[78]

I simply cannot imagine that not a single officer in the entire Army clearly grasps our situation. If the officers are not all bewitched, the day has to come when the Nazi Party will be stopped. Defeat then would be inevitable, of course, but that would be deliverance for millions of people from the most terrible tyranny ever in the history of mankind.

Hopefully it is superfluous to say no one who helped this devilish Nazi system may play a role in Germany's future. We cannot repeat 1918 and give another chance to those who led the German people into so much trouble. They cannot cloak their wolf's nature with sheepskin and pretend they were but harmless helpers – as little by little they take over the next government. Unremitting hardness must prevail: whoever went along with the Nazis has to disappear without pity. The time of Friedrich Ebert with its terrible weaknesses has to be an admonishment for the times to come.[79]

The German people must acknowledge there is no superior race.

Hate between races has to be suppressed with the most stringent means.

Whoever by word or writing wants to pit the German people against other races should be punished by death!

If the German people respect other people, they will certainly be respected too.

The German people have to learn they can never change their position by power politics.

We can solve the problems of humanity only with decent attitudes, respect for the rights of others, and acknowledgment of justice.

December 6, 1941

The army still fights for Hitler's tyranny and the Nazi pigsty! When will enlightenment come?

Reich Protector [Reinhard Heydrich] complains Czech officials in the Protectorate of Bohemia and Moravia too often refer to themselves as Czechs in their correspondence. "This designation is not in accord with the German legislature's pronounced wishes and is also politically undesirable," he states.

So, what actually is will not be allowed to appear as such. The "Protector" protects the Czechs by teaching them they are not Czechs. With such antics, the Nazis make policy.

A poverty of intellect without example.

December 7, 1941

We often hear the opinion, especially from soldiers, "we have to win the war; otherwise we will be in a lot of trouble." This, too, is a Nazi trick. Even during the decline they play around with dumb people's minds. First they turn the entire world against us, and then they say to the miserable people, "You have to fight or you are lost." [. . .]

December 8, 1941

While diplomatic talks were being held between the Ambassador of Japan in Washington and the American Secretary of State, the Japanese air force attacked American stations in the Pacific. A good student of Germany, Japan shows its mean and dishonest character to the world. Finally, finally, we have clear fronts. It will soon be raining declarations of war.

Will the isolationists in the USA now open their eyes? What a delusion these cowardly people were under. How can you stand on the sidelines claiming neutrality during this gigantic fight for human dignity and freedom – when in actuality that places you on the side of the terrorist nations? Now Germany, Japan, and Italy will no longer be able to escape their well-earned fate.

The hard judgment of history will be pronounced.

Ninety-nine percent guilty in Germany!

December 9, 1941

A lady from Düsseldorf, quartered in Laubach with the Frey family, expressed her feelings about the war the Japanese have instigated in the Far East: "Is it not wonderful, this new war?"

There are many examples of this brutal Aryan to be found in warmongering Germany. They believe the war in the Pacific will take a load off Germany. During World War I it was similar. Then too they shouted jubilantly to the world, "We are still taking declarations of war here." We will have to feel much stronger effects of the war in our country before all Germans have had enough of it.

December 10, 1941

It is delightful to see how Nazi Party members gain new courage from Japan's early successes. Dr. Goebbels, most of all, celebrates Japanese victories with great fanfare. What does Germany gain if Japan attacks Hawaii, the Philippines, and the Malacca Peninsula? There is no reason for the Nazis to dance with glee. It would be a different matter if the Japanese had raised their sword against Russia in Siberia; then you could talk about Germany's burden being lightened in the East. Japan has yet to do us this favor. [...]

When this tyranny by Nazi big shots has broken down, and I am asked which Nazi requirement gave me the biggest headache, I will say without hesitation it was the greeting, "Heil Hitler." This criminal of all criminals forces even those people he has suppressed to worship him daily in greeting. Something like this has never happened in world history. This is unique.

December 12, 1941

Hitler and Mussolini have declared war on the USA! With my attitude it is not necessary to add a commentary to this. Whom God wants to destroy, he strikes with blindness.

Any objective or normal person, even one favorable toward Germany, would have to conclude these declarations will prolong the war. In fact the war can end only in the total defeat of the Axis members (Germany, Italy, and Japan). However, if anyone supposes the majority of the German public agrees with me on this, he is in for a disappointment.

It is a hard punishment to have been born in Germany. These people have become completely insane over the early Japanese successes, which have wreaked havoc among them. Their minds must indeed be lost, or it would not be possible for so many of our "national comrades" to declare with absolute conviction Germany's victory will now come much quicker! I am really shaken by this kind of idiocy and could cry aloud at such nonsense. Yet it was our opponents who created the basis for this mental attitude of so many Germans. Their principal military leaders show immense incompetence. It was plain stupidity to offer up battleships as a gift to Japanese bombers. The American fleet should never have been allowed to hang around some island in order to be massacred. If the Hawaiian Islands cannot be defended with long-distance artillery, heavy bombers, and numerous fighter planes, it would be better to leave the islands to the opponent. The same is true for the English fleet at Singapore, where the English let Japanese bombers destroy their largest battleships, Prince of Wales and Repulse. Where were the carriers to protect these battleships; and where were the fighter planes from Malacca? A sad chapter for the English "Empire"!

I do not want merely to criticize without also adding what I would do as commander of the English and American forces. Everyone usually waits until things are over and then says, "I would have done it this way." But before the main battles begin I want to say how I would do it.

America, England, China, and Russia have tremendous strategic opportunities if they attack in the right places. Attack, gentlemen! Attack the weak spots of the Germans, Italians, and the Japanese. The latter have already spent much of their strength, which was a crucial mistake. So cut these Japs into pieces. [. . .]

I would lead a general attack against Norway and Finland to maintain connection with Russia. Canadian and American troops would reinforce Russian troops in Murmansk and Archangel – and together roll up the entire front. And arm the Norwegians. Attack Sweden for its swinish behavior throughout the world. These Swedish curs are supplying Germany with iron ore!

Hopefully, hopefully, there is at least one man in America with halfway reasonable ideas. Please, God, help us a little and give the American officers the necessary guts and common sense. Go after these enemies of humanity: Germany, Italy, and Japan!

December 13, 1941

A mental disorder besets the "higher" circles. Former Laubach Chief Judge Zimmermann's widow thinks it is laughable for anyone to believe the war will take longer because Germany declared war on America. "We will win even sooner," said this lady with the greatest conviction. One is disarmed by such logic.

A rare visit: the wife of our chief judge came to my office because of some matters with her taxes. The following dialogue ensued:

I said: "Well, Frau Schmitt, I was right the war with Russia would become quite irksome."

Frau Schmitt: "That is not so."

I replied: "Our front in the East is wavering; it was a big mistake to go so deeply into Russia before the beginning of winter."

Frau Schmitt: "The Eastern Front is holding steady; we will advance in the spring." She added she had received a letter from an acquaintance stationed near Tikhvin on the Russian front. This soldier wrote the enemy forces were comprised mainly of children and graybeards, and the Germans were ten times better prepared for the coming winter than the Russians!

My response was that this soldier would not be writing to her any more from Tikhvin. (The Russians reconquered Tikhvin.) And to myself I thought: If our soldiers truly believe the untruthful, arrogant, and simplistic reports that retreats are merely a change in position in order to better crush the Russians, my heart goes out to them.

I could see in this woman's face my remarks were uncomfortable for her. These people have become so bound to National Socialism, which has promised much to them, even the smallest defeat is wished away.

The army report does not announce anything about retreats on the Eastern Front. Do these men believe in miracles? The exhausted army can no longer show resistance of any consequence. The troops need a long rest. There probably are no reserves left after these terrible battles before Moscow. The moment is here when each mistake they made earlier comes to fruition.

My dear generals, why did you not warn Corporal – and Supreme Commander of the Armed Forces – Adolf Hitler before he unleashed his megalomaniacal notion of conquering the world? Could it possibly be one or the other of you deliberately kept quiet? Who knows the souls of these "aristocratic" National Socialist army leaders?

Take care in whom you trust.

Now the German troops in Africa, Italy, Yugoslavia, Greece, France, Belgium, Poland, Denmark, and Norway must see how their comrades return from Russia infested with lice, full of bitterness, apathetic, heads bowed, forced to abandon their positions, able to rest only when the enemy permits it. Units are split up and out of touch with each other. "Is this division at a stopping point? Where will the enemy attack again? Is our rearguard still intact?" Those are the questions.

The army is approaching difficult days, and the German people know nothing about it. Christmas 1941 will not be merry.

December 14, 1941

It is Sunday. Just a while ago a bunch of young people passed the house, bellowing out this song:

"We will march further on, even if everything falls into pieces.
Today Germany belongs to us; tomorrow the whole world."

These conceited, empty-headed kids cannot help it if they were misused by insane egotists. The main guilt lies with the Party and the Reich leaders. The first thing to be done after this war is to teach the educators some humanity; only then can the uncivilized young people be helped. A different Germany has to arise, a moral Germany, a Germany that can be called a land of culture in which artists and scientists can freely create and work. Today I can only say the great men of our past lived in vain. Raw power replaces art and science. Germany can and will become healthy when we can rightly say about our leaders in every field: "These are noble men; see that you follow their example."

Until then much blood will flow. I am not completely convinced that from the bloodbath a German will arise who disenfranchises his Teutonic nature and the examples of heroic myths. The germs of this sickness are so deep it will take many years to form a new human type – of which other countries will say: "The German is a decent person."

December 15, 1941

It is reported that in some areas Jews are being transported somewhere. They are permitted to take a little money and about 60 pounds in baggage.[80] The Nazis are proud of their animal protection laws. But the suffering they cause the Jews proves they treat Jews worse than animals. This cruel, despicable, and sadistic treatment against the Jews that has lasted now several years – with its final goal of extermination – is the biggest stain on the honor of Germany. They will never be able to erase these crimes.[81]

The Local Group Leaders have been granted tremendous power. Clerk Becker is supposed to be promoted to senior clerk, but it cannot take place without the Nazi Party's recommendation. Local Group Leader Pott had to attest to Becker's character, especially about his political convictions and his attitude toward the Church. Because the Party does not want officials who have connections to the Church, Pott told Becker that in his recommendation he characterized him as a person who did not attend church!

But when English bombers strike a church, Goebbels cries with crocodile tears. Hypocrite!

Of course such matters are never discussed in public. The Nazis attack the Church in an insidious and cunning way. Despite that, a large number of Protestant pastors have conscripted themselves with all their hearts to this Party that is so much an enemy of Christianity. They are the same type of pastor who in the previous war belonged to the warmongering Fatherland

Party and went from one house to another to collect signatures in its favor. Pastor [Theodor] Nebel in Laubach is an example.

If these Protestant ministers had only been concerned to take care of their parishioners and to really represent Christian teachings, the defection from the Church would not have occurred in such great measure. The education of ministers leaves extremely much to be desired. None should be ordained who is not completely convinced of the teachings of Christendom. Those seeking just to earn a livelihood should be disqualified.

December 16, 1941

ON THE EASTERN FRONT

Berlin, December 14.

[...] The Russian winter's onset has made it almost impossible for quite some time to launch extensive offensive operations in the East. The employment of German army units is characterized therefore in the past week by numerous local engagements along the lengthy Eastern Front. Every day the enemy tries again and again to push up against the German lines at many points or to break through, using the cover of fog, the advantage of night, and all their weaponry. However, our soldiers bloodily beat back the Bolsheviks' reinforced attacks using at times tanks, heavy artillery, and airplanes. By the way, for now and for yet awhile it will not be the possession of this or that piece of land that is crucial, but only the fact that the enemy, as weather conditions and the terrain permit, is under the gun and suffers heavy losses of men, weapons, and equipment. The important thing is not obtaining or maintaining any particular place or point, but the occupation of wide positions favorable for tactical reasons or for the quartering of troops. [...]

Source: "An der Ostfront," *Frankfurter Zeitung*, December 16, 1941, p. 2.

The above "clarification" of today's meaningless army report is peculiar. Suddenly the Russian winter plays a role. The Russian army, supposedly destroyed – or so it had been in word and writing – does not worry about winter or the German army's urgent need to rest. "The important thing is not obtaining or maintaining any particular place or point, but the occupation of wide positions favorable for tactical reasons or for the quartering of troops." The writer of these commentaries has an immature mind. When he is looking for a favorable position for defense it will always be near a village or city, whichever fits his narrative – but these same places become unimportant when they no longer suit him. He reads it any way he likes.[82] I can personally attest that the failed offensive at Moscow parallels the lost Battle of the Marne, and that is the unvarnished truth.[83] However, this truth is a severe blow for the Germans because the Army High Command reports thoroughly convinced them there could be no doubt about final victory. For the great majority of the German people, *belief in victory* is and has been enormous. That has been the bulwark of National Socialism.

December 18, 1941

The Nazis are enraptured by the Japanese victories, which serve as a replacement for their own missing successes. How myopic. The Japanese do not lift a finger in favor of Germany; otherwise they would be attacking Russians in Siberia.

The yellow bandits behaved toward their allies in World War I (England, etc.) just as they do today for their friend Germany.[84] For their do-nothing actions at that time, these yellow tricksters received Tsingtao and the Pacific Islands of Mariana and the Carolines – without having fired one shot for their allies. They were just passive or neutral.

Germany deserves this. It chose Italy and Japan for its allies. I would never have made a pact with these two countries. First, because of their behavior in 1914–18, and then because they are nations from whom no support can be expected.

A pact with England would appeal to me very much. Germany could make do with a small fleet and would be cured of the idea "our future lies on the water."[85] So far this "future" lies primarily on the seabed.

[. . .]

December 21, 1941

The same Führer Headquarters that used grandiose and over-exaggerated reports since the Russian campaign began – to increase the people's belief in victory – finds itself, after six months of intense battles, forced to release the following declaration and excuse:

ARMED FORCES REPORT FROM FÜHRER HEADQUARTERS, DECEMBER 17, 1941

Supreme Command of the Armed Forces bulletin:

In the course of the transition from offensive operations to maintaining defensive lines during the winter months, various Eastern Front sections will undergo necessary improvements and shortening at this time according to schedule.

Source: "Wehrmachtberichte vom 17. Dez.," *HF-Abend,*
December 18, 1941, p. 2.

[. . .]

It is understandable the creator of such reports at Führer Headquarters (who I assume is Adolf Hitler) would seek to use all means to suppress the truth. I took part in "improvements at the front" in France in 1914. Of course, we soldiers called movements to the rear simply "retreat." What is there to be covered up? In time even the dumbest Nazi will recognize these official embellishments. [. . .]

The shortage in all necessities has led to bartering. To obtain additional rations, people with something to barter follow the law of self-preservation. The farmer who goes to an "honest" city merchant with his fresh farm produce will never return home empty-handed. Merchandise wins out over money. It was different in the last war when paper currency was able to induce money-hungry farmers to furnish us with food. Bartering of merchandise is the way to do it today. The officials are trying to stop the devaluation of the economy, but there is no success in sight. Both the self-sufficient and the controlled economy are preparing for defeat in this war, which hopefully will have a sobering and cleansing effect for all time. [. . .]

December 22, 1941

Six months of war with Russia. The General Staff's goal to destroy the Russian army has not succeeded so far. The change in the Supreme Command proves not everything was calculated from the beginning (as the Führer once insisted). The Russians constantly dodged engagements, but now they are starting their counter-attack. The German army finds itself in an unenviable situation at the beginning of this winter.

Now the infallible leader Adolf Hitler is Oberste Befehlshaber, having made himself the head of the Army High Command. He alone has responsibility for all fronts. Now his believers will expect him to go down in history as "the savior of Germany." In a few weeks or months I will take a position on this feeble hope.

General Field Marshal von Brauchitsch was relieved of his post. On February 4, 1938, this general had replaced von Fritsch, who would not go along with Hitler's policies.[86] Brauchitsch, one of the many worthless characters, submitted himself like a slave to Corporal Hitler. His fall is a great punishment for Hitler accomplices. How different it could have been if after the removal of true soldiers like Fritsch no officers could have been found to play the role of German Officer Corps traitor. It has been hard to find a man of character since 1933.

December 23, 1941

I want to take a position about the initial Japanese successes. It is surprising they are able to land everywhere when the English have not been able yet to do the same in Norway, Belgium, Holland, France, or Italy. Both England and America carried out hapless politics before the war and acted myopically. In order to be rid of the Communist Russians, the miserable capitalists of both countries supported the over-armament of Japan, Italy, and Germany. In this lies the hidden secret why the Americans and English failed to act. Germany would not have been in a position to attack Europe had it not received the necessary raw materials from England and America.

This is true, is it not, Mister Lindbergh?[87] You know the score, don't you?

I would have found it very regrettable if the USA had not finally been awakened. Japan is a pike in a carp pond. That is good. Have you had a good sleep, you Americans?

To rid the Japanese of their power politics will require a lot of effort. It would have been easier years ago and substantially cheaper if China and Chiang Kai-shek had been helped with every means. Now it is vital to give China and Russia complete support. When will the blind democracies open their eyes?

December 25, 1941

First day of Christmas.

On December 19, "in recognition of an inner calling," Hitler personally took over the office of Commander-in-Chief over all the armed forces. The final sentence of his address to the soldiers of 1941 is as follows: "The Lord God will not refuse victory to his bravest soldiers."[88] I think the Lord God will know what he has to do. The National Socialist Lord God (Adolf Hitler) has signed his own death warrant. There is no escape. Now he cannot make an army general a scapegoat. We shall see.

Wartime Christmas! Peace on earth is still far away. Is real peace possible at all? I say yes. I believe in a moral world order yet to come. But the conditions for this world order have first to be created. If this succeeds then all the sacrifices in this greatest of all wars will not have been in vain.

This new order can have its basis only in law, justice, and compliance with treaties. The small nations must have full freedom and enjoy all human rights. Within each nation the basic laws have to be laid down irrevocably, especially to guarantee individual freedom. Friendship among nations requires as its substructure a fair distribution of natural resources. All nations must renounce despotism and be subject to world order. The inclination of individual nations, for instance Germany, to create a world empire is to be removed, which can be done if raw materials are used (under supervision!) only for friendly objectives and not for military purposes.

Open or disguised suppression of races or populations must be abolished.

December 27, 1941

Yesterday the army report stated Benghazi, the capital of Cyrenaica, was being evacuated according to plan. The phrase, "according to plan," plays a considerable role in these reports. What is it supposed to mean? Nobody can prove if it is true or not. Even when the opponent dictates the move – as being done now in North Africa – this pretense of "according to plan" is presented to the listening believers.

The people are "by necessity" lied to "according to plan." [. . .]

1942

January 1, 1942

One year ago, on January 1, 1941, the "Führer" made a special appeal to the National Socialists and Party comrades – he did not address me! – and he gave an order of the day to the armed forces. [. . .] "The year 1941 will bring about the completion of the greatest victory in our history!"[1]

Now 1941 has passed without the prophesied "greatest victory in our history." Germany cannot win this war with big phrases and admonitions. Not to mention the war was already lost before it even started. Several miracles would have to happen now if Germany is even to come out of this melee with its skin intact.

It is impossible for Germany to win this war. This bloodthirsty Adolf Hitler, dictator of Europe, inventor of total war, cannot and may not win this war.[2] He has inflicted unspeakable pain with his brutal despotism, not only upon foreign nations but also on his own people. His career, built upon great disregard of Right, and through cruel methods of suppression, has brought only unhappiness to the world.

When will this insanity end? When will a deserved fate overtake this lunatic?

January 2, 1942

Japan is on the prowl in the Pacific and has landed troops in the Philippines, Borneo, and the Malacca Peninsula. In its lust for power Japan makes the same mistakes as Germany. It can hold these islands only if it has a superior fleet. Its fleet would have to be stronger than those of England and America combined.

These passing Japanese victories will not be of long duration. The situation in the Far East will change when the Mediterranean fighting ends in favor of England. The USA will give Japan the right answer, and with a permanent effect. It needs but a little time.

January 3, 1942

With a lack of German victories, the entire Nazi press, on orders from above, commenced a hysterical applause for the yellow rogues' piratical

12. Jan. 1942.

"völk. Beobachter"

Tschungking-Truppen bei Tschangscha aufgerieben.

Tokio, 6. Januar

47

Über die erfolgreichen Kämpfe der japanischen Truppen bei Tschangscha in der chinesischen Provinz Hunan bringt Domei eine längere Übersicht. Danach wurde Tschangscha von den japanischen Truppen vollständig besetzt, nachdem letztere seit dem 1. Januar mit dem 10. Armeekorps der Tschungking-Truppen, das sich aus der 3., 10. und 90. Division zusammensetzte, Straßenkämpfe ausgefochten hatten. Das genannte Armeekorps wurde völlig aufgerieben. Es verlor 19 000 Tote und 7000 Gefangene. Eine Menge Kriegsmaterial wurde erbeutet. Mehrere Bunker und militärische Ziele innerhalb und außerhalb der Stadt wurden vollständig zerstört.

attacks. With a distorted visage they piece together their slimy drivel. It is really disgusting to see such undignified behavior. These Aryans are not at all ashamed to adorn themselves with foreign Japanese feathers. They have to present victories to the people no matter where they come from – without the smallest word about their own defeats. What grandiose modesty! The explanatory commentaries following the army reports are now considered unnecessary by the gentlemen in the Ministry of Propaganda.

January 4, 1942

Two weeks ago Dr. Goebbels broadcast an urgent radio appeal (on December 19) to the entire German nation. In moving words he described the deprivations of the fighting front; he indicated the Home Front would not deserve one quiet hour if only one single soldier had to do without sufficient clothing for the hardships of winter. He asked the Home Front to help and to bring the winter clothing to the collection points between December 27 and January 4.

I had been of the perhaps quixotic view that army administration had fully equipped the troops. All the proud reports in the media had led me to assume (and eased my concerns) that my Führer had "calculated everything beforehand." [. . .]

January 9, 1942

Judge Boländer has been drafted, beginning January 17. I wonder if he will think of what I told him around a year ago when he told me emphatically we had the best relations with Russia. "You will march against Russia," I responded with a substantially different opinion. Germany was capable of continuing this war only by robbing one state after another. The English fleet's blockade was being felt more and more, so Germany could get nothing without stealing. Attacking England would not do much good; they have to import most things, and nothing would be left for us. Hence the aggression against Russia, and we will learn eventually about our true motive. The "fight against Bolshevism" is just a ridiculous phrase like everything else National Socialism presents to delude humanity. They have had plenty of takers for their lies, but the light of dawn is slowly approaching.

[. . .]

January 11, 1942

How subdued our army reports have become! If anyone later makes it his calling to critically examine the army announcements during the Russian campaign, posterity will have trouble believing it was done like this. Arrogance and bragging are so unworthy of a true soldier. The propagandists do not leave one good hair standing on the opponent's head. The Russian leaders and their subjects are painted with every bad attribute a soldier can have. [...] Now our "glorious" army has to leave piece after piece of the conquered terrain to this "incapable," "collapsed," and "destroyed" enemy. Before the fall comes Pride. But it is more than arrogant pride. To underestimate one's opponent like this is a mental affliction.

But anyone who expects people to learn from this Russian experience will be greatly disappointed. I see that everywhere. I make every effort to tell my acquaintances the United States will achieve such great things we will not be able to make any effective defense. Mainly I am met with disbelieving faces. Can it really be true our enemy will one day show us he knows how to handle weapons too?

What can I do? It is exasperating. I want to raise concerns about German might and power among my friends, but it is easier to storm a bunker. Dear Lord, why have you made the skulls of the thick-skinned so impenetrable?

January 12, 1942

Inspector Paul stopped by our office to tell me he was to be drafted into the engineer corps. (He was born in 1908.) He is no longer deferred from military service and shows enthusiasm. Full of hope, he said his cousin, recovering in Giessen from a wound, is convinced of a coming German victory. There can be no doubt of any kind when it comes to Germany's victory.

I could not determine if his conviction about victory was especially emphasized for my benefit, but Paul is completely convinced of the army's invincibility, and it is futile to say anything to him to the contrary. Hopefully, now that he is an engineer, he will have a chance to become more closely acquainted with the other side of things, and my own.

CHUNGKING TROOPS BY CHANGSHA EXHAUSTED

Tokyo, January 6, 1942.

Domei News Agency brings an extended look at the Japanese troops' successful battles in Changsha in the Chinese province of Hunan Gang. Changsha was fully occupied after the Japanese fought street battles beginning January 1 with the Chungking troops, composed of the Chinese Tenth Army Corps 3rd, 10th, and 90th divisions. The Army Corps was fully wiped out. Its casualties were 19,000 dead and 7,000 taken prisoner. A large amount of war material was captured. Several bunkers and military targets within and outside the city were completely destroyed.

Source: "Tschungking-Truppen bei Tschangscha aufgerieben," *VB-Süd*,
January 7, 1942, p. 1.

Posterity may see in this article an example of how the German people were lied to – because the opposite of the above is true. The Japanese suffered a huge loss in Changsha. The "wiped out" Chinese are fighting just as victoriously as the "destroyed" Russian army.[3]

[. . .]

January 24, 1942

Our soldiers in the East have been fighting without interruption since June 22, 1941. First it was heat, dust, and shortness of water; then it was rain, mud, and bad roads. Now it is snow and cold. There was hardly a break in the fighting. For the infantry, there were continuous marches, one after another. Whoever among the leadership's high and supreme ranks had the idea there would be something like a winter rest and the so urgently needed respite for the troops will have a sobering disappointment. The Russians care nothing about the Germans' need for rest. There will be no breathing space, and this means victory for Russia.

I assumed from the beginning the Russian General Staff would use time and space as weapons and keep their reserves in the background. If the Russians have sufficient strength, it will prove catastrophic for the army, similar to what Napoleon's army suffered in 1812.

[. . .]

January 30, 1942

According to a January 6, 1942, confidential memorandum from the minister of justice, the agricultural bureaucracy's fuel quota has been shortened in order to fulfill fuel requirements at the front. The cutbacks are so big they will gravely decrease the allotment for official vehicles not involved in food production or manufacture. Our bailiff, for instance, will not receive any more fuel.

The Party circles were informed yesterday evening that a commission will inspect all basements for potato supplies. They are looking for surplus potatoes! Considering this situation it is quite remarkable the unified German press made fun of Churchill's recent statement in the lower house of parliament: "We are just able to keep our heads above water."[4]

I do not know how this alleged pronouncement by Churchill is to be understood because I do not know the context. Acknowledging England's weakness so openly, though, verifies England's lack of preparation for war and underscores that until now that nation did not put forth its best possible effort. A "World Empire" really should appear differently. It is pitiful to see how England prepared its defense. Where are the submarines to protect the Dominion? I would recommend to England they hire German and Japanese consultants for the English navy. You cannot bring forth heroic deeds with the attitude of a shopkeeper.

February 1, 1942

Every Sunday they arrive with their collection cans and lists. Instead of a chicken in the pot, it is money out of your pocket. National Comrades, give the Nazis everything you have, and you can keep the rest for yourselves. Whoever gives his oath to Adolf Hitler has nothing that belongs to himself.

But if there is any German who loves his country more than do all of these tormentors put together, and who wants to see his country saved from the consequences of an insane politics of despotism, he is a "Public Enemy" in the eyes of the Nazi Party Germans and is treated accordingly. [. . .]

February 4, 1942

Frau [Marie] Rühl told Frau Jochem today her son Willi wrote about retreating 120 kilometers in the East in order to move into "winter quarters." But these winter quarters lasted barely three days. On January 30, 1942, in his speech at the Sports Palace, Hitler dressed up the news in the following way: "The enemy has advanced by a few kilometers in a few places." And he added, "In the spring we will crush the Soviets."[5]

The "Soviets" have been officially destroyed and crushed so many times such announcements make no impression at all on me. I suspect the Russians also will attack. We will see!

[. . .]

February 12, 1942

General Rommel's successes refresh the minds of those war-tired Germans who may have begun to lose confidence in victory.[6] What can I say to these people in the face of such pathetic "efforts" by the English? [...] The English cannot even assemble a troop contingent in their African colonies that might be in the position to beat General Rommel's troops. There is no justification to call England a world power. [...]

February 13, 1942

Here we go again. A teacher who is from nearby Grünberg expresses loudly and clearly on the train the British Empire will be completely destroyed within four months. The drum beating of our propaganda machine claims another victim. If a teacher no longer has his own opinion, what kind of attitude should simple people have?

England's failures everywhere in the world naturally support the supposition it is on its last legs. One has to be a really big opponent of the Nazis to preserve a last ray of hope. I tell myself England and America are putting everything upon the playing card "Time" – Germany's weak point. We in Germany have no time. Things are getting worse here by the hour. Every aspect of material and human reserves is almost completely exhausted. We are not far from the conditions of 1918. Under such circumstances I think it is very possible our opponents have yet to play out their trump cards.

February 16, 1942

The Japanese have conquered Singapore! It was supposed to have been one of England's strongest naval bases. They also have landed at Sumatra. The Japanese can land where they want to; nobody has given them any energetic resistance. They have left untouched only Java and Australia; but how much longer will that be? Japan has to continue to attack, of course, if it wants to stabilize previous conquests. Will these robbers finally get a good smack on the hand?

A lack of ideals – especially among the English – is the real reason for their failure on all war fronts. China has been at war with Japan for five years, and England went ahead and closed the Burma Road for a period of time to shipments of war material. What should we say to that? This is a crime. Instead of supporting China with every possible means, simple-minded England created difficulties for the Chinese. Why did they not immediately (that is, five years ago) train Chinese as pilots in England and America?

Even if they did not employ these foresighted measures, they at least should have erected fortifications of all kinds in the English possessions. I can assure England that under a German government, Singapore would not have fallen within a single week. [. . .]

February 23, 1942

All guilt is avenged on earth! The Laubach SA leader and persecutor of Jews, the teacher Albert Haas, is dead.[7] Now he has received his payment for all his bad deeds. Hopefully the remaining cohorts will go the same way. None of them may remain. If that happens I will believe in divine justice.

[. . .]

March 9–26, 1942

Vacation in Freudenstadt. As we did last year, we took room and meals at Gasthof Dreikönig, whose proprietor is Max Finkbeiner. The food was plentiful and good despite the difficult conditions. Just a few spa customers are here in Freudenstadt. On the other hand, there are many sick and wounded armed forces personnel. The major hotels (Palmenwald, Waldesruhe, Waldeck, Teucheleswald, Rappen, Adler, etc.), and the hospices and sanatoriums have been converted into field hospitals. Business life is languishing because of the lack of merchandise. Many businesses have closed (with official permission) on account of the military draft, or because of sickness. Others are open for a few hours only; for instance, from 3–6 p.m. We see samples in the show windows that are not for sale; or there are empty decorated boxes or empty bottles. All in all, a gloomy picture.

On March 20 we learned about the prospect of a reduction in food rations. Only 300 grams of meat or cold cuts per week! The Führer once asserted he had the right to require sacrifices because he himself was ready to accept any personal sacrifice. If now the idea to starve to death came into his head, I would not want to take away his right to ask all his fellow fighters to do the same.

April 11, 1942

The minister of justice's edict of April 1 is a new order for reporting court proceedings. It says the work of justice must be represented in the press as "the true mirror of life in Germany" and reflect the seriousness of the tasks the people have to fulfill.

So how are we to bring about this true reflected image? The Nazis are in no way embarrassed: the minister simply forbids unrestricted reporting of court proceedings and replaces it with exclusively official reporting. Newspaper reports, court proceedings, and documents can have only the official wording. The publication of court proceedings is now under the Reich Ministry of Justice and the Ministry of Propaganda. [...]

April 13, 1942

Some artful dodgers here signed up for the artillery because it is generally considered the infantry suffers the greatest losses; the artillery is better protected. This obituary proves artillery men within the infantry are killed – exactly the same as in 1914–18.

It is remarkable this lieutenant was a company commander at such a young age. The obituary's brevity is commendable.

Artillery Lieutenant Albert Kehrberger
Company Leader in an infantry regiment
Born July 17, 1921, died Feb. 25, 1942
Parents: Hans and Elsa Kehrberger, née Pippig; Sister: Helga Kehrberger.
Our request is to please refrain from statements of condolences.
                                        Source: VB-Süd, April 9, 1942, p. 6.

[...] This year, 1942, can shake hands with 1917, when our leaders made fun of the USA. The year after that, 1918, the Americans became the decisive factor. We had nothing left in 1918 to throw on the scale to tip the balance in our favor. Today is similar, to say the least.

April 17, 1942

A lady from Dortmund is hoping the English will soon starve to death! She would do well to worry we do not end up with major difficulties feeding ourselves. But it is easier to embrace the opposite hope. Most people have the minds of infants.

April 20, 1942!

He is 53 years old today, the "Führer" of the German people – the most horrible person in Germany's history. "And the most horrible of horrors is man in his insanity" wrote the poet Schiller. What would he have written had he lived in this era of an insane Hitler?

Who will be able to tell our progeny about this rat-catching pied piper, Adolf Hitler, with his absolute terribleness – he, the sole culprit in the mass murder that began in 1939? A great number of helpers, of course, share the guilt: stirrup holders, bootlickers, and fellow travelers without conscience and character.

I feel the turning point will show up soon. The attackers will come from the ranks of the attacked, along the entire line, in all of Europe. Perhaps the overture will begin in just days. The English and American planes will initiate the attack. The coming clear nights will bring unwelcome visitors to the German people. What we inflicted on others will be given back to us. Retributive justice: "What you do to me, I will do to you."

April 27, 1942

Yesterday, on Sunday April 26, the All Powerful One spoke in the Reichstag to the representatives. The puppets were permitted to rise from their seats and unequivocally confirm the last Enabling Act.[8] A new epoch. The Party is completely in power. Might over Right to the highest degree. They have finally buried the so-called independent judges (who existed since 1933 merely on paper). Nazi outcries against officials – and especially against those in the justice system – are only to be understood by those who can look behind the scenes. Here and there were still a few men who insisted on their honestly obtained rights. Hitler rooted them out yesterday. "There are no rights, only duties." That is how he droned on in the convention hall, and the audience applauded in homage![9]

Since the Jews cannot be presented to the people as scapegoats now, another group has been chosen: the officials are now the scapegoats. I have had much opportunity to "admire" those in the justice system who became more Pope than the Pope himself, an unbelievably large number of submissive and toady knaves, especially among the judges. And now, with typical Nazi gratitude, they are thrown to the people to devour. The beasts need something to sink their teeth into when things do not go right. Yes, you confederates and sycophants, that is how it is. Submissiveness receives its well-earned punishment. The whore "Justice" is treated as her behavior deserved from the beginning. In 1933 they all went along, and today they are under the heel. I love it!

Just keep going, Adolf Hitler. Nobody could do it better. Your herd of sheep is very patient. And keep praising the infantry. They will let themselves be killed for their supreme warlord with even greater enthusiasm.

These people are crazy!

April 28, 1942

"That was a wonderful speech by the Führer," said Pastor Goldmann about Hitler's Reichstag speech. Although this fine Laubach minister has no more rights, he is especially happy anyway. [...]

April 29, 1942

Now Bormann, Himmler, and Sauckel are governing.[10] Sauckel should be called *Saukerl* [filthy wretch]. Have fun, gentlemen. The apex has been reached; it cannot go any higher. All that remains is the descent.

If the future Germany cannot prove to the world it has nothing in common with the present mentality, it will never recover. All the people in Germany responsible in any way for the present situation must be cleaned out. The guilty must fall. Justice must come away with an immense victory. Justice demands all criminals whose guilt has been determined without doubt have to pay for the crimes they committed.

100,000 RM REWARD

French General Giraud has fled from a German prisoner-of-war camp

Berlin, April 25.

French General Giraud, who was placed in a German prisoner-of-war camp, has escaped from the Königstein Fortress. Because of his health condition the general was given greater freedom of movement. He took advantage of this accommodation to escape.

Anyone who is involved with helping the general in his escape will be punished with death. A reward of 100,000 RM has been set for the general's capture. General Giraud is 1.82–1.85 m tall, slender build, with gray hair and gray mustache, and speaks German with a French accent. All armed forces posts and police stations will receive updated reports.

Source: "100 000 RM. Belohnung," *HLZ,* April 26, 1942, p. 2.

This must have been a valuable general.[11] Who helped him to break free? High rewards seldom lead to anything getting resolved, which probably will be the same here. By the time the announcements appeared in the newspapers, the general was no doubt across the mountains in Switzerland. You can peacefully travel throughout Germany wearing an officer's uniform and driving an army vehicle.

May 1, 1942

According to the April 26 decree of the Greater German Reichstag, published in *Reichsgesetzblatt*, I, 1942, page 247, Führer Adolf Hitler, without being bound to existing laws, comprises in his person the following:

1. Leader of the Nation.
2. Supreme Commander of the Armed Forces.
3. Head of Government and the Supreme Holder of Executive Authority.
4. Supreme Judicial Authority.
5. Leader of the Party.

In short: God Almighty of Germany.

I have in front of me two small volumes about the Napoleonic era: *Germany in its Deepest Humiliation* and *The Misery of Foreign Rule*.[12] It is strange how sensitive the German people were when they themselves were the suffering party in Napoleon's time. Now Germans are enthusiastic about the oppression of other people and show not the least sympathy for the suffering of those in the conquered countries. What we demanded for ourselves 130 years ago – delivery from foreign demagoguery – all of Europe can demand with total justification from us. Our entire conduct has shown a brutal and unfeeling egotism for which we will be made to pay.

[. . .]

May 3, 1942

If anyone thought the German people would rise against the dictator Hitler, I can say the whole world would be wrong on this point, just as the world was wrong about the extent of German armament before 1939. Just as Napoleon could not be deposed at the height of his power, it is love's labor's lost to think to erase Hitler's reign with words. Napoleon was ousted only by defeat on the battlefield. This will be the case with Hitler. Only military defeat can bring about a change.[13]

Hitler duped the entire world. He had the great unbelievable luck to meet with weak and vacillating opponents, cowardly people who knew nothing of idealism or had a feeling for solidarity, who did not possess honor and love for freedom. Bribed by Hitler, the politicians in Norway, Hungary, and Romania blew on the same horn as their lord and master. Incompetent General Staffs along the entire opposite line had fleets for parades but not for battle. A spirit of a small tradesman is not statesmanship. Except for Germany and Japan, this describes the world from 1939–1942. The Japanese meet nowhere with significant resistance. Even on that side of the globe the entire Allied nations are incapable of concentrating their forces at one point in order to beat the Japanese and destroy the mystique of invincibility.

When will our opponents attack? They have talked about it enough. How can the German people come to their senses if they see that Great Britain and America's attitude is diametrically opposite their own? Will a heavyweight fighter let himself be beaten by an opponent who only rolls his eyes at him? Or does it require a good punch? [. . .]

May 6, 1942

[. . .] I want to write down a collection of my thoughts about the times since 1933. I am beginning the manuscript now. This writing will give my progeny a look into the period of my lowest humiliation as a human being. If I get it done I will perhaps try to publish it as a book. The title could be "Out of an Insane Asylum," or simply "An Insane Asylum." "The Pied Piper from Braunau on the Inn" would be quite charming.[14]

I will not rack my brain about that today. All in good time. On to work!

[. . .]

May 15, 1942

Göring, at the head of the Council of Ministers for the Defense of the Reich, published a proclamation on April 10, 1942, about government service minimum work time. The minimum for officials is fifty-six hours a week. "Just as a soldier at the front, despite deprivation and dangers, knows no limit to his services, every official has to realize nothing should remain undone in his daily work. There will be no more leisure for Saturday afternoon and Sunday."[15]

Thus the humane order of Marshal Göring. I really enjoy such orders. They possess historical value. Those who told me before 1933, "Things have to be changed," now have their due. Yes, you idiots, now things have truly changed. Prosit!

May 20, 1942

Dr. Scriba's decree of yesterday:[16]

Effective on May 21, 1942, the work hours for justice officials are determined as follows:

Monday–Friday: 7–1 and 2:30–6:30.
Saturday: 7–1 and 3–5.
Sunday: 10–noon.

With such measures the men on high want to win the war. Just keep going – nothing to eat and more work: the National Socialist common good. "Heil Hitler!"

[. . .]

May 22, 1942

The German press is a chapter in itself. Like salesmen at a book fair, publishers push to the forefront everything the believers desire. Following are some headlines that appeared in the *Völkischer Beobachter* from May 14–21.

A GREATER VICTORY FOR GERMAN WEAPONS

THE BREAKTHROUGH BATTLE OF KERCH IS DECIDED

STUKAS CUT FURROWS THROUGH THE AIR NON-STOP

[. . .]

And in red letters the *Völkischer Beobachter* published this quote (from a speech by Hermann Göring) on May 22, 1942:

A STEEL-LIKE HARDNESS GUARANTEES FINAL VICTORY

As an aside, there is still some talk about Roosevelt. My pen refuses to repeat it. The "drunkard" Churchill has somewhat disappeared in the background and the entire editorial diarrhea is poured over Roosevelt. In December 1941 Japan attacked America. Then Germany declared war on America. In spite of those events, Roosevelt's "sick brain" was responsible for this war. "Roosevelt is a cowardly subject who is beyond all imagination," the writer said, and added the Americans would have done well "to have put their sick president in an asylum instead of in the White House." Thus it goes day by day. The "embarrassing stupidity of Roosevelt" is a tender flower of German newspaper filth.[17]

Why this childish smearing? The opponent will not be shaken. The lowest low in German journalism has been reached. No trace of culture. [. . .]

May 23, 1942

THE REICH WOMEN'S LEADER IN THE REGIONAL BRIDES SCHOOL

Pirmasens, May 18, 1942.

On her trip through the Westmark region, the Reich Women's Leader Scholtz-Klink visited the Brides School in Pirmasens, where over 300 women officials within the National Socialist Women's League had prepared a warm welcome for her. Along with the Regional Women's League Leader, and with the District Leader and District Women's League Leader, she made an extended inspection of the school. The journey through the region was concluded by Frau Scholtz-Klink's visit to Metz, where she spoke at a large rally to the Lothringen women.

Source: "Die Reichsfrauenführerin in der Gaubräuteschule," *VB-Süd*,
May 19, 1942, p. 4.

The Brides School is mainly for the pregnant "brides" of SS men. The German people are preached to day and night not to take trips, but yet in Pirmasens three hundred women assembled to prepare a wonderful reception for the Nazi women's leader.[18] For this circus there are sufficient materials and railroads available. [. . .]

On May 21 Marshal Göring said during a ceremonial act of state in the new Chancellery Building's Mosaic Hall, "This war has to be endured, no matter how long it will last."[19] With that, Göring placed himself in the category of defeatists who predict a long war.

May 25, 1942

Pentecost Monday, a holiday. Excursion to Schotten.

The heavy rain made us cancel a hike to the Hoherodskopf peak [in our mountain range]. We went to five restaurants, trying – without success – to buy lunch. In Adler Restaurant we managed a bowl of thin soup. Germany, you have changed enormously! The National Socialist goblet is not yet completely empty. Only after the last drop is the end near. Before that, we will be eating rutabaga roots.

USA WARSHIPS FLEE FROM JAPANESE PLANES

Tokyo, May 18, 1942.

As reliably reported, on Friday morning the Japanese air force sighted a hostile fleet 500 nautical miles east of Salomon Island traveling in a westerly direction consisting of the North American aircraft carriers "Hornet" and "Enterprise," as well as some cruisers and destroyers. When the enemy discovered the Japanese airplanes, they turned away toward the east without positioning themselves to fight. Japanese naval experts see in the sudden appearance of two aircraft carriers in these bodies of water the indirect confirmation of the loss of the North American aircraft carriers "Saratoga" and "Yorktown" in the Battle of the Coral Sea. [...]

Source: "USA.-Kriegsschiffe reißen vor japanischen Flugzeugen aus," *VB*,
May 19, 1942.

Japanese reporting is a completely obvious swindle. Not even Goebbels dares to serve such stuff to the German people. It is the most blatant idiocy to say US warships had run away from Japanese airplanes. The Japanese insist they have sunk two carriers. The Americans deny any losses. Now Japanese storytellers say they have seen two other carriers, and that was for them an indirect confirmation of the loss of Saratoga and Yorktown.[20] The Tokyo Fairy Tale Department's crazy assertions would astound even the inmates of a mental institution.

May 26, 1942

[...] After temporarily returning to perform his duties, District Leader Backhaus in Giessen has once again fallen "ill." He is said to have played a certain role in the mayor of Steinbach's imprisonment. The egg-batter pancakes were not able to remove the district leader; now the sausage packets may have been his undoing. It is all too obvious how the Party greats have retained their former body circumference despite three years of war.

May 27, 1942

The Giessen surveyor, Gontrum, hopes the English soon will have their tongues drooping with hunger. That is a typical example of the attitude of many Germans. Do not think about the possibility that hunger might soon cause us many problems. We have plenty of reason, considering our food situation, to worry about what is at our own front door. But no, it is more satisfying to allow other people to hunger and collapse.

May 28, 1942

Polish and Jewish women who are pregnant, lying in childbed, or nursing their children will no longer receive supplementary food. That is according to the Nutrition and Agriculture Minister's May 24 decree. The Reich health leader has indicated repeatedly in circulars and during conventions additional food stuffs for sick Jewish people could be recommended only after strict investigation.

This probably can be put in the chapter "Extermination of Jews and Poles." [...]

My wife and I were of the opinion from the beginning Germany would lose this war. We often were out on a limb all by ourselves. Currently the belief in victory is once again given a boost. The exaggerated army reports about the battles on the Kerch Peninsula [Crimea] and near Kharkov bring new courage to those who had their heads hanging down. The hope barometer is rising. The Nazis well know the psyche of the people. But still all these tricks are worthless. What shall be won by them? The enemy cannot be shaken by such manipulations.

May 29, 1942

Today the court attendant Scherdt came in and brought with him five posters inscribed as follows:

IN THIS ROOM IT IS THE DUTY OF EVERYONE TO ACT AND SPEAK WITH POLITENESS.

This poster is supposed to be hung in every office. Proof positive we have no lack of paper.

If the people in charge would show a good example, especially if those on the radio would show themselves as educated and polite, the general public would probably take pains also to be civil. Since 1933 the Party broadcasts have been far from civil. It seems most did not have a good upbringing.[21]

May 30, 1942

Why cannot Germany win this war? Because our naval fleet and air force are smaller than the combined forces of England and America. Because air attacks on Germany throughout 1942 will result in damages that will considerably interrupt our war production. Because if the English and the Americans launch an attack on the continent all suppressed populations will revolt, and the instability will bring about the collapse of Hitler's New Order. "Someday we will not know in which direction to shoot," I wrote earlier. In the general turmoil there will, of course, be a revolution in Germany. "Hitler, a disaster for Germany."[22] All of the small-minded people will say they always knew National Socialism would end in this manner and that none of them had ever been a National Socialist. In reality, only one percent of Germans at most were true opponents of Hitlerism. The remaining ninety-nine percent actively took part in everything or at least bowed spinelessly under the yoke of the NSDAP, tame as lambs. I have met so very few "men" I could house them in a single small room.

Hopefully there are at least among the emigrants who left Germany some courageous and determined men because only they will be in a position at the end of the war to bring some order into this pigsty. It will not be over without loss of blood. Those circles who presented us with the Second World War must not have an opportunity to burden the world with their insane ideas for a third time. What was not done in the November days of 1918 has to be done this time. And the main thing must be continued and strict observations of all creatures who have not learned anything from the two world wars. At the smallest attempt to disturb the peace in any manner, we have to intercede without pity. Above all, racial hatred has to be exterminated. It has to be impossible for all eternity for the Germans to treat other people as they have the Jews and Poles, in a sadistic manner, arranging their systematic eradication.

A special report has informed us the battle for Kharkov is over and we captured over 250,000 Russians. The enemy suffered the bloodiest losses. Nothing was said about our own casualty figures. The number of prisoners is probably like the amount of tonnage we sank in the ocean: there is no upper limit. How long would it take to count 250,000 prisoners?

May 31, 1942

Newspapers constantly report German U-boat successes along the North American coast. I truly recognize the amazing accomplishment of our submarines, but it is more amazing we have not heard anything about the American submarines operating close to the Japanese coast, or English submarines operating in the Baltic. Why this incapability in our opponents?

Nevertheless, the submarine war close to the gates of North America is a major political mistake. At the beginning of the war, the average American did not feel like getting involved in the European conflict. President Roosevelt had to continually rouse his people and steer their attention to the danger he recognized. The German side marked him as a warmonger. Now the Germans give the dumbest American clear proof Roosevelt's instinct was very good. The deeds of German U-boats work better than the words of prophetic American politicians. Those who designated the American continent a danger zone are not making it better for us by attacking there. German U-boats may sink more ships, but they will not prevent large-scale attacks by English and American bombers on German industrial cities.

June 1, 1942

Dr. [Robert] Barth, former mayor of Mainz and a first lieutenant in the army, has been killed in action at the Eastern Front. Before the "Seizure of Power" Dr. Barth was an assistant judge in the Mainz courthouse. I knew him as being a fanatic. He was a ruthless academic and just as much of a power politician. A fighter in the Freikorps, Dr. Barth is to be counted along with Reventlow and company. During the First World War such people united under the company name "Fatherland Party." They wanted to extend the war. This man had wanted to become an active officer, but because the 100,000-man army during the Republic could take just a limited number of men, Dr. Barth became a lawyer.[23] His hatred was for all those responsible [in the Weimar government] for keeping him from becoming an active officer. [...]

June 2, 1942

Former Mayor [Julius Johann] Boehm from Laubach passed me yesterday afternoon on Friedrich Street. He stopped and shouted at me in a loud voice: "Heil Hitler." Apparently I had answered his greeting too weakly. This same man a few years earlier hollered after me on Wetterfeld Street after I had greeted him with "Good Day."

"You say, 'Heil Hitler,' young man!"[24]

Unfortunately in both cases I could not counter with a fitting repartee – for obvious reasons. Hopefully God keeps us alive for some time yet so after the war I can revisit this matter.

The Supreme Command tells us English pilots have carried out "terror attacks" on Cologne and in doing so have hit civilian residential areas. For them to talk about "terror attacks" is the apex of insolence and ridiculousness. It is childish and naïve to start speaking about terror attacks. There were times we used our air force with an unprecedented ruthlessness to destroy thousands of people without considering the views of cultured humanity. We were still in possession of our full power and the opponent could not retaliate in the same manner. Germany was brutal and insolent. Today the tide has turned, and here we are with such stupid frivolities about "terror." What is being done to the German people is divine judgment. They have to feel on their own bodies what they did to other people in their arrogant enthusiasm. Germans! Remember Poland, Holland, France, Yugoslavia, England, and Russia! The German pilots wreaked havoc in these countries. Who laid waste Russia and Rotterdam? Who destroyed London and made ashes out of it? (Or so our newspapers reported.) Who wanted to eradicate the English cities? Was that not the Führer Hitler? Does not all of Germany rejoice about the "heroic deeds of the pilots"?

And all of a sudden these jokers turn around and talk about "terror." If they would keep quiet and take it, one could still have some respect for them. But it is asking too much to expect dignity from sadistic criminals.

[. . .]

June 6, 1942

Over the last few days the citizens of Laubach with houses close to Ramsberg Hill were entertained morning to night by the "lovely" monotone sounds of signal horns. The leaders of Hitler Youth are assembled here not to help the farmers but to train in military matters. This is called premilitary education. The militarization of our youth begins at the age of ten. Poor German people!

June 8, 1942

SHD BECOMES THE AIR DEFENSE POLICE

June 1, 1942.

The Security and Assistance Service Organization, which the German people already know by their courageous action during the air raids, will make the change from June 1, 1942, by the order of the Reich Marshal and Commander-in-Chief of the Luftwaffe and under the jurisdiction of the SS Reich Leader and Chief of the German police. The SHD is subordinate to the regular police and from today will be known as the "Air Defense Police."

Source: "SHD wird Luftschutzpolizei," *HF-Abend,* June 1, 1942, p. 3.

Himmler has taken the Security and Assistance Service [SHD, Sicherheits- und Hilfsdienst] under his wing. There are good reasons for this. Some folks among the SHD ranks are not much interested in National Socialism. During air raids they are the ones remaining out on the streets, and sometimes during air alarms provocative sentences are written on walls. Now the SS supervises the SHD. The SS sure has its hands full to take care of its own security. Someday this cunningly created system will collapse like a house of cards. You cannot put an SS man at the side of every European. How does the saying go? "Neither horse nor knight secure the steep heights where princes repose."[25]

The free man's love for his government is alone the guarantee of order and security. All measures of suppression create counter pressure. [. . .]

The radio blares out its special reports with fanfares and sounds of marching. Ta-ra, ta-ra! Theater, nothing but theater. The people must be aroused. Victory after victory. The flutes are "the quiet certainty in the final victory." Quite true; they will likely be heard at victory. But in the cold light of day this final victory is very far away. The USA and England must first be conquered. For almost three years we have been making our drive against "Engeland" and we never seem to get there; such a faraway land, this "Engeland." Yet to the *Engeln* [angels] many have already gone.[26]

June 9, 1942

I wanted to become a land owner, so I went to the Solms castle to buy a piece of property from the Count of Solms-Laubach.[27] The piece is about 600 square meters on the Ramsberg. Yesterday I received a response from the count saying he "presently could not manage the sale of the desired piece of property since building on the property was out of the question during the war."

His reason does not sit well with me because I could have begun installing a garden. It would have been much more truthful if the count or his consultant had just briefly told me we do not sell anything in the present situation because we cannot do anything with the money. Everybody has money today – but there is almost nothing to buy. Money has lost its charm. Another aspect of this Nazi era.[28] [. . .]

June 10, 1942

[. . .]

DISTRICT LEADER SCHÖNE KILLED IN ACTION

Frankfurt am Main, June 5, 1942.

District Leader Schöne of Oberlahn-Usingen, a sergeant and officer candidate, died in a field hospital in the East after a difficult and critical illness. District Leader Schöne belonged to the National Socialist movement from 1923 and was outstanding in the fight to cleanse Frankfurt of its Red and Jewish low-lifes. [. . .] He showed himself in all of his political positions to be a loyal follower of Adolf Hitler. He proved his idealism as a soldier of the Führer in his fight for freedom for our people, in which he was awarded the Iron Cross for his courageous, exemplary behavior under hostile fire.

Source: "Kreisleiter Schöne im Felde gestorben," HLZ, June 6, 1942, p. 2.

Nazis are masters at twisting things. From a sadist they make an idealist. From a fiend they fabricate a devoted follower of Adolf Hitler. Without doubt District Leader Schöne had been especially "excellent," as is shown by his political development. The type of a relentless brutal person "who was outstanding in the fight to cleanse Frankfurt of Red [Communist] and Jewish low-lifes." This too is the art of twisting because the real low-lifes, Nazis, remained in Frankfurt and enjoyed the booty.

The retribution that came to District Leader Schöne will not neglect the remaining Nazi bandits. I would like to solemnly swear to that today. [. . .]

June 12, 1942

When I tell acquaintances I am convinced England and America will attack Germany soon, I always meet with incredulity. Judge Hornef does not believe the English are able to undertake an attack. So far no one – except my wife – fully agrees with my opinion. Even those who do not contradict my arguments inwardly embrace the official view the English are incapable of doing anything of consequence against us.

The effect of German propaganda is extremely long lasting. And counter propaganda lacks evidence. Common sense is on its own and not greatly represented. The one thing definitely proven is people are forgetful. Hitler writes in Chapter 6 of *Mein Kampf*, "The receptivity of the great masses is very limited, their intelligence is small, but their power of forgetting is enormous."[29] And their forgetfulness is widespread. Twenty-five years ago the USA entered the First World War. All public figures made fun of America. It was disputed that American soldiers would ever come to Europe, but in 1918 the American army made the difference in every respect: morally and honestly. [. . .]

People in neighboring countries also pay homage to Nazi propaganda. Professor van Genechten personifies the National Socialist "worker," and he is threshing phrases like grain.[30] It is always the same game. One clears his throat and spits, and the others follow suit. With assurances by this bought-and-paid-for professor, the Dutch Nazis can look forward to a great and splendid future for Holland at the side of mighty Germany. Holland was a free country. Under the wings of Hitler it is a slave state. Only a major scoundrel can behave as this repulsive professor. Phooey! He should be put in chains.

June 16, 1942

It is instructive to cast a glance at an old newspaper. In 1940, on November 12, the *Hamburger Fremdenblatt* published an article by Lieutenant Colonel Benary about Russia's defensive strength. Because Russian Minister of Foreign Affairs Molotov was in Berlin "to enhance friendly relations," the newspapers were permitted to write the truth. The German people were meant to see Russia was a noteworthy partner. After we invaded Russia, the Russian army, according to Goebbels, was just a wild gang – whatever suits the propaganda.

Lieutenant Colonel Benary believed Russia's armament was huge and its defensive strength was founded on the vastness of its territory, riches of raw material, and the number of its people. Among other things he wrote:

The depth of its space has always been Russia's best protection. It lets the power of invading armies drain away. Russia became the scourge of Napoleon. Even today under the specter of long-distance airplanes it offers great possibilities of evasion, so that Russia is the only country in Europe that knows its war industry would remain undisturbed by enemy air raids. Also it is one of the few countries in the world that does not have to worry about supplies of necessary raw materials or the depletion of its sources – coal, ore, oil, and whatever is desired for armament. Everything exists in great abundance within the homeland. And the food supply economy is no less. There grows enough grain between the Baltic and the Pacific, with plenty of grazing cattle, to feed the population and the army. There definitely is no lack of people. Millions and again millions are ready to carry weapons, to manufacture weapons, to produce raw material, and to resupply food stuffs.[31]

Even a Russian could not have documented this better. Lieutenant Colonel Benary has evaluated Russia correctly in my opinion. And in actuality, the Russian army today offers extremely stiff resistance. German army victories have to be gained by resorting to deception and surprise attacks. One must wonder why the aggressive German politicians and generals were not better informed. [. . .]

June 17, 1942

A visible change has occurred in the newspaper world from 1940–1942. The *Hamburger Fremdenblatt* used to publish an average of eight to ten pages in each issue; today there are at most four pages. Obituaries used to be printed in a large layout. Now they take one sixth of the space. Yes, we have become more modest. The paper supply may likely run out. What luck if such newspapers were no longer available. The voracious believers would no longer have the "accomplishments" from Dr. Goebbels and his cohorts to bring up.

June 18, 1942

Only a megalomaniac fanatic could unleash such a war. In just four more days it will be one year we have been battling Russia. On September 1, 1939, Hitler said in the Reichstag [of the pact with Russia], "We have therefore decided to enter an agreement which makes it impossible for us to use any force against each other in the future." On November 9, 1940, we were assured Commissar Molotov's visit to Berlin had deepened the friendly personal relationship between Russia and Germany.[32] But in fact the dagger was already being sharpened to stab our non-aggression-pact partner in the back. On June 22,

1941, seven months after the reassurance of friendship, Hitler commanded the German troops to attack Russia. "Friendship" lasted from August 1939 to June 1941.

June 19, 1942

Dr. Goebbels frequently shouted to the world that National Socialism was not export merchandise. The opposite is true. Dr. Wahl, director of Hamburg municipal library, has brought together the various translations of *Mein Kampf* in an exhibition. Nazi newspapers brag *Mein Kampf* has been published in all cultural languages and could be compared only with the Bible for distribution.

"It is necessary to remember, especially during the war, that the German fight for power has its basis in the battle for the mind," writes the reporter H. P. about this book exhibition.

I always believed the "adoration of power" prevailing in Germany is what has kept the world from getting any rest. If the world is to have peace, it will have to remove this barbaric spirit from the minds of Germans.

A difficult task! But it is worthy of the sweat of the whole world.

Hugo Lindenmayer, the bank director, said goodbye to me today by telephone. He is starting a job in the Ukraine. Year after year, even before the war, the local bank in Laubach displayed a German Labor Front poster with the announcement, "We March Together." This was not completely true because Herr Director (born in 1900) was lucky enough to "march together" neither in the previous war nor in this war. Now he is headed close to the front and finally will be able to pursue some political studies.

I am sorry I cannot feel badly for him. Heil Hitler![33]

Willi Rühl, allegedly the son of a French prisoner of war from the First World War, has been promoted to lieutenant. He was active at the beginning of the war. He also was conspicuously active during the Jewish pogrom.[34]

June 20, 1942

The Nazis do not love him. Whom? Roosevelt, the man in the photo.

Franklin Roosevelt
Source: AFP/Getty Images

Why does the Führer talk about a crazy Roosevelt? Because the "crazy one" correctly saw through the Führer and his movement from the beginning. Very unfortunately a large part of the American people failed in the worst manner, and therefore America itself is now in the war – and truly in a war of unbelievable extent. The overly-clever American egotists who do not want to worry about the remainder of the world until they feel their own backsides getting warmed are getting an education.

June 23, 1942

The barber, Karl Pfeifer, born in 1924 in Laubach, and the electrician apprentice, Ernst Puissant, born in 1925, were sentenced to juvenile prison by the Juvenile Delinquent Court in Giessen on June 2 for causing bodily harm followed by death. Pfeifer was sentenced to two to four years, and Puissant to eighteen months. The convicted men beat their comrade, Adolf Jäger, late in the night of October 16, 1941, on the road from Grünberg to Laubach. Jäger died the same night as a consequence of the beating.[35] Pfeifer, Puissant, and Jäger belonged to the Hitler Youth marching band. The motive for the attack was not clear. During the proceedings the defendants' great brutality, cowardice, and crass deceit were revealed.

In two words: Hitler Youth!

These characteristics of the young culprits can be found in the entire population.

The attacks on the countries now occupied by German troops are also evidence of brutality and cowardice. Added to this are the deceitful reasons for the German crimes; for example, in Russia we were only pre-empting an attack!

June 24, 1942

When the war enthusiasm thermometer shows a worrisome low, the English are always invoked to raise the temperature. The already announced general offensive against Russia has not yet happened, so as a replacement we have victory announcements from North Africa. General Erwin Rommel has beaten the English and secured Tobruk and has been promoted to General Field Marshal.[36] When Rommel was stationed here in Laubach in 1940 [commanding the Führer's Escort Battalion] he was a Generalmajor assigned to Führer Headquarters. Since 1940, thus in merely two years, he became Generalleutnant, General, Generaloberst, and now Generalfeldmarschall![37]

I am sorry to have to tell the English their North Africa campaign shows a pitiful lack of understanding of warfare. I cannot comprehend why they do not use their African colonies better. [...] Hitler has been able to bring hundreds of thousands of Frenchmen into Germany to work. It is a colossal embarrassment England does not know what to do with its millions of people in its African colonies.

Why are Egypt and Abyssinia not used for defense?

[...]

July 4, 1942

Our successes in Africa and on the Crimea Peninsula have considerably enforced the people's confidence in final victory. Even if no one is breaking out into loud song (on account of our food situation) hope still exists that one or the other enemy will give in. Block Leader Walter expressed it this way: "The Russians will now certainly come around with a peace offer." [...]

July 18, 1942

Tonight at 8:00 is a big special-request concert in Laubach for the Red Cross's war effort. It is at the Solmser Hof restaurant. An "event" for

Laubach. It is greatly advertised. The Local Group Leader visits the government offices to raise enthusiasm. Printed invitations appear at every house.[38]

Dear Music Lover!

You certainly must have noticed one of your favorite melodies among the rich selections offered here you would enjoy hearing again with pleasure. This wish can quickly be fulfilled. You need to make a donation of not less than 3 RM which will go to the German Red Cross war relief. But you can make a combined request with your friends, acquaintances, co-workers, company, associations, etc. with a collective donation of not less than 15 RM. The contributors will be announced during the request program.

So make your decision right away!

Fill out the attached form as soon as possible and give it to your block leader or the block warden. Your request must be received no later than July 14 in order that all the preparations can be made. Until then your donation can be made at the NSV payment office or with the block warden where you will receive a receipt for the payment.

Secure your tickets in time!

Advance purchase available through all local chapter office heads and administrators for the price of 2 RM. [...]

Donation collectors move from house to house: smallest donation, 3 marks. Ticket, 2 marks. We donate 5 marks, do not buy a ticket, and do not request anything. The little town is in good spirits. Of course, there will be standing room only.

The master of ceremonies announced the specific donations. That is a rich morsel for "friends" and acquaintances: material for gossip for several days. Everybody is upset Dr. Massing donated just 10 marks. The little war profiteers naturally show off: lumber factory Schmidt, 50 marks; weaver Rühl, 50 marks; stonemason Rühl, 50 marks; grocery store owner Justus, 30 marks.

One feels so important. Small people!

July 19, 1942

The butcher, Herr Reidt, does not believe the United States will attack in Europe – he and many others. Reidt is not a Nazi, but he is a militarist and naturally desires the German Wehrmacht's victory.

August 10, 1942

A new regulation from the Supreme Command:

TATTOOING SOVIET PRISONERS OF WAR

Chief, Prisoner-of-War Administration. Berlin Schoneberg, July 20, 1942, Badensche #51.

1. Soviet prisoners of war are to be marked by a distinctive and endurable tattoo.
2. The tattoo consists of an acute angle of 45 degrees, open downward, each side about one centimeter (^). It is placed on the left half of the buttocks, one hand-width from the anal opening. Lancets are already available in each troop. Chinese ink will be used as a coloring pigment . . .

More directions follow, and then this:

Since at the present time there is not sufficient practical experience regarding the tattoo's durability, it is to be checked after fourteen days, then four weeks, and after a quarter of a year. If necessary the tattoo is to be repeated.

The completed first marking is to be noted in each prisoner's personal record, in the Special Marks section, by a drawing of an inverted angle (^) and the date – and also the date that it has to be done over again.

Very inventive! If the enemy on his part would put a swastika on both buttock halves of each German prisoner we will have perfect world order. Later on during mutual salutation and to ensure proper identification they will show each other their asses.

This measure indicates the Supreme Command of the German Armed Forces either has a lot of Chinese ink or anticipates a long war.

The world has learned over the centuries how to inspire soldiers. The German is unusually ambitious, sensitive to praise, and enthusiastic about special recognition. He will be more than just a little proud if he can have one little star, one little ribbon, or one medal more than his neighbor. The Führer recognized "his" people's weakness and used it to the utmost. Medals and awards are handed out continuously. [. . .]

August 11, 1942

"Even the attempt is punishable" is the title of Reich Minister Dr. Goebbels's article in the newspaper *Das Reich*. He addresses the question of our opponents establishing a second front. In his usual style he ridicules the English, saying it would be a pleasure for Germany to see English troops on the European continent. "We bid the English a cordial welcome. Hopefully they will bring along a few Americans."[39] Goebbels's tone is impudent and infantile. He poses as the strong man, but the truly strong do not brag of their strength. [...] When they do come, it will not be with golf clubs or tennis rackets. Despite Goebbels's opinion, they first will rain bombs. Then all types of weapon will be used according to each situation. That is how I imagine things. And if the enemy is not led only by incapable people, they will be victorious. They probably will say after the deed is done, "We were jackasses not to have done this sooner." [...] If the enemy lands paratroopers any place in Germany, they can with skillful leadership do infinite damage. They would be especially successful near prisoner-of-war camps. Telephone and power installations, factories, railroad crossings, railroad installations, supply depots have to be destroyed. Forests have to be set on fire. I will never understand why no Rhine bridges have been destroyed or the ship traffic obstructed. Railroad traffic on both sides of the Rhine near Bingen can be paralyzed using little effort, especially in Bingerbrück and Rüdesheim. Allied transport airplanes could block ship traffic at the so-called Bingerloch [a narrow area of the river] by dropping stones, iron pieces, and so forth. Nothing of this has happened yet, but it can still come.

I assume the general attack will occur in September; therefore we will have to expect heavy air attacks soon.

August 12, 1942

We have a God-given politician and strategist in our midst: Judge [Heinrich] Bischoff from Alsfeld. So far this thirty-seven-year-old "indispensable" has been able to ponder the German army's glory while remaining in the hinterland.[40] Naturally he is prepared with not just a handful of exaggerations. "In the Caucasus the Russians will be cut off from oil, and because their army is motorized they will be finished." Thus speaks Herr Bischoff. He will not consider my objection that Russia possesses oil also in the Ural region and in Siberia. Some especially interesting opinions of this academic should be written down:

"We have to cut off the American capacity for armament. We have to keep America from transporting war material to the fronts." (I object: "It will not be easy for us to prevent American airplanes from flying to England." And Bischoff: "That does not matter.")

"In the Caucasus we and the Turks will attack from two sides and cut off the Russians."

"If we had killed all the Jews, this war would not have come."[41] (If there had not been one Jew in the whole world Hitler would have still attacked Poland and would have wanted to steal land in the East. For precaution, I only thought that.)

This justice official provides a look into the soul of a real German academician. Hopefully I will have the opportunity to write a few extra sketches.

August 13, 1942

English airplanes attacked Mainz in the night of August 11–12.[42] When we found out about it yesterday morning, I tried to speak by telephone with Mainz, but the post office could not establish a connection. During the day we learned through telephone conversations with people in the outlying districts that the raid had been intense. Various public buildings, tax offices, post offices, and the railroad station are said to be destroyed. We have to wait for more definite news because we know great exaggerations occur in such cases.

We just received a registered letter and a telegram from Mainz. "Everyone is well. Katie." At least the worry about relatives is over. Katie described what occurred in broad strokes. According to her, it must have been a horrible night. It is really sad the nice ones also have to suffer. But those who were happy about the air raids on England cannot be punished brutally enough. The German people have to feel firsthand what war means. Until now they could wreak havoc and bring death and destruction to foreign countries with impunity.

There will be a cruel accounting, but this fate is earned. There are men among the German people who could bring about a change, but nobody moves. Therefore it is completely justified that the entire German people – without any exceptions – be held to account. The punishment has to be implacable and effective.

[. . .]

August 17, 1942

In 1933, on May 17, Adolf Hitler said this in his "peace speech":

The generation of this young Germany that so far in its lifetime has known only hardship, woe, and the misery of its own people has suffered too much from this madness to want to inflict it upon others. Our nationalism in principle obligates us to keep a general world view. While we are devoted in boundless love and faith to our own people and culture, we respect at the same time the national rights of other people on these same grounds, and we want with all our hearts to live with them in peace and friendship.[43]

Thus spoke this pied piper and phrase-thresher in 1933. The wolf clothed himself in sheepskin because he was not fully armed. He played the peace-loving statesman concerned with the well-being of humanity. In 1939 Hitler showed his true nature without shame. The world allowed itself to be deceived. I am proud I was not one of them. At no time have I been at the side of Hitler.

August 18, 1942

A busy Dr. Wellmann, in charge of the Darmstadt justice ministry's news section, informed media representatives on August 15, "The Federal Justice Ministry press chief declares it is unsuitable to have press releases about police officials being punished for exceeding their authority in the course of official investigations . . . Reporting in the daily papers concerning this type of criminal procedure is to be suppressed, by order of the Reich Ministry of Propaganda."

Many things are unsuitable for newspaper reporting in this exemplary state. Herr Goebbels, a specialist in ferreting things out before 1933, now invents the greatest tactics for covering things up. He shies from the light as though it were the plague. It is absurd to talk about "free press" reporting.

August 21, 1942

During a rally in Slovakia, President Tiso, a man we particularly need to remember, said this: "If Germany had not helped us in previous years, things would have been bad in Slovakia."[44] This follower has suddenly disclosed why his country sides with Germany. Germany not only "helped" with foodstuffs, but Dr. Tiso likely received correspondingly high sums of money for his "loyalty." Slovakia used to export merchandise, but today it has to accept alms. This is the "New Order" benediction. No country we have voluntarily or involuntarily brought to our side brings us any advantages. But a huge amount of Germans let themselves be fooled into thinking the conquered countries are supplying us.

August 22, 1942

The wife of our local Farm Leader in Münster declares, "We will have everything again in huge amounts after the war." This and other phrases are presented to the people so they can live in hope and console themselves. The Church consoles with heaven; the Party consoles with promises and empty phrases. It is difficult for me not to start swinging around with a club.

The wife of a soldier at the front is convinced every fighter will be given a cottage [on conquered land]. The hopes based on conquering territory in the East are so deeply rooted no one can argue against them. Faith indeed moves mountains. The Nazis have the propaganda ministry and the Nuremberg funnel at their disposal. Nothing is lacking anywhere. How blessed to be a believing Nazi: an easy life and an easy death, and no spirit to give up.

Everyone views this victorious war optimistically and gives no thought to peace. I am firmly convinced peace will bring a painful awakening. Peace will be terrible.

August 23, 1942

Now Brazil has declared war on us. The unlimited submarine war is a detriment for Germany. Forget everything and do not learn anything. Hitler widely accused the Kaiser's government in *Mein Kampf* for making "enemies of God and the world."[45] He, the most ingenious of all, has done it even better. [...] German U-boats sank several Brazilian ships, but Brazil waited a long time before declaring war. Their declaration has not impressed the arrogant Germans at all, who understand only the language of force. Therefore as punishment for destroying those ships, Germany should receive a lot of damage. As you do to me, so I do to you. Brazilian airplanes flown from England could do a lot; and they could drop leaflets along with the bombs: "You owe this to your Führer."

The Führer must be the first to carry the responsibility for every one of the misdeeds.

August 24, 1942

I became uneasy during a conversation with Judge Bischoff. The only person who can exceed the way this man handles the most complex problems of war is an armchair general seated at his favorite table in a pub in the hinterland far away from any army post. Bischoff is an optimist of the purest water. As far as he is concerned the Americans and English are already checkmated. They have no room left to wage an offensive. Bischoff is totally convinced we will take "the island." The island is England.

I can only respond weakly because Bischoff immediately links my response to enemy propaganda. To be safe I have to restrain myself. When I mentioned Brazil's declaration of war, he called it ridiculous. "The whole of America cannot do anything to us at all." "The entire American shipping is handcuffed by Japan." "America will never recover the islands it lost in the Pacific." In this sing-song way, this indispensable droned on with his convictions.

Bischoff is a pure type of a molded Nazi: arrogance personified. Such people elevate the silliest bombastic phrases to sacred poetry. It is terrible to have to talk to such idiots. This type knows, of course, a lost war would do away with them. They cling fanatically to Goebbels's wisdom and resent any critic who is guided by intelligence. Well, I have to let all this go for now. At the opportune time I will pull this little general by his necktie. I will not protect any of these academics. The slimy way these people subjugated themselves to the Nazi potentates, and the way they helped to further the process of making the German people into dummies is a real shame. People in these circles, with their schooling, their studies, and their professional training should not have to run after every false prophet. They probably are to be blamed the most for Germany's collapse; they had to know it was simply impossible to use force against so much of the world.

August 25, 1942

The Reichsführer-SS [Heinrich Himmler] has a security service [Sicherheitsdienst, SD]. The SD has recently been tasked with gathering news on matters concerning the "effect of official measures on the population's mood."[46] This security service, its personnel and organization, is a Party institution. The almighty Party – with the Almighty at the head – fights for its existence to the last breath. The Party big shots believe their organizations can prevent a repeat performance of November 9, 1918. They do not suspect situations can arise that can blow them away like chaff: for example, enemy armies pushing into Germany. Much time will pass before that happens, but I will count on it.

August 26, 1942

The developers of the German language were no doubt proud of themselves when they created "Kurzschrift" for the Greek word "stenography." Their happiness must be short-lived. The Führer proclaimed that from now on "Kurzschrift" will no longer be used. We must use "stenography" instead. (*Deutsche Justiz*, 1942 p. 543.)

A leader has so many concerns. [. . .]

August 27, 1942

Deputy Justice Minister Schlegelberger has retired. Dr. Otto Thierack has been named Reich Minister of Justice. This SA brigade leader has been given special authority by Adolf Hitler:[47]

Therefore I ask and authorize the Reich Minister of Justice to initiate a National Socialist Administration of Justice according to my interpretation and instructions, in concordance with the Reich Minister and Chief of the Reich Chancellery, and with the head of the Party Chancellery, and to fulfill all measures necessary for this end.

In doing so he can deviate from existing law.

Signed: Adolf Hitler. Führer Headquarters, August 20, 1942.

Countersigned: Dr. Lammers, Reich Minister and Chief of the Reich Chancellery.[48]

Now it can start. They can "deviate from existing law." The constitutional state has finally been buried. Crime is trump. Arbitrariness is law.

Who will sweep up the shards? [. . .]

August 28, 1942

We begin the fourth year of war in a few days. What was it Dr. Goebbels said in the foreword to his book, *From the Imperial Court to the Chancellery?*

With an instinctive confidence did the Führer go his way. He alone was never deceived. He was always right. He never permitted himself to be seduced by the advantage or disadvantage of the moment. Like a servant of God he fulfilled the law that was given him. And thus in the highest and best sense he fulfilled his historic mission.[49]

This Mephisto and ultra-liar Goebbels had every reason to elevate his Adolf Hitler to divinity because a ministerial post was waving at him; therefore, the oily phrases. One thing is correct: Hitler was not mistaken about the German people's mental condition. He also was not mistaken about the industrialists' unscrupulous attitude and underhandedness. Nor was he wrong to expect a lot of money to come in when he promised to crush the unions.

He also managed with his hatred of Communism to deceive the best and highest office-holders in the whole world. But he was not fully content with matters beyond the borders of Germany, so he picked up the card "War" and played it. That was his downfall. And all of his friends and donors will fall with him into the abyss.

These jackals must never be allowed to rise again.

I want to be there in that fight.

August 29, 1942

Even the NSDAP's opponents (or just the envious) will have to admit constant activity and indescribable fanaticism have kept not only Nazi members but also the entire nation in a continuous state of bated breath. Now they are initiating even more so-called "Appeals." Attendance at these local appeals is "one's duty." In other words, they are mandatory meetings, as in the military. The cell leaders, Association of German Officials representatives, and the high-level German Labor Front leaders are all there. And the district chairman gives a speech. He reminds the audience before everything else of the duties every individual political leader and every Party member has to fulfill.

[...] Today the German people have the greatest decision in their history. Millions are at the front, fulfilling their duty heroically. Millions are working in the fields and in the factories to supply the bread at home and the weapons for the front. Therefore we will act ruthlessly against those who propose to undermine unity. Frederick the Great created the Order of the Officers and the Order of the Officials. The Führer created for the German people the Order of the NSDAP, which will carry forth his ideas and philosophies into distant time. This signifies both an admonition and the highest obligation for all political leaders. Only someone who believes in himself can turn others into believers. And he who is himself ablaze can ignite others. Germany is the NSDAP, and the NSDAP is Germany. And even after a thousand years, it shall be said: My leader is Adolf Hitler!

The listeners get up "spontaneously" from their seats when the speech ends, and after the Sieg Heil greeting to the Führer, they "enthusiastically" sing the national anthem.

This happens not only in one place or in one meeting. No. All across Germany they go about it according to the same recipe: everywhere the same phrases, everywhere the same drama. The Nazis convince themselves in this hysterical fashion that the enemy has already lost the war. According to their proven system this has to be repeated every hour in order for them – and even the enemy – to finally believe it.

The "thousand years" slogan plays an enormous part. And Frederick the Great must always be invoked.[50] This is the whipped cream on the cake. And at the same time they fill the grumblers with fear and horror. In doing so the Nazis believe they have erected an invincible Home Front. They glue and splice together the Home Front folk with every possible means. They are completely convinced that under their glorious leadership and with the aid of their remedies a collapse like November 9, 1918, is simply not possible. [. . .]

August 30, 1942

The author, S. von M., wrote an article titled "Differences" for the August 8 issue of *Hamburger Fremdenblatt*. What this imbecile squashed together out of confused nonsense really beggars description. From a lack of tonnage he jumps to a lack of steel. And of all things, the United States is supposedly experiencing a lack of steel:

The largest contract by the Navy Commission in Washington for two hundred Liberty ships had to be canceled in spite of expensive research . . . The Todd Shipyard has to relinquish the steel apportioned to it because it was needed in other places . . . Other armament enterprises are facing closure, and newly erected factories have been inactive for several months already. Some of them probably will never be used. Even steel production by factories that worked for the Lend and Lease program had to limit their production by fifty percent.[51]

This is but a taste from this splendid article. During a war everybody has to expect somebody will lie to him, but this swindle is really a little bit too much.[52] The press during the 1914–18 war also could take credit for some respectable "performances," but in this war the unified press has celebrated true orgies. I hope this scourge will be eradicated after the war. It will not do to let these scoundrels who would poison us go unpunished.

To the gallows with them!

August 31, 1942

German Law! During criminal proceedings against Germans we have to use every possibility to get along without Poles or Jews as witnesses. If the testimony of a Pole or a Jew cannot be circumvented, he still may not appear in court as a witness against Germans; his testimony has to be taken by an official or an appointed judge. Criminal reports submitted by Poles or Jews against Germans can justify action only when sufficient reasons exist that a procedure is necessary.[53]

Imagine what would happen if a Pole denounced a Party bigwig. What district attorney would proceed with the indictment?

Jews and Poles are completely without rights!

It really is deeply regrettable there are Germans who have sunk so low they do not accord the most basic human rights to other people. Furthermore, it is deeply regrettable the decent members of the German nation will have to suffer greatly when the retribution comes.

September 1, 1942

Three years of war are behind us. The fourth year has begun. On September 1, 1939, Hitler gave the signal to begin the war. After years of preparations an excuse was found to attack the Poles. It was supposed to have been a lightning-fast war. We have experienced the results. Adolf Hitler was capable of frivolously picking a quarrel to start this war with all its horrors, but at this point he is not in a position to end it. This is the tragedy of what is happening. It has turned into a battle of "To be or not to be," not only for the Nazis but the entire German people.

This war was unnecessary because it was not going to solve any of mankind's problems any more than other wars. The "master race" used force to erect a "Greater German Empire" and ruthlessly prevail over other nations. The power mongers were not content with historical developments. Plunder and annihilation was what the Nazis wanted. They named it, "creating Lebensraum" – increasing their living space.

Well then, fate must take its course. We can never again talk about law and justice if there is no penance for the abominations that have been taking place since 1933. The whole world should take note of that.

September 2, 1942

[. . .] What is justice today? "When a judgment represents the feeling for justice which is held by the people," states the new Minister of Justice Dr. Thierack. Gentlemen of the NSDAP, please tell me in what manner you determine the people's perception or feeling for justice? The majority say nothing: the people have no freedom to express an opinion. And yet this conjuror, Thierack, knows exactly what the people's opinion is.

If they give a rousing speech in the Sports Palace in Berlin, and the controlled attendants scream and applaud, this demonstration is not an expression for establishing law. The masses are served a huge swindle. The special stress given to "the people's inner feeling for justice" is to make the brainless ones think the tyrant is giving their ideas consideration. The almighty judge never comes in contact with the real people; he has his accomplices carry out the hocus-pocus. Therefore who are the "people"? The "opinion of the people" is manufactured in the Ministry of Propaganda; and the people's "feeling for the law" is produced in vague phrases on order of leading Nazi judges. In this insane asylum no one knows in from out anymore.

Not even a soccer game can be played without referees and rules. Yet the judge is now supposed to judge without being governed by law. For an uncorrupted, courageous judge, who has not taken bribes and who is honest, this situation is simply horrible. He may do what he wants, but it will be definitely wrong. It is impossible for a judge to always do just as the Führer or the minister of justice wants.

I am curious how this comedy will develop.

September 3, 1942

A professor in Bonn (a lawyer) once demonstrated to his students "a sense of justice." He presented a case and then he asked for the solution in such a way each student had to answer with just yes or no. The play began. "Yes, no, no, yes, yes, no, yes, no, no, yes, yes," and so forth. At the end the professor said, "I thank you, gentlemen. Now you know what 'a sense of justice' is."

The following judgment has absolutely nothing to do with "justice":

DECISION [. . .]. The movable and immobile possessions of the Jewish couple Hirsch – Otto Julius Israel Hirsch, born October 20, 1863, in Mainz, died May 21, 1942, in Mainz, and Melanie Tara Hirsch, born Roos, October 6, 1872, in Speyer, living in Mainz at 47 Schuster Street – are requisitioned in favor of the German Reich.

There are no laws in effect against this edict.

Darmstadt, August 24, 1942.

Gestapo Headquarters, Darmstadt. Signed by proxy: Fentz.

Source: "Beschluß," *HLZ*, August 30, 1942, p. 6.

Providence, to which Hitler so frequently alludes, has thwarted the Third Reich's plans. The Hirsch couple's possessions, and all the others on Schuster Street, have been completely destroyed by the air raid of August 12 and 13, 1942.[54]

Property unjustly gained will do you no good!

September 4, 1942

From reports we have received so far, we have learned Mainz suffered greatly from the air attacks, especially the inner city. The same is the case in Cologne and Karlsruhe. It appears the English have promised themselves something from that – do they seek to break the population's resistance? If my assumption is correct, then I have to feel sorry for anyone who has such a notion in his head. Destroying the houses in Mainz will not shake up the front or the war machine in any way. [. . .]

If they want to paralyze Hitler's war machine they have to make powerful and concentrated attacks against key objectives. From the beginning I never thought much of scattered attacks. In effect these are merely mosquito bites. How would it have been if during the past three years every attack had been on the Ruhr valley? In such a case would the Ruhr still be able to supply Italy with coal? The English have not made a single attack against the harbor at Kehl, a very important transit point for coal shipped to Italy. It almost looks as if they are purposely avoiding those attacks so the war could take a long time. I am reluctant to think only incapability and foolishness predominate in our enemies.

September 7, 1942

On Saturday and Sunday we were in Mainz to see the air raid damage. At first glance when approaching the city from the railroad bridge you do not get the impression one third of the city has been destroyed. Mainly the inner city is demolished. [. . .] Therefore it was an attack against the population. There were 1,958 houses destroyed or heavily damaged, among them 161 restaurants. It is said the enemy dropped 460 concussion and about 40,000 incendiary bombs during those two nights. According to the experts the damage to buildings is estimated at 600 million marks.

Without doubt the destruction is great, but this will not influence the war. If the English authorities believe such attacks might lead to a change in their favor then they have been extremely ill-advised. If the entire city of Mainz were turned into a heap of rubble the war would calmly continue.

The companies that manufacture war material remain untouched, for instance the Opel Works in Russelsheim-am-Main. And the regional traffic installations were not bombed: the railroad yards in Giessen, Friedberg, Frankfurt am Main, Hoechst, Main Bischhofsheim, Mainz, Wiesbaden, Offenbach, and so forth. And the electric power station in Wölfersheim. Most of these installations have no flak protection whatsoever.[55]

With our enemies conducting such warfare, this war can only become a permanent thing. One cannot understand it. I wonder if they will explain it to us later on.

[. . .]

September 16, 1942

In the last few days the Jews from this region have been removed. The families Strauss and Heynemann were taken from Laubach. I heard from a reliable source all the Jews were taken to Poland and murdered there by SS brigades.[56]

This cruelty is horrible. Such atrocities will never be able to be erased from the book of humanity. Our murderous regime has for all times besmirched the name "Germany." It is unfathomable for a decent German that no one can stop the activities of these Hitler bandits.

September 17, 1942

In an article, "What They May Expect," the September 10 *Schwarze Korps* addresses the settlement in the East.[57] The author asserts, "The entire nation expresses an immense interest in the settlement of the East." As far as the western part of Germany is concerned, this assertion is an "immense" lie. I have never met a person interested in the territories in the East. The opposite is true. Everyone who has anything to do at the great Eastern Front, who is forced to be there, is eager to return back home – and today rather than tomorrow. Be that as it may, this assertion about "immense" interest serves to support the war against Russia. I do not mean to deny there might be people in some areas who for some reason or another would consider the

East as a future area for settling. But the leaders have no luck with their propaganda here. [...]

How and where will Hitler come to an end? I do not want to be a prophet on this point. Hopefully Hitler remains alive up to the final destruction. The storytellers must be denied their material because it is clear they would use an early death as an excuse for the bad ending: "If only Hitler had not been killed, we never would have lost this war." That would be the leitmotiv of all the history falsifiers.

"With Hitler into the abyss." That is what I wish for the German nation.

September 21, 1942

Slowly the light of day approaches. Of seventeen war dead whose deaths are published in the September 19 issue of *Hamburger Fremdenblatt*, only three died "for the Führer," and but one of them died "for the beloved Führer." This is remarkable.

September 25, 1942

CLEARING SOUTHEAST EUROPE OF JEWS

The following report comes from the *Berliner Börsen-Zeitung*, No. 424, September 8, 1942, about the scheduled purging of Jews in Southeast Europe:

Five years ago everybody would have thought it impossible the end of the Jews in Southeast Europe could come about as quickly as it in fact happened. All states along the Danube have, after the example of Greater Germany, begun to limit the parasitic presence of Jews, to eliminate Jewish influence and to push Jews out of their own sphere of living.

Slovakia followed the example of Greater Germany with the goal to completely free itself of Jews. Since 1939 it systematically encouraged Jews to leave, and in the spring of 1942 it started with the expulsion of Jews. Of 89,000 Jews, 65,000 were moved out in transports, 6,000 have fled to Hungary and 18,000 are awaiting transportation.

Hungary, which is especially plagued by Jews, and counts 800,000 Jews, not considering those who have converted and Jews of mixed parentage, has embarked on a complicated path for gradual expulsion of Jews and has already attained worthwhile results. The large number and the extensive settlement of Jews in all areas of life make this work especially difficult in Hungary but also urgent. The cultural life as far as theater, movies, and writing are concerned is already completely purged of Jews.

Croatia has completely eliminated its close to 60,000 Jews from the national life and has utilized them for necessary labor on the Adriatic island of Tag.

Serbia and the Banat are free of Jews and they are the first areas in Southeast Europe where there are no more Jews at all.

Bulgaria has energetically prevented all possibilities of influence on Bulgarian life by about 80,000 Jews and has separated them strictly; their marking with a Jewish star is in progress.

Two years ago Romania had almost as many Jews as Hungary and still counts, apart from Transnistria, Bessarabia and Buchenland, 272,000 Jews; in Buchenland 16,000, while Bessarabia is free of Jews. About 112,000 Jews are in camps in Transnistria. Almost a third of the Jews, 98,000, are living in Bucharest. Their expulsion is being prepared.

This concise overview shows the significant progress: in one year there will be no more Jews in Slovakia, Croatia, Serbia, and Romania. The dangerous internal enemy is being methodically eliminated.

Source: "Die Bereinigung Südosteuropas von Juden," Deutsche Justiz, Edition A, vol. 10, no. 38, September 18, 1942, p. 611.

To where [are they being transported]? This so-called "clearing" Europe of Jews will remain a dark chapter in the history of mankind.[58] If we in Europe are so far gone we simply eliminate people, then Europe is irretrievably lost. Today it is the Jews; tomorrow it will be another weak tribe that is exterminated. The Nazis say the Jews have "settled in." Have not Germans also "settled in" everywhere in the whole world? And even now, are not the Germans in the process of creating living space in the East in order "to settle in" there?

The Berliner Börsen-Zeitung prophesies, "Within one year there will not be one Jew left in Slovakia, Croatia, Serbia, or Romania." Perhaps also not one German! What hysterical screaming this newspaper would start if some country were to expel and transport the "settled in" Germans. The Europeans should be told they do not create a New Order in this way. Somewhere, somehow the growing nations of Europe will collide. For example, Slovakia is in the heart of Europe. To where will Slovakia spread? The relocation of 90,000 Jews in Slovakia is a small means to create space for their own increase. After a relatively short time the governing masters are faced with the same problem. Whom will they then remove? As I said, that is not how it works. I almost forgot that the Nazis can eradicate the Russians. Then, however, there would be space for a few years.

Our era is just awful.

According to my opinion there is but one possibility to restrain the desire for expansion of the nations: birth control. I immediately hear the nationalists screaming. Every nation feels it has the right to create as many children as possible – that is particularly true for Germany – and then to claim a lack of space and resolve the problem by eliminating its neighbors. If the neighbor is not willing to be gobbled up, then one puts a "defensive war" into action. Presently we have reached this point.

[. . .]

October 15, 1942

[. . .]

JAPANESE 32 KM FROM PORT MORESBY

Berlin, October 3, 1942.

After difficult hand-to-hand combat the Japanese in New Guinea threw the Australians back to their initial positions. The Australians received heavy losses in their vain attempt to halt the Japanese advance on the Port Moresby capital. The Japanese won six kilometers, putting them just 32 kilometers from this important Australian base.

Source: "Japaner 32 km vor Port Moresby," HLZ, October 4, 1942, p. 2.

Goebbels sets the tone in the newspapers, and the Führer cannot lag behind. Now we want to turn our attention to this area around New Guinea and see whether and when the Japanese will conquer it. I suspect more extensive combat will soon take place in Africa and in the Pacific. England and America must eventually, finally, take the offensive. They have demanded much patience of the nations to whom they had assured their support and that still await their deliverance.

October 17, 1942

In the Laubach train station ticket office I spoke with the building inspector, [Heinrich] Schmier, and others about the war's duration. He said the situation will change because we have forced Russia to its knees. I responded, "You will never experience the day we force Russia to its knees. Take note I have said that today." Propaganda has disordered the people's brains.

[. . .]

October 22, 1942

The rumor mongers in the Party offices are again at work. Judge Bischoff said soldiers home on furlough are being told where they have to report in case of an armistice or special peace with Russia. The same rumor circulates in Laubach. A soldier supposedly said it on the train. They are once again manufacturing a new ray of hope. In doing so they want to convince us the German people need only keep going for a little while longer until the enemy, according to the rumor manufacturers, is finished.

[...]

October 25, 1942

In recent times much has been spoken and written about the unsurpassed courage, battle-readiness, determination in the face of death, and radiant heroism of all German soldiers. A war reporter writes, "Death has long since lost its horror for the soldier on the front; it is accepted as fate and as an edict of what cannot be changed. It marches along as a cohort in every company and nobody knows when he will meet him."[59]

Death is drawn here as a matter of course. The fighters' thoughts and feelings are not disclosed. No one is allowed to write what kind of imaginings and feelings are moving them. The sacrificial lamb has to keep quiet. The reporter reports from the rear, far from the shooting.

Poor German nation!

[...]

October 28, 1942

Twenty years ago the Fascist Party in Italy marched to Rome and put an end to the democratic system of government. The king and the army were standing at ease when the Fascists suddenly became owner of the nation. The army, of course – exactly as in Germany – was completely orientated toward fascism, with its leading officers (for instance De Bono and Balbo) counted among Mussolini's closest cohorts. The Blackshirts (armed battle units) were the carriers of the revolution, and in the evening of October 28, 1922, Mussolini was empowered to form the government. The same process as on January 30, 1933, in Germany.

We know where Mussolini has led Italy – to Abyssinia and into war. The Africa adventure was costly, resulting only in losses. Their participation in the present war will have no different result. The Italian nation will be taught a lesson for the "indescribable exultation" they once felt at the victory of fascism.

October 29, 1942

[. . .] The SS brigades are maintaining an active campaign to persuade Hitler Youth members to enter the armed SS at an earlier age. The SS agents can sign the young people's forms without the parents' consent. Many seduced youth are drafted into the army in this manner at the age of seventeen. Not a few of them, by the time they are eighteen, are awarded a "heroic death" – as seen in the obituary here:

> **Helmut Wiegand**, War volunteer, SS Private First Class in a police battalion. Holder of the Silver Infantry Assault Badge.
> For Führer and Fatherland, our dearly beloved, good son, brother, grandson and nephew, at the flourishing age of 18, and after being severely wounded in the East on Sep. 19, 1942, died a hero's death.
> In deep anguish: August Wiegand and wife Johanna, née Weilbächer, sister Liselotte, all family members. Mainz (Pankratiusstr. 20 pt.), Hochheim, Wiesbaden.

Still a child and already a dead "hero." The Nazi bandits not only kill the children of other nations, they do not stop at their own progeny.

[. . .]

October 31, 1942

[. . .] Hopefully the people will be permanently reminded of this war. It will be an immense task to restrain the Germans' characteristic for conquering, and to steer them toward peaceful matters, particulary considering how the youth have been contaminated through and through by the spirit of Hitler.

[. . .]

November 4, 1942

The increase in children's deaths has been obvious to me for some time already. There are numerous obituaries in *Hessische Landes-Zeitung*, especially in the Darmstadt area. Here too the war is a direct cause. In normal times there is one physician for every 2000–3000 people. The army's need for doctors is so great there are places where 15,000 inhabitants have to get by with one doctor.

[. . .] A big mouth is the most outstanding characteristic of these unique Nazi creatures. Not one of them is an exception – even the officers are infected by it. One month ago, on October 3, General Field Marshal Rommel spoke in Berlin in front of the German and foreign press about the events in the North African theater. Among other things Rommel said this:

I can say with pride we have taken away the positions the English conquered in the Mediterranean. They succeeded twice in pushing forward to the Cyrenaica, but thanks to the valor of our troops we got the upper hand after a heavy fight, even though they outnumbered our military power. But the quality of our troops and leadership gave us the victory. When history later reports these events, the world will perhaps be surprised with what small forces we managed to beat the English and push them far beyond the borders of Egypt. Today we are 100 kilometers from Alexandria and Cairo and have the gates of Egypt in our hand – and indeed with the intention to take action. We did not go there to eventually be pushed back. You can depend on this, that in Africa as well as here, what we have, we keep.[60]

Such pronounced bluster. This kind of high-toned speaking is really grave. Even a victor should be a little more modest, especially when tomorrow he could be beaten again. There is no doubt Rommel's push to Egypt was certainly a great military effort. The defeat of England is downright disheartening. In spite of everything the finish is lacking in Rommel's effort. Why did Rommel stop 100 kilometers before Alexandria and Cairo? Probably because his army does not have the necessary momentum. The Italian army also was stuck some time ago at the Egyptian border and destroyed. I do not believe it is justified militarily to conduct a war at this place (100 kilometers from Alexandria) that is such a distance from the supply lines. The expenditure of strength on the German and Italian side is much too great and the results equal zero.

This African theater has been elevated to an important subject much more than necessary because it is a question of Italian prestige. The division of our own forces is especially evident now: a useless waste of men and material. And in the end it did not help the Italians at all. Italian North Africa is also going to the devil. America is continuously sending troops to Africa and to the Near East. Something is going on there. Perhaps we will be enlightened about it soon.

November 6, 1942

Field Marshal Rommel told the world he had the gate of Egypt in his hand and he intended to take action. Barely one month has passed since this declaration, and already special reports inform the people about a defensive action – not an offensive – near El Alamein.[61]

The war reporter Rudolf Kettlein lets loose his bragging from North Africa in *Hessische Landes-Zeitung*, November 5: "Let the Tommy come. We will beat him back." He concludes his report with these words:

The British offensive is not yet ended. Bitter fighting is still going on. They fight tenaciously for every meter of ground. The battle is fierce. It demands everything from our soldiers. But the "hour of retribution" about which the English Eighth Army commander, Montgomery, spoke will never arrive. More than ever our soldiers will vouch for what General Rommel said: "What they have, they keep."

This is the war reporter's conviction. I think the outcome depends more on the English Eighth Army's momentum. The greatest bravery will not help against a superiority of tanks and airplanes. The German army itself has proved this more than once. Now they feel firsthand the effect of their strategy.

Today the enemy is the stronger one. Fate!

November 7, 1942

After exerting so much effort fighting the Christian religion, the Nazis felt they had to present something godlike to the population. Years of painstaking work in creating a Lord God resulted in Hitler. I would like to record here how this is done in our daily lives. A certain Dr. Edzard Hobbing wrote the following in an article, "The Goal is in Sight," in *Hessische Landes-Zeitung*.

When it is announced in foreign countries that a speech by the Führer will be broadcast over the radio, there are countless people who hate to miss the broadcast, even though they hardly understand one word of German and only seldom grasp the idea of the talk. At the sound of the Führer's deep voice they listen in fascination and are soon enchanted. A radiant power exudes not only from the Führer's eyes but also from his voice. People become subject to the magic of this commanding organ. Many listeners from abroad agree it is the voice of a man who knows his own mind.

[. . .]

Foresight: that is what characterizes the Führer's entire policy since the Seizure of Power. Nothing finds him unprepared and nobody knows better than he a good start into the war is already a half-won war – because he ascertains the best starting points for the important decisions. With a cool calmness and with certainty of his goal the Führer steers toward the main decisions, which for him lies in the final confrontation with England. At the present time there is probably no governmental or military leadership that plans so imaginatively, cleverly, and realistically, but also prepares and executes as calmly as that in Germany.

Dr. Hobbing concludes his article with these comments about the enemy:

What England and America lost in a flash at the beginning of the war, no eternity shall return to them. Even if both of them wish in hindsight they had had a plan and pursued a particular line, they must bear the consequences that they had calculated badly and completely misjudged the enemy. Their unfortunate beginning in this war will produce an effect that carries all the way to the conflict's end.   Source: "Das Ziel im Auge," HLZ, October 4, 1942, p. 2.

One should be grateful to the Nazis that they talk openly about having prepared for the war. For me the name Hitler was always synonymous with war. All his talks about "peace" were just to fool the neighboring countries, which were promptly duped. You can see here also how foolish so-called statesmen can be.

With true Nazi recklessness the author dismisses England and the USA. What these countries have lost at the beginning of the war "no eternity shall return to them." So Dr. Hobbing would like! Such a knave should be thrashed for hours. I am curious whether something will be done against such creatures. If they can do their mischief without being punished, it will never get better in the world.

Gutenberg, your printing press has been defiled![62]

November 9, 1942

The positions near El Alamein have been breached and heavy fighting is taking place in the Mersa Matruh area, say the reports. Naturally the enemy has the all too familiar "high losses." Our own losses are kept quiet. The Italian reports are always a bit closer to the truth. Whenever the Italians mention hard fighting, they are preparing the Italian people for bad news. I have noticed that often.

The braggart Rommel has found someone to tame him. Where are the boastful speeches from the Sports Palace? "What we have, we keep"? Rommel the windbag!

CONTINUATION OF HEAVY FIGHTING IN NORTH EGYPT

Berlin, November 8, 1942.

The British continued their advance in northern Egypt on November 7 in the area of Mersa Matruh with heavy tank attacks. According to Supreme Command reports the combined defensive fire of the German and Italian forces caused high losses and considerable failures of tanks, guns, and vehicles of all kinds. In repeated counter-attacks the enemy lines were broken in several places and numerous prisoners were taken. However, the enemy keeps sending new units into the fire, and the struggle continues in full fury.

On the night of November 8 German and Italian hunter- and fighter-plane squadrons continued their attacks on columns of marching British soldiers in the coastal region eastwards of Fuka. The targets were clearly visible in the glow of flares. Armored and vehicle columns were attacked in several waves that continued until morning. Blazing fires and violent explosions testified to the heavy blows that fell upon the British this night.

Source: "Fortdauer der schweren Kämpfe in Nordägypten" *HLZ,*
November 9, 1942, p. 2.

[. . .]

On November 8, yesterday, American and English troops landed in French North Africa. The convoluted wording in the news report about it shows they tried to obscure the facts. No whining will help. The Americans are there! This is an extremely unpleasant position for the gentlemen in Berlin. This will be of far-reaching significance. This is the beginning of an attack against Italy. Herr Mussolini, make out your last will and testament! At long last, a heartening piece of news. Now the war becomes interesting.

A question to Hitler: How was it possible troops could be transported freely from America to Africa? Where were your submarines, Herr Hitler?

A question to Göring: A few days ago you said the Americans were merely bluffing. Is the landing in North Africa a bluff?

A question to Dr. Dietrich, press chief: You wrote in "The Battle for Tonnage" it was not possible for the enemy to undertake large-scale military operations because of transport difficulties. Where did the Americans find transports for their landing in Africa?

If one would write down all of the Party blockheads' arrogance, it would fill volumes. Particularly during the fighting, they took great satisfaction elevating German glory by lying, insulting, or spitting on the opponent without interruption. We repeatedly heard from Hitler's lips our enemies were zeros, fools, gangsters, Mafia bosses, crooks, crazy, retarded, drunkards, and so forth. When he spits out such phlegm all the other little Hitlers do it too – though sometimes a bit more elegantly.

[. . .]

November 14, 1942

Frau Dietz from Giessen said to Frau Metzger, "Hitler has been sent to us by God." These people have a strange idea about God, a name much misused in this war. Wars are started with "God," and "God" is called upon to bless Germans with victory.

In a letter we received from Katie she writes, "They are very believing in Mainz, like children at Christmas time." She means the belief in Hitler.

[. . .]

November 17, 1942

I expressed my opinion to Judge Bischoff that we have to take seriously the American and British landings in North Africa, and Bischoff replied the enemy had committed a big mistake because their supply lines were in jeopardy. Even if that were not the case, he added, final victory is still certain for us.

This was a moment where I had to keep quiet. My colleague, Delp, from Darmstadt, who knows Bischoff, cautioned me to be careful. Bischoff is an old Party member and was a regiment leader in the Hitler Youth. It is self-evident this man has to win the war.

If in a short while no German or Italian is running freely about in Africa, I want to see what the Party propaganda will say. Of course they will find a bandage for this wound. They will fight with lies and deception to the last breath. That is part of their nature. Their soul was black, is black, and will remain black even in defeat.

November 20, 1942

[. . .] As soon as the Americans and English, supported by the French colonists, control the complete coast of Africa, Italy's hour of fate will have arrived. The dream of an Italian empire by this robber state is finished. We will find out Italy is not able to mount a successful resistance.

Let us not forget the Eastern Front. The German army is engaged in all of Europe, and now it has to turn its attention to South Europe. We will have to expand into that part of France we had not needed to occupy yet. Having to support Italy is the second disadvantage of the American landing in Africa.

Plus the German army needs to initiate a holding action at the Eastern Front – if the Russians allow. If Russia is able to bring up its reserves for a concentrated attack – which I believe it will – it is possible the Eastern Front will present some surprises for us. For example, our front in the Caucasus is extremely vulnerable. Our push toward – and through – the Caucasus should have been successful; Georgia and Azerbaijan should have been conquered. But we were stuck halfway in! A definite failure! Holding onto those present positions just for reason of prestige is first-rate military insanity! Only a stubborn Führer Headquarters would do anything like that. Personally, though, this is agreeable to me. The necessary German defeats are prepared in this manner. [. . .]

Reich Field Marshal Göring, who is well-liked by many Germans because of his folksy manner of speech, gave a talk at the Berlin Sports Palace at the Thanksgiving celebration on October 4. "Who brings much will bring something to everyone," Göring said, and his listeners were ecstatic.

THE USA CANNOT IMPRESS US WITH BLUFF

[. . .] I am the last one to underestimate the American arsenal. In certain areas the Americans have technical skill, and without doubt they have production capabilities. We know they make a colossal number of automobiles, and the radio and razor blade belong to their special accomplishments. In these three areas they undoubtedly have huge success. But that is quite another thing in comparison to what is needed in a war. And even if I do not underestimate them in that regard, I know exactly what enormous difficulties must be overcome in building an arsenal. [. . .]

Never forget: America has written quite largely a word – written monstrously large – and this word is called Bluff. It was always made in the biggest way, from the president down to the nigger. (Applause from the audience.)

As for some other achievements – I do not say there are no skilled or brave American soldiers – these achievements have so far been in other areas. We know of some of their strange ambitions. Whoever can wobble on a dance floor for 72 hours with contorted limbs and a completely dumbfounded look and rolling eyes will be crowned with a prize, and whoever can throw someone else into a mud pit during a boxing and wrestling match will also be a national hero. Here they busy themselves in areas that are totally alien to us and have absolutely nothing to do with soldiering. And from such things they can hardly derive a true and genuine confidence in victory.

Göring is much mistaken. The landing in Africa is no bluff. Since the Führer always presents himself as a prophet to "his" people, Göring has to do something in this respect too. And so he predicts the future:

[. . .] Things will be better from today on because we hold the territories with fertile soil. Now it is but a question of organization. They can accuse us of anything they want – but not of poor organization. The general chaos is not with us but with them over there. (Stormy and prolonged applause.)

Source: "Aus der Einigkeit des deutschen Volkes wird des Reiches Größe und Freiheit erwachsen," HLZ, October 6, 1942, p. 3.

Thus: things will be ever better! We will wait calmly. It can be verified only in the future.

November 21, 1942

Forestry Superintendent Zimmer from Laubach, who works in the East as a forester and is presently home on vacation, said to Senior Secretary Becker: "The Russians will starve to death this winter." When Becker did not agree, Zimmer repeated his assertion with a tone of absolute conviction.

Is it not sad all these college graduates have lost their minds? Or is it they never had any?

November 22, 1942

The lack of transport ships in the American and English camps is a popular theme in the German newspapers. The writers can lie and swindle to their hearts' content, and not even one person in Germany is in a position to check their assertions. They give the U-boats credit for accomplishments they have not earned and are not in the position to earn. The U-boat commander reports the "successes"; the Navy High Command rounds the figures upwards; the propaganda ministry improves the result – and the special report is born. In the meantime the enemy uses its "sunken" ships to bring troop after troop to the war theaters. [. . .]

November 24, 1942

[. . .]

TIME AND SPACE ARE OUR ALLIES

Berlin, October 5 1942. (Wire report from our Berlin editorial staff).

[. . .] The continuation of the war for us will be less difficult than before. The reason for that lies in the circumstance that the enemy's plan to starve us out, upon which their entire plan of warfare was built, must be considered now, even by the enemy, as having finally failed. Materially the Reich is completely secured for the war's duration. Time is on our side. And also space has become an ally of Germany. The production of food and raw material in the conquered territories works against our enemies' warfare. Subsequently, it can only benefit us.

Source: "Zeit und Raum unsere Verbündeten," *HLZ*, October 6, 1942, p. 1.

It is amusing to see what these Nazi liars brew together. It can no longer be denied the war will last longer than what the "glorious Führer" surmised in 1939. Now all of a sudden "Time" is an ally for Germany. Not only time but also space – territory. As if the enemy had no territory. Every day the enemy gains more of it. Entire continents are at their disposal: America, Africa, and Australia, and not just a little space in Asia. These Nazi ninnies do not have to consider that at all, of course. "Space and time are on our side." Who dares to disagree? Method: Adolf Hitler.

Only a simpleton can assert time is on Germany's side. As for the vaunted "space," that is actually a disadvantage for Germany. The downfall comes from this stolen territory. The delusions of these Hitlerians cannot be surpassed. In their language they call them Belief, Trust, and Certainty of Victory.

November 25, 1942

DECISION [...]. The mobile and immobile possessions of the deceased Jew Maximilian Franz Israel Carlebach, born Sep. 2, 1883 in Mainz, last residence in Mainz, Ersgrubenweg 7, are seized in favor of the German Reich.
There are no laws for appeal against this decision.
Gestapo Headquarters, Darmstadt. Nov. 11, 1942. Signed: Mohr.
                                        Source: "Beschluss," *HLZ*, November 17, 1942, p. 6.

If sometime in the future the property of the National Socialist enemies of mankind is requisitioned, the executors can use the edict mentioned here as a guide.[63] It is time these Nazi sadists are stopped so the whole world can breathe a sigh of relief.

[...]

November 27, 1942

There was a rally this past Sunday in Laubach's Traube restaurant. The disingenuous speaker talked about *Freiheit, Recht und Brot*. A strange topic. I do not know what the speaker told the faithful, but there is no "liberty" or "justice" in Germany, and the "bread" is so bad people can hardly eat it. That would be all I would say about these three subjects.

"Friedel Schumann and Senior Squad Leader Trawnik can look back upon ten years as street collectors for the Winter Help Work." *Source:* "Reichsstrassensammlung," *HF-Abend*, November 23, 1942, p. 5.

The landmark of Hitler's Germany (a country of beggars) is the collection can. Many "Old Fighters" devote themselves to the activity of collecting with great enthusiasm. They must be earning something from this. Before the so-called "Seizure of Power," the Nazis characterized themselves as the noblest of idealists. After coming to power they showed themselves as the vilest materialists and egotists. The correct description of them is not National Socialists but National Egotists.

November 28, 1942

I think it is time to critically evaluate Germany's military position. What does a panoramic view show us? At the moment the German army is fighting at Stalingrad, the Caucasus, Libya, and Tunisia. The Russians have attacked us on the Eastern Front in a place that is quite dangerous, according to my view: northwest of Stalingrad. No one can make any sense out of the German army reports, so it is presently impossible to get a clear picture of the strategic situation. But it is clear our troops in the area of Stalingrad and in the Caucasus are in great danger.

The megalomania of our army command knows no limits. How can a General Staff be so imprudent as to keep launching attacks at Stalingrad and in the Caucasus when the English and American armies are approaching from the south? They have sacrificed hundreds of thousands of German soldiers these past months instead of saving every man for defense. Our front should have been radically realigned last winter. Now doom approaches with giant steps – just before another Russian winter!

[...]

November 30, 1942

The Nazi chief of the propaganda ministry publishes a "weekly maxim" [*Wochenspruch*] to which every office subscribes. [...] While paper is supposed to be saved in every nook and cranny, the Party has sole permission to waste it. If something could be achieved with this propaganda, one could condone it. These maxims are printed on high quality paper and are supposed to adorn the walls in the offices. I pick one at random:[64]

**Courageous initiative and quick action
are most often half the success**. Dr. Goebbels.

Is Dr. Goebbels's assertion really true? Yes and no. Instead of "half the success" by quick action, I believe total success by "considering before daring" is better. In this war Hitler has shown courageous initiative and quick action; however, the second half of his success is still pending.

The property of a Jew has been transferred to the German Reich (Reich Finance Authority) just on the basis of a simple requisition. A stroke of the pen is sufficient. German law! (The document is filed in my Ruppertsburg 269 folder.)

Pastor Goldmann in Laubach is a fanatical Nazi. A clergyman and the Antichrist Hitler make a strange team. Payment for the pastor's despicable attitude has to be set after the fact. The judgment should be loss of pension. That is justice.

December 1, 1942

When I asked Judge Bischoff this morning what he thought about Toulon, he gruffly responded it did not concern him, and he said he expected me to say only defeatist things about it.[65]

It is time now for me to be careful.

I have to wait until the "defeatists" have won. Then we will talk!

December 2, 1942

"I hate the Jews; they have to be eradicated. The Jews are to blame for all wars," said "Judge" Bischoff with the strongest emphasis.

Bismarck started the wars of 1864, 1866, and 1870–71. Was he also a Jew? Was Napoleon a Jew? Was Alexander the Great a Jew?

Bischoff mentioned he had belonged to the "Oberland" Freikorps brigade, which was politically close to the German Nationals. To a response from me, Bischoff said, "The Jews work consciously toward the goal of creating wars so they can make blood money from the fighting."

When I replied, "Krupp-Essen earns money from the war," the calm talking was over. He thought I had a very strange mental attitude which he had noticed frequently before.

This Bischoff is a man who was a member of a dueling fraternity, who later moved about in the German National waters and then embraced the NSDAP. His way of thinking advanced further in the Nazi "Workers'" Party. All former German Fatherland Party members, chauvinists, and anti-Semites do their damage in this hodge-podge NSDAP. Outwardly their banner reads National Socialist. Inwardly: Mean Sons of Bitches.

These people, contemptuous of human rights, nurtured to be a master race, were entrenched in heresies which they now just spout out. Will it ever be possible to cure such creatures? I believe that to be completely impossible. Only the utmost severity and pitiless hardness has to be employed. There is also a punitive and vengeful God, and we must act according to this God.

[. . .]

December 10, 1942

[. . .] From an article, "A Stab in the Heart of France," in *Das Schwarze Korps* of December 10:

The traitors and their followers not only have gambled away the colonial empire and broken their word [by scuttling the French fleet in Toulon], they not only have done things they personally thought would supposedly benefit France, they also have cut off the motherland from her most important base for living, North Africa, and in so doing made feeding the French nation a completely doubtful and difficult problem to solve.[66]

The paper admits feeding France will be a difficult problem. The whole extent of France is occupied by German troops. Therefore for the first time in this war Germany will not be able to rob others for food but will have to supply their troops from Germany.

It is easily understandable why the National Socialists are not happy with the French "traitors." However, we were elated when the German navy scuttled its own fleet in Scapa Flow in 1919. But we consider the same behavior by another country a crime. I forgot: there is no objectivity in Germany.

If there had been any men of stature in France after that country's collapse in 1940, they would have marched off in the only possible direction. To save themselves [to fight again], they should have gone to Africa! Officers, pilots, merchant ships, and warships should have hurried to Africa. That would have been the only correct thing to do. Unfortunately there were only poor creatures in the leadership. An old imbecile named Pétain. Laughable figure. [. . .]

If France wants to be saved it has to be enthusiastically on the side of England and America without any limitation. Every Frenchman who makes deals with Hitler is a common scoundrel.

Just now the old tinsmith [Friedrich] Döll, with whom caution has to be taken, came to see me. I asked him about the situation. He said with conviction, "My hope is we win this war. I do not believe we will lose it. I am completely confident and very happy about the special report yesterday about sunken ships."

Look at this, Goebbels, you have undeniable successes. The special reports do not touch me in the least, but the people believe in the U-boat successes and place all their hopes on the sinking of ships. It is the task of the Nazi propaganda and the unified press to repeatedly refresh these hopes. Someone like me has but one weapon: patience.

When a German soldier is captured, some families feel immense joy – this, despite the prevalent impression our soldiers are supposed to die with enthusiasm for their dearly loved Führer:

HANS WOELK
I want to tell all our friends and acquaintances the happy news that my dear fiancé, and a good son-in-law, a mechanic in Motorized Transport, is still alive and is a prisoner of war in a British prison camp. In immeasurable happiness, Juliane Sonntag and parents. Hamburg. 20, Lenhartzstr. 23, December 1942.

Source: HF-Abend, December 4, 1942, p. 4.

December 11, 1942

[. . .] In my character as a carper and defeatist I have been able to see more clearly than has the entire Party. Just a few days ago Judge Hornef frankly admitted he had been disappointed greatly about Russia and that, in any case, my opinion about Russia's strength was correct. If the Russians could have been fought with flim-flam, speeches, exaggerations, and lies, the war would have long been ended.

December 12, 1942

The Reich Minister of Justice published a new confidential guideline on November 5, 1942, about the number of deaths occurring in prisons.

Subject: Procedures in the event of deaths in prisons.
   It is no longer necessary to ask the next of kin about burial arrangements for anyone who dies in prison convicted of high treason, treason, or of any other crime committed for political reasons, or if they are Jews or Poles. [. . .] In cases where it is still permissible for the next of kin to be involved, burial of the corpse will still take place at the seat of the institution.

There must be a large number of mysterious deaths if such measures have to be put in place. Burial on the prison grounds is doubtless supposed to make the examination of the body more difficult.

December 14, 1942

The more stimulating and inflammatory Hitler's speeches are, the more they impress these primitive-thinking people. All his speeches are geared to the broad masses whose mental level is not high. It is great enjoyment for the savage gang whenever he mentions lots of "destruction" and "eradication." I have often heard people say with satisfaction: "Hitler has told them again."

December 15, 1942

The NS Women's League leader, Fräulein [Pauline] Fritsch, again made an effort to excel and to shine at the general public's expense. On the second day of the Christmas holiday the inhabitants of Laubach are supposed to host wounded soldiers as guests. This terrorist and Hitlerist Fritsch well knows the apportioned food rations are short, while the armed forces, on the other hand, are always well supplied. The people are therefore expected to give to the soldiers of their little food supply even though the soldiers are much better taken care of than the civilian population. By this, Fritsch is only concerned with becoming part of the inner circle and getting the War Service Medal (the prolongation-of-the-war medal)!

"Bestürzung." This is a popular word that recurs all the time. It reigns throughout the world at every occurrence. For example, "Dismay" reigns with our enemies because of Germany's success with its submarines or England's and America's diminishing ship tonnage. I have in front of me an old newspaper with an article, "Bestürzung in Neuyork." It says, "The dismay in New York over the unstoppable advance of German troops in the East becomes greater and greater."[67] There is also "Dismay in Australia over Japanese victories." On every continent Bestürzung prevails. At least this is how the newspaper reporter, sitting at his desk in his apartment in Germany, pictures it. Exaggerations and superlatives are the tools of our German press. How dumb are such machinations? How does it benefit us to keep wishing for things to happen inside our enemies' countries that are not going to happen? How often have we wished for England's destruction, their people to starve, to fall into ruin, and other beautiful things? England still lives and it will thrive. [. . .]

December 16, 1942

The striking number of children's deaths, compared to peacetime, is continuing. The following three obituaries appeared in the December 9 issue of *Hessische Landes-Zeitung*:

Hannelore Berta
Our child and good little sister, the love of our heart, at the tender age of 2 ¼ years, according to God's inexplicable decree, passed away on December 2, 1942, after a short, serious illness. [. . .]
Family Karl Palm. Darmstadt, Karlsstrasse 73.

Renatchen
3 years old, is forever asleep.
In deep anguish: Sergeant Major of the Security Police Walter Wille and wife.
Darmstadt, December 6, 1942.
Funeral: Today at 2:15 p.m. at Wald Cemetery

Wolfgang
At the age of 4 ¾, suddenly and unexpectedly our entire happiness, our beloved
and good son, was torn away.
In inexpressible anguish: Heinrich Seibel, military judge, presently in armed
forces, on leave, and wife Johanna, née Orth, and little sister Waltraud. [...]

The Eastern Front has demanded the second victim from our local population. The first was [former mayor] Högy. Now the National Socialist nurse,
Lilli Boehm (former mayor Boehm's daughter), died suddenly in
Lithuania.[68] This family supplied many enthusiastic National Socialists and
no doubt this sacrifice is gladly given for the concept "Adolf Hitler." The
deceased's half-sister is Frau [Margarethe] Desch, Party member Number #1
in Laubach. Another sister, Frau Haack, is active as a leader in the Nazi
Women's League.

For a Nazi nurse, *Weltanschauung* (world view) is especially important.
[...] The soul of a nurse has to be "aligned," as it is called in Nazi jargon. The
main task they will learn is probably how to dispatch sick and old people into
a better hereafter.

December 17, 1942

[...] Adolf Hitler is the most cunning criminal of all time. He is Satan and the
devil in one person. He is the bloodiest tyrant filled up with cruelty and
unremitting hardness. He, who seduces, inveigles, lies to, and cheats the
nation has won millions of adherents and makes them into fanatical fighters
for his heresies, which are nothing other than a conglomerate of ideas stolen
from other fanatics. He is a copier of the purest water. Nothing he brought
forth has grown on its own dung pile. Nevertheless, he enthused even
scholars and scientists.

All this is incomprehensible – but true.

Over the course of twenty years Hitler was free to do whatever he wanted.
Men, women, and children danced according to his tune. He reigned not
only in Germany. No, in all of Europe he set the tone. His whip snapped in
every country. His poison was offered everywhere in the world – and taken.
He was permitted to tear up treaties, to break the given word, to invade other

countries, to plunder and steal other people's goods – and everything received enthusiastic applause from his followers. The more fanatical and cruel he was, the higher rose the enthusiasm. The frenzy often bordered on madness.

Hitler was permitted to begin war after war, to lead millions to slaughter, and nobody hurt him. How is that to be explained?

There is just one single explanation: All this had to happen. This Hitler has risen to be a glaring example of abomination for mankind. For me he has always been what he was: a brigand, a beast!

This individual carries all of the responsibility. But we may not forget he had many helpers. Accomplices, assistants! Let us not forget those of the so-called intelligentsia who clung to Hitler's coattails and became 150-percent Nazis and who acted even more wildly than their lord and master. Also let us not forget the academics (judges, lawyers, physicians, etc.) who always behaved as the worst anti-Semites – from professional jealousy!

[...]

December 21, 1942

[...] Japan can be sure it will lose its exposed positions one after the other. It is not capable of getting transport ships to the endangered areas in a timely and practical way to provide the needed materials and troops. They will learn the difference between their sneak attacks and the coming attacks by America and England. It was no big feat to ambush the islands in the Pacific and the poorly defended areas in Asia. But to keep those areas and to defend them, that is the more difficult task. As soon as the American and English fleets are superior to Japan's in the Pacific, it will be all over for the Japanese. I have never had the least doubt the strength of the attacked nations will increase.

It appears, however, the drama in Europe will take place first. After Italy and Germany are taken care of, then God help the Japanese. And then what I told my colleague Curschmann in Mainz many years ago will be fulfilled: "After Germany, Italy, and Japan are destroyed, there will be peace on Earth." That this declaration was taken badly (as my colleague Kaster confirmed) does not change anything of its correctness. Kaster urgently warned me not to make such statements in front of former acquaintances because people had turned toward Hitlerism and they could become dangerous. I will not fail to remind Herr Chief Inspector Curschmann at the correct time. In the meantime, during this interlude, I have made notes of things that will serve to support memory.

It will soon be time to record the injustices and crimes which have occurred in the local district in order that retribution can be carried out.

Case 1: Matter of murder: Oppenheimer in Langsdorf (perpetrators in Nonnenroth and Ettingshausen).[69]

Case 2: Hussel in Ruppertsburg (persecution of Jews).

Case 3: Pogrom of Jews in Laubach (November 9, 1938).[70]

Hahn the swindler (obtained house at ridiculously low price, interest free).

Lind in Ruppertsburg (threatened ropes were on hand to hang those who voted against Hitler).

Scherdt (!) the informer. And Stotz, who teaches the population to say "Heil Hitler."

Brunner Jr. and wife (same as above).

Mönnig, the National Socialist Welfare boss, stole a rabbit that was donated for the NSV because "nobody had asked about it."

Henze walked around with his chums and installed newspaper boxes with a banner, "The Jews are our downfall."[71] (In reality the Nazis are the greatest downfall for Germany).

Reuter burned the black-red-gold flag! [Social Democratic Party flag]

Willi Rühl, the main vandal in the destruction of Jewish property.

December 22, 1942

When Ludwig Heck visited us some weeks ago as a sergeant from the Eastern Front, he was full of praise about our impregnable positions.[72] Apparently this is preached continuously to the soldiers until finally even those who should have a critical attitude toward the war – based on their face-to-face association with anti-Nazis – nevertheless believe the propaganda. When I mentioned to him the coming total collapse of our German army he was not even remotely convinced by my words.

What happened to this soldier is just as it happened to the vast majority of the German nation. Even if one like me could talk with the tongue of angels, it would not have any effect. The people are not amenable to reasonable considerations. Only when the water runs into their mouths will they realize they are close to drowning.

The German soldiers are very arrogant and underestimate their enemies!

December 25, 1942

The fourth Christmas of the war!

We received a Christmas tree through the Municipal Forestry Department. But that is all. Were it not for the three days off (Friday, Saturday, and Sunday), nobody would feel anything about "Christmas." The customary gifts are completely lacking because nothing really is available in the stores. For clothes, linens, and other articles of daily use you need either a requisition or coupon "points." In most cases, however, nothing can be bought despite the requisitions. For two months already I have been looking for a pair of slippers. But nothing! The requisition has to be renewed because it becomes invalid after two months. This is really a "great" time!

We endure all this in the knowledge that by the end of 1943 we will be free of the Hitler tyranny. We still do not suppose happy times will come. We know much is going to happen to us Germans (no matter whether we were Nazis or not). However, it is a well-deserved fate. This soothes all those who feel themselves to be free of blame. We count ourselves among those in the first line. We (my wife and I) were the fiercest opponents of the Nazi heresy and of the Party comrades. Perhaps Providence will reward us for this one day. That nothing significant has befallen us during times past and in spite of dangerous moments is proof God is on our side (on the side of the Kellner family)!

[...]

December 31, 1942

Every year Adolf Hitler has made a New Year's proclamation to the armed forces and to the Party:

December 31, 1939: "With such soldiers, Germany must win. May the year 1940 bring the decision. But whatever will happen, victory will be ours."

December 31, 1940: "Soldiers of the National Socialist armed forces of the Greater German Reich! The year 1941 will bring about the completion of the greatest victory in our history."

December 31, 1941: "1942 will have to bring the decision. We all want to ask this from the Lord God – for the saving of our people and the nations allied with us."[73]

The year 1942 is coming to its end today and the decisive victory desired by Hitler has in no way come about. Not once were we able to reach our strategic goals. Stalingrad, the Volga, and the oil in the Caucasus are still in Russian hands. The Russian offensive is in full swing, and things can happen elsewhere that may have devastating consequences.

With these prospects Germany enters into 1943.

1943

January 1, 1943

The year has begun that I repeatedly insisted would bring the end of the war. Germany was lucky in this war in a manner never known before in history. The high point in 1940 was reached with the complete conquest of France. The successes against Russia were also great, but the crowning finish is lacking. By no means is Russia conquered. In the vast reaches of Russia lies the germ for the final collapse of Germany – because the army is completely incapable of mounting the efforts required of it this year. On all fronts and in the occupied countries, flames will shoot up everywhere from embers glowing in the ashes, and this will bring about a collapse such as the world has never experienced. That is my prediction.

"I never saw anyone come to a happy end who had received the gifts of the gods constantly with full hands."[1] Alexander the Great was poisoned, Jesus was crucified, Hannibal committed suicide, Julius Caesar was murdered, and Napoleon died in captivity. Therefore why should Adolf Hitler end in happiness? It appeared God wanted to make an exception until Satan grabbed Corporal Hitler by his collar and dragged him toward ruling the entire world. But he will never reach the goal. Whoever adores power will be removed by power. Whoever gives his time to peaceful works will reap earthly happiness. Peace on Earth to those with whom He is pleased!

Adolf Hitler always wanted to fight. Now he has it in gigantic proportions. Hitler is no longer able to control this fight. It is over.

January 5, 1943

The petroleum wholesaler Otto A. Fritz from Giessen is a great barroom strategist. Such men always possess an oversized mouth. A few days ago he said to G. Becker, "Our troops are pulling back a little bit in the East, but they will regain the lost territory in the spring." It would be appropriate to put such people in the front line so every day they would be able to storm ahead and conquer.

14. Jan. 1943.

15. Jan. 1943.

N. S. D. A. P.
Kreisleitung Wetterau
Giessen
Schliessfach 139

(stamp: Nationalsoz. Deutsche Arbeiterpartei — Kreisleitung Wetterau — Gau Hessen-Nassau)

T in deutschland

G. S. Formular Nr. 4. (Muster 80, § 488.)

January 7, 1943

[. . .] For over twenty years already the poison of the Hitler heresy has dropped upon the German people's brains. For over twenty years he has preached hate and enforced the "will to power."[2] The goal of nationalizing the broad masses was reached by a brutal and fanatically one-sided focus. Objectivity and humanity were removed. Adolf Hitler and his Party trained the German people to be extreme nationalists. Fanaticism and hysteria became the pledge of the National Socialist creed. Was it not hysteria when the mass of people screamed "Hail Victory" endlessly in unison [*Sieg Heil, Sieg Heil*]? "We want to see our Führer!" "Führer, you command, we follow." "For this we thank our Führer." The masses were possessed by a fanaticism as never seen previously in the most vivid imagination. Will and power intoxicated the people. Visions of power and bragging awakened thunderous applause and standing ovations. Ruthless attacks on every adversary and the destruction of others were elevated to the most desired goals – and no voice dared to contradict them.

The National Socialist idea was elevated to a religion for the German masses. Intolerant of everything else and fanatically convinced of their own right: that is National Socialism!

January 9, 1943

Little children in a National Socialist kindergarten have to learn the follow-ing saying:

> "Fold your hands; let your head sink,
> And always on the Führer think."[3]

With time, the Lord God Number 2 will be created.

January 13, 1943

Even the specialist would be surprised at the bureaucracy's incomparable tenacity and mighty energy as it works toward any goal it has started. Regardless of whether the work has anything to do with the war situation, it primarily is to keep the bureaucrats in the rear and away from the battlefront. Many Party comrades pretend in this manner to be "indispensable." There are positions, offices, and command posts that make the already bloated official apparatus completely incomprehensible to the layman. The offices remain stubbornly in existence for their own purposes, become bigger, and can no longer be shut down.

The SS is especially masterful in creating new posts and subsidiary posts. This is mainly for political reasons to strengthen the inner front. Yesterday I came across two SS members (of military age) who were not on the front but worked here for the railroad. Within the SS organization is a sub-office called Reich Commissioner to Strengthen German National Characteristics. Its directives are truly a laugh. [...] This agency deals with the establishment of German farms in the annexed Eastern territories, Styria and Carniola, and in Alsace and Lorraine. Everybody knows this war is in no way finished; even the most optimistic Party member cannot say how peace will look someday. Yet they occupy themselves with the settlement of Germans in territories that do not yet belong to Germany in any way. The pelt is being distributed before the deer has been shot. This is National Socialist planning![4]

[...]

January 15, 1943

District Leader Backhaus in Giessen (a former post office official from Hamburg) asked the judicial office for a list of people who had left their Church. The Party once again works for the emptying of churches. Those who have some kind of an official position are under a lot of pressure. Yesterday Area Farm Leader Metzger from Röthges had me notarize his declaration of withdrawal from the Church.

In fact National Socialism and Christendom are completely incompatible. Because of their international position, the churches are hated by the Nazis. Anybody may go to church, as he wants to, but I myself do not belong to any church; therefore I can express my neutral opinion as an outsider.[5] I do agree with Christian moral teachings. But according to my opinion it is not necessary to belong to a church that uses power politics. I left the Evangelical Church because it and a great many of their ministers behaved un-Christianly during the war years of 1914–18. Both in word and writing they constantly called for a peace by force [continuing the war for better surrender terms], and they did that in the leading Christian circles. Also in this war you can observe the Church in Germany does not take a position about the terrible atrocities committed against the Jews.[6]

Unfortunately Christianity has not been able to educate people about peace or about restraining the wildest instincts; but it still has to be recognized Christianity brings about much grace for the individual. It brings consolation and strength in the time of need and affliction. At any rate Christianity should have never been fought officially the way the Nazis like to do it, in the manner of assassination. In the future we must have freedom for religious philosophy. The state has to act with an informed wisdom and uncompromised morality. If a nation respects the laws of morality internally and externally, the citizens will restrain their animal instincts.

January 18, 1943

[. . .] Since mid-1942 the Russian army leadership has been very good. The offensive actions since November are excellent and could not be better. Has it ever happened in the annals of war that the siege army (near Stalingrad) is itself put to siege and disappears from the earth?[7] The Russians brought this about in the fight against the Sixth German Army. In general, Stalingrad will remain a glorious chapter in Russian history.

The stubborn German highest-in-command, Adolf Hitler, is fixed like one possessed to the points reached: a victim of prestige. If the Russians can maintain their strength of advance for some time longer (which I do not doubt they can) there will be a dramatic turn in the theater of war in Russia. Hitler believed he made a mistake last winter trying to supply the army across far distances to the front. This time he wanted to be smarter, so he moved supply depots close to the fighting troops. When the Russians advanced, these depots fell immediately into their hands. This loss can never be made up. Russia is continuously supported by America and England and now is enormously ahead of the game.

Hitler does not dare tell the truth to the German nation, even approximately. A few days ago, for the first time, the army reports said the German army at Stalingrad is under attack "from all sides."[8] That the German army has been encircled is still not being told. This is more than stupid. Someday the truth will come to the light of day.

How these Nazis fight for their stay of execution!

January 19, 1943

The "Old Fighter" Heinrich Haack's wife is still convinced we will take Stalingrad in the spring. She said that to Alice Schmidt. These political wives are thrilled when we are "taking," and they do not even ask themselves whether the husbands, who are in Stalingrad, get hurt. Frau Haack will be surprised when she finds out the truth, which is, "Stalingrad is Russian and will remain Russian." [. . .]

January 20, 1943

Party member Scherdt told Heinrich Becker: "After the war, those who have not participated can expect something." This Nazi terrorist has a towering rage against non-Party members who manage to achieve things for themselves. This imbecile has us especially close to his heart. He makes no secret of his hateful feelings. He does not greet my wife at all; he ignores me unless he has to come in contact with me on an official basis.[9] The enthusiasm of this late-blooming National Socialist comes from attending a Party Congress in Nuremberg, from which he returned as a completely converted man. The events, the pomp, and the Party glamour had made a deep impression on him. Anyone who had gone to the rally and seen what was there, said Scherdt, would have been equally convinced. His example easily shows why the Party rallies are put up with extraordinary care. The objective justifies the means. The simple Party comrade is overwhelmed by the splendor of flags, the martial entrance of the different factions (the SA, the SS, the National Socialist Motor Corps NSKK, Hitler Youth, and so forth), the drama, and the many speeches. The outward show, expressing the strengths and power of National Socialism, has to replace the internal emptiness. The soul of the silly attendant Scherdt was not the only one caught in this manner; no, many intellectuals also became victims of the glamorous spectacle. What parades are for the military, Party rallies are for the NSDAP. For those who cannot be there for the presentations, the press steps in as a consoling force. Their colorful overly exaggerated feature articles bring those who had to stay at home a replacement in words. That of course increases the longing to actually be at a rally someday.

[. . .]

January 28, 1943

Hilde Conrad says the German troops in Stalingrad are to blame for their defeat. This Nazi wife will shift the blame to the soldiers. The Führer, of course, is infallible and untouchable.

Who commanded the troops to hold on and refused to order them out of the Stalingrad area in time? The Supreme Commander. His pride was the reason for the senseless sacrifice of twenty encircled divisions. On September 30, 1942, Hitler said to stormy and turbulent applause from his listeners at the Sports Palace, "We will take Stalingrad; you can count on it . . . The city of Stalingrad itself in particular will be occupied, and you can be convinced no man shall move away from this place."[10]

Only because Hitler wanted to take possession of Stalingrad and hold onto it, hundreds of thousands of soldiers were driven to their deaths. The Russians cared nothing for Hitler's bluster; despite the assertions of Supreme Commander Hitler, they threw the German troops out of Stalingrad and its surroundings.

NOW MORE THAN EVER!

[...] The homeland will never know the likes of the heroic behavior of the fighters at Stalingrad. We can offer our unbounded gratitude for this immense debt we owe to every single fighter at Stalingrad, and that is but a weak repayment; we promise that come what may, be it the hardest of difficulties, we shall defy all strokes of fate, unbowed before all tribulations that remain ahead of us. The name Stalingrad should, must, and will pull us upward if destiny and the war's changing circumstances bring dark and dangerous hours. And the name of Stalingrad from now on will be connected to the phrase, "Now more than ever!" The real total war that begins for us right now encompasses the last man and last woman in all their activities. More than ever right now there is but one thing: victory, for which the heroes of Stalingrad fought, suffered, and died!

Source: "Nun erst recht!" *HLZ*, January 27, 1943, p. 1.

Stalingrad has been sacrificed for nothing, and these heroic songs change nothing at all about that. It makes no sense to have twenty divisions destroyed in order to praise the heroism of German soldiers. What was done in and around Stalingrad was a useless waste of human lives and can only be called madness. When it was known in the fall of 1942 that the strategic goal of surrounding the Russian army in Stalingrad could not be reached, there was just one sensible decision: abandon the dangerous position.

Now the dance begins! The Stalingrad drama will not help to do away with the incapable German leadership. Whoever thought otherwise does not know the Nazis. Now the real Total War begins, as the reporters in the newspapers proclaim. I had been thinking the total war actually began in 1939. But that must have been a mistake. The NSDAP leaders are completely beside themselves trying to cope with the Russian successes, not knowing up from down. All the newspaper scribblers, barroom strategists, and speakers have been mobilized to bring by word and by writing the German nation's will to fight at full blast. [...]

January 29, 1943

Stalingrad has broken all records when it comes to the German soldiers' slavish obedience in going to their own annihilation. No nation in the whole world would submit to such an insane order as Hitler gave his troops before Stalingrad: Hold out, even in the lost positions.

Similar things are happening within the civilian population. Males from 16 to 65 and females from 17 to 45 are being mobilized for the war machine. Here also is blind obedience to the last breath. Even before this, every healthy person was somehow utilized. This last effort is supposed to protect the Nazis from the accusation of not having tried everything. Even if an army could still be scratched together from all the different institutions, this would in no way change our catastrophic situation. By the time this reserve force can be put together, the army's losses will have again increased in such a way these freshly drafted men would barely fill in the gaps instead of increasing the numbers. [...]

This winter, the Russians are attacking on the entire Eastern Front and are causing the whole front to move. It is possible a catastrophe will develop for the Germans if the Red Army maintains sufficient momentum for the next few weeks. I believe the worst threat to the German positions in the Ukraine is in the Voronezh area. From the upper Don to the middle of the Dnieper there is a distance of 400–500 kilometers to overcome. But the Russians have a firm hold of the upper and middle Don area and are already approaching the Donets River in a wide front. Furthermore the Russians can use the majority of their Stalingrad troops to relieve the Ukraine, and they have to march only about 300–400 kilometers.

The German Supreme Command committed the fateful mistake of clinging everywhere instead of a timely retreat to suitable positions and securing sufficient reserves for operative actions; now it is impossible in the middle of winter and under enemy threat. The loss of men and material cannot be made up overnight.

[...]

February 1, 1943

Frau [Bertha] Döll, the headmaster's wife, cannot understand why other nations are against us since we only wanted to bring about good (!) things. Such idiocy is much more widespread than one would assume. The majority of the German people have neither intelligence nor any feeling for justice.

February 2, 1943

The battle in and around Stalingrad found its end today at 4 o'clock. The drama is over! The Sixth Army under General Field Marshal Paulus no longer exists. More than 300,000 men are dead or in captivity.

Hitler demanded the troops sacrifice themselves to the last man. Of the "one hundred percent" generals, twenty-four of them preferred to walk alive into a Russian prisoner-of-war camp. A hero's death is just for the stupid.

The German army under the "the most brilliant commander of all time" (as Hitler was called after the victory over France), has suffered the greatest defeat of all time. Why? Because the "brilliant commander" had not the faintest idea of real strategy. On account of his ego he desperately wanted to hold the positions in and around Stalingrad with everything possible. On Sep. 30, 1942, in the Berlin Sports Palace, he had boastfully announced to the world, "We will take Stalingrad and no man will ever move us from this place." For that, hundreds of thousands were fanatically and senselessly sacrificed. "We" will take is what this fool screamed, but he and the other screamers remained quietly in the rear.

Now the bosses and the propagandists are filled with bluster, attempting with arrogant tirades to cover up the shame called "Stalingrad" and to rouse up the dim-witted population again to use their last strength for more production.

DEAR FELLOW COUNTRYMEN!

The Total War and You

[...] Total War calls out: mobilize all your forces, direct the last man and woman toward the needs of war. Now we all have to do only what serves the hard and relentless fight; and we all must set aside everything – and be this even in the smallest things of everyday life – that hinders the will to fight and the decision for victory by the individual and the entire population. There is no other choice: either victory or downfall, freedom or Bolshevism, a break-through into a shining future or a plunge into a dark void. The heroic struggle of our soldiers at Stalingrad stands before us as a shining beacon and a compelling reminder to the German homeland and European world. [...] Today the power of our hearts, minds, and fists, the entire resolute determination, blazing anger, and unflinching readiness of our people must serve but one major purpose: total war at the front and in the homeland until the enemy is put down forever.

Source: "Lieber Volksgenosse," HLZ, January 28,1943, p. 3.

[...]

Total war! The conscription of the entire nation! The irreversible last hope. This helps nothing. Patchwork, that's all. What Goebbels once shouted about

America's help for England excellently fits all the measures being taken in the face of the bad situation on the Eastern Front. We are "too late." We cannot face the victorious Russian army with improvisations. The Russians are being led excellently, and such leadership will not be shaken by our relief measures.

I will not dispute many German men still at home could be sent to the front. But men alone are not sufficient. The quality of these emergency fighters leaves much to be desired in this fourth year of war. The soldier needs weapons – and more weapons. During the past two months the German army lost enormous amounts of war material. The remaining material undergoes great abuse in a retreat at this time of year. The soldiers' uniforms and shoes become damaged and cannot be replaced in large quantities. Whoever considers all these matters will be convinced, as I am, Germany's situation begins to change into a disaster.

[. . .]

February 8, 1943

In order to strengthen and renew the sinking courage and the confidence in victory, the press and the Party are putting forth desperate efforts. Planned assemblies, rallies, and training sessions are supposed to help to attain final victory. [. . .]

Yesterday the local area head officials were called to Hungen in order to receive the "last rites." The local area speaker was there, as well as the veterinarian Dr. Erb from Lech, and also Mine Inspector Carl Dietrich from Lardenbach, who is the training director. As I was told, the area speaker was not distressed at all and gushed about victories on all fronts. Dr. Erb is supposed to have spoken more soberly and talked about the importance of unifying our efforts. To him it was most important to maintain the population's morale. He asked the audience to watch for those trying to diminish the good morale by rumors or defeatist talk. One should then get an irreproachable witness and call the Gestapo! All Party members have this point of view: it concerns "To be or not to be" and therefore "We" have to be victorious. This is really understandable when they have conscripted themselves so sincerely to the Party. [. . .]

In my character as a defeatist I should point out there is no great longing within the ranks of officials and Party bosses to place themselves at the Eastern Front. They talk about war effort and remain serenely where they are. They should be made to set a good example. I mean it: an entire army made up of Party comrades, fireside warriors, traveling speakers, officials, journalists, and propagandists could be assembled. The Party and its factions are not necessary for everyday living. In the past, wars were led without these groups. Please gentlemen, up to the front!

(My call remains without result.)

FRATERNIZATION WITH A PRISONER OF WAR

Else Wingert, 22, of Darmstadt, wife of an army member, has fraternized in a particularly serious manner at her place of employment with a French prisoner of war. And in the course of these shameless and ignoble relationships she has for a time even supported him in attempts to escape. The Special Court in Darmstadt gave the perpetrator of this crime one year and five months in the penitentiary.[11]

February 12, 1943

"We will take Stalingrad again," said the wife of farmer Diehl in Ruppertsburg to her brother August Högy. The terrible losses the German army suffered in Stalingrad make no impression whatsoever on this peasant. I would know a good remedy to quiet these reconquest fanatics. Everyone who wants to retake the territories the German army relinquished should immediately be given a weapon and sent to the Eastern Front. It is not impressive to leave the conquering to others. A person should do everything for himself.

[. . .]

February 15, 1943

[. . .]

An article appeared in the South German edition of *Völkischer Beobachter* on February 6: "Bridgehead Tunisia," by Lieutenant Colonel A. von Olberg. He makes a huge effort to depict Rommel's retreat as strategic, and he is enthusiastic about the bridgehead Tunisia. I am placing here the conclusion of this article.

All of Tunisia is now quite strong and well secured, with well-equipped troops, providing a large bridgehead on the Mediterranean Sea, effectively extending the maritime strategy triangle to the south. This overall position is able to serve as a support for all military tasks which may fall to the Southern

Front of the Axis in times to come. It not only separates the Mediterranean into two parts, it pushes itself as a barrier between the direct ocean connections for the army of Montgomery and secures the total European southern flank. Therefore it also prevents every possibility of an enemy landing in Italy.

Source: "Brückenkopf Tunis," *VB-Süd*, February 6, 1943, p. 3.

This bridgehead is no match for a concentrated air attack. I assume the enemy has delayed a landing in Europe only until they remove the bridgehead. When they have taken care of the supply situation, the landing will commence.

February 16, 1943

The merchant Reiss from Breitenbach feels it his duty as a Party member to educate his customers politically. A few days ago in his outlet in Laubach he said, "We have to win the war, and we will win it. This year is the year of decision. It will be a difficult year. This year we have to be done with Russia. As enemies, England and America are not difficult. England has to import seventy-five percent of its food and we will completely cut them off. It is self-evident America will then retire to its own continent."

These are the current views of a Party member who belongs in a mental institution.

February 18, 1943

"VICTORY AT ANY PRICE"

Presentation by the Reich Speaker in the District of Wetterau

[...] Prince zu Schaumburg-Lippe will speak in Giessen on February 20 at 8 p.m. in the university auditorium. The entire population today more than ever has the need to become informed about the current situation from the mouths of chosen officials. Therefore no one must fail to attend the meetings.

Source: Oberhessische Tageszeitung, February 11, 1943, p. 3.

The Regional Speakers, Work Effort Speakers, and other Reich speakers traverse the country as emissaries of Adolf Hitler to serve the people mush concocted by Joseph Goebbels. Did the ancient Germanic tribes have speakers too? Or did they show themselves more as fighters with weapons? [...] Reich Speaker Prince zu Schaumburg-Lippe has a bullet-proof post. Better to speak for Hitler than to die for him, thinks this prince. But the accounting is approaching. It would have been smarter if the prince had kept quiet at this point in time. In his role as an accomplice, he will be held to account just as much as the other perpetrators, abettors, confederates, and helpers.[12] Everyone who has knowingly helped is responsible for the Third Reich's deeds.

February 19, 1943

Reich Minister Dr. Goebbels was let loose upon the public on February 18 in the Berlin Sports Palace to justify conducting total warfare. [...] At the close of his speech Goebbels said, "Now we have to come to the decision to subjugate everything else to the war. This is the demand of the hour. And therefore the watchword is, 'Now nation arise and storm break loose!'"[13] According to the newspaper report, the minister's last words were drowned by never-ending applause.

   "Now nation arise!" That would be the correct thing to do. Not to prolong the war but to immediately bring this insane war to an end.

[...]

March 9, 1943

Starting tomorrow, March 10, I have the honor and the unlikely pleasure of working three days per week at the judicial office in Altenstadt (on the Frankfurt–Lauterbach railway line). My notes will become sparser because without doubt my time initially will be limited. The war has found its way to me. Quite undeserved. Did anyone ask?[14]

[...]

April 13, 1943

On April 12 Führer Headquarters reported our troops withdrew from the Tunisian cities Sfax and Kairouan "in keeping with planned movements."[15] Our inventive National Socialists are wonderful at euphemisms. For what is really a retreat they use a little bit of imagination and offer us "planned movement." On the other hand, if our enemy is in retreat, Goebbels's trumpets blow a never-ending victory fanfare. We Germans, however, break off from the enemy solely "under the pressure of the enemy's larger forces" – and we are able to do that, naturally, without the enemy noticing. We are such daredevils! [. . .]

April 14, 1943

DEATH PENALTY FOR A RADIO CRIMINAL

Vienna, April 12, 1943.

Oskar Uebel, 47, of Vienna, was sentenced by the Special Court in Vienna to ten years in prison for radio crimes. The senior Reich prosecutor threw out the verdict and returned the case to the Special Court. In its new judgment the Special Court determined Uebel listened continuously to enemy radio broadcasts in his apartment with several young people on thirty to forty occasions and then discussed with them, in a manner detrimental to Germany, what they heard. He compiled and distributed the information. The Special Court considered it an especially severe case in the sense of Paragraph 2 of the orders concerning radio broadcasts which carries the death penalty. Therefore he was sentenced to death. The sentence has already been carried out.

Source: "Todesstrafe für Rundfunkverbrecher," *HLZ*, April 13, 1943, p. 2.

Ten years in prison for a "radio crime"! But that was not punishment enough for the senior Reich prosecutor, who did not rest until he found a court that would give the death sentence.[16] Just think: the death penalty for listening to a foreign broadcast! It is inconceivable any other country in the world would give out such a punishment for listening to a German broadcast. This terror regime has given itself a gruesome monument into the distant future.[17]

Will there not be retribution, Herr Reich Prosecutor?

April 25, 1943

The "Atlantic Wall" is presently a favorite topic in the press and on the radio for rousing the people.[18] The philistines are told they can feel completely secure in Fortress Europe. "The impenetrable and unconquerable wall of concrete and iron" reaching from the North Cape to the Spanish border is presented to the astounded Europeans in words and pictures and has approximately the same ranking as the Maginot Line had for a sleeping France – which believed it was safe because of it. The Mareth Line in southeastern Tunisia was also presented as impregnable, and in a few days it was in the possession of the English.

Aufn.: O.T.-Kriegsberichterstaffel (Sch)

VÖLKISCHER BEOBACHTER

16. 4. 1943.

Atlantik-wall

Ragende Burgen
aus Stahl und Beton

Unüberwindliche
Abwehrfront vom Mittelmeer
bis zum Nordkap

*

Die Batterie Todt, eine der Fernkampfbatterien, die am Atlantikwall von der OT. erbaut wurden.
PK.-Aufn.: OT.-Kriegsberichter Maier (PBZ)

Freitag, 16. April 1943 * Nr. 106 * Seite 6

In ununterbrochener Folge ziehen sich an der Atlantikküste die von den Männern der Organisation Todt in rastloser Arbeit geschaffenen Befestigungsanlagen und Verteidigungsworke entlang und machen sie zu einer für jeden Feind unangreifbaren Festung. Eine der zahlreichen Fernkampfbatterien am Atlantikwall

The exact same media that convinced us the Maginot Line could not help the French now tells us miraculous things about the Atlantic Wall. Not only does it contradict all military rules to reveal military installations to unauthorized people, but it is embarrassingly dumb to suppose such tactics will frighten and worry our opponents.

Even as a temporary measure, there is nothing simple about transforming even a small space into a fortification of unconquerable proportions. No reasonable person would believe a "fortification" – or even a line of defense resembling a fortification – could be erected along the thousands of kilometers of the Atlantic coast. Such a fabulous "fortification" is merely a sham of false facts. Or using a modern expression: a bluff. Nothing changes this truth even if certain "neutral" gentlemen are invited to this wonderful Atlantic Wall to inspect various sections of it. This theater is completely unnecessary. Everybody knows the German army administration has been erecting modern fortifications at many strategic points since 1940. Every child on the other side knows this too. Therefore the enemy will not look to make his landing at the most strongly defended coastal positions. At one time a German General Staff believed they could overlook this rule, and they brought about the 1916 tragedy of Verdun.[19] The English are not so inclined to do away with established military laws. Up to now they have not attacked because they were not ready with their preparations – and because we Germans have not been softened up enough yet.

I have no doubt at all that somewhere on our incredibly far-reaching battle lines there will be an attack on the European continent and it will succeed. Germany cannot be stronger everywhere than the attacker. [. . .]

At all times and in all countries it was forbidden to record fortification installations. We, the invincible Germans, take the liberty of showing photographs of our fortifications (even in the middle of a war) in order to scare the enemy.[20]

April 26, 1943

[. . .]

On the Führer's birthday [April 20], the "commitment of youth" takes place everywhere in the Reich. Boys and girls ten years old are initiated in the Hitler Youth on this day with corresponding pomp and circumstance. The military career of Germans begins at age ten. The children do not know much about the "power" and the "honor" of Germany at this age, but at least they get a uniform. At ten they feel the breath of militarism and are not released from its claws until the mass grave.

THE MOST RECENT AGE GROUP

[. . .] A word from the Führer to the boys and girls reminds us a Germany of power, honor, order, and loyalty can exist only if the boys and girls practice and live these virtues of the Reich, that the greatness of our Reich has its roots in the discipline of our youth, and the youth must fulfill the Führer's wishes and expectations for the future of Germany. The Reich Youth Leader also offers a personal message to the incoming ten-year-olds that is repeated throughout the muster areas by the training leaders.

The sword pledge for the young boys (*Jungvolk*) is this:

"Pimpfe are hard, quiet, and faithful. Pimpfe are comrades!
To the Pimpfe, honor is above all!"

And the girls repeat their guiding principles:

"Jungmädel, be comrades, be faithful, obedient, brave, and tight-lipped!
Jungmädel, take care of your honor!"

The enrollment of the ten-year-olds will conclude with handshakes during the roll call. This solemn occasion ends with a chorus or communal singing of "Now carry the drum before us."

Source: "Der jüngste Lehrgang," VB-Süd, April 18, 1943, p. 3.

[. . .]

May 11, 1943

The *Völkischer Beobachter* of May 10, 1943, omits things about the battle in Tunisia. Naturally, the writer says the Axis troops covered themselves with the highest glory. The Nazi press knows its readers; otherwise they could not print such bullshit. "The Axis troops continue the task of engaging large numbers of opposing battle forces," babbles this newspaper idiot. A strange assignment [for the troops].[21] A much smaller fighting force would have been sufficient for such a tactic. But bridgehead Tunis was defended with large German forces. There were even heavy losses of ships. Having 200,000 men in Tunisia proves the Germans considered the area very important militarily. The English and American victory there has decisive importance for the overall situation, particularly as they now can travel securely in the Mediterranean along the African coast. North Africa in enemy hands represents a major threat to Italy and the entire Southern Front in general. [. . .]

May 23, 1943

ENEMY AIRCRAFT SHOT DOWN

The civilian population around the German Bight suffered losses during the enemy's daytime air raid. Greater damage was done to the municipal areas of Wilhelmshaven and Emden. German fighter planes and navy flak guns shot down 17 attacking four-engine bombers. Two German fighters were lost in dogfights. Four enemy aircraft were destroyed at Einflügen in the occupied western region.

Source: "35 Feindflugzeuge abgeschossen," *VB-Süd*, May 23, 1943, p. 2.

Yesterday the Supreme Command publicized daytime air raids on Germany. They say great damage has resulted. The time of "small property damage" appears to belong to the past. When the English began with their nighttime attacks, the newspapers made snide remarks about night pirates and cowardly pilots afraid of daylight. I am sure the daytime attacks will not suit these same people any better.

THE COASTAL REGION OF ATTU PURGED

Tokyo, May 22, 1943.

Major-General Nakao Yahagi, Imperial Headquarters press department spokesman, explained that the Japanese troops on the island of Attu are offering a determined resistance to numerically superior American troops, whose numbers are still increasing. His opening remarks were that the enemy began landing their tanks and other heavy weapons on May 16. Yahagi further stated the Japanese troops are in the process of purging the enemy from the coastal landing area, and there are no more hostile troops there.

    The enemy force consisted of a division, with tanks and heavy guns, supported by strong naval and air units. Yahagi added that the Japanese armed forces have inflicted heavy losses on the enemy despite intense bombardments by planes and artillery.

Source: "Das Küstengebiet von Attu gesäubert," *VB-Süd*, May 23, 1943, p. 1.

Lying is the order of the day during a war, even though no war has ever been won by it. I see the Japanese as excellent swindlers. What these yellow gangsters bring forth exceeds our European power of imagination. Perhaps lying is a noble virtue in Asia. I do not know. This newspaper article shows how the Imperial Japanese Headquarters does it. They assert on May 22 the Japanese troops are busy with the cleanup of a section of Attu [of the Aleutian Islands] and no more enemies are present. Every reader here gets the idea American landing attempts there have failed. But one week later the same headquarters uses an abundance of phrases to give us a different reality. With a lot of self-flattery and cheap heroic songs, they inform the listening world Japanese troops are no longer present on Attu. There might be insane Japanese who become intoxicated with the thought the Battle of Attu will be "written in gold letters in the history book of Japanese warfare." For me, however, it is a sober fact the Americans have driven out the Japanese.[22] Japan will experience still many more unsavory events of this kind. [. . .]

The collapse of France in 1940 was a real puzzle for many people throughout the world. Probably just as many today cannot understand the behavior of Pétain, Laval, and their consorts.[23] Germany attacked, robbed, plundered, and fully occupied France. In spite of that there are still Frenchmen completely on the side of Hitler. The German foreign minister has thanked the French Admiral Esteva for using his position as French Resident-General of Tunisia for "facilitating the conduct of the war for the Axis powers."[24] That is a kind of fame, Monsieur Esteva, of a sad nature. We see the same mind-set in France that infected the German army and navy in the Weimar Republic: democracies doing unusually little for their own safety. Where were the democratic generals and officers? Nowhere to be seen! This iniquity has found a hard and bitter punishment. Weak democracies like these produce demagogues like Mussolini and Hitler. Will the German people learn something from this?

[. . .]

June 11, 1943

The German nation was consoled for the lost battle at Stalingrad with promises of a spring offensive. These consolers are never embarrassed to use a con man's technique of infinite promises to strengthen over-rated expectations in single-minded optimists. We see their suggestions every day in the newspapers that people need to have only a strong attitude to gain victory. Here are headlines from the *Hessische Landes-Zeitung* of June 6–9:

OUR PRODUCTION IN ARMAMENT IS GIGANTIC! WE ARE INVINCIBLE
[. . .]
HOLD YOUR BREATH DURING THE LAST QUARTER HOUR!
GERMANY'S CERTAINTY IN VICTORY RESTS ON VERY SOLID BASIS
WE ARE SUPERIOR TO THE ENEMY IN THE WAR OF NERVES [. . .]

This is how the German people are worked over. Unless the people subject these daily effusions to a rational critique, they will be filled with an indestructible faith in ultimate victory. [. . .]

The headlines in the June 10 *Hessische Landes-Zeitung* declare: "Pantelleria and Lampedusa are Showing a Tough Resistance. A Damper for Anglo-American Invasion Fever." [...]

The Pantelleria and Lampedusa islands will be in English and American hands in the shortest time. That is crystal clear. Italy's desperate situation is not going to change because the Germans engaged some enemy reconnaissance patrol on the island of Lampedusa in some puffed up "action."

THE PROUDEST ANSWER

Rome, June 10, 1943.

The American General Spaatz's demand to the occupiers of the fortified island of Pantelleria to surrender remains unanswered. Pantelleria fights on despite coming under no fewer than five sea-to-shore artillery bombardments since May 9, and more than 140 air attacks. The attacks have increased to an average of 12 per day and 9 attacks per night. Although these attacks caused much damage, the strong coastal defense against the most recent attack has clearly shown they are in no way defeated. The Italian High Command reports 15 aircraft were shot down on Tuesday, bringing the total to 116 these past months.

June 12, 1943

"Yesterday on their proud horse, and today shot through the chest."[25] One can rightly say that about the island fortification of Pantelleria. Despite the scribbling of Nazi and Fascist writers, the enemy now sits on this island. The thirst for glory, the Nazis' conceit, and their blustering words are weak fortifications for defense. It is but a small leap now to Sicily and to Italy. I have no doubt Italy is lost. It is not defensible at all and is collapsing in every respect: economically, politically, and militarily. [. . .]

The Fascists of all countries are similar: birds of a feather and stubborn as goats. What they have in their heads cannot be dislodged. The German press chief made a fool of himself in October 1942 with his assertion the Allies would not have enough ship transports for a large military operation. A few days into the following month, the English and Americans landed in North Africa. What should it mean today if an idiot on a Spanish newspaper asserts there are no Allied ships available for a large-style invasion? The Falangists, Fascists, and National Socialists are naturally hoping and wishing an invasion of Europe is impossible "because of a lack of shipping capacity." It is always the same song: underestimate the enemy.

Quiet down, you Fascists: the Allies have all the ships needed for an invasion! [. . .]

June 14, 1943

We now have the themes for heroic songs and cheap heroic stories: "The last bullet," "the last radio transmission," and "the last grenade."

THE LAST RADIO TRANSMISSION

Berlin, May 15, 1943.

The heroic struggle to the last bullet of the German troops on African soil can be seen in a large number of combat reports and also in many short radio transmissions. The German and Italian people and their friends greet in profound comradeship these heroic soldiers who have given the world an example of self-sacrifice, perseverance and an ardent love for the homeland. Even the opponents, who finally were able to overcome the Axis at the African front through an enormous array of manpower and weapons, and with enormous losses to themselves, must recognize the German-Italian forces' bravery.

Even the last radio messages of trapped German units expressed unbowed fighting spirits and their unbreakable ties with the homeland. Such was radioed by the commander of the airport area east of Tunis in the early morning hours of May 13: "Yesterday we had two enemy attacks, damaged ten tanks, and captured ten prisoners. We will hold until the ammunition runs out. We have a good position and hope to be the last ones remaining. You will receive ongoing messages until this transmitter no longer works. We send our most heartfelt congratulations and greetings to our mothers and wives for Mother's Day on May 16 from Africa." A short time later this brave combat troop signed off with this final radio transmission: "Long live the Führer, long live our homeland!"

Source: "Der letzte Funkspruch," *HF-Morgen*, May 16, 1943, p. 1.

[...]

Any halfway reasonable person can see German troops in Africa are in a lost position. If Italy with its almost fifty million citizens cannot success-fully defend its stolen territory, Germany should not make any major effort in this adventure. The irrational ambition of Mussolini and his collaborators has suffered its deserved defeat. We can only hope it is so complete and final the Italians will be stopped forever in their larcenous handiwork. [...]

MURDERS IN FRANCE

Paris, May 17, 1943.

On Sunday, Mayor Raymond Dirr of Perrefitte was murdered. He was waiting at the bus stop when a car with two young men came to a halt in front of him. One jumped out and fired two shots at the mayor. The perpetrators in the car had been waiting for Dirr on a side street and then carried out their obviously long-planned attack as the surprised mayor, who had no sense of the impend-ing danger, read his newspaper. They escaped undetected.

On Friday the medical doctor Michel Guerin was stabbed in Portier. He had been called by someone unknown by him to treat a sick person. When he went through the door, four men set upon him with knives and injured him so badly he passed away on Saturday.

The two victims were active members of the Doriot Party that has many goals in common with the German Nazi Party they emulate. These two crimes show the ruthlessness of those foreigners coming from revolutionary circles. [...]

Source: "Morde in Frankreich," *HF-Abend*, May 17, 1943, p. 2.

The Doriot political party members are getting a foretaste of what is going to happen to them when their patron saint Hitler has disappeared from France.[26] France has never sunk so low as it is under the regime of Pétain–Laval and Company. One can never find a Frenchman who worked more intimately with the NSDAP.

A little character might have been shown at least after the collapse, but scoundrels do not have character. Laval and cohorts believed in the victory of Hitler and wanted to receive from his hand gratitude for their subservience and collaboration. What do such individuals care about their homeland? Money is the only determining factor. Settling accounts with these vile creatures must be radical. None of them may remain.

The Italian army report of June 12 rejoices Lampedusa Island is still resisting. The report literally states, "The enemy conducted renewed and strong attacks from the air and from the sea against the small contingent in Lampedusa that refused the demand for surrender and showed heroic resistance."[27] We know from experience when it comes to the Italians that their reports of "heroic resistance" take place shortly before the surrender. Why should it not be the same in this case? Without convolutions there is nothing.

June 16, 1943

Two men I did not know were sitting with me at the table in the Stockheim waiting room talking about enemy casualties. They believed the enemies' losses, especially of English pilots, would have to become burdensome soon. One believed measures would be undertaken against England, and when we occupied it, peace would prevail. It is downright torture to sit there and hear such wisdom and have to be quiet instead of offering enlightenment. [...]

June 17, 1943

Dr. Goebbels inspected the damaged areas in Essen and spoke at a meeting of the Party leadership.[28] His focus was on the air war. He admitted the air raids were both a material and psychological burden for the German people. He promised what the population had to suffer would be forgotten soon after the war. New streets and new city layouts would rise from the ruins. The English were only temporarily in a better situation than we were, he said. Their attacks would be able to do considerable but not decisive damage. Our submarine warfare had them by the throat. Here the English can be hurt in a fatal way. After a certain time the U-boats' damage to the English would have long-lasting material effect. But everything is based on our nation being able to keep up its morale – which the recent situation requires during the English air war. [...]

Dr. Goebbels thus comforts residents in the heavily damaged areas. What they have experienced will be forgotten soon after the war (about the same way they will forget the Nazis' many promises). He also uses the submarine warfare to soothe them. But he makes success contingent on the German people quietly letting the air raids happen while keeping their good attitude. The main thing is Attitude and Readiness, even if the entire Ruhr area is destroyed: Ready to die for Goebbels and consorts!

June 18, 1943

The glorifiers of the war are silent about the shady side of wartime. It is therefore necessary to concern myself with what the people are doing.

Kassel, June 15, 1943.

Two unfaithful German wives, ages 34 and 40, had invited two young foreign laborers to their apartment. When they made coffee they apparently forgot to close the gas jets. The next morning other people in the building smelled the strong odor of gas. When they broke down the door, they found all four people poisoned by gas. Three could not be saved. Only a 19-year-old Belgian escaped with his life.

The much-admired German women have miserably failed. The poet should be a little bit more careful and not sing so many exuberant songs of praise for women in general. To be quiet is better than praising. Considering the laws of nature, perhaps the real culprits are those responsible for the war; but apart from that, one should work toward the goal of educating people in peacetime about the abundant immorality that exists during wartime. There might then be very few who are enchanted with war. [. . .]

Europe does not possess the necessary natural resources to produce the required war needs over a long period. The Nazis will never admit that because strangely enough they insist "time and space" are acting for Germany. In the era of slogans nobody should be surprised "Zeit und Raum" are the new expressions being used as weapons. An article with that title, showing time and space are working for us, is in the *Das Schwarze Korps* paper of June 17. But the Russians own even more space. What does that signify? This is part of the article:

TIME AND SPACE

Basically we need to do nothing else but defend ourselves and employ heavy attacks against the enemy to put him on the defensive until he collapses. [. . .]

The enemy has already recognized that so-called Fortress Europe is indeed not a fortress that can be overcome simply in a matter of time. He is going to realize time is rather on our side, and the region itself is united with us. Such a handicap leaves open for him but one way: speed of action. He must launch a successful attack, and indeed an immediate one this very year. If he fails, he has missed obtaining the victory. We can remain on the defensive as long as necessary, but he will not be able to withdraw into a defensive posture. For him, standing still is always defeat because Europe is regaining strength. And all the while, time is expiring for the Jewish seducers of the enemy population, the extra time they counted upon before the relentless danger of anti-Semitism finally reaches them.

After Stalingrad we learned to see the war through different eyes. [. . .]

Source: "Zeit und Raum," *Das Schwarzes Korps*, vol. 9, no. 24, June 17, 1943.

All of a sudden defense is praised as a means for final victory. If only somebody had demanded that from the "most ingenious strategist of all time" in September 1939. For God's sake! Until now defense was equated with high treason! For the Germans, attack was always the best defense. Now they have discovered all of a sudden we can defend ourselves until the enemy collapses.

[. . .]

June 22, 1943

[. . .] Willi Leidner, a former SS man and now a sergeant, talked with senior secretary Metzger.[29] Leidner works in Litzmannstadt [Łódź] at the clothing office. He believes the war will last years. For such people in a safe position the war cannot last long enough. He thought Hitler would move to a castle in Posen [Poznań] after the war. If only this Nazi is not wrong.

On June 18 and 19, Reich Minister Dr. Goebbels visited areas attacked by British planes and gave a speech in Wuppertal and Dortmund. What he said in Wuppertal follows:

NUMEROUS MURDERED DEFENSELESS VICTIMS OF TERRORISM CALL OUT AGAINST AN INHUMAN ENEMY

[. . .] I stand here as an accuser before the people of the world. I accuse the enemy of conducting a brutal air terror for no reason other than to terrify a defenseless civilian population as a way of forcing them to betray their nation. Such an attempt can never succeed, and such cowardly deeds will bring only eternal shame on those whose governments carry out such abhorrent and malicious warfare against women, old people, and children. [...] This method of airborne terror comes from the sick minds of plutocrats who would destroy the world. The Führer tried everything to avoid the war, and when it was forced upon him, to wage it in a humane manner. [...]

> Source: "Zahlreiche wehrlos gemordete Terroropfer klagen einen unmenschlichen Feind an," *HLZ*, June 19, 1943, p. 1.

Dr. Goebbels's speech might have had a certain effect upon the world if Germany had not used its own air force so ruthlessly. What were Germany's intentions in 1940 when the air force made repeated heavy attacks on England? Dr. Goebbels has but to read what he and his press wrote during that time. The entire nation was beside itself then, waiting for the report England had disappeared from the earth. It is miserable dishonesty today – now that Germany feels the pain – to place all the guilt on the enemy. Wretched society!

AN ARMADA OF REVENGE WILL RISE

Minister Goebbels spoke in Dortmund / Leadership has reasons to wait to retaliate

[...] A tremendous outpouring of consent greeted Minister Goebbels when he announced "an armada of revenge will rise," and he knew exactly the month in which they would begin to strike. Until then it was important to be patient, to hate the enemy, not to look to the right and left, but only to act and live as required for the good of the German people. [...]

> Source: "Eine Armada der Rache wird entstehen," *HLZ*, June 20, 1943, p. 1.

So far the "Armada of Revenge" is just a threat. Very often children use threats as a weapon. But if it is true Germany is manufacturing heavy bombers in large numbers, this will not keep our opponents from bombing us thoroughly right now. This seems to be the crux of the matter. Our destroyed cities will not be restored by our acts of revenge.

June 24, 1943

When the German air force conducted heavy attacks against England in 1940, the High Command must have expected a certain effect. It will have to be found out in some future confession whether they thought to destroy industry or to ruin the English people's nerves to make them more desirous of peace.

England's air offensive is part of the overall attack against the continent. I do not believe the attacks are exclusively to weaken the German people. They have a plan to disturb and paralyze the total war machine. The bombardment of city centers could lead, however, to the supposition their goal is mostly to target the people. But the war industry, in the first place, is comprised of people. If their homes and those of the suppliers are bombed the industry will be disrupted in a way not to be underestimated. Since no official in Germany will tell us the amount of real damage to industrial buildings, the arms industry's current situation is not known. But it is hard to believe the assertion no decline in production has occurred. Everywhere the air raids are disturbing the factories and traffic lanes. Not even counting the loss of human lives, there is doubtless a regression in production output. Nobody will ever admit that officially.

We can do nothing but let the drama play out until the day when even the fattest lie can no longer cover up the demise.

It is unspeakably sad that Germany has run into such a dead end from which an escape appears to be, as far as one can tell, no longer possible.

June 26, 1943

A wounded soldier in the convalescing hospital in Laubach – in a wing of the Solmser Hof Inn – has been punished with fourteen days arrest because he had undertaken nightly excursions.[30] He was caught when leaving the house at 12 Im Hain Street at four in the morning. It was not the only time; he admitted he had dared to make the same excursion four times before. Who was the partner? The young wife of the teacher, Herr Kaiser, who presently is in the army. Frau Kaiser does her community work in the hospital kitchen and apparently has fallen in love with the soldier. Opportunity makes the thief.

I mention this case only because the academic circles like very much to feel superior to other people. They have no reason for that at all. In our little town of Laubach, which has just 1,800 inhabitants, and among them only a small number of academic families (it might be twelve), I know not less than four women who are anything but pure. The wife of the teacher Kammer is particularly wild. [...]

June 27, 1943

I am surprised we are permitted to know the USA had prepared for the war against Japan. Just recently it was reported a 2,700-kilometer highway was completed in Canada to connect the United States with Alaska. This has to be embarrassing for those who publicly told the German people fairy tales about our enemy's lack of raw materials. One time it was a lack of rubber, then oil, and then it was labor, and so forth. Now we read oil-rich America has discovered new oil fields and swims in oil. Lies have short legs.

A NEW OIL PIPELINE THROUGH ALASKA

Berlin, June 24, 1943.

For some months Americans have been at work in Alaska to build a highway from the Canadian border to the Bering Sea. Tens of thousands of workers are employed day and night in order to complete this in the shortest possible time and to facilitate the supply of arms, ammunition, and food to Americans who are struggling in the Aleutians. Now a special correspondent from the "Daily Telegraph" of Whitehorse (Yukon) reports that immediately following the completion of this highway an oil pipeline will be built, which reveals the new road's full military significance. They have indeed discovered that the Mackenzie River oil fields surpass in oil wealth all geological calculations many times over. After its complete development, these should be among the largest oil fields of the American mainland. [...]

Source: "Eine neue Oelleitung durch Alaska," *HLZ*, June 25, 1943, p. 2.

[...]

The wonderful education of our youth through Hitler Youth results in more stringent laws *against* youth – for the "protection of the youth":

VARIETY SHOWS AND CABARETS FORBIDDEN FOR YOUNG PEOPLE

New Police Regulations for the Protection of Youth
[...] Previously young people's behavior decided to what extent they would be kept away from shooting galleries and game arcades, and discouraged from public dance marathons and the like. New police regulations can override that. In particular, minors under the age of 18 are forbidden to remain on the streets and in the squares, or any other public place, after dark. Minors under the age of 16 may not be unaccompanied in cafes after 9 p.m. Furthermore, attending the cinema after 9 p.m. without parents is prohibited. It should be noted non-rated films should not be attended even with the parents. The restrictions on alcohol consumption and the ban on smoking in public have been carried over unchanged to emphasize today as yesterday the importance of maintaining the health of youth. [...] The regulation provides for fines and imprisonment against dilatory and unco-operative guardians, business owners, and operators.

Source: "Varietés und Kabaretts für Jugendliche verboten,"
HLZ, June 25, 1943, p. 4.

And Herr Goebbels shouted: "Youth is always right."

June 28, 1943

[. . .]

HARDNESS AND DIGNITY

Munich, May 22.

We Germans know we are the envy of many other nations in the world for our hardness. That is the impression given by all our soldiers in this war. As the soldier fights in the field, and as the worker does his duty at home, so can be seen the degree of a people's hardness. This is true in any assessment of our people. From our origins and history these soldierly qualities were forged, and now are more perfectly developed under the influence of total war. And at the same time we see such qualities decreasing in the people who come against us.

Soldierly qualities mean not only fortitude and the power to resist but to have the internal state of the mind complement the outward expression. Life in our time has its own style; a person is complete only when his internal hardness is combined with an external dignity that is natural and unperturbed. In the greatest moments in human history, when unshakable courage achieved the highest deeds, testimony also recorded the highest degree of human dignity in those involved. Thus we see our soldiers facing the enemy today as the masters of the battlefield just as much in the military success as in the human posture. [. . .]

Source: "Härte und Würde," *VB-Süd*, May 23, 1943, p. 2.

The National Socialists have been more than a little conceited about their "hardness." The entire education of youth since 1933 was geared toward completely hardening the population. However, even a cursory observation shows this hardness is nothing more than crudeness and insensitivity. The German people are not envied for these attributes – as this author asserts in this article – but they are hated from the depths of one's soul.

The youth were educated according to military precepts in order to raise a type of human with distinctively soldierly characteristics. Young people were constantly preached to about becoming as hard as Krupp steel.[31] And the results can be seen in the way our army treats the populations in the occupied areas, as well as the treatment of prisoners at the beginning of the Russian campaign.

The atrocities against the Jews are the result of this praised hardness – an extremely sad chapter in the bloody German history.

"We see our soldiers facing the enemy today as the masters of the battlefield," says the article writer. They were not "mastering" the battlefields at

Stalingrad and in Africa. And as for the "comportment" our soldiers displayed when they were being marched into Russian and English prisoner-of-war camps, I cannot even imagine it. As for "dignity," I do not see much of that around me. The people behave much more like defendants when the court has adjoined for deliberations; they are sitting in expectation of the decision to come in a depressed mood and with dark forebodings. That is reality.

THE BLACK MARKET

Munich, June 24, 1943.

We know everyone realizes there is a black market. It would be an illusion to assume it is lacking anywhere. In every era when certain merchandise was hard to get, a secret market arose. We in Germany know there is one here and there are those who frequent the market to obtain the illegal additional goods to be found there. But the German people's morals are not characterized by this but rather by the smooth and well-functioning rationing system. What we may demand is available to us. [. . .]

That the black market has existed forever in the Soviet Union for the few advantaged – the Jews and their helpers – should be noted only as an aside. But also in England, the population's anger against the black market is increasing. Bartering and trading of material in short supply have taken such volume that the hate against the Jews there, which is smoldering below the surface, frequently erupts. Therefore, the Spectator magazine writes that one would do the public a big service to openly declare the Jewish population in Great Britain had reached the highest record of black market crimes. [. . .]

Every nation has a black market it deserves. The German people do not know at all what trouble and what discouragement have been saved to them with the disappearance of the Jewish black market in Germany.

Source: "Der schwarze Markt," *VB-Süd*, June 25, 1943, p. 1.

[. . .] The secret black market is a result of the lack and shortage of goods, and the Nazis have not been able to stop these activities, not even with draconian means. The swipe against the Jews in this article is completely out of place because there are no Jews in Germany any more. And still the black market is here. The Jews are no worse than people are in general. It is just that these Nazi hypocrites do not want to see the beam in their own eyes.

Anyone in Germany whose food supplies are limited only to what is apportioned cannot be far from complete debilitation. The instinct for self-preservation, which applies to everybody, may force one to disregard the laws and seek repeatedly and carefully how to get the necessary food.

July 6, 1943

NSDAP PUBLIC RALLY IN DARMSTADT

This war was wantonly declared by our enemies because of our rein-
corporation of Danzig into the German Reich along with the corridor
to that German city. The instigators behind the start of war were the
Jews. The International Jew has the illusion he can achieve world
domination by rousing the plutocrats and Bolsheviks, already in bondage and dependent upon him, to destroy the German people. The Jew
is the creator of world chaos. His intention to crush Germany will
never succeed. We are positioned with our total power to vigorously
defend ourselves. Through the unsurpassed bravery of our soldiers, the
onslaught by our enemies encountering the powerful effectiveness of
our armies and the joyful work effort of our Home Front forces will
fail. We all participate! We all help! And that is necessary to secure the
future of Germany. Victory will be ours! [...]

Source: "Sieg oder bolschewistisches Chaos!" *HLZ*, July 7, 1943, p. 3.

The Nazis cannot be cured. They think their methods from the so-called
Time of Struggle can win this war. [...] The "total power," "unsurpassed
bravery," "powerful effectiveness," and "joyful effort" are all things that
found a safe place in the mouths of every Party speaker. Slogans are not
practical weapons, though, to stop an enemy's attack. And yet there are still
those among the people inebriated by Party bigwig speeches. The hangover
will be tremendous.

31 TERROR BOMBERS SHOT DOWN OVER WEST GERMANY

17 Soviet landing boats sunk in the area of Kuban

[...] British bombers flew last night over western German territory and
attacked several cities with numerous explosive and incendiary bombs,
including particularly Wuppertal-Elberfeld and Remscheid. The inhabitants' losses within the affected cities are heavy. So far 31 enemy bombers
shot down were located. The enemy lost an additional eight airplanes during
a daylight attack against the western areas. [...]

Source: "Über Westdeutschland 31 Terrorbomber abgeschossen,"
VB-Süd, June 26, 1943, p. 2.

If the Supreme Command characterizes the casualties in the cities
Wuppertal-Elberfeld and Remscheid as "heavy," then the number of people
killed must be considerable. I really would like to know what Marshal
Hermann Göring thinks today because it was he who in August and

September 1939 declared the industrial area would not be subjected to a single enemy bomb. How much foolish stuff has been said already in the Third Reich? This simplistic chatter could always find enthusiastic listeners. Just think of the storms of applause that always began when the talker's mouth was really overflowing.

"We will eradicate their cities," screamed Adolf Hitler. He meant in England. There are cities today that have been "eradicated" – but they are, in fact, in Germany. The Nazis greatly value strengthening penal law in regards to "intent": the perpetrator's criminal intention is to be viewed as a decisive factor. Adolf Hitler intended to eradicate the English cities, although he has not yet been able to bring it about. The intention of the perpetrator, though, is what matters.

GERMANY WILL NEVER CAPITULATE

Gauleiter Sauckel spoke in southwest Germany to a major corporation

Strasbourg, June 20, 1943.

'Germany will never capitulate!" [...] With a poignant appeal to the working men and women, to managers and engineers, to all creative members working with their head or their hands, to continue their never-tiring belief in Germany's final victory and to give the last ounce of devotion to duty and working zeal, Regional Director Sauckel closed to a thunderous rallying cry as he repeated his strong conviction in the coming victory.

Source: "Deutschland wird niemals kapitulieren," *VB-Süd*,
June 21, 1943, p. 2.

Whoever knows the Nazi mind is not surprised Germany will never capitulate and compromise will not be a factor. As long as the Nazis are in charge, there will never be a settlement. I was convinced from the beginning our present leadership would rather sacrifice the entire nation than give in.

The German people should really be ready to expect something. The time will come when the nation realizes the revolution in 1918 saved it from much suffering. At least Germany was not destroyed then. If it had offered further senseless resistance in 1918, Germany would have been finished. The "stab in the back" was in reality a saving grace. This time the false prophets have the word. We shall see. [...]

July 7, 1943

THEY WANT TO DESTROY GERMANY'S CULTURAL MONUMENTS

Besides Cologne Cathedral, so far 133 churches destroyed,
494 badly damaged[32] [. . .]

How many churches and other cultural monuments have the German armed forces destroyed? Who destroyed all the synagogues in Germany and in the occupied territories? Those who announced the total war are not entitled to levy any complaint. When the German airmen launched bomb raids in Spain, Poland, Holland, Belgium, France, Yugoslavia, etc., they certainly did not seek out and only hit military targets. Whoever glorifies war must also bear the blows. C'est la guerre!

ALWAYS PUT INTO PRACTICE THE PARTY'S PROGRAM

The Gauleiter spoke at inauguration of Pres. Schwebel's government in Wiesbaden[33]

The worst swindlers of all time, after having ruled for over ten years, refer today to their "Party Program."[34] Of all their many promises, the Nazis have kept only one: the eradication of the Jews. The rest: catchphrases.

July 8, 1943

FROM FÜHRER HEADQUARTERS, JULY 7.

Supreme Command of the Armed Forces bulletin:

The Soviets launched serious attacks with their strongest units in the area of Belgorod and south of Orel these past weeks and failed. In contrast, our troops were effectively supported by the air force, even for offensive attacks. It was possible to break deep into the enemy positions and inflict heavy losses on the enemy. Army troops alone destroyed or disabled about 300 enemy tanks, some of the latest design. [. . .]

Source: "300 Panzer, 637 Flugzeuge vernichtet," *HLZ,* July 8, 1943, p. 1.

Shamefully, the German offensive in the East is represented as a defensive counter-strike. In any case, I am surprised our criminal Supreme Command in the East starts another attack and creates useless victims. This bulletin was calculated for just the moment everyone was expecting an attack by our foes in the south of Europe.[35]

July 11, 1943

DETERMINED RESISTANCE IN SICILY

Rome, July 10, 1943.

The Italian Armed Forces report of Saturday has the following text:

Last night the enemy began the attack on Sicily with support of sea and air forces and parachute troops. Our combined forces met the enemy action with determined resistance. Battles are in process along the southern coastal strip. The enemy air force attacked built-up areas throughout Sicily.

Source: "Entschlossener Widerstand auf Sizilien," *HLZ*, July 11, 1943, p. 1.

[...]

The American and English attack against Italy has started! The world will now be given the opportunity to admire "Fortress Europe" and the "South Wall," as well as the Italians' "iron determination"! The scanty information does not allow any assessment yet of the situation. One is certain of this, though: The enemy has landed. So this landing could not be prevented; neither the air force nor the land forces were able to stop it. Actually, I should be pleased because I have always held the opinion our enemies can land everywhere they want. Where were the U-boats and the Fascist braggarts? [...] The Italian people have the "Duce" to thank for the critical situation. This looter of corpses wanted to walk off with easy spoils in 1940. Mussolini was blind enough to have been fooled by the moment. A real statesman would have had the foresight to remain neutral at least.

The Italians tolerated the Mussolini regime all this time, and for that they must be punished.

July 12, 1943

[. . .]

How fundamentally a military situation can change. A cry for defense is all that remains of the Fascist dictators' bombastic and imperialistic plans of conquest. Now they cling to the defense works on the coasts of Italy. A look at the map shows there is hardly a country more difficult to defend than Italy. It is impossible to fortify Italy's coasts against every serious attack. And because such a defense is impossible, the Americans and English of course will conquer Italy. I have not the slightest doubt.

The Anglo-Saxons do not need to be afraid of any "strategic reserves" because it will soon turn out there are hardly any such reserves left. When Europe's defense burns at all corners, we will have to seek the "reserves" with the stable lamp. The "strategic reserves" are an extremely poor consolation.

[. . .]

July 18, 1943

German troops are making more senseless victims by fighting on the island of Sicily. The landed English and Americans can be hindered for some days, but this changes nothing of the end result; the island will be in the enemies' hands soon. The Germans have granted help to their Italian ally to retain some prestige. This is merely a gesture that will lead the Italians to offer useless resistance. Germany is engaged so strongly in the East and in Europe that its limited support in Italy will not suffice to hold back the strong opponents.

There is but one possibility for Italy: Surrender! Even if Mussolini and comrades inspire their supporters to a desperate resistance, the final success of these efforts will merely be devastated towns and landscapes. I expect a revolution against the Fascist regime. The Italian people hopefully will rouse themselves to this.

July 20, 1943

[. . .]

The people believed there would be no Party nepotism with the National Socialists. That is, until the Nazis were at the helm. Then beast of prey instincts developed. Running after jobs and the hunt for positions started like never before. Every restraint was finally shoved aside and membership in the NSDAP was required for any good position. They started with a swindle and continued with deceit. It is lucky there is a limit to everything. The Party reveler will yet experience much grief, and some will be deeply sorry for their materialistic strivings.

The Führer signed a document regarding a civil service bureaucratic status:

HEINRICH BACKHAUS, District Leader of the NSDAP, is now President of the Hessian Fire Insurance Chamber.

Source: Hessisches Regierungsblatt, no. 8 of 1943, February 24, 1943.

Where is the law to protect the civil service? [. . .] Anyway, District Leader Backhaus did not get a chance to enjoy his civil service status for long. He died before then.

And the others will follow him.

And rightly so![36]

July 26, 1943

The Axis is now broken!

Mussolini has resigned![37]

This dictator is out of business. He has disappeared from the stage. The Fascist charade is over. The people are left with the pieces. If this tyrant chieftain had raged and lived within his national boundaries, it would merely have been a matter for the Italian people to decide whether or not they wanted to obey him. Since megalomania rules over moderation in such violent men, the rest of the world was also affected. The Italian Lord God, the Duce, is no longer a part of the Berlin–Rome "Axis"! Interesting days will come. What will Dr. Goebbels say to this?

CHANGE OF GOVERNMENT IN ITALY

Mussolini has stepped down as head of government – Prime Minister
Marshal Badoglio is appointed his successor

Romo, July 26, 1943

As the Stefani Press Agency announced on Sunday night, the King and
Emperor of Italy has accepted Benito Mussolini's resignation from the office
of head of government and prime minister. He has appointed Marshal of
Italy Pietro Badoglio as the successor. One assumes this change in government is due to the Duce's health, as he was ill recently.

Source: "Regierungswechsel in Italien," *HLZ,* July 27, 1943, p. 1.

An inglorious departure of a man addicted to glory! "One assumes"
Mussolini has fallen ill. "One" has lost the words. Hitler's friend and ally
has, of course, been ill, but mentally ill, and for more than 20 years already.
This experience unmistakably means a severe shock for National Socialism.

REGULATIONS ISSUED BY THE NEW HEAD
OF GOVERNMENT

From dusk to dawn there will be a curfew. No civilian may be outside his
living quarters during these hours. Public offices of all kinds, music halls,
theaters, cinemas, gyms, etc. must be kept closed during the hours of curfew.
Under all circumstances, it is at all times forbidden that more than three
people gather in public or in enclosed spaces to talk. Hanging printed labels,
manuscripts or propaganda of any kind is prohibited in public places. The
carrying of weapons is forbidden to the population. All Italians who leave
their homes must carry identity papers with a photograph. They must show
their identity cards to military and official authorities when requested. [. . .]

The Italian people presumably will not be delighted with the announcement
that the war goes on. The war goes on, of course, until the surrender. This
stopgap new government cannot have a long life. The announced martial law
over Italy indicates things ferment and seethe in Italy. If no basic change in
politics is intended, then it is not clear to the distant observer why Mussolini
had to vanish into thin air. Perhaps Marshal Badoglio thinks the soldiers will
show a greater enthusiasm now under his command than ever before?

[. . .]

July 28, 1943

If I were French, I would describe the present government head, Laval, as the
worst kind of villain. On July 5, 1943, at a French press conference, he said:

There are many French who believe one day we will be saved by the United States, by England, and, in their exuberance, by Giraud and de Gaulle. I do not share these illusions. The German army will not be beaten. Europe will not be defeated by armed might wherever they come from. These illusions of a German defeat, which so many Frenchmen have, can only cause a deadly crisis for our country.[38]

Laval, therefore, wishes for the victory of Germany and its oppression of France. Let not a single word be lost about this fact: France would be swept away for all time by a German victory.

It could not be possible to sink morally lower than Laval. Even if he, from some innate inability, is not able to get an idea of what is coming, he then at least should have enough character to impose silence upon himself. It will be the task of the hopeful Frenchmen to get rid of this Laval and like-minded people and to build up a free France.

Laval would be much surprised, by the way, if he could read the thoughts of many Germans. The number is definitely growing of those who are convinced of Germany's defeat. "The German army will not be beaten" is a dumb comment, the cackling of propaganda. [. . .]

WEEKLY NEWSREEL

It is a pity we cannot bring the German Wochenschau to the people of our enemy because then they would have to recognize from the powerful voice of facts it is pointless for them to waste their hopes on their statesmen's illusions and phrases. Just the latest film strips of recent events attest yet again to the inexhaustible power of Germany and its allies. This material strength, associated with sacrifice, faith, and trust gives reason for the confidence in victory the Führer expressed on January 30, 1942, on the entire German people's behalf. The enthusiasm and the cheering surrounding Adolf Hitler – captured on film by the camera in the Berlin Sports Palace – is an irrefutable document of the German people's great attitude, and how this attitude reveals itself in detail is shown in the incomparable examples of heroism and bravery of his soldiers.

German propaganda has brought all technological aids into its service. The film industry and the illustrated newspapers are tireless preachers of the German army's "glory," "heroic courage," and "bravery." It is a waste of time to seek a presentation that invokes a thoughtful approach to an issue or has any critical commentary. The images show only perfect victories and first-class heroes. A dead German soldier will never be seen; no wrecked German airplane either. Jack-of-all-trades Goebbels and his assistants know perfectly what the arrogant German bourgeoisie would like to see. The weekly newsreel must of course never be absent in the cinemas. The moviegoer is infused with enthusiasm for Germany's "inexhaustible strength" and later goes to bed relaxed, dreaming of, as he considers it, the inevitable final victory.[39] [...]

Just within the last few days, regarding the reorganization of Italy's government, I saw again the compulsion to hope. My opinion about Italy is clear and definite: the fall of Mussolini is the beginning of the end. Fascism is ruined. The consequences for Germany and the states allied with it are not yet to be foreseen; but in any case this will accelerate the end of the war.

But what do I hear in my surroundings? Primarily considerable surprise, then hesitance, dark premonitions, shaking the head, and attempts to grasp at another straw. Hopes are not missing. They are even far-reaching, as if Mussolini's downfall could be beneficial for Germany. But a depressed atmosphere generally rules, waiting on something redemptive. A lack of comments in the newspapers is striking: only repetitions of official Italian reports. No obituaries for the departing friend.

Could Joseph Goebbels have lost his balance? This would be the first time. What a turn!

[...]

July 31, 1943

[...] Extravagant praise [for Mussolini] has been muffled. This is called "back to reality." The "ingenious" man, the "best" man, has burst like a soap bubble. And the Italian people do not have the slightest intention of flocking to "Il Duce." He too had to learn power is merely a temporary protective agent. He shares the destiny of all tyrants, and no one learns anything from it.

Mussolini was the master of the revolutionaries. Hitler is his clever pupil: a copyist, as he admitted in his book. Mussolini wanted a 1,000-year empire. Hitler also talked foolishly of a 1,000-year empire. Mussolini's empire lasted 20 years. Hitler's empire is 10 years old!

How long will it yet live?

With the enemy standing before the gates and preparing to step over the borders of Germany, the Third Reich's hour of death approaches. The Nazis will do everything to prolong this war. The German soldier has it in his hand to abbreviate the sufferings. An end to terror!

August 1, 1943

In spite of everything the propaganda still lives and continues to dispense illusions. Now it demonstrates for us how the landing in Sicily is a costly matter for our enemies:[40]

SEVERE BLOWS
STRONG ENEMY LOSSES IN SICILY [. . .]

And it must be hammered into us that Russia's attacks are shattered:

HUGE LOSSES OF SOVIET WEAPONS
IMMENSE TANK BATTLE IN THE AREA FROM BELGOROD
TO OREL [. . .]

The endangered zones are reinforced:

FORTRESS CRETE – A FIRE-BREATHING ISLAND
SOUTHEAST RAMPART GROWS EVER STRONGER

The propaganda tries to cause disagreement between the opponents:

THE SOVIETS DEMAND EFFECTIVE RELIEF
ENGLAND BELONGS TO THE USA! [. . .]

The others are the ones who are worried:

ENGLISH ANXIOUS ABOUT THE WAR SITUATION
DISTRESS OF THE AMERICAN WORKERS

If we do not have any victories, then our distant friend has them:

**JAPAN'S AIR FORCE SUCCESS
JAPAN'S SUCCESS**

Propaganda heals all wounds!

Die gefährdeten Inseln werden stark gemacht!

Abwehrbereiter Vorposten im Südosten

Festung Kreta – eine feuerspeiende Insel

Südostwall immer stärker

So propagierende versucht Uneinigkeit unter den Gegnern hervorzurufen:

Die Sowjets fordern wirksame Entlastung

„England gehört den USA!"

Die USA. kämpfen bis zum letzten englischen Schiff

USA. und England machen sich die Erdpole streitig

USA.-Luftwaffe kann Tschungking nicht helfen

Die Sorgen sind bei den andern:

13. 7. 1943

Englische Beklemmung über die Kriegslage

Not der amerikanischen Arbeiter

Wenn wir keine Siege haben, dann hat sie aber den fernen Freund:

Japanischer Fliegererfolg

Japanischer Erfolg

Die Propaganda hält alle Stunden!

[...]

August 7, 1943

What are the people saying? In general the mood is not rosy. It is difficult to assess how most feel because too few express their opinion unreservedly. Fear still guards the forest. Those of us who are regime opponents have no further doubt about Germany's defeat; however, it is not possible to determine the percentage of optimists versus pessimists. The number of the hopeful is still considerable. Hope seems indestructible. When I must hear today the "strike" against England is to be expected soon (they give the date of August 17), then it is surely impossible for a sensible person to say anything else about this. Nothing is gained presenting common sense to the mentally ill. [. . .]

August 8, 1943

The Nazis still contrive to make something from a defeat.

OVER 300,000 SOVIETS BLED TO DEATH BEFORE OREL SINCE JULY 5

Breakwater Orel has served its purpose – Immense attrition
of Soviet forces –
Clearing prepared for weeks and schedule being followed

Berlin, August 5.

On the night of August 5 our troops evacuated the city of Orel. Having been prepared for weeks, this measure is part of our great mobility and control of our defensive operations. Our army units settle only where they can create the basis for effective counter-attacks against extreme resistance, but otherwise they wear down the enemy by dodging and counter-attacking the Bolsheviks' flanks and rear lines to destroy the enemy's offensive forces. [. . .]

Source: "Vor Orel verbluteten seit dem 5. Juli weit über 300,000 Sowjets,"
HLZ, August 6, 1943, p. 1.

The opponents' gigantic losses are announced to comfort the German people. [. . .] No human soul cares about the German losses.

The "strategic purpose" has been fulfilled at Orel. That is the childish and naïve way they paraphrase defeat. They will tell us next, perhaps, we abandoned the entire Eastern Front because the area no longer has value because we destroyed it! I would not be astonished if that or similar reasons were used for new "shortenings of the front."

Africa fulfilled its purpose. Sicily, too. The fallen have fulfilled their purpose. So, German people, be happy you are sacrificed so carefully, correctly, and usefully!

Also fulfilling their purpose are the awards handed out in large quantities to promote ambitions. Hitler knows the Germans and is not stingy. He knows the decorated soldiers will want to distinguish themselves repeatedly, right up to the moment of their "heroic death." [. . .]

Lance-Corporal Schiemann, awarded the Knight's Cross on April 8, 1943, was killed in battle at the Eastern Front on July 13.

Source: HLZ, August 3, 1943, p. 2.

Master Sergeant Willi Zahn, platoon leader in a Pomeranian Grenadier Regiment, was posthumously awarded the Knight's Cross of the Iron Cross on July 18. He found a hero's death on July 16 in the battles south of Orel.

Source: HLZ, August 5, 1943, p. 2.

When a lance-corporal or sergeant is honored (the potentates like to show they make no distinction between enlisted and officers) their joy is seldom long-lasting. Lance-corporal Schiemann carried the Knight's Cross for two and a half months before he died, and Staff Sergeant Zahn did not live long enough to experience the ceremony. Military leaders know many of the soldiers being honored at all the fronts will likely not survive the war – so the Führer patronizingly distributes the Knight's Cross and other badges as compensation and does it with much fanfare.

The recent newsreel:

TIGERS ROLL FORWARD – THE PICTURE OF THE BATTLE OF OREL

Over 7,000 Bolshevik battle tanks were captured or destroyed in three weeks of this fierce warfare of attrition. What this fact signifies is shown in the recent weekly newsreel about the Battle of Orel. Our "Tigers" roll forward and put the Soviet tanks to flight. In the roar of battle, weapon is wielded against weapon, and the individual steers the fight and makes the decision. A colossal pictorial impression is made when our mortar batteries begin to speak, when lightning from the mouths of the guns flashes diagonally across the screen through the fog and gives the landscape a fantastic face that no painter could employ any better in creating a symbol of powerful war. And the camera leads our eye over the battlefield, out over the corpses of the Soviets, over destroyed tanks. Over and over again, everything is drowned out by the impact of shells and the roar of airplanes, and we recognize the magnitude of this battle.

A navy reporter sent an interesting film strip of a submarine tanker's departure from port and the ensuing supply of a submarine on the high seas. Calculating at any moment upon the possible emergence of enemy forces, everything had to be done quickly and accurately. One sees yet again how each man in this war knows and masters every technical apparatus and weapon, and one recognizes yet again with what degree of certainty and superiority the men set themselves to work even in the most difficult of situations.

Of the homeland we are shown the happy life of children at the Baltic Sea and the enthusiastic reception in Lübeck of our combat troops. German youth from different countries are seen performing their national service, and not the least of those images that capture our attention is a meeting of our military leaders and ministers at Hitler's headquarters.

Source: "Tiger rollen vor – Das Bild der Schlacht bei Orel," *HLZ*,
August 7, 1943, p. 3.

The weekly newsreel totally fulfills the average guy's dreams. He gets to see Russian corpses and happy faces at home.

For how much longer?

August 11, 1943

For a change, I want to write something of myself. Last night was warlike. We went to bed at 9:30 and were awakened shortly after midnight by an intense rumbling. We clearly heard bombs exploding and anti-aircraft guns. I suspected it was in Frankfurt or surroundings. It continued until 2:00 a.m. The alarm clock went off at 3:45, and the night was already past. I took the 4:57 train to Hungen. After almost an hour of waiting, I went on to Stockheim, waiting there for an hour and fifteen minutes. Finally on to Altenstadt, where I arrived at 8:25 a.m. Every week on Wednesday I am here for three days. I live there in August Holzapfel's inn. He also has a farm. The vicinity is rural and with moderate war activity.

I found out the planes had not attacked Frankfurt but Nuremberg. The previous night, planes went to Mannheim. South Germany seems to be having its turn. The newspapers have already found the right twist, inspired, of course, by the master juggler Goebbels:

> We have prepared ourselves even for terror from the skies. Those of us in the rear will confront reality coolly and unemotionally! As is well known everywhere and in all cases, one may strike back against terror and protect his belongings. No one on the other side should have any illusions we shall become weak. We are prepared for any action and any sacrifice because it is about the Reich's existence and our people's lives. The more courageously we face the real dangers, the easier we will limit them to a manageable level. The moment of truth has arrived for us. The terror makes us even harder and instills an irrepressible hatred against those who have provoked an

inhumane war against non-combatant civilians. No one on the enemy side should believe we will idly watch the rabid bombing terror. Our time will come again. When? We shall leave that to the Führer. We are accustomed not to talk but to act, and at the appropriate time. [...]

Source: "Kühl und nüchtern den Dingen ins Auge sehen," *HLZ*,
August 8, 1943, p. 3.

The Germans must remain courageous, cool, and rational – even if all their belongings and their homes are completely reduced to a heap of rubble. So expects the government. The main thing is to stand the test! And with that, iron discipline and unshakeable steadfastness is demanded. Then will come the hour of retribution.

For the moment, however, retribution is just on paper, which inflicts no harm at all. It is inexpensive to put off the people with promises. I have heard a number of Party members these past few days repeating the various propaganda hints, bringing into the mixture some mysterious preparations for the "strike" against England. This comes from on high. The Local Group Leader in Hainchen told me about a meeting of officials in Büdingen that took place some days ago. Regional Leader [Emil] Görner had sharp words for those Party members who prefer to creep away into a mouse-hole. He demanded they have the courage of their convictions and fight everyone who exhibits even a lukewarm behavior. The officials are to pay particularly attention to any gossips, and to emphasize courage to the population, and to ensure high spirits. Officials should, if necessary, proceed physically against fickle persons or opponents of the Party – exactly as was done before 1933. No Party member would be prosecuted legally in such a case, added the Büdingen Regional Leader!

[...]

August 17, 1943

Afternoon. Roaring noise. The sound of airplanes. High in the sky are three massive groups of planes. German or hostile? It is a mystery, but since they are flying very high I bet they are Americans. [Pauline and I] try to count them and get up to 180 planes. They are coming from the east and heading west. Were they at Nuremberg? A strange situation. The enemy moves in the skies above Germany as though he were at home. Who actually controls Germany's air space?

August 18, 1943

On the trip to Altenstadt, I learned the enemy bombers had been to Schweinfurt. Several German fighter pilots attacked them near Nidda but without success. Two fighters were shot down. The pilot (an officer) parachuted from the plane and injured both his legs. He was taken to the military hospital in Bad Salzhausen. In the Stockheim waiting room, I got into a conversation with a traveler. It turned out he was a long-time Nazi Party member. His remarks had a pessimistic coloring. He said frankly an aerial attack in broad daylight had laid hold of his beliefs. The "Old Fighter" realized Germany is too weak to successfully fend off the enemy pilots. So even the oldest Party comrades begin to lose their faith in the omnipotent Hitler. However, the appearance of a single swallow does not mean summer has arrived. This will still require patience. [. . .] Daily papers and radio broadcasts imaginatively lend their efforts to bolster faith in final victory. The dangerous setbacks suffered at all fronts change nothing in the confident depiction of the situation. "Do not waver": that is the slogan of every speaker and correspondent. Defeats are transformed into great achievements and retreats all take place according to "a planned schedule." Obfuscation is the order of the day, and words of comfort are administered in abundant quantities. A glance at the newspapers shows us the nature of the propaganda. The key words and headlines are taken from the *Hessische Landes-Zeitung* [August 15–19, 1943]:

[. . .]

IN THE LAST WEEK NEARLY 2,000 SOVIET TANKS DESTROYED

HIGH BLOODY LOSSES OF THE BOLSHEVIKS

SERIOUS DEFEAT OF USA AIR FORCE IN THE PACIFIC

THE OPPONENTS HAVE FOOD SUPPLY DIFFICULTIES IN SICILY

JAPAN'S FIGHTING ABILITY IS UNASSAILABLE

ENEMY SUPPLIES FOR SICILY SUNK IN THE MEDITERRANEAN

SOVIETS BLOODILY REPULSED AT ALL FRONTS

August 19, 1943

Official reports in Büdingen state three German fighter aircraft were shot down by American bombers in the Büdingen region the day before yesterday. Yet the Armed Forces report speaks of only one pilot shot down.[41] German planes were also undoubtedly shot down in the attacked areas of Schweinfurt and Regensburg. In instances like these, the Supreme Command reports are considered irreproachable. But what do they gain with such insolent lies? The enemy knows who was shot down, and the German air bases know which of their comrades did not return.

August 25, 1943

The Armed Forces report announced the "scheduled" evacuation of Kharkov. Lately the name Kharkov has been cautiously avoided. It is always the "area of Belgorod" or "southwest of Belgorod." This way the radio and newspapers hope to present Kharkov as an affair of second rank. [...] Kharkov's importance can easily be recognized from the great efforts our army exerted to conquer this city and then to futilely defend it. Why downgrade a position we once valued? Because we have given up this key position for good.

It is little comfort for us to hear the Russians did not succeed in making a strategic breakthrough. Did the Russians even want to break through at this time? That will happen, though. When the Russians have the necessary momentum, they will push us back little by little. Five kilometers a day will result in five hundred kilometers in one hundred days. The continued attenuation of our front is the prerequisite for Russia's successful breakthrough.

August 26, 1943

In the Stockheim waiting room I heard the radio report about the change in our government. Heinrich Himmler is Reich Minister of the Interior! This is the last resort, the last rites. Himmler can do no more than he has already done. And he has done a lot. Now the most radical men are in all positions. My opinion: when you bend a bow with too much pressure, it can only break, and nothing else. The situation now approaches its end, slowly but surely.

August 28, 1943

On Wednesday evening, August 25, I was visiting the family of assistant justice inspector Hühn in Stammheim [near Altenstadt]. A teacher named Bergk was there, and with Bergk were his relatives from Mainz, a bailiff and his wife. It was inevitable our conversation would eventually turn to the war. I was really shocked by the village schoolteacher Bergk's way of thinking. He is the type of person who mounts the wrong horse, and when the horse starts limping and has no chance at all of winning the race, he refuses to acknowledge it under any circumstance. Bergk enthusiastically described his unwavering conviction our retaliatory measures against England will succeed. At present that is the favorite topic of all the revenge-seeking armchair generals at home. I mentioned that even with the implementation of such wishful thinking, English air raids upon Germany would not be eliminated. We would just be returning harm for harm against the English. Our major concern should be to prevent bombardment of the German cities. But there is no miracle drug for that. Fighter pilots and anti-aircraft artillery are weapons that can be used against the hostile bombers, but they really are no more than defensive tools.

The conversation included Italy. If Mussolini had eliminated the Italian king and the Pope, said Bergk, the Duce would have remained a winner. As his highest trump, Bergk played out the assertion Mussolini would be reinstated by Germany to further fight at our side with his Blackshirt squadrons.

(Nothing is so dense, it cannot find its audience.)

My response was Italy had three years of opportunity to test its military capabilities, and the Italian people were tired of war. That made no visible impression upon the herald of the latest wisdom. Such people simply do not want to think; they prefer making it through each day going from one hope to the other. Even at the grave's edge, they will plant one more hope. One must resign himself to it.

[. . .]

August 31, 1943

Dr. Joseph Goebbels wrote a few days ago about "The Realities of War." I quote some notable sentences:

[. . .] Where have a people ever had an equally favorable position for victory on the eve of the fifth year of a war as huge as ours today? The fronts are unshaken. Despite the enemy terror bombing, the homeland has grown both in morale and in material. A stream of war materials leaves our factories. A new offensive weapon against the enemy's air war is under construction. Day and night, countless hardworking hands are working at it. We are yet tasked with a hard test of patience, but it will pay off one day.[42]

Dr. Goebbels is consoling. He makes mysterious insinuations.[43] Those who believe in miracles have once again received an injection. Goebbels alone still dares to step up onto the platform and comfort the people with words. Hitler, Göring, and consorts are silent. Their silence has already lasted for some time, over six months. It would be asking too much that they also speak about their false prophecies or the German defeats.

September 1, 1943

The fifth year of war has begun!

We were reminded during the night of Goebbels's "Realities of War." Between midnight and 2:00 a.m. endless columns of enemy airplanes flew over Laubach. Berlin was bombarded. The destruction of German cities continues. The war also goes merrily on at the other fronts even though no prospect exists for it to be decided in Germany's favor.

Our rulers are too cowardly to resign. Fate, run your course!

Judge Boländer, who is home on leave in Grünberg, visited me today. His unit is at present in Crimea. Boländer was a big optimist. Today, however, his head was hanging. He readily admitted I had been right in all my points. This insight comes too late. The academics should have been wiser in 1933 and not have dismissed opinions from people like me with a contemptuous smile. I really ought to be immensely proud all the judges who work with me attach great value to hearing my opinions about the war situation.

September 2, 1943

As if to confirm what I wrote yesterday about Judge Boländer, Judge Bischoff came by today. He is training in Hersfeld as a driver. Immediately after the greetings, he said abruptly, "Things are not going well at the front. I believe Kellner had it right."

Late, very late, comes the realization!

Neither of these men had a seasoned political judgment. I do not want to maintain neither understood anything; that would be exaggerated. But I could determine neither had imaginative power. They prayed simply for what the National Socialist authority drummed into them. Instead of thinking critically, they believed blindly. That is an extremely regrettable circumstance, since it directly concerns those who could have been leaders in thinking straight.

September 3, 1943

We are living through eventful days on the whole line. Heavy fighting has been underway at the Eastern Front since July 5. It is likely the Russians gained considerable ground in Orel, Kursk, Belgorod, and Kharkov. Führer Headquarters and the German people fool themselves with the notion the Russians actually failed because they "did not break through and roll up the German front." It is a strange turn of events in the war, though, that instead of our troops destroying the Russian army, they are pleased they at least have kept the Russian army from breaking through. Germany's leaders probably never considered such a circumstance.

Also, it is rather feeble to take comfort in the shortening of the front and the creation of new reserves. The enemy likewise has reserves.

FROM FÜHRER HEADQUARTERS, AUGUST 30, 1943.

Supreme Command of the Armed Forces bulletin:

Despite the Soviets' numerical superiority in men and matériel in the heavy battles that have continued almost without interruption in the East since July 5, they have not managed to break through the front anywhere and to push back the German forces. Even when the enemy, regardless of its heavy losses, threw new units into the area of battle where it had achieved some break-through, the counter-attacks and the dogged defense of our incomparable fighting infantry, superbly supported by the other branches, succeeded yet again in recovering territory and holding the line. Where evasive action was taken, it was done in good order and after the destruction of anything of importance to the enemy, and always with the purpose of shortening the front lines and to gain new resources.

Also yesterday saw heavy defensive fighting in the Eastern Front's southern sector. The completely destroyed Taganrog was evacuated on schedule.

Source: "Zwei Tanker versenkt," *HF-Abend*, August 30, 1943, p. 1.

The Russians are west of Belgorod and Kharkov, and they are gaining ground toward North Ukraine. It is possible they can undertake further offensive operations from there, which by itself could bring big changes to the entire strategic situation. Breaking through the front is not the only necessary way of bringing about our defeat. The Russians are drawing us out by intelligent maneuvers. That is their tactic on the way to their goal.

KING BORIS

Sofia, August 30, 1943.

On Saturday, August 28, at 8 p.m., Prime Minister and Minister of Foreign Affairs Professor Filott read the following proclamation:

His Majesty the king, Zar Boris III, the Unifier, passed away after a short and difficult illness today, August 28, 1943, at 4:22 p.m., within the circle of his family. The pain of Bulgaria and the Bulgarian people is immense. We all have the holy duty to fulfill his legacy in the way shown by him, proceeding with unity and without swerving from the course.

Source: "König Boris," *HF-Abend*, August 30, 1943, p. 1.

A faithful servant of Adolf Hitler, King Boris, died suddenly. In both the last war and this war, Bulgaria placed itself on the wrong horse. Rulers simply ignore the people's voice, but it is the people – here, the Bulgarian people – who pay the cost. The stupidity of people knows no bounds. Why can a tyrant be able to force his will on everyone else?

STATE OF EMERGENCY IN DENMARK

Copenhagen, August 30, 1943.

The Commander-in-Chief of the German troops in Denmark has imposed a state of emergency to safeguard the Danish coast and protect against any activity by enemy agents. The necessary measures have been carried out. There have been no major incidents.

Source: "Ausnahmezustand in Dänemark," *HF-Abend*, August 30, 1943, p. 1.

The "New Order" in Europe, invented by the Nazis, is being shaken. The oppressed people have not lost their desire for freedom and will soon be able to reclaim it. With English and Canadian troops in southern Italy, "Fortress Europe" in the south becomes a war zone. [. . .]

September 8, 1943

On September 3, according to Italy's Armed Forces report, the enemy tried to land on the coast and was pushed back. On September 8, today,
    Italy has unconditionally surrendered!
    The beginning of the end is here! Now the liars in the Italian armed forces command do not need to exercise their dirty office any longer. Italy's surrender is of tremendous importance, and its consequences will be seen in the coming days.

On the other hand, the Nazi presses will remain confident up to the last breath. From the September 3 *Hamburger Tageblatt*:

"'Shrinking hope in the enemy camp,' declares the Argentine newspaper, *Pampero*, having determined through its observations Germany will go on the counteroffensive in the fifth war year and secure the ultimate victory."[44]

Of all things, a newspaper in Argentina calculates Germany's final victory. [...]

September 10, 1943

The Giessen Council ordered the mayors in its jurisdiction to stop the "rumors" about Italy and reassure the public. The calming sedatives to be administered are pathetic. The people are to be told a Fascist Italian government was established that will further fight at the German side, and our Führer would soon speak about it. Ach! This is the Führer who spoke so much in the past and promised so much that not much more remains to be said. [...]

September 11, 1943

The Badoglio government has surrendered [to the Allies]. German troops are disarming the Italian army.[45] There are fights in some places between German and Italian troops, but they are likely to be of short duration. Mussolini will be freed by German units.

The landed English and American troops progress slowly. Both forces lack zeal. What the enemy exhibits is not impressive. Russians advance faster under heavy fighting near the Donets Basin than do the English in Calabria without any effective resistance.

It is certain Germany has thrown additional troops into Italy. Badoglio's intention to bring Italy out of the war has failed. Italy now becomes a theater of war. Hitler has managed again, for the time being, to keep the war away from the southern border of Greater Germany.

It will depend on how our allies Bulgaria, Romania, and Hungary behave in the next weeks. An objective assumption, one without emotion, is Italy's example will have no effect on the other countries. Continued advances by the Russians, though, will have an effect. And perhaps Turkey will finally step forward [and join the Allies] in the belated way Italy joined Germany in 1940. The smell of carcasses will bring them in.

England and the USA's next chess move is finally coming due. The Balkans probably will work out well for them as it did in 1918. The Allies can count upon the population's support in this area. That is where a parallel can be made to the chain of events of 1918. At the end of September of that year Bulgaria entered into a separate surrender. Turkey followed on October 30, 1918. Nonetheless, the "stab in the back" [*Dolchstoss*] legend found many followers after the war. Even if the German army had offered further resistance after November 9, 1918, the British–French Orient army would have invaded Austria by way of Hungary. This most vulnerable point in the southern part of the Kaiser's Reich was simply disregarded by the Dolchstoss liars and later on was never mentioned at all.

Hopefully, there is no Dolchstoss in this war, and hopefully Adolf Hitler really fights until "five minutes after 12 o'clock." Then the coming screamers for revenge will have little possibility of saying, "If only we had fought on for another 14 days."

I, however, can say, "If only you had never started a war."

September 12, 1943

[. . .] The Russian successes are substantial. They have reconquered the areas around Orel, Belgorod, Kharkov, Voroshilovgrad, Gorlovka, Makiyivka, Stalino [Donetsk], Taganrog, and Mariupol. The entire Donets Basin is in their hands; the industrial area in this region alone would be a success of special significance. The ultimate consequences of their victories, however, will be on a large scale. The raid against Kiev and the Dnieper will cause the Crimea to be vacated, and the Ukraine will be reclaimed by its owners! Mind you, in summer 1943!

Autumn and winter are at the door. Since even the Nazis admit the Russians are superior in the winter, one need not be a prophet to forecast the German army will slowly but steadily be thrown out of Russia.

September 13, 1943

I almost forgot to mention the Führer's speech of September 10. It took the collapse of Italy to open his mouth. Hitler focused on Italy's broken compact with Germany and gave it the following significance: "Militarily, the loss of Italy means little because the fighting in that country was supported and carried for months primarily by German forces. We will continue this fight now free from all burdening inhibitions."[46] Furthermore, Hitler said:

I already explained on September 1, 1939, in the Reichstag that neither time nor force of arms will ever defeat the German people. Since then, primarily by our own strength, the enemy was pushed back more than 1,000 kilometers from the German borders. Only in the air is the German homeland susceptible to terrorism. However, also here the technical and organizational conditions are developing – not only to stop these terrorist raids, but also, through other and effective measures, to retaliate. Because of tactical necessities in this enormous fateful fight, it may be that we are forced now and then to give up some part of the front, or to evade a special threat. Yet, the fully developed steel forged by the German homeland will never break, and through the heroism and the blood of our soldiers, the Reich will be protected.

The speech ended as follows:

In view of the extraordinary proceedings in Italy, strong measures are being undertaken to defend German interests. As far as they concern Italy, they already run now according to plan and successfully. The example of Yugoslavia's betrayal gave us before this a wholesome cleansing and valuable understanding.

The fate of Italy, however, may be for all of us a lesson to never renounce, in hours of the hardest distress and the bitterest emergency, the requirement of national honor, to stand with our confederates with a believing heart, and to fulfill faithfully the obligations imposed upon us. The nation that withstands this testing before divine Providence will in the end receive from the Almighty the wages of the laurel wreath of victory and thus increase the value of its existence. This must and will be, in every circumstance, Germany.

This speech, given after a long period of silence, is an appeal, in the hour of fate, to persevere. Nothing is said to the people about the Eastern Front, or about the submarine failures – or about victory and peace being in sight. The earlier bold prophecies are held in check. Only dark hints are made about "retribution" for the air terror. Of the former descriptions of applause and rejoicing after his speeches, nothing was presented.

The seriousness of the hour exhorts us!

The collapse of Italy is because one man, Mussolini, determined the politics of Italy. This autocrat did not foresee the Italian people's limitations of strength but instead acted merely on his megalomaniacal ideas. That is his guilt. If now Hitler and consorts spit out poison and gall because in Italy there were men who wanted to end the war, it is only because such actions are, from Hitler's point of view, beyond comprehension. He raves over the "breaking of the trust." It can be objected, however, a certain Herr Hitler also broke the trust on June 22, 1941, when he broke the alliance with Russia. Of that there is no doubt. The lame excuse that Russia had been ready to attack Germany is an allegation – and nothing more.

September 14, 1943

[. . .] The Führer mentioned in his speech of September 10, 1943, the "technical and organizational conditions are developing" in order to meet the hostile air raids with appropriate measures. According to Hitler's statement, "the conditions are in the process of arising."

For a long time, Goebbels has been threatening retaliation. From all of that, it is clear Germany is presently not in the position to defend itself against the air raids, or to undertake counter-attacks. The situation is very embarrassing for those in charge. The only thing left is to console themselves, though they should not be waiting on miraculous things to occur. It is always cooked up the same way. The expectations in the First World War involved airships, heavy cannon ("Big Bertha"), and submarines.[47] With what final success? Everything was for nothing! Why would it be different this time?

Is it not possible our opponents also have expectations, an improvement here or there, or a new invention? Naturally, we may not speak about that. One certainty is this: the enemy air force does not become weaker but stronger – stronger every day. That alone is bad enough.

September 15, 1943

When Mussolini was forced to retire, the new government of Marshal Badoglio placed him under arrest, and it was not known what became of him. But now stories are coming from around the world Mussolini has been freed from prison by a special commando unit of SS and paratroops.[48] This rescue operation with its sensational success has invigorated the German people. Our enemies display little understanding about the feelings of the masses. The initiative shown by Germany here is compelling. The English and Americans make sophisticated calculations, but they lack any impetus from military actions. They make no impression at all on the German people.

In any case, it is inexcusable carelessness if every major Fascist is not immediately put into prison. That should have been a prerequisite for concluding any negotiations for an armistice.

I regard General Eisenhower as incompetent.[49] Quicker action in North Africa could have avoided the campaign in Tunisia. The enterprise in Sicily was pitiful because the German troops' retreat to South Italy was not cut off. Landing at Salerno is not to be understood because landing at Lazio would have been better and cut off the supplies to our troops in South Italy. Moreover, our opponents are so feeble in their air war. The moment their attacks begin to have effects (Hamburg, for example), they let up. No attacks have taken place since September 6.

What is the opponent thinking? Neither side is going to win this war just with phrases. Lay it on! More courage, gentlemen! So far, only the Germans, Greeks, Japanese, and Russians have real achievements. All others are light-weights, starting with the Belgians and their King Leopold III heading the list, right on up to the Italians, who let themselves be disarmed by the Germans without offering any resistance.[50]

There even were people who could not muster the courage to offer any kind of passive resistance.

September 20, 1943

DEATH PENALTY FOR TREASONOUS DEFEATIST

Berlin, September 2, 1943.

The 52-year-old Councilor Theodor Korselt from Rostock was executed August 25, 1943, having been sentenced to death by the People's Court for aiding the enemy and subversion. By his defeatist talk and spreading rumors to adversely affect the German people's morale, Korselt betrayed the fighting front. For traitors guilty of betraying the people, only the death penalty is applicable.

> *Source:* "Todesstrafe für verräterischen Defaitisten," *VB-Süd*, September 3, 1943, p. 8.

[...]

EXECUTED FOR AIDING THE ENEMY

Düsseldorf, September 14, 1943.

The pianist Karl Robert Kreiten, 27, from Düsseldorf, was executed on September 7, 1943, having been sentenced to death by the People's Court for aiding the enemy and subversion.

Using the worst incitements, defamations, and exaggerations, Kreiten tried to adversely influence a national comrade in her loyal and confident posture and thereby showed himself to be outside the people's community [*Volksgemeinschaft*].[51]

> *Source:* "Wegen Feindbegünstigung hingerichtet," *HLZ*, September 15, 1943, p. 1.

Heinrich Himmler at work!

What type of "work" must Himmler and his cohorts be up to in the German-occupied areas if here at home citizens can be condemned to death for something they said? It is highly dangerous to speak the truth. Such draconian measures underscore the terrible situation in which we find ourselves. When our enemies allow even the sharpest public criticism, they display strength. With us in Germany, thinking is a dangerous thing.

September 21, 1943

We are undergoing major changes in straightening out the front and repositioning our units, according to the army reports. Particularly interesting is the September 19 report from Führer Headquarters:

For the past two weeks around Salerno, ongoing heavy battles have kept the British and American landing forces from achieving their anticipated operational success. They did not succeed in cutting off the German divisions in South Italy. In the face of far superior numbers of enemy forces, our troops prevented each attempt to expand the landing area. Despite the strong fire coming from the enemy ships' guns, our counter-attack pushed their forces to the coastal edge.

The report concludes with this statement:

After the German forces in South Italy united, our troops pulled back from the enemy according to plan and put together a shorter defensive line.[52]

Thus in the course of a single breath the report tells us the enemy had no operational success and the German troops pulled back from the enemy according to plan. The impartial observer will come to the clear conclusion the German troops lost the Battle of Salerno in Italy. In such a way will the war be lost – "according to plan."

BEARER OF THE KNIGHT'S CROSS MET A HEROIC DEATH

First Lieutenant Josef Lang, a company commander in an engineering battalion, had received the Knight's Cross of the Iron Cross for outstanding bravery in the western campaign. As a sergeant, he safely led four men in an operation to blow up the enemy bridge over the Aisne Canal. Although two engineers fell while approaching the open terrain, he rushed forward with the other two, cut through the barbed wires under heavy enemy fire, and destroyed the bridge with an explosive charge. Now, this exemplary officer has succumbed to a wound sustained in a battle at the Eastern Front.

Lieutenant Lang, son of the cutler Lawrence Lang, was born on February 20, 1914, in Stetten on the Danube (in the vicinity of Tuttlingen). He attended elementary and vocational school and learned masonry. Later, he volunteered for military service and in 1934 entered Engineer Battalion 5 in Ulm. He was transferred to Engineer Battalion 15 and moved onto the field of battle. In 1940 he was promoted to sergeant, and in 1942 to lieutenant.

Source: "Ritterkreuzträger starben den Heldentod," *VB-Süd*,
August 30, 1943, p. 2.

Long before the "Seizure of Power," Hitler said in a meeting he would not promote the most capable people to leading positions but the most devoted Party members. Those who are particularly preferred in the armed forces are the daredevils. They are promoted and given honors and awards. The apogee is a hero's death. The obituary for First Lieutenant Lang shows he was a technical sergeant in 1940, but today he is a dead first lieutenant. [. . .]

September 27, 1943

Yesterday, Sunday, [Pauline and I] were invited to Dr. Weber's house in Grünberg for coffee. The Heutzenröder family also was there. Frau Heutzenröder, wearing the Party badge, declared not a single railroad track, or even a bolt, would be left behind in Russia as the Germans retreated. Every objection of mine was futile. One can only regard such people as simply having lost their reason. This sort can be instructed only at the end, when they clearly and distinctly see the living rubble of their hopes lying before them. Until then, it is necessary to practice further patience. Patience, and again patience.

October 10, 1943

Sunday trip to Bad Nauheim. Wonderful weather. A summer day in autumn. We also visited the cemetery and had an opportunity to see the WWI graves of the soldiers from Bad Nauheim. The famous "Honor Memorial" was covered for the most part in ivy. Very many graves were but small mounds of earth without decoration. That is uncommonly sad, particularly for a state like the Third Reich that so tendentiously exalts the deeds of its armed forces. "When the Moor has done his part, he is simply forgotten."[53]

The "thanks of the fatherland" is assuredly yours, it was said in the First World War. We now have had the opportunity to view this thanks.

October 14, 1943

Three o'clock in the afternoon in Altenstadt. The roar of airplane engines can be heard. An attack is being played out high in the sky. For the first time I am able to witness German fighter planes on the attack. Two American bombers are brought down in flames, breaking into pieces. After the crash of the airplane that fell in the forest between Rommelhausen and Obereu, a violent explosion took place and strong smoke clouds ascended. Twelve parachutes are visible. A third plunging airplane, which spiraled downward very fast to the earth, was for certain a German fighter.[54]

October 15, 1943

At least five to six American bombers were shot down in the vicinity of Altenstadt. A soldier from the Altenstadt airfield told me today German fighter pilots stationed in Hannover refuel here. The wrecks of several airplanes and the corpses of airmen are in the Langenbergheim forest. The pilot from the fallen German plane saved himself by a parachute jump.

The deputy mayor of Höchst on the Nidder reported to the Altenstadt administration office the troops' mood was confident.[55] In approximately two weeks a miracle would happen, an officer said.

I regret not being able to believe in miracles.

October 16, 1943

If part of the German people, and in particular soldiers, remain convinced of victory and still believe in "retribution" and other miraculous things, it is entirely the fault of our enemies' incomprehensible way of fighting. Those people seem to have no esprit de corps. One might even come up with the notion the English and their allies do not want to win. Measured in terms of Germany's and Russia's achievements, the English and Americans have shown nothing impressive so far. It nearly looks like what the Nazi propaganda has so often stated, that the English want to let Germany and Russia cut each other to ribbons and then appear on the battlefields at the end without having struck a blow.

The lack of an idealistic motivation will be costly for the English nation in times to come. For now, the English may consider their cold calculations as smart, but they had better think about when Russia may want to repay them for their hesitant attitude. The English have sufficient troops in the mother-land, in North Africa, and in the Near East, but they will not undertake to relieve Russia. Their slow crawl through Italy is truly wretched. That can be only deliberate.

October 26, 1943

Every Monday the judicial officers of Upper Hesse must meet in Giessen for continuing education courses. We are in the middle of war, and the National Socialist Administration of Justice thinks it can afford to torment older officials with courses.[56] During a recess, I was called to Regional Court President Jacobi's office where he proceeded to give me a lecture. He said, among other things, Local Group Leader Pott in Laubach com-plained the Laubach District Court was not enthusiastic enough. Pott also complained against me personally. He stated my door was often closed to collectors, and he had the impression I was doing it deliberately. My objection that the collectors simply should have returned when I was available did not satisfy President Jacobi. He said I had the obligation as a civil servant to set a good example, and if I was going to be away when they collect on Sundays for war victims, I had to bring my donations in advance to the appropriate place!

This small slice of life of a "national comrade" in the Third Reich might present a lesson for coming generations never to tolerate a tyranny. [. . .]

November 1, 1943

SERIOUS ATTACK BY A FOREIGN WORKER

A foreign worker on a farm in the Biberach district attacked the farmer's two daughters in the morning in the stable and stabbed them with a knife in the chest and back, inflicting mortal injuries. Then he set fires, burning much of the property, whereupon the author of the deed fled into the forest and hanged himself from a tree, apparently having made preparations earlier for that. The heinous act caused strong outrage among the population.

Who brought foreign workers into Germany to perform hard labor and sent German workers to the Eastern Front to be used as cannon fodder? The Supreme Commander of the Third Reich bears the sole blame for such occurrences. In many cases the brutal treatment of foreign workers creates the reason for these vengeful actions.

November 2, 1943

In "Return to the Dnieper," the army reporter Eugen Feederle writes, "The German soldier, without batting an eyelash, carries out the decision to retreat, and he believes fervently in the coming settlement of accounts with the enemy." Herr Reporter regards it as his special task to make retreat at the front, or the shortening of the front, a wisely calculated move by the German High Command. He speaks even of a "free choice in a self-imposed time-table" and suggests the path to a counter-attack is clearly visible.[57]

The propagandists manage to elevate the continued retreat in the East to a brilliant achievement by the German army. It is the same whether we triumph or are struck down; the Nazis make a gigantic affair of it. However, the Nazis employ quite another method when it comes to our opponents. When the English General Alexander in Burma had to retreat, from then on the Nazi press called him the "retreat general."[58] But for the ingenious Commander-in-Chief Hitler, it is not a retreat but just a practical breaking off or shortening of the front. [...]

November 9, 1943

The Führer spoke in Munich to his "Old Guard."[59] Some items from his speech:

[...] The fight in the East is the heaviest which the German people have ever had to go through. What our men bear there, cannot be compared at all with what our opponents suffer. This is the last attempt to bring the German front to collapse, but as always in world history the last battle alone brings about the decision. This battle will be won by the people with the greatest inner values, the greatest persistence, and the greatest zeal. What I therefore ask of the German soldiers is immense ... In barely two or three years after the end of war all our buildings will be rebuilt again, so the enemy may destroy as much as they want ... They may believe it or not, the hour of retribution will come. (A storm of rejoicing without precedent rose up. The ovation lasted several minutes, with roars everywhere, constantly renewing itself, and cries of "Der Führer!") ...

Even if we do not reach America at the moment, then God be thanked there lies a state within reach nevertheless. And we will hold ourselves to that. (Again stormy applause erupts.) ...

Let this war last for as long a time as it will, Germany will never capitulate! (Strong applause.) ...

We will never repeat the error of 1918; that is, that at a quarter to twelve we will lay down our weapons. Whereupon one can rely on this: the one who lays down the weapons at the end will be Germany – five minutes after twelve! (Stormy applause.)
...

German people, be completely assured, whatever comes we will master it! At the end victory stands! (For several minutes, showers of applause.) . . .

I know throughout all these entire years, it is the women of our nation wherein reside my most fanatical followers. Hail victory! [*Sieg Heil!*]

As to the war situation in general, the losses of men and material, or in what way the victory of Germany will be achieved, Adolf Hitler said nothing. His intention to fight until "five minutes after twelve" was clear to me already in 1933. That Adolf Hitler could watch as an entire people go down, about that I had never a doubt. A tyrant is simply a tyrant.

November 12, 1943

THE DONETS BASIN IS COMPLETELY USELESS

Berlin, November 11.

The particular goal of the Soviets' summer and autumn offensive this year was the Donets Basin coal mines and ironworks. A great cry of triumph arose in the Anglo-American press when the Soviets recaptured the Donets Basin. Now the "Times" reports meekly from Moscow that Soviet experts to their sorrow found the Germans had rendered Donets's industry completely useless before their departure. Not a single steel mill escaped the destruction; all blast furnaces, rolling mills and coke ovens were carefully destroyed so that reconstruction will require a very long time. Furthermore the Germans managed to carry away many valuable machines. The hopes the Soviets placed on using the industry in the Donets Basin have been thoroughly disappointed.

Source: "Das Donezbecken völlig unbrauchbar," *HLZ*, November 12, 1943, p. 2.

German soldiers boast about destroying the Russian military and industrial plants – and also some residential property of the long-suffering Russian people. There are some humane soldiers conducting this war who abhor such things. Unfortunately they are a small minority. [. . .]

November 18, 1943

BEARER OF OAK LEAVES RECEIVES A FARMSTEAD

Posen, October 24, 1943.

In a highly significant act that will settle frontline soldiers in recovered German territory in the East, Regional Leader and Reich Governor Greiser presented to Oak Leaves bearer Chief District Leader of Hitler Youth Captain Gerhard Hein a farm in Wollheim in the district of Gniezno [Poland]. In the presence of leaders from the Party, state, and army, Regional Leader and Reich Governor Greiser made this solemn act as a way of marking the upcoming settlement tasks in Wartheland.

The long-established German farmers of this land, so said the Regional Leader, have always been fighters for the preservation of their nationality and their economic existence, just as the many hundreds of thousands of evacuees, who, following the call of their Führer, have positioned themselves in the past years as a front row of national fighting farmers. Now we add the new – and yet so ancient – Teutonic German type of military farmer, who shall merge with the already established settlers in the coming years and decades to create a new type of the politically combative farmer. By providing land for our wounded veterans, the beginning has been made. [. . .]

Source: "Eichenlaubträger erhält Bauernhof," VB-Süd, October 25, p. 2.

The Nazis plan ahead. They already are thinking of "later" positions for the fighters at the front. The Regional Leader gives a "gift" to a fellow Party comrade who is presently a captain. The gift is a farm in Gniezno, Poland. But to whom does this farm belong? What happened to the owner? These questions interest neither the donor nor the recipient.

The Germanic armed peasant of the past, the soldier-farmer, is again to rise. Today's ruling powers know the stolen land must be defended and those they seduce into taking the gifts will be grateful to them. Naturally the leaders do not become settlers themselves but once again place the credulous front-line fighters' lives in jeopardy. The soldiers who heedlessly believe they are receiving gifts will come to realize property wrongly acquired will not prosper. [. . .]

November 19, 1943

Frau Desch, wife of innkeeper Hermann Desch, denounced Captain Menz for making insulting remarks about Adolf Hitler. Menz is the Laubach Support Services Officer. (In civilian life he had been a court bailiff in Frankfurt.) The military court in Berlin sentenced Captain Menz to three years in prison. An office worker named Frank, a cashier at the Laubach military hospital, was an additional witness and countersigned the charges.

[. . .]

November 22, 1943

Adolf Hitler addressed the subject of women in his November 9 speech. He called women his fanatic supporters and referred to an American magazine that said German women were the worst thing about National Socialism.

THE PARTY AND WOMEN

An American newspaper recently wrote that the worst part of National Socialism is the women, that National Socialism obviously does more for German women than for other folks. It has elevated them socially and brought them together into strong organizations. It sends cultured women into the factories to take jobs, so that they may take vacations, and so on. And the newspaper concludes they could not do that in the democracies. And because they cannot do that, they will have to exterminate National Socialist women in the future because they have become fanatics and cannot be re-educated.

That is correct! I know in all these years it has been especially the women from among the people who have been my most fanatical followers. And let this continue to an even greater extent in the future. The women, together with the men, must support the movement even in the difficult times.

When bombing raids come, it is the Party above all that takes the trouble to see order is maintained, and everything that can be done is done. Can you imagine at all, my Party comrades, that we could have suffered and endured for even a single month of the First World War what we have now shouldered for years? Can you imagine that? That is to the credit of the bold education of our people. That is to the credit of the National Socialist faith. (Loud applause interrupts the Führer.) As long as this power remains, we need not despair, but to the contrary, we may look to the future with proud confidence.

I have come here for only a few hours to speak to you, my followers of long standing. Tomorrow I must return, and I will take with me a beautiful memory of my comrades-in-arms and of our Time of Struggle. And you must leave here with the fanatical confidence and fanatical belief that nothing else at all can exist for us but our victory. That is why we are fighting, that is why many have already died, that is why even others will make the supreme sacrifice. That is why generations will live, not only now but in the future. Our nation will be richly rewarded for the blood that is shed here today. Millions of people will be granted an existence in new homelands.

For that we remember all those of our comrades who as National Socialist fighters paved the way for a greater fatherland and for a greater German people.

To our National Socialist Party and our German Reich, Sieg Heil![60]

Are the magazine's views and Hitler's response correct? The male fanatic can be placed on the same level with the female fanatic. But for Hitler this was naturally a welcome opportunity to give praise to his Party's women and to spur them to further "deeds." Simple-minded people are sensitive to praise. Anyhow, the American magazine editors will have formed their opinion solely from German propaganda material. There is not one illustrated newspaper in Germany that does not somehow place girls and women in the foreground: laughing girls as assistants, or engaged in sports, women shown as workers, and mothers radiating joy with their playful children. Sunshine, nothing but sunshine – that is National Socialist propaganda. Both the homeland and the foreign countries have been smoothly taken in by this propaganda. The gentle sex did not notice at all they became slave girls under the Nazi regime. On one point, however, women have unrestrained liberty, in the area of eroticism. Is that why women switched themselves over to National Socialism with their entire being?

I certainly know many women who want nothing to do with the NSDAP, primarily those within the Church. But the question up front is why do so many women have such a fanaticism for the Party? What attracted them? That is not simple to answer. Exaggerated nationalism doubtlessly had a strong effect. Certain mythic ideas made an impression. Women are easily attracted to the hero cult, and then this cult reinforces the attraction. Apart from that, the NSDAP program is extensive and multiform. Who offers much, offers everyone something. And if the individual is asked, "What moved you to become a National Socialist," he or she for the most part does not know how to explain it.

National Socialism is a disease, a plague. Perhaps that is the best explanation. Anyhow, hysterical women are completely determined Party members. These women urgently want to have themselves in the spotlight and have decided only the Party gives them the opportunity to follow their hearts' desire – to harangue their fellow citizens. From this then the fanatical followers develop, just as Hitler needs.

November 23, 1943

If someday the rest of the world reproves the German people for giving in to the rule of Hitler, it will be good to remember this death sentence:

DEATH PENALTY FOR THREE PARASITES

The Mohrlüder siblings, who own a home in Nordstemmen, denied lodgings to people displaced by the bombing in Hannover, even though their house has ten rooms. After being pressed, the Mohrlüders set out a soiled mattress in their vestibule and offered it to a couple from Hannover who, with their child, were supposed to spend the night there. The investigation of their incredible behavior led to the discovery that the Mohrlüders were outrageous hoarders whose stocks filled an entire guest room. The special court of Hannover has sentenced Heinrich Mohrlüder, 52, Frieda Mohrlüder, 65, and Marta Mohrlüder, 54, to death as parasites of the people.

Source: "Todesstrafe für drei Volksschädlinge," *HF-Abend*,
November 15, 1943, p. 2.

There is no paragraph in the German penal code on which this judgment is based. Nevertheless a death sentence was given for "public parasites." Everyone who rebels in any possible way against National Socialist regulations is immediately an "enemy of the people" or a "public parasite." This designation is sufficient to mark people in Germany as candidates for death. It does not require special explanations from me how such judgments spread terror. Evoking terror by acts of violence serves to intimidate an entire people. Hitler and Company's art of governing depends on the continued application of force. It is by this system of terrorism the NSDAP prevails.

I can only repeat something I realized from the beginning. This kind of government, this vainglorious and exaggerated One Thousand Year Reich, cannot in any way be eliminated from the inside out. Hitler can fall only by a lost war. Otherwise by nothing. Any German who opposes this system cannot say so outright, or without further notice he would be easily finished off.

Hitler is not embarrassed at all to let daily death sentences be carried out. I am convinced the death of the entire German population would not even impress him. He could see eighty million Germans die and still turn to his friend, Dr. Joseph Goebbels, and say, "You see Joseph, this has never happened before me, and it will never happen again after me: I am the most ingenious mass murderer of all times."

[. . .]

November 25, 1943

These past two days, November 23–24, the Supreme Command of the Armed Forces issued reports about the air attacks against Berlin. Conditions have fundamentally changed. Germany tirelessly sang the praises of the German pilots who attacked England in 1940, and London in particular. I well remember the enormous enthusiasm prevailing throughout the population for continuous air raids against England. They could not have been more insane. I never heard anything from them about "terrorist raids."

> British bomber formations conducted a heavy terrorist raid into the evening hours of yesterday against the Reich capital. The dropping of numerous explosive and incendiary bombs caused devastation in several parts of the city. A number of irreplaceable cultural sites were destroyed. The population had losses.

> Source: "Großer Abwehrerfolg an der Smolensker Rollbahn," HLZ, November 24, 1943, p. 1.

> The Reich capital was attacked again in the evening of November 23 by strong British bomber formations. This new terrorist attack caused damage in several districts. In addition to residential areas, many public buildings, including churches, welfare institutions, and cultural sites were destroyed. Despite difficult conditions, fighter unit and air defense artillery shot down 19 enemy aircraft.

> Source: "Sowjetkräfte eingeschlossen," HF-Abend, November 24, 1943, p. 1.

Because the opponent is paying us back with interest for what we did to him, suddenly we are victims of "terrorist raids." You, National Socialists: Air raids are a part of war. If you really thought differently, you would not have sent your planes against Poland, Norway, Holland, Belgium, France etc. Besides, is not "Total War" yet another of your own inventions? So why this pitiful pretense?

Harald von Scheidt-Weschpfennig

Lieutenant and Company Leader in a Grenadier Regiment. Holder of the Iron Cross 1 and 2, and the Wound Badge,
For his beloved Fatherland, my hopeful, courageous son [. . .] died at the age of 19.
In deep anguish: Frau Elisabeth v. Scheidt-Weschpfennig [. . .].

> Source: HLZ, November 21, 1943, p. 8.

A company leader at merely nineteen years of age! A minor promoted before his elders. That gives cause for serious reflection.

Only cannon fodder? And nothing else?

Dear Fatherland, listen! I mean only good for you!

[. . .]

December 2, 1943

During the war a joyful event. Can there be such a thing? Today we received a letter from our daughter-in-law, Freda Kellner, from New Haven, Connecticut. It came by way of the German Red Cross in Berlin through the International Red Cross in Geneva. Freda writes that all goes well, and a third child, a boy, has been born, who is fourteen months old.[61] The letter, which is allowed to have only twenty-five words, is dated August 19, 1942! It has thus taken fifteen months to come into our hands. We answered immediately, likewise twenty-five words. When will this letter arrive in the USA? Before the end of the war? No one knows. We hope our son and his family receive this sign of life from us soon.

December 3, 1943

Gloomy weather brings forth gloomy thoughts. For those people unwavering from the beginning, as I was, convinced Germany would never win this war, for them a look into coming developments is a terrible affair. I see such deep darkness in the future I have to give all my efforts to preserve the last bit of optimism. Perhaps my belief that a ray of hope will somehow come out of America gives me a reason to keep my head high, at least to some degree.

By no means does one have to be a prophet of doom to imagine a dark future. How could it be at all different? The imbroglio that will occur among the German populace is alone reason enough to look ahead with deep concern. If the more decent Germans are not ready to establish a justice of full atonement and to heal the people's spirit, Germany is forever lost.

[...]

December 5, 1943

[...]

ITALIAN JEWS INTO THE CONCENTRATION CAMPS

Rome, December 1, 1943.

All Jews living in Italy, no matter what their nationality, must be sent to concentration camps, it became known on Wednesday, according to a police ordinance sent to all provincial heads. Their entire mobile and immobile

possessions are immediately seized, to be appropriated later – so states the
same ordinance. The Republic will divide these properties among those who
have suffered from the bombing. All half-Jews – as has been decided – were
to be under sharp police surveillance. [. . .]

Source: "Italiens Juden ins Konzentrationslager," *HLZ,*
December 2, 1943, p. 1.

Senseless and cruel? Those are not the correct names for these Fascist
crimes.[62] These beasts simply no longer realize how such vile actions
they perpetrate bring them down so low. Perhaps in the Fascist reasoning this is known as "heroic deeds." We do not know what goes on in
sick minds.

December 8, 1943

Mussolini. *Source:* Detail from Keystone/Hulton Archive/Getty Images.

This is the "Duce." This is the man, this Italian with his megalomania
and crazy ideas who has brought the Italians to the edge of the abyss.
The Italian people must pay the cost because they did not have the
courage to defend their democratic rights before the bill came due.
[. . .]

December 9, 1943

Otto Burk

On November 18, 1943, our beloved son and brother, Captain Otto Burk, was killed on the Eastern Front at the head of the regiment he was commanding.
Age 28
Holder of the German Golden Wound Badge, Iron Cross 1 and 2, the Panzer Assault Badge, and Eastern Front Medal.
Arnold Burk, MD, and wife Lotte, née Strasser; Martin Burk, cadet-sergeant; Klaus Burk, Lieutenant.

If a 28-year-old captain is a regimental commander, there is an uncommon shortage of staff officers. That shortage cannot be solved if large numbers of potential officers (officer candidates) are sent to the front lines. These young cadets wind up as platoon leaders, and most will die for "Volk und Führer" within their period of probation.

COUNT REVENTLOW HAS DIED

Berlin, November 22, 1943.

In Munich, the well-known Pan-Germanic pioneer, the National Socialist author and journalist, Count Ernst zu Reventlow, died at the age of 74. With the passing of Reichstag Deputy Count Ernst zu Reventlow on November 20, the National Socialist movement has lost one of its earliest and most valuable protagonists. [...]

Source: "Graf Reventlow gestorben," *VB-Süd*, November 23, 1943, p. 2.

Count Reventlow was already accountable to every German – before and during the First World War – for his animal lusting after power. The heavy suffering and damage brought about by Kaiser Wilhelm II owed much to Reventlow's concept of the German Empire's superiority. This type of person, with his exaggerated nationalistic convictions, generates intolerance, arrogance, strife, and war. The organizations that established themselves by saber rattling and caused the entire world to go after Germany prayed to power and identified war as a healing agent for the people. They even went so far as to declare war was decreed by God, and a long period of peace would be a national mishap for Germany.

This Count Reventlow (formerly a naval officer) was a warmonger, war fanatic, and glorifier of war, who brutally championed the right of the strongest, and therefore always demanded a "vigorous" foreign politics. This chauvinist did not fall victim to the people's anger in the revolutionary days of 1918, and that encouraged Reventlow to reshape his politics into a more presentable form for the people. Like every other extreme national politician, he found his way to the National Socialist German Workers' Party. He, the scion of old hereditary nobility, from then on embraced "socialism"! It was plain to be seen the NSDAP leaders intended to shape their socialism into a special format; otherwise these noblemen would not have so completely gone over to them.

National Socialism is the greatest swindle of all times, using the word "socialism" in its name to beguile the working masses. I once read (in 1933 or 1934) an article by Count Reventlow in a trade union newspaper, where he said the workers before 1933 had been blinded and deceived by their union leaders! Of all people, the Count an advisor to the German workplace!

It is unfortunate Count Reventlow died before the end (what he hoped would be "final victory"). Or did he perhaps anticipate the things yet to come and make his getaway: furtively, silently, and quietly? Deserted?

December 10, 1943

[...]

Sometimes a person is inclined to believe there is no prevailing heaven. But from time to time people see there is indeed revenge. The Party boss, Julius Weber, had to have a leg amputated in the First World War, but that was not enough of a warning for him – he still could not be an enthusiastic lover of peace. So he dedicated himself to Adolf Hitler, although Weber knew the nation's seducer would do everything to start an even more tremendous world war. For his deeds, Weber has the single most fitting award: two sons killed in battle. But that is how heaps of medals can be handed out at receptions. And there is the satisfaction of having provided actual sacrifices for the Führer. Heil Hitler! [...]

The conferences held by the Allied statesmen in Cairo and Tehran have moved the Nazis to an impotent rage.[63] For some time German propaganda insisted the competing interests of Russia, England, and the USA would one day benefit Germany. There was also heavy speculation about disunity among the enemy. Now that these last hopes have shattered, we get the temper tantrums. In the *Völkischer Beobachter* of December 6, Karl

Neuscheler wrote an editorial, "Unconditional Surrender," in which he unleashes a vulgar torrent of abuse.

"UNCONDITIONAL SURRENDER"

The pathetic political notions of our enemy culminated in Casablanca with noticeable obstinacy and persistence after all sides constantly repeated the formula, "Unconditional Surrender." [...] They press on with their fighting, using cheap methods: lies, unashamed defamations, murder, extortion, terror, robbery, and underhandedness of every form. They try to appear as saints, prophets, and world saviors, anointed by heaven, to command as they wished over the people and earth's possessions. And whoever is not convinced of their resemblance to God and wants to determine his own rights and way of life, is maligned, enslaved, or removed.

Source: "Bedingungslose Kapitulation," *VB-Süd*, December 6, 1943, p. 1.

I do not know if it is stupid and ridiculous, as the article writer says, for our enemies to declare Germany must surrender unconditionally. Given the balance of power, it seems impossible Germany can dictate the peace to its enemies. If Germany, for any reason, cannot continue fighting any longer, we know it will not be allowed to set any conditions. The enemy will set them. That is the meaning of "unconditional surrender," and indeed it is based on the German nation's conduct since 1933.

[...]

December 12, 1943

Today is Sunday, not a day of rest for the Nazis. At 1:45 in the afternoon the air defense unit assembles on Stifts Street. I belong to Block 10. We have to assemble in work clothes, gas masks, and air defense equipment. On the way there, I borrow a rope so I can have something to hold in my hand. Men and women appear. The wives are dressed in male clothing. The air defense team gathers in front of the former night quarters for travelers. We take our positions. An automobile appears. From it emerges a uniformed and decorated man from Giessen. Greetings from the local air defense leader. He lets it be known the community of Laubach has provided a small house for the air defense forces. Then words from the high dignitary from Giessen. Of his performance I can hear only bits and pieces. For example, whoever tries to save his own skin during the danger of an aircraft attack will be considered a fugitive. In between all this my feet begin to get cold.

I always take the opportunity to stay in the background, resolved to be prepared for the end of the "celebration" and slowly but surely take off. I disappear in an opposite direction.

Why these alarms for nothing? Because the air defense department and air defense officials must find justification for their existence. The office holder does everything in the same manner as the National Socialists. Then they report how it was a fantastic event that mobilized everyone, and how it all went wonderfully well. That is National Socialism!

[...]

December 14, 1943

[...]

THE SOLDIERS' YOUNGEST HELPERS

The soldiers' very best comrades, the onlookers who have long since become a household name, happy to be involved with protecting the homeland, stand within the exclusive community of their batteries: our "Hitler Jugend Luftwaffe helpers." The blue-gray uniforms with the HJ armband and the blue Luftwaffe eagle belong to the familiar street scene, like all other uniforms. But one thing they have over the other uniforms is they represent two formations: they have remained Hitler Youth, and stand also as such in the ranks of the soldiers. [...]

Source: "Jüngste Helfer der Soldaten," VB-Süd, December 9, 1943, p. 5.

We often read in the newspapers the Bolshevik children and old men were being made to fight, which supposedly signified the Russians had irrevocably used up their last reserves of troops. For some time (according to plan, naturally) Germany has been teaching high school students to operate anti-aircraft flak guns. Under the category, "Air Force assisted by Hitler Youth," the children wear military uniforms and become used to handling the artillery.

Fifteen- and sixteen-year-old children as warriors! If the war still continues to last for a long time, perhaps infants also will be used. Total war! [...]

For the observer it is uncommonly difficult to figure out Turkey's position at the conclusion of the [Cairo] conference. Until now Turkey has been proclaiming its strict neutrality, in spite of its duty toward England. According to their treaty, Turkey should have unfurled its banner and joined England. But as the war began to play out in the Mediterranean, Turkey completed a non-aggression pact with Germany and Bulgaria, and supposedly was going to maintain a good relationship with Russia. Now a meeting comes about in Cairo with Roosevelt, Churchill, and President Inönü of Turkey. That is significant. Turkey is inclined today toward the Allies. Turkey was cautious and waited for the moment that revealed which side would give it the least risk. [. . .]

December 15, 1943

[. . .] The secret weapons and the fairy tale about "retribution" are not measures that will show any effect. But that does not prevent the Party from implanting this belief in their comrades. Just a few days ago I heard conversations in the waiting rooms in Hungen and Stockheim about the "retribution." In Hungen a Party member from Ulrichstein sitting opposite a non-commissioned officer had the impression the retribution was definitely on its way. He had heard it from a worker who was working on a secret weapon. The expression on the sergeant's face showed his doubt. In Stockheim a farmer said quietly to the railroad attendant the war would be ended victoriously in four weeks – to the day. The attendant said, "Hopefully." The continuing absence of German victories is the reason so many people are now convinced Germany cannot at all win this war. People like me, who from the outset were convinced of a German defeat – or who wished for Germany's defeat – were a small minority. Most Party members, though, are still optimistic. But I do know some who are thinking skeptically about the end of the war. The incorrigible philistines, idiots, and sundry collection of crooks will believe in their "Führer" Adolf Hitler up until the last minute. Our opponents have not done much to shake these beliefs. This is the state of affairs today.

December 17, 1943

STONE AND CONCRETE FLY THROUGH THE AIR

Harbor walls, piers, and quays at small ports in Italy that have no more value for us are systematically blown up to make landings in the back of our front impossible.

Source: "Steine und Betonklötze flogen durch die Luft," *HF-Abend*,
December 13, 1943.

In this photograph they destroy stone and concrete, but they also destroy non-military facilities and residential homes. This destruction may delay and hinder the enemy a bit, but it cannot stop our enemies' forward advance. That was made absolutely clear in Russia. Since July we have systematically blown up everything, and the Russians still press forward. It will be the same in Italy. In the end it is only senseless destruction.

Because a number of stubborn Fascists will not see the war was already lost before it even got started, our partners' lands will be just as devastated as the lands of our opponents. At the head is "the great Duce." We must console

ourselves somehow. It will be this way until the spirit that dominated Italy
and Germany has expired.

December 21, 1943

The war becomes perceptible here in Upper Hesse. Last night, December
20, aerial combat took place between German night-fighters and English
bombers. Some English airplanes were shot down, among them one
between Laubach and Weickartshain near Pestburg. Six bodies (five in
the airplane and one nearby) were found and were buried in the Laubach
cemetery.[64]

We probably will be collecting English airplanes because we are continuously overflown, although usually they are not challenged. Only lately
German night-fighters are tracking them.

SOVIET RUSSIA HAS FAMINE

Lisbon, December 17, 1943.

In today's Soviet Russia the bitter agony of hunger comes as regularly
as the dawn. "The average Russian lives on less than two pounds of
food per day," notes the American magazine "Time." Of this, half have
black bread; the rest have potatoes, cabbage, etc. Sugar is scarce, and
butter is almost completely unavailable. The women work 66 hours a
week, and the men 84 hours; the children work harder now than the
adults did before the war.

Source: "Sowjetrußland hungert," HLZ, December 18, 1943, p. 2.

It is quite popular in Germany to talk about our opponents' food shortages.
Our stomachs do not become any fuller because of it, but the people need to
be constantly reminded they must hold out just until the others are starved to
death.

AN INEFFICIENT WAY TO PRODUCE FOOD

"Potatoes, sauerkraut, and celery are not for rabbits." *Source:* "Blindgänger der Erzeugungsschlacht," *HLZ,* December 18, 1943, p. 3.

Our food situation is rather tight. Various posters are hung up suggesting the authorities are greatly striving to provide everything edible for the human diet. Now the battle against home-bred caged rabbits has begun. Here and there someone breeds rabbits so he can quietly enjoy some extra meat. Perhaps grains are being used for the hares in urban areas, which could instead be put to use for people. But generally the rabbits are fed waste. Nevertheless, we now have propaganda against the caged bunnies.

1400 HUNDREDWEIGHT POTATO LOSS IN THE REGION

The economical and most careful use of potatoes, especially in densely populated districts, is a need of the hour. We must take the stand that really not a single potato may be lost. Because of the large number of households in our region, if every one of these households loses only a single potato per year, we have an annual loss of 1400 hundredweight of potatoes.

Source: "1400 Zentner Kartoffelverlust im Gaugebiet," *HLZ,* December 18, 1943, p. 3.

Attention is already being directed at every single potato. We are not far from being in the supposed situation of hunger in Russia.

December 24, 1943

The fifth war-Christmas stands at the door. During the First World War we "celebrated" Christmas just four times. Mankind is to be deeply pitied it cannot establish a rule of law that guarantees real peace. True respect for the neighbor's rights would bring peace without further ado. The lawbreaker must be brought to account – through legal means.

If all spiritually high-minded men would restrain their animal instincts and set a good example for the remaining citizens by respecting their rights, would not peace be possible? The enthusiastic warmonger must be replaced by an uncompromising friend of peace.

This Christmas will be unusually modest. There is no possibility for buying gifts. Our expenditures allow 30 pfennigs for a small Christmas tree! For "Peace on Earth" we continue always to wait. Our "Führer" will fight until five minutes past twelve; therefore the war will continue. He can bring no peace. The drive for self-preservation compels him to go further with this war. Hitler fights out of desperation!

[. . .]

ROMMEL AT THE ATLANTIC WALL

Berlin, December 19.

General Field Marshal Rommel, whom the Führer assigned to oversee the defensive readiness of Fortress Europe, meets with General Field Marshal von Rundstedt in his headquarters during Rommel's inspection trip through Denmark. In the middle of the visit, alongside discussions of the fight against the Western powers, the highly decorated Field Marshals prolonged their inspection trip to examine the Atlantic Wall's defensive strength and the intervention force's striking power, a force already in position.

Source: "Rommel am Atlantikwall," *HLZ*, December 20, 1943, p. 1.

General Field Marshal Rommel, the great retreater, who at one time had "the gates of Egypt" in his hand, is nevertheless the propaganda machine's darling and is being brought out of mothballs. His blemished fame will fill the forgetful ones with hope. But Rommel and von Rundstedt, as well as the fabled Atlantic Wall, will not be able to repel the forthcoming American and English attacks. The "intervention force's striking power" will have to retreat before the striking power of the unfolding superiority of our enemy. The

German army is no match for simultaneous attacks from the east, west, and south. No Rommel and no von Rundstedt – or anyone else who might be considered – can change that fact.[65]

The well-deserved final defeat moves closer. The end of terror!

[...]

December 30, 1943

"THE GERMAN MOTHER" – FIVE YEARS OF THE CROSS OF HONOR

Five years ago, on December 16, 1938, the Führer issued an ordinance, the substance of which is found in a single sentence: "As a visible sign of the German people's appreciation to mothers of large families, I establish the Cross of Honor of the German Mother." The veneration of motherhood, deeply rooted in the German character, forms an especially strong and intimate bond between the front and the home, sanctioned for the first time in the history of our people by the Reich. [...]

Source: "'Der deutschen Mutter' – Fünf Jahre Ehrenkreuz," VB-Süd, December 16, 1943, p. 5.

Mothers with many children receive the German people's appreciation with the Cross of Honor of the German Mother. The creators and presenters of this medal care not at all about honoring mothers. Their strategy is to encourage mothers to strive for the Cross of Honor by producing more children. The Nazis need them for cannon fodder. That is the only reason and purpose to honor children-rich mothers. A high population is a prerequisite for imperialistic politics, and a regime abounding with children leads unmistakably to war under the motto, "People without enough space to live." Millions of mothers then lose their sons in war, and millions of wives lose their husbands. That is the downside of medals for mothers!

December 31, 1943

Yet another year of war belongs to the past, and it did not bring us an end. It seemed but common sense to think the combined forces of our opponents could have finished the war this year. That did not happen. England and America could have positioned their forces in a way to bring a collapse of

German resistance. It may be that political reasons are behind such behavior of these countries.

So what is the situation as seen from our perspective? The Russian army approaches the borders of Poland, Hungary, and Romania. The two German allies (Hungary and Romania) will be asking themselves some serious questions quite soon: will they resist and be destroyed, or will they separate from Germany? Our troops in the East are in dire distress, and they are also under siege in the conquered countries in all of Europe, from north to south! None of the officers involved disputed this "genius" undertaking of conquest. No general was to be found who refused to take part in such nonsense.[66] A sad wartime story!

1944

January 1, 1944

Every year the German people have been overwhelmed with exhortations by their rulers. Here are some excerpts from the Führer's appeal today [. . .] that concluded with these words:

The year 1944 will place hard and difficult demands on all Germans. The gigantic war taking place will approach a crisis this year. We have complete confidence we will successfully come through. Our one prayer to the Lord God should not be that He present us with victory, but that He weigh us justly according to our boldness, our bravery, our diligence, and also our sacrifices. He knows the goal of our struggle. It is nothing less than to safeguard our people, whom He Himself created. Our readiness for sacrifice, our diligence in our tasks will be revealed to Him. We are prepared to give all and to do all in the service of our goal. He will continue to test us justly, until He is ready to pass judgment. Our duty is to strive not to appear too lightly in His eyes but to experience the gracious judgment called "victory," and through that bring meaning to life.

Source: "Autruf des Führers an das deutsche Volk," *HF-Morgen*, January 1, 1944, pp. 1f.

The Lord God, who was cursed by every professional National Socialist, is beseeched in their greatest distress. An exceptional hypocrisy!

In his Order of the Day to the German soldiers [. . .] Adolf Hitler claims the Russians did not reach their goals. He seeks comfort in what the Russians have not yet reached – but they will get there in the coming weeks. An objective observer must admit the Russians achieved utterly remarkable successes in 1943. Ceaseless fighting from Stalingrad to the Polish border is a significant achievement.

The Order of the Day contained once again prophecy: "The plutocratic world of the West may undertake their threatened invasion wherever they want to. It will fail!"[1]

Hitler is curt: the invasion will fail, and that is that. [. . .]

Das Reich schließt mit nachstehenden Worten:

Das Herrgott, das von vielen Nationalsozialisten braußtümmig gelästert worden ist, das wird jetzt in der höchsten Not von dem Führer angerufen.

Eine ungewöhnliche Heuchelei!

> Das Jahr 1944 wird harte und schwere Forderungen an alle Deutschen stellen. Das ungeheure Kriegsgeschehen wird sich in diesem Jahre der Krise nähern. Wir haben das volle Vertrauen, daß wir sie erfolgreich überstehen. Unser einziges Gebet an den Herrgott soll nicht sein, daß er uns den Sieg schenkt, sondern daß er uns gerecht abwägen möge in unserm Mut, in unserer Tapferkeit, in unserem Fleiß und nach unseren Opfern. Das Ziel unseres Kampfes ist ihm bekannt. Es ist kein anderes, als unserem Volke, das er selbst geschaffen hat, das Dasein zu erhalten. Unsere Opferwilligkeit, unser Fleiß werden ihm nicht verborgen bleiben. Wir sind bereit, alles zu geben und alles zu tun, um dem zu dienen. Seine Gerechtigkeit wird uns so lange prüfen, bis er sein Urteil sprechen kann. Unsere Pflicht ist es, dafür zu sorgen, daß wir vor seinen Augen als nicht zu leicht erscheinen, sondern jenen gnädigen Richterspruch erfahren, der „Sieg" heißt und damit das Leben bedeutet!

Der Tagesbefehl für die deutschen Soldaten bringt u. a. die nachfolgenden markanten Stellen:

> Trotzdem gibt es gar keinen Zweifel darüber, daß dieses größte Krisenjahr in unserer Geschichte, von dem die Engländer und die Bolschewisten felsenfest überzeugt waren, daß es mit einem vollkommenen deutschen Zusammenbruch enden wird, ein großer geschichtlicher Erfolg geworden ist. Es mögen die Kämpfe im Osten noch so schwer gewesen und weiterhin schwer sein: der Bolschewismus hat sein Ziel nicht erreicht. Es mag die plutokratische Welt im Westen ihren angedrohten Landeversuch unternehmen, wo sie will: er wird scheitern! Der Versuch, die deutsche Heimat zu zermürben, führt zum Gegenteil ihre Absicht, die deutsche Kriegsproduktion auszuschalten, wird zuschanden gemacht. Unser Widerstand wird nicht geringer werden, sondern er wird im Jahre 1944 erfolgreicher sein.

> Das Jahr 1943 ist nun zu Ende! Es hat den Gegnern nicht nur verweigert, was sie sich erhofften, sondern im Gegenteil zu ihrer, vielleicht schwersten Enttäuschung geführt.
>
> Das Jahr 1944 wird ein sehr hartes sein. Unsere gemeinsame Aufgabe ist es aber, in ihm die Periode der reinen Verteidigung wieder zu überwinden und dem Gegner mit schweren Schlägen solange zuzusetzen, bis endlich die Stunde kommt, da die Vorsehung dem Volke den Sieg geben kann, das ihn am meisten verdient. Wenn ich aber den Blick auf Euch, meine deutschen Soldaten, werfe. Euer Heldentum, Eure Tapferkeit und Euren Mut bedenke und die Opfer und Leistungen der Heimat abwäge, dann wird meine Zuversicht zur unerschütterlichen Gewißheit: Mehr kann ein Volk leisten, erdulden und ertragen. Wenn daher die Vorsehung das Leben als Preis demjenigen schenkt, der es am tapfersten erkämpft und verteidigt, dann wird unser Volk die Gnade vor demjenigen finden, der als gerechter Richter zu allen Zeiten immer noch jenen den Sieg gab, der seiner am meisten würdig war. In diesem Kampf um Sein oder Nichtsein wird am Ende Deutschland siegen!

Adolf Hitler bestätigt, daß die Russen ihr „Ziel" nicht erreicht hätten. Er mag sich trösten, weil die Russen noch nicht erreicht haben, das werden sie in den kommenden Wochen erreichen. Der sachliche Beobachter wird zugeben müssen, daß die Russen im Jahre 1943 äußerst beachtliche Erfolge errangen. Von Stalingrad bis zur polnischen Grenze in fortgesetzten Siegen ist immerhin eine bedeutende Leistung.

Der Tagesbefehl enthält auch wieder einmal eine Prophezeiung:

„Es mag die plutokratische Welt im Westen ihren angedrohten Landeversuch unternehmen, wo sie will: er wird scheitern!"

Hitler ist Gott verbunden, der Landeversuch scheitert, damit basta.

January 9, 1944

From time to time our newspapers publish information about the living conditions in the Soviet Union based on reports from their correspondents in neutral countries. A headline:

HOT WATER WITH BREAD – HOW A PERSON LIVES IN THE SOVIET UNION

For years heavy deficiencies in merchandise have led to widespread poverty. The worker plods along until he drops.[2]

For the most part the "neutral" journalists will paint the darkest picture because their clients would not pay them otherwise. The most beloved portrayal is that the entire Russian nation is on the brink of extinction: monthly rations of butter and fats have sunk to 100 grams; fruit, milk, and sugar are not available; breakfast consists of hot water and bread; lunch is some cabbage soup, and so forth. In addition, the Soviet authorities realize they cannot control any of this. In short, they have entered into impoverishment in Soviet Russia. [. . .]

There is not a single journalist who can give a perfectly factual report about conditions in Russia at this time. Everything spoken or written is from one side or the other with the clear intent of coloring it. Who dares to assert he knows everything going on in Russia? Who knows anything about the Urals or Western Siberia? Our soldiers know only the destroyed areas of battle, and they form these self-serving portraits. They and the German people want a complete breakdown in Russia so the war would end. The press nurtures these hopes.

The supposedly despairing spirits in the USSR are countered by certain facts. Russia began offensive operations in July 1943 without hindrance; it is making continuous and fierce progress this winter chasing German troops off its territory. West of Kiev the Russians have already pushed past the Polish borders of 1939. Their advance around Berdychev and Kirovograd at the Bug and Dniester Rivers will cut through the German troops and lead to the capture of Ukraine.

Despite what we might like, death from starvation does not appear close in Russia. Weapons endanger the enemy while wishes merely awaken illusions.

January 13, 1944

123 SHOT DOWN

Führer Headquarters, January 12, 1944.

In the early morning hours of January 11 North American bombers attacked several locations in central Germany. Due to the immediate onset of German defensive attacks the attack did not have an effect. According to the still incomplete messages by German fighter planes and anti-aircraft batteries throughout the Reich and the occupied western regions, 123 North American airplanes within the massed groups of four-engine bombers were shot down. The casualties of additional aircraft could not be confirmed due to nightfall. The exceptionally high loss of enemy aircraft and crews is compared to previous reports about the loss of the crews of two German fighter planes. Seven other crews are missing.

Source: "123 Abschüsse," *HF-Abend*, January 12, 1944, p. 1.

A Special Report from Führer Headquarters. For some time it had become quiet in the victor's kitchen, but now they offer welcome news to the folk about a large air battle – although the results are not exactly known yet. The daily slogan everywhere is "Shoot them down!" Many people think the German forces will stop the airplane raids. For me it is clear the opponent has sufficient airplanes and pilots. The Americans and English presently are concentrating their war efforts solely in the air. When they planned the campaign, they no doubt realized they would have losses, so their casualties are no consolation for us.

The report strangely omits the exact places that were attacked. What does it mean, "some places in central Germany"? From this we can conclude strategically important facilities were hit.

January 14, 1944

The Atlantic Wall in word and image is a popular topic of our propaganda, convincing the people it will cause fear and terror in our enemies. In reality, this is just a bluff. It is impossible to turn the entire Atlantic coastline into an impenetrable rampart. Not to mention we have no specific reason to think the fortified areas will be attacked. I would vote on South France, North Italy, or the Balkans as the first goal of an attack. Then the Atlantic Wall will fall automatically. Besides, they can fly over it. [. . .]

Even if the reigning tyrant is your wife's father, it is dangerous to have an opinion contrary to his. Mussolini allowed his son-in-law, Galeazzo Ciano, to be executed.[3] The executions also will claim Fascism, which these men served for many years, as a victim. For this reason I find it difficult to feel sorry for any Fascist member. In addition, discarding their own policies at the end did not alter the outcome. In reality, the only thing they wanted was to save their own skins. [. . .]

DEFENSES READY AT THE CHANNEL COASTLINE

A built-in cliff-top artillery emplacement at the Atlantic Wall. *Source:* "Abwehrbereite Kanalküste," *HF-Abend*, January 3, 1944, p. 5.

"FIRST WIN, THEN TRAVEL," say the posters at all the train stations. Naturally that does not apply to NSDAP big shots. The regional propaganda leaders, the most indispensable Party comrades throughout the entire Reich, will travel to Berlin to receive the usual "preparation" for the continuation of the brainwashing – the "unanimous commitment" and the "resolute will to victory," which no Party assembly has yet been without. If war could be won by such tactics, Dr. Goebbels would have received victory laurels long ago.

Why do these propaganda leaders not meet at the Eastern Front? Because the war is for the inferior "national" comrades, the Volksgenossen. Is that not so?

January 15, 1944

Last night the radio announcer said, "German troops have evacuated Stepan, 500 kilometers east of Katowice." Stepan is in Volhynia, a part of Poland before 1939. The report intends to assure the worried minds Russians are still far from the German border. What a turn! For an entire year the masters bragged about maintaining a 2,000-kilometer distance between the homeland and the front. Today they take refuge in deceit. Only 370 kilometers separate Stepan from the East Prussian border! To Silesia is approximately 500 kilometers. That is today, but how close will the Russians be tomorrow, the day after tomorrow, and in the coming weeks?

The announcer did not refer to Greater Germany – not a word about our expanded territory with its supposedly German cities. That is because Russian troops are getting nearer to these cities, in increasing tempo. If the radio announced the distance from where the advancing Russians have penetrated the front to the cities of Lviv, Krakow, and Warsaw, it would evoke a cry of panic in Eastern Germany. Instead they mention Katowice and the 500 kilometers.

Sedatives work only for a short period of time. It is extremely bad for German troops at the Eastern Front. The breakthrough in the center, at the Pripyat marshes, has ruptured the German lines and allows the Russians to undertake risky operations. Our thoughtless seizure of positions at the Dnieper bend was a major folly. Only a corporal could do such a thing. Where are the clever generals?

[. . .]

January 26, 1944

There have been endless "victorious" defensive battles since July 1943. German defeats do not exist. The word "retreat" has been eradicated. For its replacement we have "scheduled shortening of the front" or "alignment," and these movements occur "undetected" by the enemy. We are to know that the abandoned territories are worthless. (Mainly because they are now destroyed or ravaged.) The enemy attacks are always "cut up" or "parried"; their advances are "constrained" or "sealed tight"; and attempts to break through are "caught." Such language by the Supreme Command of the Armed Forces requires deciphering. Not everyone can.

They record the numbers of prisoners of war, and the captured or destroyed tanks and artillery pieces. But only as it regards the enemy. Our losses are coyly concealed. For four years, the Nazis have placed such details before the German people, and many are still intoxicated by the numbers they read. Only a few think about the true state of things.

The army reports refer to battles "southwest" of Leningrad.[4] "Southwest" is a loose term that does not tell us how much conquered area we have abandoned. We were still reporting our shelling of Leningrad to the end of last month. We had to give up our siege, and the Russians are marching against Estonia – which is southwest of Leningrad. If the Russians have broken through Germany's heavily fortified positions at Leningrad, they are providing evidence of what more can be expected.

As the Russians achieve these victories in their military campaigns, political changes will not be far behind. Germany's allies, Finland, Hungary, Romania, and Bulgaria, reshape their friendship in relation to the ongoing war situation. So every German troop division has been ordered to hold its position at all costs, to delay the possibility of the Axis partners – who so far continue to believe Germany will be saved by some miracle – from switching sides. Once the last hope disappears and these countries become part of the theater of war, a change can occur with a furious speed that will expedite the end.

Until then the domestic propaganda, the Party's Führer Corps and many other organizations, and the entire network of Nazi associations, work in the usual way. Reich Commissioner and Regional Leader Sprenger offered these words on January 23 at a regional assembly: "For the entire German people, the Führer has given a categorical order which is called Victory! Germany remains invincible if it is true to itself." Sprenger said in conclusion, "The Führer will win. Long live the Führer!"[5] [...]

RAMMED AND YET LANDED SMOOTHLY

Berlin, January 21, 1944.

During the terrorist attack on the capital last night, Prince of Sayn-Wittgenstein, among the most successful German night-fighters and the bearer of Oak Leaves, performed a special achievement. After winning three engagements in a short time, his plane was hit by an enemy fighter while attacking a fourth bomber. Because of the heavy damage sustained by his plane, Major Prince Wittgenstein had to cancel the dogfight. However, he managed to land his plane smoothly despite the odds.

Source: "Gerammt und glatt gelandet," *Darmstädter Zeitung* [*DZ*], January 22, 1944, p. 1.

Yesterday the prince was a great heroic pilot. Today dead. The army reported several days ago Major Prince von Sayn-Wittgenstein, a *Nachtjäger* ["night-hunter" fighter pilot], did not return from a flight. One after another dies for the Führer.

January 28, 1944

CAPTAIN MEURER KILLED IN ACTION

After a fierce dogfight against several terrorist bombers, such as he had emerged victoriously from so often before, Captain Manfred Meurer, commander of a night-fighter squadron and bearer of Oak Leaves, was killed. [...] Up to his heroic death Meurer had been victorious in fifteen battles. Along with the air force, which has lost one of its best, Hamburg mourns one of its bravest sons.

Source: "Hauptmann Meurer gefallen," *HF-Abend*, January 28, 1944, p. 1.

The night-fighter pilots are becoming especially famous in these times and have produced a new hopefulness. Fame is short-lived. According to the *Hamburger Fremdenblatt* Captain Meurer was filled with a strong confidence in victory. The newspaper quotes a passage from a letter by this pilot: "The Tommy will get his just deserts for his terror politics, born of his arrogance for his supposed unassailability. Every success we achieve in the face of our burning homeland provides special satisfaction for us and motivates us again and again to the highest personal performance."

I do not believe the English in 1940 felt they were unassailable. German pilots had the upper hand in the air then and were not interested in England's cries of woe. [...]

"OUR RETRIBUTION WILL BE BRUTAL"

Paris, January 8, 1944.

The newly appointed Secretary General for the Maintenance of Public Security, Joseph Darnand, has sent a declaration to the weekly magazine "Je suis partout" that one can expect every effort will be taken in France against terrorism [by the underground resistance].

Darnand said: "The time of indulgence is over. Five months the French militia has taken the murderers' blows without striking back. The terror just further increased. It is aimed at all the political parties, all professions, all individuals, even those who thought themselves secure from the 'friendly' machine guns. We have organized ourselves for battle. Our retribution will be brutal." [...]

Source: "Unser Gegenschlag wird brutal sein," DZ, January 9, 1944, p. 2.

When the French occupied part of Germany after the First World War, from 1918–30, Germans in the Rhineland who flirted with the French were not much beloved by their fellow citizens. Those who resisted the French occupation (for example, Schlageter) were raised to the status of national heroes.[6] Exactly the same comparison exists today in France. One can well understand why freedom-loving Frenchmen would turn against the politics of Pétain and Company. Their desire for freedom cannot be suppressed with gentle means, so terror is employed: terror against terror. The declaration of brutal reprisals is a characteristic of Fascism and National Socialism. In all probability these brutal fanatics will one day become the victim of brutality.

[...]

February 5, 1944

NOT ONLY ON THE FRONT DOES THE ENEMY STAND

No! He has also crept in among us. Like a shadow he follows you, German man, and you, German Woman! He spies on you and hears every word you speak! He is difficult to recognize and hard to seize, but he is there! In our midst. Every day brings us new and bloody evidence. Therefore, look around you! Be silent!

Source: "Nicht nur an der Front," DZ, January 30, 1944, p. 3.

The newspapers, kiosks, offices, train stations, railroad cars, store windows, and so forth display posters with the figure in black along with the warning,

Nicht nur an der Front

"The enemy is listening." The number of "enemies" must be unusually large if warnings must be given this way. Or is there another goal? The command, "Be silent!" makes me wonder if they want to create such anxiety the people will be afraid to speak at all. Be silent! The dictator wants the least said about hardship, misery, despair, destruction, death, and defeat. Therefore: "Be silent!"

The enemy that has "crept in among us" could also be the foreign worker. Except these have not crept in but were dragged into the Reich through compulsion and force. I do not doubt the actual enemy used this wonderful opportunity to smuggle in spies with these workers. It was not done so easily in the other war, 1914–18. In any case, the Nazis' governing skills wield this slogan "enemy spies" as an excellent tool. The tactic of obfuscation: the propaganda disguises the true situation and bewitches the German folk. In spite of that, truth comes through. Slowly – but surely!

The folk have been waiting for the "retribution," and so something had to be done. And it was: German air raids on London.

Supreme Command of the Armed Forces Bulletin:

The British try to minimize the effect of the German nighttime air raids on London on January 21–22 and 29–30 by deliberately giving wrong information about the number of attacking German airplanes and the resulting damages. Contrary to their report, more than 900 airplanes participated in the attack, with 750 of them attacking London with over 1,000 metric tons of explosive bombs and incendiaries. The remaining airplanes carried out diversionary attacks on southeastern England. According to reports from our crews making observations at low altitudes of both attacks, huge fires and destruction can be seen in the city of London.

Source: "Schwere Verluste der angreifenden Sowjets," *DZ,*
February 3, 1944, p. 1.

Will it be any easier now for the citizens of Berlin to bear English attacks? Will anyone here question the German attacks' ferocity and brutality? In either case, it is rather conspicuous 900 airplanes suddenly can be employed when only a weak German air force flew over London these last months. It would have seemed more plausible if the amount of airplanes had increased progressively during that time: 100, 200, 300, 400, etc. Why did they wait until it was 900? It is hardly possible in this war to hear the pure truth. But even suppose the alleged number of 900 is true, that will not keep the English and Americans from continuing their own attacks.

Yesterday afternoon, on Friday, February 4, I had the opportunity in Altenstadt to observe American airplanes attacking Frankfurt. Neither our flak nor our pilots prevented it. The American squadrons were sovereign in their course, ruling the air. And there was quite a difference between yesterday's attack and the American attacks against Schweinfurt (east of Frankfurt) this past autumn. Then too the bombers made a strong attack as they passed over Frankfurt's air space, but their own losses were high. Yesterday the American bombers were backed up by their fighter planes. That may have been the reason German fighters stayed away. Or do we have to be frugal now with our airplanes and crews? [. . .]

Field Marshal Rommel inspected the Atlantic Wall a few weeks past. And now Senior General Jodl provides his assessment.[7] Not long ago the threatened attack against the coast was called an English bluff. Subsequently, it became known that American and Canadian troops were transported to England. Our army felt the need to instill fear in our enemies, so they declared the enemy would survive "no more than nine hours" on the mainland. Now we are in the third phase. The Supreme Command expects an attack and believes it will be a successful landing, so they share with us how they have created a deeply structured backfield defense zone.

If the enemy decides to attack these built-up positions, our troops will come under an unusually heavy air bombardment. The enemy will attack only after the German defense is weakened. Then it will come – and indeed from all sides.

VÖLKISCHER BEOBACHTER *19.7.44*

Im Rahmen seiner Besichtigungsreise zu den Westbefestigungen stattete Generalfeldmarschall R o m m e l (links) dem Oberbefehlshaber West, Generalfeldmarschall v o n R u n d s t e d t (rechts), in dessen Hauptquartier einen Besuch ab
PK.-Aufn.: Kriegsberichter Jesse (Sch)

"During his inspection trip to the western fortifications, General Field Marshal Rommel (left) visits the Commander-in-Chief West, General Field Marshal von Rundstedt (right), in his headquarters."

February 6, 1944

EISENHOWER AND CO.

Stockholm, Early February 1944.

The How, When and Where of the promised "second front" our enemies have tossed out loudly on and off now for two years still lies in the darkness of the future of this war. The only thing for certain is never before in the history of modern times has a large-scale military campaign ever been surrounded by such publicity. It is not only quite unusual but also stands in contradiction of the military principle that surprise can signify half the success. It is astonishing, for example, that the exact composition of the supreme command intended to lead this enterprise has already been announced. Downright amazing is the way strategic, tactical, and geographic possibilities of this action are treated in the hostile press with a comprehensiveness that could fill many volumes. In reality this is a deliberate commotion, courtesy of Eisenhower and Company, produced with the thoroughness of advertising bosses preparing the central marketplace for a new item, an important component of the company – or at least it is so designated by our enemy.

The close fusion of such clamor and warfare runs like a red thread through the entire Anglo-American methodology. It has been found in the way they have initially directed their often grotesque and quite vocal confirmation of the broad context in this war of nerves. This onslaught against the moral resistance of the masses behind the fighting front, which has gone on with great perseverance and undeniable talent of the Anglo Saxon's specialty in the art of war, includes also the permanent campaign of rumors and false reports about the brutal air terror, and finally the broad depiction of forthcoming actions. This attempt to shape the enemy's morale by fantastic and impressive descriptions and pre-announcements to wear them down and, if possible, form a kind of fatalistic fright paralysis, even before they have to take the risk-heavy actions, corresponds to the rest of the oft-repeated British and North American tactics on the battlefield. What they do in battle with the massed deployment of material, with air and artillery bombardments before moving the infantry forward, is a rehearsal, over and over, for the broader fight; they prepare themselves in the war of nerves, for when they must face the dreaded military campaign to come; they test and probe themselves, searching for courage and cheering on that fearful leap into the great adventure they are promoting.

Source: "Eisenhower & Co.," *HF-Abend*, February 2, 1944, p. 1.

This news critic is correct from the standpoint of those people who futilely hoped for an English–American attack to liberate them from German occupation. We can only imagine the thoughts of those waiting all this time for the "help" promised them at the beginning of the war. Not promised by minor politicians but leading statesmen.

There was a time when it was highly unusual to advertise a military plan an entire year in advance and to discuss it openly in full detail. A German proverb says, "A good beginning is half the battle." The Americans and British seem to follow other proverbs. On September 21, 1943, Prime Minister Churchill gave a speech in Parliament and said the following in regards to the "Second Front":

"One day, when we and our American allies judge it to be the right time, this front will be thrown open and the mass invasion of the continent from the west, in combination with the invasion from the south, will begin ... The House may be absolutely certain that His Majesty's present Government will never be swayed or overborne by any uninstructed agitation however natural, or pressure however well meant, in matters of this kind. We will not be forced or cajoled into undertaking vast operations of war against our better judgment in order to gain political unanimity or a cheer from any quarter. The bloodiest portion – make no mistake about it – of this war for Great Britain and the United States lies ahead of us. Neither the House nor the Government will shrink from that ordeal. We shall not grudge any sacrifice for the common cause. I myself regard it as a matter of personal honor to act only with the conviction of success founded upon the highest professional advice at our disposal, in operations of the first magnitude."[8]

The right time has not yet been there. [...]

GERMAN CAVALRY AT THE EASTERN FRONT

The repositioning between Lake Ilmen and Lake Peipus

[...] For a long time already the withdrawals between Lake Ilmen and Lake Peipus served the general shortening of the front in the Eastern Front's north sector. After breaking off the siege of Leningrad, the German military leadership could put no value on defending the extensive marshland between Lake Ilmen and the Gulf of Finland. Accordingly, as is apparent from the note by the Wehrmacht report, marching orders to the rear were issued that have brought the abandonment of this militarily unimportant terrain with it.

Source: "Deutsche Kavallerie an der Ostfront," DZ, February 11, 1944, p. 1.

For two and a half years this area was occupied by German troops. For two and a half years fortifications were built at Lake Ilmen. Ten thousand determined young men were killed in hard-fought battles, and despite that the dirty Nazi speaks of "unimportant terrain."
[...]

February 23, 1944

Increased aircraft activity! Day and night it buzzes and hums. It appears, though, this is still just the overture to the threatened invasion. Mister Churchill had indeed pronounced, "When the autumn leaves fall," but it is the right of states-men to hand out all sorts of twaddle and to lie under the blue heavens.

How do the people behave now? On my train travels I have the opportu-nity to hear "the voice of the people." I can say immediately the propaganda has again booked an initial success. The masses are hypnotized by the numbers of downed aircraft. The numbers are prudently given only for the English and American bombers. People are thereby content: the enemy cannot afford such losses over the long run; it will have to give up the fight. Hope is indestructible, regardless of bad experiences.

Whenever possible I point out the opponents have become stronger not weaker. No one believes me. I also say their losses do not interest me at all. I want to hear about the German losses. That makes little impression on most listeners, who simply do not want to know the reality of anything. They do not think; they prefer to give in to the obsession of sipping the sweet propaganda, which takes them by the hand. Yes, the German people are a unique race. I look forward to the total disillusionment. [. . .]

February 29, 1944

Today is our son's birthday. Once every four years.[9] His thoughts will turn to Germany. He will be thinking his parents were smarter than the majority of the German people who blindly subscribed to the World Conqueror Hitler and the New Idea – poor mentally ill people!

March 3, 1944

HERMANN GÖRING: "THE AIR FORCE WILL ANSWER THE ENEMY WITH NEW FORCES AND NEW WEAPONS"

Reich Marshal's Order of the Day on the "Day of the Luftwaffe"

Berlin, March 2, 1944.

Comrades, in defiance of all the cruel terror bombing, the splendid morale of the German people is for us the highest obligation. With new forces and new weapons we will give the enemy the answer it deserves. I trust in you and I know the Führer can count on the air force in the time of great decisions.

Filled with unwavering confidence in victory we commemorate this day in endless gratitude of love for our comrades taken by the enemy and for our soldiers at the front fighting for Germany's great future who lost their lives for the homeland. Their sacrifice is the great imperative for us.

Comrades, we greet the Führer! Hail, my Luftwaffe!"

Source: "Hermann Göring: Die Luftwaffe wird mit neuen Kräften und neuen Waffen dem Feind antworten," *DZ*, March 2, 1944, p. 1.

What did Herr Reich Marshal say on August 9, 1939? "We will not allow a single bomb to be dropped by enemy planes on the Ruhr district."[10] What did I say to the prattlers who worshiped him? "Do you have iron curtains that will be dropped from the sky to keep enemy planes from flying into Germany?" I belonged to the disgusting "defeatists" and was accordingly treated. All of the Nazis regarded me with suspicious eyes because I exercised (as Herr Mönnig wrote to District Leader Backhaus) "a bad influence on the people of Laubach."

And so the fight continues, as it has without interruption since the "Seizure of Power," against the ignorance of the masses. Most Hitler believers are still welded together, but the main feature is yet to come.

March 4, 1944

HIGH HONORS FOR THE CHERKASY FIGHTERS

Führer Headquarters, February 24, 1944.

The Führer has awarded a large number of medals for high bravery to military members after completion of the breakthrough at western Cherkasy. [...]

Source: "Hohe Auszeichnungen für Tscherkassy-Kämpfer," *DZ*, February 25, 1944, p. 1.

The Russians claim they succeeded in surrounding and destroying ten German divisions in the area west of Kaniv-Cherkasy. The German Supreme Command says these divisions fought their way through. Who tells the truth?[11] Presenting high honors to the superior officers proves nothing because it is possible to fly them in small groups out of the Russian cauldron. They are decorated for implementing the pigheaded instruction to hold out at all costs. For this slavish obedience the Führer rewarded them. What reward did the many infantrymen who were sacrificed in the cauldron receive, senselessly sacrificed because the area is in Russian hands? These pitiable battle victims do not even get a simple wooden cross or a bundle of twigs on their mass grave.

The Bolshevik scare goes around again. Here is a servant who copies his master, Dr. Goebbels. The writer hauls out the entire register of his skills. He depicts the

Bolsheviks' reign of terror in the bloodiest colors to highlight his true purpose, which comes in the final paragraph: he wants to mobilize Europe against Russia.

ESTONIA STANDS AT THE NARVA

by Robert Krötz

It is still not too late. But it is high time there to see where it burns. It burns at the Narva. A European forward post is in danger. The Estonians are already struggling. Will the others, the wise people in Paris, Stockholm, and Brussels, be shamed by the Estonian fishermen and farmers into realizing this is now their moment?

Source: "Estland steht an der Narwa," *VB-Süd*, February 25, 1944, p. 1.

What would Robert Krötz have written in 1939 when Germany secured a pact with Russia, or on June 22, 1941, when Hitler invaded Russia without even declaring war?[12] Germany's rulers carry the sole blame for the invasion that compelled the Russians to carry out this enormous defensive fight against us. All guilt is avenged on earth! [. . .]

"The Führer has given Prof. Dr. Theo Morell, physician and researcher, the Knight's Cross of the War Merit Cross. Prof. Morell, the Führer's physician since 1936, has earned special recognition for decades of work as a pioneer in the field of vitamin and hormone research." *Photo:* Press-Hoffmann. *Source:* original from *VB-Süd*, March 2, 1944, p. 3. Reproduction: Ullstein Bild/Getty Images.

The former Austrian laborer and First World War corporal, Adolf Hitler, has come far. He fought for socialism, and today, in the manner of former emperors and kings, he has a personal physician. There is no doubt the socialism aspect was splendidly resolved both for "Führer" Hitler and for "personal physician" Dr. Morell.[13] The fat circumference of the calorie-pig, Professor Dr. Morell, is proof nothing remains to be desired within the National Socialist rationing card system. Heil Hitler!!

[...]

March 11, 1944

[...]

The English attack us at night and the Americans in the daytime. Lately there have been no massive daytime attacks. In the past week they used large formations to attack and bomb mainly industrial towns with aircraft factories. The strategy is to damage aircraft production and at the same time decimate Germany's air defense – meaning our fighter pilots. There is a method in that. When the English land invasion finally begins, Germany's air defense will have been so weakened it will not be able to contribute in any crucial way. [...]

The Nazis call out, "protect your children from bombing terror." They should themselves have carefully considered that in 1939. Terror bombing is stopped only by peace. Peace nourished, discord abated. How this war affects children is shown in the following obituaries:[14]

> Infinitely heavy sorrows have stricken our hearts.
> In an air raid on Hamburg in the night of July 27–28, 1943, I lost my dearly beloved, devoted wife, **Marie Planthaber,** née Schulz, 57 years old, and my never-to-be-forgotten daughter, **Marie Pantelmann**, née Planthaber, 36 years old,
>
> and my grandchildren,
> **Sonja,** 18
> **Ursula,** 17
> **Harald,** 10
> **Werner,** 4
> In deep sorrow: Hans Planthaber, Sr., Harald Pantelmann, [...]
> Hamburg, Breitenfelder Str. 21/27

> Only now have we received cruel confirmation that our dear, kindhearted and hard-working daughter, **Johanna Wolf**, née Hansen, 33,
> and her four lovely children,
> **Marga,** 12

Klauss, 5
Peter, 3
Heiner, 2
had to lose their young lives in the night of July 27–28, 1943.
Deeply despondent parents, Max Bindszus and wife, née Hokemeyer [. . .]
Hamburg, Düppelstrasse 41, III.

After a long wait we now have the sad certainty that the terrorist raid on July 27–28, 1943, has taken away our Lieselotte's dear and irreplaceable parents and brothers and sisters, our beloved children and grandchildren, our beloved sister and brother-in-law who have all fallen victim.
Walter Lohse, 38
Therese Lohse, née Trapp, 33,
Ingrid, 9
Anneliese, 7
Walter, 5
Werner, 2
Painful feelings of loss and grief from their little Lieselotte; Martha Lohse, widow née Specht; Rudolf Trapp and wife, née Pohlmann; Sergeant Walter Trapp, prisoner in America, also wife and little Anke; Sgt. R. Trapp; Soldier Hans Trapp and all relatives.
Glückstadt, Nordmarkerstr. 29; Hamburg 22, Osterbeckstrasse 102, near Pohlmann.

Not only in Hamburg have many children become victims of this senseless war; the war has wreaked havoc and given us mass graves in cities and villages everywhere in Germany. [. . .]

March 12, 1944

[. . .]

"THE GERMAN ARMY IS INVINCIBLE"

Paris, March 4, 1944.

On the occasion of a reception for the French Chamber of Trade chairman, Prime Minister Laval gave a speech in which he said the German army could not be defeated as it has significant reserves. Laval briefly mentioned the dissidents and declared that those who would leave the country would be responsible for a Bolshevik takeover in the event of an "Allied" victory. What has occurred in Algiers was only a prelude of what you would get to see in France. Finally said Laval, he would do everything in an attempt to save France.

Source: "'Deutsche Armee unbesiegbar' / Eine Ansprache Lavals,"
VB-Süd, March 5, 1944, p. 2.

Again the wish is father of the thought. When France in 1940 was totally crushed, with partial responsibility going to the Laval circle, immediately there crept the looter of corpses, Pierre Laval, under the wings of the supposed winner, Adolf Hitler. Laval and cohorts submitted, and they did not care a damn about their fatherland. They came to power and were tolerated by Germany. It is readily understandable the firm Laval & Company fervently longs for the final victory of Germany and also believes to the last in this victory. Without this victory by Germany, the life of Laval and the other egotists will find a terrible end.

[. . .]

March 17, 1944

[. . .] In order to strengthen the German mind in National Socialist thinking – in particular the German soldier – a special Propaganda-Kampagne (PK) was created. There are a considerable number of war reports in this campaign. Below is the beginning and conclusion of a PK report by the war journalist, Herbert Wiedemann:

PORTRAIT OF A YOUNG MAN

(PK) In the first weeks of the New Year, the youngest in the flight squadron, twenty-year-old Corporal Werner, was killed in the air. This life was plain and simple, and to glorify it as unusual would be a falsification. He had neither Goethe's Faust nor Nietzsche's Zarathustra in his backpack. It is not acceptable to measure his ideals against the yearning of Alcibiades; his youthful impetuosities had no ancient comparison. He lacked those titanic presumptions one gives to Germans in our literature. Not hubris, but real simplicity was his distinctive trait. Is not simplicity a virtue? Is not faithful devotion an adornment of youth? It seems to us that nothing in a fighting nation could be more precious than such unostentatious young men. This early consummate life of a pilot is an example – for many of his kind . . .

When his engine failed, we found on his desk two parcels, carefully tied, for his girlfriend. The demise of people with early achievements is nothing like a special glory, yet it is comforting to know we Germans are not poor in such unassuming youth, who give all to their beliefs with heart and deed. Hölderlin, the poet of the Germans, calls to us from the Stygian twilight: "We have won the battle! Live on high, O Fatherland and do not count the dead! For you, my love, not one too many has fallen."

Out of every 100 boys, 99 say they want to be pilots – providing the parents' influence is excluded. In earlier times they would have wanted to become legionnaires. The young boy loves adventure and does not think of the dangers. It is easy play for those who want to entice these young fellows. Because of a lack of experience, the boy is quickly inspired. Flying is accordingly glamorized and the enthusiasts approach in bright streams, like moths to a beam of light.

The article says Corporal Werner was killed. Did he want to die? Probably not. He likely thought, "Why me?"

Is there anything great or heroic in this event? Can we speak here of "devotion" or "fulfillment?" Not at all. Yet with these terms youth is beguiled. And they die for them, not suspecting they all died for nothing.

[. . .]

March 21, 1944

Yesterday evening the speaker on the German shortwave radio announced that our government requested Sweden to send us a six month supply of ball bearings within the next eight weeks. We had ordered them to overcome production shortage caused by the air raids.

Sweden is responsible for the useless extension of this war. Perhaps a careful investigation would show Sweden carries the principal debt for both world wars. At the least, without Swedish ore supplies, Germany could not have carried out either war to such a long duration.[15] When I say Sweden, I mean the big income earners and capitalists of that country.

March 22, 1944

Professor Theo Morell, born July 22, 1886, in Trais-Münzenberg (Upper Hesse), personal physician to the Führer, has belonged to this narrow circle since spring 1936. In the weekly *Das Reich*, Professor Morell says, "I was at the Führer's side during all the campaigns and even the time before. But fortunately Providence would have it I only rarely needed to go into action."[16]

I hope Providence understands it needs to allow the Führer to live until the end of this war because it would be cruel to have to hear, "If the Führer had remained alive, we never would have lost the war." Let us all experience the end together.

March 23, 1944

The war reporter, Otto Hermann, describes in a Ministry of Propaganda special report German measures being taken in the Netherlands to counter a British–American invasion. To defend against an enemy invasion, part of the Netherlands will be flooded! The population was already evacuated from the frontline area some time ago. The fertile soil will become a swamp. The war reporter consoled those concerned in the following manner: "For the farmer, this consequence of the war is a hard blow, but the sacrifice he must make for the security of Europe is small compared with what is at stake. If the English and Americans succeed with their invasion adventure to weaken the German Eastern Front in a way that allows the Soviets to break through, Europe would be lost, and the Dutch farmer would be left with a miserable slave existence at best."[17]

If war reporter Otto Hermann believes German troops overran Holland in 1940 because of European interests, why were the Germans allied with the "dangerous" Russians in that period, 1939–40? Why, before the entire world, did the Führer praise the alliance with Russia as a great deed?
[. . .]

March 29, 1944

[. . .] Advancing Russian armies from northern and central Ukraine have already crossed the Bug and Dniester Rivers and now stand at the Prut River. Therefore, fighting is already underway in Bessarabia and Bukovina! German troops first crossed the Prut River on June 22, 1941. Today they are back to their starting point. That is a military drama of the first order, without example in history! With a pride that cannot be surpassed, the German army attacked Russia without warning. "Providence" has pronounced its judgment, and history will yet proclaim it!
[. . .]

April 5, 1944

Reich Minister of Justice Dr. Thierack spoke on the radio on March 25 about the tasks placed before the German judiciary in the war. In addition, he objected to the mavericks among the German people who use the enemy's speeches to disseminate false news reports to undermine the faith in victory. He said this about them:

We call them defeatists. These creatures attend to the business of our enemy and fall upon the backs of those fighting at the front. Here there can be no consideration. The law well understands here how to differentiate between a national comrade who sometimes loses his nerves during a night of bombing, and a public enemy who wants to undermine, in a planned way, our people's will for victory. And here, too, and directly here, applies the saying: "The higher the position, the greater the responsibility." We owe it to our comrades at the front, for their sacrifices and their confidence in the homeland, not to fail to exterminate such elements before they continue to scatter their poison. Thus we constantly see the judiciary in watchful readiness in the war in all areas of life. The German people can rely on their judiciary.[18]

The Party big shot, Dr. Thierack, uses the key word "defeatist" to open a campaign against the pessimist or alarmist. He wants to "exterminate" this sort of people. To that, one can only recommend this man destroy everyone who might still be equipped with even a partially healthy human understanding. It was not the people the Justice Minister calls "mavericks" who shook the "faith in victory." The military leaders did that with their glaring mistakes. [. . .]

[. . .]

April 15, 1944

I was ordered to go to Hotel Burghof at 8 a.m. today for a military physical examination. The command came by postcard from the Giessen military district. All the men in Laubach born from 1884–88 were required to do this. It is an outlandish situation when a grandfather in his sixtieth year is called up for military service. The leading officer there (colonel and commander) let me know the examination results: "Provisionally capable for the war."

The justice administration made a motion to have my classification reset as "indispensable," which provides for a postponement only until October 31, 1944. Will the die be cast by then? Who is able to predict it with certainty? Because of the English and Americans' unhurried war tactics, nobody can predict when this hateful war will end. Landing their troops in the Balkans or elsewhere would expedite the end. I cannot understand why our opponents do not attack. Have they been bluffed by our propaganda, or are they convinced they can slowly bleed the Germans to death? And why no concentrated attacks? If our opponents are looking to walk over corpses and rubble, this will last for some time yet. The Nazis hold onto power. A democratic Germany would have already thrown in the towel, but the leader of today's Germany will fight up to the last infantryman.

I heard the following graffiti was scribbled on a railroad car:

> Adolf calls old men to save the nation.
> And this is what he calls retaliation?[19]

April 21, 1944

Once upon a time a civil administration in the Reich Commission in Ukraine employed many, many indispensable and noble Party comrades. But now a "confidential" memorandum from the Chief Regional Court President in Darmstadt about legal assistance from the Ukraine Commission, says, "All requests for legal assistance that require the Reich Commission in Ukraine's co-operation are to be directed to the Public Prosecutor's Office with the German High Court of Rovno, presently in Frankfurt on the Oder, Fürstenwalder Post Road 80."

They could not hold on to their governing powers. They went there expecting to have immediately returned "home to the Reich" without pre-paratory intermediate steps. These German conquerors saw themselves in their bold dreams as masters of the East. Now the administrators are fleeing back from whence they came. The troops, too, must leave the conquered area in disappointment, though this is done more slowly than with the civil administrations. Tremendous ground has already been given up from Stalingrad to Ternopol. Much of the war material and all the graves remain in the enemy's hands.

Major attacks by the Bolsheviks were made simultaneously from the areas of Kerch to the west. Here also our troops withdrew from the persistent heavy fighting, in which the Soviets incurred serious casualties. After destroying every important war installation in the city of Kerch, the troops pulled back to the earlier prepared positions in the Isthmus of Akmonai. Meanwhile, the German and Romanian troops, acting with great mobility, led battles in the rear toward the west and south.

Source: "Die schweren Kämpfe auf der Krim," *VB-Süd*, April 16, 1944, p. 2.

The assurance that the important war material in Kerch was destroyed may make some Party members feel better. But that is small comfort considering how all of the sacrifices to conquer the Crimea were for nothing. [...]

OUR FALLEN

by Jakob Sprenger

With painful sadness in these past days we have buried our dead. [...] Nearly 1,600 men, women and children fell victim in the month of March to the enemies' terrorist attacks on the regional capital of Frankfurt am Main. So far a total of 4,363 defenseless people were murdered by a sadistic enemy in this area. They fell victim to an enemy who is deluded enough to believe he can get closer to his aim of this war by terrorizing the civilian population. The enemy kills women and children in the assumption that lowly cowardice might be greater than the German people's compelling requirement of honor.

Source: "Unseren Gefallenen," *DZ*, April 27, 1944, p. 1.

Regional Leader Jakob Sprenger has forgotten what the entire German press wrote in 1940 about our bomb attacks on England. There were no limits to the satisfaction. The desire and goal was to have "London in rubble and ashes." It failed not because of any considerations of humanity but the lack of enough military ability. What rejoicing would have broken out in the Sports Palace in Berlin with the announcement: "London has disappeared from the earth"? A storm of applause without comparison would have been the accompanying music.

Only those who condemned in principle the use of the air force are justified to raise their voice against the bombing war! Who tested their air force in the civil war in Spain and heaped upon its squadrons praise and fame? Who boasted no one could catch up to the German Luftwaffe's great head start? Was that not Air Marshal Göring?

It badly suits these men to pour forth tears because the enemy surpassed us and uses air raids the way we did or the way we wanted to do – if only we could have. Germany is not going to awaken the compassion of mankind. The actions of our own pilots prevent that. [...]

April 30, 1944

Obituaries of children have been appearing for a long time in nearly every daily newspaper edition. They too are war victims. A lack of doctors and medical supplies prevents rapid assistance. Doctors are in such demand they often must leave even some of the most urgent calls unanswered. In one of our small neighboring villages two children died on one day because the physician could not get there immediately.

Peterle, at the age of 2 ¼ years. God the Almighty suddenly and unexpectedly took our good, dear child, brother and grandson after a one-day illness.

In deep anguish: Georg Heiligenthal and wife Else, née Heider, and little sisters and all relatives. Darmstadt, Gutenbergstrasse 66, in April 1944.

Funeral: Saturday, April 22, 11:30 a.m., in the Old Cemetery, Nieder-Ramstädter Strasse.

Wilfried, at the tender age of 7 months. All of our sunshine, our dear and delightful child passed away suddenly and unexpectedly.

On behalf of the bereaved: Sergeant Wilhelm Aessinger, presently in the East, and wife Liesel, née Reitz, and child.

Funeral: Saturday, April 22, 11 a.m., in the Old Cemetery, Nieder-Ramstädter Strasse.

Johannachen, at the tender age of 5 years. After a short, serious illness, our good dear, beloved child and grandchild passed away unexpectedly on April 18.

In deep heartbreak: Frau Maria Kögel, widow, née Huthmann, and all relatives. Pfungstadt, April 21, 1944.

Funeral: April 22, 1944 at 3 p.m. From the cemetery gate. Consecration 10 minutes earlier.

Source: DZ, April 21, 1944, p. 4.

The war enthusiasts are not worried about these deaths, nor are they overly concerned about those who die a "heroic death" for the Führer, whether on the battleground or in an air raid. People have been made almost callous by the continued, increasing losses. One speaks about casualties as if the death of soldiers was the most understandable thing in the world. One died yesterday, another today, and already forgotten tomorrow. Everyone still thinks only about himself.

This world has become terrible. Ripe for the downfall.

May 1, 1944

When we went to visit the Seeleke family in Bad Nauheim and wandered through the streets of this world-famous city of spas, we could not avoid seeing the sad reality. Each step, each glance showed us mercilessly we are in the fifth year of war. This is a tragedy. Most shops are closed, partly because the owner was drafted into the armed forces, partly on government orders. A bookshop offers just covers of the books. A poster declares, "Only for those with bomb damage." Some things might be seen in a shop window, but they are mostly window displays or items in a clearance sale. Cheap souvenirs are still found here and there. All in all it is a picture of disconsolation. One can say we are at the eve of doom. [. . .]

They have earned their place in the Nazi royal court:

FORESTRY USE OF HIKERS

In order to remedy the lack of workers for the management of our forest, hikers readily put themselves at the forest authority's disposal. The Darmstadt Odenwald club therefore converted a planned hike for last Sunday into the first working group sent to the forest rangers' office in the Frankenstein district. At the Frankenstein rest area Ranger Trautmann awaited the 43 assistants, among them Forester Hesse, the Odenwald club leader. In five hours of hard work, the Riedenberg height was newly replanted to the helpers' satisfaction and the joy of the forest service, which was represented by Forester Bechtel.

Source: "Forsteinsatz der Wanderer," *DZ*, April 19, 1944, p. 3.

Ingratiating oneself in such a manner is not heroic, but it is common among those who curry the sole blessed Party's favor. In former times, one spoke of "manly pride before princely thrones," which even then was so meagerly represented.[20]

[. . .]

May 6, 1944

The commotion over Rommel:

"EVERY DIVISION IS A FORTRESS": ROMMEL AT THE ATLANTIC WALL

"What do you do when the enemy, without any sound, lands with gliders in the night in the middle of the battery?" the field marshal asked a battery commander. The captain pointed to the trenches, to the machine-gun nests. But the field marshal was not satisfied. He said, "Pay attention to what I say. I am assuming the enemy is silently approaching us ..." Then he gave practical directives to make sure any landing by paratroopers from the air would fail from the outset. He concluded by saying: "Always remember, one must expect the unexpected daily and hourly. We can never be finished with our preparations; there is absolutely no 'finished' with us."

During this trip, even during meal breaks, we heard no conversations that digressed from mines, barricades, obstacles, and guns. We once saw a wonderful meadow with colorful spring flowers under a beautiful sky: an idyll of peace. "Wonderful!" exclaimed the field marshal. "Wonderful," we repeated, lost in the sight. But he added, "Wonderful, if one considers eighty thousand mines lie under those flowers!" [. . .]

Source: "Jede Division eine Festung: Rommel im Atlantikwall,"
HF-Abend, April 15, 1944, p. 2.

It is likely the English are aware the Atlantic Coast has strongly defended areas. The question is only whether they are going to do us Germans a favor and attack those places where General Field Marshal Rommel erected his main fortifications. According to an ancient military rule, the opponent should be attacked at his weakest point.

Fortress Europe also has weak places. Except we guard against speaking about them.

It is quite conceivable "Fortress" Europe will be shaken from the inside out by airborne troops who are joined by the people in the occupied countries. I believe Yugoslavians could prevail over the German troops stationed in their country without receiving substantial support from the outside.

Prisoners of war and foreign workers likewise signify a large risk. If the storm breaks from all sides, a rapid situation could develop in which Germany would stand powerless. The Party organization will be of no help then. The white flag will have to be hoisted. I have no objection if the Party comrades fight to the last breath, even to five minutes past 12 o'clock.

Sometimes it seems to me as though it were already midnight. [. . .]

Our nephew, Erwin Ganglberger, who completed his work service a few days ago, was drafted into the Feldherrnhalle Division. We know with what methods the reserves of this division are trained to be tomorrow's "heroes."[21] [. . .]

May 11, 1944

The Führer's decree of April 25 about the military and work service obligations for stateless people is published in the *Reich Law Gazette*. From now on, stateless people who are in Reich territory can be used for military service and the Reich's work service the same as German citizens.[22] Germany is no longer so very particular. Now even the stateless person may sacrifice himself for Germany. The reserves must be sparse; otherwise they would not fall back upon the stateless people.

Once again there are many threats. The press threatens, Goebbels threatens, and the "famous" Field Marshal Rommel threatens. In Africa, before his major retreat, Rommel spoke strong words. Today he emits faint sounds of rage. After an inspection trip in the West, Rommel declared:

The German soldier knows his clear combat mission today. He is tried and proven, he has new weapons in his hand, and he is determined to provide the utmost resistance. The collision at the German coastal front will be dreadful for the enemy. I am convinced every individual German soldier will then make his contribution to the retribution he owes the Anglo-American ghoul for its criminal and bestial air warfare against our homeland.[23]

Much has been written and said about the "Invasion," "Atlantic Wall," and "Coastal Front." One would like to proclaim, "Let us finally see the action." Then the proof will be furnished whether the legendary Atlantic Wall is to be breached or not. In the East the Russians defeated the strongest fortifications. Why should that not be possible in the West? We will soon see!

In the May 9 *Darmstädter Zeitung* this is written:

> Through the reports about the Atlantic Wall we experience the defensive readiness of this most enormous protective cordon of all times. We admire the many and confounding systems of the trenches, crossbars and barricades, of the bunkers and machine gun emplacements, the threatening, elongated muzzles of the super-heavy cannon – and we understand the nervous mood on the British island, where they hope in vain to grate the German people's nerves by the shouting about invasion and "second front."[24]

May 12, 1944

The *Giessener Zeitung* of May 8 brings the following noteworthy notice:

> **Laubach.** The boys' troop of Jungstammes V116 met in Wetterfeld. The day began with a march through Laubach and Freienseen. Whoever sees these young boys singing knows why the enemy has not been able to bring us to our knees after five years of war. After cooking dinner together, a singing contest began, to which marching and games were added, by which Troops 21 and 32 were tried and tested.

Thus, we have evidence for Germany's ultimate victory. The Laubach boys in the Hitler Youth still sing. Because of this overwhelming fact, the enemy will not defeat us. But if the youth on the enemy side also sing as an indication of their victory, what then? The call is somewhat complicated.

> **Karl-Heinz Weisser**, Party Member, SS Lieutenant and Company Leader in an infantry regiment. Holder of the Iron Cross 1 and 2, and the Infantry Assault and Wound Badges.
> December 23, 1924 to January 14, 1944
> Our beloved youngest son found a hero's death in the difficult defensive battle in the East, just as his brother, **SS Wolfgang Weisser** (July 4, 1921 – August 21,

1941), corporal in an infantry regiment and holder of the Iron Cross 2, who took part in the western campaign, also was killed in action at the Eastern Front. [...]

Wolfgang Förster, Party Member, SS Second Lieutenant and Battalion Leader in an SS Panzer Grenadier Regiment. Holder of the Iron Cross 2, Infantry Assault Badge, Eastern Front Medal, and Wound Badge.
For Germany's future, and true to his oath to the flag, my only beloved and ever hopeful son, our dear nephew and cousin, died a hero's death at the Eastern Front.
August 14, 1921 to March 22, 1944 [...]

A nineteen-year-old company leader and a twenty-two-year-old battalion leader! That may scarcely be surpassed. The "best army in the world" has very young "Führers." [...]

The English will rejoice when they learn the *Hamburger Fremdenblatt* military editors consider the Supreme Command bulletin about Crimea's evacuation a "proud" report.[25] Thereby the English retreat from Dunkirk likewise becomes a glorious deed. A mass of words to explain or excuse a retreat or evacuation after it has taken place makes no impression on the impartial observer. A strategic evacuation of the Crimea would have been done in a timely fashion and without fierce fighting. After using everything they had militarily, the German troops were forced to leave the Crimea. The Germans had camped before Sevastopol [in South Crimea] for ten months before they conquered it. The Russians reconquered this strong fortress in a few days. By any measure that was an outstanding achievement. How does one now respond to the claim the German army in the Crimea was stabilizing the entire front? Does that include the dead and the prisoners? And does this now free up the Russian troops?
[...]

May 23, 1944

Court Bailiff Brunner expressed his opinion today in the office about the war's duration. Irritated by the contradictions of those present, he said with special emphasis, "The war is not going to end this year, nor is it going to end next year. And you can write that down." And so I herewith grant Herr Brunner that favor. When the war first began, the entire population believed in a rapid end; and today many contemporaries go to the opposite extreme and see no conclusion to the fighting coming at all.

The momentary quiet in the East and the West leads many to assume our enemies will not undertake anything crucial. I am steadfastly convinced of the opposite. I have no doubt at all about forthcoming large-scale attacks on all fronts. If the English and Americans give up their timid attitude and skillfully attack, first of all with airborne troops, it is quite possible a relatively rapid German collapse will take place. Naturally, it is a prerequisite our opponents give heed to this saying, "A good beginning is half the battle." Miserable landings (as in Italy) do not bring about a quick end. The number is increasing of those who begin to realize they must put an end to terror or have terror without end.

Gentlemen, bring it to an end.

[. . .]

May 27, 1944

[. . .] It required just a few days for the English and Americans to show the Pontine Marshes were no obstacle to their advance. They are already fighting in the mountainous regions past the swamps. So the German army's deliberate and senseless flooding of the marshes harmed only the Italian people, our allies.

[. . .]

June 5, 1944

GARRISON OF CISTERNA PUSHES BACK ALL ATTACKS
FANATICAL GERMAN SPIRIT IN DEFENSE AT CASSINO

All reports such as these are now worthless.[26] American troops pushed into Rome yesterday, on June 4. This Allied success has the utmost significance because the German Supreme Command had built defenses south of Rome and heavy fighting raged there for months.

June 6, 1944

FINALLY!

With the utmost inner excitement we heard the announcement today landings were made on the northern French coast.[27]

The German people react very differently to this momentous event because a large portion of them get their knowledge entirely from German radio announcements or the press. And what do they offer?

Hope that the German army will conquer the interlopers. That is strongly presented, and no one should be surprised. Dr. Goebbels and his large staff took care the public was informed and prepared in the wished-for way. The following excerpt certifies with what pride the Nazi hacks perform their trade:

Berlin, June 6, 1944.

On June 5 the announcement was issued from Führer Headquarters that the year of the invasion will bring a crushing defeat to the enemy at the place he has chosen to invade. In the early hours of June 6 the British and Americans began an attack on Europe at the northern French coast. Their enterprise is and remains now, immediately and directly, strongly overshadowed by the threatening prophecy from Führer Headquarters. The German people hear the news of the invasion's beginning with deep seriousness, which it is entitled to, but also with the imperturbable certainty we will victoriously emerge from this enormous struggle over liberty, the future of the nation, and the existence of Western culture.

Source: "Die entscheidende Schlacht im Westen hat begonnen,"
DZ, June 7, 1944, p. 1.

The Führer has once again risen to the heights of prophecy. On June 5, one day before the attack, he prophesied a crushing defeat for the enemy. What all has this man prophesied in the course of this war? But yet his errors do not deter him from continuing with his favorite hobby right up to the end.

And as does the master, so do the followers:[28]

NOW WE HAVE THEM FINALLY BEFORE OUR SWORD!

Shining justification of the German strategy /
The enemy came where we expected him

WE ARE PREPARING FOR THEM A HOT RECEPTION!

Declared Reich Press Chief Dr. Dietrich about the enemy landing

THE SURPRISE DID NOT SUCCEED

Immediate onset of Defense – Heavy fighting between
Cherbourg and Le Havre [. . .]

General Field Marshal von Rundstedt, Commander-in-Chief of the West. *Source:*
Bettmann/Contributor/Getty Images.

FROM FÜHRER HEADQUARTERS, JUNE 6, 1944.

Supreme Command of the Armed Forces bulletin:

Last night the enemy began his long-prepared and anticipated attack on
Western Europe.

Initiated by heavy air attacks on our coastal defenses, they dropped
airborne troops at several points of the northern French coast between Le
Havre and Cherbourg and landed at the same time, supported by strong
naval forces from the sea. Fierce battles are in progress at the landing sites
along the coast.

Source: DZ, June 7, 1944, p. 1.

CHURCHILL ON THE INVASION

Geneva, June 7, 1944.

As Reuters reported, Churchill came on Tuesday to speak in the House
about the invasion. He said the invasion of the European continent began in
the previous night and continued into the early morning hours of Tuesday.

He further stated the battle will continually grow in scope and intensity, and indeed for many weeks.

[...]

June 10, 1944

Adolf Hitler on September 30, 1942:

Whether or not Mr. Churchill has selected with his military intelligence the first place where he wants to begin the "second front," I can assure him of this in any case: it makes no difference at all which place he chooses because it will only be a matter of luck if he remains nine hours ashore! (Thunderous laughing [from the audience].)[29] [...]

And today? Like the silence in the forest! Only one, the Regional Leader and master of Berlin's ruins, Dr. Joseph Goebbels, still shoots his mouth off.

At present we have three fronts: Russia, Italy, and France. Further fronts are approaching!

June 15, 1944

For ten days the invasion battle in the West, in Normandy, has been under way. Sentiments differ, depending on what expectations were linked to the beginning of the invasion. Regarded from my point of view, the following facts are to be considered:

1. German pilots were not able to disrupt the enemies' preparations in the English ports.
2. The German navy was not able to stop the English from crossing the Channel to France.
3. The Normandy coast defenders could not prevent the landing in France.

[...] The Party's immediate worry is that the German people do not become anxious. The Party claptrap circulated from town to town is supposed to make the people optimistic. It was said the enemy's landing would be welcomed because our troops would have a better opportunity to strike the enemy. That is still believed, at least by those who have a lot of confidence in the German troops.

The war correspondent, Dr. Schaefer, held a talk yesterday on the radio. According to him the landing is a failure. The ports of Cherbourg and Le

Havre are not even threatened, and the enemy must be in possession of the ports if his enterprise is to be crowned with success.

The present situation in the combat area in Normandy is not far enough advanced to shake the believers among the Germans. Our military reports read very confidently. Most people cling to them, and almost everyone draws a small remnant of hope from them.

In point of fact, for those here who wanted an end to the war, the landing was not massive enough to accomplish that. [...]

EACH GERMAN SOLDIER IS A FORTRESS!

Like an eagle's nest, the paratroopers' machine gun positions, fixed between rocks and ruins, overlook the southern Italian battlefield. In these bastions, the superior individual fighters continually break up the waves of the enemy's superior strength.

War Correspondent Uecker.

These "fortresses" in South Italy could have been eliminated had the major military commander made landings in central Italy or even in northern Italy – from bases in Sardinia and Corsica.

The turnaround will presumably come only if the Russians go on the attack along the entire Eastern Front.

THE FINNISH ARMY REPORT

Helsinki, June 11, 1944.

According to the Finnish Armed Forces report of June 10, Russia began a general offensive in the early hours of yesterday on the Karelian Isthmus, supported by heavy artillery fire and strong air squadrons. The attacks, which were made at various points, were broken off except for a few small limited incursions. The enemy suffered significant casualties. Ten tanks were destroyed. Our fighter pilots and anti-aircraft artillery shot down 24 enemy planes. The fighting continues. Patrols are active along the front lines.

Source: "Der finnische Heeresbericht," *VB-Nord,* June 12, 1944, p. 3.

The beginning was made on the Karelian Isthmus. It should not be surprising that the Finnish army report did not tell the Finns the truth. Lies have short legs though, and it will not take a long time before the Finnish people notice what is going on. Why this hokum?

June 16, 1944

"FIGHT AND WIN, IF WE WANT TO LIVE."

State Secretary Dr. Naumann about the Invasion

Berlin, June 12, 1944.

[...] "We stand before the greatest onslaught of this war and must survive. It is a war of life and death for the entire nation. Therefore we must fight," called out State Secretary Dr. Naumann, to the enthusiastic approval of his listeners. "Fight and win, if we want to live!" Fighting to a victorious end is the German leadership's uncompromising decision. And they have the best soldiers and the most diligent and courageous people behind them. [...]

Source: "Kämpfen und siegen, wenn wir leben wollen," *VB-Nord,*
June 13, 1944, p. 2.

[...] State Secretary Dr. Naumann from the Reich Ministry for Propaganda knows the best approach.[30] When he says to the people, "We must fight," what he wants is to prepare them to fight up to the last breath. "We" means "the people" when it comes to fighting. But when it refers to staying alive, then "We" means the Party big shots. If Germany wins the war, then naturally the Party shall claim all the credit. If Germany loses, then it will be "all the other Germans" who are to blame.

The following headlines from June 6–17 about the fighting in France (Normandy) show how the "Leadership" is handling the propaganda.[31]

THE MAJORITY OF ENEMY BRIDGEHEADS ANNIHILATED: HEAVIEST LOSSES OF LANDING FORCES

SLAUGHTER IN NORMANDY

SUBDUED SPIRITS IN LONDON

CALL FOR SOVIET ASSISTANCE

NO TRACE OF ENTHUSIASM IN THE USA FOR INVASION [...]

[...]

June 20, 1944

Today, deputy judge Holzschuh wanted me to describe the strategic situation as I see it. I told him I was convinced Russia would soon begin large-scale attacks – by June 22 at the latest. The first battles will commemorate the German assault of three years ago and will take place in the North: Estonia, Latvia, and Lithuania. A primary aim included in this would be the liberation of White Russia [Belarus].

I am looking forward to seeing if I correctly assessed the military situation. Until now, I saw clearly almost without exception – although I did err, now and then, in haste. I had not sufficiently realized the English, those cold calculators, wanted to ensure every tiny detail was carefully considered. In 1940 Churchill said it is not enough to prepare, but one must really prepare! Thus even in 1940 the authorities in England had not thought seriously yet of a total deployment. While the greatest struggles were occurring in Russia and Germany, millions of soldiers in England (Englishmen, Americans, Canadians, and many others) were resting on laurels yet to be achieved. That is not warfare!

The delay in Italy is clearly evident. They landed in Sicily on July 10, 1943. They were in Calabria on September 3 and in Naples on September 9, 1943. Rome was not taken until June 4, 1944. Nearly an entire year fought in Italy, and even now they have not reached northern Italy. An Englishman will never be able to tell me why it was not possible to use more troops in Italy.

June 21, 1944

What is happening? The philistines are hopeful again. The "retribution," in which they no longer believed, has begun:

FROM FÜHRER HEADQUARTERS, JUNE 16, 1944.

Supreme Command of the Armed Forces bulletin:

Last night and this morning, South England and the regions around London were struck with new explosives of the heaviest caliber.

Source: "Gegen London und Südengland," *VB-Nord*, June 17, 1944, p. 1.

For sure, this military report is concise and simple, but yet it is a feast for the propaganda ministry, which has since come up with victory messages and special reports. Goebbels must make something from it, and so he does – and not sparingly:[32]

NEW EXLOSIVES OF THE HEAVIEST CALIBER AGAINST LONDON AND SOUTH ENGLAND [...]

MASSIVE DESTRUCTIVE FIRE ON LONDON NEARLY WITHOUT CEASE

THE EFFECT IN LONDON FAR STRONGER THAN IN AUTUMN 1940

ENGLISH DEFENSE SO FAR FUTILE [...]

ENGLISH FLAK IN VAIN AGAINST THE GERMAN EXPLOSIVES

Berlin, June 18, 1944.

The British believe they can use flak to stop the heavy attacks of the new German weapon, not previously experienced in this war, which began Friday night against London and other South England cities. In their dismay they even sent up fighter pilots against the pilotless, remote-controlled explosives. Over the entire southeast coast of England was a fire wall of hundreds of searchlights and ten thousand anti-aircraft flak guns. But the hope remained elusive of being able to destroy the explosives in the air. The sky was fire-red, with huge clouds of smoke, from the targets that were hit. Throughout the day numerous other projectiles fell. At varying altitudes they flew to London and parts of South England. New fires arose and mushrooms of smoke penetrated the low-hanging clouds. Even from a distance of over 200 km, they showed our reconnaissance aircraft the way.

> Source: "Vergebliches englisches Flakfeuer gegen die deutschen Sprengkörper," VB-Nord, June 19, 1944, p. 1.

Propaganda has thus spoken. Now we want to wait for the "miracle weapon" effects. Apparently it concerns a flying bomb or air torpedo, undoubtedly causing destruction – completely indiscriminately. Whether the effect, however, is stronger than with concentrated bombing raids, I would like to doubt.

All attention on England and no one thinks of Russia. Where is the "miracle weapon" against the Russians? With the coming offensive by Russia, it will help Germany little to go hunting with explosives across the Channel to England.

June 22, 1944

[. . .] Barely three days have passed since the Party comrades and common folk were raised to high rapture, and the cold water comes rushing in. The people are told not to exaggerate their hopes because the new weapon is aimed only at England. What did I say! With so many people enchanted by the prospect of Endsieg that was to come after England's complete destruction, the propaganda machine was not very nice to deflate their pretty dream so quickly. [. . .]

The effect on the average German may be drawn from the following remark. In a second-class compartment on the train from Laubach to Hungen, an evacuee said to his wife, "If England collapses, the war is over in six months." [. . .]

The inexperienced reader cannot in any way discover the actual situation from the Armed Forces reports. Every day it is "all attacks are returned or repelled." In reality, the Russian troops have already pushed through and captured the entire Karelian Isthmus and Vyborg [Viipuri]. The Russians also conquered the Finnish positions between Lake Ladoga and Lake Onega. Finland's situation is hopeless. But that is not to be discerned from the newspaper reports. There it says:

> It is true Vyborg, the old border fortress of Finland and capital city of Karelian, is newly threatened. But the Finns' will is unbroken, fierce resistance is given, and the enemy in forward positions is being held to a standstill. Strong streams of additional reserves are employed despite heavy enemy air attacks on supply lines.
>
> *Source:* "Heldentod des erfolgreichsten finnischen Jagdfliegers," *VB-Nord,*
> June 21, 1944, p. 3.

The "fierce resistance" leads to new senseless victims. It borders already on insanity to assume Finland can successfully defend itself with the present balance of power. Finland had one requirement only: friendship with Russia and not with Hitler!

June 23, 1944

FLOODING OF THE NETHERLANDS' COASTAL REGION

Where once greenhouses and fruitful meadows were, can now be seen just wide surfaces of water. Too shallow for inflatables and too deep for infantry, here is an almost insurmountable safety barrier to our positions and tank works.

Source: VB-Nord, June 21, 1944, p. 6.

"Where once greenhouses and fruitful meadows were," which also supplied Germany, is now just an area of water. Is it still possible anyone in Germany is surprised hate grows day by day against the Germans in the occupied countries? That is a component of the "New" Europe!

June 25, 1944

[. . .]

HEROIC RESISTANCE OF THE DEFENDERS AT CHERBOURG

From Führer Headquarters, June 26, 1944.

The brave garrison of Cherbourg, under the command of Lieutenant General von Schlieben, together with strong navy and air force contingents, is since yesterday in fierce urban warfare within the city and at the waterfront. Two calls of the enemy to stop fighting and surrender the fortress were not answered. The port and all important war plants are blown up. At the fortress commander's command post, and at the arsenal, a simultaneous defensive fire broke up the enemy's attacks.

Source: "Heroischer Widerstand der Verteidiger von Cherbourg" *VB-Nord*,
June 27, 1944, p. 1.

June 27, 1944

We repeatedly go through the same pretense as at Stalingrad. The German troops are led into situations that offer no prospects and are uselessly sacrificed. Whether Cherbourg falls into American hands on the siege's first or fourth day really remains the same thing. Every German soldier who fell in Cherbourg died for the insane Supreme Command of the Armed Forces.

FIERCE GERMAN RESISTANCE

Berlin, June 27, 1944.

The new Soviet offensive, which began on June 22, has been cut off in some places, and in other places the attacker has had some success. The units of the so-called First and Second Belorussian Front broke into the German positions. The Soviet term "front" as it refers to a larger military unit is hard to translate. According to the number of forces deployed it means something between an army group and army. The garrison of Vitebsk is in a difficult situation. The Soviet pressure is continuing and appears to be spread out evenly from northeast and southeast against the German front's projecting bulge.

Source: "Erbitterter deutscher Widerstand," *VB-Nord*, June 28, 1944, p. 1.

My prediction was fulfilled exactly as stated. The new offensive was generally expected, but everyone believed Romania would be the theater. My deliberations made me think the opposite because Romanian oil fields were already under attack by English and American airplanes stationed in Italy. The middle and northern part of the Eastern Front are now in the Russian zone. In effect, they are liberated. There are signs of great strategic successes there, not only the liberation of Estonia, Latvia, Lithuania, and Belarus, but also Russia's threat against East Prussia.

The last hour of Germany's army in the East has struck!

July 4, 1944

[...] German troops on all fronts are too weak to be able to defend themselves effectively. The army's situation is extremely bad, particularly in the East. In just twelve days, the Russians conquered all the strong positions of Vitebsk, Orsha, Mogilev, Minsk, and Polozk. The Russian armies are closing on Latvia, Lithuania, and East Prussia, and any moment will be at the borders of Latvia and Lithuania. That is a truly delicate situation for our army because if they relinquish the Baltic region of Germany, rescue becomes impossible. The development in the coming days and weeks will confirm my suppositions. The initiative is fully and wholly in the hands of our enemies, who no longer relent. When a weak place is strengthened by our Supreme Command, there immediately arises at some other place further risk of a gap. Eventually the breaks in the line can no longer be filled – quite apart from the fact that you cannot improvise in all directions. Serious errors were made in the overall German strategy; for five years the Supreme Command has demonstrated every kind of military and political ineptitude.

Those who act contrary to common sense cannot complain when they are punished by fate.

July 5, 1944

INCREASING EFFECT OF THE V-1[33]

Given the disastrous defeat in the vast "Lebensraum" in the East, the propagandists must prevent the mood barometer from falling below zero. They do not have much to choose from, so less is being put out. The new miracle weapon is called V-1. The "V" is for *Vergeltung* (retribution/revenge). The number "1" is to suggest more such weapons are to be expected. For the time being, the V-1 is to be used with a cumulative effect. It is difficult to get more information about this; it is left to the individual's fancy to imagine what the effect is.[34]

When in the past the luck of war turned toward our enemy, the propaganda always gave us refuge in new weapons. I recall the "Tiger" and "Panther" tanks – and also the assault gun, "Ferdinand."[35]

NEW GERMAN ANTI-TANK WEAPONS PANZERFAUST AND PANZERSCHRECK [TANK PUNCH AND TANK SHOCK][36]

One joker said "V" in V-1 stands for *Verzweiflung* [desperation]. Not bad. Another took the saying, "Lies have short legs," and turned it into "The liar (Goebbels) has a short leg."

[...]

July 9, 1944

The Party members' confidence is not yet shaken. Yesterday, Hauck, the Local Group Leader from Hainchen, mentioned the Americans and English had been destroyed on the Cherbourg peninsula. He believes unswervingly in the Führer and final victory. Nothing can be done in this instance, as reasonable considerations are impossible with such Party members. Their blind faith in Hitler rules over reason and understanding.

July 14, 1944

The *Darmstädter Zeitung* of June 22 published an essay by Hans Hertel: "Three Years of War in the East." [...] This Nazi is so dazzled by the propaganda of his lord and master, Dr. Goebbels, he believes Russia is incapable of anything further. The Supreme Command likewise underestimates the Russian forces. I cannot understand that. For me it is certain

Russia will launch a final and decisive attack as soon as the Allies complete their landing in the West. The Nazis will yet learn about Russia's offensive capabilities. Too late, however.

[...]

July 24, 1944

July 20, 1944!

TRAITORS WANTED TO MURDER ADOLF HITLER
THE FÜHRER LIVES
DEATH FOR THE CLIQUE OF ASSASSINS![37]

OFFICIAL REPORT ON THE ASSASSINATION ATTEMPT

Führer Headquarters, July 20, 1944.

An explosive attack against the Führer was committed today. Seriously injured at the scene were Lieutenant General Schmundt, Colonel Brand, and staff member Berger.

Minor injuries were received by General Jodl; Generals Korten, Buhle, Bodenschatz, Heusinger, Scherff; the Admirals Voss, von Puttkammer; Sea Captain Assmann, and Lieutenant Colonel Borgmann.

The Führer, except for minor burns and bruises, suffered no injuries. He immediately started working again and, as expected, received the Duce for a lengthy discussion.

The Reich Marshal went to the Führer's side quickly after the attack.

Source: "Amtliche Mitteilung über das Attentat," *DZ*, July 21, 1944, p. 1.

ADOLF HITLER'S SPEECH TO THE GERMAN PEOPLE THE
BACKGROUND OF THE MURDER PLANS

Betrayal by small clique of generals operating as the enemy's agents

The Führer presented this evening the following speech over the radio to the German people:

German men and women:

I do not know how many times an attempt on my life has been planned and carried out. If I address you today, I do so for two reasons: first, so you can hear my voice and know I am uninjured and well; second, so you can hear the details about a crime unequalled in German history. An extremely small clique of ambitious, unscrupulous and also criminally stupid officers concocted a plot to remove me and at the same time to kill the entire

German Supreme Command staff. The bomb placed by Colonel Graf von Stauffenberg exploded two meters from me toward my right side. It seriously wounded several of my dear collaborators, and one was killed. Except for minor cuts and bruises and burns I am entirely unhurt. I consider this to be a confirmation of the task Providence has handed me, and I will continue in pursuit of my life's goal, as I have done up to now. I can solemnly state before the entire nation that since the day I moved into Wilhelmstrasse I have been guided by one thought only: to do my duty to the best of my knowledge and ability. And when it became clear to me that war was inevitable and could no longer be postponed, I lived only for my people in all of my work and concerns throughout countless days and sleepless nights.

At the hour when the German army is waging a very hard fight, a very small group of people, similar to what occurred in Italy, appeared in Germany thinking they could thrust a dagger into our backs the way they did in 1918. But this time they made a huge mistake. They assumed they had succeeded in killing me, but I am disproving that at this moment, as I speak to you, my dear fellow countrymen. The circle is quite small in which these would-be usurpers reside. They have nothing to do with the German armed forces, and particularly nothing to do with the German army. It is a very small clique of criminal elements. They will be exterminated mercilessly. [. . .]

Source: "Die Hintergründe des Mordplans," *VB-Nord*, July 22, 1944, p. 1.

[. . .]

THE PLOT IS COMPLETELY SMASHED

Berlin, July 21, 1944.

As the German News Agency has learned, the criminal conspiracy of the officer clique has been completely smashed. Some ringleaders killed themselves after the failure of their attack, some were shot by firing squads of army battalions. Among those shot is the assassin Colonel Count von Stauffenberg. No other incidents have occurred. The remaining culprits will be held responsible for their behavior.

Source: "Das Komplott völlig zusammengebrochen," *DZ*, July 21, 1944, p. 1.

[. . .]

July 27, 1944

[. . .]

We have heard what the ruling Party greats had to say about the assassination attempt. What would I say? My first thoughts were occupied with the manner and way the event was communicated. The first official report concealed the course of events and the perpetrators' names. The Führer spoke of a "completely small clique" of officers. The German press agency reported the ringleaders were executed by army battalions. One might think battalions would not have been necessary against a "completely small clique"! The bomb, allegedly put in place by Colonel Count von Stauffenberg, exploded two meters away from the Führer. The Führer remained intact. That is the quintessential point of the entire story. Who now still doubts the Führer is protected by "Providence"? Thus a visible miracle happened, and that is all that matters. The people must derive from the reports the conviction that the Führer, after this rescue, shall be recompensed at the end with victories.

Because the continued retreat in the East is likely to diminish the faith in the Führer, the director of this drama announced that the assassination attempt plotters were generals who had been under investigation for cowardly and bad leadership in the field. These generals are then readily regarded as scapegoats, and the motive for the incident is provided.

If the attack actually had been arranged and implemented only by officers, then it was an amateurish enterprise. A revolution can be promising only on the broadest basis. A revolution only of officers is a stillbirth.

By the way, I welcome the rescue of the Führer because for tactical reasons he must remain alive to the bitter end. It must not be possible for his death to be used as an excuse in the future. He must remain until there is no more way out, until Providence itself would not be able to come to his side to help him.

[. . .]

August 2, 1944

[. . .]

On June 22, German troops were still in the upper Dnieper area. But by the end of July the Russians had already reached the Vistula River south of Warsaw! Naturally, that can neither be hushed up nor excused. But the propagandists must nevertheless do something! The Party gossip is that German forces are coming together and setting up strong forces somewhere in the interior, to put a final halt to the enemy at a place determined by the Führer. Once again there is a ray of hope for those who will get nothing else.

August 3, 1944

[. . .]

The adversary who was so crushed he would never rise again – according to Adolf Hitler's statement in October 1941 – is presently displaying amazing combat strength before the gates of East Prussia, as well as in the Vistula region and in Galicia. No German soldier stands any longer on Russian territory. At the least, that is a masterly achievement by the Russians, which is without example in the past.

What can our German paper-strategists put up against that? Dr. Goebbels announced the irrevocable, final, absolute mobilization to establish new divisions for the Eastern Front. It is preached to the German people every-where that new forces (already existing and newly formed) will shortly perform a counter-attack – but, of course, the assembly of all these forces requires still some more time, so the people must merely have patience and provide complete co-operation. To what extent the total mobilization will postpone the collapse cannot easily be judged. The sole determining factor is whether the opponents give the German General Staff enough time.

DR. GOEBBELS ORDERS: NO MORE PRETENSE WORK

YOUR WORKMANSHIP BELONGS TO THE NATION

In agreement with Dr. Goebbels, the Reich Plenipotentiary for Total War, Regional Leader Sauckel, as Plenipotentiary for the Allocation of Labor, promulgated a regulation on the use of labor in sham employment.[. . .] Whoever within this fighting nation withholds his labor or other aid that might be rendered is the enemy!

Source: "Deine Arbeitskraft gehört der Nation," VB-Nord, July 30, 1944, p. 2.

[. . .]

Strange! The Nazis knew sham employment existed and they failed to stop it? How would it be, by the way, to give all the Party bigwigs real employment at the front?

August 4, 1944

[. . .]

Besides the regulation against sham employment, a further measure regarding total efforts for the war entered into force on July 30: raising the age bracket for female workers to 45–50. All women between the end of their forty-fifth and the end of their fiftieth year are now subject to the legal obligation to register for work assignment.[38]

The Nazis take the view that these women, compared with younger women, have led a nearly peacetime existence.

My opinion: I have absolutely no doubt a full utilization of reserves is possible in Germany if it is ruthlessly accessed. However, these radical measures should have been done several years ago. People who have to be pressed today into war assignments are those with very little inspiration, and above everything else they are unskilled. [. . .]

SEARCH FOR ACCOMPLICE IN ASSASSINATION ATTEMPT ON THE FÜHRER

Karl Goerdeler. *Photo:* Presse-Hoffmann.

Berlin, August 1, 1944.

On account of his complicity in the assassination attempt on the Führer on July 20, 1944, he has become a fugitive since that day: Chief Mayor (retired) Dr. Carl Goerdeler, born July 31, 1884 in Schneidemühl, was last living in Leipzig.

For information leading to his capture, a reward of 1,000,000 RM is posted. All persons who can provide any information are asked to report to the nearest police authority.

Source: "Wegen Mittäterschaft am Attentat auf den Führer gesucht," *VB-Nord*, August 3, 1944.

[. . .] The Nazis masterfully perfected artful representations of deceit. In all nooks and crannies, they preach the "believer's faith." And the number of those who still fanatically believe in miracles is large. The July 20 assassination attempt supplied new material to all preachers of miracles. In the Geist Inn at Altenhain, the railroad official Nickel from Mücke loudly and clearly announced his inspired feelings: "Hitler is an envoy of God who will bring us final victory. We must only believe, and faith shall make us inwardly and outwardly strong." Nickel said also if he lost his son, he would consider him a sacrifice for his fatherland. [. . .]

[. . .]

August 15, 1944

[. . .] The labor offices certainly will seize yet another large number of workers to register in their lists. And the military district commands, with the help of their faith healer, likewise will find many previous "indispensables." But all of these measures were taken much too late to change anything in Germany's favor at the different theaters of war. It especially should be noted the enemies' reserves (above all, England's and America's) are already available to intervene immediately in the fight. Furthermore, do not forget German troops have registered enormous losses of people and material since June 1944. Just filling in the gaps will require a large effort. Going beyond that to set up entirely new divisions is just not possible at all. People might still be available, but you cannot make much of a start with soldiers who have no weapons. And for that, raw materials are necessary; and there the problem is absolutely enormous.

The war is lost for Germany. I do not mean lost today or tomorrow. It was already lost in 1943. It should have been ended then.

[. . .]

August 20, 1944

[. . .]

Another Allied landing, this time on the coast of southern France between Toulon and Cannes on August 15. The "most ingenious general of all times" was outwitted once again by our opponents, the "military idiots." [. . .] This landing has greatest strategic importance. The German troops in South France are lost. The Frenchmen will rise, and the Allies will be able to go to Germany by way of the Rhone Valley, as well as to Italy by way of the Riviera.

It is humorous that with this less than pleasant situation, the Party, which scatters rumors, says we intentionally allow enemy troops to come in, to be better able to destroy them! And that is believed! There is nothing so dumb it cannot find an audience.

STUFF EVERY CHATTERBOX'S MOUTH

Talkers are traitors! – Severe penalties for divulging state secrets

[...] The 49-year-old Sergeant K. had to pick up a secret piece of equipment in a military department. While in a waiting room, he said, "Things are happening with the V-1." One of those present asked, "What have you to do with V-1?" Sergeant K. told all the important details of this weapon, and also spoke of new experiments, mentioned places of manufacture and delivery companies. He also spoke about the stages of development of other weapons. While he was speaking, several other people joined to listen, including two temporary employees. Nevertheless, K. was unconcerned and continued talking. He was sentenced to death. [...]

Source: "Stopft allen Schwätzern den Mund!" DZ, August 17, 1944, p. 1.

The chief executioner Himmler is concerned! But the sergeant who was condemned to death spoke only about inconsequential matters to other Germans. The V-1 weapon was clearly shown in the German illustrated magazine, Die Wehrmacht.[39] I have no doubt the English are informed in every detail about the V-1's construction, and England considers it sense-less to create a similar weapon. Their bombers are incomparably better than the V-1 toy. Besides, how much longer can the V-1 be fired at England? Its days are numbered. American tanks are already close to Paris. From Paris to the V-1 firing ramps is not far. And yet, because of such an idiotic weapon, our soldiers are condemned to death or put into prison, on the exaggerated grounds they had betrayed "secrets." The idiocy stands in full bloom.

What has not been raised to "secret"? And yet foreign workers and prisoners work in all the factories, and there are plenty of captured German soldiers to tell everything they know. Many military "secrets" appear in the photographs taken by enemy pilots. Here in Laubach we all know about the factory built in the neighboring town of Freienseen that was also a "secret." Do reasonable people believe such a "secret" will remain hidden to the enemy?[40]

THE OPPONENT HAS TO HURRY – WE ARE FIGHTING FOR TIME

The demonstration of our new weapons has alarmed the enemy[41]

Granted, it is possible Germany may be superior to the other powers in weapon technology. We were once superior in the air; our submarines and ground troops were superior in every way to all others. But since then, our adversaries, who indeed were unprepared, caught up with us and overtook us. The crucial pillars of this war are strategy, people, and material. No particular weapon will be decisive – our rifle versus theirs, cannon versus cannon, plane versus plane, tank versus tank. Who has the most people and the largest quantity of war material? We can see right now in France who is superior: battles north, south, and all over France. Germany is not at all able to confront the enemy everywhere with the necessary strength. That is the determining factor – not the possession of winged bombs and other mysterious weapons in small quantities. Also, even if it were possible to magically come up with some extra divisions and weapons, they could not fill in the gaps that developed in the East and the West over these last months. It is not enough to establish any kind of equilibrium. No. We would have to achieve predominance, superiority. Germany simply is not able to do that. Even a corporal in Berlin must see that. Unfortunately, Hitler is determined to see nothing. In his stubborn narrow-mindedness lies the tragedy of all that has happened in Germany. But the entire nation's complicity is beyond doubt. The main culprits are those who eliminated democracy in Germany or even tacitly helped the dictator to achieve his victories. [. . .]

August 22, 1944

LIEUTENANT GENERAL DITTMAR ON THE MILITARY SITUATION

Adding new formations in the East –
thinning out the front in the West
Berlin, August 17, 1944.

[. . .] It requires very skillful operations on our part to counter the danger. But we must not overlook the fact that a thinning out of the battle fronts, as it is now occurring, may also provide chances for effective counter-attacks, which give us time, as we are primarily engaged in future weapons technological developments that will give us renewed prospects.

Source: "Generalleutnant Dittmar zur militärischen Lage," *DZ,*
August 18, 1944, p. 2.

An army general broadcasting over the radio in 1944 has it far more difficult than in the successful years of 1939 and 1940.[42] [...] According to Dittmar, a new supply of units to the East will change the combat situation. Here he is greatly deceiving himself. Since their offensive of June 22, 1944 (just two months ago), the Russians have covered 400–600 kilometers. Obviously the Russian army's final challenge – invading Germany – cannot be done with empty ammunition cars. They need to organize the entire supply and the traffic routes. That is why their recent advance on so many positions was stopped – except for localized attacks along the Russian border. The Russian trumpets will soon sound to resume their offensive.

As for the combat situation in the West, Dittmar does say it is difficult, but he would not be a genuine Third Reich general if he did not offer us "comfort" and "hope for improvement." He writes about counter-attacks, gaining time, and weapon-technology developments.

The Nazi Party is likewise consoling its followers with the future. Standardized reports are handed out at Party meetings, and the members have the task to spread the subject matter further. The same hopes are parroted everywhere. Judge [Erich] Zimmermann's wife told me she places her trust in the "V-2" because something must come from it. Judge Schmitt's wife asserted we would allow the English and Americans to come into Germany and then destroy them.

Party slogans are haunting every head. There will be an awakening!

An evacuee from Frankfurt said her husband had collected and turned in numerous leaflets – without reading them. It is strictly forbidden to read leaflets. And so it continues. With such Germans, Adolf Hitler can fight right up to the end.

A nation of cattle!

August 25, 1944

ST. MALO IS FANATICALLY DEFENDED

The Commandant Knows Just One Thing: No Surrender!

OAK LEAF CLUSTER FOR THE DEFENDERS OF ST. MALO[43]

[...]

Führer Headquarters, August 18, 1944.

The St. Malo fortress commander, Colonel Andreas von Aulock, sent a radio message on the afternoon of August 18 to the Führer: "My Führer, the Battle of St. Malo will be brought to an end today or tomorrow. Under the heaviest bombardment one position after another falls in ruins. We are going down, so let this be a fight to the end. The Lord God holds his hand protectively over you! Long live our Führer!"

The Führer answered with the following radio message:
"To the St. Malo fortress commander, Colonel von Aulock.
   I thank you and your heroic men on my behalf and on the behalf of the German people. Your name will go down in history forever.
   Adolf Hitler."

Source: "Gehen wir unter, so soll es nur nach Kampf bis zum letzten sein,"
VB-Süd, August 19, 1944, p. 1.

After this Nazi officer received from his "Führer" Oak Leaves for his Knight's Cross of the Iron Cross, he surrendered and was put in prison. Hundreds of soldiers had to lose their lives for the senseless and useless defense in Brittany of the St. Malo fortress so Herr Commandant could be decorated. The "heroic" defense was merely for that.

Whoever implements Hitler's insane instructions is promoted or decorated. In former times one knew only of rewarding the winner. Today slavish obedience in situations offering no prospects is praised as the greatest heroism. The ambitious officers do not have any sense of responsibility for their men. They believe they shall "enter into history as heroes."

The path that leads from hero to villain is not long.

[...]

August 27, 1944

MAXIMUM DEPLOYMENT OF FORCES

By General Field Marshal von Brauchitsch

July 20, 1944, was the darkest day in the history of the German army. Men who wore the honorable uniform of the German soldier became criminals and assassins. Had their backstabbing succeeded, it could have ended in the nation's downfall. There is no denying this and it cannot be glossed over or excused.

The army itself nipped this plan in the bud. They have executed the unworthy individuals and have crushed all internal and external groups associated with them. Their names have been erased. Along with the deep thankfulness for the wonderul rescue of the Führer, rage and shame fill every honorable soldier. [. . .]

Source: "Höchster Krafteinsatz," *VB-Süd*, August 20, 1944, p. 1.

Adolf Hitler's opinion on this topic differs substantially from General Field Marshal von Brauchitsch's. He states in *Mein Kampf*, [. . .] "a state authority is entitled to demand respect and protection only when it meets the interests of a people, or at least does not harm them. There can be no such thing as state authority as an end in itself, for, if there were, every tyranny in this world would be unassailable and sacred. If, by the instrument of governmental power, a nationality is led toward its destruction, then rebellion is not only the right of every member of such a people – it is his duty."[44] [. . .]

FROM PARIS TO NORMANDY

"German troops and columns of vehicles march down the Champs-Élysees in Paris to the front in Normandy. The Parisians give the withdrawing German soldiers, who even now fight for them and their home, flowers along the way."

The war correspondent Mielke apparently thinks his compatriots are even dumber than he is.[45] He will not convince reasonable people the French population is "enthusiastic" about German troops with such posed photographs. The small detachment of soldiers is not marching to the front lines, as he says, wearing their caps and without their gear. The flower-carrying women and girls, who no doubt were brought in from a nearby market along the way, are not making preparations to give the flowers to the troops.

It is extremely sad how the German people allow themselves to be lied to and deceived with such means and by such fumblers. Pitiful swindlers! [...]

INTENSIFIED HUNTING OF WILD BOARS

The increase in wild boars, due to the war situation, must be reduced to a tolerable level. Although the successes in killing boars were higher last year, they were not enough to keep the game damage within tolerable limits. [...]
Source: "Verstärkter Abschuß von Schwarzwild," *VB-Süd,* August 21, 1944, p. 5.

Dr. Goebbels is going to have to understand many [non-war related] job positions are essential and cannot be eliminated. To ensure the ruling Party does not collapse because its members lack employment – which would be a grave danger for the beloved fatherland and the existence of the Aryan race – all of the following bureaucracies will be involved in granting authorization for hunters who want to be able to shoot more wild boars:

Reich Minister for Nutrition
Reich Hunting Master
Office for National Nourishing
Regional Hunting Master or Forest Authority
and the Regional Leader.

Did our opponents think, even in this fifth year of war, we had no more reserves?

August 29, 1944

> **Ernst Adolf**, my son,was born to me today as a legacy to my husband, Ernst Langer, First Lieutenant in a Panzer Regiment, killed in action in March in the administrative district of Jauer-Katzbach, Poland.
> Maria Langer, née Hibbeler. [. . .]
>
> *Source:* VB-Nord, August 22, 1944, p. 5.

The Nazi language has a slogan for each of life's events. The birth of a child after the soldier-father's death is a "legacy." The legacy recipients someday may think it would have been better not to have received their "legacy" at such cost. [. . .]

Newspapers will be reduced to four pages beginning September 1. That will affect the obituaries in particular. Until now, the survivors could allow their feelings free rein. [. . .]

September 1, 1944

[. . .]

The military situation in the western theater changed enormously in the last month. At the beginning of August, fighting was going on in the areas of Avranches and Caen, and at the end of August the Allies had already crossed

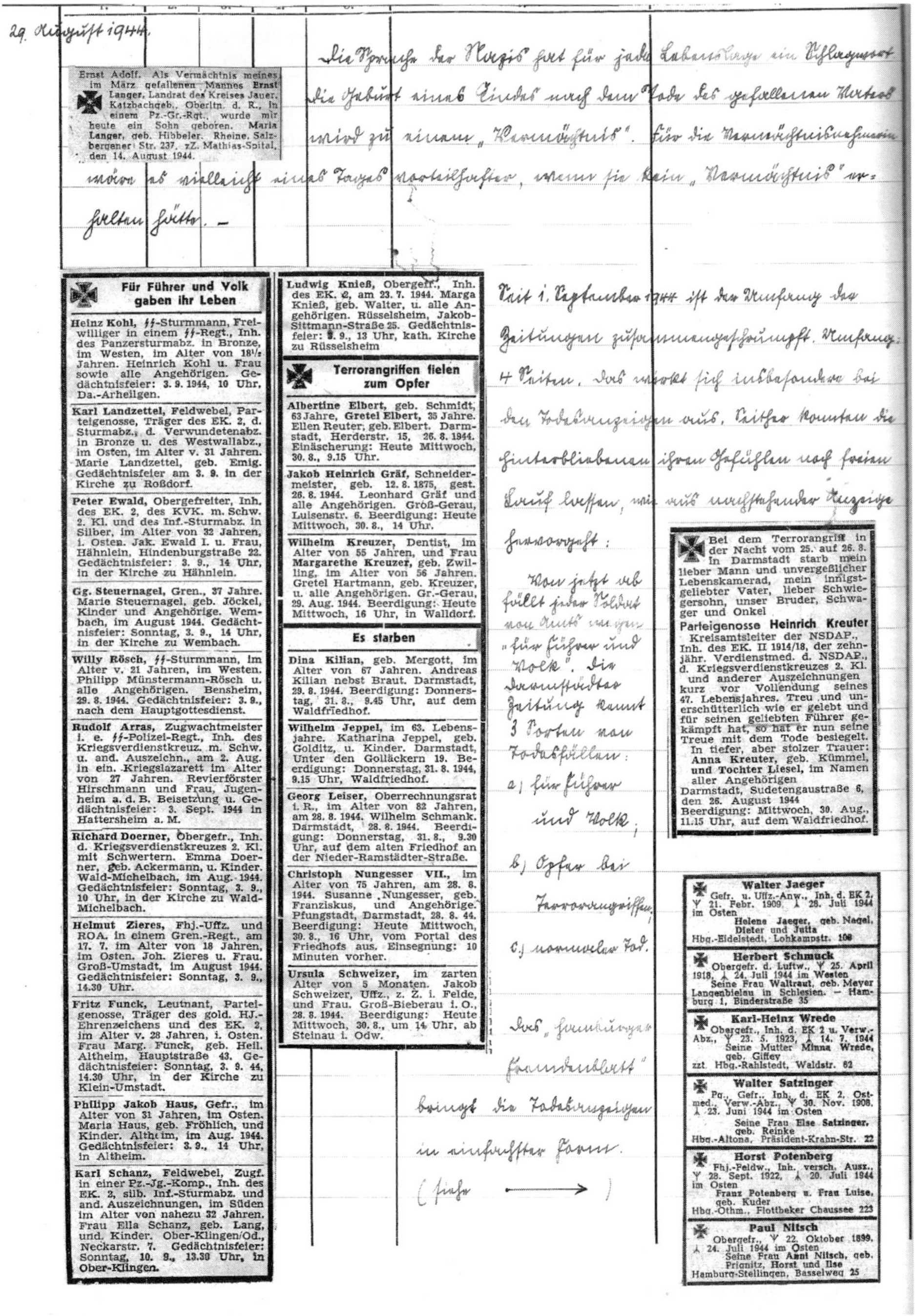

29. August 1944.

Die Sprache der Nazis hat für jede Lebenslage ein Schlagwort. Die Geburt eines Kindes nach dem Tode des gefallenen Vaters wird zu einem „Vermächtnis". Für die Vermächtnisnehmerin wäre es vielleicht eines Tages vorteilhafter, wenn sie kein „Vermächtnis" erhalten hätte. –

Ernst Adolf. Als Vermächtnis meines im März gefallenen Mannes **Ernst Langer**, Landrat des Kreises Jauer, Katzbachgeb., Oberltn. d. R., in einem Pz.-Gr.-Rgt., wurde mir heute ein Sohn geboren. **Maria Langer**, geb. Hibbeler. Rheine, Salzbergener Str. 237, zZ. Mathias-Spital, den 14. August 1944.

Seit 1. September 1944 ist der Umfang der Zeitungen zusammengeschrumpft. Umfang: 4 Seiten. Das wirkt sich insbesondere bei den Todesanzeigen aus. Bisher konnten die Hinterbliebenen ihren Gefühlen noch freien Lauf lassen, wie aus nachstehender Anzeige hervorgeht:

Von jetzt ab fällt jeder Soldat von Amts wegen „für Führer und Volk". Die Darmstädter Zeitung kennt 3 Sorten von Todesfällen: a) für Führer und Volk, b) Opfer bei Terrorangriffen, c) normaler Tod.

Das „Hamburger Fremdenblatt" bringt die Todesanzeigen in einfachster Form. (siehe →)

Für Führer und Volk gaben ihr Leben

Heinz Kohl, ꟻꟻ-Sturmmann, Freiwilliger in einem ꟻꟻ-Regt., Inh. des Panzersturmabz. in Bronze, im Westen, im Alter von 18½ Jahren. Heinrich Kohl u. Frau sowie alle Angehörigen. Gedächtnisfeier: 3. 9. 1944, 10 Uhr, Da.-Arheilgen.

Karl Landzettel, Feldwebel, Parteigenosse, Träger des EK. 2, d. Sturmabz., d. Verwundetenabz. in Bronze u. des Westwallabz., im Osten, im Alter v. 31 Jahren. Marie Landzettel, geb. Emig. Gedächtnisfeier am 3. 9. in der Kirche zu Roßdorf.

Peter Ewald, Obergefreiter, Inh. des EK. 2, des KVK. m. Schw. 2. Kl. und des Inf.-Sturmabz. in Silber, im Alter von 32 Jahren, i. Osten. Jak. Ewald I. u. Frau, Hähnlein, Hindenburgstraße 22. Gedächtnisfeier: 3. 9., 14 Uhr, in der Kirche zu Hähnlein.

Gg. Steuernagel, Gren., 37 Jahre. Marie Steuernagel, geb. Jöckel, Kinder und Angehörige. Wembach, im August 1944. Gedächtnisfeier: Sonntag, 3. 9., 14 Uhr, in der Kirche zu Wembach.

Willy Rösch, ꟻꟻ-Sturmmann, im Alter v. 21 Jahren, im Westen. Philipp Münstermann-Rösch u. alle Angehörigen. Bensheim, 29. 8. 1944. Gedächtnisfeier: 3. 9., nach dem Hauptgottesdienst.

Rudolf Arras, Zugwachtmeister i. e. ꟻꟻ-Polizei-Regt., Inh. des Kriegsverdienstkreuz. m. Schw. u. and. Auszeichn., am 2. Aug. in ein. Kriegslazarett im Alter von 27 Jahren. Revierförster Hirschmann und Frau, Jugenheim a. d. B. Beisetzung u. Gedächtnisfeier: 3. Sept. 1944 in Hattersheim a. M.

Richard Doerner, Obergefr., Inh. d. Kriegsverdienstkreuzes 2. Kl. mit Schwertern. Emma Doerner, geb. Ackermann, u. Kinder. Wald-Michelbach, im Aug. 1944. Gedächtnisfeier: Sonntag, 3. 9., 10 Uhr, in der Kirche zu Wald-Michelbach.

Helmut Zieres, Fhj.-Uffz. und ROA. in einem Gren.-Regt., am 17. 7. im Alter von 18 Jahren, im Osten. Joh. Zieres u. Frau. Groß-Umstadt, im August 1944. Gedächtnisfeier: Sonntag, 3. 9., 14.30 Uhr.

Fritz Funck, Leutnant, Parteigenosse, Träger des gold. HJ.-Ehrenzeichens und des EK. 2, im Alter v. 28 Jahren, i. Osten. Frau Marg. Funck, geb. Heil. Altheim, Hauptstraße 43. Gedächtnisfeier: Sonntag, 3. 9. 44, 14.30 Uhr, in der Kirche zu Klein-Umstadt.

Philipp Jakob Haus, Gefr., im Alter von 31 Jahren, im Osten. Maria Haus, geb. Fröhlich, und Kinder. Altheim, im Aug. 1944. Gedächtnisfeier: 3. 9., 14 Uhr, in Altheim.

Karl Schanz, Feldwebel, Zugf. in einer Pz.-Jg.-Komp., Inh. des EK. 2, silb. Inf.-Sturmabz. und and. Auszeichnungen, im Süden im Alter von nahezu 32 Jahren. Frau Ella Schanz, geb. Lang, und Kinder. Ober-Klingen/Od., Neckarstr. 7. Gedächtnisfeier: Sonntag, 10. 9., 13.30 Uhr, in Ober-Klingen.

Ludwig Kneiß, Obergefr., Inh. des EK. 2, am 23. 7. 1944. Marga Kneiß, geb. Walter, u. alle Angehörigen. Rüsselsheim, Jakob-Sittmann-Straße 25. Gedächtnisfeier: 3. 9., 13 Uhr, kath. Kirche zu Rüsselsheim

Terrorangriffen fielen zum Opfer

Albertine Elbert, geb. Schmidt, 63 Jahre, **Gretel Elbert,** 35 Jahre. Ellen Reuter, geb. Elbert. Darmstadt, Herderstr. 15, 26. 8. 1944. Einäscherung: Heute Mittwoch, 30. 8., 9.15 Uhr.

Jakob Heinrich Gräf, Schneidermeister, geb. 12. 8. 1875, gest. 26. 8. 1944. Leonhard Gräf und alle Angehörigen. Groß-Gerau, Luisenstr. 6. Beerdigung: Heute Mittwoch, 30. 8., 14 Uhr.

Wilhelm Kreuzer, Dentist, im Alter von 55 Jahren, und Frau **Margarethe Kreuzer,** geb. Zwilling, im Alter von 56 Jahren. Gretel Hartmann, geb. Kreuzer, u. alle Angehörigen. Gr.-Gerau, 29. Aug. 1944. Beerdigung: Heute Mittwoch, 16 Uhr, in Walldorf.

Es starben

Dina Kilian, geb. Mergott, im Alter von 67 Jahren. Andreas Kilian nebst Braut. Darmstadt, 29. 8. 1944. Beerdigung: Donnerstag, 31. 8., 9.45 Uhr, auf dem Waldfriedhof.

Wilhelm Jeppel, im 63. Lebensjahre. Katharina Jeppel, geb. Golditz, u. Kinder. Darmstadt, Unter den Golläckern 19. Beerdigung: Donnerstag, 31. 8. 1944, 9.15 Uhr, Waldfriedhof.

Georg Leiser, Oberrechnungsrat i. R., im Alter von 82 Jahren, am 28. 8. 1944. Wilhelm Schmank. Darmstadt, 28. 8. 1944. Beerdigung: Donnerstag, 31. 8., 9.30 Uhr, auf dem alten Friedhof an der Nieder-Ramstädter-Straße.

Christoph Nungesser VII., im Alter von 75 Jahren, am 28. 8. 1944. Susanne Nungesser, geb. Franziskus, und Angehörige. Pfungstadt, Darmstadt, 28. 8. 44. Beerdigung: Heute Mittwoch, 30. 8., 16 Uhr, vom Portal des Friedhofs aus. Einsegnung: 10 Minuten vorher.

Ursula Schweizer, im zarten Alter von 5 Monaten. Jakob Schweizer, Uffz., z. Z. i. Felde, und Frau. Groß-Bieberau i. O., 28. 8. 1944. Beerdigung: Heute Mittwoch, 30. 8., um 14 Uhr, ab Steinau i. Odw.

Bei dem Terrorangriff in der Nacht vom 25. auf 26. 8. in Darmstadt starb mein lieber Mann und unvergeßlicher Lebenskamerad, mein innigstgeliebter Vater, lieber Schwiegersohn, unser Bruder, Schwager und Onkel

Parteigenosse Heinrich Kreuter

Kreisamtsleiter der NSDAP., Inh. des EK. II 1914/18, der zehnjähr. Verdienstmed. d. NSDAP., d. Kriegsverdienstkreuzes 2. Kl. und anderer Auszeichnungen kurz vor Vollendung seines 47. Lebensjahres. Treu und unerschütterlich wie er gelebt und für seinen geliebten Führer gekämpft hat, so hat er nun seine Treue mit dem Tode besiegelt.

In tiefer, aber stolzer Trauer: **Anna Kreuter,** geb. Kümmel, **und Tochter Liesel,** im Namen aller Angehörigen

Darmstadt, Sudetengaustraße 6, den 26. August 1944

Beerdigung: Mittwoch, 30. Aug., 11.15 Uhr, auf dem Waldfriedhof.

Walter Jaeger
Gefr. u. Uffz.-Anw., Inh. d. EK 2, ✱ 21. Febr. 1909, ✝ 28. Juli 1944 im Osten
Helene Jaeger, geb. Nagel, Dieter und Jutta
Hbg.-Eidelstedt, Lohkampstr. 108

Herbert Schmuck
Obergefr. d. Luftw., ✱ 25. April 1918, ✝ 24. Juli 1944 im Westen
Seine Frau Waltraut, geb. Meyer
Langenbielau in Schlesien. – Hamburg 1, Binderstraße 35

Karl-Heinz Wrede
Obergefr., Inh. d. EK 2 u. Verw.-Abz., ✱ 23. 5. 1923, ✝ 14. 7. 1944
Seine Mutter Minna Wrede, geb. Giffey
zzt. Hbg.-Rahlstedt, Waldstr. 82

Walter Satzinger
Pg., Gefr., Inh. d. EK 2, Ostmed., Verw.-Abz., ✱ 30. Nov. 1908, ✝ 23. Juni 1944 im Osten
Seine Frau Else Satzinger, geb. Reinke
Hbg.-Altona, Präsident-Krahn-Str. 22

Horst Potenberg
Fhj.-Feldw., Inh. versch. Ausz., ✱ 28. Sept. 1922, ✝ 20. Juli 1944 im Osten
Franz Potenberg u. Frau Luise, geb. Kuder
Hbg.-Othm., Flottbeker Chaussee 223

Paul Nitsch
Obergefr., ✱ 22. Oktober 1899, ✝ 24. Juli 1944 im Osten
Seine Frau Anni Nitsch, geb. Prignitz, Horst und Ilse
Hamburg-Stellingen, Basselweg 25

the Seine, Somme, and Marne. It would not be uninteresting, therefore, to submit a closer retrospective view of the reporting. The reporters say nothing about the German army's unusually serious situation.

BRADLEY'S MAKESHIFT STRATEGY UNDER STRONG GERMAN PRESSURE

The American thrust toward Normandy and to the north

[. . .] It could be interesting to see how the American military leadership will respond to the German advance. Meanwhile, the Americans have resolved this issue by turning more to the north of Le Mans. Thus, they hope to get behind the German basic front. Their plan is either to cut off the German rear lines of defense – or at least to eliminate the threat from the German troops at Avranches. The American spiral movements reveal how the enemy leadership focuses its plans on the circumstances of the day and does not operate according to a predetermined campaign. A glance at the map shows that although the American makeshift strategy brings surprises, it also poses many dangers for them. [. . .]

Source: "Bradleys Augenblicksstrategie unter starkem deutschen Druck,"
DZ, August 13, 1944, p. 1.

[. . .]

While earlier reports in August referred to the narrow gap at the front at Avranches, the German troops' defensive readiness, the cordoning of Caen, and the Americans being cautious about surprise attacks on their flanks, the wire reports since August 20 seem not to address the current situation as much. The propaganda ministry's hopes – and perhaps also those of the mystical-minded persons at the Supreme Command – lie in the future. The people are continually assuaged by the German counter-attacks, the mass of new weapons, and the gain in time.

NEW OVERTAKING ATTEMPTS BY THE AMERICANS

Valiant resistance of our units in Romania

Berlin, August 29

We can now recognize the North Americans' strategic design connected to its Seine crossing south of Paris. Their new heavy tank attack on a broad front to the north, on the line from Chalons sur Marne to Chateau Thierry – as spelled out in a Wehrmacht report – has the task of attacking our southern flank and achieving a breakthrough in the direction of Amiens. The enemy hopes to cut off the rear lines connecting those German divisions that have formed a strong and often futile defensive line in the area of Rouen and the lower Seine. Against this advance are German soldiers who have engaged the enemy in fierce battles at the Marne. [. . .]

Source: "Neue Überholungsversuche der Amerikaner," *DZ*, August 30, 1944, p. 1.

LIEUTENANT GENERAL DITTMAR IN HIS RADIO BROADCAST: THE ENORMOUS STRUGGLE CONTINUES

The command to fight to the finish for our people shows our highest purpose

Berlin, August 30, 1944. [. . .]

Developments in these weeks may have awakened in our enemies the hope that the hour of their goal to bring about Germany's military downfall is no longer in the distant future but merely a few weeks away. We have in two months lost a substantial part of our first year's conquests, which we believed was firmly in our hands and was regarded as a desirable broadening of the economic base of our warfare. France for the most part has slipped out of our hands. We are in heavy fighting in the important remaining territories, both on the coast and in northeastern and eastern France. [. . .]

Source: "Der gewaltige Kampf geht weiter," *DZ*, August 31, 1944, p. 1.

It does indeed sound heroic when a radio-general without weapons recommends a fight to the finish: bayonets and hand-to-hand combat. I believe, however, a bayonet against the American tank corps is not well balanced in reality. Put away your bayonet, Herr Lieutenant General Dittmar! Long live the V-8, which will be a stick with a white cloth![46]

September 3, 1944

[. . .]

What headlines do we now see in the German newspapers?[47]

THE ENEMY UNDERSTANDS: GERMANY WILL NEVER SURRENDER!

TO WIN TIME MEANS TO WIN EVERYTHING [. . .]

EACH DAY THE V-1 DESTROYS 17,000 BUILDINGS IN ENGLAND

How long will the V-1, this retribution bomb, continue to be fired at England? Our opponents have the notion to take North France and

Belgium into their possession. They will locate the launching platforms for these flying bombs, and then another hope is ended – one of the last and final hopes. Someday the history of this war will note the V-1 stood for Versager-1 [Loser's Weapon]!

September 7, 1944

[. . .]

A new achievement of National Socialism. They have made 60 hours the minimum workweek for the burdened people of Germany. There are some enterprises where the employees must work even longer. A slave existence. How it could be worse cannot be imagined. Nevertheless, "Heil Hitler" shouters have not yet become extinct. The soul of the German peasant knows nothing about the love of liberty. [. . .]

German troops marched into Belgium in 1914 and 1940, in both cases without a declaration of war. We occupied that country from 1914–18 and again 1940–44, shedding much blood on Belgian soil and heavily afflicting the people. Inexpressible misery and great sorrow prevailed in these war years. But that made no impression on many Flemish politicians in Belgium who go arm in arm with their nation's oppressor, Führer Adolf Hitler.[48] The Belgian people must clear up this intellectual confusion and not allow fools, with their fixed ideas, to bring the entire country into disarray, to create unrest and make preparations to sow new discord. Now it is the foolish seduction of the Flemish youth, expecting them to sacrifice themselves [fighting for Germany], a thing that can be found only in sick minds.

What is it the Flemish want? They want their culture not to be disturbed by anyone. But an independent Flanders is in no way viable. It must align itself with a neighboring state. [. . .]

Léon Degrelle is a Belgian who created the Walloon Legion for the Führer and fights with this troop at the side of Germany against the Russians.[49] What did Russia ever do to the Walloons? It would be a more natural affair if Degrelle and his freedom fighters had arisen against Germany. That would be understood in the rest of the world. But no reasonable person will understand this unbelievable behavior by the Führer's Walloon candidate. The day approaches when the Degrelle bogeyman will disappear from the soil of Belgium, and free Belgium will establish a monument of disgrace to this rogue.

DANGEROUS INSTIGATOR EXECUTED

Berlin, August 30, 1944.

Johann Kalla, 52, from Kreuzenfeld/Loben, who already in 1941 had been punished by the Special Court for subversive remarks, used his position as an insurance agent to repeat enemy lies and make defeatist comments to wives and mothers of soldiers in order to make them more inclined to purchase insurance policies. Soldiers' wives brought this dangerous agitator to the authorities' attention so that they could put a stop to his dirty handiwork. The People's Court has sentenced this public vermin to death. The verdict has already been enforced.

Source: "Gefährlicher Hetzer hingerichtet," DZ, August 31, 1944, p. 2.

Whoever in Germany criticizes Nazi government methods or shows alarm about Germany is a "public enemy" or a "public vermin." The real spoilers and public vermin are the accusers and judges against innocent people. [...]

FINLAND ON A DANGEROUS COURSE

Breaking off relations with Germany. Accepts Soviet conditions

September 3, 1944.

The Finnish government has, according to information from the government in Helsinki, decided to break off relations with Germany to be in accord with the conditions imposed by the Soviet Union as a basis for negotiation with the enemy. In a speech, the Finnish Prime Minister tried to explain the motives of this behavior, suggesting a strong Anglo-American influence on the Finnish government resolutions. Finland's previous companion in arms, Germany, was not unprepared for Finland's decision. [...]

Source: "Finnland auf gefährlicher Bahn," DZ, September 3, 1944, p. 1.

September 16, 1944

When German troops were forced to withdraw from a large city or area they had occupied for a long time, and when that area was then occupied by enemy troops, the newspapers would report famine had broken out.

HUNGER AND HIGH PRICES IN PARIS[50]

FLORENCE: "A STARVING CITY"

Geneva, September 15, 1944.

[...] The reporter asked a number of women about the food conditions for their families. One said she had not yet seen even a speck of what the Anglo-Americans announced they would distribute. No bread at all has been allocated yet. Another said she had received twice in eight days a tiny bread ration and some dried vegetables. To be supplied with water, each family had to queue up daily from three to four hours. [. . .]

> *Source:* "Florenz – eine hungernde Stadt," *VB-Süd*,
> September 16–17, 1944, p. 2.

These tendentious reports are intended to prove our enemies possess no organizational ability. And the reports are useful to pressure the German people to a greater resistance, so that what happened to the people in the areas conquered by the Allies will not happen to them.

Through a coincidence, we discovered the "famine" in the evacuated areas can be attributed to the Germans. Upon leaving Krakow, Hellwig sent to the courthouse address fifteen packages that contained mostly food and beverages. Because the packages arrived in bad condition, the contents were visible, and we reproached Hellwig for taking things from there that were already available to him here. Thereupon, Hellwig clarified for us that when the camps in Krakow had to be evacuated, all the goods were removed, too. On orders from above! So wherever time was available for an evacuation, it was promptly ensured all supplies would disappear. In this way the propaganda's "famine" is caused.

Everything the Germans allowed to occur in the foreign countries will fall back upon Germany. This retribution will not be absent. The German people must pay a heavy penalty for all the horribleness committed in their name.

"VB" SPLINTER BOMB

In an August 23 terrorist attack on the surroundings of Weimar, the Buchenwald concentration camp was hit by numerous splinter bombs. Among the dead prisoners are the former Reichstag deputies Breitscheid and Thälmann.

> *Source:* "'VB.'-Splitter," *VB-Süd*, September 16–17, 1944, p. 2.

The first announcement about the August 23 "terror attack" on the Buchenwald concentration camp came today, September 16. It is extremely strange this information is made known three weeks after the fact. Perhaps it may come out sometime who really arranged this attack. It seems unlikely our enemies would want to kill the NSDAP's political opponents.[51]

AIRBORNE LANDING IN HOLLAND: BLOCKED

The above headline is what the *Hamburger Fremdenblatt* announced in large letters on September 18, 1944. Since the decrease in movements by the

German army, the word "block" is found in frequent use. Despite our troops constantly applying this "blocking" our opponents push ever closer to and across the German borders. To "block" apparently does not prevent in any way the advance of the Allies' armies.

FROM FÜHRER HEADQUARTERS, SEPTEMBER 18, 1944.

Supreme Command of the Armed Forces bulletin:

Yesterday afternoon after strong air attacks, paratroopers and glider troops landed behind our front, focusing on the area of Arnhem, Nijmegen, and Eindhoven. Later in the day ground units attacked between Antwerp and Maastricht to connect with the dropped troops. Fierce fighting developed, particularly in the Neerpelt area, during which the enemy was able to make few territorial gains to the north. Concentrated counter-attacks are being carried out against the enemy's airborne forces. Our troops are still in a heavy defensive battle with strong enemy forces between Maastricht and Aachen. Numerous weaker enemy attacks in other Western Front sectors were smashed.

The army report of September 18 makes it known airborne landings in Holland took place, and counter-attacks were made. From this it does not appear the landing was "blocked"[52] The newspaper strategists continue to go a step further than the Supreme Command. If the English or Americans landed successfully in Holland, I have no doubt whatsoever this enterprise will have the greatest significance for developments in the western theater. The landing places in Arnhem, Nijmegen, and Eindhoven are west of the Ruhr district. The Ruhr can be outflanked from Arnhem and Nijmegen and seized. Westphalia will show up soon as a theater of war.

Below is the conclusion of a news article, "The Enemy at the Gates," in the September 9, 1944, issue of *Darmstädter Zeitung.*

It must be stated explicitly we have no reason to describe the Reich's position in this battle as really bleak. It is serious, which we know, and there is not the slightest reason to gloss over that. The enemy's advance to Aachen, Eisenhower's new preparations for attacks, and developments in the East speak just as clearly as harsh language. But we still have every reason to calmly and quietly look into the future and not let the pressing cares of the day get us down. We believe unwaveringly a people so decent and idealistic, so brave, loyal and willing to make sacrifices, so full of poise and discipline as the German, cannot be defeated, particularly that the winner in this struggle will be those who work and fight like no other. Of this people and nation, to which we have the honor to belong, we may be unspeakably proud! [. . .]

No nation is lost that has good leadership, and no nation needs to abandon a good thing as long as its leaders do not give up. However, these leaders do not even think to give up, but are committed to the utmost to fight and through that always really lead! As long as we have this leadership, nothing is lost, but every chance for us remains preserved. [...]

> *Source:* "Der Feind vor den Toren," *DZ*, September 9–10, 1944, p. 1.

[...]

September 22, 1944

[...]

Here are the nations no longer part of the fraternity-in-arms with Germany: Italy, Romania, Bulgaria, and Finland. Only Hungary has not yet found a way out of the war. But how does that look in the near future? Hungary has no possibility of successfully defending itself when Romania no longer fights for Germany. It would be absolute suicide for Hungary not to immediately lay down its weapons. The Russian troops are in the position to advance into Hungary from north, east, and south. Germany has no consideration for the predicament of its "national comrades" there. German propaganda will speak only of their "betrayal" and forecast the disintegration of Hungary in the coming Bolshevik chaos.

"Churchill is already writing victory on the wall. We have a small note about that to make in the margin." Illustration: Mjölnir. *Source: VB-Nord*, August 23, 1944, p. 2.

The German comic papers and cartoonists would be in quite a quandary if there were no Churchill. Despite all the mockery – or precisely because of it – Churchill is and remains the English politician who correctly recognized Hitler's intentions.

[. . .]

October 1, 1944

THOSE WHO EVADE EMPLOYMENT

Ernst Gaetke, 58, from Würzburg had to answer before the Special Court for a crime against the Emergency Service Ordinance. In early September Gaetke received his call-up orders to a position on the border, and he was also assigned to a transport train. Before the transport arrived at its destination, Gaetke left the train without reasonable grounds and could not be reached. Instead he inquired at the next station about a train back to Würzburg, and he unceremoniously left for home. The accused was sentenced to six months in prison for this behavior.

As a Party member and a political leader, Gaetke was supposed to present himself as having an exemplary commitment to the emergency regulation. Before his hearing in court, the Party ejected him from its membership. [. . .]

Source: "Wer sich dem Einsatz entzieht," *VB-Süd*, September 30, 1944, p. 5.

Here they caught one of those who stayed safely in the rear while he preached at every opportunity how maximum employment was needed for everyone. To be a political leader is to have an excellent life insurance. Many had the bright idea to make themselves "indispensable," and for the Party to stay in the background while running the war. [. . .]

The Allies' breakthrough at Avranches has led to the conquest of France and Belgium. I do not think General Eisenhower is planning to carry out his invasion of Germany without taking a pause. It would be possible sooner if revolution broke out in Germany and the armed forces ceased their defense. Invading Germany requires a huge concentration of forces. Such an enterprise requires an enormous supply, and this supply must be brought over the water. That takes time.

October 7, 1944

DÖNITZ: NEW SHIPS AND WEAPONS

Thanks and appreciation for the Home Front's creative work

[. . .] Admiral Dönitz said clearly and unambiguously what would happen to the German people if they surrendered, if they were disarmed and had to wait with bare hands for whatever the subhumans decided to do with them. We would be ashamed in light of those who had fallen for us, and ashamed when our children and grandchildren would someday tell us: You were too cowardly, and we now have to pay for your not having been hard enough and able to endure more.

Thank God the unanimous unity of our people makes it impossible for us to concede and give in. For us, there is only the path of standing and fighting and striking back ruthlessly. There is no middle way. We must stand together. The people make the weapons and the soldiers fight. We must stand together fanatically. This is our greatest strength. And we all need to employ the same fanaticism in following our Führer, a man of unique greatness who combines the profound humanity of a warm heart with vast knowledge, skills, and an iron will. There is no one to be followed with more love than this unique man. A leadership that is harder than fate will ultimately and always win." [. . .]

Source: "Dönitz: neue Schiffe und Waffen," *VB-Süd*, September 25, 1944, p. 1.

Admiral of the Fleet Dönitz, who once was convinced victory would be achieved with U-boats, clamors for new ships and weapons. For sixty-one months we could not defeat our adversaries with the old ships and the old weapons, but the fleet admiral now believes a change can be realized by his fanatical appeal?

Out of a sense of panic, these people who would lengthen the war call for help and hope in miracles. But these miracles never happen. The battlefield mastermind, Adolf Hitler, has brought the end, with Germany surrounded on all sides. In this phase the leadership cannot give way because it would signify the end of Hitlerism and the end of everyone who took part. Because of this, a war that is already lost will continue until enemy armies march through Germany and stop the war machine. [. . .]

Some opinions of my contemporaries, parts of discussions by fellow travelers that took place in a train compartment en route from Hungen to Nidda:

"We will soon turn the tables on them." (That is, the German troops will soon proceed to victory.)

"The war must not end now, otherwise we are lost. It must continue yet for a while." (A sergeant said that to a soldier.)

October 16, 1944

BITTER AWAKENING IN BULGARIA

Call of National Government – Rather death than dishonor

Berlin, September 17, 1944. The Bulgarian National Government's Minister for Education and Propaganda Christo Staneff called out in a National Bulgarian radio program for the Bulgarian people to sharply settle accounts with the traitors, whose shamelessness and political short-sightedness have driven Bulgaria into the arms of the Soviet Union and Bolshevism. Bolshevism is already endeavoring to dominate the entire spiritual and material substance of the Bulgarian people. [...]

Source: "Bitteres Erwachen in Bulgarien," *DZ*, September 18, 1944, p. 2.

The "bitter awakening" will occur first of all in the ranks of the Bulgarian Nazis, and with good reason. Those politicians who pushed Bulgaria for the second time in twenty-five years to be on Germany's side in a war must disappear from the scene. The Bulgarian ruling powers believed they could enrich themselves at the expense of Yugoslavia and Greece. Common low-down thieves! For the alliance with Germany, Macedonia and Thrace were to fall as a gift into Bulgaria's lap. Such was not merely the fruits of German victory in the Balkans but rather also the wages of robber-captain Hitler and his robber-accomplice King Boris. All of this was prepared long beforehand. In a *Das Schwarze Korps* article, "The Classic Example," of September 21, the author rages about Bulgaria dropping out of the Axis and says, among other things, "Bulgaria possessed a powerful army, which from 1937 was armed with German assistance."[53]

Which means as far back as 1937 Germany and its henchmen were already planning to attack Russia! [...]

The "Poglavnik," the tyrant of Croatia, was invited to Führer Headquarters to receive his instructions for the coming days from his lord and master, Adolf Hitler.[54] It will turn out that instead of the Croats seeking fame fighting for Hitler up to the last breath, the German troops will end up defending the "independent" State of Croatia. But what a waste of effort that will be for our troops. The "Poglavnik" and his helpers soon will flee from Croatia. [. . .]

SWITZERLAND ADJUSTS ITS EXPORT OF WAR MATERIALS

Berlin, October 2, 1944.

As announced officially in Bern, the Swiss government has decided to stop the export of war material to all the belligerent countries with effect from October 1, 1944.

> Source: "Schweiz stellt Export von Kriegsmaterial ein," *VB-Nord*,
> October 3, 1944, p. 2.

This comes under the category, "You have come late, but you have come." A so-called "neutral" country supplying war material to a prominent warring country is a violation of neutrality.[55] If wars are to be made impossible, then this matter of supplying war material must find a solution. The classic example is Sweden. Sweden calls itself neutral, yet it supplies war material in large quantities. Could Germany have led two world wars without Swedish ore? I believe the experts will answer this question in the negative. Sweden is thus jointly guilty. Those who supported an aggressor should be treated exactly the same as the aggressor. Death to the supplier! It simply may not occur any longer that a country such as Sweden may rake in profits from the blood victims of other nations by supplying raw materials and war goods.

October 17, 1944

THE COMRADE FROM AACHEN

We know some things about Aachen, that for seven centuries it was the coronation city of German kings, and its venerable cathedral houses the great Emperor Charlemagne's tomb. A comrade from Aachen knows more. For him, this city is the epitome of home. He knows the house where he was born, the other in which he lived with his wife and children – until it was destroyed by the bombs, along with many other houses that connected him with personal matters. There was the school, and there was where his mother died; and there his business was located; there was the SA stormtroopers' local chapter, and there was the NSDAP Local Group's room where he made the clear decision to give up his long denial of the right to exist. If someone says "Aachen," everything that embraced his past life animates him and makes his eyes shine.

Today, as the city is located in the front, we avoid with the most delicate sensibility – that we surprisingly preserve under a soldier's rough exterior – to speak of Aachen in his presence. If the Wehrmacht radio report mentions Aachen, then the comrade's face no longer lights up as before, a few steep wrinkles crease his forehead, and sometimes he leaves the room to be alone with himself. [...]

Source: "Der Kamerad aus Aachen," *VB-Süd*, October 7–8, 1944, p. 1.

A huge luminous sign will have to hang over Aachen in the future with the label, "This is what we owe to our Führer." National Socialism has brought such great bliss to Germany. Hitler wanted to "eradicate" the cities of England. Now the German cities collapse into debris and ashes because a madman wants it so.

UNFALTERING WILL

Berlin, October 6, 1944.

[The enemy] will never win this victory – that is our unfaltering will. Each house will be a fortress, Dr. Goebbels said. If they think they can count on a bout of weakness in the German people, as they found in 1918, they are sorely mistaken.

Source: "Unbeugsamer Wille," *VB-Süd*, October 7–8, 1944, p. 1.

Our enemies are not the ones destroying Germany. Goebbels and his comrades are doing it. If every house becomes a fortress – as Dr. Goebbels wishes – then every house will equally be destroyed. These men want the entire German people to go down with them. [...]

October 28, 1944

THE FÜHRER'S DECREE TO CREATE THE GERMAN VOLKSSTURM

After five years of the heaviest fighting and the failure of all of our European allies, the enemies on some fronts stand near or at the German borders. They are over-exerting their forces to crush our Reich and destroy the German people and their social order. Their ultimate goal is the German people's extermination. [...]

Against the total destructive will of our Jewish-international enemies, with whom we are well acquainted, we will place the total effort of every German. To strengthen the active might of our armed forces, especially to lead the inexorable battle against our enemies wherever they choose to set foot on German soil, I summon all able-bodied German men for an all-out fight.

I hereby create the German Volkssturm in the regions of the Greater German Reich of all men capable of bearing arms, aged 16 to 60. They will defend the homeland with all weapons and material wherever it appears applicable. [. . .]

Source: "Der Erlaß des Führers," *VB-Süd*, October 20, 1944, p. 1.

In commemoration of the so-called "Battle of the Nations" – Battle of Leipzig – the National Socialist historical falsifiers saw themselves compelled to call up men from 16 to 60, capable of bearing arms, to unite in a "Volkssturm" [People's Attack Force]. As if the year 1813 could in any way possibly be compared with 1944! In 1813 Europe had to deal with the French tyrant Napoleon, who had been heavily beaten in Russia in the year 1812. Germany was allied with England and Russia against Napoleon. German youth in the army fought to free Germany and the rest of Europe from the tyrant. The German princes who had allied with Napoleon abandoned him at the Battle of Leipzig.

How does it look in 1944? The German youth fight *for* a tyrant against the remaining world. England and Russia stand at our borders as enemies. All of Germany's allies in this war have abandoned us and even fight to some degree against us.

Now at the moment when our enemies are prepared to march into Germany and strike the last blow, the National Socialist faithful have played their last card: the Volkssturm. An obvious act of insanity and the devil's invention! How can sixteen-year-old boys and sixty-year-old gray-haired men in a Volkssturm measure up against the fully equipped and victorious Allies' armies? Shall the English and American tanks be fought with pitch-forks and threshing machines?

Everywhere one hears from the wounded and those on leave that they often lack sufficient ammunition and sufficient weapons at the front. In the midst of that situation the "ingenious" Field Marshal General Hitler wants to set up yet another auxiliary army! It is absolutely time a rapid end is prepared for the Nazi ghouls, so the whole world can draw a deep breath.

Germans who consider themselves Nazi system opponents cannot under-stand why the armed forces officers do not brace themselves finally for the courageous act of refusing to obey the destroyers of Germany. There can be just one reasonable explanation for the armed forces' incomprehensible attitude: the commanders are jointly guilty for the atrocities committed and fear retaliatory measures.

Also among the crews and non-commissioned officers are many with a guilty conscience because they lived like Huns and barbarians in the foreign territories. [...]

November 6, 1944

INCITER CONDEMNED TO DEATH

Innsbruck, October 19, 1944.

Josef Axinger from Amams, near Innsbruck, had found a number of leaflets from Allied airplane raids. Instead of delivering them immediately to the nearest police station, he distributed them further with anarchist aims. In addition, he frequently listened to enemy radio broadcasts and continued to tell hostile lies with the purpose of incitement. Through such serious criminal offences Axinger made himself our enemies' accomplice. He was condemned to death by the People's Court in Berlin. The judgment has already been carried out.

Source: "Hetzer zum Tode verurteilt," *VB-Süd*, October 20, 1944, p. 4.

The wife of an office warden in Frankfurt stated some time ago in August Holzapfel's restaurant in Altenstadt that reading from handbills was strictly forbidden! The fanatical dinner-table heroes are possessed of a fixed idea. Nothing will be able to heal them from their delusion – not even defeat. They remain unteachable, and if they had the ability they would begin yet a third world war. [...]

HITLER YOUTH IN THE VOLKSSTURM

Berlin, October 30, 1944.

German youth have received the Führer's decree to establish the German Volkssturm with enthusiastic hearts and have incorporated this task in the units of their oldest comrades. The fighting youth in the West was the subject of a visit by Reich Youth Leader Artur Axmann, who called for the Hitler Youth to be in the Volkssturm and be comrades with their leaders and instructors who wear medals of valor in this war, and the youth who have been proving to be good assistants and substitutes at the front and in service for the Luftwaffe. The youth of the Greater German Reich, said Artur Axmann, have recognized the need of the hour. They stand within this war as volunteers at the front and in the homeland, the vanguard of faith, with commitment and steadfastness against the enemy's burning hatred and desire to destroy everything. [...]

Source: "Hitler-Jugend im Volkssturm," *VB-Nord*, October 31, 1944, p. 3.

The propaganda descends upon the "Volkssturm." This motley bunch is to save the fatherland. Germany always spoke with indignation and contempt of other countries' freedom fighters and referred to them as "gangs," "bandits," "partisans," and "terrorists." And what is the Volkssturm?

CHURCHILL NO LONGER WANTS TO PROPHESY

The German resistance is too tough – Admissions of a warmonger

Since the matter of the autumn leaves, the British faith in the prophetic gifts of Winston Churchill has declined considerably. Once again, as in 1942, the decisive Allied victory and peace were to come with the falling autumn leaves. Now the trees are bare, just as the Bald One hopes to avoid a sixth winter of war. Bald and scrawny and not with his usual flowery language of the prophet, Churchill had to make this admission in the House of Commons. [...]

Source: "Churchill will nicht mehr prophezeien," *VB-Nord*,
November 2, 1944, p. 1.

If our propagandists are going to make fun of the "prophet" Churchill, then they should have a small reminder about keeping things relevant and recall that every statesman more or less errs. The speeches of Hitler represent a treasure trove for such prophecies.

Looking at the situation from Germany, it is not understandable why the Allies' combined forces cannot prepare a more rapid end of the war in Europe. The snail-like fighting speed in Italy, as well as the lack of support for the Yugoslavians, is incomprehensible. Except for Russia, what is missing in Germany's enemies is a serious use of their full military power. England, in particular, appears as a country that counts on caution rather than boldness.

ONE OF THEM

Junior Squad Leader Martin Zoppelt came illegally to the Reich from his Transylvania home when the war began to take part in the German people's fight for freedom. In 1940 he was accepted into the Waffen-SS. He was in the Eastern campaign as a member of an SS Cavalry Division. He was severely wounded in August 1943 and had to have his leg amputated to the thigh. He has been in a hospital for many months listening to the radio, "listening day after day to what our thousand times damned enemies were doing to our beloved Germany." [...] It rankles him that for such a long time he has been useless. Yes, this farmer's son from Transylvania who came voluntarily to the Reich to be a soldier and bravely fight to fulfill his duty because his German conscience called on him to do that, who gave his blood and his bones, says he has not done enough. It is intolerable to him that now, disabled, he can offer nothing more to the German people. [...] "I would be overjoyed to have some employment soon, and be able to show the Russians in no way will they take this war on the cheap. Ivan may feel heady he has taken my leg in Kharkov. I am myself once again and ready, wherever it may be, to make my healed bones completely available to the fatherland." [...]

Heil Hitler! Martin Zoppelt, SS Unterscharführer, SS hospital.

The so-called "Germans in foreign lands" had no reason and no cause to take part in Adolf Hitler's predatory war. The war, which was started for these "Germans," served only to turn them into cannon fodder. The majority of these people lived in their second homeland freer, happier, and more content than do most inhabitants in the German Reich's villages and cities. The farmer's son from Transylvania mentioned in the November 2 news article illegally left his homeland in order to take part in the German people's "fight for freedom." That is what the Nazi bandits call this most scurvy of all wars, the "fight for freedom." This Martin Zoppelt is one of those crazy beings who worship a soulless utopia as long as sufficient opportunity exists to commit brutal actions. [...]

November 9, 1944

National Socialist German Workers' Party
Local Group Laubach, Hesse.
November 9, 1944.

To: Friedrich Kellner in Laubach, Friedrichstrasse 19.

In accordance with the Führer's decree of September 25, 1944, you are called up to serve in the German Volkssturm as your legally obligated duty.

I hereby summon you to the swearing-in muster on Sunday, November 12, 1944, at 1:30 p.m., in the Laubach marketplace. Suit is preferable, breeches, boots, or leggings.

Heil Hitler,
Dapper, Local Group Leader

November 12, 1944

Sunday. Indeed it has finally come that we old folks are now the ones "to be called up." We were ordered to report to the marketplace in Laubach at 1:30 this afternoon to be sworn in. In a pouring rain, the "Volkssturm" men assembled at the marketplace at the appointed hour. In the presence of Mayor Dapper, Laubach Building Inspector Schmier, who wore an official warden's uniform, assembled us in three rows and began the count.[56] The names were read out. Present were 113 men. Right turn! In lockstep, march! Direction: the castle park. The castle's northeast side was hung with large swastika banners. A podium stood in front of the outside steps. An ancient cannon, the only visible weapon, was set up next to the steps. Functioning as the performers were the Land Watch, Hitler Youth (male and female), a number of wounded, led by a sergeant, and some women in mourning clothes.

The Party flag was raised before the troops. The mayor appeared as the first speaker and at the same time conducted the swearing-in. One verse of "People to their Guns," was sung with the Volkssturm's feeble participation. Forest Master Ostheim, in Party uniform, recited a poem; then followed speeches by Schmier and the district leader. After that came the affirmation of the oath. The formal oath was spoken out, and the Volkssturm repeated it. Six men touched the Party flag with their left hand. It surpasses everything – such a charm.

Wartheländ Volkssturm, for the first time with its weapons, passes in review on "Freedom Day 1944" in the regional city of Posen. *Source:* "Wartheländischer Volkssturm," *VB-Nord*, November 8, 1944, p. 1.

This looks like a Volkssturm cleaned up for the weekly newsreel. Other than in the movies, the only thing to be seen in the regional cities and towns is a motley heap of civilians who do not possess such boots as in this photograph. This footwear, in such condition, would be useful for a field regiment for autumn and winter. As far as our other equipment and weapons are concerned, I do not even want to talk about it at all. The armed forces everywhere lack uniforms, equipment, and weapons. What is left for the Volkssturm? [...]

ARMED FORCES MEMBERS AS LUGGAGE THIEVES IN BAVARIA

On September 13, 1944, travelers on the train at the Würzburg railroad station and during the trip from there to Nuremberg had their luggage and numerous ration cards stolen by two unknown armed forces personnel. One of the thieves offered to help a woman in Würzburg carry her belongings during an air raid. The soldier disappeared into the crowd with her linen sack. Continuing to Nuremberg the lady told traveling soldiers in her compartment of her misfortune and asked them to watch over the rest of her luggage as she looked through the train for the thief. When she returned to the compartment at Nuremberg, she spotted the soldier with the sack and also a suitcase. Inside were two quilts, two men's hats, and a man's suit. On his person was a ration card case [...]. This culprit was pretending to be traveling from the Neuenahr hospital near Koblenz to Linz. For a year he had been masquerading as someone bombed out in Cologne.

Soldiers as criminals are unfortunately not an isolated phenomenon. The soldier no longer differentiates between foreign country and homeland. He continues the unrestrained shameful deeds he committed, with or without approval of his superiors, in the occupied countries. Robbery, plundering, and theft are designated as "organizing" in the soldiers' lingo. These actions are not in the punishable category but transformed into deeds given tacit consent from above. Even those who do not have much imagination can already paint the coming conditions in extremely dark colors.

Herbert Kloss, Lt. Col., Regiment Commander, Honor Roll Clasp, Iron Cross 2, and other distinctions. Our beloved last son and brother succumbed on October 29, 1944, age 29, to an illness while on campaign.
Major (ret.) Dr. Kloss and wife, née Jung; Ilse Kloss.
Presently in Dresden, Weisser Hirsch

Siegfried Richter, Lieutenant and Company Leader, Nov. 11, 1924 to Sep. 20, 1944. Our sunny son found a hero's death at the head of his company at the Eastern Front.

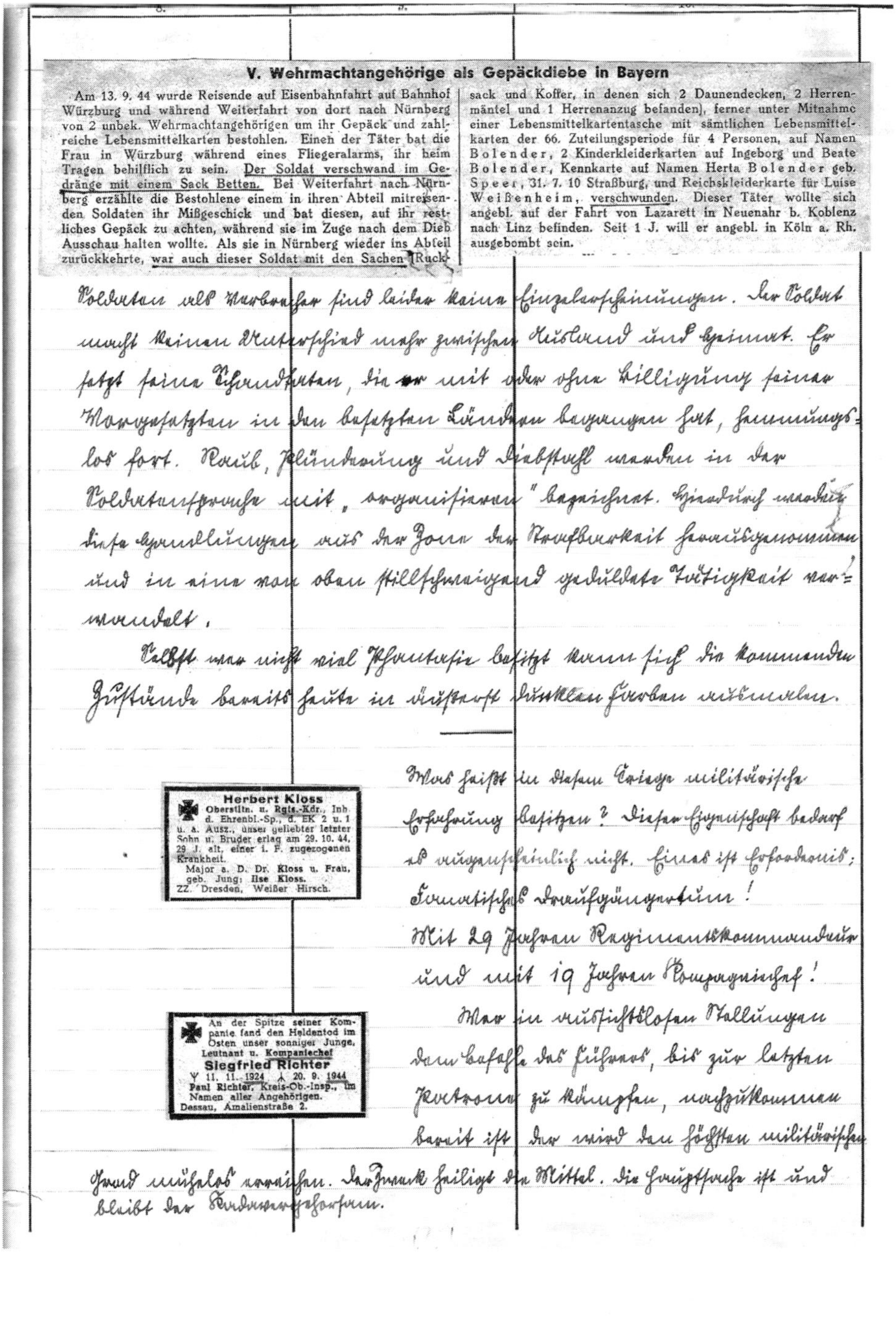

V. Wehrmachtangehörige als Gepäckdiebe in Bayern

Am 13. 9. 44 wurde Reisende auf Eisenbahnfahrt auf Bahnhof Würzburg und während Weiterfahrt von dort nach Nürnberg von 2 unbek. Wehrmachtangehörigen um ihr Gepäck und zahlreiche Lebensmittelkarten bestohlen. Einen der Täter bat die Frau in Würzburg während eines Fliegeralarms, ihr beim Tragen behilflich zu sein. Der Soldat verschwand im Gedränge mit einem Sack Betten. Bei Weiterfahrt nach Nürnberg erzählte die Bestohlene einem in ihren Abteil mitreisenden Soldaten ihr Mißgeschick und bat diesen, auf ihr restliches Gepäck zu achten, während sie im Zuge nach dem Dieb Ausschau halten wollte. Als sie in Nürnberg wieder ins Abteil zurückkehrte, war auch dieser Soldat mit den Sachen (Rucksack und Koffer, in denen sich 2 Daunendecken, 2 Herrenmäntel und 1 Herrenanzug befanden), ferner unter Mitnahme einer Lebensmittelkartentasche mit sämtlichen Lebensmittelkarten der 66. Zuteilungsperiode für 4 Personen, auf Namen Bolender, 2 Kinderkleiderkarten auf Ingeborg und Beate Bolender, Kennkarte auf Namen Herta Bolender geb. Speer, 31. 7. 10 Straßburg, und Reichskleiderkarte für Luise Weißenheim, verschwunden. Dieser Täter wollte sich angebl. auf der Fahrt von Lazarett in Neuenahr b. Koblenz nach Linz befinden. Seit 1 J. will er angebl. in Köln a. Rh. ausgebombt sein.

Soldaten als Verbrecher sind leider keine Einzelerscheinungen. Der Soldat macht keinen Unterschied mehr zwischen Ausland und Heimat. Er setzt seine Schandtaten, die er mit oder ohne Billigung seiner Vorgesetzten in den besetzten Ländern begangen hat, hemmungslos fort. Raub, Plünderung und Diebstahl werden in der Soldatensprache mit „organisieren" bezeichnet. Hierdurch werden diese Handlungen aus der Zone der Strafbarkeit herausgenommen und in eine von oben stillschweigend geduldete Tätigkeit verwandelt.

Selbst wer nicht viel Phantasie besitzt kann sich die kommenden Zustände bereits heute in äußerst dunklen Farben ausmalen.

Herbert Kloss
Oberstltn. u. Rgts.-Kdr., Inh. d. Ehrenbl.-Sp., d. EK 2 u. 1 u. a. Ausz., unser geliebter letzter Sohn u. Bruder erlag am 29. 10. 44, 29 J. alt, einer i. F. zugezogenen Krankheit.
Major a. D. Dr. Kloss u. Frau, geb. Jung; Ilse Kloss.
ZZ. Dresden, Weißer Hirsch.

Was heißt in diesem Kriege militärische Erfahrung besitzen? Dieser Eigenschaft bedarf es augenscheinlich nicht. Einzig ist Erfordernis: Fanatisches Draufgängertum!
Mit 29 Jahren Regimentskommandeur und mit 19 Jahren Kompaniechef!

An der Spitze seiner Kompanie fand den Heldentod im Osten unser sonniger Junge, Leutnant u. Kompaniechef
Siegfried Richter
11. 11. 1924 20. 9. 1944
Paul Richter, Kreis-Ob.-Insp., im Namen aller Angehörigen.
Dessau, Amalienstraße 2.

Wer in rücksichtslosen Stellungen dem Befehle des Führers, bis zur letzten Patrone zu kämpfen, nachzukommen bereit ist, der wird den höchsten militärischen Grad mühelos erreichen. Der Zweck heiligt die Mittel. Die Hauptsache ist und bleibt der Kadavergehorsam.

Paul Richter, District Senior Inspector, in the name of all family members. Dessau, Amalienstrasse 2.

Does "Needs to possess military experience," have any meaning? Apparently this war does not require this qualification. There is but one requirement: fanatical bravado – a regimental commander at twenty-nine, and a company leader at nineteen![57]

Whoever is ready to give the order to others to fight to the last bullet needs nothing other than that to become the leader – and he will easily achieve the highest military honors. The end justifies the means. The main thing is and remains blind obedience.

November 19, 1944

THE OATH OF THE HEART

[...] The enemy will have to reap what he has sown. The German Volkssturm, which in all German districts swears its allegiance to the Führer, is not our only and last but certainly our most decisive and most indestructible and noblest fighting potential because its power is firmly implanted deep in our hearts. We shall remain true to this force, as is required of us by our oath, so one day it must be said of us: "And you have indeed won!"

Source: "Volkssturm im Geist der Feldherrnhalle," *VB-Nord*, November 12, 1944, p. 1.

[...] The Volkssturm I have seen can only be called an unwilling heap of bad-tempered slaves who do not possess the slightest trace of spirit the Party leadership would so gladly like them to have. The Party will experience a fiasco with their Volkssturm that is not associated with any product of the past. [...]

The Führer's voice was not to be heard this November 9, the Holy Party's holiday. Why is the man silent when in former times he could not let his voice ring out enough? Strange affair! Where is the "Führer" of the German people in these serious hours? His substitute, Heinrich Himmler, read the Führer's proclamation, which did not bring anything new – just trite assertions that do not work convincingly because they are repeated over and over.

[...]

November 20, 1944

[...]

The world is being told the German youth have integrated themselves into the Volkssturm with "inspired hearts." Except for Reich Youth Leader Artur Axmann, few Germans will have noticed this "enthusiasm."[58] The fact is the Volkssturm is a mechanism to bring sixteen-year-olds to the front lines. Perhaps the armed forces are embarrassed to directly accept children as soldiers.

LONDON: "THE LAST CHANCE IN 1944 IS LOST"

Impact of the Soviets' Offensive Failure in East Prussia.

Enemy laments lost time in East and West.[59]

[...]

In this time of defensive victories it is a popular method to claim the other side did not achieve its goals. However, that does not change anything because the other side has already reached its goal: clamping down on Germany.

BELATED OFFENSIVE BEGINS

Eisenhower's First Large Autumn Attack

Berlin, November 11, 1944.

[...] The offensive has brought the initial successes usually achieved when an opponent accumulates a long front line of troops and military equipment at a certain point. Nomeny, east of Pont à Mousson, has been taken; and the attack has been carried forward into the Delme area. General Patton's infantry, which will lead the attack with the Third US Army, crossed the Moselle River at Thionville. Heavy fighting is occurring around Königsmachern. The actual rampart area west of Metz has not been attacked. It is clearly seen the enemy, after first avoiding the immediate area of Metz, wants to push past to the north and south of it. His ultimate goal can be seen on the map: the Saar region. [...]

The Americans and English defeated the Atlantic Wall, which was portrayed by our propaganda as unconquerable; they crossed over the Seine, Maas [Meuse] and Mosel [Moselle] Rivers; they conquered the fortresses at Maubeuge, Verdun, and Diedenhofen. And they will clear out any other obstacles in the way – even if the faithful Nazis refuse to understand that.

EISENHOWER HAS BEGUN A SECOND OFFENSIVE

Preparatory Battles

Berlin, November 16, 1944.

The name Gravelotte appeared for the first time in the Army High Command reports. General Patton has decided to attack the fortress area of Metz also from the west.

   This was not originally planned. The entire layout of the American attack shows the west of Metz was to have been spared until the city and possibly much of the Lorraine countryside had been bypassed and then cut off from the east. But this plan did not last. The two arms of Patton's pincer movements have been stopped by the German infantry and tanks at Königsmachern and Mörchingen. The German counter-pressure has prevented them from coming together. The fortress of Metz forms a semi-circle from north to west to the south, but the road to the east is left open. Thus Patton, on the seventh day of the Battle of Lorraine, must have decided to include this until now quiet area in front of his army in the field of offensive battle.

Source: "Kämpfe der Vorbereitung," *VB-Nord*, November 17, 1944, p. 2.

Whether Metz remains in German possession one day more or less is without importance in relation to the overall situation. However, it is interesting to mention to the reader that the current fighting is playing out in the "approaches" to the German west fortification system. When those positions are abandoned in the coming days, it will be said the "approaches" were not so important. The Nazis have never been without excuses. [...]

ARABS IN GERMAN UNIFORMS

Berlin, November 16, 1944.

For some time now a unit in the army has been building up a troop that in the beginning was designated as the German-Arab Legion. In this formation gathered the most active elements of Arabs living in Europe. They were dressed in German uniforms, equipped with German weapons and equipment, and trained as squad, platoon, and company leaders. The German instructors placed in this legion, the so-called permanent staff, were mostly Palestinian-Germans, who had learned the language and nature of the Arabs in previous tours of duty in Palestine, and were able to handle and understand the Arab volunteers.

   The volunteers wore a special badge on the upper left sleeve of their tunic, both the field shirt and jacket, to show their regimental unit. The background consists of the Iraq flag, which is a modification of the old Hejaz flag, with the colors black, white, green, and red, and two stars with seven rays in the upper red part. The flag's upper part has the Arabic Inscription, "Bilad al Arab al Hurrah"; and its German translation, "Free Arabia," is at the lower part of the flag. [. . .]

It is understood that, throughout their service, consideration is to be given to the Arab volunteers' cultural and "religious customs," as prescribed by the Quran to Muslims.

Source: "Araber in deutscher Uniform," VB-Nord, November 17, 1944, p. 3.

Arabs in German uniforms. Must we now create that? Have we not had enough bad experiences with foreigners? In an emergency the devil eats flies – and some Germans again have hopes. Suppose the English had incorporated these Arabs as fighting comrades. The German press would write, "The Englishmen use Arabs as cannon fodder."

The Nazis were never as solicitous about the German people's religious customs. What a pitiful band of hypocrites!

WE WILL FIGHT FANATICALLY

The new enemy offensive comes up against passionate German resistance

Darmstadt, November 17, 1944.

As the Anglo-American armored divisions raced down the French roads a few weeks after their armies had pushed through the areas we had previously occupied, and as they arrived at many points on the German border, it seemed to them they had Eisenhower's strategic objectives at their fingertips. An iron wall bade them stop. Only in a few places did the enemy succeed in setting foot on German soil, and then only with enormous sacrifices in men and material. A firm yet elastic line was built, against which there was now but a step-by-step advance. Despite all the superiority of men and weapons, the rapid advance was finally over. [. . .]

Source: "Wir werden fanatisch kämpfen," DZ, November 18–19, 1944, p. 1.

"We" will fight fanatically! Who are "we"? Not the leading Nazis, in any case, because they are not at the front lines. They are the Wehrmacht and the SS combat units, trying to defend the positions assigned to them. There may be many Germans and foreigners who cannot comprehend the German troops' combat spirit. Propaganda and the Party spirit brought this about, motivating the soldiers to the utmost tenacious resistance even in situations offering no prospects. The fanatical faith in victory is indeed still present in German soldiers. Each is convinced we must win in order not to be completely lost. Many also hope the alliance of our enemies will fracture, and we need therefore just endure to achieve victory. On the whole, the soldier is not a philosopher. Most soldiers went through the school of National Socialism, and therefore they are firmly convinced of Germany's right to rule the world.

MASTERFUL WITHDRAWAL FROM THE BALKANS

Berlin, November 20, 1944.

Almost daily the Armed Forces bulletins report the successful progress of the withdrawal of German troops in the Balkans. Since then, Romania and Bulgaria have removed themselves from the common fighting front and made themselves available as Bolshevik helpers. The German military leaders see a necessity to abandon the endangered Balkan positions and return the troops to a line where it is possible to apply active operations. This already difficult task was made more difficult by the terrain and weather conditions, but thanks to the exemplary collaboration of the army, navy, and air force, the plan could be carried out completely. [...]

Source: "Meisterhafter Rückzug aus dem Balkan," VB-Süd,
November 21, 1944, p. 2.

The Nazis are the greatest type of cover-up artists. Ever since Stalingrad they have been writing up all their defeats as successes and know the German people can be fooled into believing them. Each retreat is a masterly achievement. Each retreat is an ingenious strategic measure. The retreat is not really a retreat but a "displacement" or a "return." In the National Socialist language there are no German defeats at all, just "successes" and victorious defensive battles.

VLASOV TO RIBBENTROP: "FIGHT UNTIL THE FALL OF SOVIET TYRANNY"

Berlin, November 18, 1944.

Lieutenant General Vlasov, chairman of the Committee for the Liberation of the Russian People, sent the following telegram to Reich Foreign Minister von Ribbentrop:
[...] "I ask the Führer of the German people to make known my express assurance that the people of Russia have the indomitable will to endure the struggle until a victorious end and are not going to lay down their arms until the Bolshevik tyranny is overthrown."

Source: "Kampf bis zum Sturz der Sowjettyrannei," VB-Nord,
November 19, 1944, p. 1.

It has taken a relatively long time for Nazi propaganda to come up with such a Russian [turncoat] as General Vlasov – and this is one who allegedly was discovered among the Russian prisoners being used as cannon fodder.[60] Whether this general exists at all may be uncertain, but even if he does, a single swallow does not make a summer, nor can grasping at this one straw symbolize an entire campaign.

December 9, 1944

[. . .]

FIGHT WITHOUT A WHITE FLAG

The Regional Leader addresses the Volkssturm's Battalion leadership

Frankfurt, November 24, 1944.

[. . .] Regional Leader Sprenger concluded his speech with reference to the educational power of the role model, which deeply impressed the gathered cadets and battalion commanders. The Volkssturm leader will always live as a role model and fight. For him, the white flag, which offers surrender, is not available. He fights and dies at the Führer's command with the German armies in the East: "Now is the time we stand or fall." [. . .]

Source: "Kampf ohne weiße Fahne," DZ, November 25–26, 1944, p. 1.

Surrender is an enormous obstacle for Regional Leader Sprenger and his Party comrades as compared with the rest of the population, the national comrades. There is no way Sprenger can hoist the white flag – because that would be synonymous with his downfall. But in one way or the other Regional Leader Sprenger is going down. Winning some time provides only a short respite. He will fight for that respite; such is the attitude of every Party bigwig. Yet the mass of German people can hoist the white flag – or better said, must hoist it – because the war has been lost already for a long time. The German people do not run the risk of being destroyed. They are not going to be cut down suddenly, en masse. For thinking people it is perfectly incomprehensible that the Germans still do not take their fate into their own hands, but instead apathetically continue to carry their chains. When will the German people's unbelievable patience have an end?

December 10, 1944

Late Wednesday night of December 6, and into Thursday morning, the male inhabitants of Laubach were alerted to participate in clearing the rubble in Giessen. The alarm was heard only by some. An attack by English planes had taken place Wednesday evening against Giessen from 9–10.[61] From Ruppertsburg we could see the flashes of the attack (in the vernacular, called "Christmas trees") and the brightly illuminated area of Giessen. It was obvious incendiary bombs were primarily being dropped. The fires were visible from far away. In the morning, from the train station in Hungen, I still saw the light from the flames.

An attack on Giessen was expected for a long time because it has an important train junction. From all appearances, the enemy was in no hurry. The train tracks from the Main River to the Weser are expressly important, but only in the last weeks has the enemy begun to worry about this railroad line. For some time, fighter-bombers had been attacking the area of Upper Hesse but with little success. They came across some locomotives on the single rail lines, but the bomb craters next to the tracks confirm the bombs missed their goal. Only now have I seen some significant destruction around the Friedberg station area. But even here the number of misses is enormous. Many fields and meadows are scattered with craters, but the station still enjoys the best of health.

Despite the misses, the attacks on Frankfurt, Giessen, and Friedberg have disturbed the railway operations quite a bit, and they have been shaken. Travel on the railway has become anguish. The late train arrivals, the stay in the waiting rooms, and traveling in unheated cars make it understandable civilian travelers are ready to abandon railway travel. Whoever travels today has much to tell. [. . .]

The fighting front, moving ever closer, daily brings the English and American tactical air forces more into range. Some months ago that was different, when bombs were being dropped on the transportation facilities in France, Belgium, and Holland. The battlegrounds have shifted to the Rhine country and Saar district, and for our area the dangerous attacks begin to disrupt the railways or put them out of operation altogether. [. . .]

December 12, 1944

[. . .]

NIJMEGEN – AACHEN – SCHLETTSTADT – FÜNFKIRCHEN

The situation at the front.

Berlin, December 3, 1944.

[. . .] Canada's First Army replaces the British Army in the Meuse estuary combat zone from Nijmegen to the south. How this changes Montgomery's offensive thrust has yet to be seen. East of Aachen, the North Americans have hardly progressed, their attacks mostly contained. They slowly move in the Saar to the maneuvering area of the Siegfried Line. General Patton's Third Army troops are confronted by the cumbersome and thorny task that the divisions of Samson and Hodges have taken a crack at for more than two weeks now. [. . .]

Source: "Nimwegen – Aachen – Schlettstadt – Fünfkirchen: die Lage an den Fronten," *VB*, December 4, 1944.

Nijmegen, Aachen, Schlettstadt, and Fünfkirchen are now in enemy hands. And yet the German troops' resistance is still amazingly firm. It looks like the battles at the Western Front are evolving not unlike the trench warfare of 1914–18. That would be quite an unpleasant occurrence. Why are the opponents unable to recognize that their forces must make a decisive breakthrough? What are they waiting for, an economic and military collapse of Germany? Is Germany today still too strong for them? Or all of these? [. . .]

The trendy poet has new material: the Volkssturm. The ringing command, "Volkssturm, to your rifles," might find merely a faint echo at present because – at least in our district – no rifles at all are available. Even if the overeager ones truly wanted to run to their weapons, their demands could not be satisfied. I hope this situation remains for quite a long while yet. I do not feel an urge in me to pull with the Volkssturm against the enemy. A good reason is that a Volkssturm armed just with clubs cannot fight against a modern equipped opponent.

On Friday, December 22, I augmented my traveling adventures with another experience. I was on the Stockheim train to Giessen, and when it pulled into Nidda at 9 a.m. I had an extremely unhappy surprise when the conductor rang out, "Nidda, everyone off!" Traveling during the cold weather in an unheated car with broken wheels is bad, but far better it is to travel with difficulty than to be left behind. In order not to have to sit for hours in the cold waiting room, I decided to walk [the 20 kilometers] to Laubach. After a march of four hours, past the Borsdorf airfield, through Ulfa and Gonterskirchen, I arrived in Laubach at 1 p.m.

A CALL IN THE CRUCIAL HOUR

Defense Help from German Women and Girls

> The enemy's hatred wants to wipe out the German people. You already know the enemy is not only outside the gates of the Reich, he has already stepped across the borders in several places. Women and children were driven from their homes. Many of them have suffered unspeakably. They have become hardened in this time; they bear their fate bravely and work daily and hourly in loyalty to our country. The closer the enemy's circle was around us, the louder grew the desire of many women and girls to take an active part in the Reich's defense. Many thousands are already in the armed forces, and in our Women's Anti-Aircraft Assistants Corps we have the first inclusive women's unit in the national defense. [. . .]

Source: "Aufruf in entscheidender Stunde," VB-Süd, December 6, 1944, p. 1.

The new measure for total war employment brings women into military service. Since then, more young men have been taken into the armed forces. And more radical changes have been made for bringing older men to the fighting front. This required one last rationalization: countless men here in the rear of the fighting who are indeed essential, but not irreplaceable, shall be freed by women. Some of these men, who had wonderful interior posts, will think with nostalgia of past days, and many "brides" will help by such war service to send more men into the mass graves and enormously increase the number of other women who must remain single.

Everything the Nazis establish is ultimately directed against the people themselves, and not just a few participate enthusiastically.

When the Russians, during their big emergency in autumn 1941, mobilized their civilian reserves, including women, there were sneering remarks in our newspapers about "children, graybeards, and women with shotguns." Now the newspaper writers endeavor to show the new Armed Forces Women Assistants Corps has no similarity to the Soviet-minted "women with shotguns." Naturally, military service by German women and girls is a "special honorable service without any profanation of the feminine nature." Only the other side has "women with shotguns."

The female soldiers will help to extend the war, and they will do nothing to alter the disastrous ending.

UNCONDITIONAL RESISTANCE UNTIL GERMAN VICTORY

Munich, December 10, 1944.

[. . .] Where the Allied armies march, a single wave of disorder, upheaval of the underworld, chaos, and misery appears. Under German occupation Europe had work, food, and orderly conditions, but under the Allies' rule it is hungry, with mobs, strikes, and prison riots. It is the uprising of the underworld against Western civilization. Europe is facing the decision: victory or Bolshevik chaos! Our old slogan is still valid, a third possibility does not exist. Who wants to live must fight. [. . .]

Source: "Bedingungsloser Widerstand bis zum deutschen Endsieg," *VB-Süd*,
December 11, 1944.

1945

March 7, 1945

I have lost an unusual amount of time journeying back and forth from Laubach to Altenstadt – therefore the long pause in my diary entries. On January 19, 1945, for example, when I returned from Altenstadt to Laubach, it took no less than 14 hours, from 2:00 in the afternoon until 4:00 in the morning.

Also, our apartment in Laubach is very unpleasant for lack of sufficient warmth (there is no coke for heating) and does not energize anyone to do anything, not even hold a pen. The courthouse building is being used partly as a military hospital, and one would think the military hospital department could provide coal during the coldest days. In December and January we used wood for the fire, but the heating power of wood is not sufficient for the furnace system. Coke cannot be replaced by wood, so this winter we had a cold building.[1]

Every household is feeling the war in this regard. For the heating season 1944/45 we received approximately five cubic meters in uncut logs [about 1.4 cords]. In former times the wood was cut with a machine and then we would chop it ourselves in smaller pieces. This time the machine was unavailable. The wood cutters are in the armed forces. What to do? "If you are God's son, then help yourself," might be said here. Therefore we must saw the wood. We lose much time.

Since the beginning of February, I have been ill and unable to do my work. The strains of this winter undermined my health. The physician determined flu, heart and circulation disorders, and bronchitis. All these circumstances are to blame for the interruption in my reporting activities. And another reason: Sundays no longer belong fully and completely to me. The Volkssturm, to which I must unfortunately belong, has duty every Sunday morning.

Now some remarks on the situation from my point of view. The war has reached its high point in every aspect, if it has not already gone beyond that. The way that leads to the abyss for the German people has come even though the Party patriots continue ever to believe and hope. There are still those who

Stärker und gläubiger denn je!

Der Aufruf des Gauleiters zum Kampfjahr 1945

Nationalsozialisten!

Männer und Frauen des Gaues Hessen-Nassau!

Ein Jahr härtester Prüfungen liegt hinter uns, ein Jahr in welchem das Schicksal sich oft genug gegen uns entschied und uns härteste Belastungen auferlegte, die uns alle seelischen und physischen Kräfte abverlangten.

Das Waffenglück wandte sich von unseren Fronten. Der Bombenterror des Feindes verwüstete sadistischer denn je unsere Heimat. Mehrere unserer Verbündeten zogen die Sklaverei der Freiheit vor, und in unseren eigenen Reihen fanden sich erbärmliche Feiglinge und ehrvergessene Verräter, die unserem Volke und seinen Gefallenen die Treue brachen und als Mörder die Hand gegen unseren Führer erhoben.

Wenn wir dies alles dennoch mit standfestem Mut und ungebrochener Kampfkraft ertragen haben, so deshalb, weil uns das unabdingbare Ziel unseres Kampfes, die Freiheit unseres Volkes, jedes Opfer auferlegen darf, und weil wir darüber hinaus von der unbeirrbaren Zuversicht an die Wende unseres Geschickes erfüllt sind.

Wir haben in den vergangenen Jahren von den letzten Dingen Abschied genommen, die noch abseits des Krieges lagen. Wir taten es in dem Bewußtsein des Notwendigen. Wir wurden von den Schlägen des Schicksals zu einem Volk in Waffen geschmiedet und wissen heute, daß wir diese niemals niederlegen werden bevor unsere Heimat, das Leben unserer Frauen und Kinder und die Verwirklichung eines sozialistischen Aufbaues unserer Nation für alle Zeiten gesichert sind.

So gehen wir in das neue Kampfjahr 1945 mit dem Bewußtsein unserer Kraft, die wir in den vergangenen Monaten unter den höchsten Anforderungen unter Beweis stellten, und in der Gewißheit, daß das, was uns in der Vergangenheit nicht umbrachte, uns in der Zukunft nur stärker auf dem Plane finden wird.

Wir wissen, daß wir noch einen weiten Weg zurückzulegen haben. Er kann uns jedoch an Schwierigkeiten nicht mehr bringen, als wir bisher bereits überwunden haben. Wir wissen darüber hinaus aber, daß die Kraft unserer Waffen in immer steigendem Maße zukünftig den Mut unserer Herzen unterstützen wird.

In dieser Haltung wollen wir das neue Jahr begrüßen. Es mag von uns verlangen, was immer es will. Wir werden seine Aufgaben mit opferbereiter Tapferkeit, unbeirrbarer Gläubigkeit an den Endsieg unseres Volkes und unerschütterlicher Treue zum Führer erfüllen.

Wir werden damit zu jeder Stunde unter dem Befehl der gefallenen Männer, Frauen und Kinder aus unserer Gemeinschaft stehen, der gebieterisch fordert, daß ihr Opfer in der gesicherten Zukunft unseres Volkes und dem ewigen Bestand unseres Reiches erfüllt wird!

Heil Hitler!

Jakob Sprenger

Gauleiter und Reichsverteidigungskommissar

31. Dezember 1944 ★ Nr. 351 ★ Seite 2

Aufruf zum Jahreswechsel

Noch mehr leisten, noch beharrlicher sein!

Dr. Ley vor den politischen Leitern

Berlin, 30. Dezember.

Der Reichsorganisationsleiter der NSDAP., Dr. Ley, erläßt an die Politischen Leiter folgenden Neujahrsaufruf:

Der Führer spricht auf dem „Reichsparteitag der Freiheit" 1935: ,Die Partei hat mithin aus ihrer Organisation für die Zukunft dem deutschen Staat die oberste und allgemeine Führung zu geben.'

Das ist nun zur Tatsache geworden. Das Schicksalsjahr 1944 hat die totale Führung der NSDAP. auf allen Gebieten zum Durchbruch gebracht. Die Partei führt den Staat. Die Partei trägt die Rüstung und Produktion. Die Partei mobilisiert das Landvolk. Die Partei baut die Schutzwälle in Ost, Süd und West. Die Partei organisiert den Volkssturm. Die Partei ist die Seele des deut-

schen Widerstandes. Die Partei ist Deutschland. Adolf Hitler ist die Partei und Deutschland ist Adolf Hitler. Das ist die große, stolze Erkenntnis des Jahres 1944. Das ist der Sieg des 20. Juli und der Sieg über die Katastrophe der verhängnisvollen Monate des August und September. Die nationalsozialistische Revolution hat gesiegt und marschiert. Kameraden der nationalsozialistischen Führung, dieser herrlichste aller Siege verpflichtet:

Noch mehr zu arbeiten, noch mehr zu leisten und noch standhafter und beharrlicher zu sein als bisher. Dein Glaube sei Gehorsam, dein Bekenntnis sei Fleiß, und deine Treue sei Ausdauer und Zähigkeit! Unsere Ehre aber sei Deutschland!

Dr. Robert Ley!

[handwritten marginal notes in German cursive, partially legible]

do not want to see, who will hope right up to their funeral for a miracle from the Führer. In all other respects the number of peace-lovers grows from hour to hour.

The coming generations and the foreign countries will never understand why the German people did not stop the Party leaders by force and turn against the Party tyranny so this horrible war could be terminated. To clarify that, I would remind them the number of Party members is extremely large, particularly the Party functionaries with power. Plus millions of people fully believed in the National Socialist philosophy and were influenced by the Führer's radio broadcasts and the detailed manipulations of Party propaganda. [. . .] There is no important place in the state or in the private sector that has not been occupied by proven Party members [. . .] so wherever there might be a reaction, a Hitler guard stands. And those who are in these positions, who earn their living under Hitler, are certainly not opponents of the Hitler system. The want victory and not the defeat of Hitler because they will lose everything in a defeat, even though some of them, to disguise their black souls, have treated people somewhat more leniently. [. . .]

Today our opponents are at the Rhine in the West, and at the Oder in the East, and still I do not believe a collapse can be brought about by a popular uprising. Without assistance from outside it is not to be considered. Only the armed forces would be able to make a conclusive end. There, however, a united will is missing. The prominent officers know just as well as the Party officials they are going to be swept away when the war is lost. National Socialism and German militarism will cease to exist. Therefore the war continues until it is impossible for any further war actions. The war will end when the German troops finally run out of ammunition to fire at the advancing enemy. That is how I imagine the war will end. The opponents must continue to use their might in order to terminate the war.

Our war correspondents have already so often predicted the victorious end of this war that by now the war should have been over and forgotten. These glory-speakers continue to stick to the version of "no defeat and no giving up conquered areas." A small brochure by the SS war reporter Joachim Fernau, "The Secret of the Last Phase of the War," gives us an insight into the confused trains of thought of how the Nazis will win. He writes, among other things:

Victory. That is the word around which our thoughts continuously circle. Just peace alone is no more; there is only victory ... All of our territorial losses are unimportant. It is enough we previously held the necessary lands, which we did. Without doubt, this was the significance of the past years ... The last forceful effort is not about our strength. We have never in this war given up in a critical situation. We will pay the last price, which we still have to pay, evenly – with all means and with all our strength. The victory is really very close.[2]

So wrote this man in summer 1944. The writing on the wall was, "We must triumph." How we shall do that has not yet been spoken or written.

DISSEMINATED ENEMY NEWS – EXECUTED

Berlin, January 17, 1944.

Ferdinand Lang from Salzburg constantly listened to enemy radio reports from 1940 to 1943. He spread the hostile incitement and lies among his work comrades and tried to shake their faith in the final victory by anarchist expressions. Although his indignant fellow workers told him he was misguided, he long continued his infamous thrusts. The honorless traitor had to answer for himself before the People's Court, which condemned him to death. The judgment has already been carried out.

Source: "Ein Verräter hingerichtet," *DZ,* January 17, 1945, p. 2.

In no way are these "incitement and lies" that the government wants to keep away from their weak-nerved subjects. Lies have short legs, and soon every German will find out where the real incitement and lies came from. What the Nazis fear like the plague is the truth, the real situation becoming known. Only with a brainwashed population to whom the truth is not known can a war already lost be senselessly continued.

But the German people go on exactly the same, in the same manner of behavior from 1933–1945. Who will not listen, must feel.

STRONGER AND MORE DEVOUT THAN EVER!

The Regional Leader's Speech about the Combat Year 1945

National Socialists!
Men and women of the Region of Hesse-Nassau!
A year of the hardest tests lies behind us, a year in which fate often decided against us and imposed heavy burdens that demanded all of our mental and physical powers. The fortunes of war turned from our fronts. The enemy's terror bombing sadistically devastated our homeland more than ever.

Several of our allies preferred slavery to liberty, and among our own ranks pathetic cowards and traitors without honor, who broke from the loyalty of our people and our fallen ones, raised their hand against our Führer.

If we still have to endure all this with unwavering courage and unbroken combat strength, it is because the essential goal of our struggle, our people's freedom, imposes every sacrifice upon us, and because through our unshakeable confidence we fulfill the turn of our destiny. [. . .]

Source: "Stärker und gläubiger denn je!" *DZ,* turn of the year 1944/45, p. 1.

Believers ever! So says Jakob Sprenger. What the Führer preaches, all the big shots repeat. They owe their lives to this faith; therefore no one wavers in the faith. And they know the people well. A large quantity of believers still gathers around these corrupters and murderers of the nation. These arbitrary tyrants may defend themselves as they wish, but the hour of retribution approaches in spite of everything.

Call to the New Year

STILL MORE TO CARRY OUT, MORE REASONS TO PERSEVERE!

Dr. Ley to the political leaders

Berlin, December 30, 1944.

[. . .] The Party leads the state. The Party handles the armaments and production. The Party mobilizes the people. The Party builds the protection barriers in East, South, and West. The Party organizes the Volkssturm. The Party is the soul of German resistance. The Party is Germany. Adolf Hitler is the Party and Germany is Adolf Hitler. [. . .]

Source: "Noch mehr leisten, noch beharrlicher sein!" *VB-Nord,*
December 31, 1944, p. 2.

Dr. Ley raises the Party aloft. The Party is an almighty factor. Naturally, it is so because the Party is led by Dr. Ley and the other cronies and is used as a cover for all their prevailing desires. Dr. Ley forgot to say the Party in twelve years has brought Germany into the abyss and led millions of its citizens to extermination.

March 24, 1945

Mainz suffered a heavy air attack two months ago, on February 27, which transformed the city into rubble. Just 200 houses remain standing. Family

Fischler and Katie Ganglberger [Pauline's sisters] lost their homes and found refuge with us in Laubach. The houses in which they lived are totally destroyed, the cellars burned out. Nothing could be saved.[3]

I would not have left Mainz because, in my view, a return will be connected with substantial difficulties and at this time the return cannot be approximately determined. The Mainz inhabitants were for two days in the line of combat, but then the war for them was over. Most humans possess no courage and do not even want to accept the smallest risks, not even if it means they can be free of the Nazi yoke. The refugees run before the war and enter the combat operations. The slogan would have to read: Get out of the war!

Heinrich and Lina Fahrbach also left Mainz, and they too wanted to remain with us. After an explanation about the state of affairs here, they saw their foolishness and went back again to Mainz. I assume, however, they will not be able any longer to cross over the Rhine, since bridges along the return trip from here were blown up. The Fahrbachs left all their possessions in the lurch. Such weak-kneed foolishness is inexcusable.[4]

Party big shots caused the inhabitants from Mainz to evacuate, claiming it was a military duty and necessity for people to leave. The mighty Party did not miss to stress Mainz would be recaptured in six weeks, so the evacuation was necessary because the city would be under bombardment by the German artillery and the retaliatory weapons. This message also found believers.

Perhaps in six weeks no big shots will exist. The longer these gentlemen are at the helm, the greater the destruction and the more difficult the reconstruction will be. How long will the German armed forces still fight in this useless war? When the war is over will the German people call these prolongers of the war to account, or will they guarantee them generous pensions? After 1918 the German people failed in everything. Why should they be wiser this time?

THE KNIGHT'S CROSS FOR THE DEFENSE OF SCHNEIDEMÜHL

In heavy fighting, the garrison at Schneidemühl [Piła, Poland] held its ground against attacks from all sides by multiple and larger enemy forces. The Bolsheviks' strong attacks are bloodily fought off daily, and Soviet thrusts are eliminated or sealed off by our counter-attacks. Up to February 8, 1945, the garrison has destroyed 56 enemy tanks. At the side of the older proven fighters on the Eastern Front are members of special alert units and counter-attack units, brave and self-sacrificing, who repel the Bolshevik onslaught.

> Commander Heinrich Remlinger is the soul of the resistance. He knew
> how to unite the various means available for the defense of Schneidemühl
> into a solid fighting unit. The Führer has now awarded him the Knight's
> Cross of the Iron Cross.

After the Knight's Cross was bestowed upon him, Commander Remlinger in
the above article, the "soul of the resistance" who sacrificed many soldiers
needlessly, went tranquilly with the remainder of his crew into Russian
captivity.

Resistance today merely extends the German population's suffering and
torments. Why continue to fight? Because the war criminals have no more to
lose. The end of the war means their end. Therefore: "Fight until the last
breath!"

March 26, 1945

The Rhine has been crossed!

For the German armed forces to have destroyed the Rhine bridges, except
for the bridge to Remagen, is one of the many senseless acts during this
accursed war. Destroying the bridges did not stop the Allies. The crossing of
the Rhine in numerous places is a great achievement, facilitated by the fact,
however, that the German strategy failed completely. The instant the area
around Aachen was lost and the opponent advanced into the Eifel region, the
only purpose the positions on the Rhine's left banks could serve would be to
make possible an orderly retreat for the army in France to return across to
the right bank – and end the situation as soon as possible. The strategists
around Hitler made the direct opposite decision to what intelligent men
would do in this situation. I do not hold the view we would have been able to
hold the right Rhine bank, but the cities and villages in the Rhine country
would not have had to be so destroyed.

The situation now is that Allied troops in a relatively short time will
occupy the right bank of the Rhine, and raids into the heart of Germany
will take place from the bridgeheads of Wesel, Remagen, Boppard, and
Oppenheim.[5] For the first time in this war our Western opponents direct a
noteworthy energetic attack on a broad front.

General Patton's army group advanced in an exemplary manner from the
Mosel district into the Rhine area unhindered and crossed the Rhine at
Oppenheim. Today the American tanks are located already in the
Aschaffenburg area! And it is understood they are spreading out in all
directions. Accordingly, there will be a quick end to the war, other than

what was foreseen. Finally the Americans and English understand the Germans cannot be defeated by propaganda and the art of persuasion in the radio broadcasts but only by force of arms.

I hear rumors in circulation here that soon we will be retaliating with special weapons. The Party uses lies up to the last moment as a cover-up. Thus it intimidates the political opponents and provides its Party comrades with sedatives. It is so unbelievably simple for the current gang to lie to this German people and to lead these fools around by the nose.

March 27, 1945

The German army is on the run!

Since yesterday evening, March 26, cars heading east have been racing past our building. We could not sleep the entire night because of the noise. The "best army of the world" (as it was so often called) is fleeing back. Where, to the Weser? Oh God, you fools, you were not able to defend the Atlantic and Siegfried Line, as well as the Rhine. What do you think you can do inside Germany?

Despite what those who would prolong the war might still invent, the dissolution is complete – and it is but a short time before the war machine itself comes to a stop. Then an uncommonly serious and extremely heavy time of reconstruction begins after this worst of all wars. And there are few people who are in the clear; the war completely affected everyone's thinking and actions until the war was at its end. The hangover will last longer than the greatest doomsayers can imagine.

March 28, 1945

I made an exception at 11 a.m., and I listened briefly to the radio. The speaker said, "In Mannheim the Volkssturm and the Hitler Youth must make themselves ready for the city's defense." I can say but one thing to that: Forgive them, Father, for they know not what they do! Overall there prevails a mad disorder. Instructions are contradicted several times in the day; everything is just clashing together. Yesterday hospital patients able to walk were discharged and sent out onto the highways to an unknown fate. Here is the immediate situation: trucks of every kind with civilians and soldiers and all sorts of material rushing toward the east; people on foot carrying loads of all kinds heading in the same direction. This collective madness to rush into the unknown has already been going on for several days now. Escape! To where? Where is the goal? That is the epitome of madness![6]

Frau Marx, the No. 1 woman Nazi leader in Büdingen, told us the boys born between 1929 and 1931 were to be transported out of our area. Many boys ran off, however, and hid themselves and later returned to their parents' homes. The children are cleverer than their elders.

The prominent Giessen area bigwigs have absconded! A sublime moment! Twelve years of scurvy oppression are now over. And yet there is hardly enough inner strength left to openly express one's joy. But if the last SS bandit has now passed in review searching for the horizon, then we can draw ... (While sitting at my desk around three in the afternoon, airplanes circled overhead in pursuit of the German columns. Suddenly – as I was glancing at the sky – a bomb exploded in the post office [across the street] and a second bomb landed in the entrance to the Rühls' courtyard. The front of the court-house was damaged and all the window glass was blown out. We have minor damage in our apartment. My oil painting of the Rothenburg Plönlein is punctured. My desk is scattered with pieces of glass and ceiling tiles. The curtains and the flowers were blown inward) ... a deep breath of relief.[7]

It is a trick of fate that just a few minutes ago we were outside closing the gate. But we can hold up under everything if only we have the certainty the monster Hitler with his insatiable bloodletting and plundering will have committed soon his last shameful deed.

The last remnants of Hitler's "army" passed through here at noon like wild hordes; just like a gang of bandits, bums of the worst sort, an ode to an animal mass of Huns and barbarians.[8] Some cars appear as if they had been stolen from Gypsies on the road. Ragged soldiers attach themselves to the outside of vehicles in every position imaginable: on the running boards, on the radia-tors. "Man, horse, and wagon: the Lord has struck them," said Hitler in the autumn of 1939.[9] He was referring to the Polish army. And today?

Toward evening it becomes calm on the roads. Isolated cars in bad condition and tired hikers creep behind the departing rearguard in the direction of Freienseen. The tragedy appears to be over.

So that was what we saw passing by today, a component of the German army that left here as land grabbers to rob and plunder other countries, who piled up one shameful deed after another, violating the German name for eternity. Hopefully there will be uncontaminated participants who will tell the naked truth to future generations. That is my burning desire. Posterity must not be shown "heroes," but beasts in human form.

We are now in anticipation of the approaching Americans. It is possible that in a later time the readers of these lines will not have the correct understanding regarding our state of mind. We can hardly wait for the American troops to arrive and free us from the Hitler tyranny. For our area then, the war is over. After a long, agonizing psychological oppression finally comes the beginning of our liberation. Tomorrow the first Americans will arrive.

The coming night may not pass calmly because we do not know if the German troops will carry out a resistance or not. I am inclined to suppose no retreat skirmishes will play out here. It is possible other places through which this main road passes – Hungen, Nonnenroth, Röthges, or Grünberg – might be affected by that.

Sounds of artillery fire can be heard. I estimate the distance from us is 10–15 kilometers. The night begins. We lie down to sleep.

March 28/29, during the night

We sleep very restlessly. We can hear the bombs. The gunfire is getting closer to us. Between two and three we leave our beds and gather in the kitchen. With us are Philipp and Anna Fischler, as well as Katie Ganglberger. From time to time I go into the garden to determine the direction of the artillery and machine guns. Fortunately the rearguard action is from southwest to northwest, and in the north. In my estimation our area will be spared. We go back to bed.

March 29, 1945

Shortly after 3 p.m. there are noises on the street. Gathered in the cellar of our building are some wounded soldiers and some neighbors, cowed by Goebbels's propaganda [about the cruel Allies]. Among them, naturally, are the Party members, who do not have a clear conscience. These believe the approaching Allied soldiers will behave as the German soldiers did in Poland, etc. Their sheepish fear gives me pleasure, and I do not pass up the chance to make scornful remarks. We go outside to the courtyard entrance and see the advance guard drive by – tanks, armored cars, trucks, and jeeps.

For the first time we behold Americans. The soldiers are outstandingly equipped. Their appearance is remarkably good, well-fed. Nothing like the Germans' situation. Anyhow, the American army makes an impression of excellent, disciplined troops. I want to hope this good impression will continue to remain in the future.

March 30, 1945

The Party has left something behind: rumors. It is buzzing about that our troops are re-forming and will be back in Laubach within six weeks. Always the same nonsense, and it is always believed by some. The Party is not dead yet.

The drama's second act has begun. The occupation starts. All people involved in military service and Volkssturm duty must meet at the marketplace. I did not hear the bell signal, and because of a substantial delay I was present only at the conclusion. There was a lot of activity. Weapons, ammunition, cameras, and binoculars had to be given up. Radios had to be reported. My sword found its way to the collection table. Houses will be confiscated for military use, and the inhabitants have to leave their homes. Tears flow. The war still goes on. There is no sense in complaining if someone does not seem to have any under-standing and no feeling for the suffering of other people. I mean my fellow man. I myself have honestly earned the right to be spared all unpleasant side-effects of occupation because I fought bitterly for twelve years against the Hitler crowd. We must wait to see if I will be considered one of the good ones.

TRAITOR AT THE FIGHTING FRONT

> Because he had for years listened to the London stations regularly and then systematically spread the enemy's lies at his workplace to influence his fellow workers in treasonous ways, the traitor Paul Johannssen from Wiesbaden was condemned to death by the People's Court in Frankfurt. The judgment has already been enforced.

For five years and seven months, without interruption, [Pauline and I] used to listen to "enemy" radio broadcasts to be informed about the situation in the world. We attached no importance to the lying messages of Dr. Goebbels and Company. We heard broadcasts from the English and Americans and Russians and realized the National Socialist smoke screen was not working at least in some places. Fate willed it that we escaped great dangers. Perhaps we may yet receive more grace.

Führer Headquarters, March 11, 1945

> What lies ahead for our people, we are already seeing in large parts of the East, and in many areas of the West. What we have to do, therefore, is clear to everyone: to resist as long as necessary, and to smite the enemies until they are

exhausted at the end and yet break! Everyone in that way therefore fulfills his duty!
Adolf Hitler

Source: "Solange Widerstand leisten, bis die Feinde zerbrechen," *DZ,*
March 12, 1945, p. 1.

Here is the Führer's definitive and final retaliatory weapon: patience while the enemy becomes tired out. And what if the opponent does not become tired? A miracle-believing Nazi does not need to think about it. He leaves everything to the "ingenious" Führer.

April 10, 1945

A number of houses in Laubach were confiscated for the US Army soldiers. The inhabitants had to leave their dwellings, undoubtedly an unpleasant thing for those concerned. But it is still war and nothing can be said against such measures. It is very regrettable, however, that many Party members' houses were not taken. These people should be the first to have to pay for the war. The NSDAP opponents have the impression little has changed and the Party still governs as before, albeit invisibly. The sitting mayor, Willi Michel, was a Party comrade for ten years and is surely not about to cause woe for his former Party friends. Our population does not have a tendency toward revolution. Some still indeed believe the scattered rumors of a return of German troops and the use of new secret weapons. What can be done with such people? Exactly as in the past twelve years we have no courageous, action-loving humans. In a small community like Laubach we do not have too much to choose from. The petty-bourgeois spirit goes around. Heroes cannot be made from philistines. To this I must resign myself.

Today [my sister-in-law and her husband], Anna and Philipp Fischler, left. They are going by foot to Mainz. They were able to catch a ride in a truck from here to Bellersheim. The blacksmith [Karl] Kopp transformed the frame of a baby carriage into a handcart for them to push their bags and luggage to Mainz. At present there is no other way. Who can forecast when the railway will again be operating? Everywhere wanderers are to be seen on the roads, striving to get to their homes. This is the first step toward reconstruction. The difficulties to overcome will be tremendous. Will the German people be able to build on their own initiative a new state? Free of delusions? I am not too optimistic about this happening. Chaos is closer than reconstruction. The will to self-destruct is probably stronger than the desire for self-knowledge, which is the first step for improvement. The people's minds are contaminated. The German people in the main are mentally ill. A mental illness is difficult to heal. And that is the problem!

April 20, 1945

The war still goes on across the land in different parts of Germany. The continuation of military actions can only be called a great crime. Each victim is being created senselessly. These officers and soldiers who still fight are criminals and must be brought to account. There are too many guilty ones in this war. They are afraid of peace because they will be made to answer for their actions. They are like the criminal who is surrounded and has no way out, who fights up to the last bullet, which is intended for himself.

I have so far noticed very few penitent transgressors. Some Party members reveal in their expressions that they are not expecting anything good to happen. Others are impudent and arrogant. The upholsterer Schneidt expressed in the Wacht Cafe (in the town hall): "What did we Party comrades do? I wanted only the best!" The merchant Stotz called Germany "defenseless and without honor" now. The wife of Judge Schmitt believes we are not yet subdued.

It will be a hard piece of work to teach the German people another spirit. If the new coming government does not bring justice in with their victory, a reconstruction will be all but impossible. By justice I mean retribution and punishment for the sinners. National Socialism must be exterminated root and branch.

April 21, 1945

Today District Administrator Weber from Giessen appeared in my apartment.[10] He wanted to know if I was ready to become the mayor of Laubach. I rejected the offer for reasons of health and work. The district administrator then wanted to know why I had not become a National Socialist. I told him I knew from the beginning Hitler and his politics meant war. My further remarks were visibly too radical for the administrator, and I could see he was happy he would not have to put up with me as "mayor." If this new nation of mine cannot find better men than such past citizens, then a hope for a new foundation must be buried. Those who cannot honestly repent their committed shameful acts and supply proof to the world we can be a decent and freedom-loving nation cannot be fighters for the new Germany!

May 1, 1945

Adolf Hitler is said to be dead.[11]

The conflicting news stories are not clear as to how Hitler died. It remains to be seen whether his death is a definite reality or not. There have been no reports about the corpse.

Hitler's replacement, Fleet Admiral Dönitz, said in the broadcast Hitler had been killed at his command post in the Berlin bunker.

That is thus the beginning of creating a legend.

It is more than strange a successor was already put in place in order to continue the insanity, a proof of how slight the prospects are for an end to lunatics or criminals. Tyrants are strange monarchs. Hitler believed he could transfer his power with a pen stroke, without taking the people into account.

Adolf Hitler, "the most ingenious field marshal of all time," the all-powerful ruler over the One Thousand Year Reich – which collapsed after twelve years – has disappeared from the scene. The NSDAP has come to a total and inglorious end.

Providence, which Hitler was so fond of calling upon, has decided against him. The craziest of all political systems, the unique-leader state, has found its deserved end. History will note for eternity the German people were not able on their own initiative to shake off the National Socialist yoke. The victory of the Americans, English, and Russians was a necessary occurrence to destroy the National Socialists' delusions and plans for world domination.

May 5, 1945

Sensation upon sensation! Events rush in!

Berlin conquered by the Russians!

Hamburg in the hands of the English!

Russians and Americans meet at the Elbe!

German troops in Italy and western Austria have surrendered.

This morning the German army's surrender in Holland, Denmark, and Northwest Germany entered into force.

Disbanding on all fronts.

Only in Bohemia, Moravia, and the Danube region have the armed forces not yet ceased fighting. But that is just a question of hours. Then a cessation of hostilities will prevail in all of Europe. The once so proud German army was totally beaten on all fronts, and no one can ever dispute it. The enormous defeat of this war will hopefully help to remove the military spirit from the minds of the German people. I wish for that with all my heart. A peace-loving

Germany will again acquire friends, and those with good friends need never fear being attacked.

In memory of National Socialist propaganda I would like to present from my collection of wall posters the January 17–29, 1943, Parole der Woche [the NSDAP's watchword of the week], which is relevant today and might shed some daylight on what is occurring:

THE STRATEGIC MILITARY GENIUS OF THE FÜHRER, THE VALOR OF OUR SOLDIERS, AND THE SUPERIORITY OF WEAPONS WILL DECIDE THIS WAR!

While it is true military genius, bravery, and superiority of weapons can and will decide a war, the question is which side in this war dominated in these individual points. The Party comrades and their propaganda completely and enormously erred because of an innate Prussian arrogance and national boastfulness. It was not enough just to label the "Führer" a "strategic military genius," when he obviously could not recognize critical situations during the various stages of this war, or foresee the possibilities, or draw the correct conclusions, or make rational decisions.

The "valor" of the troops was largely based on stubborn adherence to commands while their own thinking was eliminated.

The "superiority of weapons" was a temporary phenomenon and overestimation of their own strength. Their tremendous preparation at the beginning gave them a head start, but the opponents quickly caught up and passed them.

Because reason was missing among their building blocks, all the Nazis' assertions crumbled into nothing.

May 6, 1945

Members of the Gaub family visited us and complained Herr Gaub had been assigned to retribution work because he had been a local public official. The public officials must restore the Jewish cemetery demolished by the Nazis. Frau Gaub insisted she and her husband had not taken any action against the Jews, and they felt it was an injustice to be included in the restitution. It is true Gaub, a teacher, can be counted among the harmless Party officials and was never a Nazi at heart, but he was an NSDAP member and head administrator of the radio station office. Every Party member carries the responsibility for what the Party did. It is not correct to place the entire blame on the leader, Adolf Hitler, and on the High Command.

Whoever did not reject twelve years of comradeship in the Party but benefited from the spoils gained by the Party must be in the front row to carry the load when it collapses.

Whoever did not take a stand against the mind-set that led to this war has no right ever to cry about the consequences of defeat.

Individual Nazis will be judged according to the seriousness of their own deeds, but overall the general assessment will be, "Rogues who travel together, hang together."

Today, naturally, no one wants to claim he had been a genuine Nazi. Everyone hides from responsibility. Justice will always exist to hand out retribution and punish the offender. That is also the epitome of divine justice: there is not only a loving but a punishing God.

In 1933 many people behaved exactly the opposite of today. They sought to prove, even with threadbare assertions, how they had always been National Socialists.

There are heroes and "heroes." Poor humanity!

May 7, 1945

From the Allies' radio broadcasts these past few days, we are receiving descriptions of the conditions in the German concentration camps that can only be called bestial and unforgivable. That even a single concentration camp could exist here is a dishonor to our culture. Here humans were tortured and killed because in the opinion of some sadist or criminal they were not perfect Nazis. Common informers were able to get the unfortunate victims of their vindictiveness thrown into the notorious camps.

These abuses during the despotic rule of Adolf Hitler and his devoted bandits will remain into the far reaches of time as a glaring warning signal in the history books of mankind. Another one of their "high achievements"!

In the broadcast I heard foreign speakers who want to impose upon the entire German people the blame for the conditions in the concentration camps. I would like to insert a caveat against such an unfair evaluation in which every German who offered active or passive resistance is being condemned as likewise guilty. That is not logic on the accusers' part.

If this kind of blanket justice were applied against the decent people in the USA when Negroes are lynched there, it would be most abhorrent. It definitely would not be reasonable for anyone to assert every inhabitant of the United States of America is responsible for such acts of violence.

In the concentration camp case, only the really guilty ones who are responsible can be called to account. Those who conceived and created the camps, and all those who put the people into the camps and tortured and killed them are guilty.

There is a very large circle of Germans who have the moral debt for the atrocities in the concentration camps: primarily all NSDAP Party members, as well as all who favored the National Socialist system.[12]

No one can say he did not know about the secret state police and its coercive acts of violence. The institution of the Gestapo will remain an everlasting disgrace. The Gestapo could use every forceful measure: there was no legal protection for liberty or property. Innocent people were taken into detention without investigation or court proceedings simply because they mentioned other world views. The Gestapo's brutality and ruthlessness remained unpunished because there was no other place where complaints could be made. The Gestapo's rule of terror was sacrosanct. Whoever got into the Gestapo's claws, and for any reason, was out of favor or even framed, was subjected to a form of capricious injustice – without any mercy. That was the greatest disgrace to civilization ever devised.

May 8, 1945

Adolf Hitler announced at every possible opportunity, "There will not be another November 9, 1918" – the day the German Revolution broke out. On November 11, 1918, the armistice of Compiègne was concluded. Germany's military, political, and economic situation had become hopeless. The people had held out up to the last breath. Military strength was depleted, raw materials were used up, and the food supplies had sunk beneath the minimum subsistence level. The revolution accelerated the completion of the war, but the collapse would have come rapidly even without the popular uprising. The "November criminals" (the Nazis' name for the group that caused the revolution) actually had helped to safeguard German territory from an invasion. But they did not harvest the German people's thanks. Those interested in getting revenge immediately after the war obscured the truth, creating the false legend that if the revolutionaries had not "stabbed their own people in the back," the First World War would not have been lost – or at the least, extending the war could have bought better armistice terms. Many Germans believed the war of 1914–18 could have been won through continued fighting. Few revisionists seem to recall our allies (Austria-Hungary, Bulgaria, and Turkey) had already stopped fighting in September and October 1918! Under such circumstances victory for Germany was impossible. Nevertheless, the people were besotted and fooled – most especially by the military, whose officers must have known the real situation and should have been able to act on better knowledge.

Was the past to be instructive? No, not in any way. The 1939–1945 war has shown that Prussian militarism, in its innate obstinacy, remained unteachable. But the lesson of May 8, 1945, is an excellent one. The Supreme Command of Germany's Armed Forces, along with the entire German armed forces, surrendered unconditionally to the Allies.

The once so very proud and "invincible" German armed forces had no other way out than an inglorious capitulation!

The arrogant, boastful German army commanders, following a rulebook for bunglers, led the German army into the deepest abyss.

We can count on the fact that even this time they will not have the courage to honor the truth. They will entrench themselves behind their oath to obey their leader, and thus place the blame for all of the misconceived orders on their Commander-in-Chief: Corporal Adolf Hitler.

The German General Staff, which deserved the full measure of blame for the defeat in 1918, masterfully understood how to clear themselves of responsibility and keep Prussian militarism alive as an infallible instrument, which enabled them to prepare behind the scenes for the Second World War.

Adolf Hitler was the dolt who was presented to the German people as a genius and a national God. The wire-pullers and minions heaped upon themselves job positions and badges as thanks for their worthwhile obedience.

Adolf Hitler never would have been in a position to lead this accursed war were it not for an extremely large number of unscrupulous accomplices at his side. These involved not only the General Staff and high-ranking officers but also managers of major industries, scholars, and diplomats. The men in the propaganda ministry and the press may not be forgotten either.

If now, after the collapse, any of these lackeys of Adolf Hitler has the insolence to want to be considered as a harmless onlooker, then one can only wish he immediately feel the scourge of avenging mankind. Whoever supported the arbitrary dictator Adolf Hitler with advice and deed so that he could provoke the Second World War will be considered jointly guilty.

Whoever in foolish arrogance or from defiance still believes Corporal Adolf Hitler was right about turning Germany into a heap of rubble must be designated a despicable scoundrel.

Whoever cries about having lost the totalitarian system or wants to resurrect National Socialism is to be treated as an incorrigible lunatic.

The reasonable and insightful Germans who opposed twelve years of National Socialist terror with an active or passive resistance may feel pride and satisfaction over the fact their fight was not futile, and the conclusion of the events justified their attitude in every instance.

May 17, 1945

The newly appointed Mayor Heinrich Schmidt invited me to the mayor's office because I was to become his deputy mayor.[13] I was present when Fräulein Thea Wachtel arrived. She wanted to find out if her father could be taken out of American detention and if she could take his place, because he was innocent, and it was she who worked for the NSDAP. At that point, the painter [Robert Ludwig] Erbes came into the office, and Fräulein Wachtel said, "You, Herr Erbes – you alone are to blame that my father is in prison. You were not a National Socialist – and you are not a German either!"

It is typical of the mental condition of those who are in the so-called "National" circles to label everybody as non-German or even a traitor who challenges their political attitudes. If it were a high honor to be German, then such a remark would be an affront. But under the present circumstances, it is an unpleasant burden to have to count oneself among the Germans.

[Translator's note: On May 31, 1945, two weeks after his final diary entry, Friedrich pasted the following news article, "Message of Hope," on a blank page. It relates directly to his May 7, 1945 entry].

MESSAGE OF HOPE

London, May 31, 1945.

The archbishop of Canterbury, Dr. G.F. Fisher, expressed himself in a pastoral letter to his Diocese about Germany and the German people. The archbishop said: "We may not forget there are Germans who opposed National Socialism and had been put in concentration camps to suffer. These Germans were ashamed of their own people and are deeply humiliated. We did not do everything only by defeating Germany. For many years to come we must fulfill the difficult and responsible task to direct the life of the Germans and to lead them on neighborly trains of thought. The unbearable revelations of the conditions in the concentration camps affected us not only deeply but gave evidence to our eyes how deeply the German people had sunk. It is not possible to exonerate the entire nation of the joint knowledge and the tolerance of terrible cruelties. It is difficult after knowing the whole circumstances not to condemn the entire race. But we may not be carried away in that regard; we may not ignore the fact that there were also Germans who did fight against the evil, however few there may have been, and who suffered for their fight against the enormous evil. Directly on these few lies our hope for the German people's rehabilitation and moral uplifting.

Source: "London: Botschaft der Hoffnung," *Frankfurter Presse,*
May 31, 1945, p. 4.

ACKNOWLEDGMENTS

The completion of my work with the diary owes much to the patience and graciousness of my wife, Bev, who in 1970 met my grandfather and realized the significance of both his life and his writings. Our daughters, Tristen and Erin, helped to proofread the diary, as did Mr. Christian Boehm. My research was facilitated by the helpful staff of our three local libraries: Clara B. Mounce Public Library in Bryan; Larry J. Ringer Library in College Station; and the Sterling C. Evans Library at Texas A&M University.

I am grateful to President George H.W. Bush, who helped bring the diary to the attention of the administrators of his Presidential Library and Museum in College Station, Texas, where in 2005 Director Warren Finch and Curator Patricia Burchfield made it available to the public for the first time. The director of the Dwight D. Eisenhower Presidential Library and Museum, Karl Weissenbach, followed with an exhibition of the diary in Abilene, Kansas. Other exhibitions took place at Holocaust Museum Houston, thanks to the efforts of Edith Mincberg and Susan Myers; and at the Friedrich Ebert Foundation in Berlin and Bonn, under the direction of Anke Fuchs.

Photographic exhibitions of diary pages, documents, and family photos were presented in 2005 at the Museum Fridericianum in Laubach through the efforts of Klemens Hogen-Ostlender, Kurt Stein, and Elisabeth Rößler; in 2007 at the Stora (Great) Synagogue in Stockholm, Sweden, inspired by Helga Sporrong and made possible by Lars Raij; in 2008 at the Dag Hammarskjöld Auditorium, United Nations Headquarters in New York, thanks to Yoon Yeocheol, Kiyo Akasaka and Kimberly Mann. My thanks also go to producer and director Arnie Zipursky and Fern Levitt of CCI Entertainment Toronto, whose documentary film, "My Opposition: The Diaries of Friedrich Kellner," was given a special screening in the Hammarskjöld Auditorium at the UN to commemorate the seventieth anniversary of Kristallnacht.

For their help in preparing the complete and unabridged version of the diary in 2011, I am grateful to my co-editors of the German edition: Sascha Feuchert and Erwin Leibfried of Justus Liebig University, Jörg Riecke of Heidelberg University, and Markus Roth, deputy head of Arbeitsstelle

Holocaustliteratur at Justus Liebig University whose associates and student members also assisted: Andrea Löw, Elizabeth Turvold, Diana Nusko, and Charlotte Kitzinger; Hanna Ashour, Aleksandra Bąk, Anika Binsch, Manuel Emmerich, Stefanie Füchter, Kathy Gareis, Anna Kiniorska-Michel, Birgit Maria Körner, Jelena Li, Nikola Medenwald, Andreas Pfeifer, Nassrin Sadeghi, Birgit Schmitges, Christiane Weber, Julia Wilke, and others. I also thank publisher Thedel von Wallmoden, editor Hajo Gevers, and staff members of Wallstein Verlag, Göttingen, Germany, for their commitment to the German book's success. Klemens Hogen-Ostlender of the *Giessener Anzeiger* contributed to our efforts with a multi-year series of incisive newspaper articles about the diary and its author.

For this Cambridge University edition, I thank Prof. Alan Steinweis for his substantial and perceptive Foreword, which illustrates the context of Friedrich Kellner's surroundings. I appreciate the impressive work of the Content Manager Ian McIver and his Cambridge colleagues in design and production, and the copy-editing of Damian Love, that have transformed my manuscript into a book. And I am especially indebted to Executive Publisher Michael Watson for his early recognition of the diary's significance and for introducing its possibilities to the Cambridge Press Syndicate. I received notice of the Syndicate members' approval, and that of Publishing Director Ella Colvin's, with deep appreciation, knowing how much my grandfather would have been honored to have his work associated with such an illustrious institution.

NOTES

Foreword

1. The province, which received this name in 1918, was also often referred to by its historical designation of Hesse-Darmstadt. It should not be confused with the neighboring region of Hesse-Nassau, which was under Prussian administration until 1945. Since 1949, major portions of both regions have been part of the German federal state known simply as Hesse.

2. Hessischen Landesamts für geschichtliche Landeskunde, Landesgeschichtliches Informationssystem Hessen: Historisches Ortslexikon, entry for Laubach, www.lagis-hessen.de (accessed February 24, 2017).

3. "Die Wahlen zum Reichstag am 31. Juli und 6. November 1932 und am 5. März 1933," *Statistik des deutschen Reichs*, vol. 434 (Berlin: Verlag für Sozialpolitik, 1935), pp. 8, 67; *Die Ergebnisse der Landtagswahl am 19. Juli 1932 und der Reichstagswahl am 31. Juli 1932 im Volksstaat Hessennach einzelnen Gemeinden*, ed. Landesstatistisches Amt Hessen (Darmstadt: Hessischer Staatsverlag, 1932), pp. 48–49; Richard F. Hamilton, *Who Voted for Hitler?* (Princeton University Press, 1982), pp. 40–43; Jürgen Falter, *Hitlers Wähler* (Munich: Beck, 1991), pp. 160–63.

4. Statistisches Reichsamt, *Volkszählung: Die Bevölkerung des deutschen Reichs nach den Ergebnissen der Volkszählung 1939*, 4 vols. in 1, *Statistik des deutschen Reichs*, vol. 552 (Berlin: Verlag für Sozialpolitik, 1941–43), vol. I, pp. 186, 188.

5. Hamilton, *Who Voted for Hitler*; and Thomas Childers, *The Nazi Voter: The Social Foundations of Fascism in Germany, 1919–1933* (Chapel Hill: University of North Carolina Press, 1983).

6. Paul Arnsberg, *Die jüdischen Gemeinden in Hessen: Anfang – Untergang – Neubeginn*, 2 vols. (Frankfurt am Main: Societäts-Verlag, 1971), vol. I, pp. 478–79.

7. Menahem Kaufman, "The Daily Life of the Village and Country Jews in Hessen from Hitler's Ascent to Power to November 1938," *Yad Vashem Studies*, 12 (1992), 147–98.

8. Hansjörg Pötzsch, *Antisemitismus in der Region: Antisemitische Erscheinungsformen in Sachsen, Hessen, Hessen-Nassau und Braunschweig 1870–1914* (Wiesbaden: Kommission für die Geschichte der Juden in Hessen, 2000).

9. Markus Müller, *Die Christlich-Nationale Bauern- und Landvolkpartei 1928–1933* (Düsseldorf: Droste, 2001), pp. 508–13.

10. Having first been appointed Gauleiter of Gau Hesse-Nassau-South in 1927, Sprenger's authority increased considerably in 1933 when his Gau was

combined with the neighboring Gau Hesse-Darmstadt to form the larger Gau Hesse-Nassau, with Frankfurt as its capital and largest city. This Gau included territories located both in the People's State of Hessen as well as in Prussian Hesse-Nassau.

11. Stephanie Zibell, *Jakob Sprenger (1884–1945): NS-Gauleiter und Reichsstatthalter in Hessen* (Darmstadt: Hessische Historische Kommission, 1999), p. 424,

12. Uta George et al. (eds.), *Hadamar. Heilstätte, Tötungsanstalt, Therapiezentrum* (Marburg: Jonas, 2006).

13. Winfried Süß, "Dezentralisierter Krankenmord: Zum Verhältnis von Zentralgewalt und Regionalgewalten in der 'Euthanasie' seit 1942," in Jürgen John, Horst Möller, and Thomas Schaarschmidt (eds.), *Die NS-Gaue: Regionale Mittelinstanzen im zentralistischen "Führerstaat"* (Munich: Oldenbourg, 2007), pp. 123–35 (at p. 128).

14. Monica Kingreen, "'Die Aktion zur kalten Erledigung der Mischehen' – die reichsweit singuläre systematische Verschleppung und Ermordung jüdischer Mischehepartner im NSDAP-Gau Hessen-Nassau 1942/1943," in Alfred Gottwaldt, Norbert Kampe, and Peter Klein (eds.), *NS-Gewaltherrschaft: Beiträge zur historischen Forschung und juristischen Aufarbeitung* (Berlin: Edition Hentrich, 2005), pp. 187–201; for further details about the end of the Jewish community in Laubach and the ultimate fate of the town's Jewish residents, see Monica Kingreen, "Die Opfer des Holocaust aus Laubach und Ruppertsburg," in Hanno Müler (ed.), *Juden in Laubach und Ruppertsburg* (Neustadt an der Aisch: Schmidt, 2015), pp. 177–90.

15. Landgericht Giessen, Trial judgment (pogrom in Laubach, November 10, 1938), December 10, 1948, 2 KLs 19/48, Archive of the Institut für Zeitgeschichte, Munich, Gg 01.10.

16. Alan E. Steinweis, *Kristallnacht 1938* (Cambridge, MA: Belknap Press, 2009).

17. Frank Bajohr, "German Responses to the Persecution of the Jews as Reflected in Three Collections of Secret Reports," in Susanna Schrafstetter and Alan E. Steinweis, eds., *The Germans and the Holocaust: Popular Responses to the Persecution and Murder of the Jews* (New York: Berghahn, 2015), pp. 41–58; Peter Longerich, *"Davon haben wir nichts gewusst!" Die Deutschen und die Judenverfolgung 1933–1945* (Munich: Siedler, 2006).

18. Ulrike Puvogel and Stefanie Endlich, *Gedenkstätten für die Opfer des Nationalsozialismus: Eine Dokumentation*, vol. I, 2nd edn. (Bonn: Bundeszentrale für politische Bildung, 1995), p. 337.

19. "Aktiver Widerstand," handwritten list compiled by Friedrich Kellner at the end of the war, private collection of Robert Scott Kellner.

20. Heinz Boberach (ed.), *Meldungen aus dem Reich 1938–1945: Die geheimen Lageberichte des Sicherheitsdienstes der SS*, 18 vols. (Herrsching: Pawlak, 1984). Important studies of popular responses to Nazi rule include Ian Kershaw, *Popular Opinion and Political Dissent in the Third Reich: Bavaria 1933–1945,*

rev. edn. (Oxford University Press, 2002); and Detlev Peukert, *Inside Nazi Germany: Conformity, Opposition, and Racism in Everyday Life*, trans. Richard Deveson (New Haven, CT: Yale University Press, 1989).

21. Axel Ulrich, "'Weg mit Hitler!': Politischer Widerstand gegen das 'Dritte Reich' im Rhein-Main-Gebiet," in Renate Knigge-Tesche (ed.), *Politischer Widerstand gegen die NS-Diktatur in Hessen: Ausgewählte Aspekte* (Wiesbaden: Hessische Landeszentrale für politische Bildung, 2007), pp. 6–40.

22. Axel Ulrich and Stephanie Zibell, "Wilhelm Leuschner und sein antinazistisches Vertrauensleutennetzwerk," in Wolfgang Form, Theo Schiller, and Lothar Seitz (eds.), *NS-Justiz in Hessen: Verfolgung, Kontinuitäten, Erbe* (Marburg: Historische Kommission für Hessen, 2015), pp. 293–334.

23. Wilhelm Form, "Politische NS-Justiz in Hessen – ein Überblick," in Form, Schiller, and Seitz (eds.), *NS-Justiz in Hessen*, pp. 77–104 (at pp. 91–92, 99–101).

24. Harold Hirsch, "Das Sondergericht Darmstadt. Zwischen vorauseilendem Gehorsam und widerstrebender Gefolgschaft," in Form, Schiller, and Seitz, *NS-Justiz in Hessen*, pp. 105–48.

Preface

1. Helmut Lölhöffel, "Der deutsche Patriot," *Süddeutsche Zeitung*, June 14, 2011; Elke Schmitter, "Das Gedächtnis gibt nach," *Der Spiegel*, vol. 40, October 1, 2011, pp. 154–55; *Damals*, 12 (2011), p. 62.

2. "Interview mit Richard von Weizsäcker: "Ich habe das Wort Auschwitz nicht vor dem Frühjahr 1945 gehört," *Spiegel Online, Panorama*, March 6, 2005.

3. Diary, May 30, 1942. (The original diary and all of Friedrich Kellner's documents and letters are privately held by Robert Scott Kellner in College Station, Texas).

4. Diary, October 7, 1939.

5. New York State Department of Health, Marriage License, Registered no. 1871, March 9, 1937.

6. Federal Bureau of Investigation, Internal Security, Alien Enemy Control, File no. 100–3219, Originating Norfolk, Virginia, April 8 – November 12, 1943.

7. David I. Epstein, *Home: Life in the Jewish Home for Children* (Ithaca, NY: WORDPRO, 2006), 75–76.

8. Department of the Army, Report of Death, AGO Form DA 52–1, Final Report no. A-1628, February 12, 1954.

9. Der Regierungspräsident in Darmstadt, Wiedergutmachungsbeschied, Nr. 2235, July 19, 1966.

10. Reconstructions of conversations are based on my notes from lengthy oral histories and general discussions with Friedrich and Pauline Kellner, and interviews with others who knew them. The most productive talks took place

in 1968 and 1970, but I also include memories from 1960. In instances where I use quotes from letters and other documents, I make specific reference to them.

11. November 10, 1959, letter from Kellner to Bürgermeister Desch, resigning from office. Also Desch's response of November 11, 1959.

12. Letter from Ludwig Heck, dated December 18, 1976.

13. Christian Children's Fund magazine, *Sponsorworld*, vol. 2, no. 1 (Summer 1983). "Village of Hope," *Bryan/College Station Eagle*, February 15, 1984, p. 1; "A&M Fund Drive aims to Educate Youths Toiling in Colombian Mines," *Houston Chronicle*, April 28, 1985, Sec. 3, p. 2.

14. Military Personnel Records, St. Louis, Missouri, Fred William Kellner, Army Serial Number 31407827.

15. *Journal of the United Nations*, Programme of Meetings and Agenda, no. 2008/219, Saturday November 8, 2008.

16. Wolfgang Stumme, *Der Mainzer Hauptfriedhof: Menschen und ihre letzte Ruhestätten* (Ingelheim: Leinpfad Verlag, 2010), 90–93. Also, "Ehrengrab für Friedrich Kellner" (Grave of honor for Friedrich Kellner), *Mainz Allgemeine Zeitung*, July 31, 2012.

17. Klemens Hogen-Ostlender, "Neue Adresse auch für die Gesamtschule: Die Laubacher Friedrich-Kellner-Strasse wird von der Andree Allee bis zum Felix-Klipstein-Weg führen" (A new address also for the high school: the Friedrich Kellner Street in Laubach will go from Andree Allee to Felix Klipstein Way), *Giessener Anzeiger*, January 15, 2013, p. 27.

Biographical Narrative

1. Georg Friedrich Kellner (July 7, 1862 – November 8, 1926); Barbara Wilhelmine Vaigle (November 17, 1858 – September 23, 1925).

2. Friedrich Karl Ludwig Emil Preuss (July 18, 1859 – September 26, 1936); Johanna Karolina Martin (January 22, 1861 – October 7, 1944).

3. Wolfgang Balzer, "Mainz – eine Stadt und ihr Militär," *Mainz: Vierteljahreshefte für Kultur, Politik, Wirtschaft und Geschichte*, vol. IV (Mainz: Bonewitz Communication, 1988), pp. 125ff.

4. In 1960 the Social Democratic Party of Germany gave Kellner a certificate marking forty years of membership.

5. Diary, January 15, 1943.

6. Adolf Hitler, *Mein Kampf*, trans. Ralph Manheim, intro. by Konrad Heiden (Boston, MA: Houghton Mifflin, 1962), p. 338. Hereafter cited as Hitler, *Mein Kampf*. Kellner's references to *Mein Kampf* are to the 1930 edition that combined both volumes in a single book. The first volume of *Mein Kampf* was published in 1925 and the second volume followed in 1926, both published by Franz Eher Nachfolger GmbH, Munich. Ralph Manheim's translation is based on the 1930 German edition.

7. "Tagebücher gegen den Terror" (Diaries against Terror), *Mainz Allgemeine Zeitung*, September 24, 2005, p. 14. Kellner uses a similar expression in his diary entry of November 7, 1942.

8. Diary, April 21, 1945.

9. Diary, October 31, 1942.

10. Diary, October 11, 1939.

11. Diary, December 21, 1942.

12. Diary, September 17, 1939.

13. Helge Braunroth, Sascha Feuchert, and Alfred Schäfer (eds.), *1925–2000: 75 Jahre Sozialdemokratische Partei Laubach, Dokumentation zum 75jährigen Bestehen des Ortsvereins Laubach der Sozialdemokratischen Partei Deutschlands* (Giessen: Druckkollektiv, 2000), p. 57. In the region of Schotten, which includes Laubach, more than 70 percent of the vote was cast for the NSDAP. Eckhart G. Franz, "Volksstaat Hessen 1918–1945" in Walter Heinemeyer (ed.), *Handbuch der hessischen Geschichte*, vol. IV: *Hessen im Deutschen Bund und im neuen Deutschen Reich (1806) 1815 bis 1945.* (Elwert: Marburg, 2000), p. 916.

14. Announced at the annual Nazi rally in Nuremberg in September 1935, the two "Nuremberg laws" were the Reichsbürgergesetz (citizenship law) depriving Jews of their German citizenship, and the Schutze (protection) law to protect German blood and German honor, which prohibited marriage between Jews and Aryans.

15. Diary, October 13, 1939.

16. Salli Heynemann (spelled Heinemann in the diary) (1879–1942) was a Jewish storeowner in Laubach. His wife was Hulda Hortense née Haas (1879–1942). John Peter Abt, PhD, who lives in San Diego, California, reports that his parents seldom discussed the past or the fate of his grandparents. Dr. Abt knew, though, that his father had been in a serious altercation with the police in 1935. (Correspondence between John Peter Abt and Robert Scott Kellner, dating from 2003.) In 1942 Salli and Hulda Heynemann were sent from Laubach to a concentration camp in Poland and murdered.

17. Pre-war writings, September 26, 1938. This phrase was used in the title for the publication of the Kellner diary in Germany, *"Vernebelt, verdunkelt sind alle Hirne": Tagebücher 1939–1945*, ed. Sascha Feuchert, Robert Martin Scott Kellner, et al. (Göttingen: Wallstein Verlag, 2011).

18. Kellner kept a list of his active resistance and another list of his passive resistance. His travels to France to mail these letters are recorded in his active resistance list.

19. Diary, May 11, 1940.

20. Many school administrators and teachers encouraged their pupils to participate in the harassment of Jews, particularly on the second day, November 10, 1938. "Significant numbers of German youths engaged in physical attacks on Jews and their property. In most cases they had been

mobilized by local officials of the Hitler Youth or by their schools. Classes of schoolchildren were marched from their schools and set loose on Jewish targets, encouraged by their teachers." Steinweis, *Kristallnacht*, p. 60.

21. Dr. Ludwig Richard Schmitt (1898–1947), chief judge, lived upstairs in the courthouse with his wife and three children. A Nazi Party member and soldier in the army reserves, Schmitt constantly badgered Kellner to join the Nazi Party. Schmitt was called into the army at the beginning of the Polish campaign but was often home on leave.

22. Diary, February 23, 1942, mentions the role of these men during Kristallnacht. Mentioned also in Wilhelm Knau's unpublished *Lebenserinnerungen*.

23. Diary entries, November 15, 1939; January 15, 1940. A few months earlier, Mayor Högy had admonished Kellner for his lack of co-operation in quartering soldiers. Letter from Otto Högy to Friedrich Kellner, November 17, 1939.

24. Diary, January 15, 1940.

25. Else Gross (1919–2012) moved to America after the war. In conversations and letter exchanges with me, she said she had not known of the diary but was not surprised. Whenever one of Hitler's speeches was being broadcast over the radio, she said Judge Schmitt or his wife would turn up the volume so that "the troublemaker Kellner" would hear it one floor below them.

26. Undated essay, "Verwandlungskünstler" (quick-change artists).

27. Hermann Johannes Colnot (1888–1959), Nazi Party member since 1933. When he assumed office in Giessen, the local newspaper wrote, "Colnot took a stand about the elimination of Jews from Germany even before the Nuremberg Law of 1935, and his articles in justice magazines became talking points for the experts." *Giessener Anzeiger*, September 3, 1939. After the war Colnot was sentenced by a Wiesbaden court to serve one and a half years in a labor camp. District Leader (Kreisleiter) Heinrich Backhaus (1888–1943) was a postal inspector who joined the NSDAP in 1925 and became Kreisleiter of the Wetterau region in 1937. "Kreisleiter Backhaus 50 Jahre alt," in *Giessener Anzeiger*, March 2, 1938.

28. Ernst Mönnig (1885–1950), Local Group Leader of the NSV (Welfare Organization). His 1937 memorandum to District Leader Heinrich Backhaus reads, "We are having continuing difficulties with Inspector Kellner, especially with collections. He very often locks his door against the collectors, and he gave nothing even for the Christmas collection. He writes letters, which are carefully phrased, as seen in the enclosed letter. Kellner wants to be in the position to do nothing. He has a married son in America. Kellner's attitude exerts a bad influence on the rest of the population, and, in our view, he should be made to disappear from Laubach."

29. Supplemental essay, February 19, 1940.

30. Hermann Desch, head of the local committee for the Colonial League, complained to District Leader Backhaus that Kellner had turned down his May 17, 1939, request to be treasurer of the group. In response to a query from Backhaus, Kellner insisted he was too busy with courthouse duties. Letter from Ortsverbandsleiter Desch, dated May 17, 1939, and Friedrich Kellner's letter to Heinrich Backhaus (and copy to Otto Pott), May 26, 1939.
31. The original is privately held in College Station, Texas. A copy of this document is in *Wiedergutmachungsakte Friedrich Kellner*, Hesse Main State Archives, Wiesbaden: HHStAW, Abt./Nr. 518/29744, Bl. 9, undated enclosure "Betr.: Antrag der Ortsgruppe Laubach der NSDAP."
32. Diary, June 16, 1941.
33. Diary, October 16, 1944.
34. Diary, July 7, 1941.
35. Katharina Maria Preuss Ganglberger (1896–1978) and Karolina Johanna Preuss Fahrbach (1889–1974).
36. Diary, October 28, 1941.
37. Diary, March 9–26, 1942.
38. Letter from Acting Mayor Otto Pott to Friedrich Kellner, dated August 14, 1943, subject "Beschlagnahme von Wohnräumen" (Confiscation of rooms).
39. Diary, August 24, 1942. Heinrich Bischoff was the judge of the inheritance court in Alsfeld and the debt relief office in Lauterbach. He was a dangerous adversary, as can be seen in numerous diary entries. During the German government's procedure in 1966 to recompense Kellner for Nazi injustices against him, Judge Bischoff was among those who attested to Kellner's integrity. *Wiedergutmachungsakte Friedrich Kellner.*
40. Item 6 in Friedrich Kellner's list of his active resistance.
41. Braunroth, Feuchert, and Schäfer (eds.), *75 Jahre Sozialdemokratische Partei Laubach*, p. 75.
42. 1965 post-war supplemental essay by Friedrich Kellner. Also Ludwig Heck's January 14, 2004 letter to Robert Scott Kellner.
43. Braunroth, Feuchert, and Schäfer (eds.), *75 Jahre Sozialdemokratische Partei Laubach*, p. 73.

Pre-War Writings

1. "Since May, there had been widespread popular anxiety in Germany about the possibility of war, made more acute by the Czech government's military mobilization in the same month." Richard J. Evans, *The Third Reich in Power, 1933–1939* (New York: Penguin, 2005), p. 674.
2. Dr. Ludwig Schmitt, chief judge of the Laubach courthouse. The Nuremberg Party Rally (*Reichsparteitag*) was a Nazi Party convention held annually from 1923 to 1938. "The rallies were a combination of open-air festival, military

display and solemn occasion. The bathetic low point was the consecration of SA banners." Michael Burleigh, *The Third Reich: A New History* (New York: Hill & Wang, 2000), p. 117.

3. Kellner is addressing Paul Joseph Goebbels (1897–1945), Reich Minister of Propaganda. Goebbels's concept of "Volksaufklärung" (Enlightening the People) was all-encompassing, including radio broadcasts and control of the press. "At his first government press conference, on 16 March [1933], he put it more plainly: it was to make the people 'think uniformly, react uniformly, and place themselves at the disposal of the government, body and soul.'" Anthony Read, *The Devil's Disciples: Hitler's Inner Circle* (New York: W.W. Norton, 2003), p. 295.

4. Johann Wolfgang von Goethe (1749–1832), from Clara's song in the play *Egmont*, III.2.

5. The Nazis' use of *Volk* (folk) in *Volksgenossen* stems from the *Völkisch* movement of the previous century that combines nationalism with racism, where the German *Volk* ideally share a pure bloodline free of Jews and other undesirables. "In NS usage it acquired first and foremost the meaning of anti-Semitic, chauvinist-nationalistic, and true to blood and species (blut- und artgemäss)." Christian Zentner and Friedemann Bedürftig (eds.), *The Encyclopedia of the Third Reich*, trans. Amy Hackett, 2 vols. (New York: Macmillan, 1991), vol. II, p. 1001.

6. The Munich Pact was signed on September 30, 1938 by the leaders of Germany, Italy, Great Britain, and France, giving Germany leave to annex Czechoslovakia's Sudetenland. Germany went on to occupy all of Czechoslovakia.

7. Friedrich Schiller (1759–1805), *Die Jungfrau von Orleans*, III.6. Goethe and Schiller were Friedrich Kellner's favorite authors. Their writings had a strong influence even beyond Germany, and their love of individual liberty was the antithesis of Nazi totalitarianism. *Friedrich Schiller, Poet of Freedom*, 3 vols., trans. William F. Wertz, et al. (New York: New Benjamin Franklin House, 1985), vol. III, p. 112.

8. Hitler, *Mein Kampf*, p. 660.

9. Ibid.

1939

1. Dictated from memory in 1968. See Preface for full explanation. An echo of these first thoughts appears in the last sentences of the December 31, 1943, entry: "None of the officers involved disputed this 'genius' undertaking of conquest. No general was to be found who refused to take part in such nonsense. A sad wartime story!"

2. Stories about the sufferings of the German minority in Poland, spread by Goebbels's propaganda ministry, and a staged raid on a German radio

transmitter in Gleiwitz (Gliwice) by Nazis dressed as Polish soldiers, gave Hitler an excuse for waging war. In concert with Germany, the Soviet Union invaded Poland from the east on September 17. Following secret protocols in the Nazi–Soviet non-aggression pact, Germany and Russia divided Poland between them. Klaus P. Fischer, *Nazi Germany: A New History* (New York: Continuum, 1995), pp. 435–40.

3. Italy had violated an earlier alliance with Germany when in 1915, one year after the beginning of World War I, Italy joined forces with France and Great Britain.

4. Japan and Germany signed an agreement on November 25, 1936, to counter the international Communist movement. Italy added its signature a year later. In 1940, this agreement evolved into the more militant Tripartite Pact where the three nations agreed to respect each other's spheres of interest and to provide assistance against any outside attack. Gerhard L. Weinberg, *A World at Arms: A Global History of World War II* (Cambridge University Press, 1994), pp. 168–70.

5. Italy conquered Abyssinia (Ethiopia) in 1936 and made it part of its East African colonies, which included Italian Somaliland and Italian Eritrea. By 1938 Italy had re-established control over its old colony, Libya. In 1939 Italy occupied Albania. These conquests, combined with Italy's control of the Dodecanese island group in the Aegean Sea, furthered Mussolini's desire to control the Mediterranean region.

6. Otto Högy (1900–42), mayor of Laubach (1928–40) and mayor of Moschin (Mosina) in occupied Poland from April 1940 until his death in October 1942.

7. At the conclusion of the Greco-Turkish war in 1922, Greece and Turkey had an exchange of populations: Turkish Christians moved to Greece, and Greek Muslims moved to Turkey. "Altogether around 1.3 million Christians and 400,000 Muslims fled between 1912 and 1923 or were driven out of their homes by 1925 under the supervision of a commission appointed by the League of Nations and headed by the Norwegian explorer and humanitarian Fridtjof Nansen." Bernard Wasserstein, *Barbarism and Civilization: A History of Europe in our Time* (Oxford University Press, 2007), p. 124.

8. In 1936 Hitler established the *Reichskolonialbund* (Reich Colonial League) to reclaim the colonies Germany had been forced to relinquish after World War I. On May 17, 1939, Kellner received a letter from the head of the Laubach branch of the Colonial League, asking him to be the treasurer of the local group. Disapproving of colonialism, and determined to avoid helping the Nazis, Kellner turned down the request.

9. Willi Wolf joined the Nazi Party in 1932 and was a member of the SS (Schutzstaffel/Protection Squadron). Ludwig Heck worked for Friedrich Kellner as a justice clerk. Kellner was under observation by Nazi authorities, and Wolf was seeking to get him in trouble for not using the required Heil

Hitler greeting. In an interview on March 24, 2009, Ludwig Heck confirmed that Kellner did not use the Hitler greeting.

10. Blackout authority was included in an air defense law passed on May 26, 1935.

11. Despite the Pact of Steel Mussolini signed with Hitler in May 1939, in which Italy was to support Germany in any defensive or aggressive war, Mussolini was fearful of the invasion of Poland and did not bring Italy into the war until June 1940. Christopher Duggan, *The Force of Destiny: A History of Italy since 1796* (New York: Houghton Mifflin, 2008), p. 516.

12. "In an attempt to force the Boer guerrillas to surrender [in the second Boer War of 1899–1902], the British military authorities in South Africa seized thousands of Boer women and children, whose menfolk were still fighting, and detained them in seventeen special camps, known as 'concentration camps'. Conditions in the camps were bad, with almost no medical facilities, and little food." Martin Gilbert, *A History of the Twentieth Century*, 2 vols. (New York: William Morrow, 1997), vol. I, p. 38.

13. *Reichspogromnacht*, nicknamed *Kristallnacht* (Night of the Broken Glass), was a nationwide attack against the Jews, co-ordinated by the Nazi government. A number of Jews were murdered, from the Nazi official estimate of less than 100 to an unofficial estimate of over 1,000 deaths; tens of thousands of Jews were sent to concentration camps; and approximately 40 million Reichsmarks of Jewish property was destroyed. Evans, *Third Reich in Power*, pp. 580–92.

14. The event was reported in a local newspaper article, "Soldaten im Städtchen" (Soldiers in a Small Town), *Heimatzeitung* [*HZ*], September 16, 1939, p. 3.

15. Kellner refers to the local SS men. He drew a line through Leidner's name but refers to him as SS in his June 22, 1943 entry. For a description of Wolf and his spying on Kellner, see note 9 above. Otto Dirlam (1911–41) graduate of the State Police Academy, SS member 1933–37, died in battle in Finland in July 1941. Stadtarchiv Laubach, VIII.8.6.25. Wilhelm Leidner (1906–43), Nazi Party member from 1936, was killed at the Eastern Front in December 1943. Stadtarchiv Laubach, XIX.5.1.71: NSDAP and VIII.8.6.25.

16. Frau Anna Becker (1888–1950) was the wife of Kellner's employee Georg Heinrich Becker.

17. Neville Chamberlain (1869–1940), British Conservative politician, prime minister 1937–40. His policy of appeasement backfired and encouraged Hitler's militant aggressiveness. The speech in the leaflets was probably the one Chamberlain gave to the British House of Commons on September 1, 1939, when Germany invaded Poland. I.C.B. Dear and M.R.D. Foot (eds.), *The Oxford Companion to World War II* (Oxford University Press, 1995), p. 202.

18. Hermann Wilhelm Göring (1893–1946), Reich minister and commander of the air force, became second-in-command of the Third Reich in 1939 when Adolf

Hitler named Göring as his successor. Read, *Devil's Disciples*, p. 483. In a rally in Berlin on September 9, 1939, Göring spoke about the Allied leaflets: "It is absurd if our opponent thinks these ridiculous pamphlets can move one single decent German to forget his duty even for one minute." *Hessische Landes-Zeitung* [*HLZ*], September 10, 1939, p. 6. Also in *Archiv der Gegenwart* [*AdG*] (1939) (Königswinter: Siegler Verlag für Zeitarchive), September 9, 1939, (K) 4218–23, quoted on p. 4222.

19. The term "Sun Politics" derives from a 1935 speech by Robert Ley (1890–1945), German Labor Front leader and member of the upper Nazi hierarchy. Ley said the Nazi Swastika represented the sun, and everything else was darkness. Ronald Smelser and Rainer Zitelmann (eds.), *Die braune Elite: 22 Biographische Skizzen* (Darmstadt: Wissenschaftliche Buchgesellschaft, 1989), p. 178.

20. Saarbrücken was under threat by a French offensive. Kellner was concerned that his sister-in-law was still remaining too near the Western Front.

21. "Spengler's elaborate effort to show that all cultures flourish and decline according to immutable laws struck a chord with the public in Germany and abroad." Eric D. Weitz, *Weimar Germany: Promise and Tragedy* (Princeton University Press, 2007), p. 334.

22. Earlier divisions of Poland came between Prussia, Austria-Hungary, and Russia between 1772 and 1795. When those powers were defeated in World War I, Poland regained its independence – only to lose it again twenty-one years later. "An 800-year old kingdom was not merely territorially truncated or temporarily occupied by its more powerful enemies and neighbors; it virtually ceased to exist." Lonnie R. Johnson, *Central Europe: Enemies, Neighbors, Friends* (New York: Oxford University Press, 1996), p. 127.

23. In vol. II, chap. 14 of *Mein Kampf*, "Eastern Orientation," Hitler insisted Germany had the right to unilaterally change its borders, and he considered Russia a good place for expansion.

24. Germany's "Michel" personifies the national character, similar to America's "Paul Bunyan" or "Uncle Sam."

25. The 1936 Eighth Party Congress in Nuremberg was called the Rally of Honor, at which the Nazis increased their denunciations of Bolshevism, a term they increasingly used as a stand-in for the Soviet Union.

26. Quote from an 1813 play, *Die Schuld*, II.5., by Amandus Gottfried Adolf Müllner.

27. Otto von Bismarck (1815–98), chancellor of the Second German Reich (1871–90), helped to unify the independent German states into the German Empire under the authority of Kaiser Wilhelm I.

28. The *Ortsgruppenleiter* was the official responsible for guiding the mayors to assure that the populace adhered to Nazi dictates. He supervised the rationing of food and other items and oversaw the creation of an effective *Volkssturm*. The Nazi hierarchy, from lowest to highest: Block Warden (*Blockwalter*), Cell

Leader (*Zellenleiter*), Local Group Leader (*Ortsgruppenleiter*), District Leader (*Kreisleiter*), Regional Leader (*Gauleiter*). Fischer, *Nazi Germany*, p. 205.

29. Kellner's employee, Georg Heinrich Becker (1880–1954).

30. German troops marched into Warsaw, Poland, on September 28, 1939. A week later, on October 5, Adolf Hitler was in Warsaw for a huge victory parade. His intentions for the Polish people were chilling: they were to be Germany's "reservoir of labour" and put to work like slaves. Jan T. Gross, *Polish Society under German Occupation: The Generalgouvernement 1939–1944* (Princeton University Press, 1979), p. 53.

31. On August 28, 1939, an order was put in place "For the temporary backup of the vital needs of the German people," which required rationing of food, clothing, tobacco, and other items. Published August 27, 1939, in the *Reichsgesetzblatt* (*RGBl; Reich Law Gazette*), part I, p. 1498.

32. "But although the formal occupation and annexation of the Baltic States took place the next summer, Stalin was already demanding military facilities in the still independent states." Chris Bellamy, *Absolute War: Soviet Russia in the Second World War* (New York: Alfred A. Knopf, 2007), p. 67.

33. Hitler's speech was published the next day under the headline, "Das Polen des Versailler Vertrages wird niemals wieder erstehen" *HLZ*, October 7, 1939, pp. 3–6.

34. "Old Fighters" were the earliest members of the National Socialist Party.

35. Kellner writes: "*Verfolgung u. Ausrottung der Juden.*" Kellner's use of *Ausrottung* (destruction, extermination, extirpation) and his descriptions of the roundup of Jews and of mass murder show that the average German (even in small towns like Laubach) was aware from the beginning of the genocide. This is echoed in the subhead of Elke Schmitter's review of the German edition of the diary: "The superb diaries of Friedrich Kellner point out what Germans could have known about Nazi terrors and the crimes committed against the Jews: quite a lot." "Das Gedächtnis gibt nach" (Memories Give Way), *Der Spiegel*, vol. 40, October 1, 2011.

36. NSV: Nationalsozialistische Volkswohlfahrt (National Socialist People's Welfare). WHW: Winterhilfswerk (Winter Aid organization). These Nazi organizations put pressure on businesses and individuals to donate money and belongings. "NSV services were partly financed by the semi-voluntary contributions of its 11 million members and . . . by the unpaid work of nearly 1 million volunteers." Zentner and Bedürftig (eds.), *Encyclopedia*, vol. II, pp. 636–37.

37. "Führer befiehl, wir folgen" was a popular propaganda slogan printed on colorful posters distributed throughout Germany. It sought to impress upon a willing audience the need to give absolute loyalty to their leader.

38. Kellner links Nazi propaganda at the Nuremberg Party Rally with an old expression, the "Nuremberg funnel," a satirical image of teaching children by

placing a funnel on their heads and pouring words into it. Franz Kaiser, *Der Nürnberger Trichter*, illus. Emeli Werzinger (Nuremberg: Sebaldus Verlag, 1946).

39. Nazi stormtroopers (*Sturmabteilung* members) were nicknamed "Brownshirts" (*Braunhemd*). Thus the nickname for the NSDAP National Headquarters building in Munich became "Braunes Haus." Zentner and Bedürftig (eds.), *Encyclopedia*, vol. i, p. 116.

40. *Kampfzeit* (Time of Struggle) is a National Socialist term for 1919–33 when they struggled for political power.

41. The Nazis relentlessly played up this theme in their weekly newspaper, *Der Stürmer* (*The Stormer/The Attacker*), where the phrase "Die Juden sind unser Unglück" appeared in bold letters on the cover. *Der Stürmer* "rapidly established itself as the place where screaming headlines introduced the most rabid attacks on Jews, full of sexual innuendo, racist caricatures, made-up accusations of ritual murder and titillating, semi-pornographic stories of Jewish men seducing innocent German girls." Richard J. Evans, *The Coming of the Third Reich* (New York: Penguin, 2004), pp. 188–89.

42. "In the spring of 1936, instances of violent assault and murder against Jews became more frequent, culminating in a riot by an angry crowd in Jaffa that left nine Jewish passersby dead . . . . . . [But there was no] need to fear that violence in Palestine would scare off potential immigrants, as Ben-Gurion had feared in 1929, for Palestine was now a land of refuge. The degree of insecurity in Palestine as a result of Arab violence was insignificant in comparison with the threat hanging over the Jews of Germany and Poland." Shabtai Teveth, *Ben Gurion and the Palestinian Arabs: From Peace to War* (Oxford University Press, 1985), pp. 152–53.

43. Anna Karolina Preuss Fischler (1891–1962), one of Pauline Kellner's three sisters.

44. Franz Jakob Preuss (1886–1963), one of Pauline Kellner's three brothers.

45. Casualty counts vary, but there were over 40,000 German casualties: at least 8,000 soldiers killed, 5,000 missing (and probably dead), and more than 27,000 wounded. Over 70,000 Polish soldiers were killed and about 130,000 wounded. Dear and Foot (eds.), *Oxford Companion*, p. 906.

46. Kellner refers to Adolf Hitler's rank in World War I: *Gefreiter* (lance-corporal, in British Army terminology). See Thomas Weber, *Hitler's First War* (Oxford University Press, 2010), p. 63. "Oh holy simplicity": Attributed to Jan Hus (1369–1415), a priest whose reformist writings were condemned as heresy. Supposedly he uttered the phrase, "O sancta simplicitas!" in contempt for someone adding brush and sticks to the bonfire as he was being burned at the stake. Georg Büchmann, *Geflügelte Worte: Der klassische Zitatenschatz*, ed. Winfried Hofmann et al. (Berlin: Ullstein, 1998), p. 347.

47. The German philosopher Bruno Bauer (1809–82) brought the Jewish question into prominence in Germany with his book *Die Judenfrage* (Braunschweig, 1843). Bauer's negative presentation of Jews prepared the ground for the Nazis' solution one hundred years later. Douglas Moggach, *The Philosophy and Politics of Bruno Bauer* (Cambridge University Press, 2003), pp. 55–62.

48. Before the Nazis formed their plan to murder the Jews of Germany and Europe, they established repressive anti-Jewish laws to encourage Jews to leave. Of the approximately half million Jews living in Germany, only about half left before it was too late. Most of their money and goods were forfeited as their ticket to freedom. The anxiety and fear of those who remained are dramatically depicted in the journals of Victor Klemperer, *I Will Bear Witness: The Nazi years 1933–1941*, trans. Martin Chalmers (New York: Modern Library, 1999).

49. Shortly after this diary entry, Himmler's head of the security police, Reinhard Heydrich (1904–42), issued the Settlement Edict, prohibiting Gypsies from leaving their homes or camping places, which was the first step in rounding up the Gypsies and sending them to concentration camps. About 25,000 German Gypsies were sent to the Auschwitz concentration camp. Tens of thousands in other countries were also targeted. Peter Longerich, *Heinrich Himmler: A Life*, trans. Jeremy Noakes and Lesley Sharpe (Oxford University Press, 2012), chap. 16, "A New Racial Order."

50. "Chamberlain verhöhnt den Frieden – Anmaßende Antwort des britischen Premierministers auf die Friedensrede des Führers – England will Deutschland vernichten," *HLZ*, October 13, 1939, p. 1.

51. Justice Inspector Karl Paul, member of the Nazi Party from 1933, had an office in the Laubach courthouse but was not one of Kellner's employees. Paul was responsible for the records on regional lawsuits.

52. The British battleship HMS *Royal Oak* was sunk on October 14, 1939, at Scapa Flow in Scotland by the German submarine U-47, commanded by Günther Prien; 833 lives were lost. One year later, Captain Prien was killed when his submarine was destroyed. Dear and Foot (eds.), *Oxford Companion*, pp. 968–69.

53. The Ottoman Empire was Germany's ally in World War I and was dissolved when the war was lost. During World War II, Turkey remained neutral until the war was well decided. In February 1945, three months before Germany surrendered, Turkey cynically joined the Allies. Weinberg, *World at Arms*, pp. 809–10.

54. Hitler was determined to reclaim all territory lost in World War I and make Germans living in those countries citizens of the expanding Third Reich. The Nazi agency *Heim ins Reich* (Home to the Reich, return home) redistributed the Baltic Germans (from Latvia, Lithuania, and Estonia) into earlier Prussian

territory reclaimed from Poland. Germans in the South Tyrol region of Italy were given the choice to return to Germany or remain in Italy and give up claims to German nationality. "After 1918, there were 7 million Germans in Austria (or German-Austrians who wanted to be German citizens), more than 3 million Germans in Czechoslovakia, and more than 1 million Germans in Poland, not to mention the hundreds of thousands of Germans in the 'linguistic islands' scattered throughout Romania and northern Yugoslavia." Johnson, *Central Europe*, p. 196.

55. Joachim von Ribbentrop (1893–1946), foreign minister 1938–45. He had no prior diplomatic experience, but as a businessman he had numerous contacts in Europe. In 1939 Ribbentrop successfully concluded the alliance with Russia. Because the Foreign Office, at his instructions, collaborated in the genocide of the Jews, Ribbentrop was condemned to death after the war and hanged. Read, *Devil's Disciples*, pp. 566–68, 923.

56. Published in *HLZ* with the headline: "Deutschlands Abrechnung mit Chamberlain: England wollte den Krieg – nun hat es ihn!" (Germany settles with Chamberlain: England wanted the war – now it has it!).

57. Karl Otto Pott (1875–1959), a local merchant who joined the Nazi Party in 1931, was Laubach's *Ortsgruppenleiter* (Local Group Leader). Stadtarchiv Laubach, XIX.5.1.77. Five months after this diary entry, Pott and Mayor Högy would interrogate Kellner about his anti-Nazi attitude and seek to have him incarcerated in a concentration camp.

58. Adolf Hitler wrote, "Only an adequately large space on this earth assures a nation of freedom of existence." *Mein Kampf*, p. 643. Germany's desire for extra territory (*Lebensraum*: living space) began decades before World War I. In 1892, under Kaiser Wilhelm II, "Germany was expanding at tremendous speed. The population was growing by almost a million souls a year, the equivalent of an entire province. There was a practical need for trade and expansion. The problem was that a united Germany had arrived too late on the scene, when most of the world had already been carved up by the great powers." Giles MacDonogh, *The Last Kaiser: The Life of Wilhelm II* (New York: St. Martin's Griffen, 2000), pp. 183–84.

59. On November 8, 1939, Hitler spoke at the annual event in the Munich Bürgerbräukeller commemorating the unsuccessful Munich Putsch of November 8–9, 1923, which was Hitler's premature attempt to seize political power. Shortly after Hitler gave his speech and left, a bomb exploded inside the beer hall in an unsuccessful assassination attempt.

60. Johann Georg Elser (1903–15), an anti-Nazi with communist sentiments, was the would-be assassin. Elser was imprisoned in the Dachau concentration camp and executed in 1945. Roger Moorhouse, *Killing Hitler: The Plots, The Assassins, and the Dictator Who Cheated Death* (New York: Bantam, 2007), pp. 49–78.

61. On February 27, 1933, the Reichstag building was set on fire. Adolf Hitler blamed the communists for the attack and called for new laws to strengthen the Nazis' control. A communist activist, Marinus van der Lubbe, was sentenced to death for causing the fire. Because the consequences of the fire benefited the Nazis politically, there was immediate but unproven speculation they had a hand in the arson. Evans, *Coming of the Third Reich*, pp. 329–31.

62. "Attentat mit einer Höllenmaschine: Die Spuren des feigen Verbrechens weisen nach England" (Assassin with infernal device: The cowardly crime is traced to England), *HLZ*, November 10, 1939.

63. "Die Opfer des ruchlosen Verbrechens, 7 tote Kameraden" (Victims of ruthless criminals, 7 dead comrades), *Völkischer Beobachter*, South Germany edition [*VB-Süd*], November 11, 1939.

64. Henriette Katz (1869–1942) and her husband, Maier, left Laubach in 1940 to live in Bad Nauheim. On September 27, 1942, they were sent to the Theresienstadt concentration camp in Czechoslovakia and killed there. Monica Kingreen, "Gewaltsam verschleppt aus Oberhessen: Die Deportationen der Juden im September 1942 und in den Jahren 1943–1945," *Mitteilungen des Oberhessischen Geschichtsvereins Giessen*, Neue Folge, 85 (2000), 5–95.

65. Heinrich Scherdt (1892–1956), Nazi Party member from 1933, was a Laubach policeman before becoming the court attendant and acting constable. In 1943 he was called into the army. After the war he was removed from his position in the courthouse but was allowed to become a policeman again from 1948–53. Stadtarchiv Laubach, XV.3.22.7, XIX.5.1.79.

66. "Finland's stand against the Soviet Union during the Winter War must remain among the most stirring in history." Eloise Engle and Lauri Paananen, *The Winter War: The Soviet Attack on Finland 1939–1940* (Mechanicsburg, PA: Stackpole, 1992), p. 148. When Germany invaded the Soviet Union in 1941, Finland became Germany's ally.

67. The Kellners were not misanthropic or stingy about helping others, but they were determined to limit aid to Nazi organizations. They were called to account because of it and almost sent to a concentration camp.

68. The German heavy cruiser *Admiral Graf Spee* was damaged by British cruisers and sought protection in the port of Montevideo, Uruguay. To keep the British from capturing his ship, Captain Hans Langsdorff scuttled it. See Richard Woodman, *The Battle of the River Plate: A Grand Delusion* (Annapolis, MD: Naval Institute Press, 2008).

69. The air battle was reported in *HLZ* on December 19, 1939. That Kellner could use British casualty figures to question the German newspaper report shows his access to foreign news broadcasts. Kellner was not deterred by the punishments (imprisonment and even execution) for listening to such broadcasts, particularly to the BBC News.

70. "Dampfer Columbus von der eigenen Besatzung versenkt" (The Steamship Columbus Sunk by its Own Crew), *HLZ*, December 21, 1939. The captain ordered the sinking to avoid capture by the British.

1940

1. One month after this diary entry, District Leader Backhaus and President Colnot of the regional court in Giessen would call Kellner to task for anti-Nazi activities.

2. "Eintopfsonntag" (single pot Sunday). The Nazis required everyone to eat an inexpensive meal on one Sunday per month between October and March and donate the money saved to the Winter Aid Association. Restaurants served only a cheap stew on those Sundays, "But you pay the price of a big meal for it, the difference going to the Winter Relief, or so they say. Actually goes into the war chest." William L. Shirer, *Berlin Diary: The Journal of a Foreign Correspondent, 1934–1941* (New York: Alfred A. Knopf, 1941), Berlin, October 22, 1939, p. 238.

3. Kellner's sister-in-law, Katie Ganglberger, and her young son, Erwin, stayed with the Kellners when Mainz was threatened by air raids. He sent her with the card payment because of a dispute he was having with the block warden, Georg Walter, who collected contributions for the NSV. The head of the local NSV chapter, Ernst Mönnig, wanted Kellner "to disappear" from Laubach.

4. A secret air defense factory was being built in Freienseen, a village adjoining Laubach. Many prisoners would be quartered there as forced labor. Others would be put to use in local agriculture.

5. The Führer Begleit Bataillon (Escort Battalion) provided security for Adolf Hitler when he traveled, especially to war zones. The escort troops arrived in Laubach on January 15, 1940 for a rest period and left on March 15, 1940. The commander, General Erwin Rommel (1891–1944), was known at this time for his bravery as a captain in World War I. "Laubach, der Gefreite Brinkforth und Generalleutnant Rommel" (Laubach, Private First Class Brinkforth and Generalleutnant Rommel), *HZ*, April 5, 1941, p. 5.

6. What Kellner does not mention here in his diary, but what he describes in a separate three-page supplemental essay, is the danger he faced a few weeks earlier, on February 19, 1940, when summoned to the Giessen Regional Court because of the block warden's complaints against him.

7. For the first eight months of the war, though the Germans were wreaking havoc, the Allies were re-arming and reluctant to send their armies into battle. That period became known as "The Phoney War."

8. The French minister of war, André Maginot, built the military fortifications from Switzerland to the Belgium and Luxembourg borders, but they proved useless against the massive Blitzkrieg Hitler launched.

9. The successor to the League of Nations has done no better: "The U.N.'s record reflects one shocking failure after another, even in the organization's earliest days." Dore Gold, *Tower of Babble: How the United Nations Has Fueled Global Chaos* (New York: Three Rivers Press, 2005), p. 3.

10. On October 12, 1937, the journalist William Shirer wrote: "The youth, led by the S.S., is fanatic. So are the middle-class *alte Kämpfer*, the "old fighters" who brawled in the streets for Hitler in the early days ... I leave Germany in this autumn of 1937 with words of a Nazi marching song still dinning in my ears: Today we own Germany, Tomorrow the whole world." *Berlin Diary*, p. 87.

11. The Alldeutschen Verband (Pan-German League), founded in 1891 in Berlin, concerned itself with German minorities in other countries (i.e., Czechoslovakia, Poland), supported German imperialistic aims, and espoused an aggressive anti-Semitism. Shelley Baranowski, *Nazi Empire: German Colonialism and Imperialism from Bismarck to Hitler* (Cambridge University Press, 2010), pp. 42–45.

12. From the Royal Air Force archives: "[Squadron 10's] first bombing raid of the war was on 19/20th March 1940, when eight Whitleys, each carrying mixed bomb loads of 1,500 lb, attacked the German minelaying seaplane base at Hornum on the island of Sylt. All returned safely." www.raf.mod.uk/history/bombercommandno10squadron.cfm

13. The Nazis persecuted Freemasons in Germany, closing their lodges, confiscating their property, and arresting the members. H. Paul Jeffers, *Freemasons: A History and Exploration of the World's Oldest Secret Society* (New York: Citadel Press, 2005), p. 161.

14. Emil Hofmann (1883–1948) murdered the American bomber pilot Captain William H. Mooney, who parachuted from his plane on December 24, 1944, and was captured alive. Hofmann was executed for this war crime on October 22, 1948. Hans-Peter Koller, *Der Fliegermord von Freienseen: Eine Dokumentation* (Giessen: Anabas Verlag, 1995), p. 72.

15. Whatever the plan was to paint the highways, it did not get past the idea stage.

16. Vyacheslav Mikhailovich Molotov (1890–1986) was on the Central Committee of the Communist Party of the Soviet Union and minister of foreign affairs.

17. "Sicherung Norwegens in vollem Gang: Blitzartige Antwort an England" (Protection of Norway Fully Underway: Rapid Response to England) and "Dänemarks Schutz" (Denmark's Defense) in *Hamburger Fremdenblatt*, evening edition [*HF-Abend*], April 9, 1940, p. 1. "While the protection of Germany's steel imports from Sweden would later be brought in as an added argument for the occupation of Norway – in the winter, when the Gulf of Bothnia was frozen, the ore was routed by train to the Norwegian port of Narvik and then by boat down the coast – the original concept was an offensive one aimed at England." Weinberg, *World at Arms*, pp. 113–14.

18. This army report was published as a news article in *HLZ*, April 11, 1940, p. 1.

19. Albert Joseph Graefling (1906–78), assessor and auxiliary judge, joined the Nazi Party in 1933. Hessisches Staatsarchiv Darmstadt (HStAD), Best. G 21 B, Nr. 1068.

20. Two months earlier Regional Court President Hermann Colnot had summoned Kellner to Giessen about his unco-operative attitude.

21. Kellner made two handwritten lists of his opposition activities: active resistance and passive resistance. What he describes in this diary entry is no. 1 on his active resistance list: "I continuously enlightened people in my surroundings by strongly stating my opposition." No. 4 on his list: "Not a single one of my employees, Becker, Metzger, Brunner, Elbe, Schüler, became Nazi Party members. This was feasible only because I, as the head justice inspector, used all my influence to strengthen them in their attitudes. If a courthouse manager were to become a Nazi Party member, the entire courthouse would become 100% National Socialist."

22. An ironic use of a phrase from a famous Nazi marching song: "Die Knechtschaft dauert nur noch kurze Zeit!" from Horst Wessel's "Die Fahne Hoch!" (The Flag Held High!). The SA stormtrooper Wessel (1907–30) was involved in numerous political brawls and eventually was shot by an assailant and killed. He was memorialized by Propaganda Minister Joseph Goebbels. Daniel Siemens, *Horst Wessel: Tod und Verklärung eines Nationalsozialisten* (Munich: Siedler Verlag, 2009), pp. 159–68.

23. Richard Walther Darré (1895–1953) was the head of the SS Race and Settlement Department (1931–38) and also Reich Minister of Food and Agriculture (1933–42). "Himmler imbibed from Darré a fixed belief in the destiny of the Nordic race, the superiority of its blood over that of the Slavs, the need to keep its blood pure, and the central role of a solid German peasantry in ensuring the future of the Germanic race." Evans, *Coming of the Third Reich*, p. 228.

24. "Captain Warburton-Lee led five destroyers into Narvikfjord and managed to sink two German destroyers, the *Heidkamp*, aboard which Commodore Bonte died, and the *Anton Schmitt*. Warburton-Lee, however, lost his life and two British destroyers in the action." Chris Mann and Christer Jörgensen, *Hitler's Arctic War: The German Campaigns in Norway, Finland, and the USSR 1940–1945* (New York: St. Martin's Press, 2003), p. 54.

25. Högy's transfer came two months after the interrogation where he threatened to turn Kellner and his wife over to the Gestapo.

26. On May 10, 1940 the German armed forces attacked Belgium, Luxembourg, and the Netherlands, and started a major tank offensive through the Ardennes toward France. Luxembourg fell immediately; the Netherlands surrendered on May 15 and Belgium on May 28. France surrendered on June 22 after only six weeks of fighting.

27. Maxime Weygand (1867–1965) surrendered to the Germans and collaborated with them under the Vichy regime. Robert O. Paxton, *Vichy France: Old Guard and New Order 1940–1944* (New York: Columbia University Press, 2001), p. 271. General Maurice Gustave Gamelin (1872–1958) had recognized the dangers of Germany's rearmament in the 1930s but was hampered by French budget cuts. His failure to stand up to Hitler in 1936, when Hitler sent three battalions into the Rhineland, encouraged Hitler to believe all of Europe was his for the taking. According to Paul Schmidt, Hitler's interpreter, Hitler said the most nerve-racking time in his life was the forty-eight hours after the march into the Rhineland. "If the French had then marched into the Rhineland, we would have had to withdraw with our tails between our legs." William L. Shirer, *The Rise and Fall of the Third Reich* (New York: Simon & Schuster, 1960), p. 293.

28. Kellner is mocking Kaiser Wilhelm II, who said on February 24, 1892: "Ich führe Euch herrlichen Zeiten entgegen" (I shall lead you on to glorious times). MacDonogh, *Last Kaiser*, p. 184.

29. On June 10, 1940, impressed by Hitler's easy victories, Mussolini declared war on France and England.

30. "The inexorable mortal enemy of the German people is and remains France . . . The final goal of their activity in foreign affairs will always be an attempt to seize possession of the Rhine border and to secure this watercourse for France by means of a dismembered and shattered Germany." Hitler, *Mein Kampf*, pp. 619–20.

31. Hermann Rauschning (1887–1982), initially a Nazi enthusiast, broke with the Nazi Party in 1934 and went to live in the United States. His 1940 book *Gespräche mit Hitler* (*Conversations with Hitler*) was a bestseller, though the authenticity of the book came into question. Eckhard Jesse, "Hermann Rauschning," in Ronald Smelser and Rainer Zitelmann (eds.), *Die braune Elite II: 21 weitere biographische Skizzen* (Darmstadt: Wissenschaftliche Buchgesellschaft, 1999), pp. 193–205.

32. "The march of victorious German troops into Paris was met with the brightest enthusiasm in Laubach. Within minutes after the special announcement, Laubach was bedecked in a parade of flags." *Grünberger Anzeiger*, June 15, 1940, p. 6.

33. The Rebstock airport was used as a military air base in World War II.

34. Dr. Oskar Hüssy (1903–64), mayor of Karlsruhe, was an "Old Fighter" who took part in the 1923 Hitler putsch in Munich. After the war he was imprisoned in France and released in 1949. Ernst Klee, *Das Personenlexikon zum Dritten Reich: Wer war was vor und nach 1945* (Frankfurt am Main: S. Fischer Verlag, 2007), p. 274.

35. *Deutsche Justiz*, Edition C, vol. 102, no. 28, July 12, 1940, 785–88.

36. Armed Forces report of August 15, 1940, in *HLZ*, August 16, 1940, p. 1.

37. *VB-Süd*, August 22, 1940, p. 1.

38. Freda Schulman Kellner (1918–2004) was the American wife of Fred William Kellner (Friedrich and Pauline's son). Another letter from her is in the December 2, 1943 entry, in which she tells her in-laws of the birth of her son, Robert Martin Scott Kellner.

39. "Glanzleistungen der deutschen Schnellboote: 57 britische Flugzeuge und 6 Zerstörer versenkt" (Masterly achievement by German speedboats: 57 British airplanes and 6 destroyers sunk), *HLZ*, September 6, 1940, p. 1.

40. "There is nothing that America can do at this moment that would be of greater help than to send fifty destroyers, except sending a hundred. The flying-boats also are of the greatest importance now in the next two months." Martin Gilbert, *Churchill and America* (New York: Free Press, 2005), p. 200.

41. "Von Hamburg abgedrängt" (Forced Away from Hamburg), *HF-Abend*, September 5, 1940, p. 9.

42. Stettin (Szczecin), the largest Polish seaport on the Baltic Sea, and approximately 400 kilometers east of Hamburg, became a major staging area for the Germans after they conquered Poland in 1939.

43. The entry of January 15, 1940, shows Kellner's awareness of the dangerous situation presented by the local leader of this NSV organization. It was necessary for him to be less obvious in his passive resistance. See the Biographical Narrative for a description of the Nazi interrogations of Kellner in February and March of 1940.

44. In a letter to Kellner dated July 2, 1937, the former Laubach mayor, Otto Högy, appointed him deputy leader of the Laubach Reich Air Defense Organization.

45. Letters from Mayor Otto Högy to Friedrich Kellner, dated June 14, 1939, and July 11, 1939, subject "Bekämpfung des Kartoffelkäfers" (Controlling potato beetles).

46. "A special monument in central Rotterdam commemorates those who died in this air attack designed to cow the civilian population, but those who set the world on fire would see their own roofs burn." Weinberg, *World at Arms*, p. 126.

47. Germany, Italy, and Japan created the Tripartite Pact on September 27, 1940, marking their spheres of influence. Germany would have supremacy in Europe; Italy would control the Mediterranean; and Japan would rule Asia. They agreed to mutually assist each other in case of an attack by any nation not affiliated with the Pact. Dear and Foot (eds.), *Oxford Companion*, p. 1123.

48. Chiang Kai-shek (1887–1975) fought a civil war against Chinese Communists, led by Mao Zedong (1893–1976). After his defeat, Chiang fled to Taiwan where he ruled dictatorially until his death. "During twenty-five years on Taiwan, operating in a microcosm of a stable and peaceful China, Chiang had his chance at nation-building, and in terms of social and economic indices he succeeded and laid the groundwork for Taiwan's leap into modernity ... Chiang's political legacy on Taiwan has

also endured, but not without controversy." Jay Taylor, *The Generalissimo: Chiang Kai-shek and the Struggle for Modern China* (Cambridge, MA: Belknap Press, 2009), p. 591.

49. "Rüstung und Ueberrüstung" (Berlin: Hesperus, 1909) was written by the Austrian pacifist Baroness Bertha von Suttner (1843–1914), who also wrote the novel *Die Waffen nieder* (*Lay Down Your Arms*) (1889). Her life's goal was to convince governments to enter into disarmament negotiations. In 1905 she received the Nobel Peace Prize. Brigitte Hamann, *Bertha von Suttner: A Life for Peace*, trans. Ann Dubsky (Syracuse University Press, 1996).

50. Beginning with Hitler's appointment as chancellor on January 30, 1933, "What is usually referred to as the 'Seizure of Power' was in reality a process that took a year and a half to complete." Hagen Schulze, *Germany: A New History*, trans. Deborah Lucas Schneider (Cambridge, MA: Harvard University Press, 1998), p. 247.

51. Walter Bechtold was to fight in the airborne invasion of Crete seven months later, where civilians were massacred for resisting the invaders. "Vier Söhne beim Heer" (Four sons in the army), *HZ*, August 5, 1941, p. 5. Christopher R. Browning would see this young man's initial dismay at having to become a murderer as having "its origins in the humane instincts that Nazism radically opposed and sought to overcome." *Ordinary Men: Reserve Police Battalion 101 and the Final Solution in Poland* (New York: Harper Perennial, 1998), p. 74.

52. The greatest casualty figures of this period came from Japan's onslaught against China, which began in 1933 with a ferocity that increased throughout the war years: "The ordinary people of the Philippines, Malaya, the Netherlands East Indies, and Burma were unlikely to have heard of the horrors of the rape of Nanking when rampaging Japanese soldiers murdered over 200,000 civilians, but they now received visual instruction on their own home territory. The use of military and civilian prisoners for bayonet practice and assorted other cruelties provided the people of Southeast Asia with a dramatic lesson on the new meaning of Bushido, the code of the Japanese warrior." Weinberg, *World at Arms*, p. 322.

53. In 1914 the Japanese took over by force the German colonies in the area of Kiautschou on the northeast coast of China, which the Chinese (under coercion) had leased to Germany in 1898. Sebastian Conrad, *German Colonialism: A Short History*, trans. Sorcha O'Hagan (Cambridge University Press, 2011), 105–07.

54. Wilhelm I annexed the French territory of Alsace-Lorraine for his German Empire in 1871. France reclaimed the territory in 1919. "There was a bigger pool of potential collaborators in Alsace than the rest of France. Much of the population had been born German and admired Bismarck's pioneering post-1870 reforms in education and social security which made the region the envy

of neighbouring French *départements*." Paul Webster, *Petain's Crime: The Complete Story of French Collaboration in the Holocaust* (Chicago, IL: Ivan R. Dee, 1999), p. 184.

55. Italy invaded Greece on October 28, 1940.

56. Great Britain guaranteed protection to Greece but withdrew its forces when the Germans attacked. The Greeks understood the necessity for a tactical retreat. "The people of Athens and at other points of evacuation seemed more concerned for the safety of their would-be rescuers than with their own fate. Greek martial honour stands undimmed." Winston S. Churchill, *The Second World War* (Boston, MA: Houghton Mifflin, 1948–53), vol. III: *The Grand Alliance*, p. 234.

57. From Winston Churchill's speech to the House of Commons on November 12, 1940: "It fell to Neville Chamberlain in one of the supreme crises of the world to be contradicted by events, to be disappointed in his hopes, and to be deceived and cheated by a wicked man." *Blood, Toil, Tears and Sweat: The Speeches of Winston Churchill*, ed. David Cannadine (Boston, MA: Houghton Mifflin, 1989), p. 194.

58. "Der italienische Einmarsch in Griechenland," *HLZ*, October 30, 1940, p. 1.

59. "Italienischer Vormarsch in 70 km Tiefe," *HLZ*, November 1, 1940, p. 1.

60. German proverb: "Wenn es dem Esel zu wohl wird, geht er aufs Eis tanzen."

1941

1. "Der Kampf geht weiter bis zum Sieg: Der italienische Ministerrat grüsst die Verteidiger von Bardia" (The fight continues until victory: The Italian Council of Ministers greets the defenders of Bardia), *VB-Süd*, January 9, 1941, p. 1.

2. Italian Army report, January 23, 1941, in *HLZ*, January 24, 1941, 2. Also as a series of reports in *AdG*, from January 23–25. The loss of Tobruk is mentioned in *AdG* (1941), January 25, 1941, (E) p. 4864.

3. "Der Fall von Tobruk," *HF-Abend*, January 27, 1941, p. 1. Field Marshal Archibald Percival Wavell (1883–1950), commander of the British Army in the Middle East, had initial success in 1940 and 1941 against the Italian forces but had to retreat before the German Africa Corps, which was sent to buttress the Italians. "I am reminded of having commented: 'Rommel has torn the new-won laurels from Wavell's brow and thrown them in the sand.' This was not a true thought, but only a passing pang." Churchill, *Second World War*, vol. III: *The Grand Alliance*, pp. 344–45.

4. Rodolfo Graziani (1882–1955), administrator of Italy's colonial possessions in North Africa, became Commander-in-Chief of Italian North Africa and Governor General of Libya in 1940 but was replaced after one year.

5. *RGBl.*, 1937, part I, No. 87, pp. 829f.: Verordnung zur Sicherstellung des Brotgetreidebedarfs, July 22, 1937.

6. Lord High Chancellor of Sweden Axel Gustafsson Oxenstierna (1583–1654) in a 1648 letter he wrote to his son Johann. The phrase is also traced to Pope Julius III (1487–1555). Büchmann, *Geflügelte Worte*, p. 373.

7. "Die breite Masse aus Dummheit oder Einfalt alles zu glauben" (The broad masses, from stupidity or simplicity, believe everything). Hitler, *Mein Kampf*, p. 324.

8. Hitler wanted Bulgaria in the Pact for another land route to Greece: "some 680,000 German troops moved from Romania into Bulgaria over three great bridges swiftly erected across the Danube by army engineers, to be ready for the drive into Greece." Read, *Devil's Disciples*, p. 679.

9. Hans Georg Fritzsche (1900–53) in the Reich Ministry for Public Enlightenment and Propaganda was widely known through his weekly radio broadcasts.

10. From Otto von Bismarck's December 5, 1876, speech in the Reichstag. Erich Eyck, *Bismarck and the German Empire* (New York: W.W. Norton, 1964), p. 246.

11. Dragisa Cvetkovic (1893–1969), Yugoslavian prime minister (1939–41).

12. When Prince Paul of Yugoslavia and his prime minster Zwetkowitsch (Cvetkovic) joined the Tripartite Pact, Great Britain arranged a coup within Yugoslavia that took both men from power. Ultimately, Hitler invaded Yugoslavia and took control.

13. When the Yugoslavian government was overthrown in March 1941, an anti-Fascist movement became active. "On March 27, Hitler decided Yugoslavia and Greece would be invaded simultaneously. In his directive No. 25 he ordered that the city of Belgrade 'will be destroyed from the air by continual night and day attack'. He also postponed the date of the invasion of the Soviet Union until June 22." Gilbert, *History of the Twentieth Century*, vol. II, p. 366.

14. The *Deutschen Wochenschau* (weekly newsreel) made Tripoli the subject of several newsreels: DW 550 (March 19, 1941), DW 551 (March 26, 1941) and DW 552 (April 2, 1941). Bundesarchiv Filmarchiv in Koblenz. www.bundesarchiv .de/bundesarchiv/organisation/abteilung_fa/index.html.en

15. On April 6, 1941, German troops marched from Bulgaria toward Greece and also attacked Yugoslavia, which capitulated on April 17. Greece fell after one month of fighting. See Mark Mazower, *Inside Hitler's Greece: The Experience of Occupation, 1941–44* (New Haven, CT: Yale University Press, 2001).

16. "Die Fronten sind klar" (The Fronts are Clear), *HLZ*, April 1, 1941, pp. 1ff.

17. The Danish envoy was Henrik Kauffmann (1888–1963), operating against the dictates of German-occupied Denmark. Bo Lidegaard, *Defiant Diplomacy* (New York: Peter Lang, 2003).

18. Hitler, *Mein Kampf*, p. 654.

19. "No propaganda was necessary to highlight the destruction of the city of Coventry, which became emblematic of the Blitz for many Britons after it was attacked by 500 German bombers on the night of 14 November 1940." Andrew Roberts, *The Storm of War: A New History of the Second World War* (New York: Harper, 2011), p. 105.

20. *HLZ*, May 10, 1941, p. 1.

21. Rudolf Hess (1894–1987) was third in command in the National Socialist hierarchy. On May 10, 1941, he took it upon himself to fly to England in order to propose a peace treaty.

22. Adolf Hitler declared in his September 1, 1939, Reichstag speech, "November 1918 will never again happen in German history." *HLZ*, September 2, 1939, p. 4. The National Socialists claimed Germany lost World War I because Jews, Communists, and others staged a revolution in November 1918 that brought the war to a premature close and forced the Kaiser to abdicate. This became known as the "stab in the back" theory. See Evans, *Coming of the Third Reich*, p. 75.

23. *Deutsches Recht Wochenausgabe*, April 26, 1941, vol. 11, no. 17, pp. 897–99, quote on p. 899. Hans Michael Frank (1900–46) was an attorney who joined the Nazis in 1923. He was Bavarian Minister of Justice (1933–34) and then Governor General of occupied Poland (1939–45). He was sentenced to death by the Nuremberg International Military Tribunal and executed. Years later, his son would write a scathing biography: Niklas Frank, *In the Shadow of the Reich* (New York: Alfred A. Knopf, 1991).

24. Günther Lütjens (1889–1941) participated in the occupation of Norway and was promoted to admiral in 1940. Of the more than 2,100 personnel onboard the *Bismarck* when it was sunk on May 27, 1941, only 115 survived. Admiral Lütjens also was killed. Niklas Zetterling and Michael Tamelander, *Bismarck: The Final Days of Germany's Greatest Battleship* (Drexel Hills, PA: Casemate, 2009).

25. Vidkun Quisling (1887–1945), Norwegian politician and army officer who created the Norwegian Fascist Party, collaborated with the Nazi occupation forces and was made prime minister in 1942. "He had believed in German National Socialism as a world power in the service of God and had made common cause with it for five difficult years." Hans Fredrik Dahl, *Quisling: A Study in Treachery*, trans. Anne-Marie Stanton-Ife (Cambridge University Press, 1999), pp. 1–2. Quisling was executed after the war, and his name became a synonym for "traitor."

26. After World War I, Iraq was governed by Great Britain. It was granted independence in 1932, though England retained military bases in the country. The pro-German prime minister, Rashid Ali al-Gaylani, was stripped of power when his rebellion failed and he was replaced by the pro-British Jamil al-Midfai. "Both Germany and Italy naturally favoured any attempt to

undermine British power in the Middle East and enlisted the support of Vichy France to this end, but the timing was such that the Axis Powers could do little to tilt the balance of forces in Iraq against Great Britain." Charles Tripp, *A History of Iraq* (Cambridge University Press, 2007), p. 102.

27. The "Heil- und Pflegeanstalt" (literally "healing and nursing institution") in Hadamar north of Wiesbaden became a murder center during the Third Reich where euthanasia programs (by poisonous gas) were carried out. Attempts to keep the killings secret did not fool the local population. "The euthanasia killings – that is, the 'systematic and secret execution' of the handicapped – were Nazi Germany's first organized mass murder, in which the killers developed their killing technique." Henry Friedlander, *The Origins of Nazi Genocide: From Euthanasia to the Final Solution* (Durham: University of North Carolina Press, 1997), p. 22.

28. Minister Goldmann was a teacher in Prussia and Saxony, and he was an NCO in World War I. He became a clergyman and joined the Nazi Party in 1931. "Silberne Hochzeit" (Silver Wedding Anniversary) in *HZ*, December 23, 1941, p. 6.

29. Julius Heinrich Dorpmüller (1869–1945), transportation minister (1937–45), shared the responsibility for transporting Jews to the death camps by train. Roderick Stackelberg (ed.), *The Routledge Companion to Nazi Germany* (New York: Routledge, 2007), p. 192.

30. On June 22, 1941, the German armed forces swiftly pushed into the Soviet Union for a war of extermination, murdering Soviet citizens and prisoners of war, and massacring Jews. "Stalin had been fooled. The superb intelligence provided by his own services, and also sincerely given by the British, had been ignored or misinterpreted, although for understandable reasons. Everyone expected some sort of ultimatum, and in the face of Soviet efforts to satisfy Germany an attack seemed hardly logical." Bellamy, *Absolute War*, p. 161.

31. "Und bist du nicht willig, so brauch' ich Gewalt!" From a line in Goethe's 1782 Ballade, "Erlkönig."

32. Helga Elbe worked as a typist for Kellner. He learned from Else Gross, Judge Schmitt's maid, that Helga was reporting on him to the judge and his wife.

33. Dr. Josef Hornef (1896–1971) was a judge in Grünberg. In 1966 Hornef would send a letter of testimony during Kellner's compensation case: "I considered him a reasonable and upright official, who stood bravely against the Nazis." *Wiedergutmachungsakte Friedrich Kellner.*

34. Winston Churchill (1874–1965) belonged to the Conservative Party. He was prime minister from 1940–45 and again from 1951–55. Anthony Eden (1897–1977) was secretary of state for war (1940–45) and prime minister (1955–57).

35. On January 20, 1940, Churchill spoke on the radio about the so-called "neutral" countries of Europe: "They bow humbly and in fear to German threats of violence, comforting themselves meanwhile with the thought that the Allies will win, that Britain and France will strictly observe all the laws and conventions, and that breaches of these laws are only to be expected from the German side. Each one hopes that if he feeds the crocodile enough, the crocodile will eat him last." Martin Gilbert, *Churchill: The Power of Words* (Boston, MA: Da Capo Press, 2012), p. 236.

36. Chamberlain may not have stated that exactly (his most famous phrase was "Peace for our time") but his actions in 1938 certainly seemed to indicate such a view. On September 27, 1938, Chamberlain explained why England would not protect Czechoslovakia from Germany: "War is a fearful thing, and we must be very clear before we embark on it that it is really the great issues that are at stake." Norman A. Graebner and Edward M. Bennett, *The Versailles Treaty and its Legacy: The Failure of the Wilsonian Vision* (Cambridge University Press, 2011), p. 180.

37. *HLZ*, May 10, 1941.

38. "Swedish accommodation of the Nazis started early. Although they resolutely refused to allow the British and French expeditionary forces to cross their territory to aid Finland in her struggle against Russia in early 1940, the Stockholm Government allowed the Germans to cross it to reinforce their army of occupation in Norway later that same year." Roberts, *Storm of War*, p. 114.

39. *Frankfurter General-Anzeiger*, "Der Kontinent im Kreuzzug," June 28, 1941, p. 1.

40. These June 29, 1941, reports by the Supreme Command of the German Armed Forces (OKW) are published in *VB-Süd*, June 30, 1941, p. 1. Also, *AdG* (1941) has six pages of reaction from England and America: 1941, June 30, 1941, pp. 5094–5100.

41. Heinrich Class (1868–1953) was president of the right-wing Pan-German League that advocated imperialism and national racism. Count Ernst zu Reventlow (1869–1943) was a naval officer and anti-Semitic writer.

42. The armistice France signed with Germany required "the French authorities in the Occupied Zone 'to conform to the regulations of the German authorities and collaborate [*zusammenarbeiten*] with them in a correct manner.'" Julian Jackson, *France: The Dark Years, 1940–1944* (New York: Oxford University Press, 2003), p. 167.

43. With his call for Germany to "wake up," Kellner is expropriating a popular Nazi slogan from "Sturmlied" (Storm Song), written by Dietrich Eckart (1868–1923), an early member of the NSDAP.

44. Georg Friedrich Kellner (1862–1926). According to normal birthday calculations, Kellner's father would have been 79 in 1941, and not 80; however,

Kellner always counted the actual day of birth as one's first "birth day" – an idiosyncrasy he explains in a humorous letter dated January 25, 1957, to his cousin Else Zauner.

45. "Stirn und Faust" (literally "forehead and fist"; i.e., brain and brawn) suggested that all workers, white-collar and blue-collar, should vote for Adolf Hitler.

46. Lieutenant Hans Philippi; the high school teacher Georg Wilhelm Kammer; and Corporal Richard von Eiff.

47. Erich Ludendorff (1865–1937) was a Prussian militarist with major responsibility for Germany's stubborn aggressiveness in World War I. He was a leader of the Völkisch movement that espoused nationalism, imperialism, and anti-Semitism, and he worked with the Nazis to foment discontent within the new democracy. In 1923 he joined Hitler in the failed Munich Putsch. Hitler was imprisoned, but Ludendorff's legendary status in World War I helped to get him acquitted of the charges. Read, *Devil's Disciples*, pp. 94–101.

48. Both sides indiscriminately murdered their prisoners. The Nazis considered the war "an ideological war of extermination," while Stalin declared in November 1941 that the Russian army's task was "to annihilate all Germans who have penetrated as occupiers, down to the last man." Bellamy, *Absolute War*, pp. 27, 29.

49. Hitler, *Mein Kampf*, pp. 625, 629.

50. A line from Section 64 of Heinrich Heine's poem "Die Heimkehr" (1823/24) in the *Buch der Lieder* (Leipzig: Hübel und Denck, undated), pp. 68–101, quote on p. 91.

51. On January 30, 1941, Hitler stated in a speech at the Sports Palace, "What are they hoping for? Help from someone? On America? I can say but one thing: we have calculated every possibility from the outset." *AdG* (1941), January 30, 1941, (A) p. 4874.

52. "Denn alle Schuld rächt sich auf Erden." A quote from Goethe's *Wilhelm Meisters theatralische Sendung*, Book 4, chap. 13: Lied des Harfenspielers. Büchmann, *Geflügelte Worte*, p. 120.

53. Nazi Party SS combat troops involved in mass murders of civilians and prisoners of war.

54. "It would go against the sound sensibilities of the German people to grant a tax exemption to the complainant, a completely Jewish institution . . . The only determining factor for this decision is our current world outlook and ideology." *Reichssteuerblatt*, August 7, 1941, vol. 31, no. 62, p. 553.

55. "Die Stunde Europas," in *Das Schwarze Korps* [*DSK*], vol. 7, no. 33, August 14, 1941, p. 1.

56. Ibid.

57. In *VB-Süd*, August 6, 1941, p. 1.

58. From the Wehrmachtbericht of August 7, 1941, as published in *HLZ*, August 8, 1941, p. 1.

59. In 1924 the name Leningrad replaced the former name, St. Petersburg. Kellner interchangeably uses both names. Leningrad is used throughout this translation.

60. Kellner went with Heinrich Fahrbach to take a photograph of the damaged building.

61. *HLZ*, September 14, 1941, p. 1. Mainz was bombed many times during the war. The bombing of September 13, 1941, was the first time it caused fatalities. Dieter Busch, *Der Luftkrieg im Raum Mainz während des Zweiten Weltkrieges 1939– 1945* (Mainz: Hase & Koehler, 1988), p. 19.

62. *RGBl*, I, September 30, 1941, p. 591. Reinhard Heydrich (1904–42) was head of the Reich Security Office before he was appointed to oversee the Protectorate of Bohemia and Moravia. As Heinrich Himmler's deputy, Heydrich helped to create the plans for murdering all Jews in German-occupied territory. His tenure in Czechoslovakia was brief. He suffered wounds from an attempted assassination in Prague and died a week later on June 4, 1942. See Robert Gerwarth, *Hitler's Hangman: The Life of Heydrich* (New Haven, CT: Yale University Press, 2011).

63. "2 million German soldiers and 2,000 tanks, backed by massive air-power, advanced on the Soviet capital in October 1941 in a fresh campaign named 'Operation Typhoon', once again encircling the Red Army forces and taking 673,000 prisoners and enormous quantities of equipment." Richard J. Evans, *The Third Reich at War* (New York: Penguin, 2009), p. 203.

64. Joseph and Helene (née Katz) Strauss owned a laundry business, which was confiscated by the local authorities. Salli and Hulda Hortense (née Haas) Heynemann owned a clothing and general store. The Heynemanns and the Strausses were forcibly deported to Poland and killed (See September 16, 1942 diary entry, and also the Biographical Narrative). Kingreen, "Gewaltsam verschleppt aus Oberhessen," p. 67.

65. "Feldzug im Osten entschieden," in *VB-Süd*, October 10, 1941, p. 1.

66. Clemens August Graf von Galen (1878–1946), Bishop of Münster. The excerpts are from von Galen's sermon of July 13, 1941, St. Lambert's Church, Münster. Despite his criticism of the regime in this sermon, Galen "nevertheless repeatedly expressed his hope for a German victory; the Nazis used patriotic passages from his pastoral letters in their campaign to enlist volunteers for the SS units recruited in Holland and other occupied countries. As long as the German armies continued their advance into Russia the German bishops maintained their calls for a German victory." Guenter Lewy, *The Catholic Church and Nazi Germany* (Boulder, CO: Da Capo Press, 2000), p. 231.

67. Richard J. Evans points out that the bishop's humanity was definitely limited regarding "other persecuted groups in German society, such as the Gypsies or the Jews. Galen said nothing about them, nor did the other representatives of the Churches, with rare exceptions." *Third Reich at War*, pp. 101–02.

68. "Ein weisser Bantuneger," *DSK*, vol. 7, no. 43, October 23, 1941, p. 5. Herbert Tingsten (1896–1973) was a Swedish political scientist and writer who warned of the dangers of National Socialism and Bolshevism. See Ingemar Hedenius, *Herbert Tingsten: Människan och demokraten* (Stockholm: Norstedt, 1974).

69. "'We ourselves will become a church,' was Goebbels's thought." Peter Longerich, *Goebbels: A Biography*, trans. Alan Bance (New York: Random House, 2015), p. 235.

70. The military commander in France, Carl-Heinrich von Stülpnagel (1886–1944), under pressure from Berlin, arranged the execution of ninety-eight hostages. Von Stülpnagel later belonged to the resistance circle that attempted to assassinate Hitler on July 20, 1944, and was sentenced to death by the People's Court.

71. Ferdinand von Schill, Johann Philipp Palm, and Andreas Hofer resisted Napoleon Bonaparte's rule over the Germans in the early 1800s. Albert Leo Schlageter (1894–1923) was active in the resistance against the French army during France's occupation of the Ruhr in 1923 and was captured and executed.

72. This is perhaps the single most important entry in the Kellner diary, an irrefutable example of how the German people, even in the small villages, knew the truth early in the war about the genocide being done in their name. "By July 1941, events elsewhere were already pushing German policy towards the Jews strongly in the direction of genocide. The preparations for the 'war of annihilation' with the Soviet Union marked, it has been noted, a 'quantum jump' into genocide. Certainly, a genocidal climate was now present as never before." Ian Kershaw, *Hitler, the Germans, and the Final Solution* (New Haven, CT: Yale University Press, 2008), p. 67.

73. Werner Mölders (1913–41), considered one of the best fighter pilots in the Luftwaffe, had been active with the Condor Legion in the Spanish Civil War. He was killed on November 22, 1941 "in a plane crash while en route to Ernst Udet's funeral." Zentner and Bedürftig (eds.), *Encyclopedia*, vol. II, p. 598.

74. *RGBl.*, part I (1941), p. 675: Verordnung über die Beschäftigung von Juden, 3.10.1941.

75. *HLZ*, November 10, 1941, pp. 1–3.

76. On November 13, 1941, the American Neutrality Act was amended to allow the arming of merchant ships. In his October 9 speech to Congress, seeking this amendment, President Roosevelt said, "We will not let Hitler prescribe the waters of the world on which our ships may travel. The American flag is not

going to be driven from the seas either by his submarines, his airplanes, or his threats. We cannot permit the affirmative defense of our rights to be annulled and diluted by sections of the Neutrality Act which have no realism in the light of unscrupulous ambitions of madmen." Franklin D. Roosevelt Presidential Library and Museum, Hyde Park, NY: www.fdrlibrary.marist.edu/_resources/images/msf/msf01448.

77. "The German troops were forced to give up Rostov-on-Don, their first serious setback on the Eastern Front." Martin Gilbert, *The Second World War: A Complete History*, rev. edn. (New York: Henry Holt, 1991), p. 265.

78. Both Werner Mölders and Helmuth Wilberg would die in separate plane crashes on the way to Ernst Udet's funeral. Wilberg was part-Jewish, but his extraordinary service to the Nazis in rebuilding the air force after World War I could not be discounted. "Hitler granted exemptions for military necessity." Bryan Mark Rigg, *Hitler's Jewish Soldiers: The Untold Story of Nazi Racial Laws and Men of Jewish Descent in the German Military* (Lawrence: University Press of Kansas, 2004), p. 177.

79. Friedrich Ebert (1871–1925), Social Democrat politician, was the first president of the Weimar Republic. He had to contend with the chaos that erupted after defeat in World War I and the Kaiser's abdication. He struck deals with anti-democratic parties in order to keep his democracy afloat. So he failed to properly punish Hitler and Ludendorff for their attempt to overthrow the government in Munich in 1923. Weitz, *Weimar Germany*, p. 28. Also Piers Brendon, *The Dark Valley: A Panorama of the 1930s* (New York: Alfred A. Knopf, 2000), p. 34. During Ebert's time in office, Friedrich Kellner was a political organizer in Mainz for the Social Democrats. In 2009 the Friedrich Ebert Stiftung (Foundation) sponsored an exhibition of the Friedrich Kellner diary in Berlin and Bonn.

80. "Most reports fail to mention any reactions, confining their comments to a cold, factual account of the 'evacuations'. In one or two instances stereotype 'approval', 'satisfaction', 'interest' of the local population is mentioned. The Nuremberg population was said to have 'noted approvingly' the first deportations from the city on 15 November 1941, and 'a great number' of Forschheim's inhabitants allegedly followed the departure of eight Jews from the town 'with interest and great satisfaction'." Kershaw, *Hitler, the Germans, and the Final Solution*, pp. 200–01.

81. In France, "police co-operation also proved indispensable to the Germans in the deportation of the Jews. Already on three occasions in 1941, the Germans had, with French police co-operation, rounded up Jews in Paris as a reprisal against Resistance attacks. These Jews were sent to internment camps, and filled the first deportation convoys that left for Auschwitz on 27 March, 5 June, and 22 June 1942, including over 1,000 French Jews. But this piecemeal policy was now to be replaced by the 'Final Solution'." Jackson, *France*, p. 217.

82. Kellner uses a Friedrich Schiller quote, "Ich merkt es wohl, vor Tische las mans anders," from *Die Piccolomini*, iv.vii. See Friedrich Schiller, *The Robbers and Wallenstein*, trans F.J. Lamport (London: Penguin, 1979), p. 303.

83. Kellner was a sergeant in the Prince Carl infantry regiment and fought in the First Battle of the Marne in September 1914. His active duty was ended by a shrapnel wound a few months later. His military passbook, which lists the several battles he participated in, is extant and privately held. The Kaiser's army had its own Blitzkrieg approach, rapidly pushing through Luxembourg and Belgium and into France for a quick takeover of Paris. But the combined French and British forces dashed their hopes at the Marne River. "By the end of October [1914] the wider German offensive had failed at enormous cost, particularly to the German volunteer corps." John Keegan, *The First World War* (New York: Alfred A. Knopf, 1999), p. 133.

84. Kellner obviously hates Japanese brutality, but his derogatory use of "yellow bandits" is not indicative of his feelings for Asians. His deep admiration for the Chinese people is seen in his diary entry of October 10, 1940: "Their truly unique courage and idealism should inspire mankind."

85. Kaiser Wilhelm II believed Germany's future lay upon the water. MacDonogh, *Last Kaiser*, p. 232.

86. Werner Baron von Fritsch (1880–1939) was the head of the Army High Command (OKH) until February 1938 and was succeeded by General Field Marshal Walther von Brauchitsch (1881–1948).

87. The American aviator Charles Lindbergh (1902–74) was the spokesman of the America First Committee (AFC) and an outspoken opponent of America's entry into the war. Despite his public persona as an American hero, Lindbergh was a racist and anti-Semite and a fervent admirer of Hitler's Germany. Max Wallace, *The American Axis: Henry Ford, Charles Lindbergh, and the Rise of the Third Reich* (New York: St. Martin's Press, 2004), p. 175.

88. "Der Führer übernimmt das Oberkommando des Heeres," *HLZ*, December 22, 1941, p. 1.

1942

1. Hitler's New Year's appeal, published under the headline, "In diesem Krieg siegt nicht das Glück, sondern das Recht!" in *HLZ*, January 2, 1941, pp. 3ff., and in *AdG* (1941), January 1, 1941, (A) pp. 4833–34. The Order of the Day is found in *VB-Süd*, January 1, 1941, p. 3, and in *AdG* (1941), January 1, 1941, (A) pp. 4834–35.

2. Erich Ludendorff's 1935 book *Der Totale Krieg* had a strong influence on Hitler. After the 1943 defeat at Stalingrad, Goebbels would press Hitler "for a move to 'total war' (to maximize every conceivable resource of hitherto unused

manpower and drastically curtail any activity not essential to the war economy) . . ." Ian Kershaw, *The End: The Defiance and Destruction of Hitler's Germany, 1944–45* (New York: Penguin, 2011), pp. 23–24.

3. Japan would succeed in capturing the city of Changsha on their fourth attempt in 1944. See John D. Plating, *The Hump: America's Strategy for Keeping China in World War II* (College Station: Texas A&M University Press, 2011).

4. "It was necessary above all to warn the house and the country of the misfortunes which impended upon us. There is no worse mistake in public leadership than to hold out false hopes soon to be swept away. The British people can face peril or misfortune with fortitude and buoyancy, but they bitterly resent being deceived or finding that those responsible for their affairs are themselves dwelling in a fool's paradise." Churchill, *Second World War*, vol. iv: *The Hinge of Fate*, pp. 61–62.

5. Published in *HLZ*, January 31, 1942, pp. 2–5.

6. Erwin Rommel was the subject of major media attention, yet he failed completely in his end goals. "The other side of the story is that German soldiers and military analysts have no particular regard for Rommel as a general . . . To men trained in the schools of Clausewitz and Moltke, the qualities Americans admire in Rommel are exactly those that merit criticism: acting on impulse, favoring spontaneity over planning, trusting to luck for logistics." Dennis Showalter, *Patton and Rommel: Men of War in the Twentieth Century* (New York: Berkley Caliber, 2005), p.3.

7. Albert Haas (1915–42), leader of the Laubach stormtroopers, received this flowery obituary in the paper: "At the age of 26, in the serious fight against Bolshevism, Lieutenant Albert Haas, holder of the Iron Cross, died a heroic death doing his soldierly duty for Führer and country. The local chapter of the Nazi Party of Laubach loses a member who was always ready, and the high-school boys have lost a proven teacher." *HZ*, February 26, 1942, p. 4. (See the Biographical Narrative for his role in the Kristallnacht pogrom.)

8. Decision of the German Reichstag of April 26, 1942, *RGBl*, Part i, 1942, No. 44, p. 247. Hitler already had dictatorial powers through the Enabling Act of March 23, 1933. This latest measure was the final step in the legislative farce that gave an aura of legal correctness to Hitler's total abrogation of the democratic process.

9. *HLZ*, April 27, 1942, p. 1.

10. Martin Bormann (1900–45) was Rudolf Hess's chief of staff and head of the Party Chancellery. After Hess fled to England, Bormann served as Hitler's chief of staff. Heinrich Himmler (1900–45) joined the NSDAP in 1925. He was made head of the Party's protection squadron, the Schutzstaffel (SS), and in 1934 brought the Gestapo (Secret Police) under his control. Among his foremost tasks was the elimination of Jews. Fritz Sauckel (1894–1946) was an

early member of the Nazi Party. He was responsible during the war for bringing foreign workers into Germany.

11. General Henri Giraud (1879–1949) was able to reach the Swiss border and from there get to Vichy, France. Because of differences with the ruling government, he lived under cover until the Allies were able to bring him to Gibraltar. "Giraud would become an idée fixe with FDR as the French alternative to de Gaulle, but the fact is he had no place in the command structure of the Army, no popular following, no organization, no program, no interest in politics, and little administrative ability. Simply put, he was an American puppet invented by FDR and the State Department to avoid having to deal with Charles de Gaulle." Jean Edward Smith, *Eisenhower in War and Peace* (New York: Random House, 2012), p. 224.

12. The anti-French pamphlet, *Deutschland in seiner tiefsten Erniedrigung*, was published anonymously in 1806 by bookseller Johann Philipp Palm. Napoleon had Palm executed. *Das Elend der Fremdherrschaft* was written by Heinrich Bechtolsheimer, Lutheran minister and historian, in 1910.

13. "Recent travellers' tales about conditions in Germany are apt to give a wrong impression. Despite food shortages and some war weariness, well informed quarters emphasise that there will be no internal revolt – at least until Nazism has been defeated on the battlefront." "Little Chance of German Revolt," *Sunday Mail*, Brisbane, Australia, September 6, 1942.

14. Kellner completed a hundred pages of his history of the Third Reich but destroyed the manuscript after the 1953 suicide of his son. Some rough-draft pages are extant, including a tribute to his wife.

15. The Council of Ministers in Defense of the Reich was to assure co-operation between business and government for the war economy. Göring's speech was printed in *Reichshaushalts- und Besoldungsblatt*, 1942, no. 11, May 12, 1942, pp. 105ff., no. 4001: Anordnung über die Mindestarbeitszeit für den öffentlichen Dienst während des Krieges.

16. Dr. Ludwig Scriba (1885–1968), Nazi Party member from 1932. In 1936 he became court president in Darmstadt, and his validation of Friedrich and Pauline Kellner's Aryan ancestry in 1938 put an end to a campaign by Laubach officials to mark them as having Jewish blood.

17. The campaign against the American president culminated in the article "Der Narr im Weissen Haus" (The Fool in the White House), *VB-Süd/Nord*, May 19, 1942, pp. 1ff. Roosevelt was called "a funny kind of human degenerate" and "a blend of malice, inferiority complex, and megalomania."

18. Gertrud Scholtz-Klink (1902–99) entered the Nazi Party in 1928 and took over the management of the NS-Frauenschaft in the Gau of Baden in 1930. In 1934, she became head of the female labor service. In 1950 Scholtz-Klink was sentenced to thirty months in prison for her war activities. "When Claudia Koonz interviewed her in 1981, she was still a confirmed Nazi offering pious excuses for her involvement and claiming

that under her rule women functioned as 'one happy family,' that no one ever resigned, and that the Nazi leaders were all perfect gentlemen." Fischer, *Nazi Germany*, pp. 357–58.

19. "Was die Front braucht, wird die Heimat geben!" (What the Front Needs, the Home Front will Provide!), *HLZ*, May 22, 1942, p. 2.

20. USS *Yorktown* was damaged on May 8, 1942, in the Battle of the Coral Sea. A month later, during the Battle of Midway, the Yorktown was sunk. The USS *Saratoga* was also in the Battle of Midway, and it continued fighting throughout the war. See Walter R. Borneman, *The Admirals: Nimitz, Halsey, Leahy, and King – The Five-Star Admirals Who Won the War at Sea* (New York: Little, Brown, 2012).

21. Two months earlier, on March 2, Mayor Högy had sent Kellner a *Ladung zum Sühneversuch* letter (Attempt at Reconciliation) regarding a complaint by Johann Günther that Kellner had called him a "foolish scoundrel." Kellner denied the accusation, considering it yet another attempt to rein him in (see diary entry for April 13, 1940), and refused to attend the reconciliation meeting. Document privately held.

22. *Hitler – ein deutsches Verhängnis* (*Hitler – a German Disaster*) by Ernst Niekisch, (Berlin: Widerstand-Verlag, 1932). Niekisch (1889–1967) joined the Social Democratic Party in 1917 but switched to the Bolsheviks. He founded and edited the journal *Widerstand* from 1927 to 1934, opposing Hitler and the Nazis. The Gestapo arrested Niekisch in 1937, and he remained in prison until the end of the war.

23. The Treaty of Versailles mandated a severe reduction in the German army, not to exceed 100,000 men.

24. Friedrich and Pauline Kellner hated to give the Hitler salute. Kellner made this notation on his passive resistance list: "Wife never greeted with 'Heil Hitler.'"

25. From the 1790 song "Heil dir im Siegerkranz" by Heinrich Harries (1762–1802), used as the national anthem of the German Empire.

26. "Engeland" is pronounced the same as "Engelland" (Angel's Land), which led to jokes at the Nazis' expense.

27. Count Georg Friedrich zu Solms (1899–1969) belonged to the conservative political environment and was a prominent member of the Stahlhelm League, a paramilitary organization associated with the right-wing German National People's Party (DNVP). Solms became a member of the Nazi Party in May 1933. Stadtarchiv Laubach, xix.5.1.77: NSDAP.

28. Kellner purchased the property a few years after the war, and in 1950 he and Pauline built their retirement home there. The original name of their street was Andree Allee. In January 2013, eighteen months after the publication of the Kellner diary in Germany, the Laubach authorities renamed the street Friedrich-Kellner-Strasse.

29. Hitler, *Mein Kampf*, p. 180.

30. Robert van Genechten (1895–1945) was a National Socialist in the Netherlands. During the German occupation he was the attorney general at the Court of Justice in The Hague. After the war he hanged himself in prison. David Littlejohn, *The Patriotic Traitors: A History of Collaboration in German-Occupied Europe, 1940–45* (London: Heinemann, 1972), p. 350.

31. "Russlands Wehrkraft" (Russia's Defensive Strength), *HF-Abend*, November 12, 1940, p. 1.

32. Hitler's Reichstag speech of September 1, 1939, published in *HLZ*, September 2, 1939, pp. 3ff. Also available in *AdG* (1939), September 1, 1939, (G) pp. 4199–200. And the article "Molotow kommt nach Berlin" (Molotov Comes to Berlin) is found in *HLZ*, November 10, 1940, p. 1.

33. Kellner returned to this entry and wrote in the margin next to it, "He [Lindenmayer] came back after only a few days."

34. Rühl would be killed in battle on May 5, 1945, in Czechoslovakia.

35. "Der Fall Jäger" (The Case of Jäger), *HZ*, November 1, 1941.

36. Rommel attacked Tobruk three times without success, which stalled his advance for months. In June 1942 he finally succeeded, but he had to withdraw when he was defeated several months later at El Alamein. "They had failed to take advantage of British overextension to turn a defensive victory into a battle of annihilation." Douglas Porch, *The Path to Victory: The Mediterranean Theater in World War II* (New York: Farrar, Straus and Giroux, 2004), p. 233.

37. The endnote for the diary entry of February 6, 1940, describes General Erwin Rommel's presence in Laubach. Rommel's promotions in equivalent American army ranks: *Generalmajor* (one-star brigadier general); *Generalleutnant* (two-star major general); *General* (three-star lieutenant general); *Generaloberst* (four star general); *Generalfeldmarschall* (general of the army).

38. The Friends of Music evening was a "Kraft durch Freude" (Strength through Joy) event. This Nazi organization provided leisure for the workers (particularly important as work hours kept getting longer).

39. *AdG* (1942), August 3, 1942, (D) p. 5582.

40. Party and non-Party members sought to avoid military duty by having their jobs marked as indispensable to the war effort. (See diary entry, January 13, 1943.)

41. A year earlier, the town of Alsfeld, where Bischoff was the judge, became free of Jews. "The *Alsfelder Oberhessische* newspaper reports: late last week the last appearance of Judaism in Alsfeld, an older woman, said farewell to our city. Alsfeld is now free of Jews." "Alsfeld judenfrei," *HZ*, November 18, 1941, p. 5.

42. At least 161 people were killed, 781 houses were completely destroyed, and many more were damaged. Busch, *Der Luftkrieg*, p. 32.

43. "Die ganze Nation hinter Adolf Hitler!" (The Entire Nation is Behind Adolf Hitler!) *VB-Nord*, May 18, 1933, p. 2.

44. "Dr. Tiso zur Judenfrage" (Dr. Tiso on the Jewish Question), *VB-Süd*, August 19, 1942, p. 4. "Father Tiso, the jowly, crew-cut president, was an enthusiastic collaborator. He sent his country's boys to fight and die alongside German soldiers on the eastern front and was generous in funneling food and mineral resources to the Nazi war machine. More damning still, his government had hastened to rid its homeland of Jews." Madeleine Albright, *Prague Winter: A Personal Story of Remembrance and War, 1937–1948* (New York: Harper Collins, 2012), p. 311.

45. The full quote is, "If the German nation wants to end a state of affairs that threatens its extermination in Europe, it must not fall into the error of the pre-War period and make enemies of God and the world; it must recognize the most dangerous enemy and strike at him with all its concentrated power." Hitler, *Mein Kampf*, p. 629.

46. The Security Service (SD) was founded in 1931 under the direction of Reinhard Heydrich and would play a leading role in the Nazis' extermination policy in the occupied territories. "After the elimination of primary enemies (1933–35) came phase two or the assault on 'racial enemies' – that is, Jews, and later, 'Asiatic inferiors.'" Fischer, *Nazi Germany*, pp. 334–35.

47. Otto Thierack (1889–1946) was a German lawyer and prosecutor. In 1936 he became president of the Nazi People's Court. In 1942 he was promoted to minister of justice. Read, *Devil's Disciples*, p. 762.

48. Published in *Deutsche Justiz*, Edition A, vol. 104, no. 35, August 28, 1942, p. 549. Hans Heinrich Lammers (1879–1962) was head of the Reich Chancellery for the entire time of the Third Reich. "When asked after the war whether he was privy to any information about the fate of the Jews, Lammers responded by saying quite innocently that he had once asked Hitler what was meant by the 'final solution' and was told that Hitler refused to discuss it, other than saying that he had given Himmler an order to evacuate the Jews. For such moral obtuseness, coupled with his readiness to put his legal rubber stamp on Hitler's criminal decrees, Lammers was sentenced at Nuremberg to twenty years in prison, but served only five years." Fischer, *Nazi Germany*, p. 312.

49. Joseph Goebbels, *Vom Kaiserhof zur Reichskanzlei: Eine historische Darstellung in Tagebuchblättern (Vom 1. Januar 1932 bis zum 1. Mai 1933)* (Munich: Zentralverlag der NSDAP Eher, 1934), p. 14.

50. In the bunker beneath the Berlin Chancellery, "Hitler's study had a picture of Frederick the Great on the wall; the Prussian King had recovered during the Seven Years' War even after the Russians had occupied Berlin, and Hitler took inspiration from his example." Evans, *Third Reich at War*, p. 722.

51. "Unterschiede," *HF-Abend*, August 8, 1942, pp. 1ff.

52. The rapid increase in manufacturing in the defense industries outstripped the ongoing increase in steel production. Despite delays, "5,601 vessels were

delivered, and additional deliveries of merchant vessels in 1939–1945 for private companies and foreign governments bring the grand total up to 5,777 vessels. Their construction consumed a total of about 25 million tons of carbon steel and engaged the labor of 640,300 workers at the peak of employment." Frederic Chapin Lane, *Ships for Victory: A History of Shipbuilding under the US Maritime Commission in World War II* (Baltimore, MD: Johns Hopkins University Press, 2001), p. 6.

53. Nr. 403: Polen und Juden in Verfahren gegen Deutsche, 7.8.1942. Available in Joseph Walk(ed.), *Das Sonderrecht für die Juden im NS-Staat: Eine Sammlung der gesetzlichen Massnahmen und Richtlinien – Inhalt und Bedeutung*, 2nd edn. (Heidelberg: C.F. Müller Verlag, 1996), p. 383.

54. Melania Hirsch, née Roos, was transported from Darmstadt on September 28, 1942, to the Theresienstadt concentration camp, where she died on January 2, 1943. Information from the Central Database of Shoah Victims' names, Yad Vashem.

55. Kellner would emend this statement two days later, writing in the margin: "The Opel Works were damaged on September 9."

56. Helene and Joseph Strauss, as well as Salli and Hulda Heynemann were deported to Poland and murdered there. Kingreen, "Gewaltsam verschleppt aus Oberhessen," p. 67. Other Jews in the vicinity of Laubach who were sent to their deaths at that same time were the widower Samuel Wallenstein of Ruppertsburg, Alexander Baum from Geilshausen, Kathinka Baum, and Sophie Baum. Jews from Upper Hesse were sent to internment camps in Giessen and Friedberg, then to the central collection center in Darmstadt, and from there to Theresienstadt and other extermination camps. Bernward Dörner, *Die Deutschen und der Holocaust: Was niemand wissen wollte, aber jeder wissen konnte* (Berlin: Propyläen, 2007), pp. 443ff.

57. "Was sie erwarten dürfen," *DSK*, vol. 8, no. 37, September 10, 1942, p. 4.

58. See Raul Hilberg, *Die Vernichtung der europäischen Juden*, 3 vols. (Frankfurt am Main: Fischer Verlag, 1991): discussion of Slovakia, pp. 766–94; Hungary, pp. 859–926; Serbia, pp. 725–37; Bulgaria, pp. 794–811; Romania, pp. 811–58. "[T]he Croatian Fascist regime had issued orders and implemented policies for genocide against Jews, Serbs and Romas even before SS-Obergruppenführer Reinhard Heydrich issued the first written operational orders to the Einsatzgruppen to kill Soviet Jews in July 1941 during Operation Barbarossa." Barry M. Lituchy (ed.), *Jasenovac and the Holocaust in Yugoslavia: Analyses and Survivor Testimonies* (New York: Jasenovac Research Institute, 2006), p. xxvi.

59. "Das grosse Leben," *HLZ*, October 13, 1942, pp. 1ff.

60. *AdG* (1942), October 3, 1942, (A) p. 5661.

61. "It may almost be said, 'Before Alamein we never had a victory. After Alamein we never had a defeat.'" Churchill, *Second World War*, vol. IV: *The Hinge of Fate*, p. 603.

62. Kellner used a similar phrase when he was campaigning in Mainz against the Nazi Party. He would hold Hitler's book, *Mein Kampf*, above his head and say: "Gutenberg, your printing press has been violated by this evil book."

63. The person in the news article, Franz Carlebach, was killed on March 14, 1942 in the Sachsenhausen concentration camp. (The Central Database of Shoah Victims' Names, Yad Vashem). Robert Mohr (1909–89), who signed the decision to confiscate his property, was head of the Darmstadt Gestapo from October 1942 until February 1944.

64. Wochenspruch der NSDAP, Issue 44 (October 25–31, 1942). The weekly maxims are available in the University of Minnesota's UMedia Archive: https://umedia.lib.umn.edu/node/42965?mode=basic.

65. Bischoff's surly remark about Toulon – that he did not want to hear any defeatist remarks from Kellner – shows the danger Friedrich Kellner faced whenever he spoke out. Toulon was an especially touchy subject that day: "The scuttling of the French Fleet at Toulon fulfilled the promise made to the British by Admiral Darlan in June 1940, and partly broken at Oran that same July, that the French Navy would never be allowed to fall into German hands." Gilbert, *Second World War*, p. 383.

66. "Dolchstoss in Frankreichs Herz," *DSK*, vol. 8, no. 50, December 10, 1942, pp. 1ff.

67. "Bestürzung in Neuyork" *HLZ*, October 10, 1941, p. 1.

68. Mayor Högy's obituary appeared in *HZ* (*Grünberger Anzeiger*), October 3, 1942. Lilli Boehm's obituary was printed in *HZ*, December 24, 1942, p. 9.

69. On June 30, 1934, members of the SS militia from the Hungen area went to nearby Langsdorf to attack Jews. They shot and killed Maurice Oppenheimer and wounded several others. After the war, five of the gunmen were sent to prison, none for longer than four years. Arnsberg, *Die jüdischen Gemeinden in Hessen*, vol. I, pp. 477ff.

70. "One of the most remarkable features of the Kristallnacht was its geographic comprehensiveness. The violence erupted not in dozens but in hundreds of communities, the vast majority of them small cities and towns where only a handful of Jews were present. . . . The list of places in which pogroms occurred on November 9 and 10 includes many towns unknown even to experienced scholars of German history, towns such as Allendorf, Bad Vilbel, Echzell, Falkenstein, Goddelau, Hungen, Illvesheim, Kirch-Beerfurth, Küstrin, Laubach . . ." Steinweis, *Kristallnacht*, p. 58.

71. Gustav Henze was a member of the NSDAP from April 1, 1931. Stadtarchiv Laubach, XIX.5.1.77: NSDAP. The newspaper boxes were for the anti-Semitic paper *Der Stürmer*, produced by Julius Streicher. On the cover of each edition was the phrase, "Die Juden sind unser Unglück" (The Jews are our misfortune).

72. Friedrich and Pauline Kellner regarded Ludwig Heck as a son, which explains Kellner's disappointment and anger about Heck's "arrogant" attitude and apparent dedication to the Nazi cause. In 2005 Heck would reveal he had the missing first notebook of Kellner's diary.

73. 1939 Appeal to the Army and Nazi Party, in *AdG* (1939), December 31, 1939, (C) p. 4366–67. 1940 Appeal to the Army, in *AdG* (1941), January 1, 1941, (A) pp. 4833–34. 1941 Appeal to the German People, in *AdG* (1942), January 1, 1942, (B) pp. 5337–38.

1943

1. From Friedrich Schiller's poem, "Der Ring des Polykrates" (*Schiller*, ed. Wertz, vol. III, p. 23).

2. Friedrich Nietzsche's 1886 unfinished work, *The Will to Power*.

3. "Händchen falten, Köpfchen senken, immer an den Führer denken."

4. Heinrich Himmler was made Reich Commissioner for the Consolidation of the Ethnic German Nation (RKFDV) with the responsibility to resettle people by race within the conquered territories.

5. On June 1, 1920, Friedrich and Pauline Kellner submitted official forms (Hessisches Amtsgericht, Mainz, SA 108/20 and SA 112/20) to the Evangelical Lutheran Church announcing their withdrawal from the Church.

6. "[T]he Protestant Church leadership of a good part of Germany – collectively, as a corporate group, and with the authority of their offices – on their own initiative implicitly endorsed the mass slaughter of Jews." Daniel Jonah Goldhagen, *Hitler's Willing Executioners: Ordinary Germans and the Holocaust* (New York: Vintage, 1997), p. 112.

7. The German Sixth Army captured almost all of Stalingrad but then found themselves encircled and under siege by the Russian army. On February 2, Stalingrad was liberated.

8. Armed Forces report, January 16, 1943: "Our troops in the area of Stalingrad, who for weeks have heroically and bravely defended against an enemy attacking from all sides, beat off strong infantry and tank attacks at great loss to the Bolsheviks. Commanders and troops gave a shining example of the German military tradition." *HLZ*, January 17, 1942, p. 1.

9. Pauline Kellner made many enemies by refusing to join any of the Nazi women's organizations. "There are to be found few wives of officials who showed the same courage," Kellner would write in a separate essay.

10. "Grossdeutschland einiger und stärker denn je" (Greater Germany is more unified and stronger than ever), *HLZ*, October 1, 1942, p. 2.

11. Source of this news article not given. The prison files on this woman were destroyed after the war. Hessische State Archives, Darmstadt: HStAD, Best. G 27 Darmstadt, Nr. 1191.

12. Prince Frederick Christian of Schaumburg-Lippe (1906–83) joined the Nazi Party in 1929 and worked with Joseph Goebbels in the propaganda ministry. He was a devoted Nazi even after the war, an early revisionist writer seeking to minimize Nazi crimes. He was held by the Americans for five years and freed in 1950. "For the princes in general, the fines were higher than was the norm for the general population. The punishments were initially harsher because both the Allies and the indigenous German authorities in the West sought to send a message about the pernicious influence of the old elite. Viewed as autocratic, illiberal, and militaristic, German aristocrats were identified as playing key roles in 'the German catastrophe' in the twentieth century." Jonathan Petropoulos, *Royals and the Reich: The Princes von Hessen in Germany* (New York: Oxford University Press, 2006), pp. 335–36.

13. *HLZ*, February 19, 1943, p. 4.

14. Kellner's exasperation is only partly tongue-in-cheek. He was almost sixty-years old, under constant watch by the authorities, working six and a half days a week, and now had to administer two courthouses 27 miles apart, requiring weekly travel and rooming at an inn. In 2010, several decades after this entry was written, the Altenstadt city magazine described Friedrich Kellner's work there: "Here with us, in a room at the Schwarzen Adler Inn, he would devote a large part of his time to his now world-famous diaries of the Hitler period." Karlheinz Malschok, "Friedrich Kellner, der Mann aus Laubach der in Altenstadt sein Leben riskierte" (Friedrich Kellner, the Man from Laubach who Risked his Life in Altenstadt), *Burgenah Altenstadt*, 2 (2010), 10–11.

15. Armed Forces report of April 12, 1943. In *HLZ*, April 13, 1943, p. 2.

16. Emil Brettle (1877–1945) was the Senior Reich Prosecutor from 1937–45. Lothar Gruchmann, *Justiz im Dritten Reich, 1933–1940: Anpassung und Unterwerfung in der Ära Gürtner* (Munich: Oldenbourg Verlag, 2001), p. 283.

17. Kellner had a personal interest in "radio crimes" and the penalty for distributing Allied leaflets. His March 30, 1945, diary entry mentions listening to foreign radio broadcasts. An item on Kellner's active resistance list shows that he kept his staff and friends constantly updated with information from the broadcasts. Another item on that list describes how he "distributed Allied leaflets in train station waiting rooms and other areas, and got them to wavering Party members."

18. "The 'Atlantic Wall,' a vast defensive barrier against potential Allied invasion and the largest construction project in wartime France, [was] constructed by labourers (many of them forced) working for French companies that made handsome profits out of such contracts." Wasserstein, *Barbarism and Civilization*, p. 332.

19. The Battle of Verdun in 1916 lasted ten months. More than 20 million artillery shells were fired back and forth, causing fatalities on both sides of over 500,000 soldiers. Keegan, *First World War*, pp. 285–86.

20. The Atlantic coast fortifications were constructed by the Todt Organization, founded by the engineer Fritz Todt (1891–1942), who died in a plane crash shortly before Hitler ordered the construction of the wall.

21. "Die schweren Kämpfe in Tunesien," *VB-Süd*, May 10, 1943, p. 1.

22. Attu is part of the Aleutian Islands off the coast of Alaska. The Japanese occupied Attu in the early part of the war, but as Kellner surmised in this diary entry, they were beaten by the American forces in May 1943. See Brian Garfield, *Thousand-Mile War: World War II in Alaska and the Aleutians* (New York: Doubleday, 1969), available in paperback reprint edition (Fairbanks: University of Alaska Press, 1995).

23. Pierre Laval (1883–1945), prime minister of the Vichy government. When Laval succeeded Pétain, he brought French policy and internal actions completely in line with Nazi Germany's, including genocide. Jackson, *France*, p. 218. After the war Laval was sentenced to death as a collaborator and executed.

24. "Der Reichsaussenminister an Esteva" *VB-Süd*, May 23, 1943, p. 2.

25. From the second stanza of Wilhelm Hauff's "Reiters Morgengesang."

26. "Jacques Doriot, the ex-Communist who was later to die fighting the Soviet Union under the banner of Nazi Germany, established his right-wing Parti Populaire Francais in 1936 in the working-class stronghold of Saint-Denis, where he continued to hold the position of mayor." Jessica Wardhaugh (ed.), *Paris and the Right in the Twentieth Century* (Newcastle-upon-Tyne: Cambridge Scholars, 2007), p. 53.

27. *HLZ*, June 14, 1943, p. 1.

28. "Bomber command had decided to saturate the Ruhr, concentrating on 'the complete destruction of four Ruhr cities,' and statistics gathered for United States Strategic Bombing Survey leave no doubt that these were all vital centers in that belt of walled cities which had bound the Ruhr since the Dark Ages with Essen as the buckle. [. . .] The Nazis had started this atrocious form of warfare. Now they were to taste it with a vengeance." William Manchester, *The Arms of Krupp 1587–1968* (Boston: Little, Brown, 1968), p. 451.

29. Heinrich Metzger was one of Kellner's employees in the courthouse. Wilhelm Leidner would be sent to the Eastern Front shortly after this diary entry was written, promoted in the field to lieutenant, and killed in action on December 31, 1943. Stadtarchiv Laubach, XIX.5.1.71: NSDAP; VIII.8.6.25.

30. Convalescing soldiers would also be quartered in the courthouse.

31. The Hitler Youth motto, "Swift as greyhounds, tough as leather and hard as Krupp steel," came from Hitler's *Mein Kampf*, p. 356.

32. Headline source: "Sie wollen die deutschen Kulturdenkmäler zerstören," *HLZ*, July 1, 1943.

33. "Das Parteiprogramm immer in die Praxis umsetzen," *HLZ*, July 1, 1943, p. 1.

34. National Socialist twenty-five point Party Program. Franz Neumann, *Behemoth: The Structure and Practice of National Socialism 1933–1944* (New York: Harper & Row, 1944).

35. "More than three thousand Allied ships and boats, large and small, were gathering for the invasion from one end of the Mediterranean to the other. [. . .] Patton's Seventh Army would land eighty thousand troops in the assault." Rick Atkinson, *The Day of Battle: The War in Sicily and Italy, 1943–1944* (New York: Henry Holt, 2007), pp. 32–33.

36. Heinrich Backhaus was behind much of the Nazis' harassment of Kellner. (See Biographical Narrative.)

37. "When the Duce went to the king on the afternoon of 25 July, Victor Emmanuel told him that the army's morale had utterly collapsed and that he had decided to appoint Marshal Badoglio as Prime Minister. Mussolini left the audience in a daze, and was promptly arrested. Later that evening a radio broadcast announced that the Duce had 'resigned' and called on the Italian people to rally round their sovereign." Duggan, *Force of Destiny*, pp. 522–23.

38. *HLZ*, July 7, 1943, p. 2.

39. In Laubach, the weekly newsreel was shown in a large room in the Traube restaurant, a ten-minute walk from the courthouse.

40. Sources for the headlines: "Empfindliche Schläge," *HF-Abend*, July 13, 1943, p. 1; "Starke Feindverluste auf Sizilien," *VB-Süd* Ausg. (2. Druck), p. 1; "Gewaltige Einbussen der Sowjetrüstung," *HF-Abend*, July 24, 1943, p. 1; "Die gewaltige Panzerschlacht im Raum von Bjelgorod bis Orel," *HF-Abend*, July 13, 1943, p. 4; "Festung Kreta – eine feuerspeiende Insel," *VB-Süd*, July 28, 1943, p. 3; "Südostwall immer stärker," *HLZ*, July 17, 1943, p. 2; "Die Sowjets fordern wirksame Entlastung," "Englische Beklemmung über die Kriegslage," *HF-Abend*, July 13, 1943, p. 1; "England gehört den USA!" *HLZ*, July 23, 1943, p. 1; "Englische Beklemmung über die Kriegslage," *HF-Abend*, July 13, 1943, p. 1; Source not located for "Distress of the American Workers" headline ("Not der amerikanischen Arbeiter"); "Japanischer Fliegererfolg," *HF-Abend*, July 13, 1943, p. 1; "Japanischer Erfolg," *HF-Abend*, July 24, 1943, p. 1.

41. Reported in *HLZ*, August 19, 1943, p. 1.

42. "Die Realitäten des Krieges," *Das Reich*, 1943, no. 34, August 22, 1943, pp. 1ff.

43. "Joseph Goebbels disseminated the slogan [*Wunderwaffen*, wonder weapons] as a response to the widespread fear of Allied military superiority: what the enemy could offer in terms of quantity, German ingenuity could offset with quality." Zentner and Bedürftig (eds.), *Encyclopedia*, vol. II, p. 1060.

44. "Schwindende Hoffnung im Feindlager," *Hamburger Tageblatt*, September 3, 1943, p. 1.

45. "Already on 10 September the German high command confirmed their ancient prejudices with a succinct communique concluding that 'the Italian armed forces no longer exist.' Up to 700,000 Italian military personnel fell into Nazi hands, most being carried off to captivity in Germany, where some would be

eventually retooled as Fascist soldiery but where the majority were destined to work as slave labourers for the Nazi war." R.J.B. Bosworth, *Mussolini's Italy: Life Under the Dictatorship, 1915–1945* (New York: Penguin, 2006), p. 504.

46. Hitler's radio broadcast of September 10, 1943, published as "Die Rede des Führers," *HLZ*, September 11, 1943, pp. 1ff.

47. Bertha Krupp (1886–1957) was the owner of Krupp Steel and the richest individual in Germany. "The world knew her as Big Bertha, because in the Kaiser's war Krupp's giant mortar had been christened for her (*die dicke Bertha*, literally 'fat Bertha') and in World War II her name had been given to the Berthawerk, a Krupp howitzer plant in Silesia built and manned by Jewish slave labor from Auschwitz, which had a Krupp automatic weapons plant within the camp, where, according to the Nuremberg testimony of one of Gustav's own employees: 'From the factory one could see the three big chimneys of the crematorium.'" Manchester, *Arms of Krupp*, p. 5.

48. "Der Führer hat dem Duce sein Wort gehalten" (The Führer Kept his Word to the Duce), *VB-Süd*, September 14, 1943, p. 1. After freeing Mussolini from captivity, Hitler made him the head of a new republic in Salo, on the west bank of Lake Garda in North Italy.

49. Dwight D. Eisenhower (1890–1969), Supreme Commander of the Allied Forces in Europe, and President of the United States (1953–61). Friedrich Kellner's impatience at Eisenhower's slow pace is understandable, but it was not due to incompetence. Eisenhower's overriding strategy was to land a huge force on the Normandy coast in 1944 and drive rapidly toward Germany's western border. His landing in Italy in 1943 had an immediate success in forcing the Italians to surrender, and his strategy in the south was "to hold what we had already gained and to force the Nazis to maintain sizable forces in that area." Dwight D. Eisenhower, *Crusade in Europe* (Baltimore, MD: Johns Hopkins University Press, 1997), p. 200.

50. Leopold III (1901–83), king of Belgium, broke his compact with the Allies and surrendered precipitously to the Germans in 1940, ensuring Germany's early victories.

51. The concept of Volksgemeinschaft preceded the Nazis. "Since World War I, the people's community had stood for reconciliation among Germans who had long been divided by class, region, and religion." The Nazis, however, used the concept to attack "internal and external enemies – Jews, profiteers, Marxists, the Allies – who allegedly obstructed national regeneration. National Socialism offered a comprehensive vision of renewal, which many Germans found appealing." Peter Fritzsche, *Life and Death in the Third Reich* (Cambridge, Mass.: Belknap Press of Harvard University Press, 2008), 38–39.

52. Armed Forces report of September 19, 1943, *HLZ*, September 20, 1943, p. 1.

53. From Friedrich Schiller, "Die Verschwörung des Fiesko zu Genua" (The Conspiracy of Fiesco of Genoa). *Schiller*, ed. Wertz, vol. III, p. 4.

54. "On 14 October 1943 a fleet of nearly 300 B-17s flew into the German Reich via Aachen. As soon as the escorting American fighters had turned back, a swarm of German fighter planes appeared, aiming cannon and rocket fire at the bombers, breaking up their formations then finishing them off singly. 220 American bombers reached Schweinfurt and caused further devastation to the ball-bearing factories, but altogether 60 were shot down and another 138 damaged." Evans, *Third Reich at War*, p. 460.

55. The Altenstadt court where Friedrich worked was located within the city hall building, which also housed the mayor's office.

56. Letter from Dr. Jakobi, President of Giessen District Court, to Justice Inspector Kellner, dated September 23, 1943, subject "Fortbildungskurse für Rechtspfleger" (Continuing courses for judicial officers).

57. "Zurück zum Dnieper," *HLZ*, October 21, 1943, pp. 1ff.

58. Harold Rupert Alexander (1891–1969) was successful in the defense of the southern coast of England against German air raids, and also against Erwin Rommel in North Africa. But it was General Alexander's lot to oversee the retreat and evacuation of British troops at Dunkirk in 1940, and to retreat from advancing Japanese forces in Burma in 1942. "Wasser in Churchills Wein," *VB-Süd*, May 21, 1942, pp. 1ff.

59. "Unsere Stärke wird den Sieg erringen!" (Our Strength will Bring us Victory) *HLZ*, November 9, 1943, pp. 1–3. News articles about Hitler's speeches often included parenthetical descriptions of the audience cheering.

60. *AdG* (1943), November 9, 1943, (E) pp. 6163–66, quote on p. 6166.

61. Editor's note: I am the child mentioned in this letter.

62. "Italiens Juden ins Konzentrationslager," *HLZ*, December 2, 1943, p. 1. "Beginning at the end of November 1943, the neo-Fascist government issued laws calling for all the Jews in Italy to be arrested and interned and their possessions confiscated. The Italian police took over from the German police for the first phase of the 'dirty work,' while the German police took on the task of organizing the deportations." Joshua D. Zimmerman, *Jews in Italy under Fascist and Nazi Rule, 1922–1945* (Cambridge University Press, 2005), p. 220.

63. The major development from the conferences was the determination to soon launch an attack on the continent to draw German troops from the Eastern Front. "Stalin reverted once again to the fact that the Red Army was counting on the execution of the landing in northern France. He was afraid that, if this operation did not take place in the month of May 1944, then it never would, because of worsening weather conditions." Robin Edmonds, *The Big Three: Churchill, Roosevelt and Stalin in Concord and Conflict* (New York: W.W. Norton, 1991), p. 356.

64. On December 20 about four hundred British bombers attacked the area of Frankfurt (forty miles south of Laubach). The Lancaster plane that crashed near Laubach belonged to the Pathfinder unit of the 8th Bomber Group, which led the bombers to their target area. Mirko Mank, *Vergilbte Akten – Verglühtes Metall: Eine Chronik des Luftkrieges im Landkreis Giessen 1939–1945*, (Cölbe-Schönstadt: Burgwald Verlag, 2007), pp. 106–13.

65. Gerd von Rundstedt (1875–1953) commanded Army Group South during the invasion of Poland and was promoted to field marshal. His initial successes in Russia ended in retreat and his forces would be routed at Normandy in June 1944.

66. This reflects back to Kellner's first diary entry, September 1, 1939: "Hitler ordered the invasion of Poland. The German officers did not object. The German troops did not rebel. The German people did not protest. Now they and the entire world will pay for their indifference to tyranny and terrorism."

1944

1. "Tagesbefehl an die deutschen Soldaten," *HF*, January 1, 1944.

2. Headline source: "Heißes Wasser mit Brot – so lebt man in der Sowjetunion" *HLZ*, December 25–26, 1943, p. 2.

3. Galeazzo Ciano, Count of Cortellazzo (1903–44), was married to Mussolini's daughter. Ciano was a member of the Fascist Supreme Council and minister of foreign affairs. He did not get along well with Germany's Foreign Minister Ribbentrop and rebelled at Italy's subservience to Adolf Hitler. "He was executed on 11 January 1944, to Ribbentrop's great satisfaction." Read, *Devil's Disciples*, p. 815. "His diaries are an important historical source for the Fascist era." Zentner and Bedürftig (eds.), *Encyclopedia*, vol. i, pp. 144–45.

4. Armed Forces report of January 24, 1944, in *Darmstädter Zeitung* [*DZ*, January 25, 1944, p. 1.

5. "Deutschland ist unbesiegbar, wenn es sich selbst treu bleibt!"(Germany is Unconquerable if it Remains True to Itself), *DZ*, January 24, 1944, p. 1. Jakob Sprenger (1884–1945), a postal clerk who joined the Nazi Party in 1922, was Gauleiter of Hesse-Nassau (1932–45). In the spring of 1945, as Allied forces were fast moving into his area of Germany, Sprenger sought to set up summary military courts in order to execute the many German soldiers fleeing for their lives. He and his wife both killed themselves when the war was lost. Kershaw, *The End*, p. 261.

6. "A few workers actively tried to sabotage the occupation; one of them, Albert Leo Schlageter, a former Free Corps soldier, was executed for his activities, and the nationalist right, led by the Nazis, quickly seized on the incident as an example of the brutality of the French and the weakness of the Berlin government, turning Schlageter into a much-publicized nationalist martyr in the process." Evans, *Coming of the Third Reich*, p. 186.

7. Alfred Jodl (1890–1946). On May 7, 1945, Jodl signed the unconditional surrender of Germany in Reims, France. Jodl's cold-blooded decisions in 1941 and 1942 to shoot Russian prisoners of war and Allied paratroopers led to his guilty verdict at Nuremberg and his execution.

8. Kellner's source for Churchill's speech is found in *AdG* (1943), September 28, 1943, (D) pp. 6111–14. This speech is available online through information provided by the Hansard Digitisation Project, led by the Directorate of Information Services of the House of Commons and the Library of the House of Lords: http://hansard.millbanksystems.com/commons/1943/sep/21/war-situation#S5CV0392P0_19430921_HOC_272.

9. Karl Friedrich Wilhelm Kellner, a.k.a. Fred William Kellner (February 29, 1916 – May 30, 1953), only child of Friedrich and Pauline, was born on leap year day, February 29, 1916. (Friedrich did not know that almost a year before this diary entry, his son had left his wife and children, come under scrutiny by the FBI, and joined the US Army to avoid prosecution. At the time of this birthday entry, Fred was on his way to duty as an MP in the Allies' prisoner-of-war camp in Chartres, France. See Preface and Biographical Narrative for details.)

10. *AdG* (1939), August 9, 1939, (F) p. 4166.

11. "All along the front, from the Pripet marshes to the Black Sea, Soviet armoured divisions were pushing through the German armies, now depleted by the transfer of more forces and equipment to the west, outflanking their defences and advancing towards the borders of Hungary and Romania." Evans, *Third Reich at War*, p. 618.

12. Robert Krötz was in the SA (1930–1940) and then in the SS, in the "Leibstandarte Adolf Hitler" (bodyguard regiment), where he also worked as a war reporter.

13. Theodor Morell (1886–1948) studied medicine in Paris and opened a private practice in Berlin around 1918. He became Adolf Hitler's personal physician in 1936 and remained with Hitler almost until the end in the bunker beneath the Berlin Chancellery. Hitler sent him away a week before committing suicide. Read, *Devil's Disciples*, p. 896.

14. Obituaries in *HF-Abend*: February 16, 1944 (Marie Planthaber), February 10 (Johanna Wolf), January 21 (Walter Lohse).

15. "The Germans were continually pressuring the Swedes to deliver more while the Allies were trying to restrict the flow." Weinberg, *World at Arms*, p. 395.

16. "Theo Morell," *Das Reich*, 1944, no. 10, March 5, 1944, p. 1.

17. "Flutwellen werden im niederländischen Raum die Invasoren empfangen" (Tidal Waves will Receive the Invaders in the Netherland Region), *DZ*, March 22, 1944, p. 2.

18. In *AdG* (1944), March 25, 1944, (E) p. 6318.

19. "Adolf zieht die Opa's ein! Soll das die Vergeltung sein?" *Vergeltung* (retribution/retaliation) was the "V" in the V-1 bombs, which were meant for "retribution" against the Allies.

20. "Männerstolz vor Fürstenthronen," from Schiller's ode, "An die Freude" (Ode to Joy) (*Schiller*, ed. Wertz, vol. I, p. 311).

21. Erwin Ganglberger (born 1925), son of Pauline Kellner's sister Katie, fought with his unit in Hungary, Czechoslovakia, and Austria. Fearing capture by the Soviets, he and what was left of his decimated unit surrendered to the Americans on May 9, 1945. He spent a month in a prisoner-of-war camp before being released. (Letter from Erwin Ganglberger to Robert Scott Kellner, dated April 5, 2010.)

22. *RGBl*, I, 5.5.1944, p. 113: "Erlass des Führers über die Wehrpflicht und die Reichsarbeitsdienstpflicht von Staatenlosen," from April 25, 1944.

23. "Marschall Rommel: 'Wir sind bereit!'" *HF-Abend*, May 9, 1944, p. 2.

24. "Die neue Wochenschau: Der Atlantikwall in Bereitschaft," *DZ*, May 9, 1944, p. 3.

25. "Nach der Räumung der Krim," *HF-Abend*, May 16, 1944, p. 1.

26. The headlines are from *DZ*, May 27, 1944, p. 2; *DZ*, May 17, 1944, p. 1. Cisterna was part of "Operation Shingle," which began in January 1944 with a landing at Anzio and Nettuno. The Allies took heavy losses in that operation. See Atkinson, *Day of Battle*.

27. Kellner wrote "Endlich!" (Finally!) in huge letters and added a vertical red pencil mark next to it for further emphasis. The Allied landing in Normandy on June 6, 1944, known as D-Day, opened the long-awaited second front that would give added strength to the Russian forces in the East and the Allies in Italy. The complex plans to land over 150,000 troops along a fifty-mile stretch of Normandy's coastline could have turned into a terrible disaster, but it did not. "The first report came from the airborne units I had visited only a few hours earlier and was most encouraging in tone. As the morning wore on it became apparent that the landing was going fairly well." Eisenhower, *Crusade in Europe*, p. 253.

28. Headlines from *DZ*, June 7, 1944, p. 1.

29. *HLZ*, October 1, 1942, pp. 2–4, quote on p. 2.

30. Werner Naumann (1909–82) joined the Nazi Party in 1928. In 1938 he was in the propaganda ministry and was eventually promoted to state secretary of the ministry.

31. Sources for the headlines: *VB-Süd*, June 8, 1944, p. 1; *VB-Süd*, June 12, 1944, pp. 1ff; "Subdued Spirits in London" and "Call For Soviet Assistance" are sub-headlines to an article entitled, "Konzentrische Angriffe auf den Gegner" (Concentrated attacks on the enemy), *VB-Süd*, June 11, 1944, p. 1; *VB-Süd*, June 16, 1944, p. 6.

32. Headline sources: *VB-Nord*, June 17, 1944, p. 1; *VB-Nord*, June 19, 1944, p. 1; *VB-Nord*, June 21, 1944, p. 1; Ibid., p. 1.

33. The headline is from *VB-Nord*, July 1, 1944, p. 1.

34. "Popular demands for retaliation against the British encouraged Hitler to squander resources equivalent to twenty-four thousand new fighters (or a functioning ground-to-air missile system) on the V1 flying bomb and V2 ballistic missiles, which never amounted to more than a vengeance-driven tokenism. Randomly destroying the odd London suburban street, however terrible for the unfortunate inhabitants, was not comparable with the Allies' destruction of entire urban districts." Burleigh, *Third Reich*, p. 747.

35. "In North Africa, then in Sicily and Italy, American tankers had regularly encountered not merely up-gunned Mark IV's but Panthers and Tigers, the former with a 75-millimeter high-velocity gun even more deadly to tanks than the vaunted 88. On the whole, the Shermans had coped – not perfectly, but they had coped, and that was enough. The 76-millimeter gun seemed an adequate response to the German innovations." Showalter, *Patton and Rommel*, pp. 379–80.

36. Panzerfaust and Panzerschreck were hand-held bazookas. *VB-Nord*, July 1, 1944, p. 6.

37. Source for the three headlines: *DZ*, July 21, 1944, p. 1. On July 20, 1944, Colonel Claus von Stauffenberg (1907–44) brought a briefcase containing a bomb into a conference room where Hitler was presiding over a meeting. Stauffenberg left the room and the bomb exploded but only wounded Hitler. Stauffenberg and his accomplices were executed. See Joachim C. Fest, *Plotting Hitler's Death: The German Resistance to Hitler 1933–1945* (London: Phoenix, 1996), pp. 255–79.

38. Dritte Verordnung über die Meldung von Männern und Frauen für Aufgaben der Reichsverteidigung, *RGBl*, I, July 28, 1944, pp. 167–68.

39. *Die Wehrmacht*, vol. 8, no. 17, August 16, 1944.

40. A bomb-proof production facility for Tachometer-Werke VDO (Vereinigte DEUTA – OTA) was built in a railway tunnel in Freienseen by Russian, Polish, French, and Belgian forced laborers. Koller, *Der Fliegermord von Freienseen*, pp. 23–27.

41. "Der Gegner hat Eile – wir ringen um Zeitgewinn" *DZ*, August 17, 1944, p. 1.

42. General Kurt Dittmar (1891–1959) was widely known for his radio broadcasts of army reports. He was imprisoned for three years after the war. Cornelius Ryan, *The Last Battle* (New York: Touchstone, 1966), p. 446.

43. Headlines: "St. Malo wird fanatisch verteidigt," *DZ*, August 16, 1941, p. 1; "Das Eichenlaub für den Verteidiger von St. Malo," *VB-Süd*, August 19, 1944, p. 1.

44. Hitler, *Mein Kampf*, pp. 95–96.

45. Probably Otto Mielke (1906–58), war journalist. He continued in his profession after 1945. Klee, *Personenlexikon*, p. 410.

46. A sarcastic reference to the series of "miracle weapons," the V-1 and V-2 flying bombs.

47. The headline sources: *DZ*, August 21, 1944, p. 1; *DZ*, August 28, 1944, p. 1; *Ibid.*, p. 1.
48. The two largest regions of Belgium, Flanders and Wallonia, are also linguistically distinct: Dutch and French. Separatist movements have existed for a long time, and the Nazis were quick to exploit internal divisions.
49. Degrelle was sentenced to death in absentia in 1945 by a Belgian court. He lived in Spain after the war under Francesco Franco's protection. Wolfgang Benz, Hermann Graml, and Hermann Weiss (eds.), *Enzyklopädie des Nationalsozialismus* (Munich: Deutscher Taschenbuch Verlag 2007), p. 906.
50. Source: *DZ*, September 4, 1944, p. 2.
51. The Allies were targeting the SS personnel and the arms depot. The newspaper report states that the Communist politician, Ernst Thälmann (1886–1944), who had vigorously campaigned against the Nazis during the 1920s, was killed in the bombing, but Thälmann had been executed a week earlier by the SS. Russell Lemmons, *Hitler's Rival: Ernst Thälmann in Myth and Memory* (Lexington: University Press of Kentucky, 2013).
52. On September 17, 1944, British and Canadian forces launched the unsuccessful "Operation Market Garden," with airborne divisions, to capture bridges at Arnhem, Nijmegen and Eindhoven in the Netherlands. Although surprised by the attack, the German General Model managed to block it. Cornelius Ryan, *A Bridge Too Far: The Classic History of the Greatest Battle of World War II* (New York: Touchstone, 1995), 154.
53. "Das klassische Beispiel," *DSK*, vol. 10, no. 38, September 21, 1944, pp. 1ff.
54. Ante Pavelic (1889–1959), Poglavnik (leader) of Croatia, founded the Ustashe independence movement and established a reign of terror particularly directed against the Serbian population. On May 17, 1941, Pavelic signed an order "for the creation of circuit summary courts to carry out mass exterminations of Jews, Serbs and Romas on the spot by Ustashe, supposedly after a trial. Tens of thousands were killed according to this law without any trial actually transpiring." Lituchy (ed.), *Jasenovac*, p. xxxvii.
55. "Switzerland's industry worked hard for Germany, substantially increasing its exports, which included arms and ammunition, during 1943 as the bombing of Germany increased her incentive to turn to the safer factories of Switzerland for products." Weinberg, *World at Arms*, p. 397.
56. Mayor Wilhelm Dapper of Grünberg was standing in for Mayor Heinrich Kopp, who had been called into the army. Stadtarchiv Grünberg, Bestand Grünberg B, xix.4.2.
57. Sources for obituaries: *VB-Nord*, November 10, 1944, p. 3, and *VB-Nord*, November 17, 1944, p. 3.
58. Artur Axmann (1913–96) joined the Hitler Youth when he was fifteen; three years later, in 1931, he joined the Nazi Party. Axmann became Reich Youth Leader in 1940. He was imprisoned after the war until 1949. Louis L. Snyder, *Encyclopedia of the Third Reich* (New York: Marlowe, 1976), p. 14.

59. Headline and subheads are from: "London: 'Die letzte Chance für 1944 verloren'," *DZ*, November 1, 1944, p. 1.
60. Andrey Andreyevich Vlasov (1901–46), Russian general, collaborated with the Nazis when he was taken prisoner in 1942.
61. The Royal Air Force Bomber Command sent 255 Lancasters and 10 Mosquitos to strike the town center and railway yards. United Kingdom National Archives: http://webarchive.nationalarchives.gov.uk/20070706011932/http:/www.raf.mod.uk/bombercommand/dec44.html. Also see Dietrich Graef, *"Hake": Angriffsziel Giessen 1944/45*, 2nd edition (Giessen: Oberhessischer Geschichtsverein, 1991), 54–147 and 186–207.

1945

1. "By November [1944], coal stocks at power stations were down by 30 per cent compared with the previous year. Many had sufficient coal for only a week. As most of the reports acknowledged, the impact of the incessant air raids on transport installations was uppermost in the production problems by late 1944." Kershaw, *The End*, p. 137.
2. "Das Geheimnis der letzten Kriegsphase" (The Secret of the Last Phase of the War) by Joachim (Achim) Fernau. Published in *DZ*, August 29, 1944, p. 1. Kellner also has part of this article in his September 3, 1944 diary entry.
3. "Mainz's city center was 80 percent destroyed by the 1.3 million incendiary sticks and twenty thousand high-explosive bombs that were dropped in 1944 and 1945. The number of casualties in the city of 158,000, with the best air-raid protection, was between 3,500 and 3,800, about double the average." Jörg Friedrich, *The Fire: The Bombing of Germany, 1940–1945*, trans. Allison Brown (New York: Columbia University Press, 2006), p. 236.
4. Many members of Pauline's family, and their spouses, had Nazi sympathies. Friedrich helped them frequently with shelter, food, and money but occasionally lost patience with them – as this entry shows. (In his October 11, 1939, entry, Kellner referred to Pauline's sister, Anna Fischler, as a "victim of National Socialist propaganda.")
5. General von Rundstedt's request to move his forces to a more sustainable position was turned down by Hitler with this terse and pessimistic comment: "It just means moving the catastrophe from one place to another." Roberts, *Storm of War*, p. 513. A popular and classic American account of this stage of the war is found in Ryan, *A Bridge Too Far*.
6. "By the end of March only 21 per cent of a sample of soldiers captured by the western Allies still professed faith in the Führer (a drop from 62 per cent at the beginning of January), while 72 per cent had none. [. . .] The defeatism was furthered, and much bitterness caused, by troops fleeing eastwards as fast as

they could go, leaving badly trained and poorly equipped Volkssturm units behind and displaying a complete lack of 'comradely' behaviour towards the wounded and civilian evacuees as they brusquely commandeered vehicles for their retreat." Kershaw, *The End*, pp. 260–61.

7. Perhaps nothing better indicates Kellner's focused dedication to recording the events beyond his own personal life than this blasé parenthetical insertion into his diary entry of a moment when he and his wife came close to being killed as he was writing in the diary. The oil painting he mentions that was damaged by a bomb fragment is now part of the Kellner Diary Exhibition, which had its most fitting display in 2010 at the Dwight D. Eisenhower Presidential Library and Museum in Abilene, Kansas, to commemorate the sixty-fifth anniversary of the Allies' liberation of Europe.

8. Friedrich and Pauline Kellner had a "front row" view: The windows of their courthouse apartment overlooked Friedrichstrasse, Laubach's main road that passed through other towns in the region.

9. From speech in Dansk. *AdG* (1939), September 19, 1939, (A) p. 4241. The phrase is from Exodus 15:21, the Pharaoh's horses, chariots and horsemen drowning in the Red Sea as Moses led the Jewish people out of Egypt.

10. Konrad Wilhelm Theodor Weber (1880–1980) was appointed on April 15, 1945, by the American military government to be the district administrator.

11. Hitler killed himself on April 30, 1945, in the bunker beneath the Reich Chancellery. Also in the bunker were Goebbels and his wife, who also killed themselves after first murdering their six children. "As a final act of institutional deceit, the remaining Nazi leaders informed the German people by radio on the evening of May 1, 1945, that 'our Führer, Adolf Hitler, fighting to the last breath against Bolshevism, fell for Germany this afternoon in his operational command post in the Reich Chancellery.'" Fischer, *Nazi Germany*, pp. 568–69.

12. "The 'Final Solution' would not have been possible without the progressive steps to exclude the Jews from German society which took place in full view of the public, in their legal form met with widespread approval, and resulted in the depersonalization and debasement of the figure of the Jew. It would not have been possible without the apathy and widespread indifference which was the common response to the propaganda of hate." Kershaw, *Hitler, The Germans and the Final Solution*, pp. 206–07.

13. In a memorandum dated August 7, 1945, Mayor Schmidt chose Friedrich Kellner to be the leading town councilman and deputy mayor.

WORKS CITED

Albright, Madeleine. *Prague Winter: A Personal Story of Remembrance and War, 1937–1948*. New York: Harper Collins, 2012.

Archiv der Gegenwart: Die weltweite Dokumentation für Politik und Wirtschaft [*AdG*]. Königswinter: Siegler Verlag für Zeitarchive, 1939–1945.

Arnsberg, Paul. *Die jüdischen Gemeinden in Hessen: Anfang – Untergang – Neubeginn*. 2 vols. Frankfurt am Main: Societäts-Verlag, 1971.

Atkinson, Rick. *The Day of Battle: The War in Sicily and Italy, 1943–1944*. New York: Henry Holt, 2007.

Bajohr, Frank. "German Responses to the Persecution of the Jews as Reflected in Three Collections of Secret Reports," in Susanna Schrafstetter and Alan E. Steinweis (eds.), *The Germans and the Holocaust: Popular Responses to the Persecution and Murder of the Jews*. New York: Berghahn, 2015. pp. 41–58.

Balzer, Wolfgang. "Mainz – eine Stadt und ihr Militär," *Mainz: Vierteljahreshefte für Kultur, Politik, Wirtschaft und Geschichte*, vol. IV. Mainz: Bonewitz Communication, 1988.

Baranowski, Shelley. *Nazi Empire: German Colonialism and Imperialism from Bismarck to Hitler*. Cambridge University Press, 2010.

Bellamy, Chris. *Absolute War: Soviet Russia in the Second World War*. New York: Alfred A. Knopf, 2007.

Benz, Wolfgang, Hermann Graml, and Hermann Weiss (eds.). *Enzyklopädie des Nationalsozialismus*. Munich: Deutscher Taschenbuch Verlag, 2007.

Boberach, Heinz (ed.). *Meldungen aus dem Reich 1938–1945: Die geheimen Lageberichte des Sicherheitsdienstes der SS*. 18 vols. Herrsching: Pawlak, 1984.

Borneman, Walter R. *The Admirals: Nimitz, Halsey, Leahy, and King – The Five-Star Admirals Who Won the War at Sea*. New York: Little, Brown, 2012.

Bosworth, R.J.B. *Mussolini's Italy: Life Under the Dictatorship, 1915–1945*. New York: Penguin, 2006.

Braunroth, Helga, Sascha Feuchert, and Alfred Schäfer (eds.). *1925–2000: 75 Jahre Sozialdemokratische Partei Laubach. Dokumentation zum 75jährigen Bestehen des Ortsvereins Laubach der Sozialdemokratischen Partei Deutschlands*. (Giessen: Druckkollektiv, 2000).

Brendon, Piers. *The Dark Valley: A Panorama of the 1930s*. New York: Alfred A. Knopf, 2000.

Browning, Christopher R. *Ordinary Men: Reserve Police Battalion 101 and the Final Solution in Poland*. New York: Harper Perennial, 1998.

Büchmann, Georg. *Geflügelte Worte: Der klassische Zitatenschatz*, ed. Winfried Hofmann et al. Berlin: Ullstein, 1998.

Burleigh, Michael. *The Third Reich: A New History*. New York: Hill & Wang, 2000.

Busch, Dieter. *Der Luftkrieg im Raum Mainz während des Zweiten Weltkrieges 1939–1945*. Mainz: Hase & Koehler, 1988.

Childers, Thomas. *The Nazi Voter: The Social Foundations of Fascism in Germany, 1919–1933*. Chapel Hill: University of North Carolina Press, 1983.

Churchill, Winston S. *Blood, Toil, Tears and Sweat: The Speeches of Winston Churchill*, ed. David Cannadine. Boston, MA: Houghton Mifflin, 1989.

    The Second World War. 6 vols. Boston, MA: Houghton Mifflin, 1948–1953.

Conrad, Sebastian. *German Colonialism: A Short History*, trans. Sorcha O'Hagan. Cambridge University Press, 2011.

Dahl, Hans Fredrik. *Quisling: A Study in Treachery*, trans. Anne-Marie Stanton-Ife. Cambridge University Press, 1999.

Dear, I.C.B. and M.R.D. Foot (eds.). *The Oxford Companion to World War II*. Oxford University Press, 1995.

Dörner, Bernward. *Die Deutschen und der Holocaust: Was niemand wissen wollte, aber jeder wissen konnte*. Berlin: Propyläen, 2007.

Duggan, Christopher. *The Force of Destiny: A History of Italy since 1796*. New York: Houghton Mifflin, 2008.

Edmonds, Robin. *The Big Three: Churchill, Roosevelt, and Stalin in Concord and Conflict*. New York: W.W. Norton, 1991.

Eisenhower, Dwight D. *Crusade in Europe*. Baltimore, MD: Johns Hopkins University Press, 1997.

Engle, Eloise and Lauri Paananen. *The Winter War: The Soviet Attack on Finland 1939–1940*. Mechanicsburg, PA: Stackpole, 1992.

Epstein, David I. *Home: Life in the Jewish Home for Children*. Ithaca, NY: WORDPRO, 2006.

Evans, Richard J. *The Coming of the Third Reich*. New York: Penguin, 2004.

    The Third Reich at War. New York: Penguin, 2009.

    The Third Reich in Power, 1933–1939. New York: Penguin, 2005.

Eyck, Erich. *Bismarck and the German Empire*. New York: W.W. Norton, 1964.

Falter, Jürgen. *Hitlers Wähler*. Munich: Beck, 1991.

Fest, Joachim C. *Plotting Hitler's Death: The German Resistance to Hitler 1933–1945*. London: Phoenix, 1996.

Fischer, Klaus P. *Nazi Germany: A New History*. New York: Continuum, 1995.

Form, Wilhelm. "Politische NS-Justiz in Hessen – ein Überblick," in Wolfgang Form, Theo Schiller, and Lothar Seitz (eds.), *NS-Justiz in Hessen: Verfolgung, Kontinuitäten, Erbe*. Marburg: Historische Kommission für Hessen, 2015. pp. 77–104.

Frank, Niklas. *In the Shadow of the Reich*. New York: Alfred A. Knopf, 1991.

Franz, Eckhart G. "Volksstaat Hessen 1918–1945," in Walter Heinemeyer (ed.), *Handbuch der hessischen Geschichte*, vol. IV: *Hessen im Deutschen Bund und im neuen Deutschen Reich (1806) 1815 bis 1945*. Elwert: Marburg, 2000.

Friedlander, Henry. *The Origins of Nazi Genocide: From Euthanasia to the Final Solution*. Durham: University of North Carolina Press, 1997.

Friedrich, Jörg. *The Fire: The Bombing of Germany, 1940–1945*, trans. Allison Brown. New York: Columbia University Press, 2006.

Fritzsche, Peter. *Life and Death in the Third Reich*. Cambridge, MA: Belknap Press, 2008.

Garfield, Brian. *Thousand-Mile War: World War II in Alaska and the Aleutians*. New York: Doubleday, 1969. Paperback reprint, Fairbanks: University of Alaska Press, 1995.

George, Uta et al.(eds.). *Hadamar: Heilstätte, Tötungsanstalt, Therapiezentrum*. Marburg: Jonas, 2006.

Gerwarth, Robert. *Hitler's Hangman: The Life of Heydrich*. New Haven, CT: Yale University Press, 2011.

Gilbert, Martin. *Churchill: The Power of Words*. Boston, MA: Da Capo Press, 2012.
Churchill and America. New York: Free Press, 2005.
A History of the Twentieth Century. 2 vols. New York: William Morrow, 1997.
The Second World War: A Complete History. Rev. edn. New York: Henry Holt, 1991.

Goebbels, Joseph. *Vom Kaiserhof zur Reichskanzlei: Eine historische Darstellung in Tagebuchblättern (Vom 1. Januar 1932 bis zum 1. Mai 1933)*. (Munich: Zentralverlag der NSDAP Eher, 1934.

Gold, Dore. *Tower of Babble: How the United Nations Has Fueled Global Chaos*. New York: Three Rivers Press, 2005.

Goldhagen, Daniel Jonah. *Hitler's Willing Executioners: Ordinary Germans and the Holocaust*. New York: Vintage, 1997.

Graebner, Norman A. and Edward M. Bennett. *The Versailles Treaty and its Legacy: The Failure of the Wilsonian Vision*. Cambridge University Press, 2011.

Graef, Dietrich. *"Hake": Angriffsziel Gießen 1944/45*. 2nd edn. Gießen: Oberhessischer Geschichtsverein, 1991.

Gross, Jan T. *Polish Society under German Occupation: The Generalgouvernement 1939–1944*. Princeton University Press, 1979.

Gruchmann, Lothar. *Justiz im Dritten Reich, 1933–1940: Anpassung und Unterwerfung in der Ära Gürtner*. Munich: Oldenbourg Verlag, 2001.

Hamann, Brigitte. *Bertha von Suttner: A Life for Peace*, trans. Ann Dubsky. Syracuse University Press, 1996.

Hamilton, Richard F. *Who Voted for Hitler?* Princeton University Press, 1982.

Hedenius, Ingemar. *Herbert Tingsten: Människan och demokraten*. Stockholm: Norstedt, 1974.

Hessischen Landesamts für geschichtliche Landeskunde. Landesgeschichtliches Informationssystem, Hessen: Historisches Ortslexikon, entry for Laubach, www.lagis-hessen.de (accessed February 24, 2017).

Hilberg, Raul. *Die Vernichtung der europäischen Juden.* 3 vols. Frankfurt am Main: Fischer Verlag, 1991.

Hirsch, Harold. "Das Sondergericht Darmstadt: Zwischen vorauseilendem Gehorsam und widerstrebender Gefolgschaft," in Wolfgang Form, Theo Schiller, and Lothar Seitz (eds.), *NS-Justiz in Hessen: Verfolgung, Kontinuitäten, Erbe.* Marburg: Historische Kommission für Hessen, 2015. pp. 105–48.

Hitler, Adolf. *Mein Kampf,* trans. Ralph Manheim. Boston, MA: Houghton Mifflin, 1962.

Jackson, Julian. *France: The Dark Years, 1940–1944.* New York: Oxford University Press, 2003.

Jeffers, H. Paul. *Freemasons: A History and Exploration of the World's Oldest Secret Society.* New York: Citadel Press, 2005.

Johnson, Lonnie R. *Central Europe: Enemies, Neighbors, Friends.* New York: Oxford University Press, 1996.

Kaiser, Franz. *Der Nürnberger Trichter.* Illus. Emeli Werzinger. Nuremberg: Sebaldus Verlag, 1946.

Kaufman, Menahem. "The Daily Life of the Village and Country Jews in Hessen from Hitler's Ascent to Power to November 1938," *Yad Vashem Studies,* 12 (1992), 147–98.

Keegan, John. *The First World War.* New York: Alfred A. Knopf, 1999.

Kellner, Friedrich. *"Vernebelt, verdunkelt sind alle Hirne": Tagebücher 1939–1945,* ed. Sascha Feuchert, Robert Martin Scott Kellner, et. al. Göttingen: Wallstein Verlag, 2011.

Kershaw, Ian. *The End: The Defiance and Destruction of Hitler's Germany, 1944–1945.* New York: Penguin, 2011.

Hitler, the Germans, and the Final Solution. New Haven, CT: Yale University Press, 2008.

Popular Opinion and Political Dissent in the Third Reich: Bavaria 1933–1945. Rev. edn. Oxford University Press, 2002.

Kingreen, Monica. "'Die Aktion zur kalten Erledigung der Mischehen' – die reichsweit singuläre systematische Verschleppung und Ermordung jüdischer Mischehepartner im NSDAP-Gau Hessen-Nassau 1942/1943," in Alfred Gottwaldt, Norbert Kampe, and Peter Klein (eds.), *NS-Gewaltherrschaft: Beiträge zur historischen Forschung und juristischen Aufarbeitung.* Berlin: Edition Hentrich, 2005. pp. 187–201.

"Gewaltsam verschleppt aus Oberhessen: Die Deportationen der Juden im September 1942 und in den Jahren 1943–1945," *Mitteilungen des Oberhessischen Geschichtsvereins Gießen,* Neue Folge, 85 (2000), 5–95.

"Die Opfer des Holocaust aus Laubach und Ruppertsburg," in Hanno Müler (ed.), *Juden in Laubach und Ruppertsburg.* Neustadt an der Aisch: Schmidt, 2015. pp. 177–90.

Klee, Ernst. *Das Personenlexikon zum Dritten Reich: Wer war was vor und nach 1945.* Frankfurt am Main: Fischer Verlag, 2007.

Klemperer, Victor. *I Will Bear Witness: The Nazi years 1933–1941*, trans. Martin Chalmers. New York: Modern Library, 1999.

Koller, Hans-Peter. *Der Fliegermord von Freienseen: Eine Dokumentation*. Anabas Verlag: Giessen, 1995.

Landesstatistisches Amt Hessen. *Die Ergebnisse der Landtagswahl am 19. Juli 1932 und der Reichstagswahl am 31. Juli 1932 im Volksstaat Hessennach einzelnen Gemeinden*. Darmstadt: Hessischer Staatsverlag, 1932.

Landgericht Giessen. Trial judgment (pogrom in Laubach, 10 November 1938). December 10, 1948, 2 KLs 19/48. Archive of the Institut für Zeitgeschichte, Munich, Gg 01.10.

Lane, Frederic Chapin. *Ships for Victory: A History of Shipbuilding under the US Maritime Commission in World War II*. Baltimore, MD: Johns Hopkins University Press, 2001.

Lemmons, Russell. *Hitler's Rival: Ernst Thälmann in Myth and Memory*. Lexington: University Press of Kentucky, 2013.

Lewy, Guenter. *The Catholic Church and Nazi Germany*. Boulder, CO: Da Capo Press, 2000.

Lidegaard, Bo. *Defiant Diplomacy*. New York: Peter Lang, 2003.

Littlejohn, David. *The Patriotic Traitors: A History of Collaboration in German-Occupied Europe 1940–45*. London: Heinemann, 1972.

Lituchy, Barry M. (ed.). *Jasenovac and the Holocaust in Yugoslavia: Analyses and Survivor Testimonies*. New York: Jasenovac Research Institute, 2006.

Longerich, Peter. *"Davon haben wir nichts gewusst!" Die Deutschen und die Judenverfolgung 1933–1945*. Munich: Siedler, 2006.

   Goebbels: A Biography, trans. Alan Bance. New York: Random House, 2015.

   Heinrich Himmler: A Life, trans. Jeremy Noakes and Lesley Sharpe. Oxford University Press, 2012.

MacDonogh, Giles. *The Last Kaiser: The Life of Wilhelm II*. New York: St. Martin's Griffen, 2000.

Malschok, Karlheinz. "Friedrich Kellner, der Mann aus Laubach der in Altenstadt sein Leben riskierte," *Burgenah Altenstadt*, 2 (2010), 10–11.

Manchester, William. *The Arms of Krupp 1587–1968*. Boston, MA: Little, Brown, 1968.

Mank, Mirko. *Vergilbte Akten – Verglühtes Metall: Eine Chronik des Luftkrieges im Landkreis Gießen 1939–1945*. Cölbe-Schönstadt: Burgwald Verlag, 2007.

Mann, Chris and Christer Jörgensen. *Hitler's Arctic War: The German Campaigns in Norway, Finland, and the USSR 1940–1945*. New York: St. Martin's Press, 2003.

Mazower, Mark. *Inside Hitler's Greece: The Experience of Occupation, 1941–44*. New Haven, CT: Yale University Press, 2001.

Moggach, Douglas. *The Philosophy and Politics of Bruno Bauer*. Cambridge University Press, 2003)

Moorhouse, Roger. *Killing Hitler: The Plots, The Assassins, and the Dictator who Cheated Death*. New York: Bantam, 2007.

Müller, Markus. *Die Christlich-Nationale Bauern- und Landvolkpartei 1928–1933.* Düsseldorf: Droste, 2001.

Neumann, Franz. *Behemoth: The Structure and Practice of National Socialism 1933–1944.* New York: Harper & Row, 1966.

Paxton, Robert O. *Vichy France: Old Guard and New Order 1940–1944.* New York: Columbia University Press, 2001.

Petropoulos, Jonathan. *Royals and the Reich: The Princes von Hessen in Germany.* New York: Oxford University Press, 2006.

Peukert, Detlev. *Inside Nazi Germany: Conformity, Opposition, and Racism in Everyday Life,* trans. Richard Deveson. New Haven, CT: Yale University Press, 1989.

Plating, John D. *The Hump: America's Strategy for Keeping China in World War II.* College Station: Texas A&M University Press, 2011.

Porch, Douglas. *The Path to Victory: The Mediterranean Theater in World War II.* New York: Farrar, Straus and Giroux, 2004.

Pötzsch, Hansjörg. *Antisemitismus in der Region: Antisemitische Erscheinungsformen in Sachsen, Hessen, Hessen-Nassau und Braunschweig 1870–1914.* Wiesbaden: Kommission für die Geschichte der Juden in Hessen, 2000.

Puvogel, Ulrike and Stefanie Endlich. *Gedenkstätten für die Opfer des Nationalsozialismus: Eine Dokumentation,* vol. I. 2nd edn. Bonn: Bundeszentrale für politische Bildung, 1995.

Read, Anthony. *The Devil's Disciples: Hitler's Inner Circle.* New York: W.W. Norton, 2003.

Rigg, Bryan Mark. *Hitler's Jewish Soldiers: The Untold Story of Nazi Racial Laws and Men of Jewish Descent in the German Military.* Lawrence: University Press of Kansas, 2004.

Roberts, Andrew. *The Storm of War: A New History of the Second World War.* New York: Harper, 2011.

Ryan, Cornelius. *A Bridge Too Far: The Classic History of the Greatest Battle of World War II.* New York: Touchstone, 1995.

The Last Battle. New York: Touchstone, 1966.

Schiller, Friedrich. *Friedrich Schiller, Poet of Freedom,* trans. William F. Wertz. 3 vols. New York: New Benjamin Franklin House, 1985.

The Robbers and Wallenstein, trans. F.J. Lamport. London: Penguin, 1979.

Schulze, Hagen. *Germany: A New History,* trans. Deborah Lucas Schneider. Cambridge, MA: Harvard University Press, 1998.

Shirer, William L. *Berlin Diary: The Journal of a Foreign Correspondent, 1934–1941.* New York: Alfred A. Knopf, 1941.

The Rise and Fall of the Third Reich. New York: Simon & Schuster, 1960.

Showalter, Dennis. *Patton and Rommel: Men of War in the Twentieth Century.* New York: Berkley Caliber, 2005.

Siemens, Daniel. *Horst Wessel: Tod und Verklärung eines Nationalsozialisten.* Munich: Siedler Verlag, 2009.

Smelser, Ronald and Rainer Zitelmann (eds.). *Die braune Elite: 22 Biographische Skizzen.* Darmstadt: Wissenschaftliche Buchgesellschaft, 1989.

(eds.) *Die braune Elite II: 21 weitere biographische Skizzen.* Darmstadt: Wissenschaftliche Buchgesellschaft, 1999.

Smith, Jean Edward. *Eisenhower in War and Peace.* New York: Random House, 2012.

Snyder, Louis L. *Encyclopedia of the Third Reich.* New York: Marlowe, 1976.

Stackelberg, Roderick (ed.). *The Routledge Companion to Nazi Germany.* New York: Routledge, 2007.

Statistisches Reichsamt. *Volkszählung: Die Bevölkerung des deutschen Reichs nach den Ergebnissen der Volkszählung 1939,* 4 vols in 1. *Statistik des deutschen Reichs,* vol. 552. Berlin: Verlag für Sozialpolitik, 1941–43.

Die Wahlen zum Reichstag am 31. Juli und 6. November 1932 und am 5. März 1933. Statistik des deutschen Reichs, vol. 434. Berlin: Verlag für Sozialpolitik, 1935.

Steinweis, Alan E. *Kristallnacht 1938.* Cambridge, MA: Belknap Press, 2009.

Stumme, Wolfgang. *Der Mainzer Hauptfriedhof: Menschen und ihre letzte Ruhestätten.* Ingelheim: Leinpfad Verlag, 2010.

Süß, Winfried. "Dezentralisierter Krankenmord: Zum Verhältnis von Zentralgewalt und Regionalgewalten in der 'Euthanasie' seit 1942," in Jürgen John, Horst Möller, and Thomas Schaarschmidt (eds.), *Die NS-Gaue: Regionale Mittelinstanzen im zentralistischen "Führerstaat."* Munich: Oldenbourg, 2007. pp. 123–35.

Taylor, Jay. *The Generalissimo: Chiang Kai-shek and the Struggle for Modern China.* Cambridge, MA: Belknap Press, 2009.

Teveth, Shabtai. *Ben Gurion and the Palestinian Arabs: From Peace to War.* Oxford University Press, 1985.

Tripp, Charles. *A History of Iraq.* Cambridge University Press, 2007.

Ulrich, Axel. "'Weg mit Hitler!': Politischer Widerstand gegen das 'Dritte Reich' im Rhein-Main-Gebiet," in Renate Knigge-Tesche (ed.), *Politischer Widerstand gegen die NS-Diktatur in Hessen: Ausgewählte Aspekte.* Wiesbaden: Hessische Landeszentrale für politische Bildung, 2007.), pp. 6–40.

Ulrich, Axel and Stephanie Zibell, "Wilhelm Leuschner und sein antinazistisches Vertrauensleutennetzwerk," in Wolfgang Form, Theo Schiller, and Lothar Seitz (eds.), *NS-Justiz in Hessen: Verfolgung, Kontinuitäten, Erbe.* Marburg: Historische Kommission für Hessen, 2015. pp. 293–334.

Walk, Joseph (ed.). *Das Sonderrecht für die Juden im NS-Staat: Eine Sammlung der gesetzlichen Massnahmen und Richtlinien – Inhalt und Bedeutung.* 2nd edn. Heidelberg: C.F. Müller Verlag, 1996.

Wallace, Max. *The American Axis: Henry Ford, Charles Lindbergh, and the Rise of the Third Reich.* New York: St. Martin's Press, 2004.

Wardhaugh, Jessica (ed.). *Paris and the Right in the Twentieth Century.* Newcastle-upon-Tyne: Cambridge Scholars, 2007.

Wasserstein, Bernard. *Barbarism and Civilization: A History of Europe in our Time.* Oxford University Press, 2007.

Weber, Thomas. *Hitler's First War.* Oxford University Press, 2010.

Webster, Paul. *Petain's Crime: The Complete Story of French Collaboration in the Holocaust.* Chicago, IL: Ivan R. Dee, 1999.

Weinberg, Gerhard L. *A World at Arms: A Global History of World War II.* Cambridge University Press, 1994.

Weitz, Eric D. *Weimar Germany: Promise and Tragedy.* Princeton University Press, 2007.

Woodman, Richard. *The Battle of the River Plate: A Grand Delusion.* Annapolis, MD: Naval Institute Press, 2008.

Zentner, Christian and Friedemann Bedürftig (eds.). *The Encyclopedia of the Third Reich*, trans. Amy Hackett. 2 vols. New York: Macmillan, 1991.

Zetterling, Niklas and Michael Tamelander. *Bismarck: The Final Days of Germany's Greatest Battleship.* Drexel Hills, PA: Casemate, 2009.

Zibell, Stephanie. *Jakob Sprenger (1884–1945): NS-Gauleiter und Reichsstatthalter in Hessen.* Darmstadt: Hessische Historische Kommission, 1999.

Zimmerman, Joshua D. *Jews in Italy under Fascist and Nazi Rule, 1922–1945.* Cambridge University Press, 2005.

Journals, Newsletters, And Magazines

Archiv der Gegenwart [*AdG*]
Deutsche Justiz: Rechtspflege und Rechtspolitik
Deutsches Recht Wochenausgabe
Reichsgesetzblatt [*RGBl.*]
Reichshaushalts- und Besoldungsblatt
Reichssteuerblatt
Parole der Woche (weekly Nazi "watchword")
Wochenspruch der NSDAP (weekly Nazi maxim, wall posters)

Newspapers

Darmstädter Zeitung [*DZ*]
Frankfurter General-Anzeiger
Frankfurter Presse
Frankfurter Zeitung
Giessener Anzeiger
Giessener Zeitung
Hamburger Fremdenblatt [*HF*; morning edition: *HF-Morgen*; evening edition: *HF-Abend*]
Hamburger Tageblatt
Heimatzeitung [*HZ*]

Hessische Landes-Zeitung [*HLZ*]
Hessisches Regierungsblatt
Oberhessische Tageszeitung
Das Reich
Das Schwarze Korps [*DSK*]
Der Stürmer
Völkischer Beobachter [*VB*; South Germany edition: *VB-Süd*; North Germany edition: *VB-Nord*]

INDEX

joins Tripartite Pact, 104
  political intervention in, 105
Yukon, 254

Zahn, Sgt. Willi, obituary, 269
Zimmer (forester), 213

Zimmermann, Frau (widow of former
  Lauhach judge), 153
Zimmermann, Frau (wife of Mainz regional
  judge), 357
Zoppelt, Martin, wounded in Kharkov, 377
Zwetkowitsch (Cvetkovic), Dragisha, 105